*Social
Problems*

Social

Frank R. Scarpitti

University of Delaware

Problems

Third Edition

Holt,
Rinehart
and
Winston

New York   Chicago   San Francisco
Dallas   Montreal   Toronto   London   Sydney

**To my wife
Ellen
and
our children
Susan
and
Jeffrey**

Library of Congress Cataloging in Publication Data

Scarpitti, Frank R.
Social problems.

Bibliographies
Includes index.
1. United States—Social conditions—1960—Addresses, essays, lectures.   2. Social problems—Addresses, essays, lectures.   I. Title.
HN59.S4   1980   362'.973   79-27274
ISBN 0-03-046736-5

Credits and Acknowledgments

Cover photo by John Simeon Block

Part 1 photo, page 23, by Eve Arnold, Magnum.

Chapter 2   Photo, page 29, courtesy of Oneida Ltd. Silversmiths. Photos, page 44: left, by Abigail Heyman, Magnum; right, by Burk Uzzle, Magnum. Photos, page 46: top, by Abigail Heyman, Magnum; middle, by Elizabeth Hamlin, Stock, Boston; bottom, courtesy of Wide World Photos. Photos, page 47: top left, by Martin Adler Levick, Black
Star; top right, by Richard Stromberg, Media House, Chicago; bottom, by Bruce Da-
vidson, Magnum. Photo, page 49, by Matt Herron, Black Star. Photo, page 51, by
Charles Gatewood, Stock, Boston. Photo, page 54, by Marc Riboud, Magnum. Photo,
page 58, by Dennis Stock, Magnum.

Chapter 3   Photos, page 72, all courtesy of UPI. Photos, page 73: top, courtesy of UPI; middle
left, courtesy of ACTION-RSVP; bottom left, courtesy of Wide World Photos; right,
courtesy of UPI. Photos, page 84: top, by Stephen Rapley; bottom, by Quentin Dodt,
Chicago Tribune. News story, page 86, copyright 1975 by Newsweek, Inc. All rights
reserved. Reprinted by permission. Drawings, page 86, by Roy Doty–Newsweek.
Photo, page 94, courtesy of UPI.

Chapter 4   Photo, page 105, reproduced from the collection of the Library of Congress. Photos,
page 118: top left, by Abigail Heyman, Magnum; top right, courtesy of UPI; middle,
by Shalmon Bernstein, Magnum; bottom left, courtesy of Illinois Bell Telephone; bottom right, courtesy of Frontier Airlines. Photos, page 119: top, by Sepp Seitz, Magnum; left, by Ronald Sherman; middle right, by Bernard Gottfryd–Newsweek; bot-

(continued on p. 648)

Preface

The third edition of *Social Problems* is designed for college courses that seek to provide the student with a comprehensive knowledge of contemporary social problems as well as an introduction to basic sociological principles and concepts. In the discussion of all social problems, the basic approach taken is sociological, although other perspectives are introduced from time to time. Since the discipline of sociology has not cornered the market on meaningful ways of viewing social phenomena, I have also drawn on economics, political science, and psychology for ideas that permit a more complete understanding of the subject matter.

Essentially, I have tried to provide a conceptual framework that will enhance the reader's ability to understand social problems. The sociology of social problems is more than a descriptive analysis of malfunctioning social institutions or social deviants. It is the application of sociological concepts and constructs to the interpretation of social problem data. In this way we are able to see how problems ranging from environmental pollution to crime have social implications and can be meaningfully analyzed by sociologists.

In providing an understanding of the sociology of social problems, it is my hope that a second goal will also be realized: to enhance the reader's ability to handle the enormously complicated problems each of us encounters as a citizen of a democracy. As educated citizens we must be concerned, for the rest of our lives, about the social problems described and discussed in this and other books. We will be called upon over and over to participate in important decisions relative to how our society should define and resolve its social problems. This places on us a special burden to be informed, to understand, to be critical, and to be involved. It is my hope that this book will serve not only to embellish the reader's scholarship but also to stimulate the type of citizenship that is essential for the preservation of a humane democracy.

By their very nature, social problems are controversial. Our values often differ as to the cause of a problem, its solution, and the extent of its ramification. I, like the reader, have my value positions, even biases. Although I have attempted to present an objective discussion of the problems covered, citing conflicting evidence and opinions in many cases, the reader may find my values slipping into a discussion periodically. Although I do not apologize, since I believe that a book of this sort cannot be completely objective or value-free, I do encourage the reader to examine the evidence presented here and elsewhere and make up his or her own mind. My hope is that this book will help the reader arrive at intelligent, informed opinions about our society's social problems.

New In This Edition

A number of additions and changes have been made in this edition to make it a more comprehensive and thorough coverage of current social problems. Of major importance is the regrouping and reordering of chapters, thus providing a more logical and integrated arrangement of topics. This new arrangement helps students to grasp the interrelatedness of problems and the application of certain theoretical principles to their analysis.

Other important changes in this edition include an entirely new chapter on aging, and new sections on sexism, terrorism, leisure, and corporate and governmental crime. In addition, population and environmental problems are now presented in one chapter.

New material has been added throughout the book, making each chapter thoroughly up to date. Whenever necessary, revisions were made to enhance accuracy and clarity and to ensure better balance.

More than half of the adapted readings in each chapter are new. Those retained were judged by users of the second edition as excellent and worthy of being kept. Charts, graphs, tables, and photographs used in this edition are either updated or new.

Organization of the Book

This edition is divided into an introduction and four major sections. The introductory chapter, "The Study of Social Problems," attempts to introduce those issues related to a sociological understanding of social problems in preparation for the theories and data which come in subsequent chapters. The next 15 chapters deal with specific social problems divided into three sections. Each section is introduced by a discussion of the theoretical issues which unify the section.

In Section I, problems related to the basic institutional spheres of American life are examined in chapters devoted to the family, education, work, the urban community, and the corporate state. Section II addresses the problems of diminishing and misused human and physical resources. This section includes discussions of poverty, ethnic, race and sex equality, health care, aging, and population and environmental crises. In Section III, the problem of social deviance is examined. Here chapters on mental illness, crime and justice, violence, variant sexuality, and substance abuse provide an opportunity for examining the personal and structural elements involved in these forms of social behavior.

Finally, the book concludes with an Epilogue and chapter on "The Future of Social Problems." Here a discussion of the problems we are likely to face in the future and how we might respond to them is presented.

Features of the Book

Many aids are used in this book to make its reading enjoyable and informative and to facilitate learning. Each chapter opens with a content outline and closes with a comprehensive summary. Within the chapter, photographs, photo essays, charts, graphs, and tables present information that supplements the text. In addition to the text, the book contains 30 short, abridged readings from sociology and allied disciplines as well as journalistic and literary sources. Many provide the reader with examples of sociological work; others, more personal than scientific, are statements by or about those whom social problems touch most closely. The readings are placed within the text to relate them directly to the material presented.

Two other learning aids appear after the last chapter. A glossary of terms used in the text attempts to present short, meaningful definitions of key words and phrases. Items were chosen for inclusion on the basis of their relevance for the study of sociology and social problems. An appendix, "Understanding Social Research," also appears at the end of the book. It is hoped that readers unfamiliar with the methods sociologists use to gather and interpret data will turn to the appendix for an explanation of basic research methods and techniques of data analysis.

Three supplements add to the usefulness of this text for teaching purposes. An accompanying set of taped interviews with a variety of knowledgeable people discussing topics covered in the text is available. Instructors will find these interviews valuable assets for stimulating student interest and fostering class discussion. An Instructor's Manual is also available to help teachers arrange their course outline and to offer suggestions for lecture topics, class discussion, and student term papers and projects. An assortment of examination questions is also available to the instructor.

Acknowledgments

Many people helped me to prepare this edition of *Social Problems*. In particular, I am grateful to Patrick Donnelly for his hard work, good humor, and loyalty. His outstanding scholarship contributed greatly to this revision. I was also fortunate in having the help of Mary Tucker, Marie Gregg, Carol Anderson, Daniel Curran, and Diane Lammey. Their consistently pleasant personalities and willingness to assist in many different ways made the past year much less difficult than it might have been.

Special thanks are also owed to Rosalind Sackoff, Senior Developmental Editor at Holt, Rinehart and Winston. Her interest and encouragement, and particularly her patience, are sincerely appreciated. I am also grateful to some six professional colleagues who reviewed the second edition of this book and furnished valuable suggestions for the revision. Their suggestions, along with those of the five additional reviewers of the draft of this edition, were very helpful and most appreciated.

Finally, I am indebted to my wife Ellen, my daughter Susan, and my son Jeffrey. They have continued to be understanding of my writer's schedule and preoccupations. Without their support and encouragement, the job would not have been possible.

F.R.S.
Newark, Delaware
January 1980

Contents

Social Problems

The Study of Social Problems

1

Anyone who reads a newspaper knows that America is a society full of problems: a child dies of lead poisoning in a city hospital; racial tensions rise as black students are bused from the inner city to suburban schools; robbery and murder occur with frightening frequency; a middle-class youth dies of a drug overdose; a large corporation plans a resort development and inspires opposition from groups organized to save the wilderness. The toll of individual misery and misfortune and the din of group conflict sometimes seem endless.

We recognize our social problems, however, and we appear to be concerned with solving them. The numerous problems of individual deviance or community disorganization, originally a major concern only in academic or social welfare circles, are now central issues in national, state, and local politics, as well as among leaders of business and industry, almost all ethnic or minority groups, and religious leaders. Crime and delinquency, poverty and unemployment, slums and urban congestion, race relations and problems of maintaining basic institutions such as the family, education, and religion have become the concerns of every political campaign since 1960. Indeed, many of the major proposals of the Kennedy, Johnson, Nixon, Ford and Carter administrations focused on issues traditionally found in standard social problems textbooks.

Nevertheless, we appear to be losing ground. All of the past and present public concern and action does not seem to be bringing us any closer to solutions to many of our major social problems. Is there less crime, delinquency, welfare, and unemployment today than a decade ago? Most assessments indicate that there is probably more. What about urban slums, congestion, drug use, alcoholism, illegitimacy, and family dependency? In spite of the most conscientious attempts to solve these problems—two decades characterized by unparalleled public and private spending, national prosperity unequaled in the history of the world, and scientific achievement almost beyond belief—the answer is the same. How can a society do more? Are some social problems insoluble—the inevitable price we must pay for the social, political, and economic systems that have served most of us so well?

In the following chapters we will examine a number of such problems and issues from a particular perspective: sociology. Not all the problems that exist in a society are the concern of sociologists, however. Like careful investigators in any field, they must discriminate between those conditions they can usefully examine and those that lie beyond their competence. Which problems are truly the *social* problems?

There is a clear distinction between private troubles on the one hand and social, or public, issues on the other. "Troubles occur within the character of the individual and within the range of his immediate relations with others; they have to do with his self and with those limited areas of social life of which he is directly and personally aware."[1] A private trouble may well cause individual suffering and misery but will not necessarily affect the entire social system. A public issue, on the other hand, is a condition that impinges negatively on large numbers of persons and has the potential to undermine and even destroy existing social institutions.[2] When one man is unemployed, we may examine his character and skills in order to alleviate his personal trouble. When a fifth of the work force is unemployed, a public issue exists, demanding reevaluation of the society's economic, political, and social policies. It is public issues with which sociologists are primarily concerned, and these issues form the basis for the study of social problems.

Social Problems: Perspectives and Definitions

How are true social problems to be identified and defined? This question has been the topic of long-standing debate among sociologists.[3] Three approaches to the identification and definition of social problems can be distinguished.

Polling for Problems

One perspective on identifying social problems is the consideration of individual perceptions of social conditions that are viewed as problematic. Certainly the opinions, attitudes, and beliefs of members of society as to what constitutes undesirable social conditions furnish a basic source of information concerning social problems. Taken alone, however, this approach has several deficiencies. Although individuals do sometimes share certain ideas, opinions, and values that result in general agreement that some social conditions represent social problems (for example, infant malnutrition), conflicting notions regarding what is or is not a social problem is the more common state of affairs. Rarely is there universal consensus about the undesirability of any social condition.

How, then, can we distinguish conditions that represent actual social problems from conditions that are simply areas of social controversy? It has been suggested by some that a kind of majority-vote criterion be employed in which the identification of social problems would be accomplished by reference to public opinion polls.[4] But this approach ties the identification of social problems directly to public awareness and to the quality of public opinion.

Public opinion is shaped and influenced by powerful interest groups in society and can only reflect certain biases held by society's "opinion makers." Thus, not everyone's values and attitudes are given equal weight in defining a social problem through opinion polls. Those persons who are in positions of power, the decision makers, are those who control the legal, economic, and political institutions. They tend typically to be white, male, middle-aged, and in the upper middle class. They are capable of influencing public opinion and structuring institutions to reflect their own particular value orientation.

Whereas these individuals exert profound influence over both the government and the communications media because of their position, they are often unaware of the problems confronting the majority of the American people. Groups within society often must actively publicize their problems in order to bring them to the attention of these decision makers. The incidence of lung disease among mine workers, for example, was long regarded as a fact of life by mine owners—and even by many workers—until intensive union action influenced the decision makers to enact legislation providing safeguards against hazardous working conditions and compensation to those affected by them. Similarly, racial and sexual discrimination were of little concern to the majority of the white male power structure until the black-power movement and the feminist movement made it impossible for the decision makers to avoid confronting the issues. Mass action is often a prerequisite for social change.

Because recognition of a social problem may result in a drastic change in the social and economic status quo, those members of society who have the capacity to effect change tend to be slow-moving and conservative in their attitudes. Slum landlords are no more enthusiastic about providing adequate housing for poor tenants than weapons manufacturers are about cutting the national defense budget. Even social workers must recognize that their jobs depend on the existence of personal and social problems. Any change in social policy is likely to have adverse effects on some portions of the population.

People in power are generally reluctant to enact changes in social policy unless they believe their own social status to be in jeopardy. During the Great Depression, for example, the threat of a socialist revolution that would change class structure and redistribute property was very disturbing to those in positions of wealth and power. By recognizing poverty as a social problem and adopting social policies to alleviate it, however, these decision makers managed effectively to stabilize their own positions in the social structure.

There is another drawback to using opinion polls to define social problems. Sometimes because of deliberate attempts to misinform the public but often because social problems are complex issues that cannot be understood without knowledge of a vast amount of information, public opinion is frequently based on faulty logic, folk beliefs, or misunderstandings. Attitudes toward marijuana use appear to rest on the premise that it is addictive or that it leads to use of addictive drugs, although neither popular belief is rooted in fact. Given these considerations, it would appear that linking the identification of social problems directly to individual opinions concerning what represents a problematic social condition may not be a fruitful approach.

A second approach defines social problems as conditions that decision makers view as undesirable *and* decide can be ameliorated by social action.[5] Conditions believed to resist corrective measures are therefore not identified as social problems. Thus the problems of the corporate state or the military-industrial complex—considered by many an inevitable outgrowth of the socioeconomic system in this country—would be considered beyond the scope of social problems analysis. Like the previous approach, this perspective largely ignores the fact that some opinions have greater weight than others. And, of course, it is largely these more influential opinions that determine whether ameliorative social action will be feasible.

Prior to the decade of the 1960s, for example, many persons believed that conditions causing millions of Americans to live in poverty represented a major national disgrace. During this period, however, concerted social action directed at improving these conditions was not evident. Accordingly, poverty was a perceived condition to some individuals but was not considered a social problem. In the early 1960s a liberal national administration declared war on poverty, and a series of remedial programs were developed to confront the conditions believed to be responsible for the problem. What changed during the early 1960s—the objective social conditions or the opinions of powerful groups that these conditions were a problem that required some type of corrective action? A more useful approach to identifying social problems would be independent of the opinions and actions of powerful social interests.

A broader perspective on social problems yields a more satisfactory definition. *Social problems are those conditions that have a negative impact on individual and social well-being, as identified by sociological analysis of the organization and functioning of a society.*[6] Rather than relying on public opinion or political interests to determine when a social condition is a social problem, this definition places that decision largely in the hands of professional experts, trained people who will use the knowledge and values of science in their assessments. On the basis of such evaluations, social problems are "conditions deemed detrimental to human well-being on the basis of reasonable evidence."[7]

Of the many social conditions one may deem detrimental to personal and social well-being, not all are serious enough to be labeled and treated as social problems. Hence, one important task of those upon whom we must rely for proper categorization of social conditions is an assessment of seriousness. According to Jerome Manis, indicators of the harmfulness of social

Correctable Conditions

Determining Negative Impact

conditions, or seriousness, are the magnitude, the severity, and the primacy of detrimental conditions.[8] *Magnitude* refers to the actual size or extent of the condition; how many people are affected. Since, for example, public notions about the extent of heroin use differ from the amount of actual use, empirical validation of its extent becomes an important requirement for determining seriousness. The *severity* of a social condition is determined by its actual harmfulness for the individual and for society. How much of a negative impact does the condition have on personal well-being, physical and emotional security, the ability of social institutions to function, and so forth. *Primacy* refers to the importance of a condition as a cause of other harmful conditions. Social conditions "that have many severe effects are more serious than those with lesser ones."[9] Poverty, for example, which it may be argued produces malnutrition, family desertion, unfit housing, and drug use, is more severe in its consequences than, say, the belief in male superiority. Although the latter may have consequences that are personally and socially detrimental, it is unlikely that they would be judged to be as severe as those produced by poverty.

The definition of social problems presented here permits a range of inquiry and investigation that facilitates understanding of the full impact of possible social problems on individuals and societies. Rather than accept popular beliefs or political pronouncements, it asks questions and relies upon empirical data for the answers. Thus conceived, the controversy concerning marijuana use as a social problem becomes a question for sociological investigation and analysis. Does it have an undesirable impact on personal security, satisfaction, or happiness? Does it act to prevent individuals from achieving their potential? Does it restrict individual freedom or available opportunities to pursue certain goals? Does it impede the functioning of individuals in society or have a detrimental impact on the basic organization of the social system? These same questions can be posed in the analysis of crime, mental illness, the corporate state, and, indeed, any conditions that individuals perceive as possible social problems.

Finding answers to such questions is obviously not easy and requires the application of judgment. But the judgment of expert analysts should be better informed than that of the general public, although it will not necessarily lead to different conclusions. The judgment of experts should be based on objective data and assessment supplemented by the values of modern science, including: "(1) individual and group survival . . .; (2) the desirability of knowledge . . .; (3) the freedom to dissent . . .; (4) the sharing of knowledge with others; (5) responsibility for actions harmful to the well-being of humanity."[10] Hence, the method and values of science, applied within the context of a specific society, can provide the sociologist with a more rationally based framework and set of guidelines for the identification and analysis of social problems.

A related approach urges that a basis for defining social problems be found in "basic presuppositions of human life."[11] Such basic suppositions derived from both science and ethics would focus upon issues related to human survival, human community, and human dignity. From consideration of each of these issues a series of postulates based upon humanistic, ethical, and scientific assumptions would emerge to set the standards against which social conditions could be measured.

In this approach, conflicting opinions and beliefs regarding social problems may also become a topic for investigation. Peter Berger emphasizes the importance of considering varying perspectives on a given social issue:

The sociological problem is not so much why some things "go wrong" from the viewpoint of the authorities and the management of the social scene, but how the whole system works in the first place. . . . Take a settlement house in a lower-class slum district trying to wean away teenagers from the publicly disapproved activities of a juvenile gang. The frame of reference within which social workers and police officers define the "problems" of this situation is constituted by the world of middle-class, respectable, publicly approved values. It is a "problem" if teenagers drive around in stolen automobiles, and it is a "solution" if instead they will play group games in a settlement house. But if one changes the frame of reference and looks at the situation from the viewpoint of the leaders of the juvenile gang, the "problems" are defined in the reverse order. . . . What is a "problem" to one social system is the normal routine of things in the other and vice versa. Loyalty and disloyalty, solidarity and deviance, are defined in contradictory terms by the representatives of the two systems. . . . The "problems" that the sociologist will want to solve concern an understanding of the entire social situation, the values and modes of action in *both* systems, and the way in which the two systems coexist in space and time. Indeed, this very ability to look at a situation from the vantage points of competing systems of interpretation is . . . one of the hallmarks of sociological consciousness.[12]

Moreover, the adoption of this broader perspective may aid in the development of a long-term view of social problems and potential solutions as opposed to the short-run, crisis management, "Band-Aid" approach all too common in popular thinking and official responses to social problems. It is becoming evident that contemporary Band-Aid approaches to the problems of crime, for example, may well force future generations to face the same problems, but on a larger scale. Even though public opinion polls indicate that more than 50 percent of the American public favor stiffer prison sentences for those convicted of crimes,[13] a long-term view of this problem suggests that the effects of such a policy (which causes the removel of a parent from the family for an extended period of time and results in bitterness and resentment when the released prisoner is unable to find legitimate employment, for example) may only exacerbate the problem of crime.

Sociology and Social Problems

Our definition of social problems as conditions having a detrimental impact on individual and social well-being as determined by scientific analysis is consistent with the orientation of sociology. It is not compatible, however, with many other approaches to social problems. In any society social problems may be approached in many different ways. Religion provides a system of values and standards of conduct to which both individual and social action might be compared. The law, embodying traditional concepts of appropriate social behavior and elaborate regulation of its conduct, also provides mechanisms by which some social conditions may be altered. With the growth of communications media, journalism and other forms of popular social criticism have often exposed conditions that otherwise would have remained hidden from the public view and unattended. Anthropology, delineating patterns of social action within and across cultures, has contributed to an understanding of social problems through analysis of the structures in which people interact.

Sociology's approach to social problems permits an understanding somewhat different from those described above. Sociologists are social scientists who study the pattern of interpersonal relationships within society. In their investigations of social problems, they collect and analyze data within the context of the society they are studying, using methods common to all science—natural and social—as well as techniques that render more rational the sometimes immense amount of data available on the problems they are concerned with. (Some of these methods are outlined in the Appendix.)

The Promise of Objectivity

Many factors complicate the efforts of the sociologist to understand social problems. In a society as complex as our own, every social problem tends to be multifaceted and interwoven with other aspects of society. Many mutually contradictory interpretations of a single set of data may thus be possible, and the causes of problem conditions are often difficult to ascertain. Since the complexity of social problems is compounded by the fact that the same conditions are often interpreted on the basis of different value perspectives, the sociologist has traditionally relied upon the scientific goal of objectivity to enhance analysis.

The promise of sociology is that it can provide objective knowledge regarding problematic social conditions. As we say in our definition of social problems, sociological analysis yields a body of knowledge that can be used to assess social problems and their consequences for human and social well-being. Sociological knowledge may furnish arguments, for example, that prostitution is less a social problem than a social controversy or that centralization and concentration of power in the economic realm is one root source of several social problems (rather than an inevitable outcome of socioeconomic development that results in the greatest good for the greatest number). Sociology thus can afford members of society a basis for judging whether the arguments and actions of powerful interest groups and individuals are rational or irrational as they pertain to social problems.

This is not to say, however, that sociology represents a panacea for understanding and solving social problems; on the contrary, sociological knowledge alone is far from sufficient to ameliorating social problems. The crucial issue is the use to which that knowledge is put. The case of the Coleman report on equality in education affords a classic example of this point.[14] The sociologists conducting the study found that children from minority backgrounds achieved the greatest levels of academic improvement when they shared classrooms with middle-class children. But the decision based on this finding—to use busing as a solution to the problem of unequal educational opportunities—was a *political* decision.

Sociology is concerned with problems that affect large numbers of people or the entire social system, and its findings bear directly on the interests of the established power structure. To some extent this power structure determines those areas of social life that will be investigated by controlling the allocation of funds for research. And, as in the case of the Coleman report, it may determine the application of sociological research findings. Given the centralization of the communications media, powerful groups are able to exercise some control over the dissemination of such findings. Research results may be used selectively to buttress arguments that certain problems are inevitable, that ameliorative programs are likely to be ineffective, or that such programs would be detrimental to other segments of society. In this sense, diagnoses of social problems and proposals for remedial measures are inextricably intertwined with political processes and power relationships, to the detriment of total objectivity.

Limits of Analysis

In addition, despite scientific training in objective analysis, sociologists cannot entirely escape from their own individual, nonscientific values, preconceptions, and biases in evaluating social problems. The great German sociologist Max Weber once suggested that the biases of social scientists should be made public along with their recommendations in order to create a relevant framework in which to evaluate their theories and interpretations.[15]

The rapidly changing nature of social phenomena further complicates the study of social problems. Conclusions that are valid today may be invalid under altered conditions tomorrow. The mere presence of the social researcher may contribute significantly to the creation of new variables in social relationships. Furthermore, the social scientist cannot control experiments in a manner comparable to that of the natural scientist. In a society geared to technological precision, these limitations sometimes cast a shadow of doubt over the efficacy of social research. It is too often felt that the findings of a sociologist's analysis, if enacted into law or implemented by public policy, should result in immediate amelioration of the conditions examined. Such a view neglects something that sociologists themselves view as given: the fluctuating nature of social phenomena.

Technology and Social Change

Sociologists tend to view the social system as a hierarchical structure, in which individual roles and statuses are interrelated so that the collective purposes of the society and the individual objectives of its members can be realized.[16] In an ideal social system one set of values would be accepted by all, and the needs, goals, and behavior of each member would be smoothly integrated with those of every other member. But in reality values and consequent behavior often differ, needs and goals of system members are not always integrated, and disharmony and friction are aspects of most societies.

One of the most important causes of social conditions of this sort in contemporary American society is the process of *social change*. A wide range of phenomena—urbanization, the population explosion, modern war—may be said to have been produced by the technological changes introduced by the industrial revolution. Sociologists, however, see them largely as the product of the changes in *social relationships* that the technological changes induced—changes in patterns of settlement and nature of work, for example—and that may themselves induce further technological changes.

Technological Enslavement?

Historically, technological progress has functioned to relieve us of many of the burdens of our daily existence—to aid us in coming to grips with our physical environment and in harnessing that environment for our own benefit. Advances in technology have permitted us to spend more time on creative pursuits and leisure-time activities. Although social problems have been associated throughout history with advances in technology, it is widely believed that technological progress has, on balance, done more good than harm. Recently, however, more and more people have begun to voice the opinion that technological advances are a mixed blessing and are themselves a basic generative force of major social problems.[17]

Doubts concerning the positive and beneficial effects of technological advances are rooted in the belief that people may be coming to play the role of servant rather than master to the technologies that have been created. The philosopher and social critic Herbert Marcuse takes this notion of technological enslavement as the central theme in his analysis of modern industrial societies in *One Dimensional Man*.[18] Marcuse sees technology as creating and perpetuating a narrow, repressive, one-dimensional society—a society in which people are dominated by their technologies and unable to conceive of alternative life-styles or systems of social organization. In a similar vein, another sociologist has noted: "Technology is created largely to solve the problems of our lives, yet the social problems in the technological society seem inevitably to become greater."[19]

The scientific-technological revolution which gained impetus during the World War II era has pervaded nearly all aspects of institutional and individual life. General social relationships as well as specific aspects of social life have been transformed in the process. The introduction of television on a mass scale, for example, has left an indelible imprint on American society. Many of our basic assumptions, values, and fundamental beliefs have been transformed during this period of rapid social change. More specific transformations in the political and economic spheres are also apparent. Technology has become fused with large-scale scientific research and big business, resulting in a centralization and concentration of power in the corporate state. Automation not only has eliminated jobs but has left whole categories of workers without a place in the occupational structure. Technology is a force which is reorganizing the conditions of social life at the same time that it is acting as a major axis of contemporary social problems.

A central characteristic of modern society is indeed an *accelerating rate of change*. Although technology is the impetus behind it, this acceleration is both a social and a psychological force:

Important new machines do more than suggest or compel changes in other machines—they suggest novel solutions to social, philosophical, even personal problems. They alter man's total intellectual environment—the way he thinks and looks at the world. . . . For while we tend to focus on only one situation at a time, the increased rate at which situations flow past us vastly complicates the entire structure of life, multiplying the number of roles we must play and the number of choices we are forced to make. This, in turn, accounts for the choking sense of complexity about contemporary life.[20]

In the face of this often bewildering complexity, the individual frequently feels alienated and unable to get a firm grasp on the events of daily life. The office worker who receives a termination notice because the company is re-structuring its management policies is at a loss to explain just why he or she is no longer employed. The mass media inform us that an international cri-sis has brought us to the brink of an awesomely destructive war; yet most of us cannot comprehend the ideologies and mentalities that have caused the crisis. In the face of this increasing complexity and continuing change, the individual, like a billiard ball, often seems propelled by external forces and unable to change the course of events. Yet change is a permanent and basic fact of life in contemporary society. Structural unemployment and social dislocations are ongoing problems, and the individual citizen may be buf-feted about by these forces without comprehending them and powerless to mediate their influence on his or her life. This feeling of personal impotence and the concomitant tendency to concede the future to fate are emerging as fundamental problems of society for the decades ahead.

Nor are these feelings without some justification. Major institutions seem to be growing more and more unresponsive to the opinions and desires of the citizenry. In large part this lack of responsiveness can be traced to a centralization and concentration of power in the political and economic realms. Technological development is one force that promotes this concen-tration of power, for technological experts and those who employ these ex-perts gain a monopoly on the specialized knowledge demanded by de-veloping technologies. And, as the English philosopher Francis Bacon has reminded us: "Knowledge is power."

The widespread use of computer technology, for example, raises the pos-sibility that policy decisions will increasingly be made in small, autono-mous centers of power:

The tendency toward planned and controlled systems has raised questions of whether the operation of a computerized government will render the average citizen ineffective in influencing policy, partly through ignorance, and increasingly through apathy . . . there is the possibility that both the definition of problems and the effec-tive solutions will be made within the constraints of the problem-solving technology. Thus the reliance on cybernetic technology minimizes the average citizen's ability to affect national policy, while at the same time limiting consideration of alternatives in national policy to those that are amenable to the problem-solving tools that are available.[21]

This type of unresponsiveness to the opinions, the interests, and the needs of the citizenry on the part of the major political and economic institutions accounts for the growing concern over the "crisis of confidence" in the dom-inant institutions in American society.

Within this setting, social problems occur and must be analyzed. Al-though feelings of personal powerlessness and alienation may dictate how we participate in and react to various social processes, they usually are not viewed as explanations of the various social problems we will be con-sidering in this book. They should be seen instead as part of the context within which certain social processes take place.

Social Processes: Insight into Social Problems

Social process refers to the manner in which groups operate, especially the ways in which individuals pattern their interaction within them. Social processes are identifiable, patterned sets of repetitive social actions that may be observed over a period of time. To understand social processes one must be aware of the availability of roles within a group, how roles are acted out, and the development and acceptance of norms as guides for behavior. Under certain conditions some social processes create circumstances that we refer to as social problems.

We cannot assume, however, that such circumstances are necessarily caused by the same social processes just because they are all called social problems. It is unrealistic to expect one explanation to fit all the conditions defined as social problems. After all, conditions such as crime, illness, pollution, worker frustration, and overpopulation have little in common except for their negative impact on individual and social well-being. It is more realistic, therefore, to accept the possibility that several social processes may be used as explanations of social problem conditions, depending upon the specific problem being analyzed. As the facts seem to fit, one or another explanation may be used to get at the root of a problem. And, at times, more than one explanation often contributes in some manner to an overall understanding of social problems. For our purposes, three social processes —value conflict, social disorganization, and deviance—will be used to help understand the social problems considered in this book.

Value Conflict

Sociologists often notice a time lag between the occurrence of a phenomenon and the change in social relationships or ideas required to accommodate it; this is called *culture lag*.[22] Advances in medical technology, for example, now make it possible to transplant the heart of a deceased patient into an otherwise normal patient with a diseased heart; however, we have yet to answer fully the question of what exactly constitutes death. Until the philosophical, religious, and scientific authorities can agree on an unequivocal definition, these advances of technology may be perceived as being out of step with the values and beliefs of society in some way. In such situations, it is the absence of change to accommodate the new technological phenomenon that creates a problem.

Whether everyone agrees on what death is seems less important than whether everyone values life. The slight qualms caused by an uncertain cultural definition of death is usually less important in society than more serious *value conflicts*. In a society composed of a heterogeneous population, the conflicting values held by disparate groups—urban versus rural, young versus old, one religious or ethnic group versus another—often play a significant role in the genesis of a social problem as well as create important obstacles to be overcome in its solution.

Significant portions of the population are socialized to accept values that are contrary to those of others. The incompatibility of such basic interests can be very deeply rooted and may instigate actual physical violence. Racial violence in the United States and religious violence in Northern Ireland are both examples of social problems growing out of value conflict. Value positions may also be a result of special interest considerations. Physicians have opposed national health insurance programs for fear such programs would jeopardize their favored economic position. In either case, whether a result of cultural commitments or special interests, value conflicts can serve as a basis for social problems.

Individuals growing up in a society of conflicting values may find it difficult to develop their own value codes unless they are firmly socialized into a value system cut off from the larger society, such as that of the Amish. Modern American society, so various in its ethnic, religious, and social makeup, contains few universal values to serve as standards in times of conflict and controversy. Indeed, as Table 1.1 shows, some of those values usually thought to be most traditional and widely accepted in our society are not accepted by substantial numbers. Among American parents asked about values they believe in and want to pass on to their children, one-fifth or more reject the belief in life after death, having sexual relations only within the marriage relationship, saving money, commitment to their country under any circumstances, and trusting those people in authority.

| | The Transmission of Values to Children | | Table 1.1 |
	Believe and Want Children To Believe %	Have Doubts but Still Want To Teach to Children %	Don't Believe and Don't Want To Pass on to Children %
It's not important to win; it's how the game is played	71	21	8
The only way to get ahead is hard work	65	31	3
Duty before pleasure	58	33	9
Any prejudice is morally wrong	51	33	15
There is life after death	51	27	21
Happiness is possible without money	50	36	13
Having sex outside of marriage is morally wrong	47	25	28
Everybody should save money even if it means doing without things right now	42	37	20
People are basically honest	37	47	16
My country right or wrong	34	41	24
People in authority know best	13	56	30

Source: "A 'New Breed' Emerges," *Family Weekly* (1978, January 1), p. 4.
NOTE: "Not sures" not included.
© The General Mills American Family Report 1976–77: *Raising Children in a Changing Society.* Reprinted by permission of General Mills, Inc., 9200 Wayzata Blvd., Minneapolis, Minn. 55440.

A recent assessment of public opinion surveys of personal, social and political values showed substantial social class differences.[23] In general, the lower middle class places more emphasis on the importance of hard work, frugality, avoiding debt, economic security and material possessions. The upper middle class, on the other hand, stressed "self-fulfillment," less emphasis on money, and making fewer sacrifices for one's children. Of equal interest, though, are the differences in social and political values. By substantial differences over the lower middle class, the upper middle class favors abortion on demand, does not believe that homosexuality and adultery are always wrong, and supports changes in traditional sex roles.

Social Disorganization

When value commitments are weak and generally ineffective, social roles and patterns of interaction become confused and lack necessary coordination. Such confusion tends to disorganize society. *Social disorganization* occurs when certain social standards and social rules lose their meaning and relevance and fail to provide predictable expectations as guidelines for social conduct. From the social disorganization perspective, society is seen as a system of "needs" that a stable complex of social institutions functions to fulfill. This simply means that in order for people to live cooperatively in groups, there are certain problems they must solve. For example, the group must acquire goods and services for consumption; it must make decisions regarding goals and priorities; it must allocate rewards and punishments in a manner consistent with these goals; it must protect itself; and it must train and socialize its members into its practices and values.[24]

Understood in this light, social institutions are patterns of behavior that have some useful consequences for solutions to these problems. The economy is an institution that functions to produce goods and services, for example. Whereas the polity functions to adjust goals and priorities, the family institution provides solutions to problems of procreation and socialization.

The stability of social institutions such as these is based on social values shared by group members. These values delimit the sanctionable properties of social behavior and provide the norms and guidelines for the patterning of social institutions. It is important to note, however, that a system of needs can be provided for by any number of institutional arrangements; American flags and apple pie can be produced by cooperatives as well as by corporations. Social values define what institutional arrangements are appropriate solutions. In so doing, they integrate the complex of social institutions into a relatively harmonious unit and reduce conflicts that may result from incongruent combinations. Such integration is thought to characterize social organization.

The inability of the social system to adequately meet individual and group needs may be traced to forces that result in a breakdown of the social values and rules on which the stability of its institutions rests. During periods of rapid social change, traditional institutions in a society (that is, the established and familiar ways of carrying on social activities and relationships) may be weakened and lose their influence over certain spheres of social life. The institution of the family, for example, has undergone changes in recent times from an extended family structure where children, parents, grandparents, and other relatives were all members of the same household unit to a nuclear family structure consisting only of parents and children. As a result, the social standards that vested the responsibility for caring for elderly citizens in the family unit have had to undergo change in recent times, resulting in a series of social problems concerning the welfare of the elderly. Social disorganization results from conditions or arrangements in which the needs and requirements of individuals or social groups are inadequately met.[25]

Social disorganization may be of three types: normlessness, culture conflict, and breakdown.[26] *Normlessness* means that no rules are available to guide conduct, whereas *culture conflict* implies that at least two sets of competing standards are available. *Breakdown* exists when adhering to available rules fails to produce the desired results, or may actually yield punishment instead. In any case, social disorganization may have personal as well as systemic consequences. Individuals may respond to social disorganization by experiencing personal disorganization, or individual stress which may result in nonconforming or deviant behavior.

For the system, social disorganization may result in change designed to alleviate the problematic elements of the situation so that the needs and requirements of groups and individuals may once again be met. On the other hand, the disorganization may be so serious as to cause the social system to break down. Since the former consequence is often very difficult to achieve and the latter is dependent upon an extensiveness and uniformity of impact that is rare, the most likely consequence of social disorganization is for the system to "continue to operate in a steady state."[27] Although elements of the social system may be disorganized, it continues to operate anyway.

Social values are put to the test in directing behavior toward the fulfillment of a society's system of needs. A successful solution of problems allows structures to remain ongoing and viable. Social disorganization may also be caused by the appearance of problems that the society does not have the capability of solving. Unsuccessful attempts generate disenchantment with values and institutions and may culminate in social disorganization. Further, as societies change they generally become more complex. As this occurs, solutions to society's problems become more difficult to organize. The more complex a society becomes, therefore, the more frequent the incidences of social disorganization will be.

Both the value conflict and social disorganization perspectives attempt to explain social problems by understanding group values, social change, rules, social institutions, and the like. The deviant behavior approach, although usually capitalizing on both the value conflict and social disorganization perspectives, attempts to understand social problems by examining the motives of those involved in the problem and society's reaction to them.

An individual whose behavior varies significantly from the social norms established for persons occupying a particular position in the social structure is often described as *deviant*.[28] Deviant behavior can be classified as either nonconformist or aberrant, however. *Nonconformists* publicly challenge existing norms, usually hoping to change them, while *aberrants* hide

Deviant Behavior

their deviant behavior to escape the penalties for violating norms they do not seek to change.

The extent to which different forms of deviant behavior represent social problems and the severity of the problems stemming from social deviance are highly variable. Criminality may be viewed by the vast majority of the members of society as a serious social problem, whereas homosexuality may be viewed as a far less serious problem by many members of society and may not be viewed as constituting a problem at all by others. Social deviance has two components: (1) the nature of a given social act and (2) the nature of the social response to that act.[29] The second—what members of society think of the behavior, how they evaluate it, and how they react to it—is as important as the first. Attention to both components of deviance leads to the recognition that there may not be consensus among the members of society that certain kinds of drug use or prostitution or homosexuality, to cite a few examples, represent deviant behavior or social problems.

Social deviance, though, is measured against norms that are relative and mutable, and conformity to one set of norms may involve nonconformity to another. Social definitions as to what constitutes deviant behavior also change over time. The increasing social acceptability of marijuana smoking and the current attempts to decriminalize this behavior represent a situation in which changing social definitions and reactions are beginning to move the act of marijuana smoking out of the realm of deviant behavior. Prior to the passage of legislation in 1914, the occasional use of heroin (that at that time was a common ingredient in many patent medicines) does not appear to have been viewed as a form of deviant behavior. Today, heroin use is considered by most people to be a serious violation of social norms. As these examples imply, the exact same behavior may at different times be largely ignored, subject to mild disapproval, or subject to severe social sanctions.

Once a person assumes a deviant role and becomes known for his or her deviant act, attribute or belief, a process of labeling usually occurs.[30] Thus, the individual becomes categorized in the minds of others who respond to him on the basis of the new label. Once the individual is labeled, official and unofficial responses to the behavior tend to isolate the person from conventional groups and force him or her to rely upon those who support the deviance. Hence, the individual's initial attraction to deviant behavior and groups is reinforced as others begin to react to him or her as a criminal or mental patient or homosexual. The community's reaction, then, is an important element in pushing the deviant toward further and more extensive deviance, while serving also to sustain deviant groups.

The nature of the societal response to various forms of norm-violating behavior in part reflects the values and beliefs of powerful groups and persons in society. As we have noted before, those who occupy strategic positions of power and authority possess a disproportionate ability to shape public conceptions and standards of right and wrong, of deviant and nondeviant.[31] The manner in which influential segments of society define a certain behavior largely determines whether that behavior will be treated as deviant or whether it will be treated as simply representing nonconformity to certain social expectations. Deviant behavior, as opposed to nonconformity, is generally viewed as a more serious threat to the social system, a problem of sufficient magnitude that society must "do something" about it.

A Web of Problems

Just as there is overlap and interrelatedness among the three dominant perspectives we are using to understand social problems, the actual social problems discussed in this text do not exist independently of one another. The conditions that give rise to any particular problem are likely to be related in a complex fashion to other problems and the conditions from which they stem. Feelings of powerlessness and apathy derived in part from the unresponsiveness of dominant social institutions to individual needs and desires are not unrelated to problems of mental illness and drug abuse. The problems that an individual experiences in the occupational realm may carry over into family life. A problem such as poverty appears to be related to the problems of family disorganization, delinquency, malnutrition, and mental disorders in ways that are still incompletely understood. Both the understanding of social problems and proposed solutions to them must take into account their overlapping causes and consequences.

An appreciation of the interrelated nature of problems at the institutional level as well as at the individual level will enhance our understanding of social problems in general. The problems of individuals do not have their basis entirely within the person; they are inextricably bound up with conditions that are external to the individual, conditions relating to the social, political, and economic structures in which the individual is embedded. One theory of crime, which emphasizes the dual components of differential social organization and differential association, affords an excellent example of sociological analysis which simultaneously considers both the collective and the individual orders.[32] This theory holds that different segments of the social structure are organized around different sets of norms and values. Thus certain segments are more likely to include and to emphasize norms and values that favor violation of the criminal law, and individuals located within such areas of the social structure are more likely to learn criminal patterns of behavior than individuals located in other areas. Sociological understanding therefore involves a cognizance of the interpenetration of the individual and collective spheres and the manner in which this interrelationship may affect social problems.

Proposed solutions not founded on a recognition of the fundamental connections between different social problems and between problems at different levels of analysis are likely to be so simplistic as to be ineffective. Proposals intended to reduce the amount of deviant behavior in our society are doomed to failure if they are based on the assumption that the causes of such behavior are located entirely within the individual. Recognizing that deviance is as much a product of social and cultural factors as it is of factors within the individual is a necessary first step toward developing rational and plausible remedies.

The Urge To Solve Social Problems

Can social problems actually be solved? Do they really lend themselves to "rational and plausible remedies"? In fact, there are those who believe that all social problems fall into two categories: those that solve themselves and those which are insoluble. This is both an optimistic and a pessimistic view. On the one hand, it implies that some social problems rectify themselves and do not require direct intervention to bring about a solution. If this is true, it does not take into account the form of the so-called solutions. In a complex industrial society like our own, we cannot often afford to allow social problems to resolve themselves in such a natural fashion. We cannot settle for whatever results as the problem runs its course—or, for that matter, tolerate the human suffering that often accompanies social problems as they grind relentlessly toward a natural solution.

On the other hand, this view implies that we are incapable of solving social problems, not because of a lack of intervention skills or, more important, a lack of commitment but because there is something intrinsic in the nature of some problems that defies solution. If this is true, then we have been wasting a great deal of time, energy, and resources that have been directed toward solving our social problems. Most Americans probably believe that it is not true, just as they reject the notion that problems solve themselves. Indeed, one observer has called solving social problems an American national characteristic: "Once an American is faced with a problem, he cannot resist the urge to try solving it."[33] This is not to imply that solving our social problems is without difficulty—difficulty of such magnitude at times that the problems may well appear insoluble. Why are social problems so difficult to solve?

We noted earlier that difficulty begins when we try to reach some consensus on what conditions to label and treat as social problems. In a heterogeneous society like our own, people are differently involved in and differently affected by existing social conditions, and definitions of what is a social problem vary accordingly. Poverty, for example, may be seen as a social evil which must be abolished at all cost, or it may be seen as a deserved situation resulting from laziness, intellectual inferiority, or the breaks of the game. When there is so much disagreement on the basic causes of a problem, it is difficult to focus on a solution that has enough support to be effective.

Solutions often create as well as solve problems. That is, an attempt to solve one social problem may actually generate or contribute to another.[34] Prohibition was an attempt to eradicate alcoholism and related problems. But it failed to do that, and it set the stage as well for the development of organized crime, a problem of some magnitude in contemporary America. Advances in medical science have succeeded in prolonging life, but they also have contributed to the problem of providing for the physical and social needs of the elderly. Although court-imposed busing has alleviated racial imbalance in the public schools, it also appears in many cases to have intensified antagonism between the races. Controlling industrial pollution has helped cleanse the air and water, but it also has forced some industries to relocate.

Of course, we should never expect to have a problem-free society. Any set of social conditions is bound to be problematic to one group or another. We may, however, on the basis of certain consensual values, detemine that certain problems are more or less severe to the society as a whole and structure intervention priorities on that basis. To most of us, death at an early age is a more important issue than the social and emotional problems created by old age. Hence, for the sake of longer life, we are willing to accept the latter problems and hope to find ways to alleviate them eventually.

On the whole, we have not been very successful in solving our social problems, especially those that do not appear amenable to technological solutions. Perhaps one reason for this is that we tend to search for technological utopias, where machines and modern technology will correct our problems without altering traditional social patterns to any appreciable degree. This may be only logical, since technology has served our society well in so many other ways; but it may also result from our unwillingness to question basic value commitments and institutional arrangements. Such questioning, of course, is difficult, especially for those whom the social system has served fairly well. Nevertheless, it may be our only hope of ridding society of some of its more persistent and debilitating social problems.

Solving social problems is not only difficult but expensive. Whether we speak of abolishing poverty, rehabilitating the criminal, or cleaning up our air and water, social action is dependent on the expenditure of public funds. Again, values, especially those of society's decision makers, play a large part in dictating whether tax dollars are expended for the solution of social problems or for other demands made on public funds.

Human values play a major role not only in the definition of certain conditions as problems and the decision to seek remedies but also in determining possible solutions. We have been unsuccessful in our attempts to solve many of our major social problems primarily because we have been unable to focus on the proper targets. The values of the majority of Americans simply exclude from the list of viable intervention strategies those that would alter traditional institutional arrangements. After all, as was stated earlier, these arrangements have served *most* of us pretty well—most of us are affluent, comfortable, secure, noncriminal, mentally healthy, receiving adequate medical care, and so on. Perhaps those who do not share these attributes are simply casualties of a complex urban-industrial society. And since it is this kind of society that has done pretty well by most of us, then social problems and some human casualties may just be the price we have to pay —until it becomes more than we can afford.

Ultimately, it is the cost of social problems that leads to reform. Drug rehabilitation programs, community public health centers, and job training centers have been provided only when maintenance of the status quo has become too costly, not just in economic terms but in terms of crime, social unrest, and a disabled population. Changes have been slow to come, but progress has been made over the years. Increasingly, the old explanations of social phenomena are giving way to more scientifically valid ones. More and more the decision makers are being forced to recognize that social problems are the product of flaws in the social structure itself and that maintenance of the status quo will not solve the problems confronting modern American society.

Summary

Our complex, rapidly changing, and multifaceted society contains many problems that are salient concerns among the populace. A sociological perspective on social problems distinguishes between private troubles (matters that may cause individual misery and suffering but do not necessarily affect substantial segments of the social system) and public issues (conditions that involve basic social institutions and have a negative impact on large numbers of people). The sociologist studying social problems is concerned not with private troubles but with matters involving the operation and functioning of major social institutions and with conditions affecting the welfare of significant portions of the population.

Social controversies involve public debate over the alleged harmfulness of a particular social condition where the manifest harm of that condition has not been firmly established. In some cases a social controversy may lead to public recognition that a certain social condition does in fact have negative consequences for substantial numbers of people.

In a diverse society there will seldom be a consensus of opinion as to what constitute social problems, mainly because opinion of this sort is strongly subject to individual values. Moreover, such values often seem to exert a disproportionate influence on public conceptions of problematic social conditions. Social problems must be identified and defined independently of the opinions and actions of powerful interest groups in the society.

Scientific criteria provide a more objective and rational approach to defining social problems than the divergent opinions and beliefs held by different groups and members of society. Thus it is preferable to define social problems as *those conditions identified by sociological analysis of the organization and functioning of a society that have a negative impact on individual and social well-being.*

Sociological knowledge, however, is not purely objective, and it does not represent a panacea for understanding and ameliorating social problems. Nor are social scientists possessed of absolute wisdom: "All that is suggested here is to permit the knowledge and values of science to identify and to assess conditions deemed harmful to . . . society."[35]

Technological advances and social change are major factors in the generation and perpetuation of social problems. Related to these broad structural factors is the trend toward growing feelings of powerlessness, apathy, and alienation among individual members of society. In the face of the complexity of American society, the concentration of power in certain of its major institutions, and the impact of social change, individuals in contemporary society often feel buffeted about by forces they cannot understand and that they are unable to modify or influence to accommodate their own needs or desires. Many of our social problems arise out of this context.

Three distinct and identifiable social processes provide perceptual frameworks for analyzing substantive social problems: value conflict, social disorganization, and deviant behavior. Each of the three provides a perspective or an approach—a framework that includes some factors and excludes others. Hence the words *process, approach,* and *framework* are used interchangeably.

The *value conflict* perspective recognizes that various groups in society may possess different and sometimes conflicting values. When the values and interests of one group clash with those held by another group, a social problem may arise. In the value conflict approach, emphasis is placed on the heterogeneity of our society; the resulting multitude of special interests and value orientations creates a situation where collisions and clashes often occur.

The *social disorganization* approach focuses on the inadequacy of a society's institutional arrangements for meeting the needs of individuals and social groups. Where this occurs, social norms that serve to regulate conduct—to prescribe desired forms of behavior and proscribe undesired forms—lose their potency. Conduct that violates the ideal normative standards of a society is more likely to occur in those areas or segments of the social structure where disorganization prevails.

Rapid social change is one root cause of much social disorganization, for during such times older norms are no longer relevant or appropriate to the changing circumstances, and new standards often have not yet emerged. In view of the accelerating rate of change in American society, social disorganization is likely to be an integral feature of certain areas of our society for some time to come.

A third explanatory framework, that of *deviant behavior,* focuses on individual conduct that violates social norms. Both the behavior of an individual and the responses of groups and other individuals to it determine the extent to which the behavior will be regarded as a serious violation of social standards. Accordingly, what in the eyes of one group violates a norm and is considered deviant is likely to be considered nondeviant by some other groups. Norms supported by powerful and influential groups have the greatest potential for determining which behaviors will be regarded as deviant. Any study of individual deviance must, of course, include an analysis of its interrelationship with the institutional structure of society.

Conditions giving rise to social problems tend to be interrelated, with overlapping causes and consequences. The interrelated nature of social problems at both the institutional and individual levels plays a major role in our understanding of social problems and of their solutions. Social problems are difficult to solve because of lack of agreement on what problems are, their causes and possible solutions. In all of these questions, human values play a major role.

Notes

[1] C. Wright Mills, *The Sociological Imagination* (New York: Oxford University Press, 1959), p. 8

[2] Ibid., p. 9.

[3] A recent discussion of the issue of social problem identification and definition is presented by

Dean D. Knudsen, "Virtues, Values and Victims: Toward a Theory of Social Problems," *Sociological Focus* 11 (August 1978), 173–184.

⁴This approach is discussed in Jerome G. Manis, "The Concept of Social Problems: Vox Populi and Sociological Analysis," *Social Problems* 21 (1974), 306–307.

⁵Earl Rubingron and Martin S. Weinberg, *The Study of Social Problems* (New York: Oxford University Press, 1971), pp. 5–6.

⁶This definition is an adaptation of one proposed by Jerome Manis, *Analyzing Social Problems* (New York: Praeger, 1976), p. 25.

⁷Ibid., p. 95.

⁸Ibid., p. 102.

⁹Ibid., p. 109.

¹⁰Manis, *The Concept of Social Problems*, p. 313.

¹¹Knudsen, *Virtues, Values and Victims: Toward a Theory of Social Problems*, p. 182.

¹²Peter L. Berger, *Invitation to Sociology: A Humanistic Perspective* (New York: Doubleday, 1963), pp. 37–38.

¹³*Gallup Opinion Index*, Report No. 123, September 1975, p. 17; Report No. 113, November 1974, p. 5.

¹⁴James S. Coleman et al., *Equality of Educational Opportunity*, U.S. Department of Health, Education, and Welfare (Washington, D.C.: Government Printing Office, 1966).

¹⁵Julien Freund, *The Sociology of Max Weber* (New York: Pantheon, 1968), pp. 48–59.

¹⁶For an authoritative treatment of social systems analysis, see Robert K. Merton, *Social Theory and Social Structure*, enl. ed. (New York: Free Press, 1968).

¹⁷A discussion of this and related issues may be found in Harrison Brown, *The Human Future Revisited* (New York: Norton, 1978); David F. Noble, *America by Design* (New York: Knopf, 1977); Langdon Winner, *Autonomous Technology* (Cambridge, Mass.: MIT Press, 1977).

¹⁸Herbert Marcuse, *One Dimensional Man* (Boston: Beacon Press, 1964).

¹⁹Jack D. Douglas, *Defining America's Social Problems* (Englewood Cliffs, N.J.: Prentice-Hall, 1974), p. 257.

²⁰Alvin Toffler, *Future Shock* (New York: Bantam Books, 1970), pp. 29, 33–34.

²¹Robert Perrucci and Marc Pilisuk, *The Triple Revolution Emerging* (Boston: Little, Brown, 1971), p. 159.

²²William F. Ogburn, *Social Change* (New York: Huebsch, 1923), pp. 200–237.

²³Everett Ladd, Jr., "The New Lines are Drawn: Class and Ideology in America," *Public Opinion* (July/August 1978), pp. 48–53.

²⁴Talcott Parsons, *The Social System* (New York: Free Press, 1951).

²⁵Robert K. Merton and Robert Nisbet, *Contemporary Social Problems* (New York: Harcourt, 1971), pp. 820–821.

²⁶Earl Rubington and Martin S. Weinberg, *The Study of Social Problems*, 2nd ed. (New York: Oxford University Press, 1977), p. 62.

²⁷Ibid., p. 63.

²⁸Merton and Nisbet, *Contemporary Social Problems*, p. 824.

²⁹For a more elaborate discussion of the deviance process, see Frank R. Scarpitti and Paul T. McFarlane, *Deviance: Action, Reaction, Interaction* (Reading, Mass.: Addison-Wesley, 1975), chap. 1.

³⁰The labeling process is discussed fully in Edwin M. Schur, *Labeling Deviant Behavior* (New York: Harper & Row, 1971).

³¹This idea is discussed more thoroughly in Richard Quinney, *The Social Reality of Crime* Boston: Little, Brown, 1970).

³²Edwin H. Sutherland and Donald R. Cressey, *Criminology*, 9th ed. (Philadelphia: Lippincott, 1974), chap. 4.

³³Russell Baker, "Observer: Unsolved Problems Needed," *New York Times*, 20 April 1965, p. 38.

³⁴Edwin M. Schur, "Recent Social Problems Tests: An Essay Review," *Social Problems* 10 (1963), 287–292.

³⁵Jerome G. Manis, "Assessing the Seriousness of Social Problems," *Social Problems* 22 (1974), 7–8.

Problems of Social Institutions

Social institutions are products of human interaction; they are ways of performing or carrying out important social activities that have become routinized, patterned, and established within a given society. These established patterns serve to shape and organize the ongoing day-to-day activities of members of society. People's activities become predictable when they follow such institutionalized patterns. Thus, for example, there is no need for each individual to learn a set of role responsibilities and expectations through actual experience because these are learned as part of the group's established and accepted ways and as such define the rights and obligations of any individual in that role. Social institutions therefore serve a crucial social function: the complexity of contemporary life is simplified immeasurably through the availability of these patterns of everyday activities.

Accordingly, institutions are the very foundation of a society. Major institutions fulfill two primary requirements of the social system. Within each institutional sphere is developed a set of norms or laws that individuals are expected to follow and which provides stability and order in social life. But institutions are also designed to satisfy basic needs of the members of society. For example, the institution of work serves to pattern the productive activities of individuals so as to provide a regular flow of needed goods and services. Without an organized way of performing work activities, individuals might engage in separate types of work which do not mesh sufficiently to provide stability in the economic realm. At the same time, work fulfills the individual's need to earn a livelihood. But, for a variety of reasons, institutions do not always fulfill these two requirements as well as they might.

Because our society is stratified, and power, wealth, and prestige are unevenly distributed, some groups are better able than others to shape institutions to serve their own interests. Groups that lack the bases of social power and the ability to shape institutions to serve their own ends are in a position of social inequality. The fact that certain segments of the population receive less than their proportionate share of the benefits of society is built into the institutional structure of a stratified society. Systematic inequalities in our basic institutions and the accompanying conflicts of values and interests among different segments of society constitute a central focus of the chapters in this section.

The nature of a society's institutions has a profound impact on the character and quality of life in the society. Since they touch the lives of large numbers of people in crucial ways, institutions are a source not only of social stability but at times of social conflict and disorganization as well. Because institutions are rooted in habits and customs, they tend to change more slowly than the conditions of life among the members of society. Owing to this institutional inertia, such changes that do occur frequently entail considerable friction and may have disorganizing consequences. On the other hand, they may also produce the conflict that is the forerunner of needed changes in the structure of society.

Major institutions in a state of disorganization or conflict are no longer able to perform the dual functions of maintaining social stability and satisfying individual needs. The result is widespread disaffection and alienation among the citizenry, with repercussions felt throughout society. In this section we shall explore the social problems that stem from conflict and disorganization in the major institutional areas of American society.

The Family

2

Trends in American Family Life
Preindustrial Families / Industrial Families

Sociological Perspectives on Family Problems
The Evolutionary Approach / The Revisionist Approach

Marriage—Ties That Bind
Divorce Rates / Creative Divorce /
Separation—Conflict Unresolved / Illegitimacy /
Single-Parent Families

The Family and Changing Sex Roles

The Changing Roles of Family Members
Wife, Mother, Housekeeper—Happily Ever After? /
Husband, Father: Provider under Pressure /
Children—Complexities of Growing Up /
Adolescent Ambivalence / Untimely Retirement

Can the Family Survive?
Legislative: A Gauge of Changing Attitudes /
Day Care: Federal Beneficence or Coercion? /
Single-Parent Adoptions / Communal Families / Open Marriage

Summary

Notes

To the producers of American television, the family's function is obvious. The depiction of American families as consumers of products and services is largely accurate.

Of late, however, television has begun to move away from the typical portrayal of family composition. The depiction of the family as father, mother, and two children—usually one boy, one girl—is still dominant, but it does not have sole possession of the airwaves. This is justifiable. Only 7 percent of all American families are composed of a father, mother, and two children. Shows with families that have several children are now presented. Single-parent households have arrived on network television. The times have changed so drastically that even cohabitation of unmarried males and females can now be portrayed in prime time.

There is mounting evidence that as a unit of social organization, the American family is unstable. More than a million couples are now divorced each year in the United States. The past 15 years has witnessed the growth of a generation gap between parents and their children; parental percepts are openly disregarded almost as soon as the children learn to talk back. Changes in sexual mores have made drastic inroads on the fidelity once presumed standard in conjugal relationships. Roles within the family structure are subject to strain. The feminist movement has challenged many of the previously accepted sex role differentiations within the family. For the first time in the history of the country, a majority of women are now officially engaged in the labor force. This combines with the more general rejection of male dominated households to result in tension and stress within families. In many cases, husbands who have traditionally been regarded as family providers are working harder than ever themselves, to the exclusion of their parental role.

Throughout our history the family's worth has preoccupied many investigators, including sociologists. Continued concern today seems justified since the family has functioned as an institution basic to almost all societies. Society entrusts it with the regulation of sexual activity and procreation, the socialization of children, and the physical care of its members and makes it the focus of psychological support and emotional security for the individual. Traditionally, of course, the family has shared these functions with other social institutions, such as the church, school, or place of work. The precarious position of the family in modern society, however, stems from the fact that the family's share of these functions has been dwindling while other institutions have taken on greater responsibilities. Typically, the stability of the family is grounded in the consensual values of its members and of society in general. The advance of industrialization has done much to throw the shared values into disarray. The family no longer functions as the center of many aspects of our lives, as it once did. One prime example is the loss of the family's function as the basic unit of work. The social problems relevant to the study of the family are the result of changing societal conditions and the inadequacy of those changes to provide for alternative measures of expression for the family. This is precisely the reason that the social disorganization approach to the study of the family will be utilized in this chapter. Divorce, separation, and illegitimacy are only a few of the problems resulting from the failure of society to assist families in adapting to modern social situations.

In the United States today, the family is left mainly with the functions of consumption and personal fulfillment and security. Yet adjustments have been slow, and alternative family structures and values—perhaps more congruent with the family's increasingly limited role in society—have not been institutionalized. As a result, many family functions have been left poorly defined, and social disorganization pervades. What are legitimate grounds for divorce? How can parents relate to children with vastly different life experiences? These are commonplace questions to which traditional social structures no longer seem to provide viable answers.

Because the lives of so many Americans revolve around the families in which they live, some understanding of changes in the family's structure and function is particularly important. Using the social disorganization perspective, this chapter will examine the problems of the family in American society and its prospects of the future that are currently being negotiated in bedrooms, courtrooms, boardrooms and legislatures.

Trends in American Family Life

The family has been an important unit of social organization in our country since its earliest day. Whereas in Latin America the first European presence was primarily a rapacious one in that the invaders intended to take what wealth they could and return to Europe, in North America the early Europeans came with the hope of colonizing and settling the land. Settlement was accomplished, for the most part, by small groups of families. The relative stability of American society, up to the present, can be partially ascribed to the establishment and reinforcement of these early family patterns.

Preindustrial Families

Much of early American family life took place within communal or utopian societies, such as that of the Puritans in New England. In Puritan families the father was vested with total authority. His wife and children were to respect and obey him in all worldly matters But the family itself was subject to the strict religious, social, and moral norms of the community. Social control was generally effective; what deviations did occur were harshly sanctioned. As the colony prospered, stresses in the communal arrangements grew greater. Deviant or dissatisfied members departed, often at the express bidding of the community. Those banished from one community founded another. But social stresses could not be altogether avoided. Lawsuits involving property rights and farming and grazing rights increased markedly, in both the new communities and the old. The communal system could not respond adequately to these problems, especially when subjected to outside pressures. With the influx of new cultural groups, family life in New England and other areas took on the character of European family life of the time.

The colonial period was one in which the institutions of property and family were virtually inseparable. The British legal systems of primogeniture and entail guaranteed that a family's landholdings would be wholly retained by its heirs. Under this system the leading families of the colonial period evolved into units with more substantial social power than legislatures, which were severely limited. Within such families the husband and father still enjoyed complete authority even though the wife might be entrusted with the actual management of the household.

The American Revolution ended primogeniture and entail. Most of the landed estates were broken up as a result, a move that gave impetus not only to national expansion but to much greater freedom within the social structure. Both of these conditions had an effect on the family patterns that were to emerge in the nineteenth century.

Ideas of communal living reappeared in the nineteenth century, and many experiments were tried. The Oneida community in New York State practiced an idealistic form of free love and held property in common; socialist experiments, such as that at New Harmony, Indiana, lasted for years in the 1840's. The Mormons, organizing themselves in response to a religious vision, practiced polygamy in all their settlements, a custom so opposed to prevailing norms they were forced to move farther westward. In Utah their settlement flourished with its polygynous family structure intact; yet legislation upholding monogamy was a condition of Utah's acceptance into the Union in 1896. From this fact alone, it is clear that the major expansion of the country and the consolidation of its enterprises were in the hands of families of another character.

The family unit that faced the challenges of settlement on the American frontier was usually of the extended type, in which three generations lived together as a single large household. In such families the authority of the

husband and father was virtually that of an Old Testament patriarch. The wife and mother was responsible for the ordering of the household and for the domestic training of female children. Grandmothers and aunts, if present, shared in these responsibilities. The children helped work the land, and because there was much to be done, large families were preferred. Typically the extended family included married children as well as their spouses.

On the frontier, the extended family was often the sole unit of social organization, sustained by strong religious beliefs, a rigid moral code, and hard cooperative work. Significantly, the family patterns of many of the European immigrants who came to America after 1840 were well suited to the frontier situation. The social structure of the communities established by Germans, Scandinavians, Poles, and others resembled the towns and villages the immigrants had left in Europe, as well as those they encountered in the New World.

Although the family patterns of the frontier were very similar to patterns developed earlier in Europe, those which accompanied the rise of American cities and towns were historically unique. New family structures developed in response to the Industrial Revolution and the growth of cities. In preindustrial society, the family had produced most of the major needs of society: food, clothing, and shelter. The coming of factory production relieved the family of most of these functions. Improved systems of transportation, most

The Oneida Community: Members of this nineteenth century commune in New York held property in common and practiced an idealistic form of free love.

Industrial Families

notably the railroad and steamboat, made possible a wider and faster distribution of goods as well, eliminating local, family-based distribution systems.

As industrialism began to usurp the production and distribution functions of the family, however, it created a growing need for labor. Prospective workers were drawn off the land and into the growing towns and cities. Farm girls were employed in early textile mills, largely because the making of cloth had been part of their domestic function at home. Mechanics and engineers were drawn to the workshops that produced the machines of the new age. Increasing numbers of men, women, and children were required to run the machines and factories of the industrial age.

By midcentury, several new trends in family life were evident. Women, no longer bound to the home, were freed from parental authority, although they were "on their honor" to respect their upbringing. The strains of this situation may account for the trend to earlier marriages that emerged at this time. It was in this period, too, that the pressure of business began to fall more heavily on the husband and father, reducing his time for participating in family life. In the growing middle classes, the responsibility for home life fell increasingly to the wife, and there were indications of growing permissiveness in child rearing—trends that became even more pronounced after the Civil War.

The war itself freed from slavery a vast number of blacks whose family life had been overwhelmingly affected by the circumstances of that institution. Slaves had been economic assets, property to be bought, sold, and even bred at will. In such conditions, any family attachments that developed were at best inconvenient. Formalized marriage was generally denied to slaves; intercourse was encouraged, however, since the children of such unions constituted additional economic assets. Fathers were not allowed to assume any familial responsibility, however, and the slave child was normally born into a family where a mother was the only parent.[1] Even among freed blacks this pattern persisted for some time. Few black fathers could support a family; there was no place for uneducated, unskilled black labor. The available work was mostly in the agricultural South and paid poorly. Consequently, the black mother, normally working as a domestic or a nursemaid, was the family provider by default.

Into the expanding industrial economy that characterized the United States after the Civil War, and into the cities which were its locus, came millions of immigrants. More and more families that immigrated after 1965 were from southern and central Europe. In family customs these immigrants—Italians and Jews and Slavic peoples—varied widely, but most came from rural villages and towns where some sort of extended family arrangement was common.

Since they could be hired for wages lower than those paid to men, many immigrant women and children found work in factories in the new country. Nonetheless, it was primarily the men who worked in the industries. When the immigrant husband was the sole provider, the wife was forced into the home, but without the community connections that had characterized her life in Europe. Child raising became primarily her responsibility, although the husband often retained the authority typical of the extended family arrangement. Combating whatever ethnic standards the immigrant mother might inculcate, however, were the schools of the period, whose policy was to Americanize the immigrant child. Under these conditions, ethnic family patterns were slowly broken down by an increasingly urbanized, industrialized environment. The national mood, if not the national policy, was assimilation. Substituted for the distinctive customs and life of the extended ethnic family was the nuclear family of the twentieth century.

Although the American family has shown itself capable of incredible strength and energy, it has also revealed unsuspected submissiveness to any external authority that challenges it. During the frontier days it amply demonstrated its ability to monitor itself and ensure its survival; but when government and business appeared and took over, it readily submitted to outside direction. There are many examples of this submission, from the effect of public education in freeing the children from family influence to the breakdown of traditional family roles due to the demands of business and professional careers. Such destruction of family cohesiveness began in small ways and proceeded by almost imperceptible degrees; many of its manifestations were entrenched and solidified before they were even noted. And in the aggregate, the consequences of industrialization finally altered the very fabric of family life and changed the traditional roles of its members.

Sociological Perspectives on Family Problems

The viewpoint we bring to bear on the problems of the family must inevitably influence the conclusions we reach. In current sociology, two broad perspectives on family problems can be distinguished: the evolutionary and the revisionist.

The Evolutionary Approach

Most sociologists maintain that the American family, though beset by formidable problems, has maintained a modicum of stability by evolving along with other institutions and accommodating itself to the changes taking place in the larger society. It continues to serve the vital functions of producing children, assuming responsibility for their early socialization, and forming the framework within which sexual activity can legitimately take place.

The modern industrial state is, of course, the major external reality to which the family has had to adjust. By demanding greater geographical mobility, industrialization rendered the extended family of earlier eras obsolete and substituted a smaller, less cumbersome unit better suited to traveling from job to job. The modern nuclear family is a more specialized unit than its predecessor, and for that reason it is even more important.[2]

These adjustments have had both positive and negative effects. The father's increased absence from the home, for instance, was at first seen as potentially disruptive but actually resulted in a democratization of family relationships. Some researchers have seen a change from an authoritarian to a corporate type of family structure.[3]

Such adjustments imply an essentially passive and melleable family structure. But one observer, sociologist William J. Goode, has modified this view somewhat by suggesting a reciprocal relationship between family and society. He believes that the family may, in fact, have been a source of independent change, and that change within it facilitated the more comprehensive changes of industrialization.[4]

The social changes of the twentieth century have further accentuated this interdependence. In a society increasingly dedicated to success and upward mobility, more and more mothers as well as fathers have been required to turn their lives outward. More married women now work than ever before in our history, sharing their husbands' preoccupation with the acquisition of greater wealth and position. The larger and more varied family units of earlier days probably also served to cushion the shocks of generational conflicts. In our urban and industrial society, children as well as parents have become subject to influences and interests outside the home. Parental authority is no longer an unquestioned fact, and open disagreement with one's elders is no longer unthinkable. In recent years this has led to what is now called the generation gap, although, in fact, such a gap may always have existed in America.

The Revisionist Approach

The revisionist, unlike the evolutionist, maintains that there is a *qualitative* difference in today's problems as compared with those of the past, reflecting a substantial and essential change in the structure and functions of the contemporary family. The revisionist believes that these problems are potentially so disruptive as to threaten the family's very survival as an institution. In the climate of contemporary life, old problems such as the generation gap, the role of women, and alienation in the family have acquired new and ominous significance.

W. F. Ogburn, one of the first to study such problems from this viewpoint, concluded that the family is in deep trouble.[5] The importance of its traditional functions—providing members with food, clothing, protection, and support against hardships and threats from the environment—could hardly be overstated. But in contemporary America, he feels, it has lost these functions and failed to assume any significant new ones. In effect, like many a good executive with a gift for organization, it has worked itself out of a job.

Whether the family will metamorphize into some new and unrecognizable form or will simply become more specialized while retaining important functions, its present milieu can best be described from the perspective of social disorganization. Modern American society is making unprecedented demands upon the family, demands to which it has yet to adapt completely, calling for new structural arrangements, new values, and new interrelations with other social institutions. For example, the fact that the nuclear family has for the most part replaced the extended family as a model structure, thus adapting to the pressures for mobility and careerism exerted by the modern economy, has created other problems. Care for the elderly, the generation gap, the expanding role of women in society, and even the nature of marriage itself all present problems that are being negotiated both informally in everyday social situations and formally in the legal and legislative institutions of our society.

The range of solutions to family problems now being explored indicates that whatever functions the family may have in the future, it will probably be characterized by a wider variety of acceptable structural arrangements. It appears that one family form cannot meet the demands of all contemporary social situations. Thus, family problems and the prospects for alleviating them can best be assessed by examining the specific components of family structures and the stresses to which society subjects them. Perhaps with this information we can begin to determine the future of the family.

Marriage—Ties That Bind

The single most important factor determining the quality of family life is the quality of the marriage that supports it. In preindustrial days, a number of basic social and economic functions served, in effect, to solder the union between husband and wife. Enlightened self-interest, if nothing else, dictated staying together under almost any circumstances.

As these functions changed, the "ties that bind" married couples changed with them. Sheer survival was no longer a paramount preoccupation, and emotional needs assumed greater importance. Marriage was now expected to supply not only security from physical want but also emotional and sexual fulfillment, as well as an antidote against the abrasiveness of contemporary life and a haven from the loneliness and isolation of city existence. It was a tall order. Increasingly, marriages have warped or broken apart under the new burdens placed on them.

Paradoxically, the changed function of marriage contains the *potential* for a more personally satisfying relationship between husband and wife; the trouble is that it has also removed certain buffers to marital conflict that the earlier extended family provided. Modern nuclear family structure often results in excessive mutual dependence of husband and wife, especially after the children are grown and gone. In such an atmosphere the importance of even minor discord can become greatly magnified. However, it is not conflict per se but *unresolved* conflict that takes its greatest toll on marriage.[6] Too often neither partner knows how to compromise; for lack of such constructive flexibility marital disputes reach a deadlock, and generally the no-man's-land of discord may begin to loom larger than the areas of agreement between husband and wife. Today's divorce trends indicate one of the ways in which such deadlocks are resolved. (See Figure 2.1 for a comparison of marriage and divorce rates.)

The problems that arise in marriage and family life apparently have not discouraged persons from entering into such relationships. As a matter of fact, more people are marrying today than 20 years ago. In 1960, it was found that 7.8 percent of all males and 7.2 percent of all females 35 and over had never been married. The rates of never-married males and females over 65 were 7.7 and 8.5 percent. By 1977, only 6.1 percent and 5.1 percent of males and females over 35 and 5.9 and 6.4 percent over 65 had never been married.[7]

The age at which people are marrying has also been changing. The first half of this century showed a steady decline in the median age at first marriage. This trend continued until the 1950s and 1960s, when it reached a plateau. Since 1960 an indication of postponing first marriages has ap-

Table 2.1 Median Age at First Marriage, by Sex: 1890 to 1977

Year	Male[1]	Female	Year	Male[a]	Female
1977	24.0	21.6	1958	22.6	20.2
1976	23.8	21.3	1957	22.6	20.3
1975	23.5	21.1	1956	22.5	20.1
1974	23.1	21.1	1955	22.6	20.2
1973	23.2	21.0	1954	23.0	20.3
1972	23.3	20.9	1953	22.8	20.2
1971	23.1	20.9	1952	23.0	20.2
1970	23.2	20.8	1951	22.9	20.4
1969	23.2	20.8	1950	22.8	20.3
1968	23.1	20.8	1949	22.7	20.3
1967	23.1	20.6	1948	23.3	20.4
1966	22.8	20.5			
1965	22.8	20.6	1947	23.7	20.5
1964	23.1	20.5	1940	24.3	21.5
1963	22.8	20.5	1930	24.3	21.3
1962	22.7	20.3	1920	24.6	21.2
1961	22.8	20.3	1910	25.1	21.6
1960	22.8	20.3	1900	25.9	21.9
1959	22.5	20.2	1890	26.1	22.0

[a] Figures for 1947 to 1977 are based on Current Population Survey data supplemented by data from the Department of Defense on marital status by age for men in the Armed Forces. Figures for earlier dates are from decennial censuses.
Source: U.S. Bureau of the Census, *Current Population Reports, Population Characteristics,* Series P-20, No. 323 (Washington, D.C.: Government Printing Office, April 1978), p. 2.

peared. Table 2.1 shows that in 1960 males tended to marry at 22.8 years and females at 20.3. By 1977, the median age at first marriage for males had risen to 24.0 years and for females to 21.6 years. The reasons behind such changes are many. The increased opportunity for women to pursue advanced degrees may postpone marriage. The woman's movement with its emphasis on establishing female independence is another. The growth of arrangements such as cohabitation and communes provide many persons with periods of time during which they can decide whether marriage, in general, or marriage to a particular person is best for them. In 1977 there were 754,000 two-person households being shared by an unrelated man and woman.[8]

Divorce Rates

In 1976 there was nearly one divorce for every two recorded marriages.[9] Add to those divorces the cases of desertion and separation, on which accurate figures are harder to come by, and one might gain a view of family change and breakup that would provide corroboration for the stand of the gloomiest prophet. But to look at these figures in isolation may be misleading, since a majority of those divorced marry again. And since single-parent families are becoming more and more common among the middle class, such figures tend to say more about marriage than about the family—two concepts no longer as inextricably linked as they were in the past. Nonetheless, consideration of the interlocking divorce and remarriage rates is essential for an overview of modern American society.

After varying periods of unhappiness and readjustment, most divorced persons eventually remarry, and the likelihood of these second marriages proving successful is almost as great as that for first marriages. Thus, the high divorce rate does not necessarily indicate disenchantment with the institution of marriage. Quite the contrary; most people have such high hopes for it that they are willing to risk a second try.

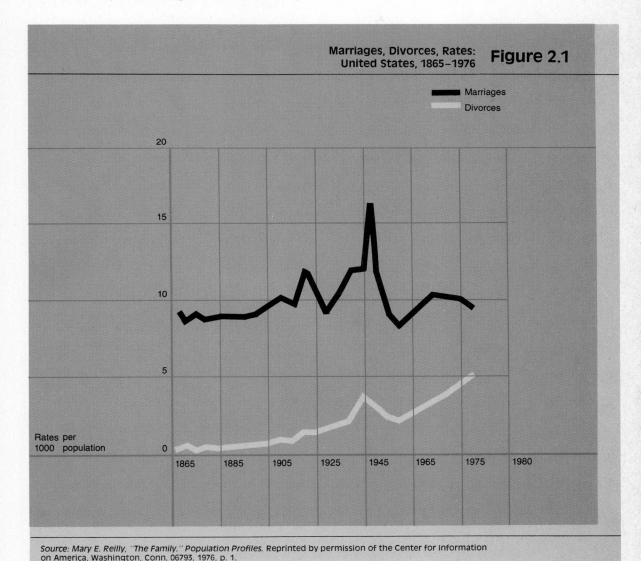

Marriages, Divorces, Rates: United States, 1865–1976 **Figure 2.1**

— Marriages
— Divorces

Rates per 1000 population

Source: Mary E. Reilly, "The Family." Population Profiles. Reprinted by permission of the Center for Information on America, Washington, Conn. 06793, 1976, p. 1.

In the past, the trend in the divorce rate has been an overall generational rise every 30 years or so (see Figure 2.1). Thus, in the 1920s, the rate was approximately 1.5 per 1000 population, which was much higher than the nineteenth century figure. In the mid-1940s, it jumped to about 2.5 per 1000 population and stayed at that figure until 1964. By 1976 it had risen to 5.0 per 1000 population.[10]

Divorce rates reflect regional, residential, racial, religious, national, class, and age influences. Of the geographical regions in the United States, the Mountain area—including Montana, Idaho, Wyoming, Colorado, New Mexico, Arizona, Utah and Nevada—has the highest divorce rate. The rate for this area is 7.3 per 1000 population. The lowest divorce rate (3.0 per 1000 population) is in the Middle Atlantic region which consists of New York, New Jersey and Pennsylvania.[11]

The rate of divorced persons residing in farm communities in 1977 is significantly less than in non–farm communities. The rate for males and females in farm areas was 2.7 and 0.8 per 1000 population, respectively. The corresponding rates for non–farm regions were 4.1 and 5.8 per 1000 population.[12]

Racial differences in divorce rates are also significant. For white males and females the divorce rates were 4.0 and 5.4 per 1000 population respectively in 1977. For blacks the rates were 4.6 per 1000 population for males and 7.7 per 1000 for females.[13]

Religion is another important variable, although one must be cautious in assuming a direct cause-and-effect relationship. The divorce rate is slightly higher among Protestants, apparently reflecting the Catholic Church's adamant stand against the dissolution of marriage. This is at least partly neutralized, however, by a higher separation figure among Catholics. Religion also seems to be a significant factor influencing divorce in religiously "mixed" marriages, but the highest rate is found among couples with no religious affiliation at all.[14]

Satisfaction with level of income and achievement—in short, status—seems to play a role as well. In a study of the relationship between a husband's income and his wife's satisfaction with his achievement as factors in marital dissolution, it was noted that wives of manual workers who considered their husbands' incomes inadequate had a higher incidence of divorce than those who were satisfied with their husband's income level.[15] Strangely enough, however, the study showed that the income of the dissolved-marriage group was actually higher than that of manual workers in the still-married group.

In other words, the crucial factor leading to divorce seems to have been the wife's dissatisfaction with the husband's achievement—and possibly her sense of being in a lower social stratum—rather than actual lack of money.

The early years of marriage produce the greatest strain and hence the highest divorce rate. In the 1920s, the third and fourth years of marriage carried the greatest divorce risk; today, 31 percent of the marriages that end in divorce last less than four years, and 66 percent lasted less than ten years.[16]

Very often, any similarity between the actual cause of divorce and the legal grounds upon which it is claimed is purely coincidental. Approximately 52 percent of all divorce cases are based on a claim of cruelty; the true reason may be desertion (only 23 percent claim this as the cause), non-support (4 percent), adultery (1 percent), or even just plain incompatibility.[17] Perhaps cruelty is a less embarrassing claim than some of the true reasons; it also tends to be more readily provable in court.

Creative Divorce

The trends of the future are difficult to predict with any accuracy, but some factors seem to point strongly toward a rise in divorce rates. Most important among them is probably the new attitude toward divorce that is developing in the country and is reflected in the following statement by Morton Hunt:

> We have not yet opened our minds to the possibilities that divorce may be a creative rather than a destructive act, that it may be a better choice for all concerned (including the children) than trying to repair a defunct marriage, and that divorcing people should be aided rather than impeded in their efforts to make the break and to live successfully in the post-marital world.[18]

If this viewpoint becomes widespread, it is likely to result in a further liberalization of divorce laws and new trends in marriage and divorce rates. More and more people are already perceiving divorce as a potentially constructive and healthy way of dealing with an otherwise intractable situation. Rather than considering it the end of the world, they see it as a gateway to a better marriage in the future or, in many cases, to more congenial alternative life-styles.

Further, the attitude that a married couple should stay together for the sake of the children is gradually giving way to the belief (borne out by research) that an unhappy marriage may be more detrimental to the emotional stability of the children involved than divorce and single-parent families.[19] Since much of the damage done to children is caused by parents' attitudes during the predivorce period, the emotional strain on children is significantly reduced if parents remain calm and amicable and include the children in discussions of the pending divorce.

Another factor that may portend increasing divorce rates is the changing attitude of women toward themselves and their relationship to the social and economic structure. Since it is becoming easier for women to support themselves and to establish reasonably fulfilling lives outside the institution of marriage, they are presumably less afraid of striking out on their own. However, it should be noted that about 35 percent of all persons living in households with a female head are living in poverty.[20] The fact is that the average working woman is still earning considerably less than her male counterpart. Furthermore, when divorce results in economic hardship, the wife and children generally experience greater hardship than the husband. In only a small percentage of cases do the courts grant alimony. In general, fathers contribute less than half the cost of child support after divorce, and court orders for alimony and child support are difficult to enforce.

Separation: Conflict Unresolved

Another large group of people involved in the dissolution of marriages is composed of the separated, about whom there is relatively little information. According to the United States census, the separation category includes those who are legally separated, those who are waiting for a divorce, and those who have been deserted (the latter being numerically the largest group). In 1977, 1.7 percent of all males aged 14 and over were legally separated as were 2.8 percent of all females.[21]

Desertion has been called the poor man's divorce. The motive behind it is, indeed, very often purely economic rather than vindictive, but this does not greatly ameliorate its harmful impact. Desertion is likely to result in many more disruptive family situations than are precipitated by divorce. Since the marital conflict is *unofficially* resolved, it remains only *half* resolved, and no legally binding provisions are made for alimony, child support, or visitation rights.

The desertion rate is particularly high among the black population — probably because of the high cost of legal divorces. This seems to be substantiated by the fact that, as the income level among black people rises, their divorce and desertion patterns become similar to those of whites.[22]

Since black men have often been victims of discriminatory employment policies, the wife in the lower-class black household has traditionally provided the economic support for the family. Frequently the entire burden of maintaining the family's emotional and psychological stability has fallen on her shoulders. With the growing strength of a black consciousness and somewhat improved opportunities, the black man has begun to claim a more active role in his own family as well as in society at large. This will undoubtedly affect future trends in desertion, divorce, and illegitimacy.

Illegitimacy

Marriage legalizes mating and defines the status of children. In some cultures, biological fatherhood is secondary to legal fatherhood. It is the inheritance of name and status that counts, and marriage facilitates the transfer of these essentials. For the most part, illegitimacy has been socially stigmatized in our American culture. Although in a comparatively open society the illegitimate child is *theoretically* as free to make his or her fortune as the child with legal status, in reality the illegitimate child is often denied the benefits of the larger social and economic structure. In addition to public ridicule, the illegitimate child may not claim the right of the father's name and inheritance, and the lack of a father is noted on official records. In 1969, only 28 states allowed an illegitimate child the right to inherit from his or her father, while only 13 allowed the child to inherit from the father's relatives. Today, more people than ever before are realizing the inherent cruelty of legally stigmatizing illegitimate children, but this liberalization of attitude has not yet produced much concrete effort to improve their lot.[23]

The crux of the problem is that the illegitimate child often lacks even a semblance of family life and thus is denied the benefits of early socialization in the home. This can adversely affect not only the individual children involved but also the families they themselves will found as adults. Without the support of parents and at least some general preparation for a role as an adult, the child is likely to be severely handicapped in developing the ability to function as a parent or a marriage partner. Seen from this vantage point, illegitimacy remains qualitatively the same problem it has been in the past. And in view of the fact that it is currently on the rise, especially among the poor, the problems connected with it cry out more urgently than ever for solution.

The number of illegitimate births recorded has more than tripled since 1950. In 1975 there were some 447,900 such births in the United States.

These births accounted for 14.2 percent of all U.S. births taking place during that year. The illegitimacy rate, which is the number of births to unmarried women per 1000 unmarried women age 15–44 has risen from 14.1 per 1000 in 1950 to 24.8 per 1000 in 1975. Among nonwhite females this rate is considerably higher, having reached a peak of 98.3 per 1000 in 1960. It has since dropped off considerably to 80.4 in 1975.[24] What impact reporting mechanisms, contraceptive use and the legalization of abortion have had and will have on these figures is still unknown.

Single-Parent Families

As a result of divorce, separation, death, and illegitimacy, single-parent families are becoming increasingly prevalent. As evidenced by the previous discussion, not all such families are a product of the same social forces. For some it represents a consciously chosen life-style, whereas for others it is a tragedy forced upon them. Nevertheless, most single-parent families confront similar social hardships.

Among other problems, the family often suffers the stigma of being labeled incomplete and unable to function properly. One view, for example, is that because there is no male role model in the black, female-headed, single-parent family, male children are demoralized and improperly socialized, and often become deviants.[25] On the other hand, if the mother has established a relationship with a man other than the father, this individual may replace the father as a role model.[26] And even when black males identify strongly with their mothers, there is little evidence of negative consequences for social aspirations. These families, for example, successfully transmit high educational aspirations to their young, although such aspirations may not be realized for other reasons.[27] The problems of these families are complicated further by discriminatory policies within other institutions.

More realistically, single-parent families are likely to experience financial problems and problems associated with limitations that are imposed on their life-styles. Because most of these families are headed by women, the problems of being a single parent become intertwined with the problems of being a woman in American society. When the mother wants to work, for example, her income is often reduced by payments that must be made to a baby-sitter. Also, women have long been discriminated against in the job market and are often paid only "supplementary incomes." In the case of divorced women, there is often the difficulty of collecting alimony and child support. One study, for example, showed that after one year 42 percent of ex-husbands were no longer making any alimony payments at all, and another 20 percent were making only partial payments.[28]

Since so many social activities are oriented toward couples, and alternative opportunities are directed toward singles, the single parent is limited in the life-style he or she can pursue. This limitation is further increased by the amount of time that the single parent must commit to raising children. Combined with the financial problems and social stigma that often accompany divorce, illegitimacy, or widowhood, these conditions tend to create loneliness, stress, and strain for the parent. In one study of divorced women with children, 62 percent reported difficulty in sleeping, 67 percent poor health, 67 percent loneliness, 32 percent memory problems, 43 percent low work efficiency, 30 percent increased smoking, and 16 percent increased drinking.[29]

The Family **39**

A phenomenon that is appearing on the American scene with greater frequency in recent years is that of commuter marriages. These are marriages in which the spouses are separated from each other for a few days each week. Such marriages are usually the result of job transfers or one spouse's finding a new job in an area too distant for a daily commute. This is a fairly new phenomenon brought about by the increase in job mobility, the tight labor market, and an increase in the rate of women in the labor force. Although the impact of these situations on children and family life has not yet been assessed, it is likely that it will be in the same direction, but with lesser severity, than the impact of single parent families.

Kenneth Woodward, Mary Lord, Frank Maier, Donna Foote and Phyllis Malamud
Saving the Family

Only a decade ago, the beleaguered American family was being written off as obsolete. As society's basic institution, it was emotionally unstable, economically weak and not up to the task of raising children—or so the experts said. Lately, however, opinions have shifted: . . .

"There is no better invention than the family, no super-substitute," says Rutgers University sociologist Sarane Boocock. The question now is not how to supplant the family, but how to support it.

That conclusion will hardly surprise most of the nation's 56.7 million families who have continued to raise their children, endure marital and economic stress and adapt with amazing grace to unprecedented social changes. . . .

Nevertheless, many parents feel increasingly harassed. Raising children has never been more costly—in time and money—and the interference from outside forces has never been more acute. Television, schools, the workplace, peer pressure and the family experts themselves have all invaded the family circle, robbing parents of much of their power without easing their responsibility. "Parents are not abdicating," says MIT psychologist Kenneth Keniston,

"they are being dethroned by forces they cannot influence, much less control." . . .

The U.S. is the only Western nation that does not have a formal family policy—the same thing, many say, as having an anti-family policy. But the impact of government and other outside agencies on the family is already so pervasive that it has provoked a grass-roots parents' revolt. The National Parents' Rights Coalition, promises that "anyone who has an impact on the family, from politicians and bureaucrats to educators and the media, will hear from us and face our power." In Washington, the Coalition of Family Organizations lobbies for tax breaks and other family support. . . .

Why is the family in trouble? One major reason is that traditions no longer dictate life patterns for most adult Americans. "Now people have more options—to get married or not, to have children or not, to stay married or not, to work or not," observes David A Goslin, who directed a study of the family for the National Academy of Sciences. "These options are really at the heart of everybody's concern." A second reason is that the sheer cost of raising a child is enough to make any potential parent pause—and current parents shudder. . . .

Finally, parents feel inceasingly powerless in the face of institutional interference. The growth of social services, health care and public education has robbed them of their traditional roles as job trainers, teachers, nurses and nurturers. And their control over their children's lives is threatened by the pervasive—and increasingly authoritative—influences of television, schools and peer groups. . . .

In their confusion, parents have increasingly turned to experts for advice—and in the process ended up relinquishing more responsibility. "We can't feed our children, discipline them, select schools, books or games for them, even, it seems, have an ordinary conversation with them without consulting someone who claims to be in the know," observes [child psychiatrist] Robert Coles. "This loss of self-respect and common sense is the principal reason why we turn to specialists, as if God had chosen to reveal Himself through them." . . .

"Various professional groups have been too eager to tell parents they weren't qualified to be parents," says Robert Mnookin, a law professor at Berkeley. "Their message is that parents just aren't competent—and the sad thing is, parents bought it." Between their own expectations and the high standards set by the experts, many parents now feel they simply cannot measure up. "When parents believe that they should be the total providers of all that a child needs . . . any suggestion of unmet needs carries with it a sense of failure," says the Rev. Eileen W. Lindner, a staff associate for youth concerns at the National Council of Churches. "The myth of the self-sufficient, independent family is one of the most oppressive forces on the American family."

That myth . . . has roots extending deep into Colonial America. From the onset, American families have been inspired by an ethos of autonomy. . . .

By the middle of the nineteenth century, however, Americans had already established the first and eventually the most powerful institutional counterpoise to the autonomous nuclear family: the compulsory, free public school. From that point on, schools were expected to do what educators assumed that families, especially those of immigrants, could not accomplish on their own—teach skills, develop work habits and instill approved social values. In the course of the following century, almost every other traditional function of the family passed out of the home and into the hands of institutions and professional providers, from care of the sick to support of the poor, from the preparation of food to instruction in leisure activities. . . .

The American family is clearly still in transition. Only about one family in four now conforms to the stereotypical image of breadwinning Dad, homemaking Mom and dependent children. Now more than half of all married women with school-age children hold some kind of job. Couples with no children under 18 now make up 47 per cent of all families, which reflects both the longevity of American couples and the increasing number of those who are delaying or forgoing having children. At the same time, increases in divorce and illegitimacy have created millions of single-parent families while the rising rate of remarriage has produced the "blended" family. "All Americans must become aware that the 'ideal' family barely exists and will never return as a significant force in American life," concludes a recent demographic profile of U.S. families by Zaida Giraldo and Jack Weatherford of the Center for the Study of the Family and the State at Duke University.

Nevertheless, there is an underlying stability to family life that often goes unnoticed. Statistics show that 98 per cent of all American children are raised in families and that, last year, 79 per cent of these were living with two parents. What's more, nearly two-thirds of all couples remain married until death, and of those who divorce, 75 per cent of the women and 83 per cent of the men remarry within three years.

The divorce rate—the highest in the world—may finally be leveling off. According to preliminary figures, the divorce rate increased only 2 per cent in 1976, compared with an annual average increase of 11.5 per cent over the past several years. And despite more relaxed attitudes toward "living in sin," only a fraction of 1 per cent of Americans admitted to cohabitation, according to a 1977 Census report—and most of them will eventually marry. "People are getting more various in their family behavior," says psychologist Arlene Skolnick of the University of California at Berkeley. "But more and more we are seeing a new commitment to child rearing and family control no matter what sort of family structure evolves."

Even so, many family structures are shaky. Thirty-eight per cent of all first marriages fail. As many as four children out of ten born in the 1970s will spend part of their childhood in a single-parent family, usually with the mother as head of the household; 17 per cent of all children under 18 are now living in single-parent families. Remarriage currently blends about 18 million stepchildren from the remnants of what used to be called "broken" families into new family units. "What was defined a decade ago as 'deviant'," observes University of Massachusetts sociologists Alice S. Rossi, "is today labeled 'variant,' in order to suggest that there is a healthy, experimental quality to current social explorations 'beyond monogamy' or 'beyond the nuclear family'."

Perhaps the most distressing development is the high tide of illegitimacy. Fifteen per cent of all births are illegitimate and more than half of all out-of-wedlock babies are born to teen-agers. Illegitimacy is particularly high among blacks: . . . And it is the illegitimate, both black and white, who are most likely to be impoverished, dependent on welfare, deprived of educational opportunities and destined to repeat the cycle with illegitimate children of their own. . . .

How should government respond to such deep-seated problems? Over the past decade, the policy debate has tended to split along classic ideological lines, with liberal Democrats pushing activist intervention and Republican conservatives resisting. . . . But positions have shifted in recent months, to the point where conservatives are now looking for ways to support family-oriented bills and liberals are abandoning such former goals as the setting up of a Federal family agency. "The last thing we need," Vice President Walter Mondale observed last year, "is for the Federal government to launch some ill-defined national crusade to 'save the family.' . . .

Instead, the Carter Administration has pledged itself to a "strong, understandable, well-considered, deeply committed, pro-family policy."

As former Health, Education and Welfare Secretary Joseph A. Califano himself told Carter in a campaign report in 1976, "The most severe threat to family life stems from unemployment and lack of an adequate income." The consequences seem clear enough—in Flint, Mich., for example, alcoholism, drug abuse and child abuse all increased when the jobless rate hit 20 per cent—but it's not as clear that employment and income-supplement programs should be designed primarily as family measures.

Kenneth Keniston, author of the five-year Carnegie Council report, "All Our Children: The American Family Under Pressure," proposes putting more money directly into the hands of poor parents—through either tax-credits, child-care vouchers or a system of child-care allowances—and thus broadening parental options. But a recent experiment in Seattle and Denver, financed by the Department of Health, Education and Welfare, showed that income maintenance given to selected black and white mothers resulted in a sharp jump in family break-ups. Ironically, the most needy wives were also the most likely to leave their husbands when given a minimum-income guarantee.

For most U.S. families, the problems are not that stark or the needs that clear. But every family is affected, to a greater or lesser degree, by the actions of government—a fact that has only recently been fully realized. Accordingly, many experts now favor a requirement for a family impact statement to assess the potential effects of all new legislation and government programs. . . .

One obvious area for family support would be help for working mothers who have not yet found a satisfactory way to combine their responsibilities to their children with the need for more income. Opinion is still divided as to how to do this. . . .

Government and corporate officials are also studying the merits of "flex-time" working hours and half-time jobs for both parents, which would allow at least one of them to be at home at all times without jeopardizing their careers. But there is a growing sentiment among some women—like child psychoanalyst Selma Fraiberg, author of "Every Child's Birthright: In Defense of Mothering"—that only a full-time mother figure can provide the nurture that children need. . . .

On the whole, most advocates of family aid favor a delicate governmental hand, with incentives and discouragements rather than direct laws and regulations. But even that approach is still debated.. . . .

In the long run, perhaps the wisest approach to the problem is to recognize that the family can best be served by nourishing those related institutions on which families have traditionally relied for primary support: neighborhoods, communities, churches and other such voluntary associations. . . .

"The most urgent thing facing us is the need to restore communities in this country," says anthropologist Margaret Mead, "—multi-generational, multi-ethnic and multi-occupational communities where you can take care of children, the old and the sick so that you don't have to segregate people by age and income into neighborhoods and institutions. The major function of a family is bringing up children to be full human beings, able to live in a world of two sexes, of different ages, of different personalities and temperaments.

There are undoubtedly millions of families that serve this function in the U.S. today, but they escape the attention of social workers and mental-health officers, who typically see only troubled families. . . .

No organizer is likely to knock on the doors of middle-class families, much less ask how the well-to-do are getting along. Yet these families, especially, suffer from both the old myth of family self-sufficiency and the modern drive for individual fulfillment. "There's a real conflict between what's good for adults and for children, and possibly even between males and females," observes sociologist Boocock. "What nurtures the family unit is in conflict with what maximizes personal development. You just can't have it both ways."

Yet as any family member knows, such conflicts are the stuff of family life—the forge in which people learn how to live in the world. The family has survived thousands of years of that sort of internal strife, along with war, famine, pestilence and tyranny. Perhaps the most encouraging thought is that with that background, it can probably outlast its new friends and their remedies as well.

Excerpts from "Saving the Family," *Newsweek*, May 15, 1978, pp. 63–73, Copyright 1978 by Newsweek, Inc. All rights reserved. Reprinted by permission.

The Family and Changing Sex Roles

The allocation of tasks, privileges, and responsibilities on the basis of sex alone is a characteristic of the status structure of most primitive societies. The study of history reveals to us, however, that sex is not a legitimate basis for stratification in modern societies. Avoiding the application of traditional sex roles in modern work and family situations is an increasingly espoused, if not enacted, social goal in the United States. The recency of this change in attitude is evidenced by the fact that the scholar Sigmund Freud, writing in this century, argued that women, by virtue of being physically weaker and equipped for bearing children, were naturally passive and designed to stay at home and be mothers.[30] Only in later years has scholarly research been directed toward discovering the extent to which "masculine" and "feminine" behavior is socially conditioned rather than biologically determined.

Although biological differences between the sexes certainly exist, and to a greater extent than in any other animal species, no instinctual, programmed responses are engineered into the brain of *Homo sapiens*. Human beings are conditioned by postnatal influences. They must be taught to feed themselves, to protect themselves, even to procreate. They must be taught which sex they belong to, though the learning begins at an early age. Studies show that a majority of $2\frac{1}{2}$-year-olds do not correctly answer the question, "Are you a little boy or a little girl?" However, by the age of 3, two-thirds to three-fourths have their sexual identities straight.[31]

Traditional sex roles are taught in the childhood years, for the most part automatically, by parents. Most girls are encouraged to be passive and obedient, boys aggressive and demanding. Boys are encouraged to prepare for professional careers, for example, through academic achievement in mathematics and the sciences. Studies have shown that in preschool and primary years, there is little difference in science achievement between boys and girls. However, during junior and senior years, boys generally do better than girls in science. Psychologists believe the difference develops because girls are usually less motivated and many have been taught to believe they are less competent. Cultural definitions of the female sex role usually have placed more emphasis upon the ability to attract a man and maintain a love relationship than on academic skills.[32]

By the time they reach maturity, therefore, both men and women are prepared for their respective roles. With the achievement of greater quality and the increasing proportion of women attending college, however, larger numbers of women are seeking employment outside the home. They have become increasingly restive within a society that dictates "careers" for married men but only "jobs" for married women and in the face of discrimination they encounter in seeking emotionally rewarding employment.

At the same time, men have been finding some aspects of the male role unsatisfying. Until the twentieth century, much prestige was attached to aggressive, warlike temperaments. However, in the nuclear age, the soldier has become a suspect figure rather than an admired one. The occupations of farmer, woodsman, frontier trapper, and explorer utilized and exemplified traditional male attributes; but these occupations are becoming obsolete. Even nineteenth century factory labor required masculine brawn. But the types of white-collar jobs that the twentieth century male must seek—whether computer analyst, certified public accountant, or "organization man"—require the very qualities traditionally considered feminine: patience, the ability to get along with people, and the capacity for routine detail.

As larger numbers of women enter the working force, men find their traditional dominance threatened. The situation can be overstated, of course. Whereas women represent a substantial proportion of all employees in teaching and clerical occupations, these are for the most part jobs with lower pay and lower status. The percentage of women in college teaching and other professions, top-level management, and political office is still small, especially by comparison with their percentage in the population. Nor, except in the field of journalism, has the percentage changed much over the last decade, despite the well-publicized activities of the women's liberation movement. Salary levels of women are generally still well below those of men, regardless of occupational level.

Nevertheless, the very fact that more women are working has combined with their changing sexual conduct and social attitudes to create an atmo-

Sexual stereotyping: Toys are both playthings and tools used to train children for traditional adult roles. (far right) Children often learn adult roles by emulating their parents. Here a young boy engages in "man's work" by helping his father paint and repair the house.

sphere in which men wonder what they must do to define themselves as men. In the nineteenth century, virility could be demonstrated by sexual prowess; now, women are expected to be almost as experienced as men. Once a couple considered a sexual relationship satisfactory if the man alone achieved an orgasm; now, the expectation is that women will derive as much satisfaction from sexual activities as men. Once women were expected to play a receptive role in both personal and professional relationships. Now a small, but perhaps growing, percentage of women initiate sexual relationships; a much larger percentage pursue careers at ever-higher levels in the work hierarchy. If the role change sought by so many women has tended to demoralize some men, it has liberated others to engage in activities traditionally considered feminine. In the present context, men can take up cooking or sewing as a hobby and not be considered effeminate.

The Changing Roles of Family Members

As the family has accommodated—or been forced to accommodate—itself to changes in the larger society, the roles of family members have been subject to change. Much of the current dissatisfaction with marriage would seem to involve uncertainty concerning these changes; change almost always produces strain.

Wife, Mother, Housekeeper: Happily Ever After?

At the present time the wife is probably the most controversial member of the family. Her function is being reevaluated in terms of the new feminine consciousness, which has already effected major changes in many spheres. Not all women were or are dissatisfied with their domestic roles, but a sizable number, especially among the educated, have felt sufficiently stifled to become the vanguard of activism for social, economic, and political change. The consequences for the family are gradually becoming dramatically visible.

Once before, a generation ago, world conditions had given women the chance for emancipation, but they did not take advantage of their opportunity. World War II had brought large numbers out of their homes for jobs and careers. But when their men returned from service, the women retreated. If this retreat caused frustration, it remained for the most part unvoiced. Although less confined by custom than her mother and grandmother had been, a married woman living in the early part of the twentieth century was still expected to find fulfillment in the role of wife and mother. Holding a routine outside job reflected adversely on her husband's abilities as a provider; having a "career"—a word always used in quotes—carried social stigma. And dissatisfaction with traditional roles implied personal deviance rather than a flaw in the social structure.

The problem worsened with the years. The woman of earlier eras had been too burdened with the work of running a large and complicated household to have much time for self-analysis, and her formal education was too limited to create much of a disparity between her potential and the actual chores that filled her days. The nuclear family structure and the socioeco-

FAMILY

Perhaps more than any other social institution, the American family has experienced great change in recent years. Traditional roles have been redefined, new life styles are being established, and customary functions of the family may no longer be taken for granted. If anything, the rapidly changing nature of family life will continue to demand flexibility and adjustment. *This page:* The pain and joy of childbirth can be a meaningful experience for both mother and father; boys can learn to cook as well as girls, family roles; women are no longer held back because they must care for young children, as this delegate to the Women's National Congress demonstrates; children will grow to adulthood in many different family environments. *Opposite page:* Sharing family responsibility may include doing the grocery shopping; for some children a great deal of nuturing and training will be done by surrogate parents and families, perhaps in day-care centers while both parents are working; the single parent family places new responsibility on the parent caring for the child; close, extended families in many cultures still provide warmth and security to their members.

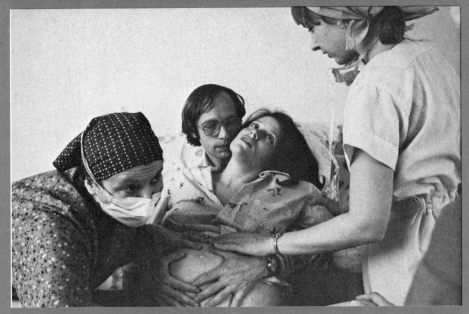

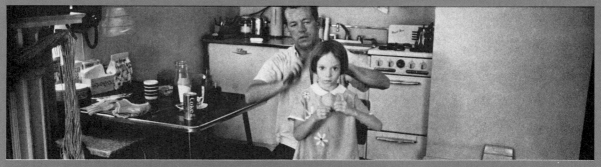

nomic conditions that fostered it changed this situation in many ways, and these changes were more intensely experienced by the wife and mother than by other family members.

As the size of the family contracted, she became aware of a new quality in her life: isolation. Her husband worked outside the home, and her children spent much time at school and with friends. The task of raising and disciplining the children was, in any case, a self-limiting one. If she had made it her sole aim in life (as her upbringing encouraged her to do), the day when the youngest child left home was tragic. The mother-housewife now became predominantly housewife—an occupation with negligible status in the outside world. Indeed, it was accorded only token acknowledgment even within the family, despite the fact that in an age of specialization she remained one of the few members of society prepared to exercise multiple functions: housekeeper, cook, laundress, governess, practical nurse, social secretary, confidante, seamstress, teacher, and chauffeur in addition to whatever professional skills she may have developed before the arrival of her children. She was not only overqualified, but, with the departure of her children, underemployed to the point of feeling expendable.

When the women's liberation movement appeared, at first only a few housewives gave it open allegiance, and not even a majority approved of it silently. Undoubtedly, many were restrained by timidity or by fear of the ridicule that some of the early radicals inspired. Many felt unequal to the competition equality might bring. But with the passage of time, the leaders became less radical and the followers less conservative. Today women in all parts of the country and of all classes seem determined to change the pattern of their own lives and that of their families.

Most significant is their wholesale return to work. Often this single change in a woman's life acts as a catalyst for many others. Far from being disruptive to the family, a wife's outside interests frequently lead to increased understanding of her husband's problems. Children soon adapt to their mother's work schedule, especially when their father participates in the household tasks. Finally, and perhaps most unexpectedly, a woman's status within her family changes for the better.[33] The return to work may lessen the number and severity of future marital problems.

Often husbands were more interested in getting their wives involved in careers than were the women themselves. . . . Resulting shared interests should help prevent a gap in understanding between husband and wife in the empty nest years. The future seems promising. It is probable that when the wife's work means challenge rather than underemployment, it can enrich the marital relationship and take some of the pressure off the intimate interdependencies of the nuclear family, pressure which led to increased marital and family problems in past years.[34]

Husband, Father: Provider under Pressure

The women's liberation movement has obviously affected not only the housewife but the husband and father as well. Although men have played what seem to be the more dominant and satisfying roles in our society, they too have been restricted to the extent that their traditional functions as masters and protectors have limited the expression of their individual needs.

Alienation from these needs has plagued men as well as women, the married as well as the single. Industrialization and technological advances have provided greater opportunity for personal achievement but have also worked against harmonious integration of the various aspects of our lives.

The pressure to compartmentalize his life has been very keenly felt by the head of the nuclear family.

At work he is expected to be—or at least to seem—impervious to the pressures of his job. In a competitive society these pressures can be great, fatiguing in mind and body. Under such circumstances, he needs a home that is a refuge, a place for rest, solitude, and escape, not active involvement and intense relationships with other family members.

When his emotional and psychological investment in his work is excessive, he may expect too much of his family without being able (or willing) to fulfill his own responsibilities toward it.

Men's liberation: Not long ago, men who enjoyed cooking for the family risked their masculine reputation. The women's liberation movement has done much to change such social sanctions.

In a chaotic and increasingly incomprehensible world, the family provides a small, relatively stable universe where "things make sense." Given work which demands emotional restraint and control, the family provides a haven for the "release" of feelings. . . . Given the tenuous relationship to the future engendered by chronic social change, children in the family provide a concrete link to the future. Given the shattering of the community, the family provides a pseudo-community which partly tells a man who he is and where he stands. Given the fragmentations of social roles on the wider scene, the family provides a narrow stage, within which life promises to be of a piece.[35]

Seen from this vantage point, a husband's acceptance of his wife's new life-style—involving, as it does, a lessening of financial pressures and increased understanding of mutual problems—becomes less surprising.

Children: Complexities of Growing Up

In the past, the family assumed the major responsibility for developing children's characters and preparing them for adulthood. This responsibility was not always successfully fulfilled; maladjusted children are not a phenomenon restricted to contemporary society. Not all children accepted their parents' values and goals, and a generation gap of some sort has probably been a characteristic common to all parent-child relationships. But, for better or worse, socialization of children was primarily the function of the family, which in a rural economy had greater opportunity to fulfill it than does the contemporary family.

Today, by contrast, other social institutions have acquired a great deal of control over children's upbringing, and the demands of modern society have further modified what socializing power the family retains. Less and less time is available for the development of close ties between parents (especially fathers) and children.

Urbanization, child labor laws, the abolishment of apprentice systems, commuting, centralized schools, zoning ordinances, the working mother, the experts' advice to be permissive, the seductive power of television for keeping children occupied, the delegation and professionalization of child care—all these manifestations of progress have operated to decrease opportunity for contact between children and parents, or, for that matter, adults in general.[36]

Growing up is therefore more complicated than it used to be. Children's needs for direction and values that can serve as a foundation for growth remain as strong as ever, but satisfaction of these needs is becoming harder to achieve. There are too many roles and alternative life-styles to make one unequivocal choice, and children may be attracted to such a variety of models that they find it impossible to achieve any cohesive self-image.[37]

Even if children were willing to base their commitments on the values and behavioral examples of their parents, which would run counter to a natural (and, to some extent, socially reinforced) rebellion against parental norms, they might still find their identity fragmented. Many parents are themselves presently experiencing confusion and doubt concerning their own roles.

In the midst of these uncertainties, children must bridge the gap between the needs of childhood and the demands of adulthood—an especially wide gap in American culture. Rather than facilitating the transition, our present culture in some ways seems to emphasize discontinuity

between childhood and adulthood. Dependence is intensely cultivated—even exploited—during childhood, whereas independence and a high degree of self-sufficiency are expected of the adult. Yet early heavy dependence on parents involves emotional dangers and may deter children from ultimately assuming responsibility for their own lives.

Of course, the problem of helping children mature into adulthood cannot be made the total responsibility of the American family. The family structure itself has been forced to accommodate other social institutions of a changing society; it is only fair to expect these institutions to assume their proper share in the socialization of children. Schools, for example, could address themselves more realistically to the transitional problems faced by children and supplement parental efforts to ensure their maturing into independence.

Only recently has youth become a social status, occupied mostly by biological adolescents, that intervenes between childhood and adulthood. Youth is a period of transition in which adolescents form adult identities, negotiating quasi-independent roles in the adult world within the context of limitations imposed on them by their sex, social class, ethnicity, and religion. Youth is often a period of experimentation and rebellion, of personal disorganization and confusion.

In youth, pervasive ambivalence toward both self and society is the rule. This ambivalence is not the same as definitive rejection of society, nor does it necessarily lead to

Adolescent Ambivalence

political activism. For ambivalence may also entail intense self-rejection, including major efforts at self-transformation employing the methodologies of personal transformation that are culturally available in any historical era; monasticism, meditation, psychoanalysis, prayer, hallucinogenic drugs, hard work, religious conversion, introspection, and so forth.[38]

One sociologist has described the situation of youth in modern American society as one of familial and cultural disorganization. Recent technological advances have fostered a changed economic system organized around the need for spending rather than the need for saving, with work occurring in bureaucratic rather than entrepreneurial settings, and consumption rather than accumulation being the major goal and source of status.[39] The family is reduced to a nuclear form consistent with the demands of the modern economic system, and the father is more frequently absent from the home, leaving the burden of early socialization on the mother. Moreover, what consistent socialization the child receives is into the cultural framework found useful by past rather than present generations—the Protestant Ethic. The Protestant Ethic is based on a system of values that prescribes hard work, austerity, independence, and materialistic accumulation as moral actions. Given the changes in our socioeconomic system, however, these are no longer useful guides to action. The irrelevance of these values, termed cultural breakdown by one observer, has "reached a point of no return when the process of socialization no longer provides the new generation with coherent reasons to become enthusiastic about becoming adult members of society.[40]

Indeed, the attitudes of modern youth toward work seem to differ considerably from the Protestant Ethic. In a recent survey of graduating college seniors, for example, only one out of five indicated that "my career will be the most important thing in my life." Over 80 percent responded favorably to the following statements: "My private life will not be sacrificed to make more money," and "I would not work for an organization that carried out policies I think are wrong."[41]

The response of American youth to their cultural milieu ranges from suicide to drug abuse to political activism.

Students are tired of rationality and things associated with it—foresight, control, discipline, the Protestant Ethic bit, grace gained only in later life—for they are hard to live with. To be irrational, to be allowed to have one ecstatic experience, even a mushy one, that is not so bad if one must live with the rational computer night and day, as these kids are beginning to have to do.[42]

But while the Protestant Ethic has apparently been rejected by youth as a culturally meaningful system of values, no alternative has yet replaced it. The beat, hippie, New Left, and other countercultural movements of the sixties, once hailed as the revitalization of romanticism, now seem to be commercialized, fragmented, and atomized. Where generational problems were once manifested as social problems and expressed through social movements, alternative life-styles, and political activism, they now seem to be privatized and disorganized, manifested mostly as a pervasive unease and as personal troubles among the nation's youth.

Can the Family Survive?

The contemporary situation of the family is a difficult one. Will the family of the future still have a meaningful role? Will it, in fact, survive at all? One sociologist has suggested that the family is obsolete and that those who assemble data on the number of marriages taking place today to prove it is still alive are prisoners of the status quo.[43]

Most of his colleagues do not go this far. Some maintain that marriage has lost its permanence since people no longer value it for its own sake, but they believe that it retains a pragmatic value if it meets the needs of the individuals involved.[44] One such function of the contemporary family may be to act as a buffer between the individual and society.[45]

Theory aside, ordinary Americans are making specific efforts to deal with their individual marital and family problems, some of which we have touched upon in previous sections. Here we will cover these and others in greater depth, since they suggest important possibilities and trends for marriage and family organization in the future.

Legislation: A Gauge of Changing Attitudes

Legislation tends to be a fairly accurate gauge of the strength of changing attitudes. The fact that controversy continues on issues such as abortion, divorce, and antidiscrimination laws creates uncertainty about future trends in these areas and suggests some possibility of backlash. But for the present the courts appear to be working toward redress of legislative imbalances that have limited women's economic freedom and social mobility.

In January 1973 the Supreme Court declared that a state could not prevent a woman from having an abortion at any time during the first three months of pregnancy, a ruling that invalidated the abortion laws of Texas and Georgia and implied the illegality of such laws in 44 other states. Although women were not granted an absolute right to abortion on demand, the ruling represents a significant challenge to the legal authority of the state and the moral authority of the church (primarily the Roman Catholic Church but also the Mormon Church) to control and define the role of women. Presumably the Supreme Court ruling will result in a lower illegitimacy rate, although one criticism of the imposed time limit is that the young and poor, who most often need an abortion after the twelfth week, will be faced with the alternatives of illegal abortion or giving birth to an illegitimate and unwanted child. It is among this group that the early signs of pregnancy are often unrecognized or hidden out of fear, and prenatal care is grossly inadequate. There should also be fewer marriages dictated by pregnancy rather than inclination. And the ruling contributes at least in theory to greater social freedom for women, since pregnancy will no longer be as powerful a deterrent to premarital sex as it once was.

Concerning divorce laws and benefits, no changes have yet been made that significantly alter the status of divorced men and women. But the National Organization for Women (NOW) is engaged in major efforts to change present divorce laws so as to provide divorced women with the req-

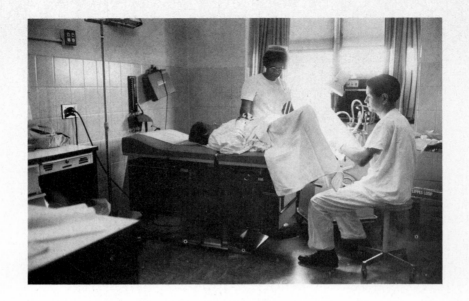

Legalized abortion: A significant gain in women's rights to determine their roles in society.

uisite job training to offset the employment disadvantages resulting from years spent at housework. Changing attitudes toward divorce are likely to bring about legislation rectifying this problem. One alternative, proposed by NOW, is a federal welfare system that would exempt any guardian or single parent of a young child from the work requirement. Another option that may become increasingly available (and indispensable) to working mothers, whether married or divorced, is the use of federally subsidized developmental child-care facilities.

In many states, however, divorce laws have been liberalized to make divorces easier to obtain. The national Uniform Marriage and Divorce Act, though not a law, has served as a model for many liberalizing changes in prescribing that there need be no grounds specified for divorce and that the marriage, rather than either individual, should be put on trial. New York, for example, has added new grounds to its traditionally stringent laws— cruelty, desertion, imprisonment for three or more years, and legal separation for a year or more—thereby expanding the legally feasible bases for divorce. A number of other states have done away with traditional grounds for divorce altogether. Already more than half of the states have passed some form of "no-fault" divorce legislation in which neither party is judged guilty of any wrongdoing.

Day Care: Federal Beneficence or Coercion?

One of the most significant responses to the problems of women who desire or need to work is the creation of day-care centers. Some observers contend that such facilities will have an effect beyond enabling women to enter the job market.

They will once and for all resolve the conflict between the child's welfare and the mother's welfare—for the centers will offer advantages that neither the nuclear middle-class family nor the economically deprived lower-class family can match. . . . The day care centers will free the suburban child from the intense and overbearing pressures of the nuclear family, and therefore fit him better for an adult life in the outside society. For the lower-class child, the centers will offer exemplary medical and dental care, the chance to use the latest educational play equipment, and the skilled guidance of experts who will help the youngster to cope with the deficiences of his own family life.[46]

Historically, day-care projects have not always fulfilled the expectations of those who promote them; nor have they satisfied the needs of those who use them. Although these public facilities are often theoretically subsidized for the poor, the federal definition of poverty prescribes such low levels of income that many families in great need are excluded from such benefits. A family with four children and an income of $8500, for example, technically not classified as poor, is required to pay the full fee.[47] The effect of such inequities is to turn day-care centers into economically segregated communities of poor children. To make matters worse, such facilities are often inadequately regulated by municipal and state governments. Staff members are not always properly trained for the responsibilities entrusted to them; nor are they, in general, employed full time.[48]

Perhaps the most serious criticism leveled at the day-care concept is that mothers, especially among the poor, may be coerced into the labor force and into using day-care facilities whether they wish to or not: "We are entering a new stage, wherein the government, under the threat of withholding relief, can compel the poor to put their children in the centers."[49]

One conceivable alternative (similar to the single-parent subsidy proposed by NOW) would be federal fund appropriations for a general family assistance program based on family size and level of income. This program, discussed more thoroughly in Chapter 10, would be comprehensive and without the stigma and oppressive regulations of public welfare. Despite the potential abuses inherent in such a concept, some believe it to be more practicable as well as constitutionally sounder than coercive day-care proposals. Mothers would have the option either to work and entrust the supervision of preschoolers to others or to stay at home and care for their children themselves until they reach school age. Some people in government and business are now considering the possibility of instituting "flex-time" working hours that would allow both parents the opportunity to work while one would always be home with the children.

Single-Parent Adoptions

The small but growing category of the single-parent family has lately been the recipient of increasing attention and recognition. This type of family unit is beginning to be considered a semipermanent or even permanent state, rather than a transitory one born of adverse circumstances. There are people who are by nature and temperament unsuited for marriage but not at all unsuited to parenthood.

It is clearly better for a child to be raised in a happy single-parent home than in an unhappy conjugal one or in an institution. If this viewpoint gains wider acceptance, and indications are that it will, it may become less difficult for single people to adopt children.

George Thorman
Living Together Unmarried

A survey of four hundred thirty-one students at the University of Texas at Austin shows that approximately 36 per cent have had a cohabitation experience that extended over a period of three to twelve months. Thirty of these couples were interviewed in depth in order that the research would reflect information that could not be obtained adequately from responses to a questionnaire. The research interviews focused on five general areas: (1) the couples' reasons for entering into the living-together arrangement; (2) the nature of the relationship at the outset; (3) areas in which problems arose during the course of the experience; (4) benefits derived from living together; (5) plans for the future or eventual outcome of the cohabitation.

The students included in the sample ranged from eighteen to thirty years of age and were distributed as follows: ten sophomores, fourteen juniors, ten seniors, and seventeen graduate students. All couples had been living together for three months or longer. Fourteen of the thirty couples had been involved in cohabitation for twelve months or longer. Fourteen of the sixty students indicated that they had been involved in more than one cohabitation experience. The remaining forty-six students were not previously involved in living together unmarried.

All couples were interviewed conjointly, and permission to tape-record the interviews was obtained in all cases. The tape recordings were monitored by the researcher and selected segments were transcribed. These interviews revealed that the vast majority of living-together couples do not enter into the relationship lightly. Three-fourths of those interviewed had strong ties of affection before they began to live together. They also had such strong feelings of personal loyalty toward one another that dating others was considered out of bounds. Moreover, since only three couples had met and immediately started living together, it is highly improbable that couples who enter living-together arrangements consider it merely casual sexual involvement without any strong emotional attachment. On the other hand, only two couples in the group of thirty were tenta-

tively or formally engaged when they began to live with each other, indicating that the arrangement is not usually considered a serious commitment to marriage. . . . Some living-together couples have rejected marriage because their parents have had a rather miserable life. A junior student revealed that his mother was now in her third marriage and also that his grandmother had been divorced three times. . . .

Most of the living-together couples we interviewed were not planning to get married in the near future, if at all. They seemed content with their present relationship and did not want to change their voluntary commitment to a formal and legally sanctioned relationship. Moreover, the living-together couples had a surprisingly good record of trouble-free relationships. They had few emotional problems, did not feel overly dependent on one another, and felt that a high degree of acceptance and understanding existed between them. The negative feeling of being trapped or being used, so frequently cited as sources of frustration and dissatisfaction among married couples, were noticeably absent from our unmarried couples.

Living-together couples also have a good sexual relationship. They report that their sexual problems are minimal. The women have only minor anxieties about getting pregnant. With very few exceptions, they stated that they would ask for an abortion if they did become pregnant. However, since the risk of getting pregnant has been greatly reduced with the use of the pill, neither partner fears that an unwanted pregnancy might alter the pattern of their lives. There are times when one or both partners have thought of having sexual adventures with other partners; but with rare exceptions, they have continued to remain extremely loyal to one another and have avoided sexual and emotional entanglements with others. Although they announce that each is free to pursue outside sexual interests, few living-together couples have done so. . . .

For most of the couples, the sexual aspect of living together is of secondary importance. The couples interviewed put a great deal of emphasis on the quality of their relationship outside of sex. They are held together by personal bonds of mutual affection and loyalty, rather than sexual attraction. . . .

Living-together couples usually move into a deep level of intimacy on all fronts, not just on the sexual front. As one partner of a living-together couple put it: "After the first six months, our relationship became much more mature. Maybe we lost some of the original romance, but I think we have really got a much better understanding of each other. . . ."

What about the practical side of living together? How do living-together couples cope with the everyday problems of survival? How do they manage to pay their bills? Most of the couples interviewed had reduced their physical needs to a minimum. They lived in low-rental housing, sharing expenses from their meager earnings and whatever money they got from their parents. Most graduate students were entirely self-sufficient. Some couples lived in co-op housing arrangements that provided cheap living quarters and meals, even though such quarters generally lacked opportunities for privacy. Some couples started living in an apartment along with a roommate and then found suitable quarters for themselves. But by and large, neither partner expressed much concern about the material aspects of their life together. . . .

Living-together couples could not be differentiated from other couples by appearance, convention, or manners. In fact, they actually represented a cross-section of the student population and did not differ from most students in family background, in intellectual interests, or in ways of living—at least within the academic community. They shared a strong conviction that the quality of their relationship and the satisfaction that they found was of far greater value then any material rewards. They valued the emotional security that could be found in a happy intimate relationship.

Most living-together couples believed the experience was beneficial to them as individuals. For some couples, cohabition provided an opportunity for emotional growth and maturity that they would not have gained through conventional dating. . . .

Couples living together put a great deal of emphasis on honesty and openness in their relationship as the prime ingredient to a successful and satisfying experience. There is a consistent rejection of the notion that "some things are better left unsaid.". . .

Living together can help a couple determine whether they are really ready for a sustained relationship, according to some of the couples we interviewed. . . . They do not live together with the express intention of determining whether they are to be married after a trial period during which they can test out their readiness to commit themselves to one another on a more permanent basis. However, some studies indicate that about one-third of living-together couples either marry or plan to marry, while about another third want to live together without considering marriage as the end in view. . . .

Some couples emphasize that living together is more compatible with the trend toward sex equality than is traditional marriage because marriage carries the implications of male supremacy and the inferior status of women. College women are especially attracted to living together because it is the hallmark of the emancipated woman, whereas getting married pegs them as joining the ranks of the unhappy women who live out their lives as wives and mothers. . . .

Why has living together become more prevalent in the past five years and what are the implications for the future of marriage? The couples themselves believe that they are involved in a search for a relationship that carries with it more intimacy and satisfaction than can be found in the "dating game." . . .

They also believe that it is hypocritical to keep up a pretense of nonsexual involvement for the sake of appearances when two people are sexually attracted and mutually consent to sleeping together and living together. . . .

Will living together lead to happier marriages? It is much too early to give a definite answer. However, cohabitation may gradually modify our conception of what marriage involves, with greater emphasis on the value of personal growth, freedom, and self-identity than we have heretofore considered to be possible. The living-together couple's life-style is quite similar to the open-marriage model, which is so often and widely discussed today. At this point, it seems reasonable to consider seriously the emergence of cohabitation as a legitimate form of relationship either as a preliminary, transitory step toward marriage or as a permanent alternative to traditional marriage that imposes no stigma on those who choose it.

Excerpts from George Thorman, "Living Together Unmarried: A Study of Thirty Couples at the University of Texas," The Humanist, March/April 1974, pp. 15–18. This article first appeared in The Humanist, March/April 1974, and is reprinted by permission.

Communal Families

An alternative to the nuclear family that radically alters the traditional roles and division of labor among partners is the cooperative or communal household. In general, communes provide for a sharing of household expenses and duties. All members participate in the task of keeping the household economically viable, either by working at an outside job, as in urban cooperatives, or by farming the land, as in some rural communes.

The idea of communes is not new in America—cooperative living was tried in certain nineteenth century rural communities—nor is it typified by any single structure or pattern of living. Some communes, for example, discourage conventional marital relationships to the point of actually requiring a group sexual arrangement, whereas others are composed of strictly monogamous couples. Cooperative life-styles also differ according to the environment—whether urban or rural—and according to the skills and backgrounds of the participants.

Child-rearing practices are equally varied. For example, in some urban groups composed of couples who primarily wish to create a supportive environment for each other and divide household expenses, child care may simply entail baby-sitting duties. In rural communes, child care, especially care of infants, is often primarily the responsibility of the mothers, although some functions may be performed collectively.[50]

As children in communes mature, they are likely to receive love and emotional support not only from their biological parents but from their communal "mothers" and "fathers" as well. Nevertheless, in the communes observed in one study the children were encouraged and expected to behave autonomously at an early age; neither parents nor other commune members were prepared to devote much time to them beyond infancy.[51]

A strikingly different attitude toward child rearing obtains among the Hutterites, one of the largest communal groups in the United States.[52] Like the Amish and Mennonites, they are Anabaptists whose lives are centered

Extending the family: In this age of the nuclear family, many have found life easier and more fulfilling in communes, where the social and economic responsibilities of day-to-day living are shared by all.

around the daily practice of their religious beliefs (including pacifism). Their religious dedication is undoubtedly a factor in the lack of crime, violence, or any observed hostility, for that matter, and the rarity of family conflict. Their religion prescribes methods of satisfying family functions and socializing children that further strengthen the spirit of harmony among them.

The Hutterites live in groups of about a dozen families on community owned farms. Almost all goods and services are provided and shared by the group, which employs scientific farming methods and modern technology in the manufacture of many of its own tools and machinery. (Despite their technical orientation, they strongly discourage the mass media in their communities.)

After their children have been weaned, they are placed in central day nurseries, where formal education begins at the age of $2\frac{1}{2}$. After-school care is the responsibility of older brothers and sisters. Between the ages of 5 and 6, the children are taken out of nursery school, given a few simple chores, and allowed to play for much of the day. Religious education (in German) and secular education (in English) begin at the age of 6, at a schoolhouse owned by the commune. Supervision and discipline after school hours are in the hands of a religious teacher. All children of the commune between the ages of 5 and 15 eat their meals in their own dining room, apart from the adults. At 15 they are baptized to signify entrance into adulthood, and from then on they are expected to assume adult roles.

It should be emphasized that the Hutterite communities grew out of a unique situation. Like members of the Israeli kibbutzim, the Hutterites share a common religious heritage and are united by common goals such as mutual economic aid and joint socialization of children. Whether similar living patterns can be established by other segments of American society is difficult to determine. The question is whether sufficient collective motivation can surmount differences in background, class, and goals.

Open Marriage

In theory, if not always in practice, the cooperative arrangement of the commune provides a framework within which husband and wife can share roles. Both participate in the raising of their children, both can contribute to the economic support of the household, and additional help is always available when needed in the form of reciprocal aid among the participants in the communal structure.

The cooperative living of the communes, then, suggests a pattern in which the family can fulfill its traditional function in new ways without excessively burdening any one member. But this is merely a structural outline. It does not necessarily eliminate marital conflict, nor does it deal with a possible resistance to role sharing. These are essentially problems of attitude and of one partner's inability or unwillingness to understand and accommodate the other's emotional and psychological growth. Traditional marriage has been a victim of such problems; open marriage is one of the most recent responses.

Nena and George O'Neill, who first suggested and systematically explored the concept, describe it as an attempt to incorporate into marriage the twin needs of relatedness and freedom, regardless of the outward form of the arrangement (such as communal living).[53] In part, it is a state of mind that not only entails but also fosters patterns of behavior resulting in a new mental outlook.

The goal is "to strip marriage of its antiquated ideals and romantic tinsel," thus enabling the one-to-one relationship to fulfill the needs for "intimacy, trust, affection, affiliation, and the validation of experience."[54] Marriage does require commitment, but, according to the O'Neills, the traditional marriage contract demands unrealistic and unreasonable commitments. Viewed in this light, every "closed" marriage is a trap that blocks separate experiences and strives for an impossible closeness—a merging of husband and wife into a single entity. Open marriage, on the other hand, provides the opportunity for mental and emotional freedom within the context of a mutually supportive relationship of trust and liking untainted by possessiveness.

Open marriage seeks to preserve the advantage of an in-depth relationship, which has become more and more necessary with manifold changes in society, while removing the restrictions that work to destroy the relationship. Although one of the most important facets of open marriage is the creation of its personal meaning by the couple involved, without regard to tradition and rules, the O'Neills suggest certain juxtapositions that can serve as guidelines in "rewriting" the marriage contract:

The Old Contract Demands	The Open Contract Offers
Ownership of the mate	Independent living
Denial of the self	Personal growth
Playing the couples game	Individual freedom
Rigid role behavior	Flexible roles
Absolute fidelity	Mutual trust
Total exclusivity	Expansion through openness[55]

Open marriage is based on living in the present, in terms of realistic expectations. It postulates privacy, open and honest communication, role flexibility, open companionship, equality, separate identities, and a trust that implies an ability to forgive and to treat the separate needs and relationships of the mate without fear, suspicion, or resentment. The most significant aspect of the open-marriage concept is its emphasis on changes that are compatible with the realities of contemporary society. It offers a way to make a viable commitment in the present without restrictive tentacles to shackle the future.

Yet open marriages cannot be seen as the solution for all. Not everyone desires to engage in such relationships. And of those that choose to try open marriages as an alternative, many fail. This may be due to internal or external problems. One spouse may have doubts about the decision to enter such a relationship. This partner may have gone along with the plan only because it was an alternative to separation or divorce. Frequently, partners will not enter an open marriage on equal footing. Background characteristics may not have prepared one spouse as well as they did the other for participating in an open marriage. Many couples find that the world around them does not encourage open marriages. Although they may strive for equality and independence, society may impose restrictions. For example, there are not as many opportunities for the female partner to establish her independence. Couples may view their roles in marriage as equal, but society may impose a "husbands are more equal than wives" sanction.[56]

These alternative forms of relationships appear to be growing in frequency. At the same time, societal attitudes towards such forms appear to be changing. Undoubtedly, the frequency of occurrence and the attitudinal change are interrelated, and the problem of which came first is a complex one. If social values regarding sexual behavior were not becoming more liberal (some call it "permissive"), many persons would probably refrain from adopting the alternative forms. On the other hand, the increasing number of persons involved in these relations probably leads to a greater societal acceptance of them. Whether these living arrangements ever come to be accepted as widely as today's nuclear family is one factor that must be considered in dealing with the question 'Can the family survive?'

Summary

Although it has always been a basic unit of social organization in American society, the family has recently shown distinct signs of strain. Analyzed from the social disorganization perspective, the family has lost many of the functions it once performed. Other institutions in society now take major responsibilities for socializing children and organizing production and recreation. Moreover, the modern family maintains functions—consumption and the fulfillment of certain of its members' personal needs—for which its traditional structures are no longer relevant. As indicated by the increase in separations and divorces, the growing generation gap, and changes in sex roles, the family is in a state of relative disorganization. While new roles and family structures are in the process of being negotiated in a variety of public and private settings, no one solution to these problems is evident.

Early American families were characterized by a man who was dominant over his wife and children, all of whom were subject to the strict puritanical standards of the community. As the country expanded in the nineteenth century, new varieties of family structure became prominent. Communal experiments were attempted but had little lasting influence. On the frontier, extended three-generation families were the basis of social organization as well as self-sufficient agents of production and socialization.

In the cities, as industrialization took hold, families no longer were the primary agents of production and distribution. Men, women, and children worked in factories and were less tied to family groupings than previously. As immigrants flowed to the United States, their extended family patterns were broken down by Americanization and industrialization. Black families were denied any legal basis until after the Civil War, and even then they were required to establish themselves with very little support from the larger society.

Urbanization, industrialization, and the growth of institutions like government and business all influenced family structure, so that by 1900 the nuclear family of the present day had begun to emerge.

Whether the present disorganized state of the family indicates simply an adaptation to change or a warning of its obsolescence is a subject of debate among social theorists. Most likely the family will survive in a variety of forms influenced by the personal needs of its members as well as by broader social forces.

The condition of marriage, within which the family usually operates, is an important factor in determining the quality of family life. Earlier in our history, marriage was generally a permanent tie. Husbands and wives fulfilled the social and economic needs of one another. Today a fast-paced, complex society fulfills these needs but creates emotional needs. Some marriages break under the strain. Divorce, separation, and desertion are increasingly common in America; but the fact that a majority of divorced persons remarry indicates that many people still rely on marriage to fulfill emotional needs.

Roles within the family are presently changing. Increased exposure to the career world during World War II, more education, and dwindling family size have all contributed to women's reevaluation of their family role. The women's liberation movement has demanded independence and respect for all women. In recognizing women's independence, men too have begun to question their role within the family, where for so long they were expected to be sole breadwinner and authority figure. Children, because of schools and their increased association with their own age groups and because of the growth and influence of communications media, are less dependent upon their families for value guidance than they once were. Familial disorganization and cultural breakdown have complicated the already precarious position of youth in society. In the absence of an acceptable value system, and therefore a reason to be enthusiastic about becoming an adult, many youths have turned to drug use, meditation, religious conversion, and so forth in response to their personal troubles. Older family members have become increasingly detached from the family unit and are forced to make lives for themselves within their own age group.

Recent Supreme Court decisions and legal changes have facilitated an expansion of women's roles in society. Day-care centers enable women to work as often and as long as men and single parents to raise a family. A more positive attitude toward divorce and more lenient divorce laws, communal living, and less parent-centered child rearing have all contributed to the development of a new flexibility within marriage and the family.

Notes

[1]F. Ivan Nye and Felix M. Berardo, *The Family: Its Structure and Interaction* (New York: Macmillan, 1973), p.92

[2]Talcott Parsons et al., *Family, Socialization and Interaction Process* (New York: Free Press, 1955), pp. 3–34.

[3]Robert O. Blood and Donald M. Wolfe, *Husbands and Wives* (New York: Free Press, 1960), pp. 47–54.

[4]William O. Goode, "Changes in Family Patterns," *The Family and Change,* ed. John Edwards (New York: Knopf, 1969), pp. 19–32.

[5]William F. Ogburn and Clark Tibbitts, "The Family and its Functions," *Recent Social Trends in the United States,* report of the President's Research Committee on Social Trends (New York: McGrawHill, 1933), pp. 661–708.

[6]Jetse Sprey, "The Family as a System in Conflict," *Journal of Marriage and the Family* 31 (1969), 699.

[7]U.S. Bureau of the Census, *Current Population Reports, Population Characteristics,* Series P-20, No. 323 (Washington D.C.: Government Printing Office, April 1978), p. 1.

[8]Ibid., pp. 1–3.

[9]U.S. Bureau of the Census, *Statistical Abstract of United States 1977,* p. 74

[10]Ibid., p. 74

[11]Ibid., p. 77

[12]U.S. Bureau of the Census, *Current Population Reports, Population Characteristics, 1978,* pp. 9–12.

[13]Ibid., pp. 7–8.

[14]Thomas P. Monahan, "Some Dimensions of Interreligious Marriages in Indiana, 1962–1967," *Social Forces* 52 (December 1973), 195–203.

[15]John Scanzoni, "A Social System Analysis of Dissolved and Existing Marriages," *Journal of Marriage and the Family* 30 (August 1968), 454.

[16]Center for Information on America, *Population Profiles, The Family,* No. 17 (Washington, Conn.: Center for Information on America, 1977), p. 8.

[17]Gerald R. Leslie, *The Family in Social Context* (New York: Oxford University Press, 1973), pp. 596–597.

[18]Morton Hunt, "Help Wanted, Divorce Counselor," *Contemporary American Family,* ed. W. Goode (Chicago: Quadrangle Books, 1971), p. 226

[19]Judson T. Landis, "A Comparison of Children from Divorced and Nondivorced Unhappy Marriages," *Family Life Coordinator* 11 (July 1962), 61–65.

[20]U.S. Bureau of the Census, *Current Population Reports, Consumer Income,* Series P-60, No. 115 (Washington, D.C.: Government Printing Office, July 1978), p. 3.

[21]U.S. Bureau of the Census, *Population Characteristics, 1978,* p. 9.

[22]Bernard Farber, *Family and Kinship in Modern Society* (Glenview, Ill.: Scott, Foresman, 1973), p. 69.

[23]Ibid., pp. 68–71.

[24]U.S. Bureau of the Census, *Statistic Abstract of the United States, 1977,* p. 61.

[25]Daniel Patrick Moynihan, *The Negro Family: The Case for National Action,* U.S. Department of Labor, Office of Planning and Research (Washington, D.C.: Government Printing Office, 1965).

[26]David Schulz, *Coming Up Black: Patterns of Ghetto Socialization* (Englewood Cliffs, N.J.: Prentice-Hall, 1968), p. 137.

[27]Denise B. Kandel, "Race, Maternal Authority, and Adolescent Aspiration," *American Journal of Sociology* 76 (May 1971), 999–1020.

[28]"The Surge in Easy Divorces—and the Problems They Bring," *U.S. News and World Report,* 22 April 1974, p. 45.

[29]William J. Goode, *Women in Divorce* (New York: Free Press, 1956), p. 186.

[30]Sigmund Freud, "Some Psychological Consequences of the Anatomical Distinction between Sexes," *Collected Papers,* vol. 5, ed. James Strachey (London: Hogarth Press, 1956), pp. 196–197.

[31]Lawrence Kohlberg, "A Cognitive-Developmental Analysis of Sex-Role Concepts," *Family in Transition,* abr. ed., ed. Arlene S. Skolnick and Jerome H. Skolnick (Boston: Little, Brown, 1971), p. 226

[32]Joy D. Osofsky and Howard J. Osofsky, "Androgyny as a Life-Style," *Family Coordinator* 21 (October 1972), 412–413.

[33]S. Ogden and N. Bradburn, "Working Wives and Marital Happiness," *American Journal of Sociology* 74 (January 1969), 407.

[34]C. Arnott, "Husbands' Attitude and Wives' Commitment to Employment," *Journal of Marriage and the Family* 34 (November 1972), 683.

[35]Kenneth Keniston, *The Uncommitted* (New York: Harcourt, 1965), pp. 258–259.

[36]Urie Bronfenbrenner, *Two Worlds of Childhood: U.S. and U.S.S.R.* (New York: Russell Sage, 1970), p. 103.

[37]Keniston, *The Uncommitted,* p. 204.

[38]Kenneth Keniston, "Youth: A 'New' Stage in Life." *The Prospect of Youth,* ed. Thomas S. Cottle (Boston: Little, Brown, 1972), p. 24.

[39]Richard Flacks, *Youth and Social Change* (Chicago: Markham, 1971), p. 21.

[40]Ibid., p. 22.

[41]U.S. Department of Labor, *Youth and the Meaning of Work,* Manpower Research Monograph No. 32 (Washington, D.C.: Government Printing Office, 1974), p. 8.

[42]Quoted in Anne MacLoed, *Growing Up in America,* National Institute of Mental Health (Washington, D. C.: Government Printing Office, 1973), p. 82.

[43]Barrington Moore, Jr., "Thoughts on the Future of the Family," *Personality and Social Life*, ed. Robert Endleman (New York: Random House, 1967), pp. 72–81.

[44]Bernard Farber, *Family Organization: An Introduction* (San Francisco: Chandler, 1964), p. 60.

[45]William O. Goode, *World Revolution and Family Patterns* (New York: Free Press, 1963), pp. 10–18.

[46]Sheila M. Rothman, "Other People's Children: The Day Care Experience in America," *Public Interest* (Winter 1973), p. 21.

[47]Ibid., p. 24.

[48]Ibid., p. 25.

[49]Ibid., p. 22.

[50]Larry L. Constantine and Joan M. Constantine, *Group Marriage* (New York: Macmillan, 1973), p. 83.

[51]Ibid., pp. 148–161.

[52]S. C. Lee and Audrey Battrud, "Marriage under a Monastic Mode of Life: A Preliminary Report on the Hutterite Family in South Dakota," *Journal of Marriage and the Family* 29 (August 1967), 512–520.

[53]Nena O'Neill and George O'Neill, *Open Marriage* (New York: M. Evans, 1972), p. 53.

[54]Ibid., p. 71.

[55]Ibid., pp. 72–73.

[56]Edward Van Deusen, Contract Cohabitation: An Alternative to Marriage (New York: Grove Press, 1974), pp. 69–71.

Education

3

Inequities in the System

Financing Education

Crisis in the Classroom

Approaching Equal Access

Equalizing Educational Funding

Curriculum Alternatives

Summary

Notes

Since the time of Socrates, education has been a major issue in every society. Socrates' battle for educational reform in Athens ended abruptly in 399 B.C. when he was sentenced to death for instilling the wrong values in his students. The harsh sentence attests to the importance that the ancient Greeks accorded to education; in our own day this issue continues to be equally crucial, even if administering hemlock to controversial educators has gone out of style.

Although the United States Constitution says nothing about public schools, the constitutions of all 50 states clearly spell out the community's duty to educate the young. By 1850 nearly all northern states had enacted free education policies, and by 1918 education in every state of the Union was not only free but compulsory as well.

The broad commitment to public education in the 1800s arose largely out of the growing need for a uniform approach to socialization for the diverse groups entering America:

Education during the nineteenth century had been increasingly viewed as an instrument of social control to be used to solve the social problems of crime, poverty, and Americanization of the immigrant. The activities of public school tended to replace the social training of other institutions, such as the family and church. One reason for the extension of school activities was the concern for all education of the great numbers of immigrants arriving from eastern and southern Europe. It was feared that without some form of Americanization immigrants would cause a rapid decay of American institutions.[1]

What was Americanization? Basically it was (and still is) a regimen of values that stressed hard work, fair play, individual initiative, upward social mobility, and monetary success. The educational system embodying these tenets was a fairly rigid one; although basic skills were taught, much of the instruction time was given over to value training such as every society has required of its educational institutions.

There were, of course, a number of children who were left out of the educational process almost entirely. Most blacks, despite the philanthropic efforts that established special institutes following the Civil War, received little training even in basic skills. Child labor in the expanding industries of the nation cut short many a school career. Most women were barred from higher education until the last decades of the nineteenth century; and even then, only the richest or the luckiest could enter the few women's colleges that had been formed.

The progressive education movement, which gathered momentum at the turn of the century, constituted a reaction to the failures of the structured schools of the time.[2] It advocated reform in classroom methods and curriculum, hoping to make students more inquisitve, creative, and actively involved in their own education. Philosopher John Dewey, a progressive, cared less for rigid socialization than for individualism and personal growth. But the progressive ideas, although generally successful in small private schools, found little acceptance in public education.

As immigration continued to increase, the size and scope of education grew rapidly. Schools had to train students for a new technological world that seemed to grow more complex each year. The educational system was forced to expand so quickly that it added to its qualities as an agent of socialization those of the bureaucratic enterprise. The net result of this rapid growth and change was that the quality of education improved in some repects for most Americans. At the same time, however, education became so oriented toward technology and rigid systems of learning that students grew more and more alienated and dissatisfied. Indeed, by the 1960s students and teachers alike claimed that public education had become dehumanizing as well as irrelevant and demanded fundamental changes.

Quality education for everyone has always been set before American society as a goal worth attaining, and over the years steps have been taken to involve all the children of the nation in the educational process. Yet many protest that equal access to quality education is still nonexistent. Blacks continue to be underrepresented in many major colleges and universities. On the other hand, when Allan Bakke sued the Regents of the University of California on the grounds that they discriminated against him because he was white, the Supreme Court declared that he had, in fact, been a victim of discrimination. The problem of equal access to quality education is the first of the education problems we shall consider in this chapter.

In the early years of our country, financing a school was one of the primary concerns of a new community, but fund raising was often difficult. Despite the country's wealth, school financing remains a difficult problem today. This will be the second aspect of the American educational system we will examine.

The substance of the values and information set forth in America's schools has been forever subject to debate, though certain trends in curriculum and policy are clear. At issue in the 1920s were such specific matters as the teaching of the theory of evolution; the current questions are much broader and more basic—for example, what are schools for? Debate in recent years has grown into social conflict taking place within educational institutions themselves. Curriculum and educational policy constitute the third problem area with which this chapter is concerned.

Both the social disorganization and the value conflict approaches offer a fruitful way of analyzing the problems related to our educational system. The former focuses on the discrepancy between what is expected of our educational institutions and how these institutions actually perform. In contemporary society, schools are expected to act as a primary socialization agent for young persons, especially in terms of adequately preparing them for future participation in the labor market. Further, schools are generally expected to provide an avenue for upward social mobility for children from a variety of backgrounds. But denial of equal educational opportunities for all and inequitable arrangements for funding schools interfere with these functions of the educational system. And social organization is inadequate whenever such a major institution fails to fulfill necessary social functions. Equality of opportunity is a major tenet of the American creed, but there is an enormous gap between the realities of the present educational system and this democratic ideal. To the extent that individuals are denied the opportunity to develop and make use of the full range of their talents and capabilities there is social disorganization.

Problems of the educational system also stem from divergent values and interest held by groups involved in or affected by the educational process. Some parents may think it desirable to maintain a curriculum that emphasizes the traditional three R's and rote learning of certain basic skills, whereas others may value a more progressive curriculum that stresses the development of independent thinking. Value conflicts are particularly visible with regard to the highly volatile issue of busing as a means of achieving school desegregation. The busing issue is a complex one, with the values of equal opportunity and neighborhood control of schools (as well as the attitudes of racial prejudice and racial harmony) colliding head on and frequently erupting into outbursts of violence.

More generally, the present system favors the privileged strata of society. Members of the middle class typically find that the current educational structure serves their interests rather well, but members of lower socioeconomic strata are often quite vocal in their condemnation of arrangements that provide poor facilities, limited opportunities, and preparation for only low-paying, low-status jobs. In these as well as other areas of the current educational system, the clash of values and interests between involved parties may generate social problems.

Inequities in the System

Although America's commitment to equal education for all its citizens has not changed in theory since the 1850s, our society has changed greatly. Advancing technology and industrialization have given rise to different educational needs, and even the idea of what constitutes education has changed drastically since the beginning of this century.

The most crucial test of this country's broad educational policy came in the 1954 Supreme Court decision *Brown* v. *Board of Education*, which ruled racial segregation in public schools unconstitutional. The Court ordered all public schools desegregated "within a reasonable time limit," thus obliging the federal government to make certain that integration was achieved throughout the country.

The issue of equal access to integrated, quality education became a national one, and it is still hotly debated today. The busing of children to distant schools—one of the most controversial methods of achieving integration—continues to arouse violent resistance in many quarters, which has slowed the process of integration, especially in the North. Nonetheless, the 1954 decision has inexorably changed not only American education but society at large as well. It was based on conclusive evidence that schooling for black children was inferior to that for whites, that black schools were financially worse off than white schools, and that the future job opportunities of black and white children were therefore wholly unequal and unfair.

Some institutions of higher learning established quota systems that would guarantee a certain percentage of classroom seats to members of minority groups. However, in 1978, the U.S. Supreme Court decided by a 5–4 vote that quotas were unacceptable.

Inequities in other social areas (particularly in housing, employment practices, public transportation, and public accommodation) soon became equally apparent to the nation. Although education had always been regarded as the "greater equalizer," black leaders, such as Martin Luther King, Jr., doubted that educational equality alone would solve the problems of their people. Even if schools were completely desegregated, this would not, for example, automatically eliminate discriminatory employment practices; and equal schooling would be of little use without equal job opportunities to follow.

Education: The Great Equalizer

More than 20 years after the historic decision, it is painfully evident that school desegregation, in spirit and in fact, has so far been largely unsuccessful. Even more disturbing, recent studies suggest that equal schooling will not in itself ensure subsequent equal occupational opportunity and income.[3]

Through the late 1950s and up to 1966, most liberal educators were convinced that if quality education were offered to everyone in our society, minorities would have equal chances to gain good employment and upward social mobility. Their two basic premises for this change in the status quo were: (1) educational opportunities must be equal in terms of finances, facilities, and faculties; and (2) integration must be sufficiently widespread to give all people access to these educational opportunities.

With these goals in mind, Congress passed the Civil Rights Act of 1964 as the foundation of President Johnson's Great Society. The act called for a report, within two years, "concerning the lack of availability of equal educational opportunities for individuals by reason of race, color, religion, or national origins in public educational institutions at all levels in the United States."[4] The resulting study, known now as the Coleman report, came as a shock to many leaders.[5] On one hand, it reported that despite the 12-year-old *Brown* decision, integration continued to be more an ideal than a reality. And on the other hand, it challenged that ideal by documenting not the difference but the *lack* of difference between black schools and white schools.[6]

The report concluded that "American public education remains largely unequal in most regions of the country, including all those where Negroes form any significant proportion of the population."[7]

But there were other findings. Segregation was found to be the rule, not the exception.[8] Yet, contrary to popular opinion, the facilities, curricula, and most of the measurable characteristics of teachers in black and white schools were quite similar. The differences in facilities, curricula, and teacher quality had little effect on either black or white students' performance on standardized tests, and the single characteristic that showed a consistent relationship to test performance was the one characteristic to which poor black children were denied access: classmates from affluent homes.[9]

In other words, the report concluded that schools did little to aid rapid upward social progress. Family background, more than education, accounted for the huge discrepancy between the achievement of blacks and whites. Many social and educational reformers had been aware of this but had believed that education would swing the pendulum toward a more equal social situation. The Coleman report, which highlighted the insignificance of educational differences between blacks and whites, raised many issues and started new controversies. If education does not further social equality, why spend millions on improving the schools? If upgrading the school system does not make a difference, what will? Even though the debate has increased, the questions have been left essentially unanswered.

In 1972 a careful review and analysis of data from many studies concerning the relationship between family background and educational and occupational achievement again generated considerable controversy among educators, policymakers, and the citizenry at large. It was found that schools are *unequal* in financial resources and facilities and that educational opportunity in the United States thus remains unequally distributed. Nonetheless, as in the Coleman study, family background was found to have a greater effect on educational achievement than any other factor. Most significant was the fact that schooling in itself was found to have minimal lasting effects on future occupational success or earnings; rather than acting as the "great equalizer," schools appear to function primarily as agents of certification and measurement. The implications of this finding for social policy are, of course, enormous. This 1972 study suggests that the most effective reform in the long run must entail a policy of income equalization, for it is economic inequities among adults, rather than educational differences among children, that are the crucial factors in determining upward economic and social mobility. Since schools can do little to bring about equality among adults, more fundamental reforms are called for:

As long as egalitarians assume that public policy cannot contribute to economic equality directly but must proceed by ingenious manipulations of marginal institutions like the schools, progress will remain glacial. If we want to move beyond this tradition, we will have to establish political control over the economic institutions that shape our society. This is what other countries usually call socialism. Anything else will end in the same disappointment as the reforms of the 1960s.[10]

Integration by Busing

The implications of these findings are evident in the problems relative to integration that have emerged in recent years. Most southern school districts have complied, de facto and de jure, with the 1954 Court decision; in fact, as can be seen in Table 3.1, the record of school integration in the South is as good or better than that of any other region of the country. In 1968, 68 percent of the South's blacks were still in all-black schools, while only 18 percent attended schools that were predominantly white. By 1972, only 8 percent of southern blacks went to all-black schools, and 40 percent were enrolled in predominantly white schools.[11] As Table 3.1 shows, the latter figure had risen to nearly 45 percent by 1974. Yet the continuing de facto segregation of residential neighborhoods meant that school segregation persisted in most regions of the country.

With the black migrations from the South to northern urban centers in the 1950s and 1960s, the makeup of many cities changed radically. By the hundreds of thousands, whites moved from the cities to the suburbs, while blacks settled in the inner cities, usually the oldest and most run-down urban areas. This pattern repeated itself across the entire country. As a result, society now faces the problem of desegregating city school systems that have 40 to 60 percent black enrollment. In many ways, the solution is more difficult now than it was 20 years ago.

Coleman has recently analyzed the impact of desegregation on metropolitan areas and concluded that current governmental policies may be producing more problems than they are solving. Desegregation plans in many areas have served to increase the rate at which whites leave the area. The long term effect runs counter to the short term effect of desegregating city schools because there are fewer white children to attend the city schools.[12] Since white parents have continued to resist integration by leaving the cities for generally more expensive suburbs, the courts have ordered school districts desegregated by taking whole regions into account: cities and their suburbs are to be considered together, with busing the mode of achieving the desired results. Decisions in 1969 and 1971 called for "good faith compliance" to the desegregation law by ordering school boards to include whole metropolitan regions in their busing plans.[13]

	Distribution of Black Student Enrollment Attending Public Schools By Geographic Area, 1974 Table 3.1					
	Continental United States	Northeast	Border States and Washington D.C.	South	Midwest	West
Total students	45,988,000					
Percent black students	14.5%					
Percent black students attending:						
0–49% minority schools	33.2%	19.0%	28.1%	44.5%	19.4%	26.6%
50–89% minority schools	26.3%	23.2%	13.5%	32.2%	18.4%	28.3%
90–100% minority schools	40.5%	57.8%	58.4%	23.4%	62.2%	45.1%

Source: U.S. Department Health, Education and Welfare, National Center for Education Statistics, *The Condition of Education, 1978 edition* (Washington, D.C.: Government Printing Office, 1978), p. 70; U.S. Department of Commerce, Bureau of the Census, *Statistical Abstract of the United States, 1977* (Washington, D.C.: Government Printing Office, 1977), p. 145.

BUSING

Busing is the only remedy the courts have recognized for equalizing the racial balance of many school districts. But while less than 1 percent of the country's children who ride buses to school are required to do so for the purpose of integration, the controversy over this small percentage has given rise to vicious and devastating bitterness. Clearly, without the commitment of the people, the American government cannot make equal opportunity more than just a great American myth. *This page:* They opened the doors—attorneys George E. C. Hayes, Thurgood Marshall, and James Nabrit, who in 1954 won the Supreme Court school desegregation suit *Brown* vs. *Board of Education;* for and against the Great American Dream— conflict over busing in Boston. *Opposite page, clockwise from top:* Enforcing equal opportunity—the doors are open, but not the minds; prelude to violence—the beating this man received on the way to pick up his daughter at school instigated a violent clash between anti-integration whites and Boston police; riding out the storm—anti-integration violence in Boston necessitated police protection for school buses; integration can work, at least for the children themselves.

In response to these recent busing mandates, a sizable number of parents are transferring their children from suburban public schools to private schools. Some observers believe that "white flight" and racial isolation will increase, at least temporarily, with the implementation of desegregation on this wider scale. The experiences of cities that have instituted desegregation plans indicate, however, that after an initial period of sometimes intense opposition, busing generally comes to be largely accepted by members of the community.

Nevertheless, opposition to busing for the purpose of achieving racial balance in the schools remains widespread. Cities in which the courts have determined that educational inequality still exists have attempted to offer alternative plans to ensure quality education for all. To date, the courts have not found any of these alternatives acceptable, and busing continues to be ordered as the remedy for educational inequality. In an attempt to circumvent court rulings, community groups and parents' committees have pressed for legislation banning the use of long-distance busing to achieve racial balance. More recently, antibusing groups have lobbied hard for a constitutional amendment to prohibit busing for the purpose of school integration.

Even Coleman appears to have changed direction from that described in his earlier work. He has now spoken out against mandatory busing. In its place he favors a plan that would allow children to choose to attend any school in their metropolitan area (city or suburb) that did not have a greater percentage of children of their particular race than their place of residence. The approach has been criticized because the schools that parents would consider better would be inundated by requests to attend. This could lead to the need to enlarge these schools at a time when taxpayers are becoming increasingly resistant to supporting public education.[14]

Lorenzo Middleton

The Effects of School Desegregation: the Debate Goes On

Do black children learn more when they go to school with whites? Will white parents move out of town rather than send their children to school with blacks? Will busing lead to better race relations?

After a quarter-century of searching for answers to these and other questions about the effects of public school desegregation, the country's social scientists have yet to reach any major conclusions that they can agree on.

The scholars' debate, peppered with bitter personal attacks among leading researchers on both sides, has made little progress since the Supreme Court outlawed dual school systems in 1954.

At that time, in the *Brown* v. *the Board of Education of Topeka* case, 35 educators, sociologists, and psychologists testified that segregation was psychologically and educationally damaging to black children. Those arguments were challenged by extensive social-science evidence presented by the other side, which held that black children were damaged even more by going to school with white children whom they considered to be their superiors.

Today, with the question of the effects of Southern desegregation still unsettled, the focus of the debate has shifted to the North, where researchers have produced volumes of data to "prove" that court-ordered busing plans have been successful or unsuccessful.

The pivotal figure in the debate has been sociologist James S. Coleman, now at the University of Chicago. He led the first large-scale, federally financed research project on desegregation in the mid-1960's, when he was at Johns Hopkins. . . .

His research has since been widely used by advocates of desegregation to support mandatory busing plans.

In 1975, however, Mr. Coleman declared that he had reassessed his original conclusions, in light of more recent research, and had concluded that mandatory desegregation had more negative than positive effects.

Mr. Coleman's widely publicized turnaround has been at the center of much of the recent academic debate on the issue, which has focused on the relationship of desegregation to the achievement gains of black children and to the rate of "white flight" from city school systems. . . .

Betsy Levin, professor of law at Duke University and chairman of the National Review Panel on School Desegregation Research, said a recent analysis of about 100 studies had found that research showing that desegregation has positive effects on the achievement of minority-group students outnumbered, three to one, those that show negative effects. . . .

Mr. Coleman, however, said he has examined the same analysis, called *Desegregation and Black Achievement*, by Robert L. Crain and Rita E. Mahard of the RAND Corporation, and found that fewer than half of the "reliable" studies in the review showed that desegregation has positive effects on achievement.

Mr. Crain and Ms. Mahard argued, meanwhile, that those showing negative effects on achievement were the "weaker studies" in their review. . . .

David J. Armor, an economist with the RAND Corporation who has found a high correlation between desegregation and white flight, says there is really no way for researchers to determine with certainty the true relationship of the two phenomena. Therefore, Mr. Armor argues, alternatives to mandatory busing plans should be adopted.

Mr. Coleman contends that the alternative is for cities to adopt voluntary school-desegregation plans in cooperation with their suburbs—plans that would allow students to attend any school in their metropolitan area, as long as their transfers would not lead to increased segregation.

Mr. Coleman's opponents, however, argue that all attempts at voluntary desegregation thus far have been failures, because of what Gard Orfield, a political scientist at the University of Illinois at Urbana, calls "the tremendous inertia of segregation in our society." . . .

White parents have refused to send their children to predominantly black schools and only a small percentage of blacks have choosen to go to white schools under voluntary plans, Mr. Orfield says. "And so," he says, "at best you have a small amount of one-way desegregation with these plans, leaving practically all the whites in all-white schools and most of the minorities in minority schools."

Mr. Coleman counters by citing the voluntary plan adopted by the Wisconsin legislature, which he says has led to the desegregation of two-thirds of the schools in Milwaukee in less than three years. Mr. Coleman agrees with Mr. Orfield that most of the predominantly black schools in the city have remained black, but he says there is nothing wrong with that.

"This belief in the inherent inferiority of an all-black school has a curiously racist flavor," Mr. Coleman argues. . . .

Mr. Orfield says Mr. Coleman's argument overlooks the court decisions, which have found segregation to be unconstitutional.

Mr. Coleman calls that argument "a fiction."

And so the two sides debate—in the courts, in scholarly papers, and in nationwide panels, such as the study group on urban school desegregation sponsored by the American Academy of Arts and Sciences. . . .

In light of the seemingly unsolvable disagreements over whether or not desegregation can work, some researchers are beginning to devote more time to studying various educational programs that have been carried out as a result of desegregation.

"This is the only research that will help the people who have to run the school systems," said Ben Williams, director of a desegregation-research effort sponsored by the Education Commission of the States.

One study now under way by Mr. William's group is an examination of the educational benefits of "magnet" schools, which have been set up under many recent desegregation plans with programs aimed at attracting students from outside those schools' normal attendence areas. . . .

James S. Coleman, whose research on public-school desegregation has made him one of the most controversial sociologists in America, is beginning a massive new study that he believes might settle many of the unanswered questions in the desegregation debate.

A professor of sociology at the University of Chicago, Mr. Coleman is also the senior study director for the university's National Opinion Research Center, which has been commissioned to do a nationwide analysis of high-school sophomores and seniors for the federal government's National Center for Education Statistics.

The researchers are planning to gather test scores and other information from 72,000 students in 50 schools this year and from 1,000 schools next year, and will follow the progress of 24,000 of those students at two-year intervals after they leave high school. . . .

The study, called "High School and Beyond," is chiefly designed to examine the effects of various high-school curricula on students who go to college and on those who go to work immediately after high school.

"But we feel it would be really foolish not to use the data from this study to further the examination of the effects of desegregation," Mr. Coleman said. . . .

His critics also agree with Mr. Coleman that many of the disagreements in the desegregation debate stem from a lack of comprehensive data on the subject.

While the 1966 study—which involved tests and surveys of 600,000 students and 60,000 teachers in 4,000 schools around the country—still remains the most extensive piece of educational research ever conducted, Mr. Coleman said his new study would provide more reliable information by tracking students over a period of years after they had been through desegregated schools. . . .

Exerpts from "The Effects of School Desegregation: the Debate Goes on," *Chronicle of Higher Education*, Nov. 6, 1978, pp. 1–5, by Lorenzo Middleton. Reprinted by permission.

The Neighborhood School— Cornerstone of Inequity

Busing will continue to be a volatile issue for some time. Antibusing groups assert that busing is too costly, unsafe, and time-consuming. They also continue to cling to the concept of the neighborhood school as a cornerstone of the community. Many who moved from the cities to the suburbs to find a sense of community solidarity want a neighborhood school and the community spirit they believe it respresents. In fact, that spirit was lost long ago when school districts became centralized. Nonetheless, even a sizable number of black civil rights leaders are now opposing busing and advocating the improvement of predominantly black schools.[15] They consider this means of achieving quality education preferable to altering the racial balance of all schools within an area.

Statistically, probusing arguments are more to the point. According to the Department of Transportation, out of the almost 19 million children— 43.5 percent of the total public school population—who are transported to school daily, *less than 1 percent* are bused to achieve integration.[16] Thus, the busing problem is really a question of how deeply rooted our commitment to integration is, or how strongly we feel about maintaining the identity of our own community or neighborhood, and not a question of our sentiments for or against busing per se: "Desegregation is not so much a technical as a political, educational, and moral concern."[17] The experiences at Central High in Little Rock, Arkansas, in 1957, George Wallace's stand against integration at the door of the University of Alabama in 1962, and the violence and resultant massive police presence in Boston and Louisville in 1975 all illustrate that desegregation is an issue so complex that it may take decades to resolve.

If full integration of class and race is to be achieved in the school systems, either communities themselves must change and become more equal or the idea of the neighborhood school must be abandoned as hopelessly out of date. Integration is a treasured principle for many people; but too few of them are actually willing to go through the steps necessary to achieve it in a manner that might really equalize education for all. And, as the social scientists note, integration per se is not synonymous with equality of opportunity.

Financing Education

For a variety of reasons, the cost of education has skyrocketed since World War II. Building costs have soared; and expenditures for facilities such as language labs, audiovisual equipment, scientific equipment, and sophisticated machinery like computers, as well as teachers' and administrators' salaries, mount each year into the billions of dollars.

One of the biggest problems facing education today is finance. Public education at all levels is paid for by tax dollars, with most of the burden falling on the state and local communities. States provide about 40 percent of all public school funding; 10 percent comes from the federal government; and the remaining 50 percent comes from local school districts, where it is almost wholly derived from property taxes.[18] There is a widely held belief that if the federal government plays too large a role in paying for education, it may also want to dictate what will be taught. And, in general, federal aid is used primarily to assist states when gross deficiencies are apparent and cannot be eliminated through state or local revenues.

Rewarding the Rich and Penalizing the Poor

Because communites vary greatly in wealth, gross inequities in the quality of school facilities and programs have plagued American education. The richer states have an obvious advantage. The higher the per capita income, the greater the amount of money that is available to be spent on schools. For instance, the estimated public school expenditure for 1974–75 per pupil in New York was $1819; in Mississippi it was $783.[19] Yet it is *within* each state that the most blatant inequalities exist. For example, in Montana in the 1974–75 school year, 24 percent of the districts within the state were spending less than $900 per pupil while 26 percent of the districts were spending more than $1500 per pupil.[20]

The 1973 Fleischman Report indicated that "A poor man in a poor district must often pay local taxes at higher rates for the inferior education of his child than the man of means in a rich district pays for the superior education of his child. Yet, incredibly, that is the situation today in most of the 50 states, and that is the case in New York."[21]

While an attempt is made to distribute state aid fairly, the fact is that in most states the districts that pay the highest property taxes get the most money. The following example illustrates the result. Two school districts only ten miles apart on Long Island, New York, vary greatly in revenue. Great Neck, a wealthy community with an enrollment of 9869, spends $2077 per year on each of its students. Levittown, far less wealthy, with an enrollment of 17,280 students, spends only $1189 per student each year. The state provides $764 per student per year in Levittown to supplement the local expenditure per student of $410, and gives each Great Neck student

$364 to supplement the much larger local expenditure of $1684 per pupil.[22] The inequality will never be made up unless the state gives far more money to the poorer community or the property tax revenue-raising system is thoroughly overhauled.

Differences between cities and suburbs are even more striking. While rich suburbs are able to build sprawling facilities complete with the newest educational aids, city schools are generally decaying. Since the white migration to the suburbs during the 1950s and 1960s was followed by the migration of corporations, the tax base of most urban centers fell enormously. Again the suburbs gained, while the cities, where money is most urgently needed for new buildings and programs, lost.

Attempts to change this situation have met with mixed results. In a 1971 landmark case, the California Supreme Court ruled that the state's system of public school finance (property taxes) "denies children the equal protection guaranteed under the Fourteenth Amendment, because it produces substantial disparities among school districts in the amount of revenue available for education."[23] The ruling was applicable only in California, but it set the stage for further litigation. In a 1973 case involving Texas schools, however, the U.S. Supreme Court ruled that education is *not* one of the rights guaranteed by the Constitution, thus declining to interfere with the state's use of property taxes for education. The case was momentous. Had the Court ruled education to be a right, nearly all the nation's $50 billion structure of public school finance would have had to be changed.[24] The California decision still holds for that state, but the only avenue now open to overhaul the school financing system is each state's highest court.

Clearly, this problem must be solved before the issue of equal access to quality education can be decided. In view of the discrepancies in educational materials, teachers' pay, and facilities, quality public education for all is still only a myth. Since the federal government manifests continued reluctance to increase its role in funding, the responsibility falls on the states to legislate new and more equitable ways of apportioning funds. Either state aid for poor school districts will have to be increased, or, more radically, each state may have to take full control of educational revenues in order to guarantee equality in distribution.

Cutbacks in Funding for Higher Education

The financial problems of colleges and universities are of a different nature. In public universities, federal and state funds supply most of the money for operating costs, while private grants finance specific projects. The 1950s and 1960s saw an increasing emphasis on technological and scientific research and development, due mainly to government fears that the Soviet Union might outstrip us in those fields. Growth and financial outlay were enormous, due to this new emphasis and also to the enormous costs of new hardware, such as lasers and computers. In 1957 expenditures for all institutions of higher education in the United States were $4.9 billion; by 1976–77 they had risen to an estimated $49.2 billion.[25]

The flow of government money to higher education began to decrease during the Vietnam War and slowed even further during the recession that began in 1970. Research grants were cut drastically, and even though Congress passed various education appropriations, President Nixon vetoed them as inflationary. Between 1968 and 1971, federal expenditures for research dropped by well over a billion dollars, with colleges and universities bearing a large share of the decrease.[26] Public institutions will survive these cutbacks because state monies will continue to underwrite operating expenses. Although universities desperately need federal funds for programs that are too expensive for the state to maintain, they can still rely on state funding to offer adequate educational programs, even at the graduate level.

The situation for private colleges is very different, however, because these institutions depend entirely on private donors and grants from foundations and the government. Having grown in response to government outlays, many private institutions have recently found themselves overextended when government aid has been withdrawn. Only a few top colleges and universities have stable endowment funds that generate money through interest accumulation and stock market growth; most of the rest are running on a one- to three-year cash supply.

Private institutions have always been more costly for students than state colleges. Even though operating costs are roughly the same, private colleges must necessarily rely far more on tuition monies than state-supported schools. In 1958 the average tuition for full-time students in private colleges was $729 per year; in state colleges the average was $192. By 1975–76 tuition in private colleges had increased to $2333 per year, while that of state institutions had risen to $563 per year.[27] Unless private universities continue to raise tuition each year (thus pricing themselves out of the reach of many able students) or recieve aid from foundations or the government, many will be forced to shut down in this decade.

Teachers Bargain for Better Pay

Although they perform an important social function, teachers in the public schools and in most universities in America have never had very high social status. In spite of the fact that they are considered professionals, teachers earn much less than doctors or lawyers. In 1976–77 the average salary for a public school classroom teacher in Mississippi was $9397, in Alaska, the average was $21,020.[28] The long vacations teachers receive are often used to rationalize their low salaries; but even when this factor is taken into account, their remuneration is low in comparison with other professions for which a similar amount of training is required.

A few decades ago, when teachers were given a salary by their board of education and had no power to bargain for higher pay, the situation was even more inequitable. Now, however, both state and municipal teachers' unions have begun to take a much firmer stance during contract talks, with some success. The average pay for all teachers in 1960 was $5000; by 1976–77 it had risen to $13,397.[29] Twenty years ago a teachers' strike would have been unthinkable. But during the past ten years, almost every large American city has experienced a teachers' strike, even though such strikes are illegal under most state laws. And on the whole, teachers' demands for more equitable wages and working conditions have been met by their local districts. Their unions, once ineffective and docile, are now powerful tools in the collective bargaining process.

The positions teachers can occupy in today's educational system are less restricted than in the past. Traditionally, elementary school teachers were women, while men dominated the faculties of colleges and universities. But with the shift in social values toward more equality in all areas, more men now teach in elementary schools and more women are on college and university faculties. The old stereotypes are beginning to fade away, and the man who teaches first grade is not as hesitant to say so as he might have been ten years ago.

Teachers will continue to press for higher salaries in the future, and suburban schools, with their greater financial resources, will be able to meet teacher demands. Urban centers will be hard pressed to compete, however, unless revenues are increased considerably. Urban teachers face many problems in the classroom, among them the violence in inner-city schools (discussed in more detail in Chapter 14). Unless school districts can pay higher wages, teachers will have little incentive to subject themselves to these problems.

Crisis in the Classroom

During the twentieth century the scope of education has grown tremendously, and its diversity today is reflected in the curriculum of nearly every school and university. The frontiers of knowledge have expanded in the areas of mathematics and the physical and social sciences. The whole world is open for study. Yet students continually complain about a dull, boring, and irrelevant school experience.

What seems to be missing from the school curriculum at all levels? Who decides what is important, and how much say should students themselves have in deciding what to study?

Frank E. Armbruster
The More We Spend, the Less Children Learn

Last school year, Americans spent far more on all levels of education than they spent for defense; for primary and secondary schooling, the bill was $75 billion, more than four times the 1960 figure. . . .

It is now clear, however, that all that money hasn't bought much. In the crudest cost-benefit terms, the more the parents have spent on schools, the less their children have learned. . . .

Many high-school graduates entering college these days cannot understand the textbooks that high-school graduates used to be able to read. . . . The Times also reported that in 1973 an estimated "19 million Americans over 16 were functionally illiterate," unable "to read job application forms, driver's license examinations and newspaper want ads" or to distinguish between medicine bottles by reading simple labels. . . .

The decline in academic performance is of growing concern to parents, who are often dismayed to find *teachers* in league with their children in resisting their demands for more effort on their studies, especially homework. . . .

The decline in academic performance is no secret in the educational community, of course, and it is common to hear educators trying to explain it in terms that are not very convincing. . . .

The most common response, however, is to point to forces operating outside the schools—to a lack of money for education, or to the underprivileged circumstances of many pupils. In light of the statistics, these excuses are highly questionable.

Examination of the pertinent data showed that

throughout this most recent period of academic decline, although there was much emphasis on the need for more money for education, there was no positive correlation between spending trends and trends in academic achievement. . . .

In fact, as money spent has increased at an ever-faster rate since the mid-60's, almost without exception, achievement has consistently fallen.

The same difficulty arises with the argument that the "changing pupil population" is the cause of their inability to handle the fundamentals and of the disruption in our schools. At the beginning of this century, the last period when large numbers of predominantly rural people swarmed into our Northern cities, urban schools in those cities took in vast numbers of pupils who spoke no English. . . .

The pupils learned to read and write, and learned basic grammar, arithmetic, history, and geography by the sixth grade—which was as far as most children went in those days. . . .

The Great Depression era again saw high student/teacher ratios (about 30 to 1) and many schools with second-generation immigrants whose parents couldn't speak English and others whose parents had finished only the sixth grade; there was little money for education "specialists" or for schools in general. Yet pupils who couldn't read by the seventh grade in those days were virtually unknown. They could also do long division, knew history and geography, could write compositions and scored some of the highest grades on ninth-grade academic achievement tests we have ever seen. . . .

Today, as in the past, poor families view basic education as a means to upward mobility; and though today's underprivileged parents may be ill-equipped to help their children with difficult schoolwork, so were such parents in the past. Other evidence suggests that home environment is not the cause of declining achievement. Some largely minority and "core-city" school systems are among the exceptions whose average achievement level has not fallen significantly. And the general decline is hardly limited to the slums. The data shows that achievement has also dropped among students from districts with more affluent homes full of books and encyclopedias, where parents have college educations, good vocabularies and provide all the advantages.

If money and home environment cannot fairly be blamed for the decline, what can? The factor that does appear to affect academic performance is the degree to which the schools sacrifice traditional disciplines and subjects for the sake of "innovative" teaching activities. . . .

This latest group of innovators . . . began to argue in the 1960s that the school system was incapable of teaching the fundamentals to America's poor children. The same school system that had taught the fundamentals to the children of immigrants . . . now presumably could not do the same for children of native-born Americans, all of whom spoke English and most of whom were at least literate. . . .

The innovators tended to see the current problems as unique and invulnerable to any past approaches to solution. Many attacked everything from homework and rote learning to curriculums that included the standard academic disciplines. . . .

Much of the innovative doctrine was questionable, if not deeply flawed. For example, the innovators claimed their approach would teach children to think (past educators would have been reluctant to say their charges lacked or had to be taught such a skill). . . .

The innovators eschew rote learning as part of the highly structured old-school "lock-step" system that squelched creativity and fostered passivity. But at least some rote learning may be essential. . . .

In some ways, the innovators seemed more concerned with theory than with the actual needs of children. . . .

Still, the philosophy of the innovators retained a seductive appeal for educators in the late 1960's and early 1970's and sometimes for reasons that did not arise directly from its dubious logic. While many dedicated teachers opposed and were even shocked by the trend, many less than totally responsible educators seemed quick to learn that down this road lay the good life. With no one looking closely at what was happening in the schools, it was possible to press the point that if the public wanted "quality education," more money would be needed. . . .

Without close scrutiny of activities inside the schools, educators can also resort to expensive but unproductive gimmickry, and thus claim to be wrestling with school problems. . . .

Meanwhile, the actual learning in our schools declines. Throughtout the school system fewer hours per day and fewer days per year are spent in school and our curriculums deteriorate. Low-academic-content electives and grade-school-level arithmetic take up dwindling high-school time once spent on the more difficult disciplines.

One high school in Connecticut had 125 electives

for a student body of 1,000. . . . Though prerequisites are often required before these electives can be taken, their diluting effect remains. . . .

One of the most discouraging aspects of this situation is that over the past decade many schools have tended to educate children for a nonexistent world. Certain things in life simply cannot be avoided or blamed on someone else; actions have personal consequences; outside the school environment one normally has to produce to be promoted; work must satisfy the needs of the economy to be profitable to the worker; many trades and professions require work that gives no credit for good intentions or being nearly accurate—much work, and advanced study, must be explicit, meticulous and correct every time; it is important to be well informed and logical, not just spontaneous and talkative. To let students believe otherwise is to mislead them dangerously—especially if they are underprivileged. . . .

A large part of the education establishment continues to avoid, if not obscure, the real issues. Too often, they still begin with the premise that educators have been doing a good job and seldom bring up comparisons of the academic achievement, or even the behavior, of current pupils of a school district with that of their predecessors. . . .

Parents should acquire an up-to-date historical record of student-body scores on standarized achievement tests administered regularly to their children, to keep track of how well their schools are doing their job and to relate these results to changes in expenditures per pupil and teachers' salaries. They should make their findings known to school administrators and school-board officials.

They should also pay close attention to curriculum. Many "specialized" courses in elementary schools are of light academic content, of little proven value, and take up a significant part of the school day. . . .

At the high-school level, pupils must know the history of our civilization and great literature in our language. They should be exposed to some higher mathematics, some real science and to at least one of the major foreign languages. They simply *must* be able to transform ideas into written material in a comprehensible and grammatically correct way. If they can't pass such courses, they should not receive a high-school diploma. . . .

In addition to the curriculum, parents and school-board trustees should examine teaching methods.

Many math and other primary-school problems might be reduced by a new emphasis on rote learning. . . . We also know how to teach children the fundamentals of grammar and how to improve their verbal skills. Diagraming sentences, essay writing and correction by teachers, and the strictly enforced use of proper grammar, grade-equivalent vocabulary and good diction at all times in school are essential. Numerical or letter-graded report cards every four weeks for elementary school, and six weeks for high school, are ways to help assure that teachers and parents will be alerted to problems a child may be having as soon as they occur, rather than later, when a child is already far behind.

Some children have always had more trouble learning than others. Some are slow starters, but if the material is not too difficult, apparently most children suddenly find themselves reading, as though a light had gone on. Promoting a child so that he must deal with more difficult material when the light has just begun to flicker may be counterproductive. . . .

It is no crime to keep a child back until "the light goes on" and he can cope with the more difficult material; it is no favor to the child to push him through and out of school without the basic skills.

These teaching methods are often thought to be "old-fashioned," as perhaps is the idea that the classroom essentially must have an orderly, well-structured, though by no means unhappy, environment. Many innovative educators may object to these methods, but until other proven techniques are developed, they are the only tried and true ones we have, and, at least in the lower grades, most current teaching staffs have the general knowledge necessary to implement them. Indeed, there are indications that moves in this direction are already under way in at least a few school districts.

It is true that, in many ways, this means returning to a system we had about 20 years and three-quarters of a trillion tax dollars ago. This is certainly a bitter pill for us to swallow, but with the welfare of a generation of youngsters at stake, we may have no other choice.

Excerpts from Frank E. Armbruster, "The More We Spend, the Less Children Learn," *New York Times Magazine,* August 28, 1977, p. 9ff. © 1977 by The New York Times Company. Reprinted by permission.

During the past few decades, many Americans believed that our sophisticated technology could solve any problem, including how to teach children. Due in part to the technological successes of endeavors such as the space program, technological utopianism has come to be a major element in American culture; more and more, emphasis has been placed on gadgets rather than on people. The dehumanizing consequences of this concept were a prime cause of the student rebellions of the 1960s. Students of that era demanded teaching relevant to current social conditions, teaching which they felt neither machines nor many of the personnel on college and high school faculties could provide.

Until fairly recently, education was controlled by relatively few administrators, who were therefore also instrumental in determining the purpose of schooling. There was also a reasonably firm consensus in the values most parents wished the schools to instill in their children. But during the 1960s, curriculum and authority in the schools became issues for heated debate. Minority groups called for more emphasis on their own concerns in the classroom, from elementary to graduate school. High school students questioned the value of their studies and the heavy emphasis placed on attending college. And all over the country college students were rebelling, challenging administrations and faculty and demanding reforms in curriculum, admissions, and educational policy. The response of many educators and reformers is summed up in Charles Silberman's introduction to *Crisis in the Classroom:* "Our bias, it should be emphasized, was not that everything that was being done was necessarily wrong; it was simply that everything now being done needs to be questioned."[30]

Elementary Schools: Creativity or Obedience?

Learning basic skills is important, of course, but the development of socially acceptable patterns of interpresonal relationships and the internalization of societal values emphasizing success and achievement have always been primary goals of the American educational system. Yet, while this emphasis on socialization is the core of elementary education and the credo of traditional authoritarian educators in America, reformers have been saying all along that this focus is wrong. Progressive educators believe schools should experiment and change and should try to change society. Authoritarians, on the other hand, view schools merely as vehicles for providing society with its necessary work force and consider experimentation and learning for its own sake irrelevant. The issue at the heart of the long-standing controversy between authoritarian and progressive educators is: Should we teach children what society wants them to learn, or should we teach them to think for themselves?

Reformers have always called for more freedom of choice in elementary education. They have maintained that a happy child who has learned to think will benefit society far more than one who has been force-fed facts and pushed into the "real world" without ever learning how to reach conclusions independently.

In an authoritarian school, children learn submissiveness as well as mathematics if they are to "succeed." In most schools they learn to direct their energies to future goals—"It will be useful some day, you'll see." They learn that the world is made up of right answers. They learn that they can be reduced to quantified equivalent, to a

Expanding the educational experience: Contemporary classrooms are no longer rigidly dominated by the teacher. Children are encouraged to question and experiment and to learn at their own pace, whether by exploring old-fashioned devices like the abacus or by working with modern technical equipment like the computer.

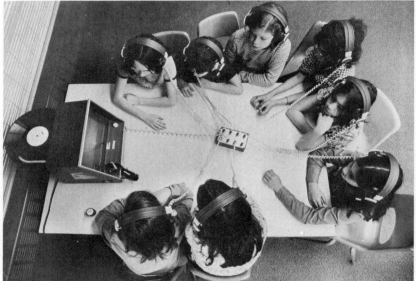

graded profile, and that this is the way to judge people. Finally, they learn to ignore their intuition and real feelings, and to replace them with strategies of "faking"—in (John) Holt's terms—in order to recieve acceptance and approval.[31]

Progressive educators stress the factors that authoritarians ignore; their emphasis is on the needs of the individual child, rather than on adherence to a rigid curriculum; they favor the development of creative, questioning minds, rather than obedient, conforming ones that are content to accept the answers provided by others.

Critics of public elementary education in the 1960s and 1970s have suggested new alternatives to the structured or teacher-oriented classroom. One such suggestion is "open classrooms," in which the teacher serves as a "resource person" offering the children many activities from which to choose. The British system, whose open classrooms have worked very well, was studied by thousands of American educators eager to institute it at home.

A number of young teacher-writers have launched attacks on our educational system in other areas. Johnathan Kozol's *Death at an Early Age* documents the harm done to children by repressive, overly bureaucratic systems.[32] John Holt's major thesis in *Why Children Fail* is basically that the schools are ruining children by teaching the wrong values, overemphasizing trivia, and not giving free rein to children's innate potential for expression.[33] Herbert Kohl, in *Thirty-Six Children*, claims that the needs of blacks and other minorities are not being met by the standard curriculum.[34]

For black children deprived of equal status in America *because* they are black, education in exclusively white values, white history, and white views of America is clearly psychologically damaging. Many standard history books discuss the entire history of black Americans in a brief paragraph or two on slavery. It is only in recent years that the civil rights movement, broad educational reforms, and enlightened thinking by a few educators have brought about some improvement in the education of minority groups. By 1969, bilingual education programs had been initiated in 76 school districts for children who spoke little or no English.[35] Black studies have become a part of many curricula, and other minorities are increasingly active in getting school districts to implement courses focused on their own ethnic cultures. The habit of American education—to force the culture of the majority on everyone—is beginning to change.

Thus, in elementary education the focus is slowly shifting from the controlled, teacher-dominated classroom to a more open, diversified setting where children are allowed to question more, to explore their individual interests, and to learn at their own pace. Most public schools are still years from the realization of that goal, but the change in thinking and values is increasingly evident.

Secondary Schools: Reinforced Repression

High school students, too old to be treated as children yet too young to be given full responsibility for their lives, have difficulty knowing how to manage themselves and interact with others. For the most part, the secondary schools do not help them; in fact, the high school years are often the most painful part of an individual's education: "Because adolescents are harder to control than younger children, secondary schools tend to be even more authoritarian and repressive than elementary schools; the values they transmit are the values of docility, passivity, conformity, and lack of trust."[36]

Perhaps because of this, the student restlessness of the 1960s filtered down from institutions of higher education, and some high schools became as frenetic as the stormiest college campus. And because the high school system was so much less open to change, the damage was more apparent. Dress codes and length of hair became important issues; drugs among high school students became a national problem; grades, rules, and college entrance exams all became targets for student revolt.

In recent years, efforts to update curriculum and school procedures often

Drawings by Roy Doty

Oregon's new high-school requirements, from refereeing to ballroom dancing: Real life takes more than English

Survival Test

Can you balance a checkbook, demonstrate first-aid techniques, answer a job advertisement, convert metric measurements to inches and feet, plan a nutritional diet, explain the advantages and disadvantages of using credit and fill out a 1040 form with perfect accuracy? If you can't do all of these things, you soon won't be able to graduate from a high school in Oregon.

Oregon's new graduation requirements are the first statewide guidelines in the U.S. that try to prepare students for real life. This year's ninth-graders, the first class to face the new tests, must demonstrate competence in dozens of these "survival" skills during the next three and a half years in order to get their diplomas in 1978. "You need more than English literature to cope with the complexities of the modern world," says Dale Parnell, the state superintendent of education who organized the guidelines.

Besides the statewide guidelines, each district has been encouraged to add a few of its own. In Salem, students will have to paraphrase an apartment-rental agreement. In Eugene, they must be able to rank a list of birth-control methods according to effectiveness, manipulate a calculator and use a road map to find the nearest entrance to a freeway from a local road. In Philomath, they will have to explain the purpose of various paycheck deductions. In Corvallis, they must officiate at two different sports games, list three suitable criteria for selecting a doctor or dentist and perform two basic dance steps.

Oregon students still must take a total of 42 required courses, including the standard academic fare. Nearly all students pass the traditional courses, but some educators are worried that many youngsters could fail the survival tests and thus not graduate. To avoid mass failures, the state education department will monitor the programs to make sure the levels of competence aren't set too high. The students themselves seem unperturbed. "The requirements are kind of dumb," says ninth-grader Anne McClintock of Corvallis. "They're basic things that kids pretty much know." Whether the same confidence could be found among Oregon's adults is an open question.

Newsweek, January 20, 1975

A problem of survival: Preparing for life in the real world.

have taken the form of investment in more technological means to accomplish a discredited task, rather than reexamination of the purpose of secondary education. What millions of students and a notable number of parents and teachers want is a whole new way of looking at the school's role in society and at its responsibilities to provide usable education.

It is not just the curriculum that will have to change [if schools are to improve], but the entire way in which high schools are organized and run. Students at present are hardly permitted, let alone encouraged, to confront either their teachers or themselves. They are given little opportunity, and no reason, to develop resolute ideas of their own about what they should learn, and in most schools they are actively discouraged from trying to test those ideas against their teachers.[37]

In this book, *Inside High School*, Philip A. Cusick has listed several important sociocultural characteristics of the school. Taken together, they provide a good overview of the repressive nature of secondary education: (1) The compartmentalization of subject matter is overspecialized. (2) The vertical organization of the school structure makes it clear that students are in subordinate positions under the control of teachers and administrators. (3) This subordinate status is made possible by the assumption on the part of the teachers that adolescents are in some way inferior. (4) These first three characteristics support, and in return are supported by, the flow of communication from top (administrators) to the bottom (students). (5) The batch processing of students takes place when teachers are responsible for large numbers of students and find it difficult to deal with them as individuals. (6) Activity in high schools is highly routinized, with times and places determined by the administrators. (7) To support the routinization of activity, an extensive array of rules and regulations is required to govern students' actions. (8) Students are expected to accept their roles on the assumption that future rewards will make it all worthwhile. (9) Finally, the physical structure of schools and classrooms supports the idea of teacher-expert-superordinate passing on specialties to students.[38]

These structures and attitudes were found to prevail in most American high schools, whether urban ghetto or middle-class suburban. Indeed, the quality of teaching itself is often so bad that little could be accomplished even with the best curriculum. Trained in bureaucratic systems, until recently, most teachers have seen little advantage in disrupting the institutions that support them by introducing innovations in teaching techniques or new subject matter. According to numerous observers, classes are boring and deadening.[39]

In the majority of school systems, individual schools are expected to adhere to curriculum plans developed by a central policymaking institutions. In a typical midwestern city, for example, there are 11 high schools. Curriculum and policy for all are established by the local board of education, although each school does have a certain degree of latitude in deciding what will or will not be studied in each class. The teachers, however, are given little choice in the matter. They may make suggestions, but actual power to implement policies and programs rests almost entirely with the board. The same situation commonly prevails throughout the country; a relatively small group of educational administrators make all decisions concerning what students are required to learn.

A great deal of the energies and monies of school districts in this country have gone into buildings rather than into improving the human environment within the educational structures. Since students spend so much time in schools, a comfortable and attractive environment is important; yet new buildings alone have not been able to provide it. Clearly, upgrading the condition, values, and spirit of education itself must occur if secondary education is to have any positive effect on students' lives.

Three indicators of the inadequacy of the present system of secondary education are found in recent figures concerning the illiteracy rate, the school dropout rate, and the scores on standardized tests. In 1976 the U.S. Office of Education released the results of a four-year study in which it was found that 23 million persons in this country are functionally illiterate. This figure can by no means be attributed solely to a failure of the schools, but by the same token it certainly does not attest to the success of the schools in teaching rudimentary skills.

The nationwide dropout rate, while on the decline, nevertheless manifests the extent of the student disaffection with current educational arrangements. (See Table 3.2 for a comparison of dropout rates in 1967 and 1973.) Offered few, if any, alternatives to conventional classroom methods and seeing little relationship between what is taught in school and the skills demanded in the job market, many students choose to drop out before completing high school (see Figure 3.1). Although alternative educational and

Table 3.2 Percent of School Dropouts
among Persons 14 to 34

	Black		White	
	Male	Female	Male	Female
1970	30.4	29.5	14.4	16.0
1976	21.3	20.3	12.8	13.7

Source: National Center for Education Statistics, *Digest of Education Statistics, 1977–78* (Washington, D.C:
Government Printing Office, 1978), p. 63.

Figure 3.1 Estimated Retention Rates, Fifth Grade through College Graduation, 1968-80

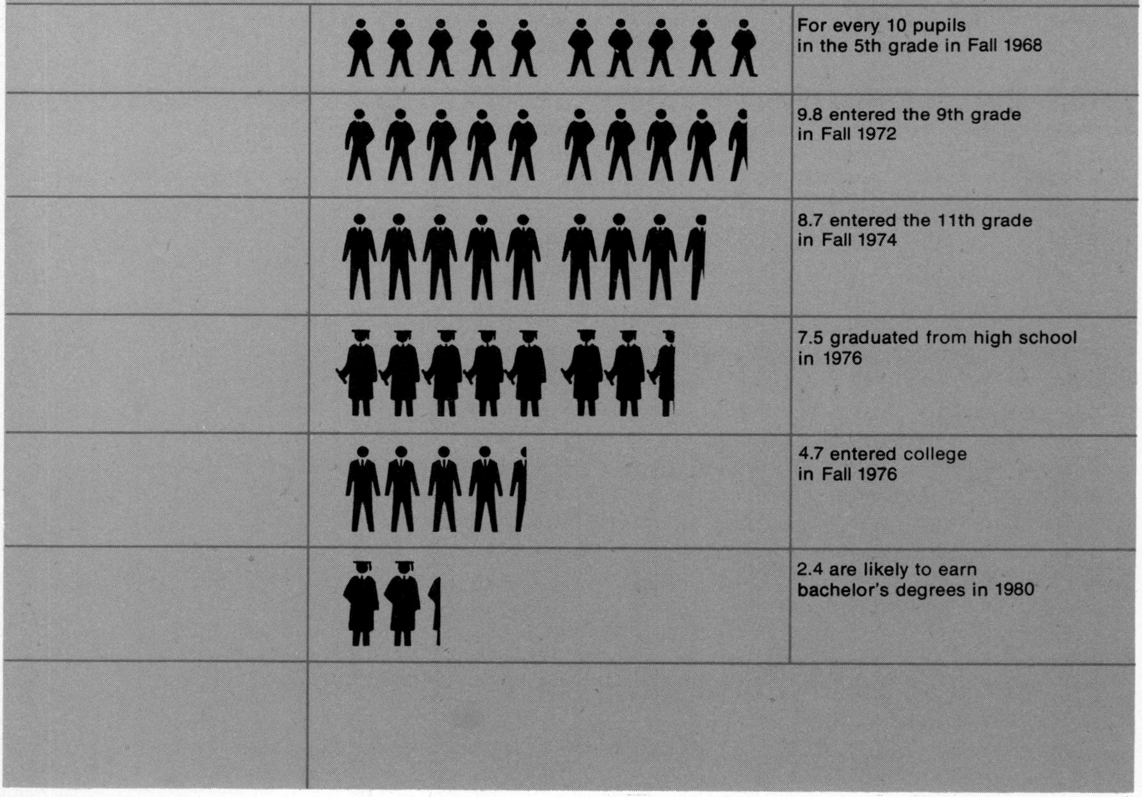

For every 10 pupils
in the 5th grade in Fall 1968

9.8 entered the 9th grade
in Fall 1972

8.7 entered the 11th grade
in Fall 1974

7.5 graduated from high school
in 1976

4.7 entered college
in Fall 1976

2.4 are likely to earn
bachelor's degrees in 1980

Source: National Center for Education Statistics, *Digest of Education Statistics, 1977—78* (Washington, D.C.:
Government Printing Office, 1978), p. 13.

on-the-job training programs have been developed on an experimental basis specifically to combat this problem, school dropouts continue to represent a significant economic liability in our society. This is especially so in light of the fact long recognized by social scientists that failure to complete high school is interwoven with other societal problems, such as crime and drug addiction.

Even for students who plan on entering college and graduate school, the educational system appears to be slipping. Scores on the two standardized college admission tests have been dropping considerably over the past decade. Table 3.3 shows that the mean score on the SAT verbal test has declined almost 40 points while the mathematics scores dropped 25 points.

Higher Education: The Finishing Touch

American colleges and universities are not often referred to as finishing schools—a term associated with elite women's schools; however, in some ways they serve a similar function. First, those who make it through the higher education system are generally thought of and treated as more adequately prepared to take on life in the "real world." The baccalaureate degree grants a certain amount of respect. Conversely, those without a college education are treated with less respect professionally and are almost always relegated to a lower social and economic status.

The growth of enrollments in two-year colleges has been much greater than in four-year schools. Most of the students enrolled in the former are in public community colleges. These colleges allow many persons who would be unable to attend four-year institutions the opportunity to obtain various skills. Though originally designed to prepare students for four-year universi-

Table 3.3

Mean Scores on Standardized Examinations 1966–67 to 1975–76

| | Mean Test Score | | | | | |
| | Scholastic Aptitude Test (SAT)[a] | | American College Testing Program (ACT) | | Graduate Record Exam (GRE)[b] | |
Year	Verbal	Mathematics	English	Mathematics	Verbal	Quantitative
1966–67	467	495	18.5	18.7	519	528
1967–68	466	494	18.1	18.3	520	527
1968–69	462	491	18.4	19.2	515	524
1969–70	460	488	18.1	19.5	503	516
1970–71	454	487	17.7	18.7	497	512
1971–72	450	482	17.6	18.6	494	508
1972–73	443	481	17.8	18.8	497	512
1973–74	440	478	17.6	18.1	492	509
1974–75	437	473	17.3	17.4	493	508
1975–76	429	470	17.2	17.1	492	511

Source: National Center for Education Statistics, *The Condition of Education, 1977* (Washington, D.C.: Government Printing Office, 1977), p. 214.
[a] For all cases attending test administrations during a testing year. Thus, an individual may be counted more than once if he or she was tested more than once in a given year. Furthermore, the cases are aggregated without regard to educational level.
[b] Since 1964–65, the volume of cases attending GRE aptitude test administrations has tripled and the proportion in social sciences has also increased.

ties and colleges, many of the two-year schools now aim to allow students to move directly into the labor force. Besides providing this career training, these schools also offer remedial work in various subjects. Many community colleges also cater to the needs of part-time students, including those people who cannot afford to go to school without working and older persons who want to take courses to enrich some aspect of their lives.[40]

After the Russians successfully launched Sputnik in 1957, most universities began to enlarge and improve their scientific and technological departments at a fast pace. America, it was felt, must never be caught off guard again, and the universities were given the responsibility of ensuring our scientific and technological preeminence. More and more highly trained people were needed not only to operate but also to refine and invent the complex machinery of the new technological era. A graduate degree became almost mandatory for a good job. Technology was seen as the key to the future; the humanities and the arts took second place.

The resultant departmentalized and specialized college curriculum that underlies the finishing school image of many institutions of higher education came under attack from students and faculty alike during the sixties. The impersonal "multiversity" or "human factory" became the target of bitter criticism. Too often, students found themselves locked into the rigid structure of their major, without a chance to study other areas of interest. The "scientific" approach to education had clearly preempted other possibilities even in the humanities courses. Frustrated and disenchanted, thousands of students rebelled or dropped out.

Inspired by the civil rights movement, alienated and rebellious students found many aspects of their educational experiences unsatisfactory and began to join forces and make their opinion known. The "silent generation" of the fifties gave way to the social and political activists of the sixties. In 1964, at the University of California in Berkeley, the Free Speech Movement pitted students against the bureaucratic administration in open confrontation. Students demanded the right to recruit members and to raise money on campus for political causes. When the administration refused permission, the first major student strike began.

As the war in Vietnam escalated under the Johnson administration, student protest became louder and more vociferous. Several campuses were disrupted by demonstrations directed at representatives of producers of war chemicals and armed forces and intelligence agencies sent to interview students. The draft issue affected most college-age men, and campuses became a natural center for resistance. ROTC, the college training program for military officers, became an important target of protest, and many colleges discontinued or modified the program to appease students and avoid violent disruptions.

By 1968 a number of campuses across the country were actually in a state of near-siege. Students were being joined by prominent public officials in their denunciation of the war and its ill effects on American society. Students for a Democratic Society, a radical group that showed its power briefly toward the end of the decade, shut down Columbia University in April 1968. Racism, complicity in the war (through contracts with the Defense Department), and an unmoving, unsympathetic administrative bureaucracy were at issue in the strikes of large numbers of students and faculty at Columbia and several other colleges. These were not just strikes, the organizers asserted, but a revolution.

In a decade's time, many students have moved from silence to bitter protest. Society was changing rapidly, and all during the 1960s college students contributed to the change.

It is not strange that students demand an education which is more relevant to their values, that they abhor war as an instrument of national policy, that they are communitarian and anti-authoritarian. These qualities, together with the beginning attempts to work out their implications in choice of life-style and in choice of careers, disprove the claim frequently voiced by officialdom that students want only to tear down—that they provide no alternatives, nothing positive. Students are filled with more anguish than rage.[41]

College youth today also demand a more flexible structure, but in a less rebellious fashion. Emphasis on future occupations and orientation toward technological fields still forms a large part of the college curriculum; but the upheavals of the 1960s have convinced administrators of the need for flexibility, and their more liberal orientation has already been reflected in curriculum changes and newly defined goals of higher education. The tranquil campuses of the late 1970s are the product of more than structural flexibility, however.

College campuses have been largely depoliticized. A number of explanations for this phenomenon have been offered. Undoubtedly, the end of the Vietnam War settled one of the major burning issues of the student movement. Another factor, possibly related to the war's end, is the career orientation of the students of the late 1970s. The economic recession has hit hard, and many students realize that prospects of employment are not as good as they once were. In order to "make it" after graduation, many students are determined to devote their time and attention to study. Others are required to work to pay the rising tuition costs and simply do not have the free time needed to engage in political activities. The tranquil campuses reflect the passing of an era of student activism unprecedented in American history and a return to more traditional education, career, and social pursuits.

Approaching Equal Access

The problem of equal access to quality education will be with us for some time to come, but improvement in the situation can already be noted. Education and employment opportunities for minorities have risen sharply during the past decade. Much still remains to be done to wipe out discrimination, but there are indications that centuries-old prejudices are beginning to change. Since education in America is almost synonymous with the concept of social mobility, the issue of equal access to the benefits and rewards of our society will have to be resolved in the schools first.

The precise effects of equal access to quality education on students are too nebulous to measure today, but Christopher Jencks and David Reisman have offered an interesting analogy:

How much of the difference between the uneducated and the educated should be attributed directly to school experiences and how much to external factors such as upbringing, intelligence, personality? A good portion of the apparent impact of schooling is, we would suggest, anticipatory socialization. Sending a child to school may be like telling him he has a rich maiden aunt and will eventually inherit a fortune. The aunt and her money have no direct effect on the child's life or growth. But the idea of the money—even if it is nonexistent—may have a considerable effect, for the child may feel he has special opportunities and responsibilities. So, too, with schooling. What actually happens from day to day in a school or college may have relatively little effect on the students—though it certainly has some effect. But a good student's knowledge that he can go to college, and that a college degree will be a passport to a good job and a comfortable standard of living, may have a significant effect on him. He is more likely to adopt the attitudes and acquire the skill he thinks he will need in the world he expects to enter.[42]

Thus, equal access to education is the beginning of a long-term and difficult social reordering, as well as an end in itself.

In the elementary and secondary grades, busing is likely to continue to be the main method of achieving integration and equal access. Recent court cases attest to government commitment to integration. In June 1973 the Supreme Court ruled that the Denver School Board discriminated against black children by gerrymandering them into a few schools. The decision clearly stated that within the city boundaries, the school board must begin to bus more extensively to combat segregation.

But the real question, busing within an entire metropolitan area, city and suburbs alike, was not decided until 1978. The courts rejected several busing plans before accepting one in which the school district of Wilmington, Delaware, was merged with the districts of the predominantly white suburban communities surrounding the city. A similar plan may also be recommended by an advisory panel to deal with the problems of segregated schools in Los Angeles and its suburbs.

Equal access at the college level has been another matter. Colleges pick and choose on demonstrated merit or talent, test scores, and a host of other criteria. Higher education has traditionally been reserved for the elite or most able. But changes are occurring here, too.

The open admissions policy in New York City and California substantially increases the chances of poor black or white students to attend college. Instituted in 1970, the program has been heatedly debated. Enrollment in the City University of New York swelled enormously after the new policy was instituted. The first year's dropout rate was 36 percent, which was very high for CUNY but about average for the country. While everyone seemed to have trouble adjusting to the new program, and many problems are still not resolved, real changes in attitude have taken place. According to the Fleischmann Report on financing education in New York State (1973), open admissions lifted morale in the high schools whose failures had made the program necessary. At Benjamin Franklin High School in East Harlem, only 10 percent of the seniors bothered to apply to CUNY before the new policy and only 1 percent were accepted. As the students discovered that they stood a real chance of getting to college, 76 percent applied.[43]

What is more important is that 48 percent of the students graduated within four years and close to 70 percent graduated after seven years. (Many of the students return after withdrawing.) Yet the future is not as bright. The financial crisis of the country has hit New York City hard, forcing CUNY officials to charge tuition for the first time in its history. This is probably one of the reasons that contributed to a decline in applications.[44]

The recent Supreme Court decision in the *Bakke* case is likely to have a significant impact on the admissions policies of many schools. Designed to help overcome a history of discrimination against racial minorities and women, many schools and businesses were providing opportunities to help them catch up and compete equally with white men. Some of the affirmative action programs established quotas that required certain proportions of positions be filled by racial minorities and women. The medical school at the University of California's Davis campus allotted 16 of its 100 positions to disadvantaged students which it defined as blacks, Chicanos, American Indians, and Asian Americans. When Allan Bakke was twice rejected by the school even though he had a higher grade point average than some disadvantaged students who were accepted, he filed a suit claiming discrimination. Appeals of lower court decisions eventually reached the U.S. Supreme Court which actually ruled on three complicated issues, all by 5–4 votes. First, they decided that Bakke should be admitted to the medical school. Second, they voted that the quota system was not an acceptable method of deciding who should be admitted. Finally, it was decided that race could be used as a factor in deciding admissions to medical schools. The rulings did not clarify the role of affirmative action programs in other settings (for example, businesses) or for other groups, such as women.[45] Discrimination suits are likely to continue in the future until the precise interpretations of this decision are rendered by courts in other cases.

Equalizing Educational Funding

Reducing the inequities in educational funding throughout each state will have to be the goal if opportunities for children are to be equalized. Since the Supreme Court has ruled that each state must find its own method of dealing with the financial problem, revision of existing laws will undoubtedly become necessary.

Developing New Sources of Revenue

The Fleischmann Report offers two feasible means of financing education for New York State; generally speaking, these proposals are applicable to other states as well. The first involves a statewide uniform-rate property tax earmarked for education. The authors of the report suggest that if this type of reform is decided on by the state, it should be introduced gradually over a five-year period. This seems to be an equitable way of approaching the problem. The second alternative concerns the role of existing nonproperty taxes in education financing—"existing state taxes on personal income, corporate net and gross income, retail sales tax, unincorporated business tax and miscellaneous state taxes."[46] These revenues, which are not usually allocated for education, could substantially improve equality in all school districts if they could be used throughout the state.

The courts have played a major role in changing the method of financing

Declining tax revenues have often meant program and personnel cuts in public education. Here, teachers, parents, and students demonstrate in Los Angeles to protest cuts in school budgets threatened by California's Proposition 13.

public elementary and secondary school education. In the *Serrano* v. *Priest* case (1971) the California Supreme Court ruled that the use of local property taxes to support schools discriminated against students in poorer school districts. Within a year of this decision, five other states were forced to alter their methods of financing public education. The reforms taking place in the late 1970s have tended toward a greater equalization of educational opportunity because of the role of state funding in guaranteeing a minimum level of support without relying solely on local taxes. As a result, public school education has improved in many of the poorer areas of major cities without imposing higher taxes on the very groups that can least afford them.[47]

Along with the revenue revision, some states are also trying to simplify and streamline the bureaucracy of public education. By decentralizing large school systems into smaller autonomous districts, it is hoped that local action in the schools will increase and communities will take more responsibility for the direction of their schools. Thus, each small district will be able to have control over curriculum, teachers, and administrators. The decentralization plan in New York City, although still in need of much work, enables Harlem to adopt one set of curricula and policies for its schools, while the Chinatown area can decide on other routes to better education. The future of decentralized systems is not clear, but they constitute an attempt to give the schools "back to the people" and should be given a chance to prove their worth.

Educational Vouchers

A much discussed alternative to local property tax funding of public schools is the educational voucher idea. Very simply, this concept would enable parents to choose a school they liked for their child and "pay" for enrollment with a state tax voucher. The parent would not actually pay for the education vouchers because state taxes would supply the revenues, with an equal amount provided for each school age child. The voucher system would hypothetically equalize opportunities for all children in public and private schools.[48]

But there are many problems. Advocates claim that the voucher system would have to be highly regulated to avoid discrimination and inequality. Yet others want the system wide open to encourage maximum variety of educational alternatives.[49] Still others maintain that children from low-income families should receive more money credit. One of the main issues in the debate over vouchers is whether both public and private schools are to be included in the plan. If all community schools are involved, the greatest possible choices would be available to parents and children. However, numerous legal complications would have to be overcome before a community-wide voucher system could be permanently accepted.

Opposition to the voucher concept is presently widespread. Most public school teachers and administrators are opposed to the idea, as are numerous other groups. They want funding to remain the same as it is now, primarily because any radical change in the system would directly affect the public school community's control over education expenditures and policy.

Voucher plans have recently been put into effect with federal assistance from the Office of Economic Opportunity. One of the test cases, in Alum Rock, California, has had mixed results. Parents were able to choose freely from a number of schools and negotiate transfers for their children to schools with programs that they desired. Knowledge of the options available to them increased as the program aged and new, innovative curricula were introduced. Yet the system also had its drawbacks. Teachers were overwhelmed with meetings and with implementing the constantly changing programs. Although the program was designed to increase the power of parents in educating their children, it increased the power of the professionals instead. Yet parents appeared content with this situation since they were more satisfied with the education their children were receiving.[49]

Curriculum Alternatives

Amid the general chaos of American education in recent years, many groups have been undertaking experiments and trying out projects designed to reform or revolutionize the existing system. At the preschool level, Head Start programs (first funded in 1965 during the Johnson administration) have aroused mixed reactions from observers. But most people who have worked in the programs feel they have enhanced general learning opportunities for participating children without requiring such strict adherence to societal norms as to dampen individual initiative.[50]

At the elementary level, many school systems have experimented successfully with open classrooms. The open classroom, however, is not easy to achieve; teachers are required to rethink their roles completely, and many older teachers react negatively to relinquishing the control they have in the traditional teacher-oriented classroom structure.

At the high school level, the past decade has seen the opening of "free" or "streetfront" schools in several urban areas. Students, teachers, and parents, disenchanted with the public school system, broke away and formed their own schools. These free schools are generally progressive, open-minded, and experimental in both curriculum and structure.[51] Many streetfront schools have sprung up in ghetto areas in an attempt to provide a relevant education for blacks who have dropped out of public schools. With foundation grants and free teaching help, they offer the best chance for advancement for many minority youths without access to an education.

Some changes have also taken place within the public high schools. Minority studies programs are now standard in most urban areas; bilingual classes are more prevalent; classes in sex education, drug education, and vocational training are more widely available than they were a decade ago. In most high schools, both the curriculum and grading systems have become more flexible. Grades have come under massive attack by reforms and pupils, because too often the grade in a course is made more important than the learning experience. The usual A to F grading system is being modified in many communities to a more moderate "pass-fail" system designed to take much of the intense competition out of the classroom.[52] It is hoped that in this way emphasis in education will turn more toward learning and exploring. Curriculum alternatives have become more realistic in other areas as well. High school systems are now offering useful technical and vocational courses for students who are not oriented toward college and who will seek employment immediately after high school.

At the college and graduate levels, students have gained a voice in certain of the programs and activities that directly affect them. Programs permitting broader and more flexible educational experiences have been implemented, and some colleges and universities have eliminated many of the traditional requirements. Although curriculum remains in the control of the faculty and administration, student demands for a loosening of the structure in their major fields of study have not gone unnoticed.

Programs leading to advanced degrees have mushroomed enormously in the past two decades. Although it now appears that we may have overproduced advanced degree holders in some disciplines, it goes without saying that as our society becomes more complex, graduate programs will have to continue to meet the increasing demand for highly trained people in all fields. Expansion has also taken place at numerous universities in adult or continuing education programs, in response to the heavy demand from people of all ages who want to take courses either for a degree or just for the enjoyment of learning.

All the reforms in our educational system are basically responses to an ever-increasing demand by members of our society for a better life. Even though there is conflict over what the "good life" and the "American dream" really are, it is safe to say that most Americans work toward their concept of that goal. Education continues to be regarded as the best means to achieve that ideal.

The need to assimilate diverse groups of immigrants into the mainstream of society helped give rise to the public school system in the United States. Authoritarian control has played a prominent part in American public education, and, despite efforts of reformers, success has often been measured by how closely a student adheres to the values and ethics of those who run the schools. These have been geared to a doctrine of upward social mobility.

The expansion and development of the educational enterprise has also led to impersonal bureaucratic school organization. Parents and communities have lost direct control of education, but students and teachers are seeking fundamental changes.

The social disorganization approach sees the origin of problems within the educational system in the failure of a major social institution to fulfill its social functions. Under present arrangements, many individuals are denied the opportunity to develop the full range of their talents and capabilities; equal educational opportunities for all members of society as preparation for the occupational world remains more an ideal than an actuality.

Problems related to the educational system are also generated when diverse groups involved in the educational enterprise hold different values and attempt to promote or defend their own particular interests—when there is value conflict. Thus, some groups may desire and actively work to maintain a structure that provides them with superior school facilities and opportunities, while other groups demand that the educational system serve the interests of all groups in society equally. Social conflict such as that currently in evidence regarding educational issues does not necessarily have a detrimental impact on the social order; conflict may act as a positive mechanism to bring about needed social change.

Three of the most important problem areas in education are equal access, financing, and curriculum. Equal access refers to equal opportunity to obtain the best possible education within any given locale and any given curriculum. Equal access is presently an unrealized ideal. Inequities in the financing of school systems in different areas are among the causes of inequality of educational opportunity. Studies have indicated, however, that equal education alone will not create equal opportunity.

Segregation has always blocked equal access to education. Although the Supreme Court outlawed school segregation in 1954, it continues to the present day and is now more prevalent in the northern urban areas than in the South. The solution most often offered for this problem is busing. The contradiction between the neighborhood school concept and integration is at the heart of the access problem. If neighborhoods remain closed and restrict their schools, integration and equality in education seem impossible.

The 1978 Supreme Court decision in the *Bakke* case, which allows for affirmative actions in principle, forbids the use of strict quota systems. Many minorities view this as a setback to their attempts to gain educational equality.

Since schools rely heavily on the property tax for financing, the amount of money spent per student becomes a function of the state's tax system and property values in the neighborhood. A pupil from a poor district will have much less spent on his or her education than a student in a wealthy neighborhood.

The costs of public education have risen sharply in recent years. With city tax bases eroding, the unionization of teachers to gain higher wages has placed big city school systems in a particularly difficult situation. Recently the Supreme Court ruled that equal education is one of the rights guaranteed by the Constitution. This decision throws the problem of equalizing revenue available for education in different districts back on the states. Many states have already taken steps to equalize the funding levels of the many districts within their boundaries.

Colleges and universities face a different type of funding problem. Federal expenditures to institutions of higher education grew enormously after World War II. But because of national priorities in the present tight economic situation, large cutbacks have been made recently, and both private and public institutions have been affected.

In American education today there is great disagreement over how and what students should learn. In elementary schools, authoritarian control is awakening. Many teachers are encouraging their students to express themselves by offering a more open, relaxed, and diversified setting in which to learn. Street schools, mini-schools, decentralization of control, and the use of educational vouchers are all being investigated as means to better ways of learning.

As student discontent has filtered down from the universities, many high school students have come to find their curricula irrelevant and dehumanizing. Administrators normally seem to see problems as matters of control and discipline; rarely have they upgraded curricula or examined the values that shape the human environment of the students. Innovations such as minority studies programs, sex education classes, and better vocational training are more available now than they used to be, but the high schools remain for the most part rigid agencies of socialization.

Student revolts of the 1960s merged political and educational issues. Today, however, many students have changed their focus of attention from broad political issues to the more personal issues of finding employment after graduation.

Notes

[1] Joel H. Spring, *Education and The Rise of the Corporate State* (Boston: Beacon Press, 1972), p. 62.

[2] Lawrence A. Crimin, *The Transformation of the School: Progressivism in American Education, 1876–1957* (New York: Random House, 1961).

[3] See James S. Coleman et al., *Equality of Educational Opportunity,* U.S. Department of Health, Education, and Welfare (Washington, D.C.: Government Printing Office, 1966); Arthur Jensen, "How Much Can We Boost IQ and Scholastic Achievement," *Harvard Educational Review*, Winter 1969, pp. 1–123; Christopher Jencks et al., *Inequality* (New York: Basic Books,

1972); Frederick Mosteller and Daniel P. Moynihan, eds., *On Equality of Educational Opportunity* (New York: Random House, 1972); William Sewell and Robert Hauser, *Education, Occupation and Earnings: Achievement in the Early Career* (New York: Academic Press, 1975).

[4]Section 402 of the Civil Rights Act of 1964.

[5]Coleman et al. *Equality of Educational Opportunity.*

[6]Ibid., p. 3.

[7]Ibid.

[8]Jencks et al., *Inequality.*

[9]Godfrey Hodgson, "Do Schools Make a Difference?" *Atlantic Monthly*, March 1973, p. 37.

[10]Jencks et al., *Inequality*, p. 265.

[11]Gordon Foster, "Desegregating Urban Schools: A Review of Techniques," *Harvard Educational Review*, February 1973, pp. 5–35; U.S. Department of Health, Education and Welfare, *Digest of Educational Statistics, 1974* (Washington, D.C.: Government Printing Office, 1974), p. 153.

[12]James Coleman, "Liberty and Equality in School Desegregation," *Social Policy*, January–February 1976, pp. 9–13.

[13]Foster, "Desegregating Urban Schools."

[14]Stanley S. Robin and James J. Bosco, "Coleman's Desegregation Research and Policy Recommendations," *School Review*, 9 (May 1976), 352–363.

[15]William Raspberry, "Busing—Is it Worth the Ride?" *Readers Digest*, September 1974, pp. 141–142.

[16]William Taylor, "Busing: Realities and Evasions," *Dissent*, Fall 1972, pp. 586–594.

[17]Foster, "Desegregating Urban Schools," p. 7.

[18]"School Taxes: Fair Enough?" *Newsweek*, 2 April 1973, p. 97.

[19]U.S. Office of Education, *Statistics of Public Schools* (Washington, D.C.: Government Printing Office, Fall 1977).

[20]National Center for Education Statistics, "The Condition of Education," (Washington, D.C.: Government Printing Office, 1977), p. 226.

[21]Manley Fleischmann et al., *The Fleischmann Report on the Quality, Cost and Financing of Elementary and Secondary Education in New York State*, Vol. 1 (New York: Viking 1973), p. 57.

[22]Ibid., p. 58.

[23]Ibid., p. 54.

[24]"School Taxes," p. 97.

[25]"The Condition of Education," p. 54.

[26]U.S. National Science Foundation, *Federal Funds for Research Development and Other Scientific Activities, Fiscal Years 1970, 1971, 1972* (Washington, D.C.: Government Printing Office, 1971), pp. 3, 11.

[27]"The Condition of Education," p. 60.

[28]National Center for Education Statistics, *Digest of Educational Statistics, 1977–78* (Washington, D.C.: Government Printing Office, 1978), p. 55.

[29]Ibid., p. 55.

[30]Charles Silberman, *Crisis in the Classroom* (New York: Random House, 1970), p. 5.

[31]Philip Bremer, "Political Knowledge and Experience in Elementary Education," *Schooling in a Corporate Society*, ed. Martin Carnoy (New York: McKay, 1972), p. 225.

[32]Jonathan Kozol, *Death at an Early Age* (Boston: Little, Brown, 1968).

[33]John Holt, *Why Children Fail* (New York: Pitman, 1967).

[34]Herbert Kohl, *Thirty-six Children* (New York: Random House, 1968).

[35]"Projects under the New Bilingual Education Program," *American Education*, October 1969, pp. 26–28.

[36]Silberman, *Crisis in the Classroom*, p. 324.

[37]Ibid., p. 336.

[38]Philip A. Cusick, *Inside High School: The Student's World* (New York: Holt, Rinehart and Winston, 1973), p. 217.

[39]See Silberman, *Crisis in the Classroom;* Cusick, *Inside High School;* and Carl Nordstrom, Edgar Z. Friedenberg, and Hilary A. Bold, *Society's Children* (New York: Random House, 1967).

[40]Leland L. Medsker, "The American Community College: Its Contribution to Higher Education," *Universities Facing the Future*, eds. W. Roy Niblett and R. Freeman Butts (San Francisco: Jossey-Bass, 1972), pp. 314–324.

[41]"Open Admissions: A Mixed Report," *Time*, 29 November 1971, pp. 50–52.

[42]Christopher Jencks and David Riesman, "On Class in America." Reprinted by permission from *The Public Interest*, No. 10 (Winter 1968), p. 84. © 1968 by National Affairs, Inc.

[43]Fleischmann et al., *The Fleischmann Report*, p. 74.

[44]John Farago and Janice Weinman, "The Decline in CUNY Applications," *Research in Higher Education* 8 (May 1978), 193–203.

[45]"The Landmark Bakke Ruling," *Newsweek,* 10 July 1978, pp. 18–31.

[46]Fleischmann et al., *The Fleischmann Report*, p. 74.

[47]Austin D. Swanson and Richard A. King, "The Impact of the Courts on the Financing of Public Schools in Large Cities," *Urban Education,* July 1976, pp. 151–166.

[48]George R. LaNoue, *Education Vouchers: Concepts and Controversies* (New York: Teachers College Press, 1972), pp. v–vii.

[49]David K. Cohen and Eleanor Farrar, "Power to the Parents?—The Story of Education Vouchers," *Public Interest,* Summer 1977, pp. 72–97.

[50]Marshall Smith and Joan Bissell, "Report Analysis: The Impact of Head Start," *Harvard Educational Review,* Winter 1970, pp. 52–105.

[51]Jonathan Kozol, *Free Schools* (Boston: Houghton Mifflin, 1972). See also "Another Look at Student Rights and the Function of Schooling: The Elizabeth Cleaners Street School," *Harvard Educational Review,* November 1970, pp. 596–627.

[52]Howard Kirschenbaum, Sidney B. Simon, and Rodney W. Napier, *Wad-Ja-Get? The Grading Game in American Education* (New York: Hart Publishing, 1971).

Work

4

Most adults in the United States spend 40 years or more of their life working eight hours a day, five days a week, with two weeks vacation and six paid holidays. Their satisfaction, or lack of it, with the work they do and the income they receive is a central experience of their lives. No other aspect of a person's life provides as much social continuity as does work. The work people do determines the material comfort and economic security that they and their families enjoy, the social milieu in which they live, and, as a result, their identity—their sense of themselves and their view of the world they live in.

The primary function of work is economic: work is the means toward the end of earning a living. Income is necessary for survival in a money economy, and without the income from their jobs most people would not be economically self-sufficient. Unions have long recognized this, and negotiations with management usually begin with wage and salary demands.

Money is a necessary reward, but by no means is it the sole meaning and purpose of work. The kind of work people do and the amount of income they receive locates them within the class structure of society. Their income determines the areas of a community in which they live and, therefore, the schools their children attend. Jobs regulate the hours of their daily lives and thus determine to some extent the people with whom they can associate. Further, their friends are often members of the group in which they work.

An individual's self-esteem is closely interwoven with work. When a job is recognized as a significant contribution to an organization or community, this is clear evidence to the worker and others of the person's value and is an important source of self-esteem. Also, as the individual achieves mastery in a job, he or she develops a feeling of competence and accomplishment, which, in turn, leads to self-confidence. Work, then, fulfills individual psychological, as well as social and economic, needs; and lack of work or the absence of meaningful and challenging work can lead to serious problems for the worker.

Society also feels the effects of work and work problems, and unemployment constitutes the largest work problem today. From an economic viewpoint, unemployment affects not only the worker, whom society must provide with some means of support in the form of welfare or unemployment benefits, but also those who contribute taxes to this support. If unemployment becomes widespread in an area, it has an economic effect on shopkeepers, banks, and property owners. In economically depressed areas where unemployment is a constant problem, the attendant ills of poverty, crime, and unstable family life constitute a state of social disorganization. When there is not enough work or when the work that does exist increasingly frustrates the workers' attempts to satisfy basic needs, society pays high economic and social costs.

Besides unemployment, another important problem in our rapidly changing technological society is worker dissatisfaction. People care profoundly about the quality of work, and significant numbers of American workers are dissatisfied with the dull, repetitive form many work tasks have assumed. They offer little challenge or autonomy. If workers believe their work is meaningless or do not consider themselves an integral part of the total operation, with opportunity for advancement based on achievement, they are discontented. Job dissatisfaction leads to lower worker productivity, which can be measured by absenteeism, turnover, wildcat strikes, sabotage, and poor quality of work. A general increase in education and economic status in our society has made the stimulation a job offers as important as the income it produces. Pay alone, though important, does not produce job satisfaction. The growing awareness of the importance of meaningful work is a fairly new social problem and reflects an overall concern with the quality of life.

In terms of social disorganization, many of the problems associated with work in our society may be seen as stemming from rapid changes in industrial technology and in the social organization of work. Trends toward task specialization and fragmentation of the work process have resulted in an occupational structure in which many types of work are neither meaningful nor fulfilling to the workers. Whole categories of workers have been displaced from the occupational structure as technological innovations have been implemented and other transformations in the economic sphere have occurred. Yet social mechanisms that might ensure a place in the occupational structure for all those who desire to work have not been developed on a scale large enough to have a substantial impact on the unemployment problem.

Work problems can also be traced to fundamental conflicts of interest between different segments of the occupational hierarchy. In America, management typically views the right to control the nature and conditions of work as its exclusive prerogative. Rank and file workers, on the other hand, often argue that they have the right to determine the conditions under which they will work. The clash between management emphases on profitability and productivity and workers' desires for reasonably fulfilling and meaningful work is a central factor in the problem of job dissatisfaction.

The Virtue of Success

The Calvinist doctrine the Puritans brought to America held that thrift, diligence, and the deferment of pleasure were virtues; work was the highest duty, idleness was evil, and worldly success was proof of salvation. Although the specific tenets of this work ethic may have lost some of their impact on worker motivation in recent years, work is still seen as a righteous means for achieving the benefits of wealth. The Protestant immigrants from northern Europe in the early part of the nineteenth century were also imbued with the same ethic, and later immigrants, too, saw work as the primary means to a better life for themselves and, particularly, their children. In America the dream of life—upward mobility in society—was to be achieved by hard work.

Individualism versus Industrialism

The early English settlers were drawn to America largely because a parcel of land for farming could be had for a very inexpensive price. During colonial days 95 percent of the population lived on subsistence farms, which each individual farmer and his wife worked autonomously. In the North, the mercantile system of the eighteenth century fostered small individual businesses run by self-employed tradesmen—merchants, artisans, and craftsmen. For both farmer and tradesman, the structure of work had an organic character. They performed a wide variety of tasks, regulated and directed the scheduling and pace of their work, and maintained control over the products of their labor. The labor force was markedly different only in the South, where relatively few land owners held large tracts of land and commanded the labor of white indentured servants and black slaves.

Industrialism is a form of social organization in which work is performed in a factory setting and on a much larger scale than were the early crafts and trades. The industrialization of America proceeded at an astounding pace; whereas in 1810 only 75,000 persons were employed in manufacturing establishments, by 1840 this number had multiplied tenfold. By the middle of the nineteenth century the factory system that would come to characterize American manufacturing was beginning to take shape. Most significantly, this period marked the separation of labor and management in the productive process, as well as the beginning of the fragmentation of work itself.

Slavery played a major role in the economic development of the nation; it made possible the production of an agricultural surplus which was sold to provide the financial capital necessary for industrial development. Although slavery grew slowly at first, and there were many more white indentured servants than slaves, the economic basis of slavery changed dramati-

In the late nineteenth and early twentieth centuries, children were exploited as a cheap and abundant labor supply. Here, a young girl is shown working in the textile industry.

cally with the invention of the cotton gin in 1793. Cotton growing became an immensely profitable enterprise due to the increase in the productivity of slave labor, and slaves eventually constituted 60 percent of the southern work force. The special importance of slavery as a mode of organizing work may well have been the work gangs formed by slave owners—a kind of agricultural version of the assembly line.[1] These gangs, working their way across fields in an organized fashion, turned out to be much more productive than individual farm workers. The forced discipline of the work gangs was soon transferred to the factory setting, with immigrant workers and children often working 74-hour weeks under grueling conditions in cotton mills and other industrial enterprises.

The Civil War hastened the consolidation of small, individually owned businesses into giant enterprises. Such men as Andrew Carnegie, John D. Rockefeller, and railroad organizer James J. Hill were the instruments of a vast money power that reorganized and enlarged America's industrial capacity. During the course of this expansion, waves of immigrant laborers were absorbed into the work force and helped build the network of railroads and canals necessary for the continued growth of the economy.

As industrialization progressed, the character of work changed and certain constraints were imposed on workers. No longer individually autonomous, they had to submit to a discipline that required them to spend a certain amount of time in their assigned places. The total work process became fragmented, with each worker performing a specialized, repetitive task. Working conditions were generally poor or unsafe, hours were long, and wages were low.

Workers: Gears in the Machine

As technology progressed, the factory system became more sophisticated. A new kind of work organization emerged—the industrial assembly line—based on the principle that specialization and task coordination would lead to greater efficiency in production. Although the idea had been put to use in slaughterhouses prior to the turn of the twentieth century, the assembly line Henry Ford developed in 1913 to produce automobiles more efficiently became the prototype of the production methods now used by most manufacturing and processing industries. It had three basic features. First, workers remained stationary and performed their operations on parts that were moved to them at optimum speed. Second, parts and partially finished products were delivered to workers mechanically on a conveyor belt in a calculated progression. Third, each operation was broken down into the simplest possible motions, because a worker could develop maximum speed only when few movements had to be repeated.

It was at this time that efficiency experts emerged in the production industries. Armed with clipboards and stopwatches, these practitioners in the school of "scientific management" attempted to transform whole factories into giant, smoothly running machines in which the workers were little more than gears. There was a science of doing work properly, they claimed, and each task was broken down into a number of steps to be performed within a specified amount of time. The job description for a pig iron shoveler, for example, specified "the size of the shovel, the bite into the pile, the weight of the scoop, the distance to walk, the arc of the swing, and the rest periods."[2] The application of scientific management principles in the factory marked a fundamental change in the conception of the workers' roles in the work process. Rather than asking how machines could be used by people more effectively, the concern was with how to fit people to machines most efficiently! Potential reactions by workers to their new roles as mere appendages of the machines were largely ignored in the quest for greater efficiency.

Automation has further refined the assembly line by adding nonhuman control mechanisms to the work process. The term *automation* first appeared in print in an article about the Ford Motor Company in *American Machinist* in 1948, where it was defined as "the art of applying mechanical devices to manipulate work pieces into and out of equipment, turn parts between operators, remove scrap, and to perform these tasks in timed sequences with the production equipment so that the line can be wholly or partially under pushbutton control at strategic stations."[3]

If mechanization, a technology based on applications of nonhuman power, and automation, a technology based on communication and nonhuman control, were the first two phases of the Industrial Revolution, the third phase is cybernation. Cybernation is the "simultaneous use of computers and automation for the organization and control of material and social processes."[4] Like the first two phases of technological development, cybernation is making significant changes in the nature of work. Sophisticated self-regulating machinery now performs welding and machining operations and monitors production quality, while computers perform clerical jobs such as billing and payroll work. Yet, although automation and cybernation have eliminated many tiresome tasks and transformed the work life of most Americans, workers must now be more subservient to machines, pacing their work with them and attempting to match their accuracy.

In our twentieth-century economy, technology has changed the kinds of work available, the organization and institutions of work, and the security of the worker. It used to be assumed that people would work their whole lives in one trade or craft. Rapidly changing technology now makes that an obsolete concept. Someone who began working in the manufacture of 78-rpm records 30 years ago must now be able to work with tapes. To continue work in the sound reproduction business, that same person will probably have to learn about quadraphonic systems.

Insecurity: A Technological Growth

Automation has affected work in several ways. First, it has eliminated many jobs. Elevator operators have virtually disappeared. Dock workers and coal miners have been replaced by automated machines. Jobs in manufacturing decreased from 34 percent of the total employment in 1950 to 21 percent in 1977. Second, automation requires a staff of technical and service personnel who have new skills and more education. Third, there is greater bureaucratization of work, and the ranks of middle managers have swelled because their knowledge of a specialized area has given them new authority. Technocrats and scientists have also moved into the business hierarchy at nearly the same level as managers. Along with that increase, the percentage of industrial workers has gradually declined since 1955.[5]

Worker insecurity is integral to the nature of work today. Whole categories of workers, such as machine operators, have only tenuous ties to the labor force. As noted in one report, "even at the present early stage of cybernation, costs have already been lowered to the point where the price of a durable machine may be as little as one-third of the current annual wage-cost of the worker it replaces."[6] Partly as a result of technological advances, job uncertainty is now a fundamental characteristic of industrialized societies, and it represents a major source of strain in the social structures of industrial nations.

Not only does technology make old skills and jobs obsolete, but the dynamics of the American economy also affect the job market. The burgeoning of employment in the space and defense industries in the 1960s, followed by a sudden and massive shrinkage of jobs in those fields in the early 1970s, came about largely because of shifts in the pattern of federal spending. Whenever the national government attempts to combat inflation by controlling wages and prices, the job market becomes even more unsettled. Workers at all levels must now live with the possibility of displacement from the work force. Of even greater consequence is the long-run problem of whether the economy will be able to provide enough jobs in the future for all those who wish to work.

The Fluctuating Work Force

Figures released by the Department of Labor show the total labor force of the United States in 1977 as numbering 97 million persons. Approximately six out of every ten persons in our society have been members of the work force throughout the post–World War II era. But although the proportion of working people to the total population has remained fairly constant, the composition of the work force and the occupational structure of our society have undergone considerable change.

The percentage of working men has declined from a high of 87 percent in 1951 to 77 percent in 1977. In contrast, the percentage of working women has risen steadily from 35 percent to 48 percent over the same period. However, women do much more work than this might indicate, for women engaged in keeping house are not counted as employed in official statistics. Working women are concentrated in fewer occupational categories than men; moreover, they are vastly overrepresented in the service and clerical categories and underrepresented in others, especially the managerial and administrative categories, where they constitute less than one-fifth of the workers in these positions. To a certain extent this distribution of female employment represents a cultural preference pattern, but it also reflects a pattern of discrimination against women workers.

White and nonwhite percentages in the labor force are not the same. The figures for 1977 show that 79 percent of white males worked as compared with 72 percent of nonwhite males. The employment rate of nonwhite women continues to exceed that of white women—50 percent as compared with 47 percent. However, as has historically been the case, minority workers tend to remain concentrated in certain occupational categories.

The Bureau of Labor Statistics uses eleven major categories in an effort to group occupations in such a way as to permit a manageable social accounting. Table 4.1 shows the distribution of the civilian labor force across these categories and illustrates that the occupational structure of our society is shifting toward professional, managerial, and other white-collar work. White-collar and service workers now comprise 63.6 percent of the work force, meaning that a smaller proportion of workers are now involved in the direct production of the tangible commodities needed by society. The increase in labor productivity as well as the rapid industrialization of American society are evidenced in the dramatic movement away from agricultural employment. Three generations ago farmers and farm laborers accounted for 42 percent of the male labor force, whereas today only 3.0 percent of the total work force is engaged in farming.

Statistical Understatement

The Bureau of Labor Statistics (BLS) is empowered with the important task of regularly collecting and reporting statistics on the labor force. The methodology of the BLS has been criticized, particularly in regard to its figures on unemployment. Unemployment will be considered later in this chapter, but it may prove useful here to explore objections to the procedures of counting and labeling the unemployed. One aspect of the criticism concerns the

	Distribution of the Labor Force by Occupation, 1954–1977	Table 4.1
	1954	*1977*
White-collar workers	38.2%	49.9%
Professional and technical workers	8.9	15.1
Managers and administrators	9.8	10.7
Sales workers	6.4	6.3
Clerical workers	13.1	17.8
Blue-collar workers	40.6	33.1
Craft and kindred workers	13.6	12.9
Operatives	20.7	11.5
Nonfarm laborers	6.3	3.7
Private household workers	2.9	1.3
Service workers	8.2	13.7
Farmers	6.0	1.6
Farm laborers	4.1	1.4

Source: From U.S. Department of Labor, Bureau of Labor Statistics, *Employment and Unemployment Trends during 1977* (Washington, D.C.: Government Printing Office, 1978), p. A-19.

fact that nonprofessionals with political ties have been employed by the BLS to release findings to the press. This situation presents the possibility that the extent of the unemployment problem may be masked or distorted through the manipulation of statistics by those who have a vested interest in the issue.

Other criticisms relate to the methods of calculating unemployment rates and to the official definition of unemployment. The BLS figures are obtained by means of regular household surveys of a sample of the population. Persons are classified as either employed, unemployed, or not in the labor force. In order to be classified as unemployed, an individual must not have worked at all during the previous week and, in addition, must have taken specific steps to obtain a job during the previous four weeks. This definition has the effect of defining out of the labor force substantial numbers of people who have given up looking for work in the belief that employment opportunities for them do not exist. These so-called "discouraged workers," variously estimated to number between .75 and 1.25 million persons, are not counted as unemployed. Thus undercounting is especially prevalent among groups whose unemployment rates are high—the young, the old, and minorities.

Moreover, the official figures take no notice of underemployment. For example, an individual who worked only one or two days at a car wash during the period of the survey is counted simply as employed. Many people in economically depressed agricultural, mining, and industrial areas are grossly underemployed, but again, the official figures list them simply as employed. Yet the economic position of someone who works only ten hours a week is really not much different from someone who is completely unemployed.

Additional sources of error arise from the methods used in obtaining the unemployment figures. Transient or highly mobile segments of the population are systematically undercounted in the household survey. The wording of the questions asked by the BLS interviewers favors a higher count of people as employed. Individuals who worked at any time during the survey period are counted as employed, regardless of whether they are currently working. Workers who are on strike are classified as employed whether or not they are receiving any income. Seasonal workers are considered employed even if the survey covers a period in which they are not working. The unemployment picture drawn by the official statistics is by no means an accurate and complete measure of the economy's success in providing jobs for all those who want to work.

An ad hoc committee comprised of many distinguished scholars and citizens has concluded that the "official figures seriously underestimate the true extent of unemployment."[7] Taking into consideration discouraged workers, underemployment, and questionable accounting procedures, the committee has estimated that four million people above and beyond those counted as officially unemployed are not working and would like to have jobs.

Classification and Class

Although a device of the BLS, the classification of jobs into professional, white-collar, blue-collar, and laborer categories is descriptive of the social and economic class hierarchy in this country. Rank in the hierarchy is related to an individual's income, social prestige, and quality of life. Despite egalitarian ideals and a semblance of democratic informality at the top of the hierarchy, the listing of work categories by the statisticians conforms so closely to the realities of the class structure in American life that socioeconomic status can be predicted from job classification.

Professionals have the highest job status and are at the top of the classification hierarchy. A professional's occupation involves general systematic knowledge, authority over clients, community interest as well as self-interest, symbolic as well as monetary rewards, self-determination of tasks, and recognition by the public and law (through licensing) of professional status.

Occupations do not remain constant with respect to professional standing. As the requirements for the licensing of members of the clergy has, in some cases, become more a matter of conscience and conviction than of seminary education and training, that occupation has become less professional. On the other hand, nurses and social workers, as well as doctors, have developed organizations that guard and set standards for the professional status of their occupations and the privileges and prerogatives of their colleagues. Such groups have become more professional in recent years.

In general, most white-collar workers differ from professionals in that they are employed by an outside agency, use practical skills, and exercise much less self-determination. Generally, white-collar workers receive annual salaries rather than hourly wages, perform tasks requiring some amount of advanced education, and are not as likely to be subject to layoffs as less prestigious blue-collar workers. Although the salaries of clerical workers and salespeople are lower than those of the better paid blue-collar workers, the close association with management, the more attractive atmosphere of the place of work, and even the clothing worn to work confer greater social prestige on the white-collar worker.

Blue-collar workers perform work that demands training and perhaps skill or craftsmanship but not higher education. They have no subordinates unless they move up to the position of foreman or line supervisor. Such positions are usually the limit of their upward mobility, and they expect no more. One study showed that nearly half of all factory workers interviewed believed that they were stuck in their jobs no matter how well they performed and that only the combination of seniority, built up over the years, and exceptional good luck could help them advance.[8]

A steel handler interviewed by Studs Terkel said that he felt he was looked down on by others because he was a manual laborer: "It's the nonrecognition by other people. To say a woman is *just* a housewife is degrading, right? . . . It's also degrading to say *just* a laborer. The difference is that a man goes out and maybe gets smashed. It isn't that the average working guy is dumb. He's tired, that's all."[9] Other interviews with blue-collar workers "revealed an almost overwhelming sense of inferiority: the worker cannot talk proudly to his children about his job, and many workers feel that they must apologize for their status."[10]

Still lower in status than blue-collar workers are the unskilled manual laborers, or day laborers. One group in this category is migrant workers. Although farming is respectable, farm labor is not. Lowest on the social ladder, migrants receive the least pay, are excluded from social security or unemployment benefits, and are paid only for hours worked. Their working conditions are not under government control, although recently efforts have been made to ensure minimum housing and sanitation standards for migrant workers.

Joblessness: Human Problems and Social Consequences

At all levels and in all categories of the work force there are people who cannot find work. Unemployment is the most serious problem of the work structure in America. While federal officials argue that we must accept a "tolerable" rate of unemployment, the percentage figures do not reveal the extent of the human problems or the social consequences of joblessness. A single percentage point can mean the difference between economic security and poverty for hundreds of thousands of families. The human fact is that, as of October 1978, 5.6 percent of the labor force or approximately 6 million people were not working because they could not find employment.

The tendency to measure the costs of unemployment in economic terms —loss of production, loss of wages, idle plant capacity—acts to obscure other important dimensions of the unemployment problem. Sociologists are now studying the relationships between increases in the unemployment rate and rates of mental disorders, suicide, alcoholism, and homicide and other types of crime. As noted in one study of workers who lost their jobs due to a factory shutdown:

The unemployed man . . . who is responsible for his own livelihood and that of others can come to feel that there is no place in industry for him. He can lose confidence in himself. In his search for a scapegoat he may take his frustration out on his family. . . . Even more likely is a feeling of bitterness toward the system that permits a man to work in a plant for many years only to be displaced from his job and to find that his age and industrial experience count against him in the job market. . . . For the older worker, particularly, lengthy unemployment is apt to be a traumatic shock.[11]

Unemployment not only threatens the economic well-being of workers and their families, but it also deprives the worker of a major source of personal identity and a feeling of doing something worthwhile. Moreover, an absence of steady employment disrupts a central mechanism by which the individual is integrated into the larger community. The impact of forced unemployment, or retirement, for those over 65 or 70 will be discussed in more detail in Chapter 10.

To assess fully all of the human factors of unemployment we must add to the number of unemployed the millions who earn so little that their income falls below the established poverty line, as well as those who are underemployed. *Underemployment* is the term used to describe workers who are working less than full-time, at a job below their level of skill or training, and for wages that are insufficient to support themselves or their family. Then, too, there are those whose primary support is derived from welfare or who are out of the labor force but wish to work. These three groups are comprised of between 10 and 30 million people who are not accounted for in the official statistics of the BLS.

Statistical Patterns of Unemployment

The official rate of unemployment climbed to a postwar high of 8.9 percent of the civilian labor force in the summer of 1975. At that time, with the economy in the midst of a serious recession, over 8 million persons were on the rolls of the unemployed. The 1975 annual average rate of unemployment was approximately 8.5 percent. Unemployment rates fluctuate with the state of the economy, and several million persons may be absorbed into the work force or displaced from it depending upon its health.

For adult men the 1975 jobless rate was 6.6 percent, while for adult women the rate was somewhat higher—7.7 percent. Teenagers (ages sixteen through nineteen)—who as a group suffer chronically high unemployment—experienced a jobless rate of 21.2 percent. In some urban areas, unemployment among minority teenagers exceeded 50 percent.

Over the past several decades, the ratio of nonwhite to white unemployment has remained at an almost constant 2 to 1. The 1977 unemployment rate for blacks and members of other minority groups was 13.1 percent; for all whites the rate was 6.2 percent. Although a variety of government programs were initiated in the 1960s for the specific purpose of reducing minority unemployment, the overall effect of these programs appears to have been minimal.

Unemployment rates also differ significantly among occupational categories. Table 4.2 shows that blue-collar workers as a whole consistently had an unemployment rate approximately double that of white-collar workers. The kinds of skills possessed by a worker greatly affect that individual's potential for finding work. A worker who has always been a coal miner, for example, is left with few marketable skills if the mines close down.

The trend reflected in Table 4.2 indicates that after the unemployment levels peaked in 1975, rates generally declined in all occupational categories. One major exception is the rate for farm workers, which continued to spiral upward to a 1977 high of 4.6 percent compared to 1.8 percent in 1971. The overall pattern of unemployment shows that the occupations least affected by the increase in 1975 were also relatively unaffected by the 1977 drop in unemployment—that is, white-collar, professional, and technical workers. The occupational groupings considered the victims of the 1975 crisis were the beneficiaries of the 1977 boom in employment—the blue-collar, craft, and kindred workers.

These statistics show a pattern of unemployment that reveals inequalities in the social structure. Joblessness is not distributed evenly across the total work force but is concentrated in specific segments of it. Sex, race, age, and occupation are primary factors in determining who is unemployed. A black youth in a blue-collar laboring job has the highest probability of being unemployed, whereas an adult white male who is a member of the professional or managerial class has the highest probability of maintaining employment. Members of the labor force who experience discrimination— whether racial, sexual, or even age discrimination—or who do not possess skills that are at a premium in the economy are the hardest hit when the overall unemployment rate rises.

Labor unions have little power to deal with unemployment. Many union contracts prohibit firing an employee except under certain conditions and specify that layoffs must be on the basis of seniority when many workers are to be laid off. Although layoffs according to seniority protect older union members, they discriminate against minority group workers who are the "last hired and first fired." On the other hand, older workers in white-collar jobs are frequently forced by management into early retirement when the unemployment rate for their occupation is high.

Unemployment Rates by Occupation: 1971, 1975, and 1977			Table 4.2
	1971	1975	1977
White-collar workers	3.8%	4.6%	4.3%
Professional and technical workers	3.3	2.9	3.0
Managers and administration	1.6	3.0	2.8
Sales workers	5.2	5.9	5.3
Clerical workers	4.5	6.4	4.9
Blue-collar workers	7.4	11.5	8.1
Craft and kindred workers	4.5	8.2	5.6
Operatives	8.6	12.7	9.5
Nonfarm laborers	10.2	16.2	12.0
Service workers	6.3	9.3	8.2
Farm workers	1.8	3.8	4.6

Source: From U.S. Department of Labor, Bureau of Labor Statistics, *The Employment Situation: August 1975* (Washington, D.C.: Government Printing Office, 1975), p. 3; *Employment and Unemployment Trends during 1977* (Washington, D.C.: Government Printing Office, 1978), p. A-15.

Causes of Unemployment

Many factors contribute to the unemployment problem in our society: shifts in consumer demands and priorities, government spending, the state of the economy, the structure of job openings, disputes between management and labor, seasonal fluctuations, automation and rapidly changing technology, and discriminatory employment practices. For the purposes of this discussion, however, we shall concentrate on the effects of three—the economy and the government, automation and technology, and discrimination.

Governmental Policies and Priorities

During the period of severe economic depression that existed during the decade of the thirties, millions of workers were unemployed. Yet, as the unemployment statistics of 1971 clearly show, even in a prosperous economic period millions of workers are still unable to find work. In the early sixties there was a change in the economic policies of the federal government, and full employment became an important priority. Employment increases with economic growth, but growth is also accompanied by inflation. Balancing the desire for full employment against the disadvantages of inflation, the federal government finally determined to hold the line on inflation and tolerate a rate of unemployment of 4 or 5 percent.

Shifts in priorities in government spending bear a constant relationship to the size and composition of the work force and are more directly visible than changes in economic policy at the highest levels. During the 1960s billions of dollars were allocated by the federal government to defense and aerospace industries. In many geographical areas huge plants were constructed and thousands of workers employed. Between 1969 and 1971, however, enormous cutbacks in federal funding to these industries caused them to reduce their work force substantially or close their operation completely. The result was a minor, though vivid, manifestation of the effects of shifts in federal spending: large-scale, long-term unemployment among professionals and technicians. Because of the high status of these people, their misfortunes were highly publicized by the news media and thus served, perhaps, to dramatize "the plight of the larger number of unemployed, nonskilled workers who may have to cope with unemployment often."[12]

Automation: Unplanned Obsolescence

Workers at the administrative, professional, and technical levels are generally not as likely to lose their jobs due to automation and rapidly changing technology as are clerical and blue-collar workers and laborers. For the most part, the operation or maintenance of computers and automatic control devices requires only skilled personnel. Thus the effect of automation is to replace many people who have low-level skills with a few high-skilled persons plus machines, as happened in the coal mining industry in the 1950s when it was greatly mechanized.

Labor unions, particularly the craft unions, have tried to protect the jobs of their membership in contract agreements. When automation has made certain jobs obsolete (as in the railroad, printing, stagecraft, and construction industries), unions have insisted that they be retained even when the work was replaced by a machine. This practice called "featherbedding" can be employed only with discretion. If the unions make work too costly, whole corporations and even industries can go out of business.

For a number of years, automation in the United States has been considered a cause for alarm, since it appears to be causing extensive changes in work. Automation and mechanization have created new jobs, as well as whole new industries, which have come into existence to manufacture and service the new machines. IBM, for instance, has grown in 20 years from a small company manufacturing office equipment into one of the largest corporations in the world, employing many thousands of people. In 1966 the National Commission of Technology, Automation, and Economic Progress issued a report calling for a manpower policy that would facilitate movement of the labor force from the farm to the city, from the South to the North, from blue-collar to white-collar positions, and from manufacturing goods to producing services.[13] These shifts were deemed necessary to meet the growing demands for skilled service personnel who could be trained to fill technical jobs in northern urban areas, as well as to prevent unemployment among the less skilled workers who might be displaced as a result of the mechanization of their jobs.

The commission's report assumed that those who had only simple manual skills would be unemployable in more sophisticated, technological industries and recommended that the federal government become an "employer of last resort" for these people. It was estimated that more than 5 million jobs could be created for them in the areas of national beautification, urban renewal, sanitation, and services in medical and educational institutions. Yet one observer has suggested that automation is not a major cause of unemployment and has little radical effect on the existing distribution of skills. He maintains that while jobs change, the level of skill does not: "The work may involve a different kind of rote, but it is still rote."[14] And current opinion concurs that aggregate demands for goods and services and government policy play a more important role in the employment situation than does automation.

Members of minority groups, who would number about one out of every ten workers at all levels if parity existed, have unemployment problems of grave dimensions. According to one study, "one out of three minority workers is unemployed, irregularly employed, or has given up looking for a job."[15] Systematic discrimination in hiring practices throughout the American economy works a far greater hardship on minority groups than social prejudice or discrimination in housing or education. According to Gunnar Myrdal's classic study on racial prejudice, *An American Dilemma*, job discrimination is the root cause of poverty among minority groups.[16] Despite the recent improvement in the situation of young educated black men, who are beginning to be hired on a par with their white counterparts, study after study has shown that qualified members of minority groups at every level have lower level jobs, receive less pay, and have higher unemployment rates than majority groups. Even after the passage of federal legislation banning discrimination on the basis of race or sex, minority workers still are

**Misusing
Minorities**

not found in many unions, are usually hired for menial jobs, and are among the first to be laid off.

A major social cost of joblessness among young members of minority groups is a loss in productivity. In a sense, they are a drain on the economy, since they make no contribution. Those aged 16 to 19 either become high school dropouts or finish high school and eventually head for a blue-collar job.

High schools tend to concentrate on the student headed for college. A recent survey found that high school guidance counselors spend twice as much time on college-related counseling as they do on vocational topics.[17] Nevertheless, over half of the high school graduates receive some form of job guidance, while less than a quarter of the dropouts receive such guidance. Vocational training is sadly neglected in our schools, and, except for apprenticeship programs in a few unions, little attention is given to training young people in skilled work. In England and the European countries, vocational training and apprenticeship programs are offered in a great number of occupations. A study sponsored by the Department of Health, Education, and Welfare, *Work in America,* determined that "where training cannot be obtained on the job, there is clearly a need for society to help young people to receive the skills they need to earn a living."[18]

Where Is Women's Work?

Although numerically not a minority group, women, because of discrimination against them in hiring practices, suffer from the same problems as minority groups: unemployment, underemployment, and lower pay for equivalent jobs. Women are prevented by occupational sex-typing from obtaining jobs for which they are qualified, they are discouraged from entering occupations and professions that have traditionally been for men only, and they have been ignored in regard to promotions despite their work records.

As of 1977 there were 40 million women in the work force, a figure representing nearly 40.5 percent of the country's entire labor force. Single women no longer predominate in the female labor force, as they did prior to World War II and in the early 1950s. Married women living with their husbands now constitute approximately 62 percent of all female workers. For most of these women the income they earn is vital to the family economy. In our society, the typical woman now marries in her early twenties, raises a family, and then enters the labor force to work for an average of 25 years.

Since work is a necessity and not a matter of choice for the majority of women, the problem of female unemployment has significant social consequences. During the past quarter century women workers have consistently had a higher rate of unemployment than men, often nearly twice as high (see Figure 4.1 for recent data). The problem of underemployment is also more serious for women workers. While slightly less than two-thirds of the men in the labor force worked 50 weeks or more in 1975, only 41.4 percent of the women jobholders were employed on a year-round basis.

For the woman worker who is also the head of a family, job discrimination and the lack of adequate employment opportunities present a special cluster of problems. Over 12 percent of all American families are now headed by women, and the proportion continues to rise with the increasing rates of divorce and separation in the 1970s. The twin roles these women

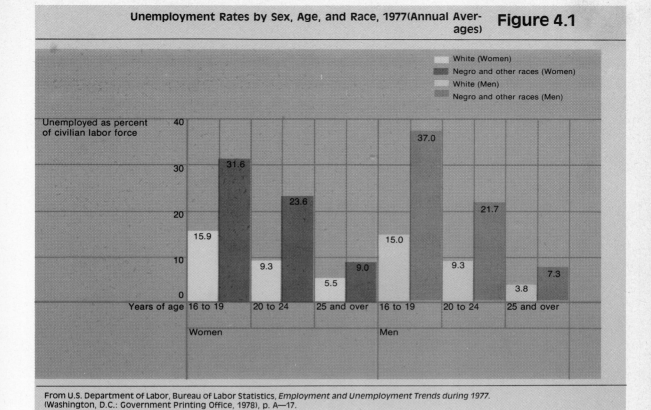

Unemployment Rates by Sex, Age, and Race, 1977 (Annual Averages) **Figure 4.1**

Legend:
- White (Women)
- Negro and other races (Women)
- White (Men)
- Negro and other races (Men)

Unemployed as percent of civilian labor force

Women:
- 16 to 19: White 15.9, Negro and other races 31.6
- 20 to 24: White 9.3, Negro and other races 23.6
- 25 and over: White 5.5, Negro and other races 9.0

Men:
- 16 to 19: White 15.0, Negro and other races 37.0
- 20 to 24: White 9.3, Negro and other races 21.7
- 25 and over: White 3.8, Negro and other races 7.3

From U.S. Department of Labor, Bureau of Labor Statistics, *Employment and Unemployment Trends during 1977.* (Washington, D.C.: Government Printing Office, 1978), p. A—17.

must play—mother and primary wage earner—constitute a significant economic liability. Where young children are present, families with a female head are much more likely to fall below the poverty line than any other type of family. The attainment of employment equality and the establishment of inexpensive day-care centers in the home community are of particular importance in reducing the economic burden carried by these women.

Occupational *sex-typing* is a term applied to a situation in which traditional expectations derived from the sex roles are associated with work roles (the association of the feminine roles of wife, mother, and housekeeper is carried into occupational categories). Thus women are largely restricted to occupations such as secretary (office wife), nurse, social worker, and schoolteacher (nurturing mother). Managerial pursuits associated with men's roles or occupations that require high-level skills are usually closed to all but a few token women. Occupational sex-typing effectively closes off many jobs and crowds women into a limited number of jobs where the pressure of excess supply lowers wages below the level that would otherwise prevail: "Once such a division of labor becomes established, it tends to be self-perpetuating since each sex is socialized, trained and counseled into certain jobs and not into others."[19] And, in fact, there is little fit between the

WOMEN AT WORK

In recent decades women have asserted their right to enter any occupation for which they are physically and intellectually qualified. Those pictured here have pioneered the way for members of their sex in all kinds of jobs previously considered the domain of men. *This page:* Miner: member of Congress; professional jockey; commercial airlines pilot; repairwoman for the phone company. *Opposite:* Policewoman; orchestra conductor; TV camerawoman; member of the armed-forces, firing an M-16.

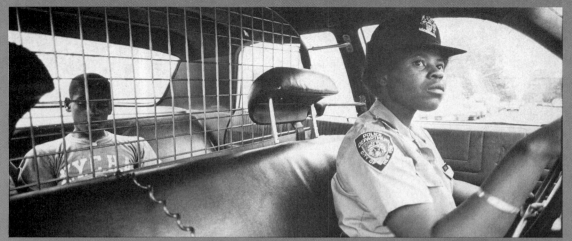

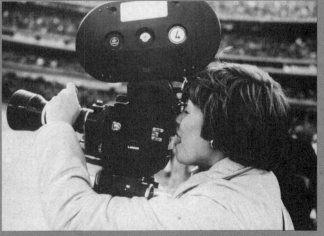

educational tracks recommended to and popular with young women on the one hand and the labor market demands and job openings on the other hand.

One study has indicated that some American women apparently choose to be part of a two-person career, remaining unemployed but experiencing achievement through participation in their husband's career. This pattern, typical of the upper middle class, "plays a particularly significant role . . . where an explicit ideology of educational equality between the sexes conflicts with an implicit inequality of occupational access."[20] In fact, it was found that some women believe the demands of their husband's job to be important in their own reluctance or inability to attempt independent careers at levels for which their education has prepared them.

Some women have been displaced by automation. The number of telephone operators dropped by almost one hundred thousand when direct-distance dialing equipment was installed. In spite of an expansion in telephone service, fewer operators needed to be hired. Much of the clerical work involving payrolls, inventories, invoicing, and sales in the banking, insurance, and retail industries has been taken over by computers, although women with appropriate training and skill can work as computer programmers, keypunch operators, tape librarians, console operators, and systems analysts. The jobs available to young women just entering the work force, however, typically require only low-level skills, so they have frequently been eliminated by automation in some fields. Unemployment rates for young women are among the highest of any group in our society (see Figure 4.1).

Discrimination against women is evident in unequal pay as well as job segregation. Federal law now requires that women be given equal pay for equal work, but on the average, women earn only about 60 percent as much as men for equal work.[21] In spite of certain gains by female workers since the upsurge of the women's movement in the 1960s, women workers remain concentrated in low-status, low-paying jobs where they lack decision-making power. A more detailed discussion of some of these issues appears in Chapter 8.

Another study of income discrepancies for women estimates that the 1960 Gross National Product would have been $105 billion larger than it was if all housekeeping wives over age 18 without preschool children had been working outside their homes.[22] The claim here is not that their productivity in the marketplace would have been greater than it was at home, but rather that the failure to value housewives' services as part of the GNP has had important consequences for the status of homemaking as well. Thus subsidies to welfare mothers could well be justified as payments for work as homemakers rather than as a handout.

Wasting Humanity

Unemployment represents a loss of human resources. Whether measured in the material loss of goods and services that might have been produced or in the loss entailed in human suffering, the cost of unemployment is high. Unused natural resources are banked for future exploitation. But the creative ability of an individual human being, when wasted, can never be recovered. Apathy attends unemployment and often inhibits a worker who should retrain and enter a different occupation. Unemployment creates anxiety and insecurity. When unemployment severs associations at work, the unemployed cease to participate in the life of the community. With neither the energy nor the disposition to make new social connections, they are, indeed, lost to the community.

Twentieth-Century Workers: Alienated Automatons?

The large numbers of working people who are dissatisfied with their jobs is a problem of major proportions in our economy. As early as the nineteenth century, Karl Marx recognized the problem of dissatisfaction in factory life. One hundred or more years ago factories were brutalizing and dangerous places where men, women, and children worked long hours under prison-like conditions. Marx, while critical of these places of work, was more concerned with the state of mind of the factory workers for whom this kind of work had no meaning. They could not identify with the goods produced, since they tended machines that were associated with only a small part of the total process of production. Lacking control over any portion of the pro-

Daniel Bell
The Changing Nature of Work

American workers have rarely vented their rage on the machine in the manner of English Luddites. Nor, surprisingly, have American trade unions ever shown serious interest in redesigning jobs or in "humanizing" work. From the start, what the American worker did seek was a reduction in the hours of work.

In the early decades of the 19th century, the hours of work customarily were, as on the farm, from "sunrise to sunset." . . .

In the years following the Civil War, the eight-hour day became the central issue for the trade unions. . . .

By 1890, however, the struggle for shorter hours had established the ten-hour day and six-day week in the majority of industries and occupations. After the turn of the century, the hours of work began to decrease in steps. By 1930 the 48-hour week had become the norm. By 1940 the 40-hour week had been established.

The trend toward a shorter work week has slowed since 1950. In that year, a worker average 41.7 hours a week, as against 39.6 hours in 1970. The real change has come not in the shorter work week but in longer vacations. Before 1940, few nonmanagerial workers received paid vacations. By 1970, two-thirds of all non-farm workers were guaranteed paid vacations, and the average for all workers was almost two weeks' vacation a year. If one includes paid holidays and sick leaves, the shrinkage in the work year has been more than three weeks in the past three decades.

The work week today seems to have reached a plateau, and it is unlikely that it will be reduced substantially in the next decade. But in the past 20 years or so, there have been four striking tranformations in the character of work and the work force.

1) *The rise of the organization man.* In 1940 about 26% of the male labor force was self-employed. By 1960 the figure had shrunk to 16%, and by 1970 to about 10%. Of the self-employed, about 1.7 million people are independent farmers; there are also 9.4 million small businesses. In all, about 75 million Americans today are wage-and-salary employees.

2) *The increase in Government employees.* In 1947, shortly after the war, slightly under 5.5 million people worked for the Government; by 1970, 13 million

people worked for the Government, or one in every six in the labor force. The major increase has not been in the Federal Government but mainly in state and local government—in large measure because these are the instruments that carry out federal programs. Between 1947 and 1970, federal employment went up about 25%, but state and local employment went up more than 250%.

3) *The growth of part-time work.* In the past decade the number of people holding part-time jobs increased from 9.8 million to 12.4 million. Much of this reflects the rise in the number of women returning to work. On the other hand, between 3 million and 4 million people "moonlight," that is, hold second jobs on some regular or substantial basis. Many millions more do occasional "extra" work.

4) *The onset of a post-industrial society.* Perhaps the most portentous change, however, is the relative decline of manufacturing and the rise of a service economy. Just as a century ago, one began to see the change from an agrarian to an industrial society, so one can now see the lineaments of a post-industrial society. Today in the U.S., 64 out of every 100 people are engaged in services; by 1980 about 70 out of every 100 will be employed in that sector. And these are new kinds of service, not those characteristic of an agrarian society (largely household servants) or an industrial economy (largely the auxilliary services of transportation and utilities, as well as some banking), but "human services" (the expansion in medical care, education and social welfare), professional and technical service (research, planning, computer systems), and the like. This has meant that the fastest growing segment of the American labor force has been the professional, college-educated people. Today the professional, technical, and managerial occupations make up 26% of the labor force, clerical workers 18%, semiskilled workers 17% and skilled workers only 13.5%.

But even within the industrial sector, there has been an extraordinary change as automation has begun to replace both unskilled and semiskilled workers. The man on the production line is giving way to the man who watches the dials or the man who comes in, as a skilled worker, to repair the machine.

Repairmen and foremen accounted for 75% of the growth in skilled jobs since 1940.

Behind these statistics is a change of greater psychological meaning—as great in its import, perhaps, as some of the first experiences of work that coded man's behavior. A pre-industrial world—whether one hunts animals or tends flocks, cuts wood or digs coal, cultivates the soil or fishes the seas—is primarily a game against nature. One's experience of this world is conditioned by the vicissitudes of the seasons, the character of the weather, the exhaustion of the soils. The forces to be overcome are tangible, if capricious. An industrial world is a game against fabricated nature. It is a world where man is hitched to the machine, overpowered by the size and power of the machine, yet also enlarged by the sense of the quantum jumps of energy that pulse through the industrial process. The forces are tangible, yet methodical and metrical. A post-industrial world, because it primarily involves services—doctor with patient, teacher with student, Government official with petitioner, research team with experimental designer—is largely a game between persons. In the daily experience of a white-collar world, nature is excluded, things are excluded. The world is entirely a social world—intangible and capricious—in which individuals encounter and have to learn how to live with one another. Not, perhaps, an easy thing.

What makes the game all the more important is that work, as Freud said, is the chief means of binding an individual to reality. The insight gains deeper meaning in modern society. In previous times, most people believed in an afterlife, in a heaven or hell. With the rise of a this-worldly attitude, the sense of death became overwhelming: work was one of the means whereby individuals staved off that consciousness of finality. The most nagging of all questions, in a world where religious beliefs are foundering, is what would happen if man lost his sense of a relationship to work.

Excerpts from Daniel Bell, "The Clock Watchers: Americans at Work," *Time*, September 8, 1975, pp. 55–57. Reprinted by permission from TIME, The Weekly Newsmagazine; copyright Time, Inc.

duction processes, they were, in fact, mere appendages of their machines. The state of these workers, with their deepest feelings separated from their daily activities, is what Marx described as alienation.[23]

Methods proclaimed as efficient in terms of human movements in production processes (introduced in 1911 by Frederick W. Taylor in his book *Principles of Scientific Management*) only further exacerbated worker alienation. Taylor's ideas were based on job analysis—breaking down each task into its simplest motions—and on time study—calculating the amount of time each movement takes. By eliminating unnecessary movements, Taylor turned men into efficient automatons. One of his earliest successes was in directing every movement of a pig iron handler named Schmidt, enabling him to handle 47.5 tons per day instead of 12.5 tons. Yet to workers this sort of success meant only a feeling of anonymity and powerlessness and an inability to identify with the finished product; in short, work became meaningless.

Alienation from work or worker dissatisfaction is seen today as a combination of four factors: (1) powerlessness—no worker control over the policies, instruments, or conditions of work; (2) meaninglessness—no feel for the relationship of a single task to the production process as a whole and no broad awareness of the utility of each operation; (3) isolation—little contact and no sense of cooperation with fellow workers; and (4) self-estrangement—boredom with monotonous repetitive work and the sense of being trapped.

Frustrated Aspirations

The problem of worker dissatisfaction has been discussed recently in the works of Frederick Herzberg, Abraham Maslow, and John Kenneth Galbraith. Each of these men classifies a system of needs and motivations related to worker satisfaction. Rapid changes in the organization of work and the attitudes toward work in our society have resulted in widespread disaffection with the conditions under which work is performed. The boring, routine, mechanical nature of many types of work often mitigates against workers' finding meaning and fulfillment in this labor. Worker alienation and the feeling of anonymity within a massive production apparatus have escalated as large-scale organizations have become common in business and industry. And when individual needs are not adequately met in the occupational sphere, the resultant problems may be viewed as manifestations of social disorganization.

Herzberg observes that there are two different kinds of work conditions related to worker satisfaction.[24] One set of conditions is concerned with the work environment—good pay, safe and sanitary conditions, and supervision with consideration for human dignity. The other set of conditions is inherent in the work itself: It must be challenging, it must provide an opportunity for accomplishment, and it must enable the worker to feel responsible for the achievement.

Maslow suggests that human needs are hierarchical and that as needs are satisfied at one level, the unsatisfied demands at the next higher level are felt as keenly as were the more basic lower-level needs.[25] He sets up the following hierarchy: first, simple physiological needs such as food and shelter; second, a need for safety and security; third, the need for friendship and affection; fourth, a desire for self-respect and the esteem of others; and fifth, a need for self-actualization—the chance to develop one's potential fully. The first and second levels of Maslow's hierarchy are similar to Herzberg's environmental factors, and the fourth and fifth levels are comparable to considerations of a sense of accomplishment.

In discussing motivation of workers in corporate organizations, Galbraith outlines a four-level hierarchy.[26] Only after the conditions of work have satisfied the motivational desires at a lower level do the desires of the next higher level operate as incentives to work. In Galbraith's system the lowest level of the hierarchy of motivation to work is simple fear of punishment, or compulsion. At the second level, money is a motivation force. The goods, services, comfort, and status that money can obtain are so extensive that financial rewards operate as intense incentives to work. Money is certainly necessary to worker satisfaction, but it is not enough alone. Galbraith proposes that the next level of motivation is identification. As human beings evaluate their own positions in relation to those of the people around them, it becomes important to them to accept the goals of their managers and to identify with the aims of their work organization. After identification has become a motivation for working, Galbraith postulates, workers desire to adapt the goals and policies of the work group to their own values. Adaptation thus serves as an additional incentive for workers whose motivation has been satisfied at the three lower levels. Lack of satisfaction at any of these levels can lead to worker alienation.

Feelings of alienation and dissatisfaction already prominent in the factories of the nineteenth and early twentieth centuries have grown more pronounced as work has become more automated. Computer control of work now extends from heavy industry jobs through lower-level white-collar jobs and even into some of the work of professionals.

Dissatisfaction among industrial workers is particularly evident in the automotive industry. In 1955 Eli Chinoy published a study of the frustrated aspirations of workers in "Autotown." In the factory he studied, 25 percent of the workers performed jobs on some kind of conveyor line. Nearly 30 percent were operating automatic or semiautomatic equipment—highly repetitive work. Only 5 percent were skilled workers. He found that nearly 80 percent of the men he interviewed had at one time considered leaving the factory. Chinoy sees their frustration as centered on the disparity between the American dream of success and the real limits to advancement in their jobs. Their work in the factory, he found, entailed "few clear-cut sequences of progressively more skilled, better-paid jobs. . . . instead, the men worked at carefully time-studied jobs in a highly rationalized industry [which] provided little opportunity to display either initiative or ability."[27]

In early 1972, prolonged worker dissatisfaction at a General Motors plant culminated in a 22-day wildcat strike after a speedup of the assembly line which allowed the workers only 36 seconds to perform their operations. The walkout was preceded by massive sabotage and was supported by most of GM's other assembly workers.[28] Although the growth of labor unions has secured for almost all industrial employees substantial benefits in the form of better wages, working conditions, and medical and pension plans, the unions have not been able to confront the industrial corporations directly on problems of job satisfaction. In most instances, industrial workers are stalled at the second level of Galbraith's hierarchy.

White-collar workers, too, face fragmented, repetitive, mechanical, meaningless tasks. Clerks, lower-level accountants, bookkeepers, secretaries, keypunch operators, telephone operators—these lower-level white-collar employees often feel cut off from advancement, in dead-end jobs. They are increasingly dissatisfied with their pay, as well as with the routine character of mechanized jobs. As the size of the organizations that employ them grows, they, like production line workers, have become anonymous cogs in the bureaucratic machinery. Two signs of their discontent are a 46 percent increase in white-collar union membership between 1958 and 1968 and a 30 percent annual turnover rate.

Professionals, too, endure a certain amount of insecurity and dissatisfaction. Among professionals and managers, 61 percent responded affirmatively to a Gallup poll statement that "they could accomplish more each day if they tried."[29] While most workers could certainly increase their productivity, the response to the statement reveals professional workers' perception of their own dissatisfaction. Even at this upper level, work could be more meaningful.

At all levels, worker dissatisfaction has significant social effects. With computerization and the invasion of technology in offices of higher management, the authority of managers who have not kept up with the new technology is threatened by the technocrats on whom they depend.[30] When profit pressures are high, these older executives undergo severe tension.

Indeed, a report done in 1972, *Work in America,* indicates that mental and physical health to some degree vary inversely with work dissatisfaction. Other studies indicate that family dissension, suspicion and hostility, escapism through drugs or drinking, and political apathy are all social costs of worker dissatisfaction.

Research and polls seem to indicate that certain groups of workers experience a disproportionate degree of dissatisfaction due to job discrimination—especially women, blacks, and youth. The rising expectations of these groups are frustrated by low wages, boredom, lack of dignity, no opportunity for progressive advancement, and little authority to direct their own work. Their demands for equality and equal opportunities often have a significant impact on society. Clearly, the quality of work and the degree of satisfaction the worker feels are vitally related to the quality of life, for both individuals and groups.

Diminishing Dissatisfaction

The major response to dissatisfaction with work conditions has come from workers themselves. From the time of its inception to the present, the trade union movement has been the most important aspect of this response. The federal government, along with state and city governments, has also taken on a share of the responsibility for solving work problems. Government programs proposed to create more jobs and to train or retrain workers in employable skills are directed toward reducing unemployment and worker dissatisfaction. In addition, some new methods of organization that

Samuel C. Florman
The Job Enrichment Mistake

Scarcely four years have passed since workers at the Vega plant in Lordstown, Ohio, went out on strike, not for more money or shorter hours, but to protest the pressure and monotony of their work on General Motors' fastest-moving assembly line. That twenty-three-day work stoppage helped make "worker alienation" a fashionable term in industrial sociological, and literary circles.

The inevitable downturn of interest in this phenomenon was heralded by a recent *Harvard Business Review* article entitled "Is Job Enrichment Just a Fad?" Only four years after Lordstown, has the battle against worker alienation been lost? Or was the battle, from the start, a sham? I believe the latter. I think that the problem of worker alienation has been overstated by social scientists who simplistically saw in the workplace a major cause of—and potential cure for—the ills of our society.

At the time of the Lordstown strike in early 1972, a stream of intriguing reports had already started arriving from Sweden, where SAAB and Volvo were trying to cope with worker discontent by experimenting with alternatives to the assembly line. Something new seemed to be in the air. At year's end the Department of Health, Education and Welfare released a study, *Work in America,* which reported that people at all levels of society were becoming increasingly dissatisfied with the quality of their working lives, to the detriment of the economic and social well-being of the nation. This study, which was widely distributed and acclaimed, provided a manifesto for the revolution that Lordstown seemed to portend. With amazing speed the concept of job enrichment spread through the worlds of journalism, academe, government, and the major corporations. In his book *The Future of the Workplace,* completed at the end of 1974, Paul Dickson concluded that "humanization of work" experiments were proving so successful that corporate executives were beginning to view them as important proprietary developments whose details were not to be shared with competitors. Changes were occurring, Dickson reported, at an increasingly

rapid rate, and these changes were no passing fad, but harbingers of things to come.

Concern for the alienated worker, in addition to spawning a host of industrial experiments, articles, studies, grants, and conferences, also inspired Studs Terkel's best-seller, *Working,* and Barbara Garson's less popular but nevertheless attention-getting *All the Livelong Day: The Meaning and Demeaning of Routine Work.* Both books were based upon numerous interviews with workers, and, in the words of the people themselves, the message seemed to be unambiguous: Americans are dissatisfied with their work. It leaves them frustrated and demoralized. They seek in their daily occupations a sense of identity, self-esteem, autonomy, and accomplishment. What they find, according to Terkel, is "daily humiliations." Their fragmented, monotonous jobs are, in Garson's view, "soul-destroying." The average worker's discontent manifests itself in fighting, swearing, absenteeism, high turnover rates, sabotage, alcoholism, drug addiction, and poor mental health. Reform of the workplace, it seemed, was one of the most critical social issues of our time.

Yet, for all this attention and concern, the author of the *Harvard Business Review* article, organizational psychologist J. Richard Hackman, reports that "job enrichment seems to be failing at least as often as it is succeeding." And further: "Even though the failures may be relatively unobtrusive now, they may soon become overwhelming." These experiments should be succeeding more often, according to Hackman, but his recipe for success is such an amalgam of wisdom and decency that it would seem to require a managerial class of supermen and saints to use it properly. As for the workers, their interest appears to be flagging. The United Auto Workers, for example, seem to have forgotten about Lordstown. In preparing for this year's contract negotiations, they are concentrating on the issues of wages and job security.

The most obvious conclusion is that a recession has occurred just in time for the ruling class to put the rebellious workers in their place. Clearly, in these uncertain times, most working Americans are less interested in fulfillment than in a living wage. But the supports of job enrichment (humanization of work, job redesign, work reform, the quality-of-work movement, et al.) claim that a more satisfying job results in improved productivity, so that it should be a management goal in bad times as well as good. In fact, this very feature has aroused the suspicions of labor-union leaders, whose lack of cooperation may be one of the main reasons for the many failed experiments. Job enrichment, according to a vice-president of the International Association of Machinists, is "a speed-up in the guise of concern for workers." Even assuming the best of motives, it is disturbing to note that job enrichment depends upon manipulation of workers by the experts. The experts maintain that the redesign of work is done in response to the desires of the workers. It is the experts, however, who determine what those desires are.

What *do* people want out of life? That is one of those questions whose answer can be shaped by the way in which the question is posed. Straightforward statistical studies find that job discontent is not high on the list of American social problems. When the Gallup poll's researchers ask "Is your work interesting?" they get 80 to 90 percent positive responses. But when researchers begin to ask more sophisticated questions, such as "What type of work would you try to get into if you could start all over again?" complaints begin to pour forth. The probing question cannot help but elicit a plaintive answer. Which of us, confronted with a sympathetic organizational psychologist, or talking into Studs Terkel's tape recorder, could resist tingeing our life's story with lamentation, particularly if that was what the questioner was looking for? Compared to the "calling" that Terkel says we are all seeking, what job could measure up?

Indeed, people are not "satisfied" with their work, nor with any other aspect of their lives. This is hardly news. But can we agree on what should be done to improve the situation? Barbara Garson sees a solution only in workers controlling their own jobs through socialism. (The widespread dissatisfaction of workers in socialist countries does not impress her.) . . . Miss Garson's workers keep contradicting her basic premise. From a woman who has turned down the job of supervisor: "I don't need the responsibility. After work I like to spend my time fixing up my house. And that's what I like to think about while I'm working." And from people with mechanical, repetitive trades:

"Flip, flip, flip . . .feels good." "You can get a good rhythm going." "You kind of get used to it." Even Garson despairs for a moment: "Maybe the reactionaries are right. Maybe some people are made for this work."

To have thought so (or, rather, to have admitted it) until recently, would indeed have marked one as a reactionary. But times are changing. The work enrichment movement appears to be running counter to another trend, the seeking of inner peace rather than ego fulfillment. In the light of this new wisdom, which advocates, among other things, the blanking of the mind in meditation for an hour each day, one can wonder who has the better of the bargain, those who are in the rat race or those who are "beneath" it. The job-enrichment enthusiasts may well have made a mistake in assuming that all people desire what social scientists want them to desire. . . .

Of course, the concept of job enrichment has much to commend it. The idea that work should provide satisfaction is a healthy one, and one worthy of future pursuit. Unfortunately, its recent manifestations exemplify our tendency to periodically identify our unhappiness with some new demon, which we then attempt to exorcise with a great blare of trumpets. . . .

Work enrichment is a fad because it was introduced with hoopla and promised a salvation it could never deliver. When the fad has passed, serious people with realistic goals will continue their efforts to increase job satisfaction. Their task will be all the harder because of the frenetic, irresponsible way in which job enrichment has been touted in the four years since Lordstown.

incorporate cooperation, decision-making power, and greater autonomy among workers have been originated and tried out in a few companies and show promise of a viable solution to worker dissatisfaction.

The Promise of Unionization

Unions have their historical roots in the nineteenth century. But the struggle for the acceptance of the union as the legitimate representative of the workers took place in the 1930s and was characterized by bitter strikes and

In union there is strength. That premise underlies the labor union movement in its attempt to balance the power of management. The merger of the AFL-CIO in 1955 was an important step in consolidating the strength of American labor unions.

hounding of union organizers by management and government alike. The early unions were organized around specialized crafts; but in the thirties whole industries, such as the automobile, mining, and electrical industries, were organized into single unions. The industrial unions not only bargained for higher wages and better working conditions but felt that the improvement of social conditions for all was an integral part of their movement.

In many sectors of the American economy, however, workers are still without union organization. Nonunion workers are at the double disadvantage of receiving lower wages and having to pay high prices for goods produced by unionized industries. The craft unions, particularly in the construction industry, have made minority membership extremely difficult, effectively preventing them from learning the necessary skills or obtaining employment.

Although unionization has not fulfilled the promise of its early days, the trade union has functioned to protect the individual worker from the misuse of management power. In some cases—for example, the International Typographical Union of printers—the sense of community among the workers is quite strong and offers some alternatives to worker dissatisfaction. Participation in union activities and recreational activities associated with the union is high, and a classic sociological study found that there was a positive relationship between participation in union activities and job satisfaction.[31]

In other cases, however, the rank and file seem to be increasingly disenchanted with the way in which their leadership represents them and with agreements reached between the union bureaucracy and industry.[32] At crucial contract negotiations, it is too often evident to them that their representatives are bargaining from a subordinate position, with union power being limited by the effectiveness of their only weapon—the strike. Since strikes are as costly to union members as to management, they are a weapon seldom used. Unions presently have no leverage to create jobs and little chance to change the structure of the work situation to improve worker satisfaction. This seeming decline in power has resulted in a change in the attitude of the new generation of workers who no longer perceive the union as a positive force in industrial relations and are therefore less receptive to unionism than were workers in the past.[33]

Total employment should be the goal of federal laws and policies concerning work, according to the report *Work in America*. That situation would obtain when anyone who wishes to work is able to find a job that is reasonably satisfying. The report rejects "full employment," an economic concept which permits 4 percent of the work force to be unemployed at any given time.

Federal Employment Strategies

In the 1930s, when 25 percent of the labor force was unemployed, President Roosevelt responded by creating jobs with public funds to employ 10 percent of the labor force. This marked the beginning of federally supported work programs. The Employment Act of 1946 committed the national government to combating unemployment in broad terms: "It is the continuing policy and responsibility of the Federal Government . . . to promote maximum employment, production, and purchasing power."[34] In spite of this policy, the rate of unemployment from 1957 to the present has seldom been less than 5 percent.

Three pieces of legislation in the early 1960s were directed at the employment problems of women and minorities: (1) the Equal Pay Act of 1963, which requires that men and women receive equal pay for equal work; (2) Title VII of the Civil Rights Act of 1964, which prohibits discrimination in hiring and promotions on the basis of sex, race, national origin, or religion; and (3) Executive Order 11246 of 1965, a "contract-compliance provision affecting companies which do business with the Government."[35] Every employer with a federal contract worth $50,000 or more must file a written affirmative action plan listing the company's "utilization rate" of minority group members in each of its job categories at each of its establishments.

Later in the 1960s two programs were established for job training: (1) WIN, the Work Incentive Program of 1967, to provide education and job training to welfare recipients; and (2) JOBS, Job Opportunities in the Business Sector, which was expected to create 338,000 jobs by June 1970 through the joint efforts of the National Alliance of Businessmen and the government. These and programs at the state and local levels have been established to alleviate unemployment among women, youth, minorities, those displaced by automation, and hard-core unemployed white males.

The programs have not been very successful. In some cases trained persons have been unable to establish contact with businesses to find openings that would fit their abilities. Many who need some kind of federal assistance do not fall into the categories specified in the laws governing the programs.

Some hastily drawn up plans were put into effect haphazardly. For example, in 1972 JOBS had enrolled only enough trainees to make up 10 percent of their 1971 goal; and WIN had only 100,000 participants rather than the expected 280,000. Furthermore, only 20 percent of WIN trainees are actually working now, and many of them are in menial jobs that pay little more than welfare.

On the other hand, the Equal Employment Opportunity Commission (created by Congress in 1964 to prevent employment discrimination) and the Department of Labor have recently reached a landmark agreement with the American Telephone and Telegraph Company concerning employment and promotion of women and minority workers. In an out-of-court settlement, AT&T agreed to pay some $38 million to 13,000 women and 2000 minority group men who allegedly suffered job discrimination, and to about 36,000 workers whose advancement in the company may have been impeded by discrimination. The company also agreed to alter its system of hiring, promoting, and transferring employees in order to upgrade the status of female and minority workers and to take steps to end sexual stereotyping in job descriptions. Men are now hired as operators and women as line and switch workers.

The federal program designed to eliminate such discrimination, known as "Affirmative Action," requires government contractors or any institution receiving federal funding to guarantee members of minority groups an equal opportunity for employment.[36] The rationale for this requirement was that numerous systems utilized to recruit for employment were inherently biased against minorities and women, even though there was no premeditated or overt discrimination on the part of the employer. The difficulties involved in inaugurating and enforcing such a program have been monumental, with the most common solution being an attempt to maintain a certain proportion of women and minorities in all job classifications. This "quota system" has become the major tactic of affirmative action, but this practice has been protested by some individuals who have labeled it "reverse discrimination." Although the U.S. Supreme Court's 1978 Bakke decision, discussed in Chapter 3, rejected the use of quotas by institutions of higher education, the Court upheld the use of racial quotas by employers in the 1979 Weber case. The impact of this decision on the future of affirmative action in employment is difficult to assess, but one may assume that it will probably increase the pressure for voluntary affirmative action programs in industry.

The concern for equality and employment opportunities will continue to be a major priority for the federal government as evidenced by the Humphrey-Hawkins "Full Employment" Bill passed by Congress in October 1978. The legislation contained several economic goals, including the attempt to reduce national unemployment to 4 percent of the labor force and to slash inflation to 3 percent by 1983 and to zero by 1988. The shortcoming of this as well as other recent legislation in the area of employment is that whereas the bill proposes a set of goals, it fails to mandate realistic programs to achieve these objectives. Undoubtedly, there will be continued efforts by the federal government to address the ideal of total employment, and it is hoped that new programs will be developed to achieve this objective.

Since job dissatisfaction is primarily rooted in the conditions of work in our society, an effective remedy may well have to include basic changes in working conditions. For blue-collar employees in particular, with the often depressing, stultifying conditions under which they work, there is ample room for improvement. Proposals for job enrichment typically involve attempts to widen the scope of the worker's duties and to provide greater variety in the types of work performed through job rotation. Many feel that when work is humanized and more flexible working conditions are implemented, employees will find more meaning in their jobs, more pride in their workmanship, and more satisfaction in their leisure.

Jobs at various stages along an assembly line are often so simple that workers are readily interchangeable. There is a growing belief that specialization may have been taken too far on the modern assembly line. In an attempt to reduce the boring, monotonous nature of automobile assembly, the Volvo and Saab motor companies in Sweden have restructured the work process through the use of work teams and job rotation. Workers change the tasks they perform frequently; a worker may assemble an entire engine one week, for example, and work on a particular section the next week. Organizing the assembly of cars in this manner reduces the fragmentation of work and gives workers an overview of the total production operation. The plan appears to be a success. Workers find their jobs more interesting and develop a sense of identification with "their" products.

Job enrichment programs have been implemented in some plants in the United States on an experimental basis, and the results are encouraging. One scholar finds that there is "some evidence that job enlargement or rotation can both reduce job discontent and increase efficiency—through improved quality and quantity of output, a more flexible work force and, less surely, reduced labor turnover." Yet he goes on to note that in the United States, "to fit machine systems to the man is an idea foreign to most employers."[37] The potential for reducing worker dissatisfaction through job redesign and enrichment thus remains a largely unexplored area.

A movement far more conspicuous and active in Europe than in the United States is worker control or democracy in the factory. The goal is not better working conditions or job enrichment, but power over production. The division of labor is both technical and social. The specialization of jobs in a factory intentionally deprives each worker of the knowledge of other aspects of the production process requisite for taking initiative or making decisions. If all the workers in a factory had the skills to do all the operations in a factory, they would not only understand the overall process but would be able to make the essential decisions regarding the production process, hiring and firing, and setting salaries.[38]

In a pet food factory in Topeka, Kansas, poor quality production, vandalism, and graffiti on the walls were diagnosed as symptoms of alienation among a younger work force. The management decided to adopt a new approach emphasizing human needs of employees for self-esteem, a sense of accomplishment, and increasing knowledge. What was needed was autonomy; workers desired to plan the work, check the quality, and change the

The Saab management agrees that variety, the spice of life and work, means happier workers and better products. Assembly teams rather than assembly lines are designed to give each individual a responsible role in production.

Bored people build bad cars. That's why we're doing away with the assembly line.

Working on an assembly line is monotonous. And boring. And after a while, some people begin not to care about their jobs anymore. So the quality of the product often suffers.

That's why, at Saab, we're replacing the assembly line with assembly teams. Groups

of just three or four people who are responsible for a particular assembly process from start to finish.

Each team makes its own decisions about who does what and when. And each team member can even do the entire assembly singlehandedly. The result: people are more involved. They care more. So there's less absenteeism, less turnover. And we have more experienced people on the job.

We're building our new 2-liter engines this way. And the doors to our Saab 99. And we're planning to use this same system to build other parts of our car as well.

It's a slower, more costly system, but we realize that the best machines and materials in the world don't mean a thing, if the person building the car doesn't care.

Saab. It's what a car should be.

design of jobs. They wanted real control, not just freedom to determine when they took their coffee breaks.

The management cut down on the work force to make each job more challenging and omitted as many specialized functions as possible. Workers learned every job at their own pace from others and proceeded up the pay scale according to their progress as judged by their fellow workers. Employees also took over hiring and firing. In terms of worker satisfaction, the results were considerable, but even more surprising was the effect on production costs. Overall costs are now considerably lower than customary in a conventional plant and quality is higher because of greater work involvement.[39]

The introduction of democracy into a Procter & Gamble factory in Lima, Ohio, had similar results.[40] Furthermore, it appears that workers who are part of a democratic process take on more activities outside the workplace. Nearly 10 percent of the work force in one such democratically run plant hold elective office in the outside community. The lesson is important: personal satisfaction and fulfillment go hand in hand with efficient production.

Shorter workweeks also seem to reduce worker dissatisfaction. One study of over a hundred companies trying the four-day, 40-hour week showed increases in worker motivation and productivity. A related concept is that of earlier retirement. At General Motors a worker can retire with an adequate pension anytime after 30 years of work. The armed forces have long had early retirement plans.

Abbreviated workweeks and shorter working lives pose the problem of leisure, however. Finding meaning and identity in leisure may prove as difficult as searching for autonomy and significance on the job. Not many of us are trained for long periods of fruitful, satisfying nonwork.

Leisure

While some historians argue that leisure has existed at all times in all civilizations, it is generally accepted that leisure, as we experience it, is an unintended consequence of the Industrial Revolution and therefore is unique to industrial and postindustrial societies. During the past century the amount of time spent at the workplace has declined progressively from an average of 65 hours per week to about 40, primarily due to advances in technology. Leisure refers to the period of surplus time when the individual is removed from the pressures of work or other related responsibilities and is free to utilize this time for relaxation, recreation, personal development, or any other purpose he or she deems appropriate.

Unfortunately, not all occupational groups have benefited equally from this increase in leisure. While white- and blue-collar workers have been the chief beneficiaries of the declining workweek and increased amounts of leisure time, approximately 23 million Americans, or 27 percent of the total labor force in 1977, worked in excess of 40 hours per week. There are several explanations why such a large portion of the population is included in this category. Among the individuals found in this situation are those who are extremely committed to their occupation or profession and who prefer working to having more free time. This type of person is commonly labeled a "workaholic." Second, certain occupations also require additional commitment and involve greater job responsibility. Professionals and executives generally have less free time and are often expected to work extended hours by "taking their job home with them in a briefcase." Farm operators, small business proprietors, and other independent workers are additional victims of this uneven distribution of leisure in the work force.

A third segment of the population included in this extended work classification are individuals in need of additional income, characteristically married males in low paying positions. Several strategies are commonly utilized to fulfill these financial needs: 1) the individual maintains a single job where he is permitted to work overtime, 2) the person can hold two or more jobs simultaneously, a practice known as "moonlighting" (in 1977, approximately 4 million workers or 5 percent of the total labor force held two or more jobs), or 3) in many cases the supplementary income is obtained by another working member of the family. (In 1977, about 48 percent of married males had wives who were employed in either a full- or part-time

LEISURE

In recent years the declining work week has meant an increase in the amount of leisure time for many Americans. Removed from the pressure of work, men and women spend their "free time" in a variety of ways. Some enjoy private leisure, those activities which they can engage in by themselves, often to improve their health or physical fitness. Others partake of public leisure, more passive ways of relaxing and enjoying themselves. Here, jogging has become an increasingly popular form of leisure and fitness; in addition to providing healthy exercise, the bicycle allows us to be mobile without gasoline or air pollution; reading a good book will always be a popular form of leisure; spending free time on the ski slopes provides vigorous outdoor activity even in the winter; an afternoon or evening at the ball park continues to attract millions of spectators each year; camping out has also become more popular in recent years, allowing the camper to experience the joys of nature while escaping the stresses of work and urban life.

job). The individual rationale for working an extended week ranges from those who find it necessary for economic survival to those who need the additional income to obtain certain special types of leisure that would be otherwise financially impossible (e.g., travel, sports car). Regardless of the reason, this practice of working overtime or moonlighting represents a significant reduction in the amount of time available for leisure activities and consequently increases the pressure of work and other relatedproblems.

The fact that the majority of U.S. workers do not fall into this overworked category and therefore have experienced a substantial increase of leisure time in recent years does not guarantee that they will "live happily ever after." For many, the existence of this free time itself is problematic, since the emergence of a leisure-oriented culture represents a direct challenge to the traditional philosophy of the Protestant Ethic. The personal conflict and uncertainty caused by this change in values is reflected in the variety of orientations toward the relationship between work and leisure exhibited in our society. The most significant approach to the work-leisure relationship continues to adhere to the traditional religious attitude emphasized within the Protestant Ethic stressing the priority of work over leisure. Work is viewed both as an instrument to economic and spiritual security, while leisure is seen as a possible obstacle in the path to wealth and salvation. A contrary orientation represents a complete reversal in values, with leisure perceived as the ultimate goal in life and work simply as a means to an end. C. Wright Mills describes this philosophy as following, "Each day men sell a little of their lives in order to buy them back each night and each weekend with the coin of 'fun.' With amusement, with love, with vicarious intimacy, they pull themselves into a sort of whole again, so that they are different men."[41] In other words, the individual is willing to sacrifice his or her labor in order to enjoy freedom later. Both of these orientations represent an attempt to isolate work and leisure into distinct spheres of activity, a social phenomenon known as "polarization."[12] In contrast, a third orientation emphasizes the need to synthesize leisure and work into a total life scheme, where the two are perceived as complementary parts of a whole, not antagonistic. This attempt to fuse work and leisure is termed integration. The particular orientation toward the work-leisure relationship an individual adheres to will generally dictate the nature and amount of time to be devoted to leisure activities.

The way in which a person spends his or her free time also varies greatly, with it often being utilized for activities other than leisure. Work-related functions are one of the major factors reducing the amount of pure leisure time on one's life. Time lost traveling to and from the place of employment, participating in parties or social gatherings with business associates and customers, or simply preparing for the next day at the office are just a few of the many work-related activities one must perform. Many other activities outside the sphere of work are also considered mandatory and therefore are marginal to what we have defined as leisure. This "obligatory nonwork" includes tasks that are not directly associated with one's profession but are not in themselves leisure activities. Repairing the house, maintaining the lawn or garden, shopping for food and other necessities, and other simple chores are examples of nonwork obligations. Outside the household, activities like participating in community or civic organizations, attending school meetings, and so on also fall into this category. For some, these activities are actually considered to be leisure, since they serve as a form of relaxation or a source of personal gratification. For numerous others, though, these duties represent an extension of work, boredom, or a total waste of precious time. From these illustrations it is apparent that the actual amount of time an individual has to use for pure leisure activities is extremely restricted.

Pure leisure-time activities assume a wide variety of forms. One broad distinction can be made between private leisure and public or mass leisure. Private leisure refers to those activities that are limited to oneself, family, or intimate friends. It can be either active or passive in nature. Some examples of the active category are jogging, tennis, horseback riding or any other activity that requires physical involvement. In recent years participation in this type of leisure has increased dramatically as the concern for health and physical fitness has evolved into a national priority. Unfortunately, the vast majority of Americans spend most of their free time in a passive manner, watching television, visiting relatives, and the like, instead of doing something that requires active involvement. Most "public" leisure is also passive in nature. Rock concerts, sporting events, and religious revivals are all events where vast numbers of people congregate to watch a performance of some kind.

The need to supply the population with various forms of leisure opportunities and activities has become a big business and has had a significant impact on the economic sphere, creating a market for numerous new organizations and occupations. The growth of the leisure industry is clearly illustrated by the fact that between 1955 and 1974 the amount of income spent by the American public on leisure activities and products increased by 550 percent, while the U.S. population during that period grew by approximately 28 percent and the Gross National Product advanced by only 80 percent.[43] The importance of leisure in the American life-style becomes evident if one considers that as long ago as 1965 the national expenditure for leisure exceeded that for medical care by approximately 500 percent. It has been increasing ever since.

The role of leisure in society will undoubtedly increase in the future as the workweek shrinks with continuing technological advances. The impact of this free time on the individual members of our society remains problematic, and the future necessitates a commitment to the resolution of leisure related problems so that this luxury can be appreciated by the entire population.

Summary

Work is the central activity in the lives of most adult men and women. People work primarily to earn a living, but the nature of the work they do also provides a sense of identity and a frame of reference from which to view the world. Further, work is a central mechanism by which individuals are integrated into the larger society. When the economy does not provide a sufficient number of jobs for the working population or when work is structured in a fashion unsatisfactory to the worker, the potency of work as a mechanism of social integration is weakened. This failure of the occupational system to meet the needs of individuals may be viewed as a manifestation of social disorganization.

The primary attitude toward work in the United States has been derived from the Protestant ethic, which held that industriousness and success were the means for salvation. This doctrine, with its emphasis on work as an obligation, was appropriate to a society of small businesses and individual entrepreneurs.

As technology grew more complex and small businesses gave way to corporations employing many thousands of people, workers lost their autonomy and often their sense of satisfaction and identification with work as well. Advances in technology have transformed the work lives of most Americans, and many categories of jobs now have a routine, monotonous, and tedious character.

Changes in values have accompanied these broader changes in the organization of work, and the values held by different segments of the occupational hierarchy have often come into conflict. Wildcat strikes, sabotage, and the production of shoddy goods may result when value conflicts are particularly acute.

The size of the labor force, the classification of jobs, and the occupational breakdowns in terms of sex, age, and race are contained in statistics on the working population compiled at regular intervals by the Bureau of Labor Statistics. The accuracy of the bureau's unemployment statistics in particular has been questioned on several grounds, and social scientists generally believe that the official figures underrepresent the true extent of unemployment.

In 1977, the work force contained 97 million people, 40.5 percent of them women. The occupational structure has been shifting in the direction of white-collar and service work. Correspondingly, the proportion of blue-collar employees has steadily declined over the past 20 years to the point where they now comprise only about one-third of the total work force. Since occupation is the main indicator of social class, the categories of professional, white collar, and blue collar are descriptive not only of different occupational experiences but also of different life-styles and degrees of social influence.

In studying work in the United States, the major social problems to be considered relate to unemployment and underemployment and their effects on different groups. The causes of unemployment are embedded not only in economic processes that determine the business cycle but in political decisions as well, any one of which may determine whether hundreds of thousands of persons will be able to find a job. The technological advances in automation and cybernetics are also responsible for the displacement of workers. Discrimination against minority groups and women makes them the principal victims of both unemployment and lower wage scales at every occupational level.

Unemployment and the attendant loss of income produces untold hardships. Prolonged unemployment commonly results in a loss of dignity and the sense of worth that comes from regular work. Unemployment is particularly hard on older workers, whom employers may be reluctant to hire when younger workers are available. The unemployed tend to drop out of community life, and in areas of widespread unemployment even those who are working are affected. The human resources wasted can never be recovered.

In response to these problems, several measures have been suggested to reduce unemployment by creating additional jobs in both the public and private sectors. Many proposals are targeted at those groups hardest hit by unemployment. Job enrichment proposals have been put forward as a means of combating the problem of worker dissatisfaction. Others have argued that a more thoroughgoing reorganization of work in our society is necessary in order to effectively remedy work-related problems. Reorganizing work may solve some problems, but it will obviously create others, including the effective use of leisure time. Although leisure is not shared equally by all workers, it has grown enormously in recent decades and must now be considered a major industry in America.

Notes

[1]Robert L. Heilbroner, "The Changing U.S. Labor Force," *Wilmington Evening Journal*, 20 January 1976. From the American Issues Forum series, copyright the regents of the University of California, 1975.

[2]Gresham M. Sykes, *Social Problems in America* (Glenview, Ill.: Scott, Foresman, 1971), p. 162.

[3]James R. Bright, "The Development of Automation," *Technology in Western Civilization*, vol. 2, ed. Melvin Kranzberg and Carroll W. Pursell (New York: Oxford University Press, 1967), p. 635.

[4]Donald N. Michael, "The Impact of Cybernation," *Technology in Western Civilization*, vol. 2, p. 655.

[5]"Where the Workers Are," *Fortune*, May 1972, p. 189.

[6]Ad Hoc Committee, "The Triple Revolution: An Appraisal of the Major U.S. Crises and Proposals for Action," *Liberation*, April 1964, p. 3.

[7]Ibid., p. 4.

[8]Robert Blauner, *Alienation and Freedom: The Factory Worker and His Industry* (Chicago: University of Chicago Press, 1964), p. 206.

[9]Studs Terkel, "A Steelworker Speaks," *Dissent*, Winter 1972, p. 11.

[10]*Work in America* (Cambridge, Mass.: MIT Press, 1973), p. 35.

[11]Richard C. Wilcock and Walter H. Franke, *Unwanted Workers* (New York: Free Press, 1963), p. 85.

[12]Douglas H. Powell and Paul F. Driscoll, "Middle Class Professionals Face Unemployment," *Society*, January/February 1973, pp. 18–26.

[13]*Report of the National Commission on Technology, Automation and Economic Progress*, in Robert MacBride, *The Automated State* (New York: Chilton, 1967), pp. 207–299.

[14]Charles Silberman and the editors of *Fortune, The Myths of Automation* (New York: Harper & Row, 1966), pp. 3, 21.

[15]*Work in America*, p. 51.

[16]Gunnar Myrdal, *An American Dilemma* (New York: Harper & Row, 1944).

[17]*Work in America*, p. 150.

[18]Ibid., p. 151.

[19]Ibid., p. 60.

[20]Hanna Papanek, "Men, Women, and Work: Reflections on the Two-Person Career," *American Journal of Sociology* 78 (1973), 852–853.

[21]U.S. Department of Labor, *U.S. Working Woman: A Chartbook* (Washington, D.C.: Government Printing Office, 1975), p. 36.

[22]Juanita Kreps, *Sex in the Marketplace: American Women at Work* (Baltimore: Johns Hopkins Press, 1971), p. 65.

[23]Isaiah Berlin, *Karl Marx: His Life and Environment* (New York: Oxford University Press, 1959), pp. 131–137.

[24]Frederick Herzberg, Bernard Mausner, and Barbara Snyderman, *The Motivation to Work* (New York: Wiley, 1959).

[25]Abraham Maslow, *Motivation and Personality* (New York: Harper & Row, 1954).

[26]John Kenneth Galbraith, *The New Industrial State* (Boston: Houghton Mifflin, 1972), pp. 141–143.

[27]Eli Chinoy, *Automobile Workers and the American Dream* (New York: Doubleday, 1955), p. 21.

[28]Emma Rothschild, "GM in More Trouble," *New York Review of Books*, 23 March 1972, p. 20.

[29]*Gallup Poll*, Report No. 94, April 1973, p. 27.

[30]Galbraith, *New Industrial State*.

[31]Seymour M. Lipset, M. A. Trow, and James S. Coleman, *Union Democracy* (New York: Free Press, 1956).

[32]James O'Connor, *The Fiscal Crisis of the State*, (New York: St. Martin's, 1973), p. 23.

[33]"Smaller Share of Workers Join Unions," *Socioeconomic Newsletter*, 3 vol. (October 1978), 3.

[34]Arthur Okun, ed., *The Battle against Unemployment* (New York: Norton, 1965), p.viii.

[35]Harvey D. Shapiro, "Women on the Line, Men at the Switchboard," *New York Times Magazine*, 20 May 1973, p. 26.

[36]U.S. Bureau of National Affairs, *The Equal Employment Opportunity Act of 1972* (Washington, D.C.: Government Printing Office, 1973), p. 14.

[37]Harold Wilensky, "Work as a Social Problem," *Social Problems*, ed. Howard S. Becker (New York: Wiley, 1966), p. 162.

[38]André Gorz, *Strategy for Labor* (Boston: Beacon Press, 1967).

[39]David Jenkins, "Democracy in the Factory," *Atlantic*, April 1973, pp. 78–83.

[40]Ibid.

[41]C. Wright Mills, *White Collar* (New York: Oxford University Press, 1951), p. 237.

[42]Stanley Parker, *"The Future of Work and Leisure,"* (New York: Praeger, 1971), p. 4.

[43]U.S. Census Bureau, *Statistical Abstract of the United States, 1976* (Washington, D.C.: Government Printing Office, 1976), pp. 10, 218, 393.

The Urban Community

5

The Urban Era

The Rise (and Fall?) of the American City

What Is a City?

Urban Problems

Federal Intervention

Proposals for Change
Revenue Sharing / Reshaping Cities / New
Communities / Neighborhood Government

Summary

Notes

Cities have a long history in organized society. It begins in 3500 B.C. with the first settlements in the Fertile Crescent of Mesopotamia—Ur and Lagash, Jericho and Babylon—and extends to the towering metropolises of modern civilization. Throughout their collective and individual histories cities have exhibited a variety of social and ecological forms, depending on the technological, cultural, economic, and political settings in which they developed.

Urban social problems, the problems of sizable numbers of people gathered together to live, to govern, and to produce and exchange goods, have been part of every form of city and are as old as cities themselves. When these problems were made manageable, cities and civilizations flourished. Then, for reasons so diverse scholars continue to argue over them, many of these civilizations—and cities—declined: "There is a significant relation between the rise and fall of empires and the rise and fall of cities; in a real sense, history is the study of urban graveyards."[1]

The historical fact today sounds something like a threat. In modern America, with its technologically sophisticated communications media, anyone who reads newspapers or watches television is constantly reminded of the problems American cities are encountering. This was particularly true in the 1960s with their massive organized demonstrations and ghetto riots. By 1968 not only journalists but politicians and community leaders were examining "the urban crisis" and proposing solutions. President Johnson's message to Congress on urban subjects that year was entitled "The Crisis of the Cities." The president of the University of California issued a statement called "What We Must Do: The University and the Urban Crisis." The bishops of the United States Catholic Conference presented "The Church's Response to the Urban Crisis."

In 1973 President Nixon, listing recent developments in urban affairs, asserted in a radio address that the hour of crisis had passed in American community life. In support of his statement, he mentioned that the rate of crime was dropping "in more than half of our major cities," civil disorders had declined, the air was getting cleaner, the number of people living in substandard housing had been cut more than 50 percent since 1960, and the business world was again investing in downtown areas.[2]

President Nixon's confidence was not shared by many representatives of urban interests. Making allowances for partisan sentiment on both sides, it seems fair to say that the optimism of the early seventies was at best premature. By 1978 we were once again seeing a rise in most forms of city crime, swelling welfare rolls, continued individual and corporate flight from the downtown areas, and, of course, financial crises threatening many large American cities with bankruptcy. Problems remain, brought about not by demonstrators or criminals but by the urban condition itself, a problematic situation that has developed out of the rapid urbanization of American society in the past century.

Since these problems are found in virtually every city, it makes little sense to focus on the unique characteristics of particular cities. Instead, it is necessary to analyze the system in which these problems arise. Historians have shown that cities began to grow when the economic system changed. As they have grown, the populations of cities have changed based on increasing competition for land use. Many of the problems related to city life in the last couple hundred years have resulted from the dynamic interplay of social and economic forces. Indeed, the problems of contemporary American cities appear closely tied to the social consequences of economic change and its often disorganizing effects.

Many of the problems described in other chapters of this book and other social problem texts are urban in nature. Most urban sociology textbooks deal with many of the same issues described in social problems courses. It is possible to argue that this convergence of subject matter in the areas of social problems and urban sociology is due simply to the fact that most people live in urban areas and therefore it could be expected that more human problems would be centered there. Such an argument is probably true, but so simple an admission accounts for neither the intensity of urban social problems nor the city's role in generating social problems. Further, it does not answer the following questions: Why do people migrate to and from cities? How do cities affect individuals? Are cities becoming obsolete in contemporary society? These are some of the questions to be addressed in this chapter.

The Urban Era

Urbanization is a worldwide phenomenon. Although cities themselves have existed for 5500 years, the urban era is of much more recent date. Sociologists make a distinction between preindustrial cities and those which have taken on their characteristic form and complexity since the advent of the Industrial Revolution. In preindustrial times, the vast majority of the population lived on farms and in small villages. Modern cities first developed between 1750 and 1850. They were capable of supporting a greater proportion of the population, because civilization had learned to utilize new sources of energy, such as coal and oil, in addition to the older sources, such as horses, oxen, and wood. Industrialization and the higher standard of living it brought to cities permitted and encouraged the development of many more specialized occupations, especially in scientific fields. Scientific contributions in turn speeded further technological advance.[3]

In the twentieth century, with the advent of the automobile and increasingly efficient systems of industrial production, a majority of the population live in urban surroundings, both in the United States and in other industrially developed countries. This shift has caused disruptions on a global scale and, consequently, the reorganization of many patterns of belief and association. The modern city has emerged as an arena in which a multiplicity of differentiated and segregated subgroups exercise competing claims for resources and the attention of the city's public institutions. Because the United States has been in the forefront of technological advance, these patterns have been particularly significant here.

City officials and national planners have made some attempt to anticipate and prepare for urban congestion and complexity; but many American institutions, designed for an earlier era, have not proved adequate to deal with our increasingly turbulent society. Today, three out of four Americans live in metropolitan areas (see Figure 5.1). That does not necessarily mean they live in a big city. Some 82 million citizens, or 39 percent of the population, live outside central cities but within the bounds of metropolitan areas. They are urban in outlook, in employment, and to a degree in social relations as well. Their problems are the urban problems that are the scope of this book: health, education, employment, income discrimination, crime, alcoholism, and drug abuse.

It is the concern of this chapter to show how the conditions of American society have been altered to accommodate the rapid urban growth and complexity produced by the social and technological changes of the past century. Especially in the urban community, these changes have created situations in which value conflicts are magnified to the extent that traditional expectations and patterns of interaction break down and a condition of social disorganization exists. As social forces work to segregate and divide urban populations on the basis of ethnicity, age, life-style, and social class, competition for scarce resources increases and cooperation among all segments of the community working for common goals is disrupted. By viewing urban social problems from the perspectives of value conflict and social disorganization, the contradictions and dysfunctions created by the structure of modern urban society can be readily understood.

Moreover, it is only with an understanding of the social and cultural heterogeneity of the city that one can analyze the variety of claims that are made on urban institutions. Indeed, the crosscurrents created by modern social structures have seemingly overwhelmed urban political and administrative units designed to serve the needs of an earlier era. Reorganization of financial, social, and governmental institutions is apparently needed, and has in some instances been undertaken. It remains to be seen, however, whether the traditional urban community can adapt quickly enough to survive.

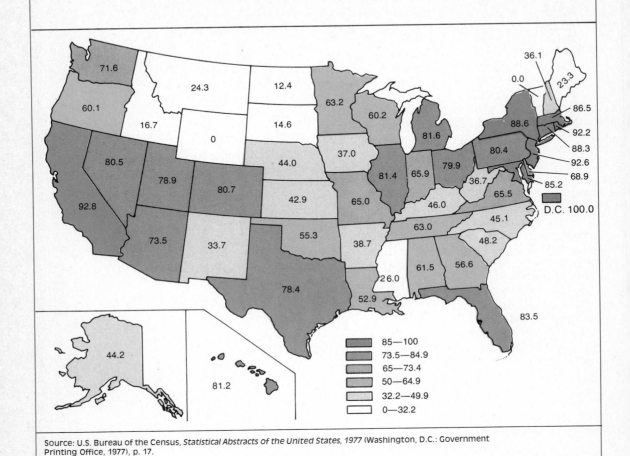

Figure 5.1 Percent of Population in Metropolitan Areas by State, 1975

Legend:
- 85—100
- 73.5—84.9
- 65—73.4
- 50—64.9
- 32.2—49.9
- 0—32.2

Source: U.S. Bureau of the Census, *Statistical Abstracts of the United States, 1977* (Washington, D.C.: Government Printing Office, 1977), p. 17.

The Rise (and Fall?) of the American City

American political thinkers and intellectuals have been suspicious of the impact of cities since the days of the founding fathers, when most Americans still lived on the land. In 1787, for example, Thomas Jefferson wrote a letter to James Madison: "Our governments will remain virtuous for centuries as long as they are chiefly agricultural. . . . When they get piled upon one another in large cities, as they are in Europe, they will become corrupt as in Europe."[4]

In their study of American intellectual attitudes, philosophers Morton and Lucia White quoted the criticism of urban society voiced not only by Jefferson, but also by Emerson, Thoreau, Melville, Poe, Henry Adams, Henry James, Louis Sullivan, Frank Lloyd Wright, and John Dewey, and suggested that "the city planner would make a grave mistake if he were to dismiss that tradition."[5] Some of these intellectuals feared that the city would fail to educate its citizens sufficiently to enable them to participate in a working democracy. Others believed the city pressures individuals toward conformity and discourages free communication. And while sociologists who have sought to analyze urban attitudes do not necessarily find data supporting these contentions, the policy of elected leaders, like that of the intellectuals, has been to praise grass-roots democracy and decry the evils of urban politics. The Jeffersonian position is traditional, found in the rhetoric of Jacksonian Democrats, theoreticians for the southern Confederacy, populists like William Jennings Bryan, and prohibitionists.[6]

Despite the concern expressed about them, American cities grew and flourished in the nineteenth century. The great seaports of the East Coast—New York, Boston, and Philadelphia—and the newer inland cities of Pittsburgh, Chicago, and St. Louis prospered as the rich resources of the Midwest and West were opened up. Spreading from Europe to America, the Industrial Revolution brought with it light and heavy industry and the mass production of industrial and consumer goods. It spurred railroad construction, money markets, and the expansion of governmental and corporate bureaucracies. Yet even before this era was fully begun, in the 1820s, the French traveler to America Alexis de Tocqueville noted that "the rabble" of New York and Philadelphia (he was referring to freed blacks and poor artisans) had already been responsible for riots. He wrote: "I venture to predict that American republics will perish from this circumstance, unless the government succeeds in creating an armed force which, while it remains under the control of the majority, will be independent of the town population and able to repress its excesses."[7]

A Population of Immigrants

In 1860 only one out of every six Americans lived in towns or cities with a population more than 8000. By 1900 the ratio was nearly one in three, and by 1920 more than half the national population was urban. People flocked from the country, abandoning their farms to the wilderness.

Another factor in urban growth was the increasing flow of immigrants. In the eighteenth century, immigrants had been principally English, Scots-Irish, and Germans who sought farmland. The nineteenth century brought an influx of Irish, starting with the potato famine of 1848, and a second wave of Germans, following the unsuccessful revolutions of 1848. Both groups became predominantly urban dwellers. The Irish were often contracted for by American employers to do coal mining, railroad construction, or other heavy labor. They settled in New York, Boston, Chicago, western Pennsylvania, and other industrial centers. The Germans settled in New York, Cincinnati, St. Louis, Baltimore, and Milwaukee. By 1855, the Irish-born made up 25 percent of New York's population, the German-born 16 percent.[8]

After the Civil War, the urban population was further augmented by waves of immigrants from south and central Europe. Czech, Hungarian, Polish, Russian, and Ukrainian peasants were also recruited as contract labor and employed in factories in northern New Jersey, Pittsburgh, Chicago, and Detroit. In the 1880s, Jews from the Austro-Hungarian Empire, Poland, and Russia, along with sizable numbers of Italians, began to arrive. The Jews assembled principally in New York; the Italians congregated in New York, Boston, and Chicago.

In the cities, members of each national group gathered together in local neighborhoods. There they could patronize restaurants and grocery stores selling their national foods, maintain family and village ties from the homeland, speak their own language, and attend churches of their native religion. They established mutual aid societies and a foreign-language press. For the most part, first-generation immigrants were confined to unskilled or semiskilled occupations. Poorly educated and unfamiliar with the English language, these immigrants adapted only gradually to American society.

Disruption of family and cultural patterns was often impossible to avoid. Old patterns often lost their hold in the process of assimilation to American life. In the context of turbulent city growth, the result was frequently family breakup, alcoholism, and delinquency.[9]

Technological advances and migration patterns have caused crucial alterations in the ecological structure of the twentieth-century city. Initially, industry and commerce located along water and rail routes; city dwellers went to work in horsecars, suburban trains, or on foot. Then the development of the automobile freed both employer and employee. Factories could be established away from rail lines, utilizing truck transport. Workers could drive to their jobs. The automobile's mode of production, the horizontal assembly line, became standard throughout industry. The new system required much larger amounts of space for its operation than did earlier means of production, so manufacturers gravitated to the suburbs, where land was cheaper. The development of heavy duty transmission lines for electricity enabled the building of factories hundreds of miles away from power sources and thus gave added impetus to this trend away from urban centers.

The invention of mechanical refrigeration, together with a vast increase in the types of inexpensive canned foods available, gave less well-to-do people much more mobility and freedom than they had previously had.[10] They could now move away from central markets, spend more money on better living accommodations, and migrate from the central cities to low-income suburbs. As early as 1930, the model of the new American urban center began to be in evidence: an increasingly decentralized unit, with teeming business districts and slums located at its center and residential and industrial suburbs expanding in ever-widening circles over the surrounding countryside.

Los Angeles was the prototype, a city that grew slowly in the era of the horsecar but by leaps and bounds after the popularization of the automobile. By 1930, prominent department stores were opening branches or relocating outside the downtown area, on Wilshire and Hollywood boulevards. Steelmakers erected furnaces in Torrance. Oil producers built refineries at El Segundo. Aviation companies constructed hangars in Santa Monica, while motion picture producers located studios in the San Fernando Valley. Plagued by competition from passenger cars, commuter railways were forced to curtail services and raise fares. With fewer and fewer customers, they eventually collapsed. Lack of public transportation caused even further decentralization.[11]

The shifts in population tell the story of change in Los Angeles. Between 1923 and 1931, when the population within ten miles of the central business district expanded 50 percent, the number of people entering downtown Los Angeles increased only 15 percent. And what was true of Los Angeles in the 1920s and 1930s has, to an increasing degree, become the pattern with other metropolitan centers across the United States. Although metropolitan areas have continued to expand, the inward drift of new arrivals to the cities has been counterbalanced by an outward drain to suburbia of residents, factories, and, in the 1960s and 1970s, white-collar employers as well.

Technology has altered the twentieth-century city in yet another way. With the development of modern transportation and communication facilities, important changes in the size, interrelatedness, and autonomy of the cities' public and private institutions have ensued. As social and spatial constraints on the level and scope of urban organizations have fallen away, institutions that were once locally oriented have become increasingly a part of and influenced by regional and national systems of specialization and control. Events occurring outside any particular city often become more important than those within, and commitment to local problems and issues is eroded by profit, political, and prestige structures located elsewhere. Although important headquarters for modern institutions may be located in the city, they and many of their employees are not really of it.

Burgeoning Suburbia

In the period between 1950 and 1970, the population of America's central cities increased by more than one-third, from 48 to 64 million; but in the same period the population of the suburban fringe more than doubled, from less than 25 million to 55 million.[12] Since 1970, however, the picture has changed somewhat. Central cities as a group have been losing population, while the areas around the cities have exhibited a less dynamic rate of population growth than in the past. The rate of increase in suburban areas has not kept pace with that in nonmetropolitan areas where population has been increasing at the rate of 1.2 percent per year from 1970 to 1976.[13] Racial variations in the rates for these areas can be seen in Figure 5.2.

This shift in population from the cities to the suburbs has been accompanied by a relocation of jobs and political power. The Bureau of Labor Statistics reported that by 1976 total employment amounted to 31 million in 30 of the country's largest standard metropolitan statistical areas.[14] (A standard metropolitan statistical area is defined by the United States Office of Management and Budget as "a county or group of contiguous counties which contains at least one central city of 50,000 inhabitants or more or 'twin cities' with a combined population of at least 50,000.") This includes jobs in the central cities as well as those in the suburban ring around the cities.

In 1972 the effects of reapportionment, based on the 1970 census, began to be felt. Some 290 members of the United States House of Representatives now came from metropolitan areas, and 145 from rural ones. Of the metropolitan total, only 100 represented districts dominated by central cities. Some 130 came from predominantly suburban areas, while the remaining 60 represented mixed districts.[15] Thus, compared to the past, the balance of political power within metropolitan areas has shifted away from central cities to the new suburbs, where residents have different concerns and are less likely to identify with the problems of the cities. The 1980 census is likely to result in a further increase in the political power of the suburbs.

Urban Ecology and the Energy Crisis

In an ecological sense, twentieth-century cities were created by a combination of centripetal and centrifugal forces. Briefly, centripetal forces are those that cause populations and institutions to concentrate and centrifugal forces are those that allow them to expand. Early urbanization in the United States occurred under the dominance of centripetal forces. Long-haul transportation innovations (trains and steamships) made it most economical for the population, industry, and institutions to cluster into the cramped quarters of central cities, and building innovations—elevators and skyscrapers—made this concentration possible. Since short-distance transportation was either not available or not economical, populations were forced to cluster tightly. Cities grew up, not out, as is evidenced by the older central cities on the East Coast. More recently the automobile and the tele-

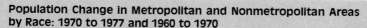

Population Change in Metropolitan and Nonmetropolitan Areas by Race: 1970 to 1977 and 1960 to 1970

Figure 5.2

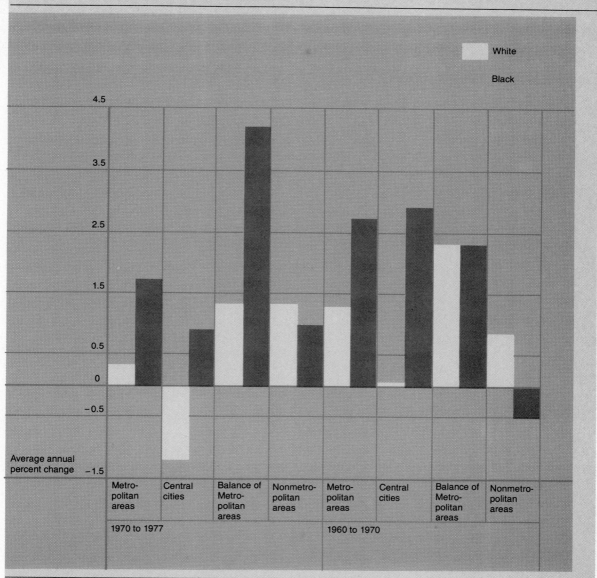

Source: U.S. Bureau of the Census, *Current Population Reports, Population Profile of the United States, 1977,* Series P-20, No. 324 (Washington, D.C.: Government Printing Office), p. 28.

phone have served as important centrifugal forces in dispersing populations by extending communications networks and making short-distance transportation economical.

A product of these counterbalancing forces, the urban scene in the United States today manifests a population increasingly concentrated in a number of urban areas nationwide but at the same time increasingly dispersed within these areas. Such "metropolitan communities" are characterized by (1) an increased division of labor among urban institutions and neighboring centers, (2) an extension of the radii of social and economic influence, (3) the dispersion of population and institutions throughout the wider region, and (4) the annexation of formerly independent towns in surrounding areas.[16]

In some regions of the country, metropolitan communities have grown so close together that the outer rings of one coincide with the outer rings of another. On the Eastern Seaboard, for example, metropolitan communities from Boston to Washington, D.C., are linked together to form a continuous urban settlement. Such a continuous band of urban and suburban development has been labeled a *megalopolis*.[17]

The metropolitan community is somewhat of an anachronism, given the present energy situation. Its industries have dispersed to the outer rings and its population to the suburbs. Through the use of the automobile it has developed specialized and dispersed land use patterns which, indeed, demand the continued use of such a transportation system. Yet it has now become apparent that the cheap energy that fueled the growth and expansion of the metropolitan community may no longer be available. The cartelization and monopolization of oil and its use as political and economic weapons, for example, have driven gasoline prices higher than many can afford and made the automobile an increasingly uneconomical means of transportation. If the costs of automobile transportation are not soon discounted, then, or alternative short-distance systems of mass transportation constructed, the centripetal forces that created the crowded structures of the past may again come to dominate.

Fluctuating Urban Populations

Seeking the advantages of proximity, transportation, and the ready availability of unskilled workers, large organizations have traditionally located in or near big cities. (Figure 5.3 shows the growth of several cities between 1940 and 1975.) In turn, unskilled labor has migrated to big cities in search of jobs. During early periods of industrialization these workers were drawn mainly from Europe, but since the 1920s, when the United States government enacted legislation limiting foreign immigration, population growth within the cities has come primarily from internal migration. The greatest number of new arrivals have been blacks from the rural South, moving to both southern and northern cities. The New York–New Jersey area has also received substantial numbers of Puerto Ricans; Chicago, Detroit, and other north central cities have attracted whites from Appalachia; in the West, Mexican-Americans long settled in the area now seek urban employment.

The black migration to eastern and northern cities began during World War I, when high-paying defense industry jobs attracted many rural blacks. However, blacks in urban centers working mostly in unskilled or semiskilled jobs were the first to be laid off and the last to be rehired in the de-

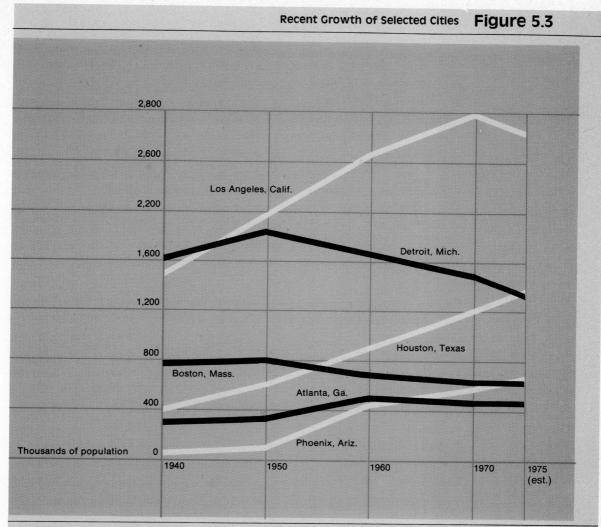

2,800

2,600

2,200

Los Angeles, Calif.

1,600

Detroit, Mich.

1,200

800

Houston, Texas

Boston, Mass.

Atlanta, Ga.

400

Phoenix, Ariz.

Thousands of population   0

1940   1950   1960   1970   1975 (est.)

Source: U.S. Bureau of the Census, *Census of Population: 1960*, **Vol. 1**, *Characteristics of the Population, Part I, United States Summary* (Washington, D.C.: Government Printing Office, 1964, 1973); and *Statistical Abstracts of the United States, 1977* (Washington D.C.: Government Printing Office, 1977), pp. 22–24.

pression of the 1930s. Despite this, black migration northward mounted anew during World War II and after. As the defense industry spread across the country, blacks also began moving westward.

In 1975, 75 percent of America's black population of 24 million lived in metropolitan areas.[18] As an indication of the concentration of black Americans in urban centers, black children now fill 97 percent of the seats in the Washington, D.C., schools. Other cities in which minorities, in most cases blacks, comprise over 50 percent of the enrollment in city school systems include Baltimore, Detroit, Chicago, Cleveland, Memphis, St. Louis, Philadelphia, and New York.[19]

Like earlier immigrant groups, blacks settled in segregated neighborhoods. But where segregation had been at least in part a matter of choice with foreign-born immigrants, blacks were forced into highly congested ghettos because of racial discrimination. One by-product of racial discrimination was that even middle-class blacks, who could afford better neighborhoods, were forced to reside in ghettos that were predominantly slums.

While blacks and others have been moving into central cities, other ethnic groups have been moving out. Yet, along with the blacks, many of these groups have not become fully assimilated into society, as it was once assumed they would. Racial and ethnic group attachments have remained important sources of identity and organization and have by no means been smoothly woven into the fabric of white Protestant culture.[20]

The proliferation of bureaucracies in the city has also brought new sources of urban cultural diversity. The growth of bureaucratic organization and the corresponding increase in the number of managerial and technological positions has brought about a juxtaposition of outward-looking cosmopolitan attitudes and bureaucratic careerism with the localism and family orientation of many more traditional city residents. Since populations tend to cluster into neighborhoods on the basis of related social characteristics, such as amount of education, life-style, stage in life cycle, and occupation,[21] modern American cities have tended to become collectivities of diverse groups reflecting these many and varied, and sometimes oppositional, values. This is the setting in which new forms of cultural pluralism have come to life. Older ethnic and social differences are combined with newer delineations of class and status in culturally and socially segregated residential areas. The resultant variety of distinct and intense interests and attitudes has significant implications for social problems.

What Is a City?

Since the early years of this century, sociologists have worked to analyze urban culture in detail. As a starting point in their efforts to interrelate technological and economic developments with other factors influencing the city's growth and distinctive character, it was necessary to isolate and define the nature of urban settlement, as opposed to a market town or fortified citadel.

Weber and Simmel

One of the earliest students of urban culture was the German sociologist Max Weber. In 1905 he summed up the fundamental attributes of a city, basing his initial definition on a comparison of the activities and institutions of cities in preindustrial Europe, the Middle East, and the Far East:

To constitute a full urban community, a settlement must display a relative predominance of trade-commercial relations with the settlement as a whole displaying the following features: (1) a fortification; (2) a market; (3) a court of its own and at least a partially autonomous law; (4) a related form of association; and (5) at least partial autonomy and autocephaly, thus also an administration by authorities in the election of whom the burghers participated.[22]

Whereas Weber approached his subject from a socioeconomic point of view, his younger friend and colleague Georg Simmel concerned himself with the psychological outlook developed by the typical city dweller:

The psychological basis of the metropolitan type of individuality consists in the intensification of nervous stimulation which results from the swift and uninterrupted changes of outer and inner stimuli. . . . With each crossing of the street, with the tempo and multiplicity of economic, occupational and social life, the city sets up a deep contrast with small town and rural life with reference to the sensory foundation of psychic life.[23.]

This phenomenon can be seen in every city but is probably magnified in New York. For example, it is estimated that a person in midtown Manhattan may encounter as many as 220,000 people within a ten-minute radius of his or her place of work.[24]

As a defense against this more complex environment, the metropolitan type, Simmel believed, became more intellectual, more rational. The fact that the city was also the center of the money economy tended to make the city dweller more matter-of-fact in dealing with people and things—a combination of formal justice and inconsiderate hardness. An intellectual and commercially oriented individual, the metropolitan type grew blasé and reserved in relations with other people. This apparent aloofness is described by psychologist Stanley Milgram as an adaptive mechanism for coping with the psychic overload of the complex environment.[25]

At the same time, the impersonality of the great metropolis granted the city dweller a unique kind and amount of personal freedom. Though often a source of loneliness and isolation, this freedom created a cosmopolitan atmosphere in which city dwellers sought increasingly to assert their independence and individuality. The extreme economic division of labor in a metropolis promoted and encouraged such differentiation. So did the fact that social relations were apt to consist of relatively brief contacts with other individuals in specialized spheres—on the job, in the home, or through membership in organizations.

The Chicago "Ecological" School

During and after World War I, a group of University of Chicago sociologists undertook to adapt and apply these theoretical formulations to the facts of the American city. The leaders of the Chicago school—Robert Park, Ernest Burgess, and Louis Wirth—wished to particularize the study of urban culture.

The first fruit of this endeavor was Park's landmark essay published in 1916, "The City: Some Suggestions for the Study of Human Behavior in the Urban Environment."[26] Park outlined possible avenues for exploration based on the assumption that the city could be understood both as a geographical entity and a moral order. Borrowing a term from the natural sciences, he maintained that cities have an *ecology*, or self-contained natural life, which tends to bring about an orderly and typical grouping of their populations and institutions. This ecology, he argued, might be examined in many ways: from the standpoint of population composition, neighborhood development, industrial and vocational specialization, social mobility, collective behavior or urban crowds, the changing influence of church, school, and family, or the effectiveness of courts, custom, party politics, and the press. Park's suggestions were extensively taken up and pursued by the "ecological" school of sociologists. Using the empirical method of postulating and substantiating hypotheses, they systematically chronicled and documented many aspects of American urban life.

The ecological approach has been used to demonstrate the varying distribution of a number of social problems. Shaw and McKay showed that for three successive decades the same areas of Chicago exhibited the highest delinquency rates.[27] These areas were located in a ring immediately surrounding the central business district. Similarly, the highest rates of schizophrenia were located in these areas.[28] The ecologists showed that these areas were those which were the older parts of the city where overall land costs were high but where multiple dwelling units served to reduce unit costs. Hence, large numbers of individuals from the lower status groups were drawn to live in this area, which came to be known as the zone of transition.

These areas undoubtedly affected the lives of the people in them. In 1938 Louis Wirth surveyed some of these findings in his essay "Urbanism as a Way of Life."[29] Wirth defined the distinctive characteristics of urban settlements as large size, population density, and social and occupational heterogeneity. He found that these characteristics, partly because of the structures of social organization required for their management, promote *segmental* and *secondary* contacts between individuals, as opposed to the *primary* contacts of folk and rural society. The urbanite described by Wirth is much like Simmel's metropolitan type. While Wirth recognized the freedom and individuality the city permits, he stressed the deleterious effect of urbanism on community life. In modern cities, where mass production techniques and the ideologies of mass communication are prevalent, he saw a leveling influence at work, destroying the social bond by catering to the statistical average rather than to the needs of unique individuals. Wirth's emotional preference was for a community where primary contacts remain important.

Characterizing Community

Some who have studied community since Wirth have questioned the extent to which a large urban settlement can be defined as a single community. One sociologist, for example, found that the population of central cities consists of not one urban type but five: (1) the cosmopolites, (2) the unmarried or childless, (3) the "ethnic villagers," (4) the deprived, and (5) the trapped and downward-mobile.[30] Of these five, he concluded that only the last two suffered from the problems Wirth described. The cosmopolites succeed in creating a distinctive life-style that makes conventional neighborhood life unnecessary. The "ethnic villagers" manage to establish their own communities through personal and social ties. For many, the city is only a temporary home; once resources for change are available, they move to the low-density, "quasi-primary" life of the suburbs. From this perspective, Wirth's diagnosis of urban life seems not so much wrong as too narrow and out of date.

Another sociologist has noted that there are ways of creating community other than by similarity of experience shared over a long time. Previously unassociated neighborhoods may be drawn together to form a sort of community when confronted with specific events.[31] A crime wave within a few blocks may cause neighbors to form local protective associations or vigilante groups. After a group of individuals have organized to confront a problem, a residuum of community organization remains and may be directed to other purposes. Interrelated but dissimilar activities—extremely important in cities, where the division of labor and the network of interdependence are highly developed—can also generate interests in common. In a city threatened by an exodus of industry, workers and employers may agree upon the need for tax incentives to encourage new industry. On the other hand, the same groups may disagree on the level of wages to be paid.

Community Fragmentation

There is little doubt, however, that urban American communities are vastly different now than they were at the time Wirth wrote. Local geographic communities are now highly specialized. Residential suburbs daily export workers. Industrial suburbs and central cities import them. Housing projects in large cities function purely as residential centers; local churches have little influence; and political bosses cannot sustain networks of supporters as they used to. College towns and resort communities attract a large proportion of part-time residents, whose attitude toward community problems may be very different from that of the natives. Communities such as retirement settlements attract a very high proportion of individuals of one age group.

Such fragmentation is even more disruptive of the community than the city Wirth described; yet, ironically, much of it can be seen as an attempt to regain the primary contacts of the village or the small town, to flee the confusion of modern city life for a simpler and more ordered existence. This search for a "purified community" has been criticized on the grounds that the inevitable conflict in cities is an opportunity for personal and social growth which does not exist in the new suburbs. The purified community of the suburbs, supported by affluence, fostered by a consumer society with an elaborate system of mass communications and persuasion, is in this view a myth bound to fail because it blinks at the inherent difficulties of social life.[32]

A Cultural Mosaic

Conditions fostering the fragmentation of the community are believed to stem from an increase in societal scale—an increase in the national interdependence of activities, in the range and content of communications, and in social integration through large-scale bureaucratic organizations.[33] The result is a greater range of activities concentrated in the city, a wider variety of available life-styles, and institutional ties that extend beyond the political boundaries of the city. That is, the technological forces that produced the twentieth-century city as a large, concentrated population have also produced within that city a wide range of cultural, social, and class-based interests. Although sometimes harmonious, or unnoticed, at other times these interests are the source of contradicting and conflicting positions with respect to urban institutions. The spectrum of class positions within the modern economy, for example, causes fundamental anxieties between the occupants of these positions. Intensifying the anxieties are differences rooted in ethnic, religious, and life-cycle identities. In one combination or another, these differences usually come together to form new hybrid subcultures, and thus the urban area becomes a cultural mosaic of different and identifiable parts rather than an undifferentiated mass.

It may be impossible to weigh precisely the advantages and disadvantages of the diversity of urban life. For persons who feel that the lives they are leading are unusual or unique, the city offers the opportunity to find others with similar life-styles. Whatever the personal quirk or eccentricity, the probability is high that someone else in the city may share it. On the other hand, cities also offer an opportunity to those who want to escape from their prior lives and life-styles. It is possible for individuals to move to cities and establish entirely new images for themselves, leaving past experiences behind. It is much easier to "pass" as someone else in cities than it is in smaller rural areas. With the reaffirmation of ethnic heritage and the formation of experimental life-styles, it is likely that in the future the diversity of the cities will increase rather than decrease.

Urban Problems

Whether conflict will result from the fragmented structure of the city depends partly on the economic situation. When resources are plentiful, all segments of the population can be offered something in terms of education, police protection, work, and political representation. When money is tight, however, priorities must be set, and power and influence play a large role in this process. It is in this situation, when the gains of one group are the losses of another, that conflict is the likely result.

We have said that urban social problems are the problems of sizable numbers of people gathered together to live, govern, and produce and exchange goods. These problems can be characterized as urban principally because most people live in urban areas. More precisely, they are the problems of a civilization. Although urban governments and institutions have often been given primary responsibility for finding the solutions to those problems, they have usually lacked the stature, resources, and structural mechanisms with which to be effective.

Autonomy, the crucial element with which Weber characterized the structure of the Western city, has been undercut by an increase in the scale of social and economic organization to the national, and even international, level. City institutions no longer have the authority or the capacity to ameliorate many of the conflicts within their bounds. The question is, of course, who does?

Although the problems of the cities at times seem endless, special attention can be focused on those conditions that in many ways underlie the difficulties of urban communities. Political power, rising costs, social order, and living conditions are outgrowths of institutional arrangements that once served cities but are now being tested and questioned.

In the United States, as elsewhere, the urban settlement developed its distinctive forms of governmental and allied institutions. The most notable is the big-city political machine, whose existence depends on the ability to control votes. Voters are organized and kept track of by a combination of party ward leaders and precinct captains. Only when voters place more value on their ballots than on favors the machine can do for them does the machine lose control. Voter indifference to issues, candidates, or principles sustains the machine.

Working class people, especially immigrants unfamiliar with American ways and institutions, have always been the mainstay of the machine. To use the terminology of the politician, the "delivery" wards are also the "river" wards, and they are a long way in both political and geographic distance from the "newspaper" wards. A delivery ward, of course, is one whose votes can be "delivered" by the machine, and a newspaper ward is one in which the voters take the newspapers' recommendations seriously. The delivery wards are the river wards because the oldest, hence poorest and most rundown parts of the city are those that lie near the warehouses and the railroad yards. Almost without exception, the lower the average income and the fewer years of schooling in a ward, the more dependable the ward's allegiance to the machine.[34]

As one moves from the lower middle class districts to those of the middle class and out to the suburbs of the upper middle class, ties to the machine become weaker and eventually cease to exist. As voters become more educated and more assimilated, they espouse the political values of "the Anglo-Saxon Protestant elite," the essence of which is that "politics should be based on public rather than private motives and accordingly should stress the virtues of honesty, impartiality and efficiency."[35] It may well be that the middle class will eventually assimilate the lower class. The resultant predominance of the middle class political ethos would probably then assure the extinction of the political machine.[36] At present, however, although machine politics has lost its dominance in many areas, there remain lower-class enclaves in some central cities and suburbs where the system flourishes.

Nonetheless, it would be a mistake to assume that because a machine elects officials to office, it necessarily controls the destiny of a community. Indeed, since the 1920s substantial research has been done by sociologists who maintain that control of most urban communities in fact resides with a power elite, a class of citizens who control a disproportionate share of a community's wealth and thus exercise a disproportionate influence on its elected officials.[37]

In recent years, the elitist model of community studies has been under attack by sociologists who argue that urban power has in fact become pluralist in character—controlled not by any one group but by a variety of interests. In a 1961 study of New Haven, one political scientist documented that community's evolution from oligarchy to pluralism between 1784 to 1960.[38] The office of mayor, he found, had from 1784 to 1842 been held almost exclusively by men from patrician backgrounds. Between 1842 and 1900, the new self-made industrialists, the entrepreneurs, took over. Since then, "explebes" rising out of working-class and lower-middle-class families of non-Anglo-Saxon origin have predominated in the office. This development has meant more sharing of actual political power than was possible in the past.

CITIES IN TROUBLE

Cities in the United States have matured, blossomed, and borne fruit. Now they slowly rot. Bound by poverty and prisoners of a hostile socioeconomic system, ghetto populations live out lives devoid of amenities more affluent Americans demand as their due. *This page:* Abandoned and dilapidated housing—the aftermath of an absentee landlord; the vandalism control squad sign on a playground reminds us that deliberate defacement and destruction contribute greatly to the city's bleakness; growing up in the ghetto—life amid litter. *Opposite page:* Gymnastics, ghetto style—evidence of the tenacity of the human spirit, even in the face of destitution and despair; garbage everywhere, even within the shadow of exclusive apartments and corporate offices.

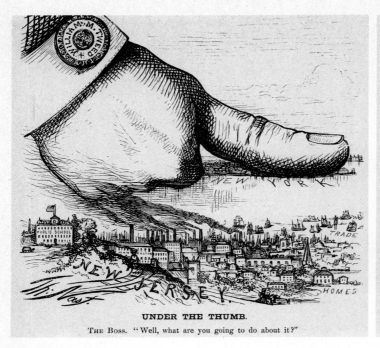

UNDER THE THUMB.

THE BOSS. "Well, what are you going to do about it?"

CLOUT

MAYOR DALEY and HIS CITY

ROARING, RAGING, CRAFTY, CORRUPT—HE'S THE GODFATHER OF BIG-CITY POLITICS AND KINGMAKER IN THE PRESIDENTIAL RACE, AND THIS IS "THE BEST DAMN BOOK THAT'S BEEN WRITTEN" ABOUT HIM! —Chicago Tribune

LEN O'CONNOR

High density urban populations of the poorly educated and illiterate provide fertile ground for the growth of political machines and big city bosses. New York under the thumb of William Tweed, 1871, and Chicago under Richard Daley, 1976.

Individual communities vary widely, of course. One recent study has attempted to reconcile the elitist theory with the pluralist theory by correlating specific variables such as population composition, size, age, and industrial makeup. Findings tabulated on community power structures in 57 cities indicate that larger cities have more diffused power structures than smaller ones, that older cities have more diffused power structures than younger ones, and finally, that growing cities are more likely to have concentrated power configurations, while stagnant and declining cities are more likely to have diffused power structures.[39]

The New Politics of Reform

Both the influence of the big-city political machine and the control exercised by the power elite have been substantially lessened by the campaigns for city government reforms inaugurated in the last half of the nineteenth century. The exact extent of improvement wrought by reformers has been subject to debate. However, there is no doubt that the introduction of merit examinations for civil service jobs deprived ward bosses of a major means of rewarding the faithful; no longer could politicians dispense low-level jobs as patronage plums. Similarly, the development of the welfare system has made the poor economically more independent and less impressed by the precinct captain's traditional means of rewarding allegiance—the Thanksgiving turkey or the extra hod of coal at Christmas.

The new style of politics, with its emphasis on honesty, impartiality, and efficiency favors a number of tendencies, including:

1. A limiting of opportunities for members of new minority groups, who in the past have risen to positions of eminence through the machine.

2. A growing demand for fresh faces—candidates who at least seem free from the taint of professionalism and who also have the technical qualifications and disinterestedness the new politics calls for.

3. An increase in professional administrators at all levels of city government.

4. An increasing identification of local, urban issues with national, ideological ones.

5. Accelerated centralization of authority, with greater emphasis on disinterested urban planning.[40]

Paying the Urban Price

Although city governments are faced with ever greater demands for services and higher standards in administration, they possess only limited financial means for providing them. As wealthier citizens emigrate to the suburbs, their houses are taken over by less affluent residents, causing neighborhoods to deteriorate. Landlords, who derive their profit from high rents and minimal investment, feel no incentive to improve their real estate to keep wealthier tenants in occupancy and within city limits.[41] A decline in the tax base of the entire community is the eventual result. At the same time, inflation, rising wages, and continued inward migration of the less affluent have increased the amount of money needed to pay for such civic services as transportation, public welfare, police services, education, sanitation, and garbage disposal.

In almost every area where services must be provided, cities are forced to do more than the suburbs, with fewer resources for raising revenue. Cities must, after all, provide services like public transport and police protection for suburban commuters as well as residents. In addition, with their higher crime rates, cities must pay a higher price for police protection. And in central cities a greater share of the population is dependent on public transportation, necessitating greater expenditures in that area as well. Then, too, city schools are expected to provide the same quality of education that suburban schools provide. But with less revenue available for their upkeep, classrooms in city schools are overcrowded and facilities are out of date.

While the tax base has declined in the cities, the cost of the vital goods and services it supports has escalated in the postwar era, as illustrated in Figure 5.4. Yet, if cities raise taxes, they risk accelerating the flight of business, industry, and residents to the suburbs. Indeed, high taxes have already caused many concerns to leave the central cities, diminishing the number of available jobs for the low-income job seekers typically concentrated in metropolitan areas.

The result is higher and higher rates of unemployment and underemployment in these areas. . . . This pattern, of job location, added to education, housing and discrimination has produced an income and poverty distribution which accentuates the disparities between city and suburb. In general, the gap between median family income in the suburb and city is increasing. Average median family income in the central cities in 1960 was $5,940 compared to $6,707 in the suburbs. . . . Estimates for 1967 are $7,813 for the central city family while for the suburban family it has increased to $9,376. Thus, the gap has increased since 1960 from a suburban advantage of $767 to a 1967 advantage of $1,446—a doubling.[42]

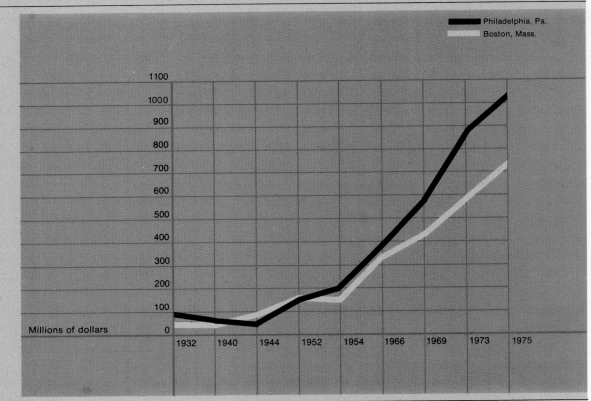

Source: U.S. Bureau of the Census, *Statistical Abstracts of the United States, 1934–1977* (Individual volumes) (Washington, D.C.: Government Printing Office).

By 1976 the median white family income had increased to $15,086 in central cities and $17,699 in areas surrounding central cities, thus increasing the gap to more than $2500. The corresponding figures for black families in central cities was $9631 and in the surrounding areas, $12,037.[43]

Yet even these median income figures do not reveal the true extent of poverty that exists in the cities. The fact that many of America's wealthiest citizens live in the cities makes the median-income figures unrealistically high. In nearly every state, welfare cases are concentrated in central cities. Much of the labor attracted to the city in search of work, or pushed into the city by the lack of jobs in the country, is unskilled and poorly paid. This population requires periodic income supplements, special kinds of education and training, and health and nutritional aid. But the unskilled and unemployed who make up an increasingly large proportion of the population of cities cannot support an adequate tax base to absorb these new social costs. Nor can the cities, where employment is in such great demand, afford to discourage corporate interests by increasing taxation.

Confronted by inflation, demands for higher wages by city employees, and the increased need for services by residents, city governments are forced to seek new methods for increasing revenues. Typically, they resort to increasing property taxes, seeking grants from state and federal governments, and borrowing. Most visible among these alternative strategies has been borrowing. As long as the economy is prosperous and employment is high, property tax assessments and federal supplements are generally sufficient to absorb most of the financial burdens. When business cycles and depressions disturb the economy, however, these resources are no longer adequate, and payment of city debts is jeopardized.

The ability of federal and state governments to provide financial assistance to cities has been limited, both legally and politically, by the "Proposition 13 movement" begun in California in the late 1970s. Across the country, a movement is being generated by taxpayers aimed at limiting government spending. In the 1978 elections 26 states had referenda on the ballot concerning tax propositions and curbs on state spending. Fifteen of these passed.[44] Although this movement claims that it is designed to limit wasteful spending and cut bureaucratic costs, many essential services also will be affected. Included in the cutbacks will be expenditures designed to alleviate the plight of the cities.

In order to meet the requirements of their limited budgets, city governments may renege on financial commitments such as salaries or pensions, cease to provide services for its dependent residents, or find new sources of revenue. The methods used by 283 cities of various sizes in 1976 can be seen in Table 5.1. Which option will be taken is probably a function of the ability of affected interest groups to mobilize and make their demands felt. City workers' unions, taxpayers' associations, corporate boards, and the poor can all be expected to exert pressure (with unequal effectiveness, of course) on the decision makers. Perhaps by observing the outcome of New York City's current financial crisis we can glean some information on the types of influence and types of solutions that can be brought to bear on city financial emergencies in the future.

Table 5.1

How 283 Cities Managed FY76 Fiscal Problems*

Local Budget Actions	City Populations 50,000 or Less	51–75,000	76–100,000	101–250,000	250,000 plus
Laid off employees or reduced work force through attrition	37%	34%	41%	44%	62%
Cut back services	24	24	32	35	43
Increased existing or levied new taxes	42	41	48	37	51
Deferred planned capital expenditures	55	59	47	51	57
Number of cities	79	54	40	57	53

Source: *The American City and County*, 93 (January 1978), p. 44.

Social Cleavage and Conflict

The existence of large, heterogeneous populations in urban centers has frequently led to conflict between different special-interest groups. Essentially, such conflicts reflect social, economic, racial, and religious cleavages within society as a whole, but they become most intense when acted out in a confined urban setting. Bus drivers and garbage collectors tie up entire urban areas in massive strikes against city authorities. Catholics and non-Catholics debate the legality of providing birth control information and devices or abortions in city hospitals. Adolescent Puerto Rican gangs engage in street fights with black or white gangs.

Ethnic minorities traditionally resolved their demands for representation in urban government through the brokerage mechanisms of the big-city political machines. Italian, Jewish, and Irish candidates were all given places on party tickets that reflected the strength of their various communities. The system was one that defused many potentially explosive conflict situations. In the postwar years, however, the newest minorities—blacks, Mexicans, and Puerto Ricans—have encountered greater difficulty in finding a voice. By and large the established central organizations have failed to respond to the needs and grievances of these new urban minorities.

Patterns of Segregation

The threat of urban crime, especially violent crime committed against the individual, has caused some city residents to form self-protection groups. Here, two young men are patrolling their community in Brooklyn.

With the outbreak of widespread rioting in the urban ghettos between 1963 and 1967, increasing study was directed toward conditions within the ghettos. The patterns of racial residential segregation have been statistically documented by sociologist Karl E. Taeuber.[45] Residential segregation has added significance because it leads to segregation in schools, libraries, parks, stores, hospitals, and a variety of other local facilities. Taeuber developed an objective index to measure residential segregation and determine the extent to which it is a result of choice, poverty, or discrimination. On his scale, an index of 80 indicated that 80 percent of a given city's blacks would

have to be relocated in white neighborhoods if the city were to achieve an integrated pattern of residence. Using census data for 207 cities, Taeuber found that his index varied from 60.4 in San Jose, California, to 98.1 in Fort Lauderdale, Florida. Half the cities had segregation indexes of 87.8 or more, half less. Moreover, by correlating income statistics, Taeuber found that discrimination, rather than poverty or choice, was the prevailing cause of segregation.

The Nature of the Ghetto

Seeking to assess the causes of and responses to the riots of 1963 to 1967, the National Advisory Commission on Civil Disorders surveyed not only population trends but also employment, family structure, and social disorganization in black neighborhoods. It found that:

1. Black incomes remained far below those of whites. Black median family income was only 58 percent of the white median in 1966.

2. Unemployment rates for blacks were still double those for whites in every category.

3. Black workers were concentrated in the lowest-skilled and lowest-

Seeking a sense of community and accomplishment denied them by middle-class society, ghetto youth form gangs, whose standards of success are within their reach.

paid occupations. These jobs often offered substandard wages, low status in the eyes of both employer and employee, little or no chance for meaningful advancement, and unpleasant or exhausting duties.

4. In 1966, 8.9 percent of all white households had a female head, but 23.7 percent of all black households had a female head, indicating that a higher percentage of black children grow up in fatherless families.

5. The relatively high incidence of prostitution, dope addiction, casual sex affairs, and crime in racial ghettos created "an environmental jungle," characterized by personal insecurity and tension.[46]

Yet a glance at similar statistics after a ten year interval reveals few improvements. In 1976 median black family income was 59 percent of the median white family income.[47] The 13 percent unemployment rate for blacks in 1977 was more than double the 6.2 percent for whites.[48] By 1976, more than 30 percent of all black families were headed by females, while this was true of only 10 percent of all white families.[49]

The social characteristics of urban residents confined to racial ghettos have been explained as the result of a "lower-class" culture, or a "culture of poverty."[50] They have also been attributed to the structural conditions of the larger society.[51] Yet many authorities believe that lower-class individuals represent only a fraction of the residential population of racial ghettos. Working-class and even some middle-class residents make up the balance. The problem of the ghettos appears to be that, as more blacks graduate from lower class to working class and subsequently to middle class, there is no space available for them to establish exclusively working- and middle-class enclaves. Because the ghettos are so restricted in area, the demand for living space is too great; and when an area "goes black," lower-class blacks move in right along with more prosperous ones and negatively influence the character of the neighborhood. Streets become littered with garbage; vandalism and the crime rate rise.

It is fear of this type of negative influence that causes conflict when racial and cultural minorities begin to expand into areas outside the ghettos. Civic associations and protective leagues protest the erection of public housing that will house low-income members of these minorities. Children are withdrawn from public schools to which blacks or other minority group children are admitted. As an alternative to these defensive reactions, white middle-class and even working-class urban residents may move to the suburbs. The incentive to move is increased by the fact that with less expensive police, transport, and welfare budgets, suburban sales and property taxes are relatively low. More money can be allotted to better-equipped schools, hospitals, and recreational facilities.

Provincial Nonpartisanship in Suburbia

Suburban residential communities develop a distinctive form of social organization and political power structure. In the suburban community, people purchase homes "with only a sidelong glance" at those who will be their neighbors to make sure that they appear to be compatible.[52] Ethnic neighborhoods do not transplant themselves; ethnic minorities become integrated with native whites and with one another.

Once people have moved in, they establish relationships on the basis of propinquity. Homeowners, concerned with maintaining the value and status image of their houses, must make sure that neighbors share their

Nat Hentoff
The Pros and Cons of City Life for Kids

I used to look at that lively part of the Saugatuck River at the edge of our former weekend refuge in Connecticut, and I would yearn to stay in what I, a city dweller, considered "the country," although we and the river were actually on the outskirts of a medium-sized town. . . .

If I had no children, I kept telling myself, I would move deeper into the country, for good. Why should my growing addiction to trees, clear air and living silences be limited to weekends and summers? . . .

"But," my wife would say, "you have a responsibility to your children. We have to stay in the city until they're grown."

Nick, our fourteen-year-old, became interested in old musical instruments a while ago and took himself to the Metropolitan Museum, where he spent an hour looking at them and hearing them on headphones. "He didn't have to depend on me to make a special trip to the city so he could go to the museum," my wife said pointedly.

Although in the city Nick has been relieved of his money by groups of older boys four times—once thrown to the ground in the process—he still wanders about, if warily. The city is an exciting place to him, quickening his curiosity. He tells us of diversely absorbing street scenes he's seen, asks questions about them, interprets the action for himself, connecting it with the news and commentaries he watches on television. He looks through *The New York Times* and the *Daily News*, and not only the sports pages. Country weekends, and small-town papers are not so stimulating.

Still, if his family is informed, as we think we are, and involved in politics and the world outside, why does it matter where Nick lives? Such a family can produce a lively child if it lives on top of a mountain. That point has been forcefully made to me in a number of the conversations I've had with my Connecticut neighbors and with other suburban and country people I have met.

"You must be crazy to stay in the city," the conversation usually begins.

"Well," I answer, "it seems to me and my wife that city kids are more quick-witted and resourceful than children in the country. Yes, some of that resourcefulness comes of being alert to danger on the streets; and I am concerned that our kids, growing up mugged, might grow up bigoted." I do tell my children that at other times in our history, other kinds of people—white people—with desperate living conditions and with many jobs closed to them, have had a high incidence of criminal behavior. But I'm not sure that sociological explanations of the causes of crime keep a kid from forming stereotypes is he's just been mugged by a member of a minority group.

My preference for the city as an enlivening place to bring up children is disputed even in the city, itself. One woman, now working in New York, tells me that she spent her first eighteen years in a small town in the Northwest. In response to my observation that kids who do not grow up in cities are likely to be insular and bland, she tells me that when she left the open spaces to attend college in the city, "I found out that I knew more about migrant workers than my dormitory neighbor from Imperial Valley and as much about Watts as most of the white students who came from Los Angeles.

"I spoke better Spanish," she instructs me sternly, "than most of my classmates, many of them from California (although I had never met more than two or three native Spanish-speaking people). Interestingly, in a school that prides itself on its high academic standards, I was one of the few entering students who brought any books to college just because I enjoyed them; I was one of the few in my dormitory who regularly read a newspaper." . . .

As for where my children live, she asks me, "What virtue is there in walking the streets in fear of your life? What cultural, social, educational goals can compensate for that? On the contrary, I am quite sure that I benefited from growing up unafraid."

I am impressed by her argument, but I am not convinced that the country or the suburbs are where I want to raise my kids. A woman I know in a Connecticut suburb moved there from New York for the sake of her children. But, she told me recently, she still harbors "this secret dream of getting back and confronting the city head-on." Her children don't want to move back, but she's not at all sure that she made the right decision for them. "The highest compliment I have ever paid my girls, twelve and sixteen," she says, "was during one of our endless discussions on the feasibility of living in the city. I told them I thought they had turned out pretty well for children who were brought up in the suburbs. You do have to work harder as a parent, I think. And yet—the thought of the life going on after 9 P.M.! There's a city vitality that dries up in the suburbs behind the shrubbery and screened porches, and that vitality is still very tempting."

But the more frequent attitude is the one expressed by another woman with whom I have been discussing the city-country dilemma. Both she and her husband are fifth-generation New Yorkers. "The benefits of raising children in New York," she says, "can't be questioned, especially with respect to the sophistication they get from living among people of mixed heritages. Unequivocally, growing up here makes one capable of living anywhere in the world."

Even so, she and her family are about to leave the city. "I don't want my young boys to get up in the morning with a lump of fear in their stomachs because on their way to school there's a strong possibility they'll be jumped. There are certainly enough pressures put on today's children without narrowing their freedom to pursue their interests. I believe in freedom from fear. We've only got one life to live, and New York will not be livable during that time. It deeply saddens me that we're leaving since no one could love New York more than we do. We weren't passing through: it's home."

She may be right about where New York and our other big cities are going. But I can't convince myself that New York is Hades, and that staying on will slowly tear away all my children's dignity and peace of mind. And if that woman is right in her conviction that growing up in New York makes one capable of living anywhere in the world, ought I to deprive my children of that extraordinary learning experience?

I am not, I concede, all that optimistic about everything a white middle-class child learns from the enormously varied, open classroom that is New York. . . .

And the truth is that my son, Nick who goes to a private school is in a privileged position in New York—until he steps out of school. Then he is sometimes, prey. Nonetheless, Nick feeds on the city that is outside the school. Despite his experiences at being heisted, he has no problems, like those experienced during the weekends in Connecticut in finding something to do. In the city, the problem is one of choosing what he wants to do. He does not have to hound his mother to drive him to the movies or to a shop that has baseball cards going back even farther than the time of Babe Ruth. He goes by himself, on foot or by subway.

The other night, I heard him on the phone with a friend as they went over an experience they had just had at the coin and stamp section of a department store. In the elevator, a group of older boys had blocked his exit. "Come on," Nick had told his friend, "let's go through." And they did.

"You saw how cool I was," Nick said on the phone. "I went right through those guys. If I'd gotten one punch, I would have run for the guard." Listening, I was pleased at his refusal to be intimidated, and more so by his good sense at having had an immediate security plan in mind. Then he said to his friend on the other end of the phone, "I wasn't scared of them. They were white."

Of course I was troubled by that observation. I realize that what I want him to learn from living in the city is not necessarily what he's going to learn. But then again, there have been tougher-looking white kids than the ones on the elevator whom he has wisely been scared of. And there are plenty of black and Spanish speaking kids among his friends.

Essentially, frustratingly, no parent, living in the city or in the country, can shape his child even approximately into the kind of adult he'd like his child to be. You do the best you can, and with regard to where you decide to live while your children are growing up, you choose between differently advantageous and differently defective alternatives.

concern; thus every block develops a social system devoted to exerting the control needed to see that houses and lawns are kept up. People join clubs, churches, and civic organizations for the purpose of finding friends. Most do not remain active in the organizations, but the organizations persist and are an important part of life in the suburbs, at least for an active minority.

In contrast to state, national, and big-city politics, suburban politics are predominantly nonpartisan.

Much of suburban politics is concerned with family-related issues. In particular, questions concerning the schools and housing attract continuing interest and attention. Occasionally in the limelight are such additional subjects as the police, recreational facilities and "corruption." In short, the politics of small communities tends to be focused on local issues. Local government in the suburbs usually pays very careful attention to the interests of its constituents.[53]

This pattern continues even when the increased concentration of the economic activity of metropolitan areas in the suburbs demands more attention to such issues as zoning and land use. By their nature, these matters often need county-wide or even region-wide consideration, but there is as yet no political organization on which the suburban constituency can focus for decisions of this kind. The result may be that, while local taxes are hotly and heavily debated, decisions about the placement of highways and the development of land will be handled at the state and federal levels, without proper attention to their local effects. Most suburbs have been unable to set standards for new development and have often become the victims of decisions that take from them the very qualities their residents moved from the city to find. These residents discover that the city has followed them and that their suburban governments are no more powerful to resist unwanted change than are the ossified structures for decision making of city governments.

Increasingly, the problems of the cities and the problems of the suburbs cannot be handled by the local governments themselves. Issues such as air and water pollution demonstrate the inability of local governments to solve a problem which originates within the legal bounds of other areas. Decisions made by suburban governments on land use and zoning affect not only the local residents but also residents of the center city whose jobs may be moved because of the decision. Clearly, fragmented local governments are incapable of managing problems that are regional in nature. The National Research Council claims that the continuation of such govenmental structures poses three major problems. It "aggravates the mismatch between resources and social needs; makes the solution of metropolitan social problems more difficult; and inhibits efficient administration of services."[54]

Federal Intervention

Since the 1930s the federal government has undertaken a variety of programs that significantly affect urban residents. Federal funds have been spent on public welfare programs, education, health, transportation, and housing supplement budgets already appropriated by state and municipal agencies. Federal spending has had diverse effects—and not always the ones anticipated.

Helping with Housing

The federal government has been especially active in home building. The Federal Home Loan Bank system established in 1932, the Home Owner's Loan Corporation and Federal Farm Mortgage Corporation of 1933, and the National Housing Act of 1934 that set up the Federal Housing Administration were all aspects of a federal policy to facilitate home ownership. The Federal Housing Administration and, to a lesser extent, the Veterans Administration functioned as incentives for single-family house construction. By insuring mortgages, they established minimum standards of construction and land use.

Federal intervention in this case encouraged land development and the resultant trend toward decentralization of population—a movement away from urban centers. Federal and state programs to encourage the construction of low-cost public housing and urban renewal programs that provide funds for development in urban centers are much more recent and quite modest in scope. Congress inaugurated federal support for public housing with the Housing Act of 1937, but large-scale urban renewal did not get under way until the Housing Act of 1949:

Urban renewal, which began in 1949, even with the large areas which have been cleared in some American cities, is small potatoes compared to the central policy of encouraging single-family home building and ownership. In contrast to some 600,000 units of public housing that have been built during the history of the public housing program and 80,000 that have been built under urban renewal, over 5,000,-000 units have been built under FHA home mortgage programs.[55]

A major part of the problem with urban renewal has been that federal funds were used to buy up tracts of inner-city land that were then sold to private developers. Given the option of using the land either for nonhousing purposes or for luxury housing, developers naturally chose the most profitable forms of construction—almost never low-income housing. One survey of the results of urban renewal found that through June 1965 the reconstruction of urban renewal land was mainly for institutional and public uses (37 percent) and commercial and industrial uses (27 percent).[56] Only 36 percent was for housing. Prior to 1963, most of the new housing was designed for upper-middle-income occupancy, reflecting the desire of city officials to attract or hold such people as residents while building up the real estate tax base.

Under new policy directives, local governments began to emphasize development of moderate- and low-income housing. Even so, by 1965 only about one-third of the new housing was for such families. Black leaders have complained that urban renewal is nothing more than "Negro removal." And in fact, 60 percent of the families displaced by urban renewal were black, although they numbered less than one-third of the population in the cities involved.

The Housing and Community Development Act of 1974 was passed in hopes of serving those groups that were most in need. However, the program falls short of its goals. By focusing on only one segment of the poor, those whose incomes are 50 percent below the median family income, it neglects many needy families. In 1974, over half of all renters with annual incomes of under $7000 were spending more than 35 percent of their income for housing.[57] In response to this, the federal government attempted what seemed to be a logical response in the form of housing allowances. It was thought that these allowances would enable poor families to rent decent housing.[58] Although well-meaning, this plan continues to ignore the most serious problem, namely, the severe shortage of low- and moderate-income rental housing in most urban areas.[59]

One of the more innovative housing programs developed by the government in the late 1970s was urban homesteading. As part of a Carter Administration housing and community development program, $15 million was allotted to a demonstration project that would permit families to purchase rundown houses for a nominal amount of money. In return, the families agree to repair the homes and live in them for a minimum of three years.[60] While it is still too early to assess the total program's success or failure, it has worked well in several large cities, including Baltimore, Philadelphia and Wilmington.[61]

By the 1960s, the focus of federal aid to the urban underprivileged had shifted from providing better housing to more comprehensive programs. With the omnibus housing bill of 1966 a Model Cities program was established that entitled cities to seek federal grants for a comprehensive attack on urban blight. These funds could be used for education, antipoverty, and social welfare programs, as well as more traditional construction programs aimed at stopping physical decay. Model Cities grants helped fund emergency street repairs, bookmobiles, ambulance services, methadone maintenance clinics for narcotics addicts, sanitation services, and day-care centers for children of working mothers. The breadth of urban problems is indicated by the variety of uses to which these federal funds have been put.

One of the goals of Model Cities was to encourage input from the local communities in the planning of programs and in setting priorities for funding. Throughout the early 1970s, Model Cities struggled to increase the level of local self-determination and to instill a desire for community organization. Yet the problems remain as we enter the 1980s, and the approaches used by Model Cities are no longer in favor.

In a free society there is no way governmental agencies can prohibit the inward migration of poor citizens to the cities. Similarly, cities can only indirectly influence the decisions of established citizens and corporations to leave or stay in the city. They can do this by offering tax incentives and other inducements to stay. Cities are municipal corporations chartered by the states. Their powers to expand their boundaries, levy taxes, and otherwise govern are limited by state laws. For grants in urban renewal and other improvement projects, they must apply to federal and state agencies. The decisions affecting them are too often made in corporation boardrooms, in state capitals—where legislators are subject to the demands of rural constituents also—and in Washington. Thus, to a very real degree, cities are incapable of directing their own destinies.

Model Cities

Proposals for Change

The most recent proposals for improving conditions in cities have called for a dual approach. On the one hand, there is the new federal policy of revenue sharing, and on the other, the argument that state governments must assume a more constructive role.[62]

Revenue Sharing

In January 1970 President Nixon proposed his revenue sharing plan, under which taxes collected by the federal government were to be funneled back to state, city, and other local governments. In the fall of 1972, Congress enacted a bill authorizing the expenditure of $30 billion over a period of five years for this purpose. The bill provided for regular increments in the amount allotted to state governments, from $1.95 billion in 1972 to $2.85 billion by 1976. In addition, it granted another $3.5 billion annually to local governments for high-priority expenditures—specifically public safety, environmental protection, and transportation. By 1977, the total outlay of the federal government for general revenue sharing was $6.8 billion.[63]

Revenue sharing was greeted initially with enthusiasm by mayors and governors; but by 1973, when the program went into effect, objections began to surface. Revenue sharing appeared to be used to replace, rather than supplement, existing urban renewal and civic improvement programs. Funds for low-income housing projects and Model Cities undertakings ceased to be available or were doled out for temporary purposes. Local officials have protested that they need revenue sharing in addition to, not in place of, the other federally funded programs. There is some indication that revenue sharing has helped both state and local officials in keeping taxes below what they otherwise would be. But cities across the country continue to face serious fiscal crises.

Reshaping Cities

Seeking to expand their tax base and develop a coordinated attack on such problems as transportation and air pollution, cities have tried to extend their boundaries or restructure their governments. Boundary extensions are regulated by state law, which tends to impede them by requiring referenda or enabling legislation. Annexation has traditionally been the most commonly proposed remedy. It has been used in recent years by Houston, Dallas, Fort Worth, San Antonio, and Oklahoma City; but it often runs into trouble where popular approval is required:

Opposition to annexation is almost always strong in the suburbs, with any one of several arguments being sufficient to secure a negative referendum vote: higher taxes, a corrupt or incompetent central city government, false promises in the delivery of services, and annexation as a devious tax-grabbing scheme. . . . In short, annexation is virtually dead in the older and larger metropolitan areas, particularly in the North and East, as a device for permitting a city to keep up with its growth.[64]

In a few cases, the boundaries of large cities have been extended to make them coterminous with county boundaries, thus permitting the consolidation of city and county governments. Baton Rouge, Jacksonville, Indianapolis, and Nashville have all used this method of restructuring their governments since World War II.

Metropolitan federations, whose city governments operate with partial independence, and limited powers delegated to the federation, have also been proposed as alternative solutions to urban problems—but almost never adopted. Although state governments have been willing to pass enabling legislation for cities wishing to consolidate with counties, they have done very little to encourage or permit the establishment of metropolitan federations in the United States. The best-known examples of metropolitan federations are the governments of Greater London and Metropolitan Toronto. In both cases the structure was established by an act of Parliament without the requirement of a popular referendum. The closest thing to a metropolitan federation in the United States is the metro government of Dade County and Miami, Florida. Voters there narrowly adopted a two-tier form of government in 1957:

In practice, Dade County's metro is more nearly a "municipalized county" than it is a federation of municipalities, since the cities as such are not represented on the board of commissioners. But even with its lawsuits, recurring referendum fights, and financial limitations, this new approach to governing a metropolitan area has offered new hope and has stimulated the imagination of many other cities.[65]

The most common reorganizational device is the special district, a semiautonomous authority set up to handle transport, housing, schools, or some other single function of government. Although special districts have proved popular with administrators, they are subject to a wide range of criticisms. For example, they separate the program under consideration from the mainstream of city affairs but make it vulnerable to the pressures of a specialized clientele; they atomize local government and make comprehensive planning of local programs a virtual impossibility.

Another approach to solving the problems of the urban center is the creation of satellite cities, or "new towns." As originally envisioned by the English social planner, Ebenezer Howard, the new town was to be a completely self-contained community in the country, near the metropolis. It would consist of not only residential but also cultural facilities, offices, and an industrial park to provide employment. In the United States, perhaps 20 communities have been built that are true new towns, all since World War II. They include Reston, Virginia; the Irvine Ranch, in Orange County, California; and Columbia, Maryland, the most successfully integrated project to date. By the time of its completion in 1980, Columbia is expected to have cost $2 billion and to house a population of 110,000 in seven villages.[66]

The late 1970s have witnessed a renewal of interest in the cities on the part of private corporations. Across the country, business of all sizes are becoming involved in the re-creation of downtown areas of big cities. One recent survey even suggests that business leaders may be more "bullish" on the future of downtown areas than the public officials authorized to govern those areas. One excellent example of the involvement of the private sector is Renaissance Center, a complex of offices and stores recently completed in the heart of Detroit. The brainchild of Henry Ford II, the chairman of Ford Motor Company, the center was built at a cost of $337 million. Much of this money was contributed by major companies, such as Ford, General Motors, and Standard Oil of Indiana. It is the hope of these and the 48 other major companies that contributed that Renaissance Center will serve as a catalyst to lure both people and other business back to Detroit.[67]

New Communities

The new town, a product of centralized social planning, is much more common to the European experience than to the American. However, a variant of the new town concept, the "new community," has received much broader application in the United States. Essentially, a new community is a new town on a smaller scale. It consists of a fairly large-scale planned development including a variety of housing types, commercial and cultural facilities, and sometimes access for industry and employment opportunities.[68]

Robert C. Embry, Jr.
Back-to-the-City Movement May Signal the End of Urban Decline

During the past two decades, large numbers of middle and upper income familes have chosen to live in suburban communities rather than in central cities. In just 10 years from 1960 to 1970, 56 of the nation's 153 cities containing over 100,000 people lost population. And, from 1970 to 1973, 87 of those 153 cities . . . lost population.

The loss of adequate housing joined with many other forces to bring about this population movement. Along with factors such as the migration of rural poor to the cities, highway construction, and the popularity of the automobile, the availability of housing has played an important role in encouraging this population shift to the suburbs.

A comparison of building permits issued in 21 metropolitan areas from 1968 to 1976 illustrates the point: in every case, areas outside the central cities showed seven-to-ten times the number of building permits than do the central cities. . . .

Today, there is a small sign of encouragement in this landscape which offers the prospect for an improvement in some city neighborhoods and perhaps also marks the end of a long period of decline.

The trend is too recent in time and too small in numbers to conclude that the migration from our cities has ended. A leveling-off of the population shift may, however, be just over the horizon for some cities.

But with this encouragement comes a concern for the low and moderate income families who stayed in the city. Our concern is that urban reinvestment may also mean the displacement of low and moderate income residents. We must consider what can be done to adjust public policy to promote diversity, to encourage this hopeful trend without doing so at the expense of these less affluent, frequently older, residents.

Urban reinvestment is essentially a rapid increase in investment—private or public or both—in an older urban residential area that usually—but not always—had experienced some decline in the past.

Some trends are clear. First, the studies of recent central city reinvestment by special census surveys from 1970 to 1974 show an across-the-board increase of 8.7% among all types of home owners: existing homeowners, newcomers, homesteaders, blacks and whites.

Second, black homeowners tended to increase their central city home repair activity both in terms of projects and expenditures more than did white central city homeowners. Further, measured as either projects or expenditures, home improvements activity was greatest among homes purchased within the last two years.

Third, there is a perceivable trend underlying much of this increase in homeownership toward a preference in cities for existing housing. During the 1970—74 study period, 80% of this reinvestment was accommodated by newly built homes and condominium. However, the trend now appears to be toward the use of existing structures. Today, 50% of the increase in homeownership in central cities is made up of existing housing.

There are some stereotypes already developing about these reinvesting homebuyers. Typically, we hear, these homebuyers are middle class white suburbanites flocking back into the city spurred by changing life styles, increased energy costs and high suburban housing costs.

Among other groups making reinvestment are young adults from both urban and suburban backgrounds buying first homes. Other reinvestors are middle class urban blacks and former tenants in apartments where rents have escalated rapidly.

Between 1972 and 1975, a full 70% of these central city homebuyers moved from within the central city. Forty-seven percent of those had formerly been renters and only 23% former homeowners.

The reinvestment process is one which has the potential for realizing not one but several important public objectives of critical concern at both the federal and local levels.

Reinvestment in existing neighborhoods can and has played an important role in increasing racial and economic integration, for strengthening the local tax base, improving the existing housing stock, using existing infrastructure, and providing an alternative to suburban expansion with its attendant environmental and energy problems. Of special importance, too, is the preservation of ethnic neighborhoods and the increasingly powerful role of neighborhood groups through preservation efforts.

Anyone looking at the dislocation problem must separate out the displacement caused by reinvestment from the turnover that takes place in any neighborhood in the absence of reinvestment.

Nationally, we know that the turnover rate is 20%. We also know that in poorer areas of our cities, the mobility rate is even higher. Therefore, in the absence of reinvestment, over half of the residents of most neighborhoods will be newcomers after four years.

Healthy reinvestment occurs when some of the newcomers are of a higher income than those leaving voluntarily. But the process becomes harmful when low income residents are forced out against their will. . . .

The dynamics which contribute to dislocation include many forces which these two cautions, there are still problems when the economic nature of a neighborhood begins to change. Moderate income tenants of single- and multi-family units may be evicted in order to rehabilitate those units for middle or upper income tenants or homeowners. Continuity in the neighborhood is threatened if young adults from the neighborhood find that housing has greatly appreciated, and they are unable to secure mortgages on suitable terms. Moderate or low income homeowners, particularly the elderly on fixed incomes, may face dramatic increases in property tax assessments.

Many homeowners may eagerly sell as reinvestment begins, thinking the knowing how much the property really is worth. Historic preservation requirements or increased code enforcement pressures may drive out long term homeowners (or tenants). Rent control may result in a conversion of moderate income rental units to high income owner-occupancy and again force out existing residents. Pressures to sell may be created by developers, realtors, or private investors. Absentee owners may hold properties without maintaining them, perhaps even not paying taxes, to "wait" for market improvements in the area.

Finally, there is the more subtle problem of dislocative influences on moderate income tenants and homeowners in terms of changing land use, employment and commercial patterns, changing neighborhood life-style and changing neighborhood networks and institutions.

While it may be a limited phenomenon, it is important to examine the specific negative impacts which can result when there is large scale displacement of existing residents.

These impacts come in many forms:
- Cost in social, economic and psychological terms to individuals forced to move and those left behind
- Racial and economic segregation
- Creation of racial and class tension
- De-stabilization of cultural/social elements of neighborhoods
- Shift of lower income and minority people into outer-city neighborhoods, or inner-ring suburbs which do not have the tax base to provide additional goods and services necessary for the dislocated
- Undermining of efforts to stimulate reinvestment by and for existing residents

The public policy must seek a balance of forces which creates and preserves heterogeneous cities with racially and economically diverse neighborhoods. While we must encourage reinvestment, we must also assure that residents of changing neighborhoods have an opportunity to reap the benefit of that change.

Clearly a vital role, not only in the success of reinvestment but also in maintaining and promoting diverse stable neighborhoods, is the participation of the neighborhood itself.

We would therefore encourage cities to begin or continue efforts to work cooperatively with neighborhoods to deal with reinvestment and other housing issues. We would propose a partnership between a city and its neighborhoods particularly where investment is occurring or is likely to soon occur.

It is encouraging to think that perhaps a corner has been turned in the decades-long struggle of the federal, state and local governments, as well as private corporations, groups and individuals to make cities more liveable places with more decent housing for all. It is critical that we continue to encourage and support this hopeful trend which may provide the foundation for revitalized heterogeneous urban centers. At the same time, however, we must be sensitive to the dynamics of reinvestment and deal with the human problems.

The American City & County, January 1978, Vol. 93, No. 1, pp. 37–38. Reprinted courtesy of American City & County Magazine.

Except for government participation in the development of the so-called Greenbelt communities during the depression (Greenbelt, Maryland; Greenhills, Ohio; and Greendale, Wisconsin), private interests have played the major role in developing new communities in the United States. Early new communities were often company towns developed by industrialists to attract labor to industrial locations. Between 1830 and 1900, for example, when this type of new community development was at its peak, the new communities of Gary, Indiana, Pullman, Illinois, and Lowell, Massachusetts, received their starts as company towns. Moreover, as of 1939, 52 out of 99 known planned communities could be classified as company towns.[69]

More recently, private speculators have played the major role in new community development. Among the major categories of participants in such efforts are the traditional builder-developers, national corporations, large landowners, the oil industry, and mortgage lenders. Early prototypes for this kind of community development include Levittown, New Jersey, and Park Forest, Illinois; California City and Valencia, in California, represent more recent efforts.[70]

Although new communities have enjoyed some degree of commercial success, they have not achieved, or attempted, comprehensive solutions to urban social problems. As a result of financing by private interests, most have not approached the broader social goals of developing low-income housing, public education, and economical land use patterns. Perhaps their utility awaits a more comprehensive planning effort by business, government, and the public to incorporate the broader spectrum of human needs and interests into their designs.

Neighborhood Government

In recent years there have been several attempts to return local control to central city neighborhoods. The late activist Saul Alinsky sought to bring pressure to bear on civic authorities by mobilizing public opinion in low-income neighborhoods in a number of cities through his Industrial Areas Federation, which included The Woodlawn Organization (TWO) in Chicago, FIGHT in Rochester, and BUILD in Buffalo. The Students for a Democratic Society (SDS) also began a number of projects for local community action in

Chicago, Cleveland, Newark, and Oakland. Their groups were primarily ideological, however, and much of their activity was of an evangelical sort.

Another, perhaps more practical, approach calls for the transfer of public authority to the neighborhood through the legal establishment of a neighborhood corporation.[71] The East Central Citizens Organization (ECCO) of Columbus, Ohio, founded in 1965 as the first such corporation, has been followed by the formation of some 70 similar neighborhood corporations in different parts of the country. ECCO is located in a poor neighborhood of Columbus one mile square, housing 6500 residents. With a 1969 budget of $202,947, consisting mainly of a grant from the U.S. Office of Economic Opportunity, it oversaw a variety of programs. Its youth center offered educational facilities, nurseries for retarded children, and adult education. Other activities sponsored by ECCO included the rehabilitation of homes in cooperation with the city government, local operation of the state employment office, health programs, and a credit union.[72]

ECCO must compete for power with other antipoverty programs spon-

The new community consists of planned development of housing, social and cultural facilities, and industrial and employment opportunities. Although successful in many ways, they have not achieved the goals that many have held for them as alternatives to urban living.

sored by the federal government, including the Columbus Community Action Agency and the Model Cities Agency. This type of bureaucratic rivalry exists in other cities as well and hinders effective planning. Some authorities believe that the best solution to the problems of cities lies not in specific programs geared toward improvement of housing, transportation, or education, but in programs intended to raise living standards across the board. Various ways to accomplish this have been suggested, including a guaranteed annual wage and a negative income tax that would enable every family's income to rise above the poverty level. However, none of these proposals has yet been enacted into law.

While the political and social change required to implement many of the neighborhood control programs proposed for urban areas demands a great deal of time and painstaking effort, some still believe these programs constitute the only sensible way to proceed. They side with Thomas Jefferson, the foe of cities, who believed the basic unit of good and safe government to be the ward, a subunit of the county. Jefferson felt that the degree of effective power internalized at each level of government should be decided on the criterion of competence.[73]

Yet many planners see the matter differently, and some economists and technologists assert that the present problems of the city are problems of transition. In their view, the technological realities of the present and future will require changes in the social and physical structure of cities along the lines of centralized authority rather than local control.

Summary

Urban problems, those of large numbers of people settled together, are as old as cities themselves; and cities have existed since 3500 B.C. The urban crisis in the United States today is a modern version of these problems, but it is complicated by the large scope and interconnected nature of modern urbanization.

The phenomenal growth of the American city has been made possible by technological advances, especially in transportation and communication, and by economic expansion. Powerful bureaucratic structures—in the form of political, economic, and social organizations that are physically clustered in the city—have expanded the scope of their interests, commitments, and activities to national and international levels. And although the number and variety of activities in the city have increased, they have simultaneously become specialized and fragmented, differentiating a number of hybrid subcultural forms that now comprise an urban mosaic.

The value conflict approach shows us how these social crosscurrents are created by the strains of modern large-scale social structures. Subcultures and interest groups are fused out of identities originated in ethnic, life-cycle, and class positions. The resulting patterns of attachments, though sometimes contributing to social stability, often form the bases for conflict and divisiveness over social issues, at times even to the extent of disorganizing the social system. The probability of conflict is increased when money, jobs, and other resources are scarce and the gains of one group become the losses of another.

Despite the suspicions of political thinkers such as Jefferson, American cities have flourished since colonial times. Fed by immigrants from rural areas and countries abroad, city populations expanded enormously during the nineteenth century. As each new wave of immigrants arrived, they gathered together in ethnic neighborhoods, often retaining their traditional social customs.

Disruption of these traditional ethnic patterns was inevitable, however, as technological changes and economic prosperity made possible a vast increase in the size of urban areas. The automobile freed both employer and employee from the concentrated city center. As industries and businesses moved out to lower-taxed land in the urban fringe, they were soon followed by city dwellers who sought the less congested living of residential suburbs. The city of the computer age is an increasingly decentralized unit, with teeming business and slum districts at its center, surrounded by ever-widening circles of industrial and residential suburbs.

The flight to the suburbs has been counterbalanced by a continued inward drift of new city dwellers. Recently, the largest immigrant group has been rural, southern blacks. Like earlier ethnic groups, they have settled in segregated communities. Because of systematic exclusion from other areas and economic distress, these black communities soon become congested ghettos marked by poverty and social discontent.

Sociologists have interpreted urban settlements by such concepts as the "cosmopolitan personality" of the urban dweller, and they continue to investigate the nature of "community" within urban areas, attempting to understand factors that affect the processes of urban life.

The American city gave rise to a distinctive form of political structure, the political machine, which for decades ruled the major cities through systems of patronage and ethnic loyalty. At the same time, much of the political power in cities over the years has resided in wealthy elites of established families and businesses, most characteristic of cities where official governmental bodies have failed to respond to pressing social ills.

As wealthy homeowners and large industries have relocated outside the city's boundaries, the city's tax base has declined drastically, making it difficult to raise sufficient revenue to maintain city services. These financial problems have come at a time of rising costs for all manner of services—transportation, sanitation, police, education, and welfare aid for a growing number of unemployed. Unable to raise funds to meet these problems, the city has turned to the state and federal governments for aid.

Since the 1930s, the federal government has assisted cities in funding services and programs dealing with welfare, education, health, transportation, and housing. The Model Cities program, begun in the 1960s, emphasized a comprehensive approach to a range of neighborhood problems, and recent revenue-sharing efforts have attempted to return more tax funds to the states and localities from which they are collected.

The recent attempt by voters in many states to control government waste by limiting government expenditures or curbing tax increases hampers the ability of states to provide the much-needed aid. The private sector is now attempting to revitalize the business districts in many major cities.

Alternatives to present modes of city organization have recently been devised in response to urban problems. Annexation of suburbs and consolidation of city-county governments are two methods intended to provide better services to city residents. Self-contained satellite cities are being built outside major urban areas. And still another attempt at dealing with urban problems involves the transfer of public authority to neighborhood governmental units.

The technological changes that made rapid urbanization possible have since been succeeded by others. It remains to be seen whether successful solutions to the urban problems of the present day can be found before the new technologies impose still more difficulties on an almost completely urbanized nation.

Notes

[1]Gideon Sjoberg, "The Origin and Evolution of Cities," *Cities: Their Origin, Growth and Human Impact* (San Francisco: W. H. Freeman, 1973), p. 24.

[2]*New York Times,* 5 March 1973, p. 1.

[3]Sjoberg, "Origin and Evolution of Cities," p. 26.

[4]Quoted in Murray S. Stedman, Jr., *Urban Politics* (Cambridge, Mass.: Winthrop Publishers, 1972), p. 21.

[5]Morton White and Lucia White, "The American Intellectual versus the American City," *Daedalus,* Winter 1961, pp. 166–178.

[6]Francis E. Rourke, "Urbanism and American Democracy," *Ethics,* July 1964, pp. 255–268.

[7]Alexis de Tocqueville, *Democracy in America,* vol. 1, trans. Henry Reeve (New York: Knopf, 1945), p. 290.

[8]Nathan Glazer and Daniel P. Moynihan, *Beyond the Melting Pot* (Cambridge, Mass.: MIT Press, 1963), p. 9.

[9]W. I. Thomas and Florian Znaniecki, *The Polish Peasant in Europe and America* (1918; reprint ed., New York: Dover, 1958).

[10]Edward C. Banfield, *The Unheavenly City* (Boston: Little, Brown, 1970), p. 25.

[11]Robert M. Fogelson, "The Fragmented Metropolis: Los Angeles, 1850–1930," *The City in American Life,* ed. Paul Kramer and Frederick L. Holborn (New York: Putnam, 1970), pp. 236, 328.

[12]U.S. Bureau of the Census, *Statistical Abstract of the United States, 93rd Ed.* (Washington, D.C.: Government Printing Office, 1972), p. 223.

[13]U.S. Bureau of the Census, Current Population Reports, *Population Profile of the United States, 1977,* Series P-20, No. 324 (Washington, D.C.: Government Printing Office, 1978), p. 26.

[14]U.S. Department of Labor, Bureau of Labor Statistics, *Geographic Profile of Employment and Unemployment, 1976* (Washington, D.C.: Government Printing Office, 1977), p. 42.

[15]Stedman, *Urban Politics,* p. 160.

[16]Robert D. McKenzie, *The Metropolitan Community* (New York: McGraw-Hill, 1933).

[17]Noel Gist and Sylvia Fava, *Urban Society,* 6th ed. (New York: Crowell, 1974), p. 91.

[18]U.S. Bureau of the Census, *Statistical Abstract of the United States, 1977* (Washington, D.C.: Government Printing Office), p. 441.

[19]Diane Ravitch, "Busing: The Solution That Has Failed to Solve," *New York Times,* 21 December 1975, Section 4, p. 3.

[20]Glazer and Moynihan, *Beyond the Melting Pot,* pp. 1–23.

[21]Eshret Skevky and Wendell Bell, *Social Area Analysis,* Stanford Sociological Series No. 1 (Stanford, Calif.: Stanford University Press, 1955).

[22]Max Weber, "The Nature of the City," *Classic Essays in the Culture of Cities,* ed. Richard Sennett (New York: Appleton, 1969), p. 38.

[23]Georg Simmel, "The Metropolis and Mental Life," *Classic Essays,* p. 38.

[24]Stanley Milgram, "The Experience of Living in Cities," *Science* 167 (13 March 1970), 1461.

[25]Ibid., pp. 1461–1468.

[26]Robert Park, "The City: Some Suggestions for the Investigation of Human Behavior in the Urban Environment," *Classic Essays.*

[27]Clifford Shaw and Henry McKay, *Juvenile Delinquency and Urban Areas* (Chicago: University of Chicago Press, 1942).

[28]Robert Paris and H. Warren Dunham, *Mental Disorders in Urban Areas* (New York: Hafner Publishing Co., 1960).

[29]Louis Wirth, "Urbanism as a Way of Life," *Classic Essays.*

[30]Herbert Gans, *People and Plans* (New York: Basic Books, 1968), pp. 48–50.

[31]James S. Coleman, "Community Disorganization and Conflict," *Contemporary Social Problems,* ed. Robert K. Merton and Robert Nisbet (New York: Harcourt, 1971), pp. 658–674.

[32]Richard Sennett, *The Uses of Disorder* (New York: Knopf, 1970), pp. 27–49.

[33]Scott Greer, *The Emerging City* (New York: Free Press, 1962).

[34]Edward C. Banfield and James Q. Wilson, *City Politics* (Cambridge, Mass.: Harvard University Press, 1963), p. 118.

[35]Ibid., p. 123.

[36]Ibid.

[37]See Robert S. Lynd and Helen M. Lynd, *Middletown* (New York: Harcourt, 1929); Floyd Hunter, *Community Power Structure* (Chapel Hill; University of North Carolina Press, 1953).

[38]Robert A. Dahl, *Who Governs? Democracy and Power in an American City* (New Haven: Yale University Press, 1961).

[39]Michael Aiken, "The Distribution of Community Power, Structural Bases and Social Consequences," *The Structure of Community Power,* ed. Michael Aiken and Paul Mott (New York: Random House, 1970), pp. 494–495.

[40]Banfield and Wilson, *City Politics,* pp. 331–335.

[41]"The Great Urban Tax Tangle," *Fortune,* March 1965, p. 106.

[42]Alan K. Campbell and Donna E. Shahala, "Problems Unsolved, Solutions Untried: The Urban Crisis," *The States and the Urban Crisis,* ed. Alan K. Campbell (Englewood Cliffs, N.J.: Prentice-Hall, 1970), p. 18.

[43]U.S. Bureau of the Census, *Statistical Abstract of the United States,* p. 441.

[44]"Issues, Issues, Issues," *Newsweek,* 20 November 1978, p. 53.

[45]Karl E. Taeuber, "Residential Segregation," *Cities: Their Origin, Growth and Human Impact,* p. 274.

[46] *Report of the National Advisory Commission on Civil Disorders* (New York: Bantam Books, 1968), pp. 251–262.

[47]U.S. Bureau of the Census, Population Profile of the United States, *1977,* p. 44.

[48]Ibid., p. 41.

[49]U.S. Bureau of the Census, *Statistical Abstract of the United States, 1977,* p. 45.

[50]Oscar Lewis, *The Children of Sanchez* (New York: Random House, 1961), pp. xi–xxxi.

[51]Charles A. Valentine, *Culture and Poverty* (Chicago: University of Chicago Press, 1968), p. 129.

[52]Gans, *People and Plans,* pp. 134–135.

[53]Stedman, *Urban Politics,* p. 163.

[54]Robert Wilson and David Schulz, *Urban Sociology* (Englewood Cliffs, N.J.: Prentice-Hall, 1978), p. 322.

[55]Nathan Glazer, "Housing Problems and Housing Policies," *Public Interest,* Spring 1970, p. 30.

[56]Morton J. Schussheim, "Housing in Perspective," *Public Interest,* Spring 1970, pp. 37–43.

[57]Ibid.

[58]Irving Welfeld, "American Housing Policy: Perverse Programs by Prudent People," *Public Interest* 48 (Summer 1977), pp. 128–144.

[59]Chester Hartman, *Housing and Social Policy* (Englewood Cliffs, N.J.: Prentice-Hall, 1974), p. 108.

[60]*Reader's Digest 1978 Almanac and Yearbook* (Pleasantville, N.Y.: The Reader's Digest Association, Inc.), p. 110.

[61]"Rebuilders of America's Cities Make Progress with Urban Coalitions," *American City and County* 93 (January 1978), pp. 31–32.

[62]Campbell and Shahala, "Problems Unsolved, Solutions Untried," p. 25.

[63]U.S. Bureau of the Census, *Statistical Abstract of the United States, 1977,* p. 300.

[64]Daniel Grant, "Urban Needs and State Response: Local Government Reorganization," *States and the Urban Crisis,* p. 67.

[65]Ibid., p. 72.

[66]Gurney Breckenfeld, *Columbia and the New Cities* (New York: Washburn, 1971), pp. 301–303.

[67]William Stevens, "Soaring Costs Threaten Huge Center for Downtown Detroit," *New York Times,* 2 March 1975, p. 47; and Azis Salpukas, "Detroit Project Gets $100-Million," *New York Times,* 15 March 1975, p. 30.

[68]Advisory Commission on Intergovernmental Relations, *Urban and Rural America: Policies for Future Growth* (Washington, D.C.: Government Printing Office, April 1968).

[69]Ibid.

[70]Ibid.

[71]Milton Kotler, *Neighborhood Government* (Indianapolis: Bobbs-Merrill, 1969), pp. 44–48.

[72]Ibid., p. 72.

[73]John Friedmann, *Transactive Planning* (New York: Doubleday Anchor, 1973), p. 219.

The Corporate State

6

Of the United States in the 1830s, a country in the first flush of democratic fervor, the French writer and historian Alexis de Tocqueville wrote:

Men there seem on a greater equality in point of fortune and intellect, or, in other words, more equal in their strength, than in any country in the world, or in any age of which history has preserved the remembrance.[1]

Yet despite a political system designed to give individuals both proper representation for their point of view and a basis for redress of grievances, prevalent among contemporary Americans is a sense of powerlessness to affect the direction of their lives in a meaningful way or even to control some of the petty annoyances of daily life. Tocqueville's promising view of American society seems not to have been fulfilled.

This feeling of impotence is not confined to the poor, the elderly, the unemployed and uneducated, or the young, but is shared by a large portion of America's middle and working classes. The student protests and widespread urban disorders of the 1960s can be seen as reactions to a political system in which power and privilege are concentrated in the hands of a very few. The events surrounding the Watergate affair have left many Americans with a deep cynicism toward major institutions and a growing distrust of national leadership. The erosion of democratic ideals is dramatically evidenced in a post-Watergate opinion poll in which 68 percent of the respondents believed that "over the past 10 years, America's leaders have consistently lied to the American people."[2]

Reactions to the growing feeling of individual powerlessness vary widely. In any given year, more than 50 percent of the electorate will choose not to vote. Another type of response has been the formation of public interest groups such as Common Cause, Ralph Nader's investigating groups, and other environmental, safety, and consumer advocate organizations. The more despairing responses are less obvious, but social scientists are now studying such behavior as shoplifting, white-collar crime, wildcat strikes, and sabotage in automobile assembly plants in this light. Such reactions reflect the growing public realization that in our political system it is not those who vote but those who possess knowledge, wealth, social position, and particularly access to officials who are able to determine priorities.[3]

Centralization and the concentration of power in a small number of dominant institutions has become a characteristic of contemporary American society. The establishment of national goals, priorities, and policies increasingly takes place within these major spheres of power. Correspondingly, the influence of the ordinary citizen in determining the direction of national affairs has diminshed. The highest-level decisions concerning, for example, military intervention in foreign countries, investment in new weapons systems versus investment in social programs, or support for an enormously expensive space program manifest little of the balance and compromise, give-and-take processes traditionally associated with democratic decision making. The structure of power in American society has undergone a radical alteration in the post–World War II period. The notions of pluralism, countervailing powers, and balance of interests characteristic of classical democratic theory are now applicable primarily to the middle levels of power.

At the highest level a power elite has emerged, consisting of those who occupy the top positions in the corporate, governmental, and military sectors.[4] It is here that major national goals are set and major policy decisions are made. The so-called 40 Committee (a group of high-level and trusted advisers to the president) is one arena within the executive branch of government where such critical decisions are made. Yet the members of this committee are executive appointees, neither elected by nor accountable to the American people.

Citizens as well as social analysts are beginning to question whether the goals and policies so established adequately reflect and serve the interests of the general public. In the words of Walter Lippmann, the eminent American political commentator:

The private individual today has come to feel rather like a deaf spectator in the back row. . . . He knows he is somehow affected by what is going on. Rules and regulations continually, taxes annually, and wars occasionally, remind him that he is being swept along by great drifts of circumstance.
Yet these public affairs are . . . for the most part invisible. They are managed, if they are managed at all, at distant centers, from behind the scenes, by unnamed powers. As a private individual . . . he lives in world which he cannot see, does not understand, and is unable to direct.[5]

In the corporate state (that is, where the institutions of government and the economy are intimately related) there is no real conspiracy among those who occupy the strategic positions of power. In fact, the individuals who sit astride major institutions are more or less interchangeable. It is important to note that the power they possess derives primarily from the positions they occupy within these institutions. The consensus arrived at by the directorate of the major spheres of power does not result from conspiratorial backroom meetings but rather from a harmony of economic interests and social and political orientations.

More direct linkages between the major institutions in the form of personnel exchanges further reinforce this harmony of interests. There seems to be a revolving door situation, wherein the top officials of government and large corporations frequently alternate positions. A lawyer for a large corporation may be appointed to a regulatory agency that has jurisdiction over the activities of his former employer. Former cabinet officials turn up on the boards of companies that had dealings with their departments, and retired military officers are appointed to the boards of companies with large defense contracts.

Institutions, not individuals, must be studied in order to gain an understanding of the present structure of power in our society. Andrew Hacker has identified a dozen of the major institutions that direct the course of American society:

General Motors Corporation
Standard Oil Company of New Jersey
American Telephone and Telegraph Company
Atomic Energy Commission
Central Intelligence Agency
Ford Foundation
National Education Association
Chase Manhattan Bank
Metropolitan Life Insurance Company
Columbia Broadcasting System
The New York Times Corporation
Merrill Lynch, Pierce, Fenner & Smith[6]

The names of the directors of most of these institutions are not commonly known to the public. Nor is there any reason to expect that their names would be common knowledge, for no single person determines the policy of such institutions. The incumbents of these positions are quite similar to those who have preceded them and those who will succeed them. Decisions are made within a bureaucratic apparatus consisting of administrators, advisers, and others who have a vested interest in the maintenance of the institution. As Hacker remarks, "If the man at the top sits at the controls, the car rides on rails he cannot move."[7]

In many instances the values and interests of elite groups clash head on with those of a great mass of the citizenry. The desire to maintain control over the course of national affairs by those who sit astride the major institutions stands in direct conflict with the interests of citizens concerned with changing the decision-making process so as to render it more responsive to a wide spectrum of needs and desires. Pursuit of maximum profits by large-scale corporations frequently leads to practices that result in the public's paying inflated prices for needed commodities. The value-conflict approach directs attention to fundamental conflicts of interest in a system characterized by centralization and concentration of power and to the problems that may be generated due to this state of affairs.

Viewed from a social disorganization framework, problems stemming from big government, corporate concentration, and the partnership between these two spheres of power can be attributed to rapid social change. As will be detailed in the following sections, the emergence of these huge organizations in their present form is a relatively recent phenomenon, which occurred largely in the post–World War II era.

It is no coincidence that large-scale problems with such organizations began at the same time. The speed at which these organizations grew made necessary adaptive measures of other social institutions difficult. Effective social mechanisms designed to balance and check the power of these organizations have not yet emerged. As a result, the lack of public accountability on the part of these enormous government and corporate bureaucracies is viewed increasingly as a condition which has a harmful impact on society. Questions concerning the legal, moral and social responsibilities of corporations are one set of problems that have not been solved. Society is not the only entity being wronged. The needs of individuals, both as citizens and as consumers, are not being adequately met by the present institutional structure. When thousands of people are having their personal lives, their careers and even their independence as individuals adversely affected by drastic changes in governmental and economic institutions, it is time to analyze what these changes are and why and how they came about.

The Development of American Business

In 1971, James M. Roche, then chairman of the board of General Motors (America's largest private corporation), attributed America's "high levels of education, health, and individual opportunity" to "our free competitive economic system." Economist John Kenneth Galbraith views the delivery of such platitudes as a basic function of modern corporate executives, who are expected periodically to affirm the virtues of free enterprise and the social responsibility of business.[8] In an address to the National Advertising Council in 1973, another corporate board chairman emphasized the need to educate the public as to how well it is served by the present business system:

I urge . . . all of us as individuals to do whatever we can to make sure that this miraculous business system of ours is not gradually crippled by a public and a Congress who do not understand it. We can do this only by educating the public about how this system works. This means that we must deepen the public's understanding of how well profits and the profit motive serve the public interest.[9]

More recently, economic policies of the Carter Administration have been attacked by the business community. In 1977 the Business Roundtable, a committee comprised of representatives of 175 major U.S. corporations, called for a decrease in government regulations of the economic affairs of the private sector. The Roundtable urged the Carter Administration to curb such interference and at the same time demanded a greater voice in forming national policy.[10]

Interestingly, the above remarks come at a time when growing numbers of citizens are questioning the virtues and the social responsibility of American big business. Apparently without regard for the kind of education referred to above, many individuals have reached their own conclusions. In testimony before the Joint Economic Committee of the Congress, a prominent public opinion analyst noted the public's "fundamental conviction that neither the close relationship between the Federal Government and the nation's big corporations nor the leadership of the Government and the nation's big corporations any longer works to protect the economic interests of the average people."[11]

The free competitive economic system extolled and defended by the representatives of the corporate establishment is in fact a myth, hardly applicable to the conditions that prevail at the present time. The early capitalists who took calculated risks in an insecure competitive market have passed from the scene, as has the market in which they built their empires. Even the economic power of such financial giants as Henry Ford, Sr., John D. Rockefeller, and J. P. Morgan has been passed on to a group that possesses the specialized knowledge and experience to make decisions appropriate to what is now a highly interdependent, rather than competitive, economic system.

Despite its theoretically laudable qualities, the market system of the mid-nineteenth century presented the entrepreneur with many problems. Raw materials had to be bid for competitively; finished products had to be sold to independent distributors, who in turn were affected by the vicissitudes of consumer demand. Price wars between competing producers threatened stable profit making. The main goal of late nineteenth- and early twentieth-century entrepreneurs was to gain control over these unpredictable aspects of the market. Through absorption of suppliers and distributors, the business organizations that were forerunners of many of today's corporate giants were able to gain a better economic foothold than their competition. Rockefeller's oil mergers of the 1870s are a classic example. During the period of economic growth and prosperity around the turn of the century, regional economies gradually merged into a nationally based economy.

An Oligopoly of Titans: Corporations

In the twentieth century, the consolidation of the automobile industry through centralization of control and administrative expertise is representative of the development of national corporations. In 1904 there were 35 American producers of automobiles. In 1909, a year after the founding of General Motors, the prototypical corporation, GM controlled twenty manufacturers of cars and auto accessories. In 1921 the costs of entry into the automotive industry were still low enough so that there were as many as 88 companies involved in the industry. Three years later, there were only 43. Although some independent companies held out against the economics of centralization until after World War II, there are today only four auto producers, who control everything from natural resources at one end of the production process to auto insurance companies at the other.

The domination of an industry by a few producers creates an oligopoly, a situation in which competition is limited and prices within an industry are determined by coordinated pricing or what is referred to as price leadership. Large producers in oligopolistic markets recognize that it is more profitable to avoid price competition, and this results in coordinated pricing. A classic illustration is again afforded by the auto industry. Several years ago Ford Motor Company announced an average price increase of 2.9 percent on its new car models. Two weeks later, however, when GM increased its new model prices by an average of 6.1 percent, Ford promptly revised its prices upward to match the GM prices, almost dollar for dollar. Chrysler soon followed suit.[12] Prices for this year's cars continue to show the same intimate relationship; only pennies separate the prices of comparable models sold by the Big Four auto companies. When oligopolistic market structures prevail, the consumer can no longer choose between different products at different prices determined by competition.

Since World War II, newer types of corporate giants have emerged. Conglomerates and multinational corporations now dominate the American economic scene. Whereas early corporations like General Motors have maintained an oligopolistic position in basically one industry, the new corporate structures are diversifying their holdings and expanding their operations into foreign countries on a massive scale. Earlier corporate mergers typically involved either direct competitors or suppliers and their customers. In the current wave of conglomerate mergers this is no longer the case; they now involve the acquisition of additional companies by a parent corporation. Today more than 70 percent of all mergers bring together entirely unrelated firms. It is now common for corporations such as International Telephone and Telegraph (ITT) to be involved not only in communications but in car rentals, insurance, and the baking of cupcakes as well.

Multinational corporations may be the most rapidly growing institutional force in the world today, penetrating many aspects of international politics and increasingly dominating the world economy. During the 1960s corporate investment in foreign countries increased dramatically, so that by 1967 fully 30 percent of U.S. corporate profits derived from overseas investments.[13] Some of the practices of the multinationals, however, such as the draining of a country's resources without concern for replenishment or conservation, have generated hostility and perpetuated the "ugly American" image in many developing countries. The domination of the Chilean economy by American multinational corporations, for example, is so extensive that it prompted the Chile Copper Corporation to place an advertisement in the *New York Times* declaring that "the decisions on Chile's resources are made in New York."[14]

America's corporate titans are so large and control so much of the business done in the country that they have a vested interest in maintaining not only sales levels but also conditions in the larger society that keep sales levels and profits high. The corporate sector is the prime beneficiary of the existing socioeconomic order; the power which these corporate titans have accumulated has resulted in an expansion of the corporate world into more and larger sectors of our national life. Moreover, their power is essentially unchecked, for the corporate sector is not subject to effective regulation by public agencies or government commissions. The large-scale business enterprises that dominate the American scene are able to do business almost without regard for the problems of private citizens or individual communities.

Concentrated Power in the Corporate Technostructure

Leadership in today's corporate world is vested in a group that Galbraith has termed the corporate technostructure.[15] The technostructure of the modern industrial corporation includes financiers and other members of the earlier entrepreneurial corporations but has in addition scientists, technicians, lawyers, and other specialized personnel. It differs from the older corporate form in that the wielder of power is no longer an identifiable person, like Ford or Morgan, but rather an anonymous group of specialists. The corporate technostructure is for the most part an impersonal entity; yet the decisions made by this group have an enormous effect on national policy and on the quality of life in America.

The most obvious characteristics of the American corporate system are its size and concentration. Indeed, many economists feel that today's corporate giants are far larger than modern technology requires for efficient operation. The five largest industrial corporations owned 11 percent of all assets used in manufacturing in 1969; the top 50 had 38 percent; and the largest 200 had 60 percent. These 200 largest corporations (out of approximately 200,000) occupy commanding positions in virtually all principal markets.[16] Between 1955 and 1970, the top 500 industrial corporations increased their total share of profits, assets, and employment in manufacturing and mining from slightly more than 40 percent to over 70 percent.[17]

This centralization is particularly advanced in one of the country's most important industries, steel production. In 1976, the largest two steel companies in the United States, U.S. Steel and Bethlehem Steel, produced 37 percent of all the steel production in America. The largest four companies produced almost 53 percent of the total steel output.[18]

Perhaps a more readily understandable illustration can be found in the fact that General Motors has annual revenues exceeding the revenues of any government except the United States, the United Kingdom, and the Soviet Union.

What do these statistics mean? They are indicative of an increasing concentration of power into fewer private hands. Major economic decisions remain essentially private ones, aimed at maintaining a favorable profit level for stockholders. Considerations of public welfare and public benefit remain secondary. For example, the public benefit derived from unpolluted air and water does not enter into computations on corporate balance sheets.

Contrived Demand: Exploiting the Consumer

The size and concentration of American corporations have many ramifications for the citizenry. Large corporations, no longer challenged by massive competition, feel little pressure to lower prices; nor do their products need to be innovative in any but the most superficial sense. Rather, emphasis is placed on maintaining the firm's share of the market. In the oligopolistic market the firms involved are large enough to absorb short-term losses in a price war; no single firm will lower prices when this will cause other firms to do likewise. Free from the traditional constraints of competitive markets, the large corporations are able to manipulate prices. It is more than coincidental that a price increase on gasoline by one major oil company is almost immediately followed by identical increases by the others. The net effect on consumers is that they have lost any power to influence prices.

Prices are often high at least in part because of the cost of advertising. Advertising often represents the only way giant corporations can distinguish their products from the very similar products offered by other firms. Since corporations are frequently unwilling to take the risks involved in manufacturing a truly different product, they must create product differences artificially through advertising. The consumer is asked to "taste the

The modern shopping mall provides beauty, comfort, food, and entertainment while we shop. Under such attractive conditions consumers run the risk of confusing shopping for essentials with recreation, and thus becoming even more susceptible to the contrived demand created by business.

difference" or "see the difference." But the satisfaction received from one product as opposed to another is largely psychological, the result of imagined rather than actual differences. Moreover, investment in advertising reduces the money available for product improvement, further diminishing the consumer's return on the dollar.

The use of advertising by large corporations is not limited to creating imagined differences between very similar products, however. Advertising is utilized to create a demand for a product in the first place, to contrive a demand for the new varieties of consumer goods that companies seek to market. The telephone industry has no need to create imagined differences. As a government-authorized monopoly it has no competition that offers a comparable service. Yet the telephone industry spends millions of dollars in advertising to convince the consumer to buy more and different varieties of its service. In the case of a new product, a carefully planned advertising campaign is usually launched well before the product itself is widely available. The implication is that the demand needs to be contrived—and this indeed seems to be true.

In earlier times, demand was largely confined to commodities that satisfied physical needs—food, shelter, clothing, and attendant goods. Although these needs obviously exist in today's consumer society, they have been supplemented by a host of contrived needs that go far beyond the necessities of life. Advertising, to a greater or lesser degree, has exploited or played upon human psychological desires, such as the desire to be accepted, to feel sexually adequate, to maintain a youthful appearance and vigor, and so on. It has become a truism on Madison Avenue that if a source of human anxiety or insecurity can be identified, it can be exploited profitably through advertising. Thus, we are continually deluged with product advertisements promising to make us look better, smell better, and be more popular.

The net effect of contrived consumer needs has been to reduce the consumer's decision-making capacity. Some contend that the exercise of America's vast industrial strength in this direction has become a burden for society. For example, the multiplicity of so-called convenience appliances so routinely sought by modern consumers has already resulted in a tremendous burden on energy resources. The archetypal consumer product, the automobile, is so involved with other aspects of American life that it has massive effects on air quality, on the physical layout of cities and towns, and on the employment of a sizable portion of America's labor force.

The acquiescence to contrived demand and the conspicuous consumption of unnecessary products are, of course, as much a product of cultural patterns and personal desires as of corporate design. The satisfaction one person obtains from the continued use of myriad electric kitchen appliances or a second and third car must be weighed against the cost to society should electricity in hospitals become curtailed because of a power shortage.

Proliferation of Government

As business organizations have grown in size and scale, so too has government, most notably at the federal level. Until fairly recent times, the federal government in the United States normally refrained from direct participation in commercial enterprise. This is not to say that government had refused a national economic role, but its role in earlier eras was not a comprehensive one stemming from any single, well-defined policy. In the nineteenth century, government did attempt to create a uniform stable currency, to protect burgeoning industry, and to promote education and agricultural advancements. However, such actions were taken in response to immediate concerns and seldom represented any long-range planning of the economic, social, or political direction of the country. Furthermore, the states retained a good deal of power, so that prior to World War II various regions were easily distinguishable in terms of their economic, social, and political features—a situation not unlike the regional development in the business world prior to the mergers that gave industry a national character.

As industries became increasingly specialized, so did the governmental bureaucracy designed to deal with the problems resulting from specialization. In the period between 1890 and 1925, government at the national level began to grow, as evidenced by the emergence of agencies such as the Interstate Commerce Commission, Federal Trade Commission, and Federal Power Commission. Governmental operations, however, remained largely unchanged. The specialized agencies, like the cabinet departments, were designed to deal with specific problems. As such, they often had overlapping jurisdictions, and the policies of one often conflicted with those of another. One could describe the United States government in this period as a feudal system comprised of petty fiefdoms of agencies, commissions, and departments, each with its own cumbersome bureaucracy.

The crisis of the Great Depression necessitated a different arrangement. Planning, although still toward limited ends, became a permanent preoccupation of government. The federal government assumed a larger, more active role in the direction of national affairs, regulating employment levels through programs such as the Civilian Conservation Corps and controlling the cash flow in the economy through the Federal Reserve Board, for example. Political power began to shift away from local and state government to national government and to become concentrated within the executive branch. During the New Deal years, appointive positions within the government, formerly filled by political cronies of the current administration, were increasingly staffed with experts and specialists. Although far from successful in curing the depression, these new people did manage to streamline and refine government bureaucracy.

During World War II and the postwar period, the federal bureaucracy, as well as the bureaucratic supporting state governments, swelled to an astonishing degree. From a federal budget equal to only about 1 percent of the Gross National Product (GNP) in 1929, recent budgets have totaled in excess of $350 billion, more than 22 percent of the GNP. (See Figures 6.1 and 6.2 for details.) (The proportion of the labor force employed by the federal government has evidenced a similar increase. New departments of the federal government were formed, including Health, Education, and Welfare; Transportation; and Housing and Urban Development. Specialized agencies like the Office of Economic Opportunity, the Central Intelligence Agency, and the Office of Management and Budget are almost numberless. In the face of this enormous size, the bewildering proliferation of bureaus, agencies, and commissions, and the volume of red tape involved in dealing with the government, individual citizens are often prompted to question what effect they can have on this massive bureaucracy and how responsive it is to their needs and desires.

Postwar Partnership: Business and Government

World War II witnessed major cooperation between big business and government. A War Production Board coordinated all industrial efforts toward wartime needs. Its director, a former business executive, reported directly to the president. Coordination succeeded not only because of the emergency, but also because the technostructures in business and government were speaking the same language.

The World War II partnership between business and government was continued into the postwar era by legislation such as the Full Employment Act (FEA) of 1946 and the National Security Act (NSA) of 1947, which greatly expanded the specific and implied activities of government in the national economic sphere. The FEA instructed the government to use "all practicable means" to maintain a high level of employment and a low rate of inflation. The NSA, especially through its National Security Resources and Research and Development boards, has been used to justify governmental actions that amount to nothing less than the financial rescue of otherwise failing firms.

This expansion in government control of the economy necessitated increased planning and coordination with corporate giants. As one observer

Figure 6.1   Government Spending Since 1950

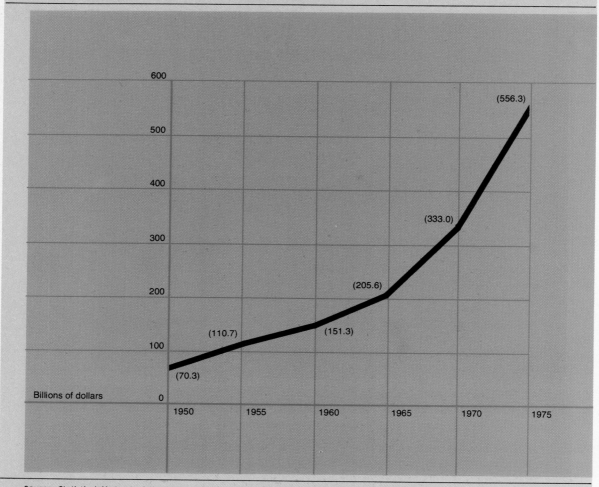

Source: *Statistical Abstract of the United States, 1977* (Washington, D.C.: Government Printing Office, 1977), p. 278.

has phrased it: "The federal government does not 'serve' business or 'regulate' business. . . . Government *is* business."[19] Most major research and development is now underwritten by the federal government. Government and the large corporations cooperate on contracts worth billions of dollars.[20] The vast majority of defense contracts are awarded without competitive bidding; not surprisingly, the recipients of these lucrative contracts are typically the major corporations. Consensus between business and government regarding major policy decisions is forged, in part, in quasi-governmental think tanks. The Rand Corporation, for example, which is well subsidized by the air force, is in a position to act as a coordinator between the government and corporate spheres.

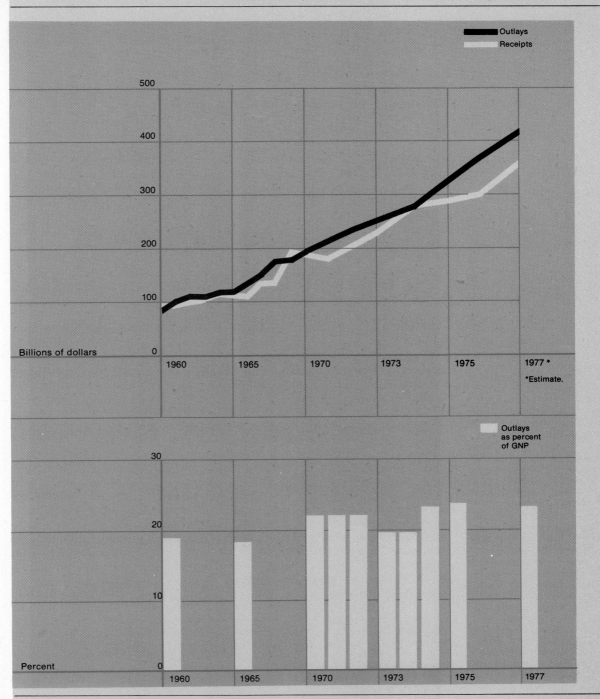

Federal Budget Receipts and Outlays: 1960 to 1977   **Figure 6.2**

Source: *Statistical Abstract of the United States, 1977* (Washington, D.C.: Government Printing Office, 1977), p. 246.

The Government and Corporations: Musical Chairs?

The intimate relationship between government and the corporate sector is the result of specific historical trends in American society. As government expenditures have risen dramatically over the past forty years, corporate suppliers have come to have a greater and greater stake in the decisions made and the goals and policies pursued by the national government. And a government with so much to manage has a keen interest in the economic survival of the corporations which supply it with so many goods and services. A steady exchange of personnel between the two sectors provides a mechanism whereby differences can be resolved and coordination and consensus achieved.

A study of presidential administrations between 1897 and 1973 revealed that at least 76 percent of all Cabinet members in that period were tied to the business community at some time prior to their appointment. There was little difference between Democratic and Republican administrations. For example, during both the Eisenhower (1953–1961) and Johnson administrations (1963–1969), 85.7 percent of the Cabinet positions were filled with persons who were interlocked with business.[21]

This phenomenon is not unique to these high positions in the executive branch of government. Professionals in the fields of environmental problems, and of food and drug, and worker safety and health hazards find that their services are in high demand by two groups, research divisions of large companies and government regulatory agencies. It is unlikely that the professionals employed by the regulatory agencies—such as the Environmental Protection Agency, the Food and Drug Administration, and the Occupational Safety and Health Administration—would want to offend future employers by citing them for violations and assessing penalties.

Many pieces of legislation are not only hampered in the enforcement stage, but bear the mark of strong corporate lobbying when the law was originally passed by Congress. For example, it is estimated that 90 percent of all the regulations and standards of the Occupational Safety and Health Administration were actually written by industries themselves prior to the enactment of the government regulations.[22]

Tax structures which allow generous tax credits and large depreciation allowances favor the corporate sector and serve to ensure its continued economic dominance. Public agencies set up to regulate oligopolistic industries soon become closely tied to the firms they are supposed to be regulating. In the words of one analyst:

The federal government—relinquishing its customary role as a foe of corporate size —is in fact now forging a New Partnership with big business. Naturally, this has many troublesome implications, but certainly it means that one can no longer be confident that government will keep the exercise of private economic power within reasonable bounds.[23]

This close relationship between government and business already works against the consumer's ability to exercise power in the marketplace; it also significantly influences the capacity of government to represent the concerns of individual citizens effectively.

Nowhere is the partnership of large corporations and the government more evident than in the military establishment. The largest hundred corporations receive approximately three-fourths of all defense contracts.[24] In 1977, there were almost one million civilians employed by the Department of Defense; this figure represents 3.5 percent of the total civilian employment in the federal government.[25] Nearly 24 percent of the Carter administration's "peacetime" budget is allocated for direct military expenditures. Without question, a sizable segment of the American economy is deeply dependent on the military for survival. (See Figure 6.3 for details on the federal budget.)

The Partnership of Defense and Industry

Shortly before leaving office in 1961, President Eisenhower warned the nation of the dangers of a "military-industrial complex," an interested cooperation between the defense industries and the military arms of government. Although the term came into general use as a result of Eisenhower's warning, the institution of which he spoke had its roots in the period immediately following World War II. The United States could not, as it had in 1918, retreat into isolation at the close of hostilities. World War II had severely crippled the industries and economies of much of the world. Two new superpowers, the United States and the Soviet Union, stepped into the military-economic void. Each had an ideology that it wanted the rest of the world to accept, and each adopted military and economic goals as a means of demonstrating its power.

The cold war both accelerated and was in turn sustained by military expenditures. The more each country spent on armaments, the greater was the perceived threat to the other country—a threat that could be met only by another round of spending. The economic results are easily measured. Some contend that the United States now has a perpetual war economy. Major segments of American industry have become so dependent on military expenditures that the GNP (and therefore the economy as a whole) would plummet drastically if weapons production were cut back significantly. The United States now exports huge quantities of military technology throughout the world; in recent years the primary consumers have shifted from Southeast Asian countries to nations in the Middle East and Africa.

During the cold war period, Charles E. Wilson, President Eisenhower's secretary of defense, declared that "what's good for General Motors is good for the United States." Wilson, previously the president of General Motors, is an example of a corporate executive who moved from being a supplier of military hardware and services to a position as procurer of military hardware and services. Several years later, Robert McNamara, president of Ford Motor Company, made a similar move under President Kennedy. Wilson and McNamara are not exceptions. Wisconsin Senator William Proxmire, a frequent critic of the defense establishment's excesses, discovered in 1969 that 100 firms involved in defense contracts employed more than

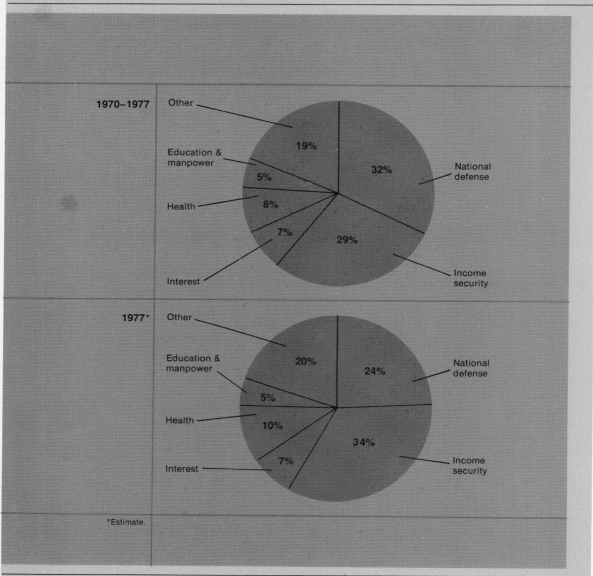

1970–1977

Other 19%

Education & manpower 5%

Health 8%

Interest 7%

National defense 32%

Income security 29%

1977*

Other 20%

Education & manpower 5%

Health 10%

Interest 7%

National defense 24%

Income security 34%

*Estimate.

Source: *Statistical Abstract of the United States, 1977* (Washington, D.C.: Government Printing Office, 1977), p. 246.

The U.S. Navy's anti-ship missile Harpoon, a product of the military-industrial complex. The GNP would plummet if weapons production were cut back significantly.

2000 ex-officers who had retired from the military at the rank of colonel (army), captain (navy), or higher. Lockheed Aircraft alone, one of the perennial defense giants, employed 210 such ex-officers.[26] Obviously, these ex-officers have rather easy access to the Pentagon and the chambers of the House Armed Services Committee. The increase in this type of interlock between corporate suppliers and the military is indicative of a "growing community of interest between the two sectors of the society."[27]

The contrived demand that operates in the private sector appears to be prevalent in the defense industry as well. How much of our defense demand is real and how much is contrived is a matter of debate. However, the so-called Pentagon lobbyists who are employed by the combined technostructure of the large corporations and the Defense Departments are ever present to provide answers to members of Congress in matters relating to the size of defense expenditures in the federal budget.

What of public opinion in relation to the size of defense expenditures? In 1970 Senator J. William Fulbright authored a book, *The Pentagon Propaganda Machine,* in which he castigated the Defense Department and military officials for "brainwashing" the American public into acceptance of a militaristic and cold war mentality.[28] This question of the influence brought to bear on public opinion by military-industrial interests has been addressed at greater length by sociologist Marc Pilisuk and former activist Tom Hayden:

The issues in the question of news management involve more than the elements of control available to the President, the State Department, the Department of Defense, the Central Intelligence Agency, or any of the major prime contractors of defense contracts. Outright control of news flow is probably less pervasive than voluntary acquiescence to the objectives of these prominent institutions of our society. Nobody has to tell the wire services when to release a story on the bearded dictator of our hemisphere. . . . In addition to a sizeable quantity of radio and television programming purchased directly by the Pentagon, an amount of service, valued to $6 million by *Variety,* is donated by the networks and by public-relations agencies for various military shows.[29]

If national survival is thought to be dependent on the various weapons systems developed and produced by large corporations, then the economic survival of these corporations is also thought to be in the national interest. The aircraft industry affords an example of the limits to which government is willing to go to support these corporate interests. In 1946 the air force, in a secret guideline that was not declassified until 1960, directed that "contracts [be] parceled out among the old established manufacturers on an equitable basis so that they may be assured enough business to perpetuate their existence."[30] Such an arrangement patently violated the spirit of the antitrust laws, for it had the effect of freezing the existing division of aircraft expenditures. It would appear that such practices have continued into the present. In 1971 the government made a $250 million loan to Lockheed Aircraft to avert its economic failure. The rationale for the loan was that if Lockheed failed, the government could not obtain certain types of military hardware without the time-consuming and expensive tooling-up of another company.

This intimate association between the huge aircraft-missile concerns and the federal government raises some important questions regarding the relationship between defense production and the civilian economy. Part of Lockheed's economic difficulties arose from its inability to meet deadlines on its civil aircraft production, particularly the L1011 Tri-Star. Although the loan to Lockheed was ostensibly made to keep it alive for defense production, in effect it allowed the firm to continue in civil aviation production. Economist Robert L. Heilbroner has described such arrangements as a "love affair" between the Pentagon and Lockheed Aircraft and has called it "the scandal of the military industrial interlock that the big contractors are now protected by the Pentagon."[31]

The alternative to bailing out Lockheed might very well have been the loss of almost 75,000 civilian jobs. Heibroner has estimated that if the Department of Defense were dismantled and no other governmental agencies spending similar amounts were installed, there would be a threefold increase in unemployment.[32] This increased unemployment would not be found primarily among ex-officers but rather among workers employed on defense-related projects. Were defense funds suddenly to dry up, the high degree of dependence of big industry on military expenditures would result in a cataclysmic economic disruption. Cutbacks in government spending in 1970 and 1971 had severe effects on the aerospace industry centered on the West Coast. The expense of a defense establishment is no longer justified solely in terms of national security; the country's very economic survival is dependent on the continued prosperity of the military-industrial sector.

Technology and Profit versus Humanity

To a certain extent, the size of the defense establishment may be seen as a reflection of national priorities:

Its cost is not only the budgeted money for these purposes, but also the shoddy education system, the poor housing, the neglected medical-care needs, the polluted streams—in short, the whole array of depletion at home and abroad due to the productive activity foregone because of the concentration of talent and capital and materials in the military sphere.[33]

The government is relatively neglectful of human services, unless they can be related to national security, national prestige, or the continued growth of large corporations and are amenable to technological solutions. The national goal of putting a man on the moon by 1970 was not primarily a scientific enterprise but rather an effort to accomplish a spectacular achievement (in competition with the Soviet Union) that would raise national prestige.

When matters having to do with the public welfare are involved, concern over the nation's prestige often seems to evaporate. The United States, for example, is the only industrial country without a comprehensive national health plan. Only when internal unrest demands it is war declared on poverty. Unlike the requirements for national defense, the needs of the poverty-stricken are not readily met by technical methods. Progress is likely to be slow; there may be no easily measured return on investment. In comparison with a public endeavor that promotes national prestige, such as the space program, solutions to poverty have little interest for technicians accustomed to results and thus to renewed funding by government.

Even in agriculture, technological problems are researched while human needs go unanswered. Government funds are spent for improvements in productive capacity—on developing special strains of hard tomatoes that are easy to harvest mechanically, though not so pleasant to eat, for example—but at the same time billions more are spent to keep a lid on agricultural production. Corporate profit taking pervades the arrangement as well. Our agricultural surplus has for years been sold to foreign nations through corporate intermediaries; yet millions of Americans are malnourished and underfed. Only after sales in large supermarkets began lagging were food stamps sold to the poor. Here again we see that the economic well-being of organizations rather than humans provides the stimulus for government programs.

Another area in which the government is called upon to weigh corporate profits versus social good is in the realm of worker safety. Some 150,000 of the country's 800,000 cotton workers suffer from a lung disease called byssinosis, which results from their exposure to cotton dust. When a standard was recommended by the Department of Labor that would force industry to spend millions of dollars to install devices that would minimize exposure to cotton dust, the Carter administration vetoed it on the basis that it was inflationary.[34] Again, profit making appears to have a higher priority than public welfare.

Profit taking in human-oriented programs also affects America's foreign relations. Many foreign assistance programs are contingent on the purchase of American products. A case in point is the Alliance for Progress, in essence an international development bank for Latin America whose deposits were supplied by the United States. If a government, say Peru, wanted to borrow money to buy bulldozers, the bulldozers had to be purchased from a United States firm, even if they could be bought more cheaply from a foreign concern. Thus what on the surface was hailed as an example of America's humanity was actually a profit-making venture.

Such a system of deriving profit is relatively benign, however, when compared to the standard operations of many multinational corporations. Many of the multinationals have been able to pay little or no taxes on their holdings in foreign countries under arrangements with the local governments. When such governments are replaced by a new group, the American firm is often in danger of losing its preferred tax status. The corporation therefore has an interest in keeping certain officials in power. The allegations that ITT enlisted the Central Intelligence Agency in an attempt to prevent the election of a Marxist president in Chile and that it was actively involved in the subsequent assassination of this democratically elected leader is a glaring case in point. Recent information suggests that the CIA has been used as a primary instrument for the implementation of corporate policy abroad.

Philip Slater
The Centralization of Political Power

The worst evils of our political system come from the centralization of power, irrespective of who holds it. It is the most naïve kind of hero-villain thinking to imagine that a new face will change a system. The major organizations in our society have seen dozens of incumbents pass through their top positions without greatly affecting the oppressiveness of their fundamental patterning. The centralization of power is rooted in paranoid motivation—to imagine that anything benign or lovely could flourish in such an environment is as illusory as the perpetual-motion machine.

Consider the power concentrated in the hands of the President of the United States. It is the power, ultimately, to decide the life or death of every living person. To give such power to a single man or group of men is to court catastrophe. Even a paragon of virtue (and what sort of virtue would pursue such evil power?) could scarcely avoid blundering eventually, simply because he would be unable to keep abreast of the enormous volume of information required to act wisely. Concentration of power means that the locus of decision making is farther and farther removed from the locus of its consequences—that decisions are based on less and less information and are more and more cut off from feedback. The President may be well-informed in an absolute sense, but relative to his arena of responsibility, he is the most ill-informed man in the United States. Fortunately, this same concentration of power contains a self-corrective. In a complex social system the power of the power-glutton is limited by the narrowness and simplicity of his own world view—reinforced by the paucity of information available to him. The more dictatorial he is, the more likely he is to lose touch with the dynamic complexity of the world around him and destory himself. Authoritarianism, as noted above, works well only in stable, homogeneous systems. Furthermore, power is symbolic, like stock market values. The minute anyone begins to doubt the power of a leader it begins to shrink.

The desire for negative power derives, as we have seen, from fear and mistrust of others—from the feeling that the world's gratifications will not be freely given, shared, or even exchanged, but must be coerced. Alexander Lowen suggests that the only people who can "handle power constructively" are those who have been "fulfilled in childhood and know how to enjoy life." But such people would not want or seek negative power. Anyone who would willingly make the kind of sacrifices required to become President of the United States must necessarily be afflicted with the need to coerce in a particularly virulent form. Such a man is precisely the person to whom such power should not be given. The power to blow up the world cannot be entrusted to anyone sick enough to seek it.

In the last analysis negative power rests on the threat of destruction. One cannot gain power by threatening to create. Anyone can create—props are not required, nor any coercion. Nor does one generally expect innovation or creativity to emerge from centers of power, which are fundamentally conservative in nature—concerned with control, with hanging on, with grasping. Those motivated to seek power tend to mistrust spontaneity, flux, creation—to believe only in what can be controlled, ensured, compelled. They are insensitive to the regenerative processes that occur in nature. They trust, in themselves, only their own defensive structure and learned skills; in others they trust only the tendency of most humans to be impressed by the canopy of status and the accouterments of power. Therefore, although they cannot innovate, it is of desperate importance to them that they stay on top of, abreast of, change. They ride the horse but cannot make it go. Government is largely a negative force—it can regulate, it can maintain, it can destroy.

But can a man who would actively seek the power of the Presidency refrain from using it under stress? If he achieves it, is he likely to tolerate restraints on it—either internally, in the form of decentralization, or externally, in the form of disarmament? International politics as it now exists grinds up millions of healthy individuals in order that the sickest ones can play a kind of chess game. Arthur Janov suggests that it is self-alienation that enables political leaders to discuss mass killing without qualms. Death is not a tragedy for those who cannot feel life. Since they themselves are dead internally, the actual death of others is unreal rather than horrifying.

A male bureaucrat once argued that women should not hold positions of responsibility because of the emotional instabilities associated with menopause, but I would rather take my chances with such a woman than with an ordinary power-hungry male. It seems astonishing that we fear menopausal lability more than the icy pathology that allows a man to order massive destruction and the killing and mutilation of hundreds of thousands of people merely to avoid being called weak, or to win points in a game of international chicken. The lust for power is the most dangerous of all sexual perversions, and the compartmentalized rationalism that often accompanies it is no cause for reassurance. The worst horrors in history have been perpetrated by "sensible," "practical" males "taking the necessary steps" to beat some symbolic opponent to a symbolic goal. . . .

Since only madmen are attracted to positions of great power, and since such people are too infatuated to diffuse and decentralize that power, how can we keep them from holding it? How can we give power to those capable of detoxifying it? An obvious although patently unpopular solution would be to choose public officials through some sort of lottery system, such as we now use to hire killers who will not volunteer for the task. The Athenians used such a method, and while it had its problems, most of them could be attributed to the prevalence of precisely the kind of egregious vanity that made it a desirable system in the first place. In the long run it is generally more useful for the person who occupies a given role to feel comfortable in it, but this depends upon power being diffused to the point where the poison is present in small enough doses to be absorbed by the average human.

The idealist who seeks high office to implement high-minded goals is thus engaged in a self-defeating effort. He who seeks such power is an enemy of the people, whatever his program. He will explain his motivation in terms of wanting to "have a real impact," but anyone who acts out of this kind of gradiosity thereby becomes part of the problem rather than part of the solution, since his behavior springs from and helps maintain the motivational core of the oppressive system in which we live.

Efforts to increase the power of a heretofore powerless group are another matter altogether, since they involve the diffusion of power, which should be the central goal of all political activity for the foreseeable future. Community organizing and public exposure of official arrogance are two of the key enterprises in this process. Power is built in large part on the concentration and manipulation of information and hence relies heavily on secrecy. "Top secret" or "highly classified" usually means, "exposure will weaken our power." The right or privacy cannot be allowed the government or any other organization in which comparable power is concentrated, since such privacy is always used by those in power to concentrate that power further. "Private" and "public" are supposed, after all, to be antithetical concepts.

The most important reason for eschewing positions of power is that social change rarely originates in power centers. Many people imagine that Washington, D.C., is "where the action is," but this is true only for power addicts. No major cultural or social innovation ever came out of the Washington political community, although many lesser ones were implemented there. Political leaders merely generalize changes that have arisen elsewhere in the society. The ideas on which new programs are based have usually been around for years. People immersed in government often seem a bit archaic—their information is screened by too many people absorbed with protecting their positions and maintaining secrecy. They are low on information pertaining to system changes, high on facts and figures plugged into rigid and antiquated frameworks. Change in America has come from technologists, businessmen, scientists, inventors, artists, musicians, blacks, street people, the media, and from day-to-day decisions made by millions of completely faceless individuals.

The proper metaphor for Washington and other power centers is the feudal castle. The inhabitants of such a castle had a purely negative function—they could sally forth and destroy, but otherwise led a parasitic existence. The castle had no energy of its own—all was drawn from the farmed lands around it. To attack the castle was absurd for anyone not driven by narcissistic motives, for all of its life lay outside. To take it was to take nothing. One could absorb all the external food and water sources and leave the castle to starve itself. The feudal lord could then sit inside and look out over "his" lands, but he would in fact have been rendered irrelevant.

Leaders do not make change, everyone does. We have been engaged for so long in dreaming of ourselves as agents of change that we have failed in the role of reactor. People are the nerve endings of social systems. If they are stupid enough stoically to bear the pain such a system inflicts upon them, the system will go right on inflicting it. Social mechanisms are mindless, undirected. Insofar as they are deprived of information about human needs and responses, they will be inhumane.

Most Western societies are like people with no sense of pain—they blunder into horrible injuries because they have lost access to vital information from their peripheries. We are the numbed and atrophied nerve endings of our societies. We have been trained to smile politely when some social institution tramples upon us, and every time we do so we give it a lesson in inhumanity.

Excerpts from pp. 153–158 of *Earthwalk* by Philip Slater, © 1974 by Philip Slater. Reprinted by permission of Doubleday & Co., Inc.

The Impotent Individual in Corporate Society

The size, complexity, and interdependence of business and government are factors that minimize the exercise of political control by the voter. Sociologist Irving L. Horowitz has suggested that in America policymaking has replaced politics. "We have," he argues, "a system in which expertise (real or imagined) displaces elective office in the legitimation of power . . . and elective offices are giving way in importance to appointive offices."[35] Few elected officials have had the power and prestige of the secretaries of state and defense in recent administrations or of the presidential aides in the Nixon administration. Government by appointed experts ceases to be either accountable to the voters or responsive to their suggestions for change.

There is no doubt that the lack of viable institutional means to affect government policy was a major cause of the demonstrations and riots of the 1960s and early 1970s. With few resources other than their indignation, people took to the streets in an effort to express their sense of injustice and to influence public opinion and government policy. However, the right to dissent—traditionally a cornerstone of democratic systems—appears to some to be more an illusion than an actuality in the wake of the killings at Kent State University in 1970 during student protests of the U.S. invasion of Cambodia.

Recent congressional testimony revealing J. Edgar Hoover's use of smear tactics against civil-rights leader Martin Luther King has further shaken the public belief that ours is a system in which the rights of the individual are cherished and protected. In light of these and other developments in government and business, serious questions are now being raised concerning the integrity of the American political system.

Voting for officials of one's choice is the traditional means in our society of choosing the priorities and policies of government and informing public officials of individual needs and desires. The Voting Rights Act of 1965 and the constitutional amendment lowering the voting age to 18 have opened this political process to more of our citizens than ever before. Yet America's voters now stay away from the polls in droves on most election days. On Election Day in 1978 only 37 percent of the eligible voters actually went to the polls to cast their ballots.[36] Many do not know the names of their elected representatives and make few attempts to influence their voting one way or another. There appears to be a growing public feeling that important decisions are arrived at in closed, smoke-filled rooms rather than in the open forum of democratic give-and-take. Increasingly, citizens are becoming aware that the "one person–one vote" maxim does not allow all to share equally in the democratic process. Persons with money to contribute to candidates and candidates with more money to spend in campaigns appear to have an advantage in the political process. In the 1972 and 1974 congressional races, candidates that spent more money than their opponents won 82 percent of the time.[37] The Watergate affair, revealing such abuses of power as the use of government agencies like the Internal Revenue Service to harass and intimidate private citizens, has only further eroded public confidence in government.

In part because of this widespread public apathy and general lack of confidence in government, the lobbyists of various special-interest groups have the ear of the legislature. Much of this is not new in American society, but as the national government has come to regulate wider and wider areas of life, government decisions have been further and further removed from the individual citizen. Increasingly, the decisions are made on the basis of a choice between expert opinions representing powerful interests within the society.

For example, few members of Congress are specialists in any legislative area. When deciding on legislation, they often need to rely on outside information. Such advice is readily offered by well-paid lobbyists representing major corporations, labor, agriculture, and other special interests. The costs of lobbying are tax deductible. Though some individuals belong to citizen lobbies that can afford to send delegations to consult with their representatives in Congress about pending legislation, most do not. The result is that few members of Congress solicit the views of their constituents except at election time. Rather, they rely on the advice of corporations, labor unions, farm associations, and the like. These to some extent represent the interests of the people, but the size and scope of corporate interests often override the legitimate demands of individuals or groups with little economic power. The dominance of corporate influence is particularly in evidence when it comes to decisions having the greatest economic consequence.

It is true that Congress was designed to balance local and national interests, and lobbying for legislation can be justified to some extent. The chief

THE CORPORATE STATE

Today's Americans seek, but seldom find, evidence of their ability to affect the course of events within society. The powerlessness of the individual is experienced at all levels of the socioeconomic hierarchy; the poor no longer suffer this misfortune alone. The frustration of those who look to government in vain for representation and recourse demands immediate attention lest it result in widespread citizen apathy, alienation, or even violence. *This page:* The federal government overlooking human needs; waiting for gasoline—is it a real crisis or the result of oil company greed and power; challenging the power structure—consumer advocate Ralph Nader testifying before Congress. *Opposite page:* Computer systems—symbol of a technological era and the life force of big business and big government; an anti-nuclear power rally demonstrates the right of citizens to protest.

executive, on the other hand, is chosen to represent the people as a whole. Yet the president works within a White House bureaucracy that has grown rapidly in recent years, especially during the administrations of Kennedy, Johnson, and Nixon. The proliferation of special executive agencies and the increase in the size of the federal bureaucracy—to 2.8 million employees in 1977—have given rise to the concept of decision by experts, many of whom come from the technostructure of corporate America. Regarding such informal structures of influence, sociologist Suzanne Keller has noted: "The tyranny of the expert over the unenlightened, though different from that of the haves over the have-nots, is nevertheless a tyranny."[38]

It is difficult to view our current governmental operations without skepticism. The rhetoric of popular sovereignty is still abundantly used, but the system of government is one in which members of Congress look to corporate advisers and supporters, where the president receives advice and much of his campaign backing from corporate executives and experts, and where regulatory commissions accede to the demands of corporate interests.

Consumers are managed, to use Galbraith's term, by the large industrial concerns that rely on the communications and advertising industries to control not only prices but, to a lesser extent, consumer demand as well. Galbraith argues that the general effect of annual corporate outlays of tens of billions of dollars for advertising "is to shift the locus of decision in the purchase of goods from the consumer where it is beyond control to the firm where it is subject to control."[39] In addition to bringing consumer demand under substantial control, advertising performs yet another important function. It provides:

a relentless propaganda on behalf of goods in general. From early morning until late at night, people are informed of the services rendered by goods—of their profound indispensability. . . . Even minor qualities of unimportant commodities are enlarged upon with a solemnity which would not be unbecoming in an announcement of the combined return of Christ and all the apostles. More important services, such as the advantages of whiter laundry, are treated with proportionately greater gravity. . . . Advertising and its related arts thus help develop the kind of man the goals of the industrial system require—one that reliably spends his income and works reliably because he is always in need of more.[40]

The citizen as voter or consumer has become the object of manipulation by organizations.

Institutionalism and Concentrated Power: Some Explanations of the Problem

The values of growth and productivity that are traditional underpinnings of corporate enterprise in America have, for the economic and political reasons described, become wed to the government's concept of its role as well. Corporate executives point to higher profits and sales in their annual reports; the government points to a rising Gross National Product as a measure of the country's performance. Such modes of thought, however, do not take into consideration the social costs of growth or of corporate and governmental policy decisions, nor do they take into account the powerlessness of individuals who wish to change these decisions through the political system. A number of sociological explanations for the present state of affairs have been put forward.

One such explanation points to the conflict of values between the vested interests of those who occupy the top positions in the major corporate and government institutions and ordinary citizens who may feel that the realization of their own goals and interests is impeded by the massive concentrations of power in a handful of institutions. Public concerns for political accountability and improving the quality of life are probably not compatible with emphasis on growth, profitability, and the desire for a strong and decisive decision-making apparatus.

Bureaucratic growth and the accompanying unresponsiveness to the needs of citizens and consumers may be viewed in part as a function of social disorganization. The massive bureaucratic organizations that dominate the contemporary American scene sometimes appear as rogue elephants, pursuing their own objectives and seemingly beyond the control of the clients they ostensibly serve. Most significantly, the development of adequate mechanisms to check and control these organizations, such as effective regulatory agencies and oversight committees, has not kept pace with the rapid growth and expansion of major corporate and government organizations.

Bureaucratic Institutionalism

Many sociologists see the close relationship between business and government as stemming from the increasingly similar structures of the two institutions. Expansion in size and concentration of resources has resulted in bureaucratic organization in both business and government. At the turn of the century Max Weber, a founder of modern sociology, noted that bureaucratic organization is one means by which institutions can efficiently collect information, arrive at decisions, and implement those decisions. The bureaucratic form of organization, Weber believed, was the structure most suited to the modern legal-rational state, which requires the universal application of rules rather than standards based on tradition and personal loyalty.[41]

In the course of arriving at their present tremendous size and concentration, however, both government and business bureaucracies underwent a transformation. Efficiency and rationality in pursuit of a goal have given way to an effort to preserve the bureaucratic structure itself, so that rather than serving simply as a means of achieving profits (in the case of the corporation) or of delivering services (in the case of government), the bureaucracy has become an end in itself. For the new bureaucracy of the corporate technostructure, profit has become as much a means for its own preservation as it is an explicit organizational goal. In the case of the government bureaucracy, the main objective has become a continual increase in jurisdictions for governmental action.

One author has demonstrated that the Federal Bureau of Narcotics was one of the most important lobbying groups seeking the criminalization of marijuana during the 1930s.[42] This drive began at a time when the FBN

Corey Rosen
How the Government Drove the Small Airlines out of Business

The federal government makes a great show of supporting the American free-enterprise spirit generally and small business in particular. There is a Small Business Adminstration and corresponding committees in Congress. But the fact is that the government neither encourages small business nor even leaves it alone; often it is actively hostile to entrepreneurs and concentrates on protecting huge, stultified corporations to small business' great disadvantage. The airline industry is an especially egregious case of the government's harassing entrepreneurs and acting precisely counter to the innovative spirit it says it's trying to promote.. . . .

At the end of World War II many returning veterans were interested in continuing to fly. Because the government wanted to sell its surplus equipment, it created a program to meet the demand. In a very short period of time, this resulted in 142 airline companies, the majority of them very small. These companies were given the status of non-scheduled carriers, meaning they could perform any irregularly scheduled air transport functions. Although they flew less than five per cent of the total passenger miles, the non-skeds proved to be a dynamic force in the industry. Their main attractions were low price and a willingness to explore new markets. Generally, they charged one half to two thirds the scheduled carriers' fares. . . .

The non-skeds expanded their low-cost concept into major markets with irregularly scheduled coach flights. These low-cost flights had been shunned by the scheduled carriers as unprofitable—for them, air travel was a luxury item only. As the non-skeds expanded this service, however, their flights became more and more regular, and the major airlines and the CAB became increasingly concerned. A secret Board memorandum in the late 1940s detailed a plan to eradicate the non-skeds under the cover of legitimate regulation: . . .

Apparently this plan was put into effect, for by 1953 the Senate Small Business Committee had concluded that the entire non-sked industry was on the verge of being wiped out by the CAB. The committee strongly denounced the Board, and called on it to create a place for the non-skeds.

What in fact happened was a slow rather than a quick death. The Board issued a series of Catch-22 regulations that made it impossible for all but a few carriers to remain in business. . . . Non-skeds were restricted at one point, for instance, to ten trips per month between any two points on an irregular basis. Rules for determining regularity were exceptionally complex: . . .

If carriers stayed within the regulations they could not make money, so their operating rights were revoked for financial insufficiency (the Board feared that economically weak carriers would cut corners on safety, although the non-skeds had an exceptional safety record during this period). If the carriers found ways to evade the regulations, they had their rights revoked for "willful violations." . . .

At the same time, the Board was conducting a lengthy investigation into the entire question or non-scheduled carriers, with an eye towards granting formal certificates of operating authority to at least some of them. The hearings lasted several years, however, and the uncertainty of the carriers' status during this time made it extremely difficult for them to attract credit. Investors naturally shied away from businesses whose right to exist could be taken away at any moment. As a result, many of the non-skeds, unable to buy new equipment because they had no capital, simply folded. One cannot even imagine the CAB allowing major carriers to go out of business because it was unable to decide what to do about a pending case. Small businesses are apparently expendable; large businesses, no matter how well or poorly managed, are apparently not.

By 1959 Board regulations and rulings—as well as poor management and a lack of market in some cases —had reduced the number of non-skeds to about 25. During the late fifties and early sixties there were a series of court cases and finally a comprehensive federal statute on the subject of non-scheduled carriers. The term "non-scheduled" was replaced by "supplemental." The CAB interpreted the new law as restricting supplementals to charter service only, and in the sixties it issued extraordinarily restrictive rules for operating those charters. One set of regulations allowed affinity-group charters only—to charter an airplane, a group had to be an organization of some sort, thus restricting the benefits of charter travel— to a tiny fraction of the flying public. . . .

The only other source of revenue for the supplementals during the sixties was military business. The military contracts with commercial carriers for a number of its air transport needs. Until 1960 this was done on a competitive-bid basis. The competition for the contracts was severe, and some carriers lost money performing them. After 1960, however, the Department of Defense and the CAB began a new policy that replaced competitive bids with long-run, minimum-rate contracts. As part of their contract obligation, airlines had to pledge to commit a certain number of their planes to the military in case of an emergency. Only a small number of carriers received the contracts. Among the supplementals, the few carriers receiving military contracts profited significantly, but those left out collapsed. . . .

The sixties, then, were trying times for the supplementals. The seventies have brought liberalized charter rules (still restrictive by European standards), but the CAB has limited the number of carriers it allows to fly those charters. Even the few that are certified have a hard time competing against the scheduled carriers, whose size and advertising make them seem more reliable to potential customers—even though they are no safer and no cheaper. The major airlines are also flying charter trips on their own, so they dominate the supplementals' turf as well as their own. And the CAB continues to give the supplementals plenty of trouble. . . .

Universal Airlines was a supplemental that suffered a fate that could not have been allowed to strike a large corporation. Universal had very limited operating rights and found that it was unable to make money. It could not get the CAB to expand its authority so in 1971 it purchased with CAB approval, a failing supplemental, American Flyers, which had the transatlantic rights Universal wanted. While delays in CAB approval caused Universal to lose much of the summer tourist business it needed, it still cornered a good share of the transatlantic market. By 1972, however, when it was in the midst of purchasing a 747, the CAB revoked Universal's transatlantic rights. As a result, Universal went out of business. The CAB had determined that there were too many carriers in the market.

Aside from the question of why the CAB should concern itself with making sure existing airline can make a profit, this case reveals a disturbing situation: the CAB approved Universal's purchase of the debt-ridden American Flyers—a purchase whose sole purpose was the acquisition of transatlantic rights—at the same time it was deciding to restrict the number of carriers in that area. American Flyers' transatlantic authority was, under the rule being developed, an almost certain casualty.

Not only has the CAB put supplementals out of business by the dozens, it has also ignored some seemingly well-qualified applicants and set up obstacles so difficult that many would-be carriers are discouraged from even thinking about applying. Many small airline company owners would like to operate as supplementals, but they see no chance of their applications being approved and they cannot afford to waste the hundreds of thousands of dollars that filing an application would cost. . . .

All this strict regulation stands in sharp contrast to the CAB's attitude towards scheduled carriers. While supplementals have been put out of business after violating CAB regulations once or twice, scheduled carriers have been found to have engaged in massive rebates and kickbacks on tickets in the North Atlantic market; have been found guilty of violating campaign finance laws; have recently been indicted for price-fixing; and have been sued for overbooking passengers. Yet they have never been threatened with an alteration of their operating rights. Non-skeds and supplementals have frequently been forced to shut down by the CAB if they were found to be financially shaky, yet when major carriers are on the verge of bankruptcy, as some have been recently, the CAB and the government scratch their heads to find ways to save them.

The loss at government hands of the entrepreneurs who run small businesses is a tragedy for this country. . . .

was undergoing a period of relative inactivity in which much of their funding was being threatened. The author suggests that in order to ensure the existence of the organization itself, the officials contrived a campaign that pictured marijuana as having major adverse effects on individuals who used it. However, at the time, there was little scientific knowledge to back up this claim.

The welfare bureaucracy, the military, and other government agencies and departments really do not want to go out of business. They have a vested interest in the persistence of the problem they were formed to control or eliminate.

Concentration of Power

Another explanation offered by sociologists relates to a concentration of power in a small number of major institutions having essentially similar interests. Power—the ability to control or command resources (including both material and nonmaterial resources)—is viewed as having become increasingly concentrated in the hands of elites who occupy the top positions in the hierarchies of these dominant institutions. The classic statement of this view was provided by the late sociologist C. Wright Mills:

> The elite are simply those who have the most of what there is to have, which is generally held to include money, power, and prestige. . . . But the elite are not simply those who have the most, for they could not "have the most" were it not for their positions in the great institutions. For such institutions are the necessary bases of power, of wealth, and of prestige. . . . No one, accordingly, can be truly powerful unless he has access to the command of major institutions.[43]

The conception of a power elite is emphatically not a conspiracy theory; it offers, rather, an explanation of the social and psychological similarities and inclinations of those who sit at the command posts of major institutions. There is a community of interest and perspective among the elite that leads to common ways of perceiving and reacting to issues. These exclusive leaders "are mutually dependent upon one another, conscious of their position in society, exercise oligarchic rule, employ methods of selective cooptation in recruitment practices, and are accountable to no one."[44]

The notion of a power elite has stimulated empirical investigations by many scholars. One such investigation has shown that through corporate investments and interlocking directorates, American corporations are effectively controlled by a relatively small number of individuals. Corporate investments enable one corporation to determine the structures and decisions of another by voting its stocks at shareholder meetings. As early as 1955 the top 200 nonfinancial companies directly owned 43 percent of the total assets of 435,000 nonfinancial corporations; these 200 were effectively controlled by a maximum of 2500 persons.[45] Although it is difficult to obtain data of this sort, there are no indications that this concentration has changed significantly in recent years.

A second mode of functioning for the elite is the interlocking directorate, the presence of directors and executives of one corporation on the boards of directors of others. A good case in point is the executive structure of the Chase Manhattan Bank. As of 1970 Chase was the second largest bank in the United States in terms of assets and deposits and had among its 24 directors the directors and/or top executives of six of the top 60 manufac-

turers in terms of sales (1970 rankings). Three of these were the chairmen of the boards of the first, sixth, and eighth ranking petroleum companies. In addition, sitting on Chase's board was the executive vice-president of American Telephone and Telegraph, America's leading corporation in terms of assets. Moreover, many of these members had previously held government office. Among the better-known board members were David Rockefeller, chairman of the board of Chase and brother of the appointed vice-president in the Ford administration; John T. Conner, chairman of the board of Allied Chemical and secretary of commerce under President Johnson; C. Douglas Dillon, chairman of U.S. & Foreign Securities Corporation and a State Department official and secretary of the treasury under Presidents Kennedy and Johnson; and William R. Hewlett, chairman of the board of Hewlett-Packard, a top defense contractor, and partner of David Packard, who served as deputy of defense in the Nixon administration.

Chase's board of directors is not unique; its makeup is comparable to that of other corporate giants. Thus there seems to be some justification for the viewpoint that actions taken by the elite, whether socially beneficial or not, "would not be the result of social control through a formal democratic structure and group participation."[46] That is, the decisions of the elite are not mandated by the great mass of citizens who comprise the base of the power pyramid in American society. This position, still the topic of ongoing debate among sociologists, represents a serious indictment of an economic and political system that is theoretically based on consumer and citizen sovereignty.

How To Reform the Power Elite

The problems of concentration and bureaucratization in business and government and the resultant powerlessness of significant numbers of the population have elicited several suggestions for change. Some proposals relate to changes in corporate policy and structure, and others point to changes in governmental structure and political life. They range from improving the operations of the business and political systems as they exist now to a fundamental reorganization of these systems.

Making the Corporate World Responsible

One suggestion for ameliorating the present situation is that corporations voluntarily devise their own standards of social responsibility. The libertarian school of economics acknowledges that corporations can take steps to improve the quality of life but will do so only if these steps can be justified in terms of increased profits over the short or long run. According to Milton Friedman, this school's most prominent spokesman, "few trends could so thoroughly undermine the very foundations of our free society as the acceptance by corporate officials of a social responsibility other than to make as much money for their stockholders as possible."[47]

Friedman's neoclassic picture of corporate responsibility and the workings of the modern economy is too much of an idealization for many scholars. Daniel Bell, for instance, has noted that the modern corporation is more than just an institution for carrying out monetary transactions; it also has a number of social functions.[48] The corporation must therefore endeavor to strike a balance between its economic role of maximizing profits and its social obligation to contribute to the improvement of the quality of life. Although Bell has provided no formula for arriving at such a balance, he has suggested areas in which corporations should weigh their responsibilities, including minority employment and environmental quality control.

The interlocking directorates described earlier do not necessarily violate current antitrust or antimonopoly laws. As long as direct competitors do not sit on each other's boards or on the boards of suppliers or customers, they may sit on the boards of putatively neutral third parties, such as banks and other financial institutions. It might be possible, through revision of the antitrust laws, to reduce the concentration of power that interlocking directorates make possible.

Critics have noted, however, that antitrust legislation that has been on the books since 1914 could be effective in accomplishing this but that it has never been adequately enforced. Current events suggest one possible reason for this lax enforcement. During the Watergate and related investigations, evidence was revealed that International Telephone and Telegraph made large campaign contributions in return for an agreement by the Nixon administration that a pending antitrust suit against ITT would be dropped.

It was also during the 1972 presidential campaign that the director of one regulatory agency, the Occupational Safety and Health Administration, in order to aid Nixon's reelection efforts, sent a memo to department heads ordering that no new controversial standards that would be costly to industry should be established.[49]

The composition and conduct of regulatory agencies might also be brought under closer scrutiny. Regulatory agencies such as the Interstate Commerce Commission, the Federal Trade Commission, the Federal Communications Commission, and the Securities and Exchange Commission have emerged largely in this century to function in those areas where the interests of government and economics meet and often clash. Designed to impose some limited amount of national control on business and trade so as to protect the public's interest, these agencies, as a result of presidential appointments, quickly fell into the hands of representatives of the private interests they were designed to control. Those with interests in broadcasting are regularly appointed to the FCC, stockbrokers to the SEC, and so on. It is no wonder, then, that these agencies are often accused of doing more to protect private interests than public interests.

Changes in the composition and effectiveness of regulatory agencies appear to be needed and probably can be accomplished only through legislative action. So long as such agencies are virtually unsupervised and so long as American presidents continue to appoint representatives of private interests, public interests will continue to be ignored. Legislation has recently been put forward to create a new independent agency, the Federal Consumer Protection Agency, to represent consumer interests before other government agencies that have regulatory power. Consumer advocate groups have been instrumental in pressing for such legislation, for the consumer's interest is indeed fragmented and grossly underrepresented within federal agencies.

Regulating the Regulatory Agencies

Power to the People

People's lobbies are citizen groups that serve as watchdogs over government and corporations. Groups such as Nader's Raiders and Common Cause search out and collect information on corporate and governmental practices that are injurious to the interests of individuals as consumers and citizens. One spectacular success was Ralph Nader's campaign against General Motors, charging that a certain car was unsafe and that GM was putting profits ahead of safety. Production of that model car was subsequently discontinued.

Such advocate groups represent the public interest through dissemination of information they have collected on corrupt, illegal, or harmful practices. They do this by providing testimony on behalf of consumers and citizens at legislative hearings and, perhaps most effectively, by initiating court action where the public interest is not being served. Significant successes have been achieved, particularly in the area of environmental pollution; environmental impact reports are now required before anyone can undertake a project that might have adverse effects on the environment.

Public interest groups, however, are not looked upon too fondly by more powerful interests in the society. If they were, tax policy might be revised so that recently organized people's lobbies, such as Common Cause and the Center for Responsive Law, would be treated more equitably. Under the present system a large corporation can deduct lobbying as a business ex-

Lasting reminders of the dependence of our economy on the automobile industry, these ribbons of concrete may not, in the final analysis, serve to enhance the quality of life.

pense, but private citizens who donate to a people's lobby that challenges corporate interests cannot deduct this contribution from their taxes.

The technique of the class action suit came into fashion in response to the high cost of court proceedings and the wide-ranging effects of corporate and governmental actions. For instance, automobiles come off the assembly lines in a series. If one auto has a defective brake system, it is likely that the other 9999 in that series will also have this defect. It is also likely that no single purchaser among the 10,000 will be able to afford the court costs to successfully pursue this grievance against the manufacturer. Through the use of class action suits, a consumer organization can sue on behalf of all 10,000. If the court finds in their favor, the manufacturer is obligated to make amends to all.

Until recently, class actions had both direct and indirect effects on corporations. Not only were several cases for product callbacks won, but several more were avoided by voluntary callbacks of defective and unsafe products. Government was just as liable as business to such action. For example, curtailment of assistance programs by administrative fiat or state legislative actions contrary to federal law were successfully challenged by Community Action Legal Services, a branch of the Office of Economic Opportunity. However, recent court decisions requiring that each injured party represented must be individually named have severely limited the use of class action suits. If class action is to continue as a viable technique, measures must be enacted to overcome this limitation.

Revamping Government

Governmental reorganization has been suggested as one means of delivering government back to the people. One proposal involves the return of some decision-making power to states and local government units in an effort to decentralize power. Under recently enacted revenue-sharing legislation, the national government redistributes some of its revenues to state and local governments for the latter to use as they decide rather than in ways determined by Washington. If revenue sharing is to be successful, however, state and local governments must also be made more responsive to citizen input.

The passage of the Campaign Reform Act of 1974 in the wake of the abuses and "laundering" of large contributions during the 1972 election was designed to limit the influence of wealthy individuals and organizations on elected officials. This legislation provided for an overall spending limit of $20 million for any single presidential candidate. A limit of $50,000 was imposed on the amount of their own or their immediate families' money they could spend. In addition, the size of any individual donation to candidates seeking federal office was limited to $1000. In 1976, however, the Supreme Court struck down the first two provisions listed above as infringements on First Amendment rights. As a result of this ruling, there are now no limits whatsoever on the amount of personal or family funds that a candidate can use in election campaigns. There is nothing to prevent a Rockefeller, for example, from spending tens of millions in family money in an effort to get himself elected. In fact, in testimony before the Senate Rules Committee, Nelson Rockefeller admitted that he spent over one million dollars of his own money to win election.[50] Few other candidates possess the resources to match such an effort. Wealthy candidates and candidates supported by wealthy interests still seem to have a significant advantage in election campaigns.

Other conditions of the Campaign Reform Act, such as the contribution disclosure provisions, represent a step in the direction of opening to public scrutiny sources of financial support that had previously been left undisclosed. In addition, presidential candidates now receive matching campaign funds from a public fund comprised of individual contributions of one dollar that can be deducted from one's annual income taxes.

Some argue that piecemeal steps will not resolve the problems. They hold that a more fundamental reorganization of our systems of business and government is needed, a reorganization that could reduce the economic and political domination of the large institutions and enlarge the role of the citizenry in the decision-making processes of government. During the National Democratic Issues Convention in the fall of 1975, serious, pragmatic members of a major political party considered for the first time proposals concerning a planned economy, public ownership of basic industries and worker management of plants, nationalized health insurance, and a program for guaranteed jobs. If one thing is certain, it is that the problems posed by the corporate state are not subject to easy or simple solutions.

Summary

In the past 30 years, the scope of American government has grown so wide, its administration so technical, and its relations with American business so close that the power of citizens to influence government policy, or even to affect the direction of their own lives, has been minimized.

In America the competitive market system has given way to a national economic life dominated by corporations. Corporations were able to absorb suppliers and distributors, thus gaining control over market insecurities. As they became larger, they also became more complex. Specialized technostructures took over each function within corporations, and the specialized knowledge and technical expertise held exclusively by members of the technostructure have served as a basis for the consolidation of economic power.

Corporations once restricted their operations to a single industry, but since World War II they have bought up diversified industries, formed conglomerates, and extended their operations abroad. Relatively few corporations control a large portion of the nation's assets and employ a large percentage of its work force. Multinational corporations, seeking tax havens and special benefits in operations abroad, also have a large potential for influencing American foreign policy.

The size and concentration of American corporations have effectively eliminated competitive pricing and seriously affected consumer choice. Much of present-day industrial production serves product needs contrived by an aggressive advertising program sponsored by industry.

Since the depression the size and scope of government operations have risen to match that of business. At that time President Roosevelt streamlined the government bureaucracy with technocrats. The result was a technostructure similar to that of business, which expanded as the economic and administrative roles of government grew wider.

Following World War II, when the cold war caused American defense expenditures to mushroom, the largest corporation received major shares of defense contracts. Over the past three decades the corporate economy has become highly dependent on government defense outlays. Interpenetration of the business and defense technostructures is typified by the entry into business of large numbers of former military men, who greatly influence the placement of defense outlays and contracts.

Besides expenditures for defense, priorities in government spending tend to go to those projects related to national prestige, such as the space program, and to those that are amenable to technical solutions. In fields such as agriculture, where technology has solved problems of production, government policy maintains attitudes toward distribution based on corporate profit taking rather than on human need.

The attempts of the government to curb corporate abuse of public commodities, such as clean air and water, are tempered by the need to prevent further inflation and to stabilize the economy. Problems that do not readily yield to technical solutions, such as poverty or the improvement of health care, are often downgraded unless political currents demand their solution.

The monetary and organizational power of technostructures in business and government has seriously affected the American political system, which depends on a legislature and executive responsive to citizens. Yet policy decisions have become increasingly dependent on the technical opinions of experts, rather than matters for public debate, and lobbying by organizations with vested interests exists on a large scale—factors that limit the effectiveness of Congress and the executive branch. Lack of institutional response to demands for changes in government and corporate policy has led to public demonstrations and to the formation of consumer movements striving for greater governmental and corporate accountability.

Fundamental value conflicts are in evidence in analyzing the social problems related to the centralization and concentration of power in our society. Elite groups are concerned with maintaining their positions of dominance and with perpetuating arrangements that permit national decision making to be carried out within the exclusive circles of those who occupy the command posts of major institutions. An affirmation of the value of a participatory democratic system and the desire for public accountability often collide head on with the interests of elite groups. In addition, the lack of responsiveness of large-scale organizations can in part be traced to their recent rapid growth, which has outstripped the capacity of existing social mechanisms to regulate their activities effectively.

Theories of bureaucracy explain the present system as the attempt by organizations to perpetuate themselves. Concentration of power theories contend that interlocking directorates between top officials of major corporations and banks, many of whom have served in government as well, place major decisions about social goals in the hands of a small group of powerful people.

Increased social responsibility on the part of corporations has been put forward as one method of alleviating the social effects of business size and concentration. Reform within the regulatory agencies of government to give them greater power to operate in the public interest has also been suggested. Attempts to make corporations and government more responsive to individuals have been the object of consumer movements and legal moves such as class action suits. Moves toward government decentralization, such as revenue sharing, and reforms in the tax system have also been proposed as possible methods for making the corporate state responsive and responsible to the average citizen.

Notes

[1] Alexis de Tocqueville, *Democracy in America,* vol. 1 (New York: Knopf, 1945), p. 55.

[2] Peter Lisagor, "Pollsters Find White House Out of Step with the Public," *Philadelphia Sunday Bulletin,* 2 November 1975, p. 12.

[3] Robert A. Dahl, *Who Governs? Democracy and Power in an American City* (New Haven: Yale University Press, 1961), p. 1.

[4] C. Wright Mills, *The Power Elite* (New York: Oxford University Press, 1959).

[5] Walter Lippmann, "What's Democracy?" *American Government in Action,* ed. Karl M. Schmidt (Belmont, Calif.: Dickenson, 1967), pp. 2–3.

[6] Andrew Hacker, "Power to Do What?" *The New Sociology,* ed. Irving L. Horowitz (New York: Oxford University Press, 1964), pp. 136–145.

[7] Ibid.

[8] John Kenneth Galbraith, *The New Industrial State,* 2d ed. (New York: New American Library, 1971), p. 104.

[9] Howard J. Morgens, "The Profit Motive and the Public Interest." Address to the Advertising Council, New York, 18 December 1973.

[10] Paul Lewis, "Businessmen Ask Curb on Growth of the Government's Interference," *New York Times,* 10 February 1977, p. 57.

[11] Lisagor, "Pollsters Find White House Out of Step," p. 12.

[12] Richard J. Barber, "The New Partnership: Big Government and Big Business," *New Republic,* 13 August 1966, pp. 17–22.

[13] Richard C. Braungart, "Multinational Corporations: A New Agendum for Community Power Research." Paper read at the 25th Annual Meeting of the Society for the Study of Social Problems, San Francisco, Calif., 23 August 1975, p. 3.

[14] Michael S. Kimmel, "The Negation of National Sovereignty: The Multinational Corporation and the World Economy," *Berkeley Journal of Sociology* 20 (1975/76), 91–111.

[15] Galbraith, *New Industrial State,* p. 84.

[16] Barber, "New Partnership," p. 17.

[17] Braungart, "Multinational Corporations," p. 3.

[18] Federal Trade Commission, Bureau of Economics, *Staff Report of the U.S. Steel Industry and Its International Rivals.* (Washington, D.C.: Government Printing Office, November 1977), pp. 51–53.

[19] Seymour Melman, *Pentagon Capitalism* (New York: McGraw-Hill, 1970), p. 22.

[20] Marc Pilisuk and Tom Hayden, "Is There a Military-Industrial Complex That Prevents Peace?" *Journal of Social Issues* 21 (July 1965), 67–117.

[21] Peter J. Freitag, "The Cabinet and Big Business: A Study of Interlocks," *Social Problems* 23(2), 137–152.

[22] Mary Jo Meisner, "OSHA: Del. Seems to Loathe It Less," (Wilmington, Del.) *Evening Journal,* 1 April 1977, p. 7.

[23] Barber, "New Partnership," p. 17.

[24] Pilisuk and Hayden, "Is There a Military-Industrial Complex?" p. 77.

[25] U.S. Department of Commerce, Bureau of the Census, *Statistical Abstract of the United States* (Washington, D.C.: Government Printing Office, 1977), p. 270.

[26] Ralph E. Lopp, "Military-Industrial Complex," *New York Times Encyclopedia Almanac 1970* (New York: New York Times, 1970), p. 736.

[27] Stanley Lieberson, "An Empirical Study of Military-Industrial Linkages," *American Journal of Sociology* 76 (January 1971), 564.

[28] J. W. Fulbright, *The Pentagon Propaganda Machine* (New York: Liveright, 1970).

[29]Pilisuk and Hayden, "Is There a Military-Industrial Complex?" pp. 85–86.

[30]Barber, "New Partnership," p. 19.

[31]Robert L. Heilbroner, "Controlling the Corporation," *In the Name of Profit,* Robert L. Heilbroner et al. (New York: Warner Paperback Library, 1973), pp. 211–212.

[32]Robert L. Heilbroner, "Military America," *New York Review of Books,* 23 July 1970, p. 2.

[33]Seymour Melman, *Our Depleted Society* (New York: Holt, Rinehart and Winston, 1965), p. 33.

[34]David Burnham, "Carter Gets Warning on Cotton Dust," *New York Times,* 1 June 1978, p. 60.

[35]Irving L. Horowitz, *Three Worlds of Development,* rev. ed. (New York: Oxford University Press, 1972), p. 149.

[36]"The New Tilt," *Newsweek,* 20 November 1978, p. 44.

[37]"Contributions, Expenditures for 1972 Races," *Congressional Quarterly Weekly Report,* 22 September 1973, pp. 2516, 3131–3137; "Contributions, Expenditures for 1974 Races," 19 April 1975, pp. 790–794.

[38]Suzanne Keller, *Beyond the Ruling Class* (New York: Random House, 1963), p. 278.

[39]Galbraith, *New Industrial State,* p. 215.

[40]Ibid., pp. 218–219.

[41]Max Weber, *From Max Weber: Essays in Sociology,* ed. H. H. Gerth and C. Wright Mills (New York: Oxford University Press, 1958), p. 216.

[42]Donald Dickson, "Bureaucracy and Morality: An Organizational Perspective on a Moral Crusade." *Social Problems* 16(2), 143–156.

[43]C. Wright Mills, *Power Elite,* p. 9.

[44]Braungart, "Multinational Corporations," p. 6.

[45]Gabriel Kolko, *Wealth and Power in America* (New York: Praeger, 1962), pp. 56–57.

[46]Ibid., pp. 68–69.

[47]Milton Friedman, *Capitalism and Freedom* (Chicago: University of Chicago Press, 1962), p. 133.

[48]Daniel Bell, "The Corporation and Society in the 1970s," *Public Interest* 24 (Summer 1971), 170.

[49]David Burnham, "U.S. Asks Delay on Dust Rule," *New York Times,* 24 May 1978, p. D1.

[50]Herbert Alexander, *Financing the 1972 Election* (Lexington, Mass.: Lexington Books, 1976), p. 397.

Problems of Human and Physical Resources

A society must have both human and physical resources in order to survive. We can afford to waste neither if we are to achieve and maintain the goals of individual well-being and social harmony. And yet we squander both, some deliberately through social policies that benefit only some members of society and others through indifference and a failure to see long-range consequences. Poverty, ethnic and race inequality, sex discrimination, poor health care, neglect of the aged, uncontrolled population growth, and environmental deterioration are all examples of wasting human and physical resources in a society which prides itself upon its exceptional standard of living. Obviously, all do not share equally in that standard of living.

Inequality refers to societal arrangements whereby certain groups or individuals are deprived of equal access to the rewards and benefits of the society. Such disparities stem largely from the system of social stratification. Although stratification occurs in all complex societies, systematic and sustained inequality is perhaps a greater problem in our society because it collides head on with the American ideal of equality for all. This ideal has never been realized in our society, and radically different views are presently held as to whether it ought to be realized and how it might be achieved.

Group conflict, at both the level of values and the level of material interests, is thus a recurrent feature of the problem of inequality. Privileged groups endorse standards of individual achievement and competition and argue that the disadvantaged "get what they deserve." Subordinate groups point to the fundamental contradiction between the value of individual achievement and the practice of systematic discrimination. Efforts by disadvantaged groups to effect a redistribution of power and benefits are met with resistance by groups attempting to defend their privileged position. Manifestations of such value conflict range from litigation in the courts in an effort to break down the barriers to equality to full-blown revolts in urban areas by the members of minority groups.

Poverty, one manifestation of inequality, affects the lives of millions of children and adults and indirectly affects many other segments of society. In American society, where poverty occurs amid affluence unmatched throughout the world, it fosters feelings of personal inadequacy, hopelessness, and despair.

Throughout American history, racial or ethnic origin, as well as sex, has been used as a basis for discrimination against individuals in education, employment, housing, and other important spheres of social life. Since members of the majority, though not necessarily consciously racist or sexist or prejudiced in attitude, benefit from the unequal status of minorities both in psychological and material terms, efforts to bring about social change to alter the position of minorities in society frequently result in conflict.

Inequality is also patently obvious in the area of health care. A disturbingly large number of Americans receive inferior medical attention, are less healthy, and have shorter life expectancies than wealthier, more privileged members of the population. Although one cannot buy health, the quality of health care is directly related to one's position within the socioeconomic structure of our society.

As Americans grow older, the problems of an aging population become more serious. Often faced with declining health, disillusionment and living on a fixed income, the aged have experienced the worst ramifications of a youth-oriented, affluent, mobile society. As their members grow they are acquiring new political power and demanding an end to their inequality.

The experiences of recent years have shown that as the American population continues to grow, certain resources essential to our standard of living will become scarce. Although the increase in the American population has been slowed, it still continues, with nearly 220 million people now living in this country. Worldwide, the picture is bleaker, since the current population of more than 4 billion is going to double in 37 years at the current growth rate. The impact of such population growth is obvious. Even if the world food supply is sufficient to feed such masses, and few believe that it will be, the effect of such growth on the world's resources and ecology may well be catastrophic. Obviously, such potential requires a reassessment of some of our traditional religious, social, and political values, as well as those dictating our consumptive patterns and present life-styles.

Social values and life-styles, political and economic considerations, and scientific and technical findings all come to bear on this set of problems, each adding a new dimension of complexity. How the existence of inequality and deprivation, the growing world population and the deterioration of the environment affect the quality of life and interact to form a cluster of critical problems will be examined in this section.

Poverty

7

Many Americans view poverty as the young regard old age—something that happens only to others, whether individuals or nations. Yet poverty is very much a part of the American scene, a fact hard to believe about the world's wealthiest nation. Poverty is a relative rather than an absolute state. America's poor may not be the emaciated skeletons that arouse horrified pity in newspaper photos of underdeveloped countries, but their plight is often quite as acute, even if less dramatically obvious. The very fact of our national wealth magnifies their condition by comparison. In most other countries, even moderate wealth is reserved for relatively few; in the United States, it constitutes the accepted middle-class standard, which the poor see portrayed as the norm in the media. Their exclusion from this norm has, as sociologists S. M. Miller and Pamela Roby have pointed out, "surreptitiously ushered in the issue of inequality in the affluent society."[1]

Such inequality extends far beyond mere inability to afford the luxuries of life. It generates a vicious cycle in which poor education leads to restricted job opportunity and thus to a reinforcement of low income and a resultant lack of the upward mobility that is one of the prized traditions of the American way of life. Low income also means poor housing, in areas of high crime and inadequate police protection, and comparatively poor health, with limited access to proper medical care.

The poor in this country are a minority, but an appreciable one; in 1976, 25.0 million Americans fell into the poverty category as defined by the federal government,[2] and $16.1 billion would have been needed to raise their incomes above the poverty level.[3]

229

These underprivileged millions represent a problem of some urgency for the entire nation. Poverty spawns a number of social problems, especially in urban areas, where the discrepancy between living standards is more obvious and causes more bitterness and despair. But neither blight nor economic stagnation is confined to the cities. Appalachia has become a synonym for catastrophic and widespread hopelessness, and many similar areas, less well publicized, exist throughout the country.

It is an odd fact that such money as the poor have frequently buys less for them than it does for the wealthy. The poor cannot economize by buying in large quantities. They cannot take advantage of seasonal sales. They have difficulty in obtaining credit; and when they do, they must pay higher interest rates because they constitute poor risks and take longer to repay loans. Finally, the tax structure, which affords the rich loopholes such as oil depletion allowances, depreciation on property and equipment, expense accounts, and numerous other legally deductible expenses, offers no benefits to those in the lowest income brackets.

Although poverty may be considered by some a result of personal failure and inadequacy,[4] it can be viewed more usefully as the product of disorganizing influences in society. American social structure creates and perpetuates conditions that impose unequal economic opportunity on millions of citizens, trapping them in a life of hardship and futility. While education is directly related to income and opportunity, it is not provided equally for all. Automation has been developed and applied without regard for its impact on employment. The American economy is structured in such a way that certain groups are consistently used as pawns to be manipulated for the purpose of economic stability. And, of course, sexual, racial, and age discrimination block opportunities and even exclude many from the chance of earning a decent living.

Poverty, like other types of inequality, is a matter of some groups being denied access to what society has taught them to want and need. It should be seen, then, as the fault of a social system whose institutions do not work equally well for all its members. During the 1960s the nation became increasingly aware of these inequities and the possibility of their developing into highly volatile political issues. Numerous programs were proposed and implemented to eliminate poverty. By the late 1970s the mood had changed and a middle-class movement aimed at curtailing government expenditures in order to fight inflation and make government more efficient became popular. The methods chosen by government officials to balance budgets and curb spending have been those that adversely affect the poor more than other groups. Cutbacks in, or the elimination of, social welfare programs most drastically affect those who can afford it the least.

The institutional responses to the problems of the poor during the 1960s and 1970s have not changed the situation. Although a number of solutions have been suggested and some have been implemented, almost all have failed. Our social system appears incapable of meeting the needs of a large segment of society, a segment that is growing in number every year. With the American economy struggling desperately to solve the problem of inflation and with pressure being exerted on government officials to cut spending, the problem of poverty does not appear to be one that will soon be solved. This chapter will analyze poverty from the social disorganization perspective, since it is a social problem that is created and is permitted to spread due to a failure of the social structure to deal with the needs of particular groups in society.

Poverty as Punishment

Several observers have pointed out a curious American harshness toward the poor. "With the emphasis on the ideology of individualism, a development which paralleled the further growth of capitalism, came not only the positive view of the successful as virtuous but also the negative or critical view of poverty as punishment for those who were not virtuous."[5] This attitude has historical roots. Eighteenth century Americans did not consider poverty a social problem. In their view, society was hierarchical, consisting of a gradation of permanently established classes. The upper classes, composed of the rich, powerful, and educated, required deference from the indigent and ignorant lower classes and in return gave them help in time of need, often on a person-to-person basis. Relief was a local matter and charity a neighborly duty. Little stigma was attached to poverty, which rich and poor alike considered part of the immutable natural law.

The winds of change originated in England in the late eighteenth century, where industrialization was beginning to produce a free labor market as well as unexpected social disorganization. The 1795 Speenhamland law, designed to establish a protected labor market, introduced the concept of the right to live and provided wage subsidies based on a scale calibrated with the price of bread, thus assuring the worker of a minimum income regardless of earnings. The result was a reinforcement of the old paternalistic

Children living in poverty— what did they do to deserve it?

system. The worker had little reason to work or to maintain quality standards. He produced barely enough to earn his minimum and received aid from the community as a supplement.

The Poor Law Reform of 1834 abolished this practice of community relief, substituting instead a publicly maintained live-in institution for the poor, where they were required to labor. Both the principle and abuses of this workhouse system spread to Jacksonian America. The surge of people into the vast western expanses had broken the colonial pattern of communities. The poor were no longer neighbors one had known for years but a group of strangers whose economic situation seemed incomprehensible in view of the New World's unlimited opportunities. It was easy to conclude that their failure and poverty were due to personal flaws—the result of vice or depravity.

The more charitable insisted that these poor people were not depraved by nature but had merely succumbed to too many temptations. Since it was thus necessary to protect them from their weaknesses, the solution offered, as in England, was to concentrate the poor within workhouses or almshouses. There, "for their own good," they were subjected to rigorous remedial discipline in the form of long hours of hard work.

The gap between theory and practice soon became evident. Since most of those assigned to almshouses were not poor due to vice but to ill health, the work regime could not be enforced; the almshouses soon degenerated into degrading human warehouses, largely populated by the remnants of successive waves of immigration. Thus, by the middle of the nineteenth century, the almshouse inmates were doubly strangers to the well-to-do American, who could identify neither with their poverty nor their alien nationalities, and, preferring to ignore the inconvenient, returned to the more genteel practice of private charity.

By the turn of the century the average American citizen's attitude was no longer as simplistic as that of counterparts a century earlier; greater understanding of the complexities of poverty generated new alternatives to institutionalization. Community social workers became active in settlement houses (neighborhood centers that furnished a variety of social services to local residents). Sociologists embarked on studies of the causes of poverty. Journalists popularized the findings of these studies, alerting their readers to the effect of urbanization and immigration, and the resulting hardships, such as disease or the early death of the family breadwinner.

As the country became more urbanized and industrialized, the number

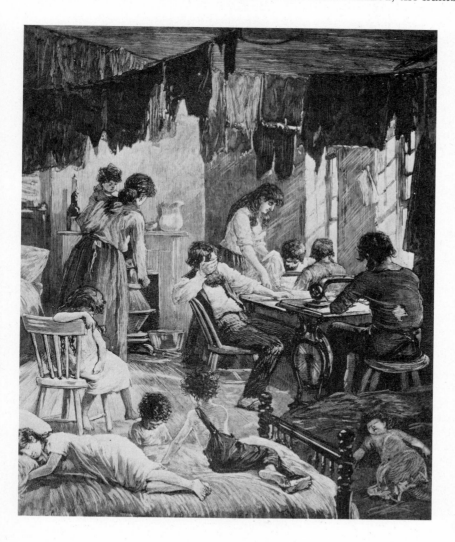

Poverty has always been part of the American picture. Shown here is a nineteenth century family confined to just one room for both living and working.

of jobs available to the untrained poor declined, and the ensuing labor surplus increased with each wave of immigration. In consequence, immigrants became a special concern of socially conscious Americans like Jacob Riis and Samuel Gompers. But much remained undone during the subsequent decades; and suddenly, in 1929, the stock market crash and the Great Depression brought a new dimension to the problem of poverty, adding large numbers to the rolls of the poor and intensifying their difficulties.

During the 1930s Roosevelt's New Deal program gradually reversed the economic catastrophe that had overtaken the country, initiating national government participation in aid to the poor and also changing the nature of public aid; a distinction was made between the unemployable, who received direct relief, and the able-bodied poor, who were put to work on federal projects. Jobs and relief funds were also made available to the states through the Social Security Act and the establishment of the Works Progress Administration (WPA). In addition, the government required employer and employee to assume responsibility for the prevention of hardship; a tax on employers provided for unemployment compensation and a tax on employees established retirement pensions.

With the advent of World War II, the country entered upon a productive period in which poverty all but disappeared from public view. The postwar boom continued into the 1950s, when alternating (and sometimes overlapping) periods of inflation and depression began to weaken the economy. It was at this point, in the 1950s, that poverty once again confronted the nation as a visible major issue.

Yet for many Americans the first major intimation of the fact that poverty had not yet been eradicated came with the publication in 1962 of Michael Harrington's *The Other America*,[6] which did much to explode the comfortable myth of egalitarian society. New dimensions of the situation of the poor were publicized; observers of the sixties described a "culture of poverty"[7] and pointed to contributing factors such as racial discrimination and widespread alienation from middle-class values.

During his brief term in office, President John F. Kennedy initiated several programs to deal with the needs of the underprivileged, both at home and abroad; but it was President Lyndon B. Johnson whose legislative program focused on a national "War on Poverty" and who related the poverty issue to the civil-rights movement. His plans were hampered by the rising costs of an escalating war in Southeast Asia, however, and only a few of his aims were to come to fruition.

In some ways our current thinking about the poor has become sophisticated, although in other ways the old ambivalence persists. This is exemplified in public response to a survey question concerning government spending for social programs. Of those who participated in a recent survey, 46 percent indicated that they would vote for a candidate who advocated increased spending, while 42 percent indicated a preference for a candidate advocating decreased spending.[8]

Many Americans still subscribe to the combination of ideas found in the Protestant work ethic and the American Dream. These concepts suggest that, with hard work and determination, all persons can achieve success. Persons are seen as masters of their own fates and fully in control of their life situations. To avoid becoming impoverished, one only needs to apply oneself fully to the task at hand. Rewards, in terms of climbing the ladder of success, will follow. Belief in these ideas largely ignores an important fact of modern day life, that our fate is to a significant degree shaped by the society that surrounds us. It is also clear that the social system in which we live puts more obstacles and hurdles in the paths of some groups than in those of others. Until these facts are recognized, the harsh attitudes towards the poor and the policies resulting from these attitudes are unlikely to change. In order to provide possible answers to the problems of poverty, it is first necessary to dispel these myths by analyzing what poverty actually is and why it exists. Only then does it make sense to begin the process of designing and implementing programs to assist the poor and to eliminate poverty.

Definitions of Poverty

Poverty, which may at first glance seem a simple and concrete term, is surprisingly hard to define. Many definitions highlight one or the other of its many dimensions; the outstanding common denominator is the implication of "not enough." But, depending on the viewpoint, "not enough" may involve a deficit of essentials, of amenities possessed by the majority, or of luxuries enjoyed by the few—poverty may mean having no food, no TV set, or no yacht.

The criteria are impossibly hard to define. Theorists often make subtle distinctions that combine economics with more abstract components by taking into account the emotional impact that accompanies these deficits. Economist John Kenneth Galbraith, for example, has included in his definition the sense of degradation from which the poor suffer: "People are poverty-stricken when their income, even if adequate for survival, falls markedly behind that of the community."[9]

Some time ago, the federal government adopted the criterion of monetary income as one of its principal yardsticks of poverty and thus established a fixed or absolute definition of poverty. This fixed-income approach defines poverty in terms of specific cash income; but the definition is often unsatisfactory, because it necessitates constant revision in accordance with rising inflation and other economic factors. In the 1950s, for example, Galbraith suggested a poverty line at $1000 cash income per family.[10] This soon became obsolete, and in 1962 Leon Keyserling suggested a poverty level of $4000 for a family of four, with an additional classification for "deprived" families—those with a cash income between $4000 and $9000.[11] This placed 46 percent of the entire population in the poor and deprived group.

None of these proposals were sufficiently objective to provide reliable figures. To remedy this, Mollie Orshansky, a social insurance research analyst with the Social Security Administration, suggested food costs as the principal criterion for a basic standard of living.[12] On an average, a third of family income is spent on food; so Orshansky established the poverty line at the minimum possible amount that should be spent for adequately nutritive food, multiplied by three. By this standard, she calculated that in 1965 approximately 34 million Americans (15 to 20 percent of the total population) were poor. The use of food expenditures as a yardstick of poverty was further facilitated by the fact that standards for acceptable nutrition had already been established by the National Research Council and cost estimates for this nutritional minimum were regularly published by the Department of Agriculture.

A relative definition of poverty considers important factors ignored by the fixed approach. This definition views the poor in terms of the standard of living enjoyed as normal by others in the society. Poverty thus is measured as some proportion of the society's lowest incomes, and it varies as incomes in the society increase or decrease. To determine such a poverty level, Victor Fuchs proposed a statistical measure—the national median family income. Families to be defined as poor are those whose income amounts to less than half the nation's median income.[13] This definition, like all relative definitions of poverty, emphasizes relative inequality rather than absolute deprivation and makes poverty impossible to eradicate in any society.

Presently, federal guidelines for classifying families and individuals as above or below the poverty line do aim to determine sufficient food needed for minimum adequate nutrition.

Families and unrelated individuals are classified as being above or below the low-income level using the poverty index adopted by a Federal Interagency Committee in 1969. This index is based on the Department of Agriculture's 1961 Economy Food Plan and reflects the different consumption requirements of families based on their size and composition, sex and age of the family head, and farm-nonfarm residence. It was determined from the Department of Agriculture's 1955 survey of food consumption that families of three or more persons spend approximately one-third of their income on food; the poverty level for these families was, therefore, set at three times the cost of the economy food plan. For small families and persons living alone, the cost of the economy food plan was multiplied by factors that were slightly higher in order to compensate for the relatively larger fixed expenses of these smaller households.[14]

This fixed-income method of defining poverty, known as the Social Security Administration's poverty index, has been criticized for taking into account only actual current income and for its exclusive reference to food, despite the well-known fact that for many of the poor (particularly blacks and large families) housing represents another critical factor. Nevertheless, using current federal standards, Figure 7.1 shows the percentage of persons falling below the poverty level from 1959 to 1974. In 1976, the poverty threshold was $5815 for a nonfarm family of four, and some 11.8 percent of the country's population fell below this level.[15]

The problem of deciding who the poor actually are is further complicated by the growing list of goods and services once considered luxuries that now are considered necessities. At one time an attempt was made to use the criterion of income balancing expenses in determining poverty levels, but this too proved unsatisfactory; with the increasing trend toward installment buying, income deficits began to show up in high-income families, who could not be considered for relief. Nor is unemployment a reliable index. The Bureau of Labor Statistics data indicate that the median 1975 income of the families of workers unemployed in the spring of 1976 was $10,411, an amount nearly double that of a nonfarm family of four designated as poor.[16]

Despite its shortcomings, the Social Security Administration's index of "poor" and "near-poor" continues to be used in those programs where one criterion of eligibility is income. These guidelines, periodically revised to re-

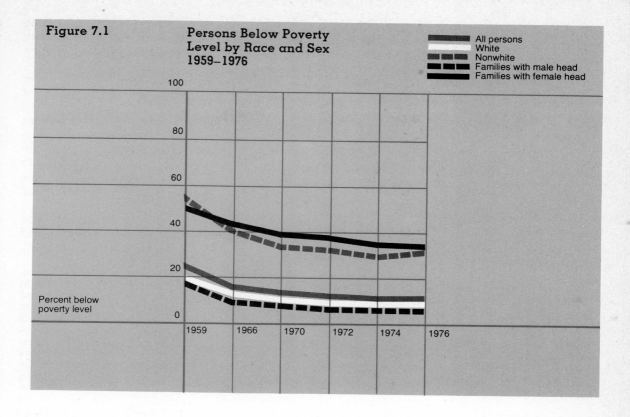

Figure 7.1 Persons Below Poverty Level by Race and Sex 1959–1976

Legend:
- All persons
- White
- Nonwhite
- Families with male head
- Families with female head

Percent below poverty level

100 80 60 40 20 0

1959 1966 1970 1972 1974 1976

flect increases in consumer prices, are also used for other purposes, such as determination of eligibility for allowances and reimbursements, data collection, and various statistical purposes.

Concepts of Poverty

Of all the definitions of poverty, those that consider it purely in economic terms have been found most inadequate. The income-deficit explanation does not, for example, do justice to relative poverty. Its deficiencies become more glaring the wider the framework in which we apply it. Lack of money may be an adequate explanation for the poverty of a welfare recipient who cannot stretch the monthly check to cover rent and food, but it is not equally adequate in explaining the position of the wealthy professional whose temporarily overextended resources delay payment of the $2500 rent on his triplex penthouse.

The poverty of a black mother unable to feed her children is not the same

POVERTY

Every era and every administration has had its own policy. Recommended remedies have ranged from punitive assignments of hard labor to total provision of life's necessities. Yet none has been very effective, and poverty continues to prey on the health and well-being of millions of people in urban and rural America. *This page:* In the 1930s the Great Depression made millions of men destitute, homeless and spiritually broken; President Roosevelt's WPA provided jobs for some 3.5 million persons. *Opposite page, clockwise from top left:* A meals-on-wheels program, one of many that provide hot, well-balanced meals to the elderly and disabled needy; unable to afford adequate health care, this man is receiving aid from VISTA nurses; the "soup kitchen," used by many charitable institutions to feed the poor in the 1930s; President Johnson signs into law the War on Poverty; a New York church distributes food to the poor and needy in the 1970s.

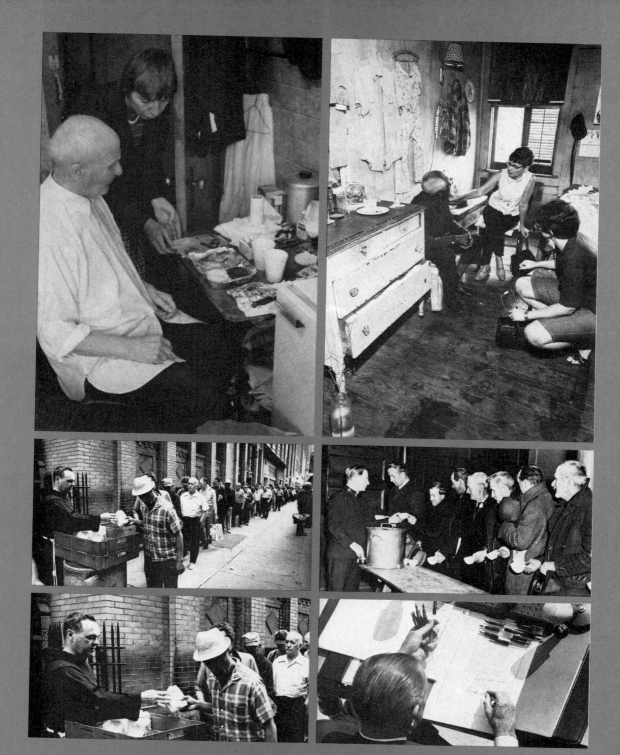

as that of a member of the upper middle class in even catastrophic financial straits, although both suffer from an absence of ready cash. The black mother is destitute; the professional is bankrupt. Destitution is a stepping-stone to nothing but further destitution; bankruptcy has often proved a stepping-stone to even greater fortune, as a number of businessmen have discovered. The enormous difference between these two hypothetical individuals brings us to a concept that has occupied many sophisticated thinkers: inequality. Some of the specific forms and effects of inequality that lend it such sociological importance deserve more detailed examination.

A Culture of Poverty

It was an anthropologist, Oscar Lewis, who studied the structure underlying the state of poverty—the set of attitudes and responses passed down from generation to generation among the poor of the United States and, in remarkably similar form, among the disadvantaged of many other countries.[17] This culture of poverty, as Lewis termed it, emerges because it provides rewards that enable the poor to adjust to their chronic deprivation and resultant despair.

A culture of poverty flourishes predominantly in societies where there is a cash economy, wage labor, and production for profit; a persistently high rate of unemployment or underemployment for unskilled labor; low wages; and a lack of social, political, or economic organization provided to serve the low-income population. Also, the dominant class in such societies normally stresses values such as the accumulation of wealth and property, upward mobility, and thrift, and explains low economic status as the result of personal incompetence or inferiority.

In response to these conditions, the poor adopt a way of life that is typified in the urban and rural slums. It consists of a multitude of interwoven social, economic, and psychological factors. Its perpetuation is natural, too, since children exposed to it from birth learn how to adapt to it very early in order to survive. The culture of poverty is both a symptom and a result of the fact that the underprivileged are denied participation in many institutions of the larger society and that those with which they are in contact often offer punitive rather than supportive experiences. Examples are the public relief system, which provides minimum subsistance at the price of dignity, pride, and privacy; or the police, who are regarded as an authority to run from in fear rather than one to turn to for help.

In fact, although the poor may pay lip service to the values of the dominant society, these values are largely irrelevant in their lives. Common-law unions are better suited than those endowed with the sanctity of legal marriage to jobless men and to women who fear being tied to unreliable providers. Poor mothers are less concerned with their children's legal status than are women of the middle and upper classes; legitimacy is not as important to them as having exclusive rights to their children if they leave the men who fathered them. Nor is the prestige of marriage as important as having exclusive rights to whatever property may have been accumulated.

Absence of financial resources prevents the disadvantaged from participating in many of society's institutions, and for these their own culture has provided substitutes. The poor, for instance, often cannot obtain loans from banks; as a result, informal credit sources are organized within their own immediate neighborhoods, often on a temporary basis.

Indeed, lack of continuity and organization are key features of the culture of poverty, which even extends to the makeup of the family. Discontinuity is visible in the brief childhood the poor have, in the frequent abandonment of wives and children, in a strong present-time orientation, and in the lack of impulse control. The thinking of the poor is not characterized by planning for the future. They know that the future will be exactly like the present; and the fact of having some kind of indigenous culture—the culture of poverty—binds them together as a social group to make that knowledge bearable.

As a conception and as a basis for social policy, the culture of poverty has received severe criticism. Detractors claim that poverty is due to a lack of money, not morals. Some would deny, for instance, that lower-class life resembles a subculture on the grounds that it does not embody a coherent design for living to which the poor subscribe.[18] Others have claimed that rather than simply rejecting dominant social values, the impossibility of achieving them forces the poor to adapt them in order to maintain a sense of self-esteem.[19] Even Oscar Lewis has clarified his position to assert that only one-fifth of all the poor fall within the bounds of the culture of poverty.[20] Finally, acknowledging the implications of the culture of poverty idea for social policy, another observer has pointed out that it places the responsibility for change on the poor, when the major obstacles to change are the economic, political, and social structures that protect the positions of the affluent.[21]

Capitalism Built on Inequality

Traditional theories of poverty tend to attribute it to a flaw in the individual; most recent theories attribute it to flaws in the social system. For socialist Michael Harrington, poverty is the result of our capitalist society's commitment to the wrong priorities. Captialism, he maintains, may have made us the richest country in the world, but it has led to an "affluence . . . so misshapen that it does not even meet the needs of the majority of the people."[22]

Capitalism is an economic system that is based on private ownership of production and requires constant growth and expansion to survive. The goal of profit maximization has relied heavily on the technological developments of recent decades. By decreasing production costs (using modern machines where people once worked) while prices are kept stable, or even raised, profits are increased. But technology does not equally affect all groups in society. The poor have been ruthlessly sacrificed to the technological progress the system has generated; and as technology advances, the number of its victims among the poor continues to grow. The unemployment brought about by technological achievements begins on the bottom rung of the ladder, the struggling blue-collar worker. And, inevitably, unemployment breeds poverty.

While acknowledging that a few reforms have alleviated some of the worst evils, Harrington insists they are stopgap measures that are overwhelmed in a welter of raw problems. In Harrington's view, the capitalistic system itself is the cause of mass poverty, and its continuance is incompatible with the solution of our national problems; relief can come only when capitalism is replaced by socialism. The inequities of capitalist class divisions built into the system are demonstrable in many areas. Harrington cites housing as one dramatic example; he points to the fact that housing shortages for the wealthy are not only improved more rapidly than those of the poor but also at the expense of housing for the poor. The same process is observable in public transportation, education, and the development of affluent suburbs at the expense of the inner cities. Poverty, in this view, is practically synonymous with the inequality upon which capitalism is built.

Poverty Put to Use

Theories have also been advanced that analyze the uses of inequality and, by extension, the reasons for its perpetuation. Sociologist Herbert Gans has isolated numerous economic, social, and political functions served by the existence of poverty to explain the continuance of poverty and inequality.[23]

First on his list of positive functions is the fact that the existence of the poor ensures a labor pool to do jobs that are repulsive, dangerous, underpaid, undignified, or menial. If there were no poor in society, these jobs would be filled only if the salaries were significantly higher than most white-collar jobs. Gans says that poverty functions to provide a low wage labor pool that is willing—or, rather, unable to be unwilling—to perform dirty work at low cost. Given the choice between no work and low welfare payments and this dirty work, the poor are coerced to "choose" these jobs.

The poor do much more than this, though. By acting as domestic workers, they make life easier for their employers and free affluent men and women for a variety of social activities. They ensure the perpetuation of higher-level occupations that either minister to the poor or protect the non-poor against them. The presence of the poor ensures the necessity of jobs for police and social workers. They use up goods that would otherwise go to waste (secondhand clothes and furniture, stale bread). Because they are powerless, they absorb the brunt of the discomfort attendant upon society's growth; land required for renewal projects, expressways, and cultural and educational facilities is usually acquired at the expense of the poor, who have no means to resist displacement. Last, they even help to solidify the present political process by providing the Democratic party with an almost guaranteed constituency.

The situation Gans has portrayed is not appealing. Fortunately, he has also suggested some solutions for it, which we shall discuss, together with governmental and other responses to poverty, in a later section of this chapter.

Who Are the Poor?

Who are the poor? Are they the lazy? Or the immoral? Popular belief would appear to impute a certain disreputability to poverty. The poor are seen by many to be capable workers who are intentionally unemployed, welfare chiselers, loose women, and social dregs in general. Myths of this sort have led to many unreasonable claims. One of the persistent myths, for example, is that the poor are poor because they are too lazy to hold a job. In looking at statistics on the poor, the inaccuracy of this claim becomes obvious. Among families living below the poverty line, 47 percent are headed by women, and most of these women under 45 years of age have dependent children. More-

Miriam Dinerman
Catch 23: Women, Work, and Welfare

Virtually all one-parent families are headed by women. These families are triply handicapped—by child care costs, lack of marketable skills, and wage and job discrimination. They are thus highly vulnerable to poverty. Does it make sense to set for the poorest—those on welfare—a policy goal of economic self-sufficiency?

Ever since the development of the Elizabethan Poor Law, public policy has struggled to separate the able-bodied poor who should help themselves from those who are incapable of self-support and who deserve public aid. In this tradition, the Social Security Act defined three categories of people as eligible for public aid because of their inability to work: the old, the blind, and children deprived of the support of a parent.

Later amendments to the act aided the caretaker parent as well—a further judgment not only that children could not and should not be self-supporting, but also that caring for them was a desirable occupation precluding economic self-support by the caretaker. In 1971 President Nixon proposed "Workfare," a program that formalized a turnabout in policy by requiring caretaker adults to be working or training for work in order to be eligible for Aid to Families with Dependent Children (AFDC). The Talmadge amendments made this policy law for parents of children over 6 years of age.

This article addresses the economic situation of one-parent families with children. There are now three major means of dealing with this issue. The first is alimony or payment of support by husbands as a result of legal or voluntary agreements when marriages break up. This has been a relatively successful device for supporting the mother and children when the father is both affluent and responsible. . . .

A second means is survivors' insurance, which is added to social security coverage to provide for dependents bereft of the support of a breadwinner through death or disablement. . . . Coverage is widespread but not total, and the benefits are least for those with a history of the poorest earnings. . . . The third device is public assistance. Its shortcomings are too [publicly] known to require listing here.

How should our society deal with poor female-headed households—of which there are an ever growing number? Why are so many so poor? Should policies encourage such women to work outside the home? Why do not more of these women work now? Is it lack of will or lack of opportunity? Were such women to work, could they earn enough to support themselves and their families? What social provision is needed, if any, to support work efforts? As more and more women in two-parent families enter the labor market, what can be expected for the heads of one-parent families? What about the children? What about dependence on the public purse? . . .

[There are increasing numbers of one-parent families and of working wives/mothers.] Working women with children are subject to special economic risks; nevertheless, more of them are entering the labor force.

Periodic surveys of the poverty population, which have been conducted since 1960 by Orshansky, document a decline in the proportion of poor families but a growth in the number and percentage of poor female-headed families. . . . Those families least able to escape from poverty—and overrepresented in the poverty population from the start in Orshansky's studies—are female-headed households with children. Current census data show the persistence of this pattern. [Escape is far easier for two-parent than for one-parent families, if young.] . . .

The typical or modal AFDC family has 2.6 children, one of whom is a preschooler. There is no father present in the home. The mother has never completed high school and has had some prior work experience, most likely as a service worker. . . .

Few persons need to be reminded that both poverty and AFDC rolls include disproportionate numbers of nonwhites. This probably reflects the fact that the unemployment rate of nonwhites is about twice that of whites, while the nonwhite family income is about 60 percent of that of white families. [Women have consistently earned about 60% of what men earn even when full-time and year-round workers are compared and even when educational levels are held constant. In 1973, women with less than eighth grade education averaged $4,303 a year for full-time year-long jobs—57% the earnings of men with comparable education.] . . .

Women appear to be at a severe disadvantage in their ability to earn, when compared with men. Black women suffer discrimination twice over and their earnings reflect this, being lower than those of comparable men *and* of comparable white women. . . .

If a woman who heads a household finds employment, she must make provision for the care of her young children. . . .

A mother who has to pay for child care faces an added cost of working. There are variations in cost, quality, availability, and types of child care preferred. . . . For a mother to purchase care for two young children, remain above the poverty line, and not need public assistance, family income *after taxes* would have to range from $6,600 to $9,800, depending on the type of care and the age of the children. How many women who head households can expect to reach such levels of earning?

A look at further date on women in AFDC and female-headed families in poverty is enlightening. More than half of each group have less than a high school education. It can therefore be predicted that they would be likely to attain median earnings of $5,037 a year if fully employed. Since a disproportionate number are nonwhite, this may be an overoptimistic figure. Twenty percent of all AFDC women had eight years or less of education and could look forward to median earnings of $4,300. . . .

The present tangle of policies is truly a Catch 23. Society defines woman's place as in the home, caring for the children, although there are signs of change. The woman is expected to raise the children should the marriage break up. Women are not encouraged to enter the job market since they are paid at just over half the rate of men. As a further discouragement for women to leave their place in the home, little has been provided in the way of alternative child care. Yet women who receive public assistance are held responsible when they fail to find jobs, fail to earn enough, and fail to provide proper child care for their children. . . . As an added irony, employers are not held responsible when they practice discrimination in hiring policies, nor is the economy blamed for its poor performance in generating jobs. In public assistance the goal of attaining or recovering economic self-sufficiency is still retained.

One policy option is to reform the existing program designed to help poor single-parent families. Federalization of AFDC—for which sporadic pressure continues—would at least equalize and, for some, raise the benefit levels as well as make eligibility requirements more uniform. . . . An alternative reform of AFDC would be to make a more fundamental change such as a tax credit or children's allowance, which is seen as a way of supplementing wages for the benefit of children, since wages are based on productivity, not on the number of dependents.

A second policy option is to create a different form of social provision for the one-parent family, recognizing that any one-parent family with young children suffers a considerable handicap in its efforts to gain an adequate income. Increasing the quantity of available child care would be one step in overcoming this handicap. However, it would help only those who already have a capacity to earn more than the cost of such care and other work-related expenses. . . .

Thus one set of policy options suggests increasing the provision of child care—through market, voluntary, or public auspices, or any combination thereof. This alone would affect the work decision of some mothers. Subsidization, a sliding fee scale, or a voucher system could increase the number and range of women able to work outside the home through this option. All variations, however, still leave the actual decision about work to each family. . . .

Another set of options lies in efforts to improve current public assistance policies and the related Work Incentive Program (WIN). It seems wise to assume that few one-patient families can realistically make it without help. . . . For those who do not or cannot work, a simplified cash assistance program might even become administratively feasible to operate. . . .

A more radical option is to redefine the tasks of caring for home and child as work. At the broadest level, any parent engaged full time in the care of children—for example, under the age of 10—would be eligible to receive a socially provided benefit in recognition of society's concern for the nurture of the next generation. This is the implicit rationale for the deduction for dependents granted in calculating the income tax. . . .

A more limited form of this option would be to provide aid solely to one-parent families, in recognition of the particular economic and other difficulties they face in rearing young children. . . .

A final option, but a slow one, is to work toward the ending of discrimination in hiring, promotion, and pay. . . .

Some of the options address the problems of proper care for children and some the ability of women to earn more adequate wages. Both areas are of concern, and clearly many policy choices should be pursued simultaneously. . . .

Our society is now in a period of retreat from social reform defended by the claim that it cannot be afforded. Society can always afford what it considers to be important. . . .

over, the heads of approximately 50 percent of all poor families worked at least some time during 1976. Of these, 45 percent of the male heads worked the full year; and of those who did not work at all, almost 70 percent were either women with household responsibilities or ill or disabled persons.[24] Another group comprising a large part of the poor are those who are forced

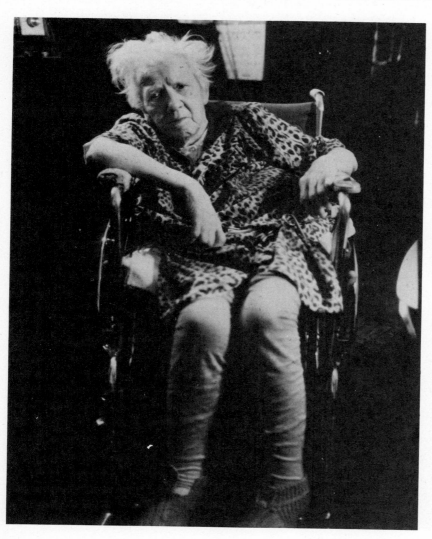

Psychological destitution —a side effect of economic destitution. The aged are often without means and without hope.

to stop working at age 65 or 70. The problems of the poor aged will be discussed in Chapter 10.

Another myth is that the welfare system breeds poverty by positively sanctioning the poor for their plight. This myth further asserts that the economic benefits of the welfare system invite childbearing—that the poor are encouraged to have more children in order to increase the real income and benefits they receive from the state. Contrary to this belief, however, a recent study reveals that women in households receiving public assistance desire fewer children than those in households without public assistance.[25] The implication is that the need for welfare is probably a consequence of an untimely childbirth rather than that childbirth is a consequence of welfare.

For the most part, poverty is not a consequence of personal incompetence; it is a social position into which many fall through personal misfortune. Poverty in America is a social fact, not the result of individual inadequacy. It is an integral part of the social order perpetuated by inequalities in the distribution of wealth, by automation, by discrimination, and by economic conditions over which no individual exercises direct control. The poor are a vulnerable population who, by the fact of their inadequate training and low economic and social status, are more susceptible to the ravages of recession and inflation than most. And this basic condition is not improving significantly.

Although one in five persons (39.9 million) was poor in the early 1960s and only one in eight (25.0 million) is considered poor today, these statistics are not as rosy as they might appear, since most of the improvement they manifest occurred in the first half of the 1960s. Thereafter conditions remained stationary for a few years. Then, in 1970, for the first time since 1959, poverty increased significantly—to 25.5 million, or 1.2 million over

Perpetuating the problem: The limited access of the poor to family planning advice leads to large families and portends more poverty for the future.

the 1969 level of 24.3 million.[26] The cause of this is not exactly known, but economists tend to lay blame on two key factors: the business slump of 1970, which reduced the number of employed as well as total working hours, and the simultaneous 6 percent rise in the cost of living.

The urban poor were the hardest hit. A 1970 analysis of the country's 100 largest metropolitan areas by the Department of Labor's Bureau of Labor Statistics indicated that the overall unemployment rate in poor urban neighborhoods had risen from 5.5 percent in 1969 to 7.6 percent in 1970.[27] Among teenagers in underprivileged neighborhoods, total unemployment rose from 19.9 percent to 24 percent. This rate reflects an increase from 27.9 percent to 35.8 percent for black teenagers and a jump from 13.8 percent to 16.3 percent among whites. In 1971 and 1972 the nationwide unemployment rate continued to fluctuate between 5 and 6 percent. By April 1975, the unemployment rate had climbed to 8.6, leaving 7.8 million people out of work, with the same groups continuing to be overrepresented among the jobless.[28] While the rate had dropped to 7.9 percent by the first few months of 1977;[29] the prospects for the 1980s are not promising. (See Figure 7.2.) The fight against inflation is likely to prevent any drastic improvements in the unemployment picture.

It is interesting to note that despite the overall growth of the economy in past decades, the relative distribution of wealth has remained almost constant. According to the Bureau of the Census, the gap between the rich and the poor remained virtually unchanged between 1947 and 1972; the wealthiest fifth of the population received 41 percent of the national income while the poorest fifth received 5.4 percent.[30] In the same period of time the top 1 percent of the population maintained control over 20 to 25 percent of the nation's total personal wealth.[31] (See Table 7.1 for a picture of the 1976 distribution of family income.)

Where Do the Poor Live?

The geographical distribution of poverty is still in a state of flux, as it has been for much of the second half of the twentieth century. Basically, the underprivileged seeking a better life continue to move from south to north, from rural environment to urban environment, from agriculture to industry.

A process of social reorganization often accompanies the geographical relocation of the poor. In the cities, racial and ethnic minorities usually live in relatively small, encapsulated neighborhoods. The concentration of large numbers of people in run-down neighborhoods breeds a special kind of big-city poverty with distinct characteristics. Crime, drug addiction, and poor mental and physical health are only a few of its components. In the United States, this is especially true of blacks, who bear the country's greatest burden of deprivation and discrimination.

Since the breakdown of the South's agricultural system in the nineteenth century, laborers engaged in agricultural work dropped from 53 percent of the population in 1870 to 27 percent in 1920, and to 5 percent in 1967. Although the poor leaving rural areas are predominantly black, many whites are also moving to the cities—especially farmers drawn there by relatively high wages. The total number of these farm emigrants dwindled during the past decade, but it still amounts to about a million people a year. Between 1959 and 1966 the number of poor farm households declined by

Figure 7.2 Unemployment Rates, 1957 to 1977

Unemployment Rates, 1957 to 1977. Percent of labor force. Values shown: 4.3, 6.8, 5.5, 5.5, 6.7, 5.6, 5.7, 5.2, 4.5, 3.8, 4.2, 4.0, 3.9, 4.9, 6.0, 5.6, 4.9, 5.6, 8.5, 7.7, 7.9.

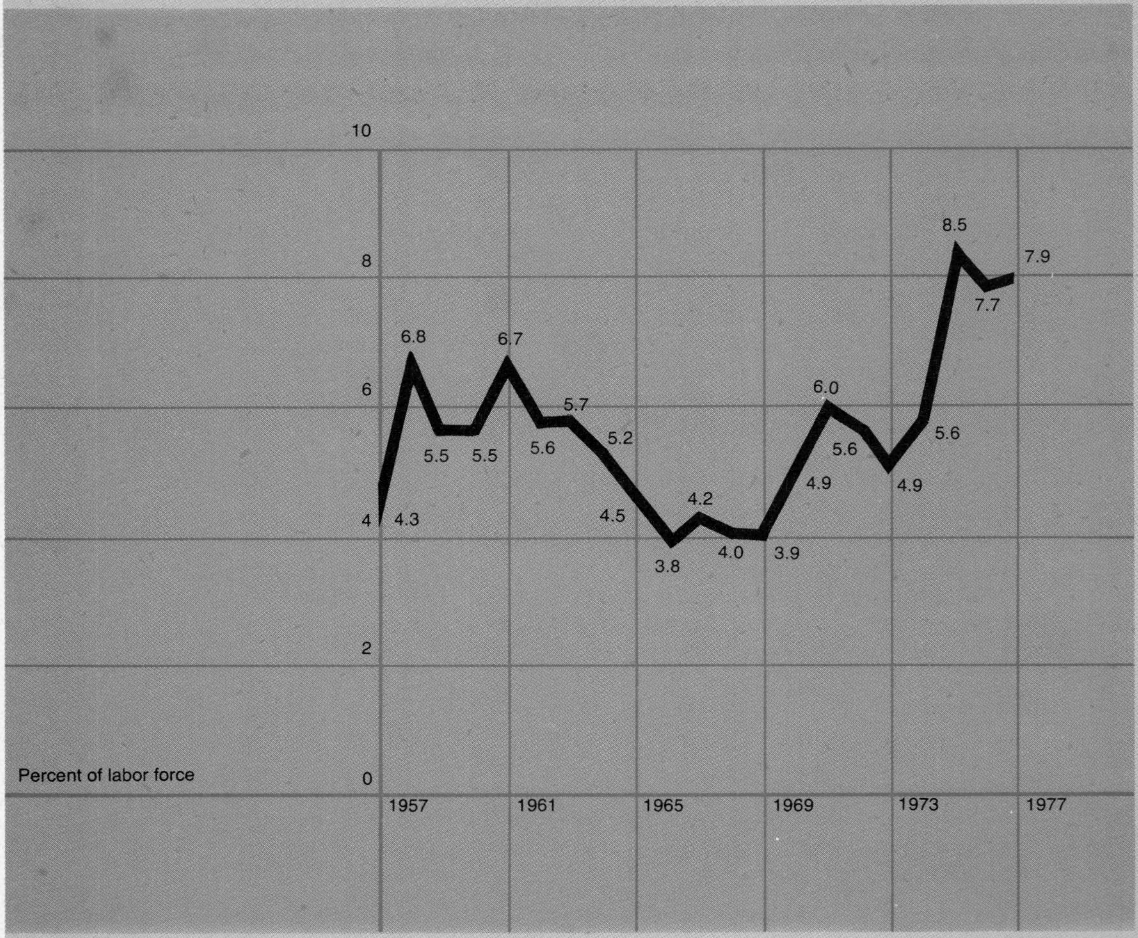

Source: *Statistical Abstract of the United States, 1961–1977* (Washington, D.C.: Government Printing Office).

two-thirds.[32] A sizable group of rural poor consists of tenant farms and sharecroppers forced to leave the land they worked because it was diverted to more profitable uses. Not all those displaced have sought their fortune in the big cities; many settled near their former homes, thus extending rural poverty to the surrounding villages and small towns. A few years ago only 25 percent of the rural poor still lived on farms.[33]

The migrant agricultural workers are perhaps the most disadvantaged of the rural poor. Their plight is described in an account published in the *New York Times*, which details the treatment of migrant black field crews hired to pick the crops on the large tomato plantations of southern Florida.[34] The workers on one plantation not far from Miami were promised the standard

	All Races	White	Nonwhite
		Percent Distribution of	**Table 7.1**
		Family Income by Race, 1976	
Under $3000	3.9	3.1	9.6
$3000–4999	6.5	5.3	14.9
$5000–5999	3.9	3.6	6.0
$6000–6999	3.9	3.7	5.8
$7000–9999	11.8	11.5	14.4
$10,000–14,999	20.2	20.5	19.2
$15,000–19,999	19.1	19.7	13.9
$20,000 and over	30.7	32.6	16.2
	100.0	100.0	100.0
Median income	$14,958	$15,537	$9821
Percent with income under $5000	10.4	8.4	24.5

Source: U.S. Bureau of the Census, *Statistical Abstract of the United States, 1977* (Washington, D.C.: Government Printing Office, 1977), p. 440.

field hand wages of 25 cents per 25-pound "lug" of tomatoes picked, payable on a weekly basis, except for two dollars given out daily for food. Although they worked ten and a half hours a day, the workers never received any wages, on the grounds that these were "owed" to the crew boss for room, board, transportation, and other expenses. Such procedures are by no means rare in Florida and other states employing migrant labor.

Barred from adequate education, health care, and any hope of future prosperity or success, the poor grow up in a discriminatory, punitive, debilitating environment.

The poverty of the rural South is old, deeply rooted and continues to exist. This large family shown standing outside their small house is representative of millions whose plight is often worse than that of the urban poor.

The problem of migrant poverty may be more severe in the Southwest, where many Mexican-Americans labor in the fields under horrible working conditions for minimal wages. Many are forced to spend the time from early spring to late fall of every year traveling from state to state planting, hoeing, and harvesting the various crops. The actual number of days they work is small relative to total working days possible. The housing that they are forced to live in is usually deplorable, as are the health and sanitation conditions around them.[35] Although earlier attempts to unionize these workers were crushed, some progress was made in the 1970s. Yet, the general conditions have not changed significantly.

Responses to Poverty

Although the Kennedy administration had already instituted a number of poverty relief measures, it was Lyndon Johnson who in 1964 declared "unconditional war on poverty in the United States" as part of his plans for the Great Society.[36] Many factors were involved in the creation of this war. Robert Haveman suggests that at least five forces were present:

. . . compassion stemming from abysmal hardship evident in pockets of the population identified by geography, culture, and race; embarrassment over the inconsistency of this hardship with the image of U.S. affluence; fear regarding the potential for violence and disruption inherent in such inequality; excitement stimulated by the call for progressive new policies by an administration with "liberal" inclinations (or at least rhetoric); and faith in the efficacy of social planning stimulated by social scientists and other academics whose public respect and influence was at its zenith.[37]

Governmental aid programs undertaken by the Johnson administration can be divided into four general categories: human resources development, social insurance, cash-income support, and income-in-kind. President Johnson's orientation favored the first type, programs that gave the poor the opportunity to help themselves rather than keeping them in perpetual bondage with "handouts." The preamble to the Economic Opportunity Act passed in August 1964 explicitly stressed the "opportunity for education and training" and the "opportunity to work," which was to be made available through the Office of Economic Opportunity (OEO).[38]

The OEO began with an allocation of $784 million; by 1972 its budget had risen to a high of $2.4 billion, declining to $1.6 billion in 1974.[39] These sums financed a great variety of programs. The Job Corps for men and women between 16 and 21, the Neighborhood Youth Corps for teenagers, the Work Experience Program for the unemployed, and the Adult Basic Education Program all provided vocational training or part-time employment. The Rural Loans and Small Business Loans Programs provided loans to farm families and small businesses, many owned by members of minority groups. The Community Action Program, the most extensive and most controversial of the OEO programs, gave financial support to local authorities for projects such as day care, remedial education, consumer education, legal aid, birth control programs, and aid to the aged. Migrant programs guaranteed to migrant workers basic necessities, such as housing and child-care facilities. The Volunteers in Service to America, better known as VISTA, was a kind of domestic Peace Corps, in which volunteers ranging in age from 18 to 80 worked on Indian reservations and in hospitals and institutions for the mentally ill, schools, urban and rural slum areas, and migrant labor camps. Head Start was a program designed to prepare disadvantaged preschoolers for regular school attendance through early education, medical care, and nutritional aid.

In addition to its major activities, OEO also ran a number of more modestly funded "special emphasis programs." The impact of OEO's Legal Services Program was considerable. Because generations of discrimination have taught the disadvantaged to distrust the legal system and its representatives, a major function of this program was the restoration of faith in our system of justice among the poverty-stricken.

The Legal Services Program was specifically designed to give the poor access to reliable legal help. It operated law offices in low-income neighborhoods all over the country, and its qualified lawyers gave assistance to numerous indigent clients. The cases handled ranged from the settlement of domestic difficulties to the successful challenge of an eviction regulation. In fact, the lawyers of the Legal Services Program actively looked for precedent-setting cases that might help to eradicate some of the inequities to which the poor have been subject. They brought suits against cities, public officials, and even OEO itself.[40] The program's educational activities gave the poor a working knowledge of the legal structure and acquainted them with their rights as citizens. Through cooperation of Legal Services lawyers and local civic groups, nearly two million people received a basic legal education.

The OEO Family Planning Program (the subject of some controversy in its early years) was added to the group of special emphasis programs in 1969. In addition to its educational functions, it provided birth control devices. These were formerly supplied only to married women living with their husbands, but policy was changed to make them available to all women.

The Office of Economic Opportunity and its local community action agencies (CAAs) constituted the first network of public agencies exclusively devoted to making a concerted attack on the whole range of problems of the underprivileged. Its system of coordination, involving federal, state, local, public, and private agencies, was designed to end fragmentation and to ensure the availability of help to all who needed it. To cite one example, its program of coordinating manpower services involved state employment services, who sent counselors to neighborhood centers to provide information on job finding. In addition, the Labor Department placed its own coordinators in the major cities to urge the state employment services to develop outreach programs of their own and to give special help to the hard-core unemployed. Out of these joint efforts developed the Concentrated Employment Program (CEP), whose purpose was to bring all manpower services under a single administration. In 1966 the same concept was used for the model cities program.

It should be expected that enterprises as numerous and far-reaching as those of OEO would include failures as well as successes. Nor are its accomplishments easy to assess, in view of the political controversy that has surrounded it. Initiated by a Democratic administration, it was widely rejected by Republicans and also aroused opposition among some southern Democrats, who feared that the programs might accelerate racial integration. President Nixon, opposed to both the philosophy and the programs of OEO, managed to reduce the agency's power by halting many of its activities or transferring them to more traditional government departments. By 1974, OEO was being phased out of existence when Nixon's budget allocated no funds to the agency for the following year.

Social Insurance Programs

Income maintenance and public assistance programs were established during Franklin Roosevelt's New Deal. Among these, the most important and comprehensive was social security or, officially, Old Age Survivors, Disability, and Health Insurance (OASDHI). Although the various programs that are part of the Social Security Administration are federal, state governments also participate in many of them and often provide supplemental benefits. Benefits are generally of two types, either cash transfers to the indigent in the form of direct payments or indirect payments for goods and services.

Cash income support programs include aid to the aged and disabled, old age assistance, veterans' pensions, and aid to families with dependent children (AFDC). AFDC is by far the most frequently criticized category of public welfare, since it allows no payment to families where a man is present.

The result in many cases has been involuntary desertion by husbands unable to work for as much money as welfare gives their wives when they are no longer part of the household. Income-in-kind programs, which provide assistance in obtaining essentials such as food, housing, and health care, include the Food Stamp Program, the Commodity Distribution Program, and Medicaid, which provides medical care for welfare recipients.

Social security is both the largest and the most successful of the income maintenance programs, since it serves two functions. Although designed as an income maintenance system, it actually provides more cash assistance to the needy than does public assistance; 35 percent of social security benefits go to poor households.[41]

Income maintenance and public assistance programs were expanded during the War on Poverty. The principal difference between the older assistance programs and those administered by OEO was in their orientation; the former were designed to alleviate "insecurity" rather than to remedy poverty and tend to benefit people with sudden economic reverses—not the chronically poor. In the words of economist James Tobin, "There is no unemployment compensation for the man who has never had a job, no OASDHI payment for the man with an insufficient history of covered employment."[42]

As Tobin indicates, the group most difficult to reach and most difficult to assist once reached consists of those known as the hard-core unemployed. Private enterprise personnel departments exist for the very purpose of screening out members of this group, which includes "undesirables" who lack education and experience, are high insurance risks, or have police records.

In 1968 President Johnson appealed to the business community to liberalize its hiring policies by hiring the hard-core unemployed, and a number of business leaders responded. Henry Ford II organized the National Alliance of Businessmen, which, in turn, organized the private jobs in a business sector program known as JOBS. Major employers in 50 large cities reacted to the program more favorably than was expected. Within six months, 165,000 new permanent jobs had been set up and approximately 40,000 filled, not including the 100,000 teenagers for whom summer jobs were found.[43] However, the number of jobs fell far short of the goals that had been set and the actual amount of training accomplished under the program appears to be minimal.[44] The recession and resulting high unemployment of the 1970s, however, has undermined progress in this area of need, and chronic unemployment continues to be a major poverty problem.

In order to be effective, aid programs must motivate the poor to help themselves. Attempts to organize the poor for action on their own behalf have been problematical, probably due to the twin handicaps of lack of education and poor health. Nonetheless, several private groups, usually headed by members of the particular diasdvantaged segment which they serve, have had some success.

One of the most active is the National Welfare Rights Organization (NWRO), which concerns itself with the improvement of the public relief system. Its primary objectives are the elimination of restrictive eligibility

The Organized Poor

requirements and the education of welfare recipients to safeguard their rights. For example, it organized a successful campaign in New York City to ensure that welfare clients received special grants to which they were entitled but which they usually had not received. Another group, the Poor People's Campaign, which grew out of Martin Luther King's Southern Christian Leadership Conference, has been less successful, probably because its concerns have ranged so widely, from hunger in Mississippi to protecting Indian hunting and fishing rights in Oregon.[45]

The long overdue organization of farm labor was realized in the early 1970s when the United Farm Workers Organizing Committee signed contracts with most of California's table grape growers. Largely responsible for the unionization of the California grape pickers was Cesar Chavez, a Mexican-American who gained national prominence in 1965 for his efforts in behalf of the farm workers. An admirer of Gandhi and dedicated to nonviolent struggle, he obtained union recognition for the California grape pickers by means of fasts, strikes, and the promotion of a national grape boycott. Since then, the lot of farm workers has improved in California, but this improvement has not yet spread to other areas. In many parts of the country agriculture still employs child labor. Farm labor has the third highest rate of work-connected deaths, and the migrant farm worker's average life expectancy is only 49 years.[46] It is possible, however, that Chavez's organization of the grape pickers will affect other segments of the agricultural labor force.

In the long run, the actions of the organized poor will immediately affect the government's responses to continued poverty. In the next pages we will evaluate the progress of government programs to date and take a look at what remains to be done.

Outlook for the Future

Almost anyone concerned with governmental programs to aid the poor agrees that they are in need of some revision, but there is great disagreement about the changes to be made. James Tobin has listed seven principal failings of the present public assistance system: inadequate coverage, anti-family incentives, inadequate benefits, incentives for uneconomic migration, disincentives to work and thrift, excessive surveillance, and inequities.[47] In his view, some of these defects could be eliminated by imposing nationwide standards of benefits and eligibility on the states, but a more far-reaching and economical move would be to establish a system totally financed and administered by the federal government.[48]

Even the most successful of the income maintenance programs—social security—could still be improved. Henry J. Aaron believes that the system could be altered to make it more efficient as a means of reducing poverty without lessening its value as the "basic retirement system" of the majority of Americans. He opposes raising benefits across the board to accomplish this and suggests instead that the poor would be better served by being freed from payroll taxes and by having their benefits determined not by the earning history of the worker but by that of the family as a whole.[49]

Nathan Glazer
Reforming Work Rather than Welfare

. . . some analysis of how we might go about dealing with the unpleasant reality of our very large population of welfare families is surely in order.

Discussions of welfare by those who politically are in the center or on the left generally take it as a cardinal principle that there is not and cannot be a relationship between work and welfare. . . . By now, however, the effort to set up an impenetrable barrier between work and welfare—part of the design of the original system—has clearly broken down.

Initially, the barrier seemed to stand firm. On the one side, according to the social security design of the 1930s, were those whose entitlement to an adequate income in the absence of work was based on contributions made while they had worked: Thus workers would receive social security when they retired, their wives and children would receive social security if they died or became disabled, and they were to receive unemployment insurance when they became unemployed. Welfare was to be a residual system, one that would decline over time as individuals gained access to work-related insurance. As we know, though, it didn't happen that way.

At the time the welfare system was first set up, the barrier may not have been considered a crucial feature, for it was not likely that welfare would be considered more desirable than work if such a choice existed. But as welfare benefits in large Northern states began to rise, welfare became an attractive alternative to work. . . .

There is a real dilemma here: The costing out of welfare benefits amounts to a great deal in public funds, but the satisfactions given by this sum to the welfare recipient do not match the satisfactions given by an income of the same size that could be freely spent. Thus we have a classic "no-win" situation, in which the welfare recipient feels she is not getting much, and the public feels it is paying out too much. But leaving this issue aside, the fact is that a welfare recipient would have to earn a substantial income to match what welfare gives.

The first problem, then, with the design of the im-penetrable barrier is that the attraction on the welfare side began to build up in the Northern and Western states, threatening an influx from the work-supported side.

The second problem was that the social distinction between those who should work and those who shouldn't began to break down. Women with young children were once not expected to work. This was not true in the South, where black women were expected to work whether they were mothers or not, and whether they had pre-school children or not, and their scanty welfare grants recognized that they would be supplementing their income through work. But in the North, a universalistic ethic and expectation prevailed, covering both black and white women: Mothers of young children should stay home to take care of them. We are all aware of the breakdown of this expectation. . . .

The third problem that developed is that the number of welfare families without male earners began to grow rapidly in the Northern and Western states in a time of relatively full employment and job availability, and this led to great concern that the welfare system was leading to the breakup of families. . . . Family breakup affects the barrier between work and welfare in a significant way. The decision whether to work or spend full time raising her children is considered by welfare authorities to be the prerogative of the mother, and the pressure on welfare mothers to work is not great, despite the rising number of working mothers in the population as a whole. But what of the men who were the fathers of these children, who may leave or are thrown out *because* of welfare? Should not the monetary returns from *their* labor support their children?

Thus the distinction between those who could not work and those who could, which the social security design of the 1940's had assumed was neatly drawn, has become complex and obscure, confusing and confounding all efforts to reform the welfare system.

For if there is a close inter-relationship between work and welfare, to improve the conditions of those on welfare—and in many states and in many respects one can make a very good case for improving their conditions—means to increase the incentives for crossing from the work side to the welfare side. . . . The key issue, as we learned again and again, was that to reduce income-tested benefits as returns from work rose meant in effect to tax returns from work so heavily as to make it economically unattractive. And we could no longer, by the late 1960's, count on traditional social or cultural pressures to make work more attractive than welfare. . . .

As a result, we in the United States are unique among developed nations for the enormous number of mothers and children that we support on welfare, that is, on a system of grants based on need and not linked to work or work effort. This is an unpleasant situation to be in. What, then, can we do about it?

I would like to suggest a line of thought which creates far more difficulty than reforming welfare, but which offers far more promise: Let us leave welfare where it is, and try to make work—the kind of work that people on welfare, or the fathers of children on welfare, might take—more attractive. . . .

. . . one benefit that comes with welfare is free health care. We have recently been faced with the ironic problem of those who, in losing their jobs, have also lost their health insurance. The problem of instituting universal health insurance so that in this respect work becomes as attractive as welfare is no simple one. Enormous as the problem is, we cannot ignore the fact that it has been solved—at least in its large dimensions—in most other developed countries, and in this respect every worker in those countries, no matter how humble, is not at a disadvantage compared to those who live on welfare or its equivalent.

A second approach to making work competitive to welfare would be to introduce in compensation for work a component related to the number of children. We do not want to confuse the workings of the market by saddling employers with the need to compensate workers with more children better than workers with none or fewer children. But most other developed nations have dealt with this problem by attaching to compensation for work a children's supplement or allowance that comes from national insurance funds. . . . We could relate children's allowances directly to wages—more than one earner in a family could divide the allowance for dependent children—or we could make them available to any head of family, whether he or she worked or not. . . . The aim would be not only to provide assistance to those with larger families, but to give value and meaning to work, because it is through work that this assistance comes.

These are perhaps the two clearest means by which the second-rate job can be made closer in worth to the first-rate job. For other possibilities the answers are less clear. Can we provide unemployment insurance for every job, even casual labor? Could we provide a one-month vacation for all such jobs, so that some of the leisure that comes with welfare could be attached to work? Could the regularity of return offered by welfare be ensured for jobs that are casual and insecure?

This is not a complete program to make poor jobs more competitive with welfare. These suggestions—universal job-linked health insurance, job-linked children's allowances, making jobs more secure and steady—are only meant to begin discussion, and to turn around our way of thinking about these problems. We have concentrated too much on improving or reforming welfare or on simply redistributing income without relating it to work. . . . We have recently seen a sign of what I believe is a better approach—the rebate to all earners of low incomes of a proportion of their earnings, to be taken from income tax if they pay it, and from the Treasury if their income tax is not large enough. This is the kind of approach to income redistribution we should find attractive. It goes to the poor, it is related to work, there is no incentive in it of any kind to prefer welfare to work, and there is a positive incentive in it to find work more attractive, for you are getting more than your wages if they are very low. . . . Presumably our ingenious economists will find some drawbacks in this scheme, but Congress' move to rebate some part of earnings and taxes for low-income earners is a step in the right direction. . . .

Perhaps the time has come when, instead of new studies of welfare reform, we should have a commission on low-income and low-benefit jobs, and consider how we may upgrade them.

Excerpts reprinted with permission of Nathan Glazer from "Reform Work, Not Welfare," *The Public Interest*, No. 40, Summer 1975. Copyright © by National Affairs, Inc.

In 1966 President Johnson's Council of Economic Advisers suggested a negative income tax as a means to reform public welfare. The concept is not new; it was proposed in the 1950s by economist Milton Friedman, who was troubled by the effect of fluctuating earnings on income tax.[50] Because of graduated tax rates, people with inconstant yearly incomes pay more taxes, in the long run, than people who earn an equivalent income in unvarying annual sums. The system is most detrimental to the poor.

Friedman's system of negative income tax would redress the balance by having the worker pay the government taxes during the worker's good-income years and the government pay the worker during the worker's bad-income years. This latter payment—from the government—is what is meant by the term *negative income tax*. Later Friedman incorporated the idea of permanent treasury payments to persons who never achieved positive income brackets. Negative income tax payments would be reduced if the worker's earnings increased, but they would never decrease to the point where increased earnings would become financially undesirable.

Among the negative income tax's advantages are its simplicity and the relative ease with which it could be incorporated into the present tax structure. Its drawbacks include the cost and the probability that it would have to subsidize some of the nonpoor in order to maintain incentives for work.

During the late 1970s and into the 1980s, it appears that the primary attempt at ameliorating the problem of poverty will be through reform of the welfare system. There are few people who suggest that welfare programs are working well in their current state. The present system not only imposes a grave financial burden on governments at all levels but is also open to abuse and corruption. The Carter administration submitted the Program for Better Jobs and Income (PBJI) to Congress in 1977. The Program has undergone a series of major revisions but the core of its proposals, a comprehensive overhaul of the welfare system, remains intact. Though there is likely to be much debate and compromise over PBJI into the 1980s, certain key elements will probably remain.

If poverty is to be overcome and those capable of working are to be self-supporting members of society, jobs must be available. When the economy is expanding, the lack of job opportunities is not a severe problem. In no-growth periods or during recessions, this becomes a severe problem, especially for the chronically unemployed, the young, and the economically marginal. Since the New Deal era, the federal government has periodically provided job opportunities for out-of-work men and women during periods of high unemployment. This has been done through tax incentives for private industry (thus encouraging expansion) and through public works projects. Since the former method of stimulating employment is unpredictable, public works projects of various sorts have become the more popular alternative. Increasingly, private citizens and public officials are coming to believe that employment is a basic right and that the federal government is responsible for guaranteeing it.

The Carter administration's proposal called for the creation of 1.4 million public service jobs. This aspect of the program would fall far short of guaranteeing a job for all unemployed persons capable of working, but it is more popular than simply increasing AFDC or food stamp expenditures. Wages for these jobs were projected at $3.72 an hour for 1981, a figure that would permit a worker to have an adequate standard of living ($7700 a year) but would encourage the search for higher paying jobs elsewhere. The jobs would be in the areas of building and repairing recreation facilities, child care, school paraprofessional assistance, and home services for the elderly and ill.[51]

For those persons who are unable to work or who are unable to find work, cash benefits would be continued. All persons below a certain income level (based on the size of the unit) would be eligible for assistance if they were classified as Not Expected to Work (NETW). The blind, the aged or disabled, and single parents with young children would be listed as NETW. All persons who were classified as Expected to Work (ETW)—single persons, childless couples, and one adult in two parent families—but could not find jobs or who had incomes below a certain level would also be eligible for cash payments.[52] The benefit proposals would be set at $4200 for a family of four, a figure still below the federally established poverty level.[53]

Federal Responsibility

Whatever the outcome of the Carter administration's proposals, it is clear that the federal government will have to assume more responsibility for helping the poor if progress is to be made. Although the three levels of government—federal, state, and local—now share fiscal responsibility for many programs designed to provide subsistence and upgrade the skills of the poor, the unequal ability of states and cities to collect taxes makes their future role doubtful.

Cities of all sizes obtain about 85 percent of their revenues through property taxes, whereas states depend largely on sales taxes, from which more than 60 percent of their revenue is derived. Since the poor must spend a much larger proportion of their income than the wealthy, sales taxes are far more punitive for them than for the rich, and are therefore called regressive taxes. The federal government, on the other hand, obtains two-thirds of its income from socalled progressive income taxes, which are graduated in relation to income. The federal income tax structure is in need of revision to eliminate inequities, but it is still fairer to more citizens than are sales and property taxes. In addition, the federal government has a much more effective machinery for collecting revenues than either the states or the cities.

A greater federal role in subsidizing the poor would ease the strain on financially beleaguered states and cities and could be funded, at least in part, by general tax reform. Plugging tax loopholes that allow the wealthy and corporations to escape paying billions of dollars in taxes each year would allow greater revenues for services to the poor. Through revenue sharing, described in Chapter 5, federal allocations for such services can be returned to local areas and administered by those closer to the problems than federal officials.

Eradicating Inequality

No treatment can be effective unless the nature of the ailment has been correctly identified. A crucial aspect of the persistence of poverty that has been given little consideration until recently is the social inequality it demonstrates. In the final analysis, eradication of poverty depends on and is almost synonymous with the eradication of inequality. It is high time, as Herbert Gans has pointed out, "to start thinking about a more egalitarian America, and to develop a model of equality that combines the traditional emphasis on the pursuit of liberty with the newly emerging need to reduce inequality."[54]

The evidence suggests that equality of opportunity cannot be a reality until all those who want opportunity are equally able to compete—held back neither by poverty-induced poor health nor lack of access to sufficient education to make them truly competitive. Under our present system, two individuals of different backgrounds but equal competence in shorthand and typing may, indeed, compete for a secretarial position; but preference will almost invariably be given to the well-groomed, well-spoken, well-educated candidate.

Methods for achieving equality have usually been collectivist, with public institutions replacing private ones as the agencies responsible for the allocation of resources. The nationalization of industry is one such method that would bring about greater equality. Because such methods could result in benefits and enrichment for officials and restrictions on the liberty of the ordinary citizens, Gans has suggested that America develop an individualistic model of equality. Such a process is complicated but feasible. It assumes that citizens are not yet ready to repress selfish desires for the public good. Instead of nationalizing industry, this model calls for a more widespread distribution of stock among the public. There would be greater equality in income but not a total equality. This would provide an incentive for individuals to strive to work harder. It also calls for a governmental bureaucracy more responsive to average citizens than to pressure groups, and for an economy in which corporations are more accountable to consumers and the public. Although some liberty would have to be surrendered in favor of greater equality, public debate would determine how much liberty should be given up in exchange for which kind of equality (social, economic, racial, or sexual).[55]

Gans has made detailed proposals for the implementation of these radical changes. But the greatest incentive lies in a point he has touched upon only tangentially: the possibility that such total restructuring toward equality would benefit the well-to-do as much as the disadvantaged, because in it lies the hope of curing the current American malaise—the poverty of spirit, with which we have all become afflicted.

Summary

Poverty is a prominent part of the American scene despite America's position as the world's wealthiest nation. The acceptance of moderate wealth as the norm in America magnifies the deprivation suffered by the poor. The American economic system, which favors the rich, prevents the condition of the poor from improving significantly.

From the social disorganization perspective, we can see that the extent and nature of poverty in America is a product of decades of rapid social, political, and economic change. Automation, discrimination, and the maintenance of extreme inequalities in the distribution of wealth are conditions that create a large vulnerable population increasingly susceptible to recession, inflation, and unemployment.

Americans look at the poor in an ambivalent way. On the one hand, they believe achievement is directly related to effort and tend to blame poverty on the poor. On the other hand, they recognize a disparity in opportunity and seek methods to help.

Defining poverty is difficult. Most definitions imply that the poor are those with "not enough." The government defines the poor as those with "not enough" monetary income. The fixed-income approach defines the poor in terms of specific cash income. The relative-income approach defines the poor in terms of the standard of living enjoyed as normal by others in the society. Defining poverty in this fashion labels the poor. It can seriously degrade those within its reach and lead them to regard their condition as a stigma.

Poverty cannot be defined in economic terms alone. Anthropologist Oscar Lewis has suggested that an essential part of it is a culture of specific attitudes and responses passed down from generation to generation. Conservative theorists have attributed poverty to flaws in the individual, whereas other theorists have attributed it to flaws in the system. Some have proposed that poverty has social uses and thus perpetuates itself. For example, the existence of the poor ensures a pool of labor for undesirable jobs.

Pinpointing the poor as a group is also difficult. They are those moving from south to north, from rural environment to urban environment, and from agriculture to industry, seeking a better life. They are those living in overcrowded, run-down, crime-infested neighborhoods. They are those receiving the worst education, food, and health care. The poor are found everywhere and because of their situation do not or cannot reverse the tide of deprivation and discrimination.

Though President Kennedy initiated numerous poverty relief measures, it was President Johnson who declared "unconditional war on poverty." The Johnson administration undertook aid programs in the areas of human resource development, social insurance, cash-income support, and income-in-kind. Income maintenance and public assistance programs, established during Roosevelt's New Deal, were expanded during the War on Poverty. To be effective, such aid programs must motivate the poor to help themselves.

Most persons concerned with governmental aid programs agree they need revision but cannot agree on what revision to make. The public welfare program, in particular, has been subject to suggestions for reform, such as Milton Friedman's negative income tax and President Carter's program for better jobs and income.

Few measures under discussion promise permanent alleviation of poverty conditions. Among programs recently instituted, revenue sharing is designed to rectify tax inequities and improve conditions in the nation's cities, where the majority of the poor live. Other measures concentrate on improving the ability of the poor to compete for job opportunities through job training programs. Increasingly, it is becoming clear that in order to eliminate poverty and inequality in the economic realm, changes in the structure of equality in the political realm are required.

[1]S. M. Miller and Pamela A. Roby, *The Future of Inequality* (New York: Basic Books, 1970), p. 5.

[2]U. S. Bureau of the Census, *Statistical Abstract of the United States, 1977* (Washington, D.C.: Government Printing Office, 1977), p. 453.

[3]Ibid., p. 456.

[4]This idea is examined in some detail in William Ryan, *Blaming the Victim* (New York: Random House/Vintage Books, 1971).

[5]Joe R. Feagin, *Subordinating the Poor* (Englewood Cliffs, N.J.: Prentice-Hall, 1975), p. 92.

[6]Michael Harrington, *The Other America: Poverty in the United States* (New York: Macmillan, 1962).

[7]Oscar Lewis, *Five Families: Mexican Case Studies in the Culture of Poverty* (New York: Basic Books, 1959).

[8]*Gallup Opinion Index*, Report No. 124 (October 1975), p. 23.

[9]John Kenneth Galbraith, *The Affluent Society* (Boston: Houghton Mifflin, 1958), p. 323.

[10]Ibid., p. 324.

[11]Leon Keyserling et al., *Poverty and Deprivation in the United States*, Conference on Economic Progress (Washington, D.C.: Government Printing Office, 1962), p. 19.

[12]Mollie Orshansky, "Counting the Poor: Another Look at the Poverty Profile," *Social Security Bulletin* 28 (January 1965), 3–26; and Mollie Orshansky, "The Shape of Poverty in 1966," *Social Security Bulletin* 31 (March 1968), 3–32.

[13]Victor Fuchs, "Toward a Theory of Poverty," *The Concepts of Poverty*, Task Force on Economic Growth and Opportunity (Washington, D.C.: U.S. Chamber of Commerce, 1956), p. 74.

[14]U.S. Bureau of the Census, "Money, Income and Poverty Status of Families and Persons in the United States, 1974," *Current Population Reports*, Series P-60, No. 99 (Washington, D.C.: Government Printing Office, July 1975), p. 3.

[15]U.S. Bureau of the Census, *Statistical Abstract of the United States, 1977*, p. 3.

[16]U.S. Bureau of the Census, "Money, Income and Poverty Status in 1975 of Families and Persons in the United States and the West Region, by Divisions and States," *Current Population Reports*, Series P-60, No. 113 (Washington, D.C.: Government Printing Office, July 1978), p. 7.

[17]Lewis, *Five Families*.

[18]Charles A. Valentine, *Culture and Poverty* (Chicago: University of Chicago Press, 1969), p. 113.

[19]Lee Rainwater, "The Lessons of Pruitt-Igoe," *Public Interest* 8 (Summer 1967), 123.

[20]Oscar Lewis, "Culture and Poverty," *Current Anthropology* 10 (April-June 1969), 181–202.

[21]Herbert Gans, "Culture and Class in the Study of Poverty," *On Understanding Poverty*, ed. Daniel Moynihan (New York: Basic Books, 1968), p. 216.

[22]Michael Harrington, "Why We Need Socialism in America," *Dissent* 76 May–June 1970), 240–303.

[23]Herbert J. Gans, "The Uses of Poverty: The Poor Pay All," *Social Policy* 2 (July–August 1971), 20–24.

[24]U.S. Bureau of the Census, *Statistical Abstract of the United States, 1977*, p. 454.

[25]Harriett B. Presser and Linda S. Salsberg, "Public Assistance and Early Family Formation: Is There a Pronatalist Effect?" *Social Problems* 23 (1975), 266–241.

[26]U.S. Bureau of the Census, *Statistical Abstract of the United States, 1975*, p. 403.

[27]U.S. Bureau of Labor Statistics, *Report for 1970* (Washington, D.C.: Government Printing Office, 1971).

[28]U.S. Bureau of the Census, *Statistical Abstract of the United States, 1975*, p. 343.

[29]U.S. Bureau of the Census, *Statistical Abstract of the U.S., 1977*, p. 395.

[30]Ibid., p. 443.

[31]Ibid., p. 464.

[32]*Economic Report of the President* (Washington, D.C.: Government Printing Office, January 1968), pp. 132–138.

[33]James Tobin, "Raising the Incomes of the Poor," *Agenda for the Nation*, ed. Kermit Gordon (Washington, D.C.: Brookings, 1968), p. 81.

[34]Wayne King, "Florida Peonage Charges Reflect Plight of Migrants," *New York Times*, 17 March 1973, p. 12.

[35]Julian Samora and Patricia Vandel Simon, *A History of the Mexican-American People* (Notre Dame, Ind.: University of Notre Dame Press, 1977), p. 149.

[36]Excerpts from a series of President Johnson's Great Society speeches are printed in Marvin E. Gettleman and David Mermelstein, *The Great Society Reader* (New York: Random House/Vintage Books, 1967), pp. 13–23.

[37]Robert Haveman, "Introduction: Poverty and Social Policy in the 1960s and 1970s—An Overview and Some Speculations," *A Decade of Federal Antipoverty Programs: Achievements, Failures and Lessons*, ed. Robert Haveman (New York: Academic Press, 1977), p. 3.

[38]Lyndon B. Johnson, "Total Victory over Poverty," *The War on Poverty: The Economic Opportunity Act of 1964*, Senate Document No. 86 (Washington, D.C.: Government Printing Office, 1964).

[39]U.S. Bureau of the Census, *Statistical Abstract of the United States, 1975*, p. 405.

[40]Louise Lander, *War on Poverty* (New York: Facts on File, 1967), pp. 131–134.

[41]Henry J. Aaron, "Income Transfer Programs," *Monthly Labor Review*, February 1969, p. 53.

[42]Tobin, "Raising the Incomes of the Poor," p. 94.

[43]James L. Sundquist, "Jobs, Training, and Welfare for the Underclass," *Agenda for the Nation*, p. 56.

[44]Sar Levitan, Garth Magnum, and Ray Marshall, *Human Resources and Labor Markets* (New York: Harper & Row, 1972), pp. 350–356.

[45]Gilbert Steiner, *The State of Welfare* (Washington, D.C.: Brookings, 1971), p. 281.

[46]James M. Pierce, "The Condition of Farm Workers and Small Farmers in 1970," *Farmworkers in Rural America*, hearings before the Senate Subcommittee on Migratory Labor (Washington, D.C.: Government Printing Office, 1972), pp. 234–236.

[47]Tobin, "Raising the Incomes of the Poor," pp. 100–101.

[48]Ibid., p. 103.

[49]Aaron, "Income Transfer Programs, pp. 53–54.

[50]Milton Friedman, *Capitalism and Freedom* (Chicago: University of Chicago Press, 1962), p. 191.

[51]Gordon L. Weil, *The Welfare Debate of 1978* (White Plains, N.Y.: Institute for Socioeconomic Studies, 1978), pp. 19–20.

[52]Ibid., p. 30.

[53]Ibid., p. 36.

[54]Herbert J. Gans, "The New Egalitarianism," *Saturday Review*, 6 May 1972, pp. 43–46.

[55]Ibid.

Race, Ethnic, and Sex Inequality

8

Human existence in any society is primarily group life. Individuals join together to meet their social, emotional, and material needs and desires more adequately and satisfactorily than they can alone. Members of any one social group develop and define boundaries that set their group off from others in society. "In-groups" are those groups with which an individual is affiliated, and those with which there is no affiliation for that individual are viewed as "out-groups." The tendency to perceive the world in terms of "we" and "they" and the human propensity to identify with, take pride in, and develop loyalty to membership groups are general processes operative in all differentiated societies.

Social scientists use the term *ethnocentrism* to refer to the belief in the superiority of one's own group over other groups in the society. As individuals develop a commitment to the values and norms of a group, they may become intolerant or even hostile toward other groups that do not share these standards and characteristics. Intolerance of out-groups is generally more intense when there are identifiable differences between groups in terms of physical appearance, religion, customs, or language. In heterogeneous societies, comprised of diverse groups having distinct cultural traditions, ethnocentrism is a common and predictable phenomenon. In the United States each new wave of foreign immigrants has been met with some hostility by older, more established social groups.

Although ethnocentric attitudes are common in heterogeneous societies, they are not necessarily the only basis for problems in group relations. Major problems also result when one group possesses sufficient power in a society to institute policies and practices that result in unequal life chances for members of other groups. Discrimination, inequality, and group conflict are the product not only of individual attitudes but also of general group processes in which the unequal distribution of power results in groups entering into relations of dominance and subordination.

Inequality and discrimination dehumanize their victims. The decision to reject the dehumanization of inequality is often a turning point in history and can have profound effects upon an entire society. In America the Indians resisted the process of dehumanization during colonial times. Similar struggles were manifest in the slave revolts of the nineteenth century. Women's groups have protested for the past 200 years against dehumanization resulting from various types of sex discrimination. Actions taken by these groups have recently culminated in the civil-rights confrontations and legislative actions of the 1950s and 1960s and the movements for political power and self-determination in the 1970s.

As America's minorities move toward self-determination, how much progress is being made against the divisiveness of prejudice and discrimination? Is American society capable of the pluralism that can accommodate so many diverse groups? Have older methods of incorporation into American life, such as assimilation, become obsolete? Is separation a realistic possibility? Can prejudice and discrimination and their attendant social problems be eliminated without violence?

Whatever answers evolve in the future, there is increasing evidence that the group conflicts that have separated America's ideals from its realities create social disorder that could rip apart an already strained collective unity. Because of this fact, a close look at the bases of racial, ethnic, and sex inequality in America has a special urgency.

Dominance and Subordination

The dominant group in American society has always been composed essentially of white Anglo-Saxon Protestants who settled this country and assumed control of its major institutions. Groups which differed physically or culturally were relegated to subordinate positions in the social structure. The sociological definition of a minority group centers around this fundamental relationship of unequal power. Such groups are "categories of people that possess imperfect access to positions of equal power and to the corollary categories of prestige and privilege in the society."[1]

American society contains racial, ethnic, and sex minorities: the racial and sex minorities differ from the dominant group in terms of some physical characteristics, while ethnic groups differ only in terms of cultural background and traditions. Minority groups have formed in our society through a variety of means. Indians were the victims of territorial conquest; they were deprived of their lands and resources and forcibly segregated into reservations or territories set apart from white society. Ethnic minorities from Europe voluntarily immigrated to America in search of a better life and to escape religious and political persecution in their native countries. Blacks were enslaved and transported to this country to serve the economic interests of members of the dominant group. The subordinate role of women was

transported to America by virtually every group. Regardless of the processes by which these groups became minorities in our society, they have all in varying degrees been excluded from full participation in major social institutions, denied certain privileges and benefits, including equal protection under the law, and relegated to inferior living conditions and social status. The democratic and egalitarian ideals of our society have had an uneasy coexistence with the concrete reality of domination.

Minority and majority relations are defined and restricted in large part by the stratification system of the society. American society has been, and continues to be, structured in a hierarchical fashion on the basis of power, prestige, and privilege. Social class, racial, ethnic and sex categories have been used as criteria for assigning members of certain groups to the lower levels of the hierarchy in our society. Owing to their greater power and prestige, members of the dominant group have had the ability to define the standards used to locate groups and individuals along this hierarchy. The amount of hostility and discrimination encountered by members of any particular minority group varies according to the nature of the differences between their group and the dominant group.

Relations between various groups in a society may take on a variety of forms, ranging from cooperation to competition, hostility, domination, and violent conflict. Individual attitudes of ethnocentrism and prejudice make it likely that hostility between groups will exist, but individual attitudes account only partially for the fact that, as one federally commissioned report has noted, America remains divided into two societies, separate and unequal.[2] Basic conflicts of interest and of group values also underlie problems in majority-minority relations.

The values that people seek are never distributed equally: in the struggle for subsistence and social rewards there are always obstacles that impede some groups more than others. Thus systematic inequality and systematic injustice are built into the very nature of stratified societies.[3]

When minority group members seek improved employment, educational opportunities, and living conditions, they threaten the privileges and advantages of the members of the dominant group. These privileges and benefits are believed by some to lie at the very heart of the continuing discrimination against minority groups.[4] Both material and status gains—generally achieved through employment—are not given up easily by majority groups and serve to reinforce feelings of group animosity and fear. In the area of race and sex, the defense of these privileges has become incorporated into the routine workings of pivotal institutions; racism and sexism have become *institutionalized*. Indeed, the perpetuation of the existing relationships of dominance and subordination is ensured by the very structure of our economic, political, and legal systems.

Poor relationships between majority and minority groups in society are complex phenomena, involving both individual elements and broader sociocultural factors. An understanding of the problems concerning race, ethnic, and sex equality requires that attention be focused on both of these levels.

Understanding Majority-Minority Relations

The study of prejudice has increased since World War II, largely in reaction to the death of six million Jewish people in Europe, the violence accompanying efforts of minorities in America and in colonial nations to regain human dignity, and the growing number of oppressed minorities making their resentments and anger known to the rest of society.

What is prejudice? The word has its roots in a Latin term meaning prejudgment. It normally implies a preconceived opinion, often an unfavorable one based on insufficient knowledge or other inadequate grounds. Although a certain amount of prejudgment is necessary for an individual to process the sheer volume of information in fast-paced complex societies, some flexibility of mind is necessary to allow for new information or a change in circumstances. Gordon W. Allport has pointed out that a prejudgment becomes a prejudice only if it cannot be reversed by new knowledge. In *The Nature of Prejudice*, he has defined prejudice as "an avertive or hostile attitude toward a person who belongs to a group, simply because he belongs to that group, and is therefore presumed to have the objectionable qualities ascribed to that group."[5] Such a preconceived and hostile attitude can be applied to people because of their race, religion, ethnic background, sex, or other kind of group membership.

Although prejudice is an *attitude* held by an individual or group, discrimination is an overt *act* that deprives members of a minority group of certain of the benefits of the society in which they live. Prejudice reflects sentiments that may be held only by an individual, but discrimination relates to the general practices within the social structure of a culture. A person may feel a prejudice and never translate it into a discriminatory action; prejudice can exist independently of discrimination, although discrimination is dependent upon prejudice.

Discrimination means "to make a distinction," which may be either in favor of or opposed to one or more persons because of membership in a group rather than individual attributes. Discriminatory behavior ignores individual merit and makes distinctions on the basis of categories presumed to be appropriate for the situation at hand.

Different levels of actions flow from prejudice, from the mild form of an ethnic slur to the most violent form of extermination.[6] The first level is a verbal expression of prejudice, such as "I don't like colored people." At the second level, the prejudiced person avoids the members of the disliked group. The third level of action resulting from prejudice is discrimination. *Segregation* enforces discrimination by law or custom, resulting in an institutionalization of prejudiced behavior—separate toilet facilities for white and black people, for example.

The fourth level brings physical abuse; members of a disliked group are attacked, as when Mexican-Americans were beaten in the streets of Los Angeles during World War II. Fifth, and most violent, is extermination; victims of prejudice are eliminated, as in pogroms and genocide. The massacres of Indians in America and the lynching of blacks after the Civil War are examples of prejudiced behavior in its most violent form.

While many groups in America have been subject to varying levels of hostility, racial, ethnic, and sex characteristics have frequently been the common denominator of these groups.

Individual Dimensions

What leads people to such brutal expressions of hostility against others simply because they belong to one group or another? In personalities exhibiting deep, character-conditioned prejudice, there is a core of insecurity; such people are afraid of themselves and their own consciousness. They fear change as well as their social environment. Unable to live with themselves or others, they organize their attitudes to match their condition; their specific prejudicial social attitudes originate in their own crippled egos.[7]

A society, as well as an individual, may exhibit psychological disorders that give rise to prejudice. Hitler used the Jews as scapegoats for Germany's misfortunes. Psychologist T. W. Adorno and his colleagues have reviewed this scapegoat mechanism at length in their study of anti-Semitism, *The Authoritarian Personality*.[8] This analysis indicates that impersonal social processes that seem beyond the control of individuals alienate people from society. These alienated persons then experience the fear and uncertainty of disorientation, which they attempt to displace onto members of a group other than their own. The victims of prejudice are thus blamed for the disorder that has been created by society's dysfunction.

In contrast to other social psychologists who suggest that prejudice is the result of deep-seated mechanisms, Milton Rokeach places emphasis on the perceived dissimilarity of belief systems. He suggests that the major determinant of prejudice is not race or ethnic membership per se. Rather, prejudice arises when individuals perceive that members of other groups have value and belief systems at variance with their own.[9] This theory allows for far greater optimism than Adorno's argument. It implies that a solution to prejudice may be found by educating individuals about others' beliefs. Increased communication between race, ethnic and sex groups might then serve to ameliorate the problem by opening previously closed minds.

Socioeconomic Factors

When psychological factors are accompanied by economic factors, the setting for violent abuse is established. Value conflict between majority and minority groups stemming from a clash of their material interests is of central importance in understanding the exploitation, oppression, and domination of minorities. For example, the interest of American settlers in the agricultural potential and mineral wealth of lands belonging to the Indians added a particular hostility to an already existing cultural discrimination. The fight for gold in California also led to increasingly violent discrimination against Mexican-Americans. A clash of economic interests seems to blur awareness of individual differences; during the period of gold excitement in California, all Mexicans, Chileans, Peruvians, and other Spanish-speaking foreigners simply became "greasers." The connection between economics, prejudice, and violence in the California experience is illustrated by the pattern of Anglo exclusion, based on economic, nationalistic, and racist attitudes, which moved quickly from suspicion to threats, violence, restrictive legislation, litigation, and back to violence.[10]

The changing economic needs of a society play a crucial role in the patterning of relationships between majority and minority groups. The institution of slavery began to wane in the South when lowered profits in the tobacco trade resulted in a switch away from that crop and made field hands unnecessary; the number of slaves increased again when cheap labor was required for the profitable development of the cotton industry. Women were encouraged to join the labor market during World War II in order to enhance production. Although they contributed valuable services to the American war effort, women were systematically discriminated against after the war when applying for the same positions they held earlier.

The routine socialization processes in our society also contribute to discrimination and intergroup hostility. Persons of different sexes and from various racial, ethnic, and cultural backgrounds tend to be socialized into different value systems, linguistic styles, and views of the world; these differences can act as a basis of hostility toward particular minorities. Thus, Spanish-speaking children may be ostracized or ridiculed by schoolmates simply because they "talk funny." This common tendency to attach special importance to cultural or physical differences typically results in group stereotyping. Social stereotypes—preconceived negative notions of how members of specific groups look, think, and behave—are learned during socialization, often from one's elders, and are usually reinforced in the mass media.

Although racial and ethnic stereotypes have often been the basis of hostility towards these groups, those pertaining to women have been equally detrimental in that they have inhibited the society. Women have typically been seen to be passive, weak, emotional, intuitive and supportive, whereas men are seen as active, strong, nonemotional and rational. Such stereotypes prevent females from achieving equal access to the educational and occupational goals available to males.

The process of socialization reinforces these racial, ethnic, and sex stereotypes and assumes that future generations will possess many of the same ideas. The social changes of the past decade have succeeded in breaking down some of these stereotypes, but for many Americans the core of ingrained ideas and attitudes remains entrenched.

The origins of hostility toward minority groups in the United States go back to European beliefs and practices at the time when America was discovered and settled. The Europeans' inability to understand peoples with dissimilar cultures, languages, religions, and racial and ethnic backgrounds contributed to discrimination so severe that it led to the virtual annihilation of the native American population and to the enslavement of Africans. European religious animosities also crossed the Atlantic to America, where those who were considered savage heathens or enemies of the majority's religion were made victims of discrimination. At the time of colonial independence, although the Constitution proclaimed individual liberty, local restrictive laws and customs rooted in Old World attitudes still applied to various minority groups, including blacks, Indians, Catholics, and Jews.[11]

Slavery and the Institution-alization of Racism

The first black slaves brought to this country in 1619 were treated like white indentured servants, able to earn their freedom after working for a time or after conversion to Christianity.[12] The economic situation soon required different arrangements, however, and Virginia enacted the first laws recognizing slavery in 1661. Gradually other colonies passed restrictive laws. Since American law was based on English law, which had no precedent for slavery, the laws that came to govern slaves in this country evolved from English property laws. Considered property, slaves had no civil rights; they were forbidden to enter contracts, their marriages were not considered legally binding, and families could be separated by the slaveholder. Slaves could be sold, given as gifts, and used as prizes and in raffles. Children inherited their status as slaves from their mothers.

After the Emancipation Proclamation and the end of the Civil War, there was a brief period in which black people held full civil rights. Thousands registered to vote, and some blacks were elected to Congress or held high state offices in the South. It seemed that the ideals of democracy might finally become reality. Once again, however, prejudices and economic forces —especially the need for cheap labor—impeded the trends to equality; the hard-won achievements of Reconstruction were destroyed. Discrimination was soon enforced by law, supported by custom, and propped up with pseudoscientific theories. During the last part of the nineteenth century, "at the very time that imperialism was sweeping the country, the doctrine of racism reached a crest of acceptability and popularity among respectable scholarly and intellectual circles."[13] Books, magazines, and other forms of communication presented preposterous arguments that black people belonged to a different species, a species lower on the evolutionary scale than the white race. Institutionalized racism became part of the American way of life.

Orientals, primarily Chinese, began migrating to the United States around 1850 as laborers and from the beginning were met with hostility. Anti-Chinese sentiment ran high in the West, especially California, and in

1882 resulted in the Chinese Exclusion Act restricting the number of Chinese immigrants. From 1902 until recently, no Chinese laborers were allowed to migrate to this country. Japanese immigrants met much the same prejudice and hostility, suffering the ultimate indignity during World War II when those on the West Coast were interned in security camps because of the fear of their disloyalty to the United States.

The black population, beginning its modern exodus from the rural South to the northern cities, also encountered the deprivations of previous immigrant groups—poor housing, inadequate schools, and economic exploitation—as well as the additional obstacle of racism. Put otherwise, nonwhite minorities have suffered the dual liabilities of class and race oppression— the former because they have occupied the lowest socioeconomic position in the society, and the latter because of the alleged inferiority of their genetic or cultural heritage. It is indeed the case, as W. E. B. DuBois predicted, that the twentieth century has seen color become one of the prime causes of social conflict.[14]

Destruction of Indian Cultures

The exact size of the indigenous population in North America at the time of the Europeans' arrival is unknown; estimates by scholars range from a low of one million to a high of ten million persons.[15] These native Americans represented diverse languages and cultures; within this diversity, however, certain similarities have been observed. Most tribes functioned democratically. They tolerated diversity among and between themselves and lived in harmony with nature.[16]

The westward expansion of European settlers and their descendants destroyed most of the original American population's way of life. By 1800 the number of Indians had been reduced to 600,000, and 50 years later it was less than half of that. Indians were killed defending their lands or died when they were forced to leave—4000 Cherokees died in 1834 on a forced march from their homeland in Georgia to reservations in Arkansas and Oklahoma.[17] Thousands of others died from starvation and disease, notably smallpox.

The story of the Sioux illustrates the process by which prejudice and economic factors led to violent forms of discrimination against the native population. The Sioux, once a proud people who hunted and led a nomadic life, were forced off their lands by the discovery of gold and a new push of European immigrants. When their reservation was established in 1889, the Sioux were designated government wards, subject to changing and contradictory policies.[18] The following year, the U.S. Army, mistakenly thinking the Sioux ceremonial dances were a preparation for warfare, massacred 200 Indian women and children and 98 disarmed warriors at Wounded Knee.[19]

The displacement of Indian people onto reservations has had profound consequences, particularly in that it has deprived them of crucial material resources and vested the administration of their affairs in a government agency. Historically, reservations were parcels of land set aside by treaty for Indian people in order to eliminate their presence from regions that whites were beginning to exploit.[20] The administrative apparatus of these reservations provided them with little, if any, just treatment.

To control and "civilize" the Indians, the reservation was placed under the jurisdiction of an Indian agent representing the authority, and supposedly the interests, of the U.S. Government. Having at his disposal both military and judicial powers, as well as control of rations, the agent was a petty tyrant who might be benevolent but was often self-serving.[21]

Today, 65 percent of all Indians live on or near reservations.[22] Setting aside lands for the exclusive use of Indians has not served them; they live in poverty and deprivation unrivaled by any other minority people. Because reservations typically have been located in remote regions that were considered undesirable by white settlers, the economic base of most Indian communities is quite limited. In fact, unemployment among males often exceeds 50 percent.[23]

The dispossesion of the Mexican-Americans paralleled that of the Indians; prejudice against the Mexicans based on cultural differences and conflicts with the economic interests of the dominant group led to violent discrimination.[24] Anglo-American attitudes toward the frontier stressed individuality and the personal benefit that could be gained from the land. The Spanish-Mexican view emphasized the community rather than the individual. Land ownership among the Mexicans involved length of occupancy and use, with less importance attached to boundaries, surveys, and grant registration— the proofs of ownership required by Anglo-Americans.

After defeat in the Mexican War, Mexican-Americans lost any grounds for argument. And they were murdered in the valley of the Rio Grande at a rate that may well have surpassed that of black lynchings around the turn of the century.[25] Like the Indians, Mexican-Americans often became impoverished outcasts in what had once been their community home.

Mexican-Americans have remained concentrated both geographically and economically. Of the 5 million Chicanos in this country, the vast majority live in the Southwest. Since World War II, the demographic trend has been an increasing movement from rural to urban areas. As with other minorities, they tend to be residentially segregated into ghettolike areas referred to as *barrios*. Occupationally, Chicanos are overwhelmingly concentrated in low-paying agricultural work.

There may be several reasons that Mexican-Americans have not been readily assimilated into the mainstream of American society. Mexicans who have immigrated to this country are primarily from the working class, with little education and few marketable skills. They have encountered widespread discrimination, not only because of their low socioeconomic status and lack of skills but because of the color of their skin as well.[26] Mexican-Americans belong to one of the few ethnic minorities in this country for which there has been practically no upward social mobility from one generation to the next.

The roots of the problem of inequality for American females go far deeper into the past than they do for the other groups discussed. The dehumanization of women also has an ironic twist in that women actually comprise a majority of the American population. Yet they are a vast minority in terms of the power and wealth that they control. Since the role of women in con-

The Dispossession of the Mexicans

The 51 Percent Minority

AMERICAN INDIANS

Perhaps no Americans have suffered more discrimination, deprivation, and hardship than the Indians, who have lost their way of life, as well as their lands, to the white invaders. *This page:* Welcoming the white race; white scalping Indian, 1873. *Opposite page:* Reservation life today—little hope of escaping from poverty; Custer in his final battle with the Sioux, 1876; Taos Pueblo Indians receive from Congress the title to land of their sacred shrine in New Mexico; protesting government treatment, past and present; some reservations have developed cottage industries to relieve their desperate economic plight; an Indian American who has escaped his tribe's poverty and works as a forester.

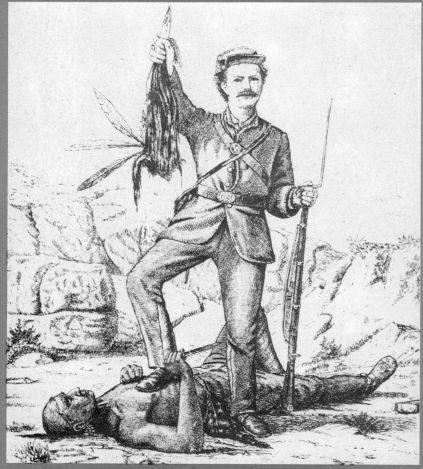

Peter Collier
The Red Man's Burden

The Alcatraz occupation is still popularly regarded as the engaging fun and games of Indian college kids. In its news coverage of the U.S. Coast Guard's feeble attempt to blockade ships running supplies to the island, one local television station found amusement in showing their films to the musical accompaniment of U.S. cavalry bugle calls. It was not so amusing to the occupiers, however. The California Indians now on the Rock know that their people were decimated from a population of 100,000 in 1850 when the gold rush settlers arrived, to about 15,000 thirty years later, and that whole tribes, languages and cultures were erased from the face of the earth. . . .

But the past is not really at issue. What is at stake today, . . . is cultural survival. . . .

The enemies are legion, and they press in from every side: the studiously ignorant politicians, the continuously negligent Department of the Interior, and the white business interests who are allowed to prey upon the reservations' manpower and resources. But as the Indian has struggled to free himself from the suffocating embrace of white history, no enemy has held the death grip more tightly than has his supposed guardian, in effect his "keeper": the Bureau of Indian Affairs.

The Bureau came into being in 1834 as a division of the War Department. Fifteen years later it was shifted to the Department of the Interior, the transition symbolizing the fact that the Indian was beginning to be seen not as a member of a sovereign, independent nation, but as a "ward," his land and life requiring constant management. This is the view that has informed the BIA for over a century. . . .

The paternalism of the BIA, endless and debilitating, is calculated to keep the Indian in a state of perpetual juvenilization, without rights, dependent upon the meagre and capricious beneficence of power. The Bureau's power over its "wards," whom it defines and treats as children, seems limitless. The BIA takes care of the Indian's money, doling it out to him when it considers his requests worthy; it determines the use of the Indian's land; it is in charge of the development of his natural resources; it relocates him from the reservation to the big city ghetto; it educates his children. It relinquishes its hold over him only reluctantly, even deciding whether or not his will is valid after he dies.

This bureaucratic paternalism hems the Indian in with an incomprehensible maze of procedures and regulations, never allowing him to know quite where he stands or what he can demand and how. Over 5000 laws, statutes and court decisions apply to the Indians alone. As one Indian student says, "Our people have to go to law school just to live a daily life." . . .

Behind the machinations of the BIA and the grander larcenies of the Department of Interior stands the Indians' final enemy, that vague sense of doom called federal policy. It has always been sinister, and no less so today than in the days when Indian tribes were nearly annihilated by the white man's gift of blankets saturated in smallpox. The current mode of attack began in the 1950's, with by far the most ominous title in the lexicon of Indian affairs: termination. Its objectives were stated innocuously in a 1953 act of Congress: "It is the policy of Congress, as rapidly as possible to make the Indians within the United States subject to the same privileges and responsibilities as are applicable to other citizens of the United States, to end their status as wards of the United States, and to grant them all of the rights and prerogatives pertaining to American citizenship. . . ." Cultural assassination always comes cloaked in such altruisms, and the crucial phrase, "to end their status as wards of the United States," was neatly circumscribed by florid rhetoric. But that phrase was the heart of the resolution, and its impact was disastrous.

Over the last two decades, the Indian has learned that he must fear most those who want to eliminate the Bureau of Indian Affairs and who make pompous statements about it being time "for this country to get out of the Indian business." A hundred and fifty years ago, perhaps, attaining such equilibrium with the red man would have been laudable; but America got into the Indian business for good when it stole a continent and put its inhabitants in land-locked jails. While the Indian knows that the BIA works against him most of the time, he also realizes its symbolic value as the embodiment of promises made in the treaties which secure his land and culture. Indian people and lands have been, and continue to be, terribly damaged by their relationship to the federal government. But their federal trust status guarantees their Indianness. And if it is terminated, they know there will be nothing left to mismanage.

The reservations which were actually terminated as a result of this sudden shift in federal policy in the

'50s provide ample warning. The Minominees of Wisconsin, for instance, whose termination began in 1954 and was completed in 1961, had a stable pattern of life which was destroyed. They owned a thriving tribally-run sawmill. They had a hospital and other community services; they had a fairly large tribal bank account. Then came termination, which made the Minominees citizens of Wisconsin and nothing more. The hospital had to close down because it didn't meet state standards; the tribal bank account was doled out to the tribesmen in per capita payments, which were quickly dissipated. The sawmill became a corporation and floundered because of mismanagement, thereby no longer providing the Minominees with jobs. The Indians were supposed to become just like everyone else in Wisconsin, but today they still stand apart as among the poorest people in the state. Much of their land, which was not taxible when held in trust, has been sold at forced auctions to make up defaulted state property taxes.

Another classic case of termination is that of the Klamaths of Oregon. As part of the proceedings in 1954, their richly-forested reservation was sold off and the receipts distributed equally among enrolled members of the tribe. The payout came to over $40,000 per person, and even before it was made the predators began to descend, offering high-interest loans and a treasure house of consumer goods. A few years after termination was accomplished, many of the Klamaths were destitute and on welfare; they had no land left, no money and no future. As one member of the tribe said, ''My grandchildren won't have anything, not even the right to call themselves Indian.''

Because of the disasters it caused, termination is now ''voluntary,'' although the Congressional resolution which authorized it has yet to be rescinded. Temporarily, at least, it has taken a backseat to the New Frontierish strategies like luring private enterprise onto the reservation and allocating meager OEO funds. However, today there are still tribes in the process of termination—several small ones in California and the Colvilles of Washington—and no attempt is made to stop the misinformation given Indians about the benefits that will result from such an option. Nor will termination ever disappear for good until Indians hold in their own hands the life and death powers over their communities which others now wield. Every time an Indian is ''successfully'' relocated in a city far from his people, it is a kind of termination, as it is when a plot of ground or the rights to water slip out of his hands. It is not necessary for Indian people to have Secretary of Interior Hickel tell them that they should ''cut the cord'' that binds them to their reservation, to know that termination exists as the final solution to the Indian Problem. . . .

Strangled in bureaucracy, swindled out of lands, forcibly alienated from his own culture, the Indian continues to be victimized by the white man's symbolism: he has been both loved and hated to death. On the one hand, the white looked out at him from his own constricted universe of acquisition and grasping egocentrism and saw a Noble Savage, an innocent at peace with his world. Here was a relic of a better time, to be protected and preserved. But on the other hand the white saw an uncivilized creature possessing, but not exploiting, great riches; the vision was conjured up of the Murdering Redskin whose bestiality provided the justification for wiping him out and taking his land. The Indian's ''plight'' has always inspired recurrent orgies of remorse, but never has it forced us to digest the implications of a nation and culture conceived in genocide. We act as if the blood-debt of the past cannot be canceled until the Indian has no future; the guiltier he has made us, the more frantic have been the attempts to make him disappear.

Yet, having paid out almost everything he had, the Indian has survived the long exercise in white schizophrenia. And there are some, like Hopi mystic Thomas Banyaka, who give out prophecies that the red man will still be here long after whites have been destroyed in a holocaust of their own making.

Excerpts from Peter Collier, ''The Red Man's Burden,'' *Ramparts*, February 1970, pp. 27–38. © Ramparts Magazine, Inc., 1970. Reprinted by permission of the author.

Slim pickings: Mexican workers have long been exploited as a cheap source of labor in the produce fields of the West. These braceros leave their families in Mexico to work ten to twelve hours a day picking fruit or vegetables.

temporary society is based on events that transcend the American experience, it is necessary to examine the historical basis of this problem.

Most aspects of society, including its labor, have always been divided at least partially on the basis of sex. This division does not imply inequality, however. Even in primitive societies, both sexes played equal roles in the struggle of the group for survival.[27] In hunting and gathering societies, the former chore was the primary responsibility of males while the latter was performed by females. Both tasks were equally important for the group.

It was not until societies moved beyond a mere subsistence level that the role of females began to change. As more goods were produced than could be immediately consumed by the producers, it became possible for an exchange of goods to occur. At this point, there developed two different worlds, the larger outside world of the whole society in which this exchange took place, and the second, more private, world of the family and home.[28] Men came to dominate the public sphere at least partially because of the necessity for women's confinement to the home during periods of frequent childbearing. Women continued to play an important role in the traditional home crafts, however, including the making of clothing, medicines, and many foods. With the development of the Industrial Revolution, though, these essential services were also removed from the home to the factories. Thus the productive functions of the home and of women was largely eliminated.

It was only at this time that women's roles became centered solely around the domestic chores of cooking, cleaning, and childrearing. With seemingly few important responsibilities left, these tasks took on new meaning and importance to women. Whereas earlier generations of females cleaned the house once every few months, daily or weekly cleanings came to be expected. Although new appliances were invented to make housework easier, they themselves became "silent imperatives to work." The phrase "The Manufacture of Housework" has been coined to describe the process by which the role of women developed into one which confined their activities to the home.[29] This development served to assure the continuation of a patriarchal family structure.

The development of this largely domestic role for women has had severe consequences on both their objective and subjective conditions. In today's economy, many women have been forced to search for jobs to supplement family incomes. Yet they meet resistance on every front. They suffer from disproportionately high unemployment and underemployment rates. (See Chapter 4, Fig. 4.1.) Females are greatly underrepresented in most of the prestigious, well-rewarded professions. In 1940, only 2.4 percent of all American lawyers were women. By 1960 this figure had risen to 3.5 and by 1970 to 4.9 percent. Women comprised only 6.5 percent of the medical profession in 1960 and 9.3 percent in 1970.[30] Although these figures have risen considerably in the past few years, they still do not come close to the 51 percent that females constitute in the general population. When women do manage to attain similar occupational levels with men, they frequently earn considerably less money.

Jane Cassels Record
Economic Rights

The becentennial celebration of the Declaration of Independence is a good time to reflect on what this document's lofty equalitarian sentiments imply for women. If the "all men" is translated into "all persons" as being created equal, what—beyond the rhetoric —does the statement mean?

The equalitarian ethic is simultaneously clear-cut and convoluted, simple and profound. Although the wording of the Equal Rights Amendment (ERA) is straightforward—equality of rights under the law shall not be denied or abridged by the United States or by any state on account of sex—the words carry an agenda of social reform which goes to the root of family, work place, and every other social institution in the land. Translating the words into the lives of Americans entails a jolting rearrangement of responsibilities and obligations, of rights and opportunities.

The revolutionary implications are best illustrated in the economic sphere. Three basic, provocative, interrelated concepts are paramount: economic independence, economic equality, and economic power. A women is *independent* to the extent that she has security and can choose her life-style. She is *equal* to the extent that she enjoys equal rights, equal opportunities, and equal achievement—and accepts equal responsibilities. She is *powerful* to the extent that she can impose her will on others.

Unless a woman has chosen her parents or grandparents wisely so as to have inherited wealth, there is no way for her to be truly independent economically without her own paycheck. For this independence she must be gainfully employed. I am not belittling the housewife's additions to the nation's output of goods and services, nor am I denying for a moment the often critical contributions made by volunteer workers in blood banks and on museum committees to the quality of American life. But since such services are given freely, they do not contribute to economic independence.

The women's liberation movement in the People's Republic of China has aroused much interest. The abominably low status of women in traditional Chinese society makes their rapid progress toward equality during the last twenty-five years truly impressive. This progress has been facilitated by two national policies.

Access to birth control services in China is easy, and exhortation to use them strong. Margaret Sanger, rather than Abraham Lincoln, should be known as the Great Emanicipator, for—whereas Lincoln liberated a few million slaves—Sanger and other birth control leaders created the means of liberating half the human race. If a woman cannot control the number and timing of her pregnancies, there is little point in discussing her liberation.

Women have made rapid progress in China for a second reason. Their expected participation in the labor force, in work earning them their own income, brings them a paycheck which—in contrast to the old days—now legally belongs to them rather than their husbands, fathers, or sons.

Americans should use any exposure to another culture to help them see their own from a different perspective. In China almost all women work outside the home. In the United States, although the participation of women in the work force has been growing rapidly since the 1930s, the majority of females between eighteen and sixty-five still are not gainfully employed or seeking paying work; hence they have no wage or salary of their own and no real economic independence.

But what about the husband who allows his wife a free hand in spending his income? The key word here is "allows." The law requires that a husband support his wife as long as she continues to provide certain services for him. The psychological setting of gifts and subsidies, however, is far different from the psychological setting of earned income. The former situation smacks of paternalism—sometimes even depotism—no matter how benevolent.

Then why not pay housewives for their work in the home? After all, if a single man requires outside help with the cleaning, cooking, and child care, he can buy these services from a professional housekeeper. But the injection of an employer-employee relationship into a marriage, with the wife as the employee, would harm rather than enhance her economic independence, to say nothing of what it would do to the marriage. Think of all those bargaining sessions on wages, hours, working conditions, and managerial rights.

There have been serious suggestions that house-wives be paid from public revenues, but this procedure would put housewives on "welfare"—hardly an appropriate strategy for increasing independence or elevating status. The only equalitarian solution to the stove and diaper problem is for the husband and wife to share equally the activities and responsibilities of people maintenance.

Equality in the home meshes with the question of economic equality. Economic equality has many faces: for example, equal rights, equal opportunity, equal responsibility, and equal achievement. Economic rights include the right to own property, borrow money, and open charge accounts in one's own name. Economic opportunity includes access not merely to jobs but to education and training programs, promotions, and job security. In these two spheres—rights and opportunities—discrimination against women has been scandalous. That some progress is being made should not cause a slack in our efforts to eliminate every single vestige of prejudice. Passing the ERA is a symbolic step in this direction.

Our preoccupation with winning equal rights and equal opportunities should not obscure the other two faces of economic equality: equal responsibility and equal achievement. Women must accept the same responsibilities for supporting their families that men do. This proposition assumes that women will have the same economic opportunities as men, and that men will share equally the tasks and responsibilities associated with housewifery and motherhood.

Childbearing is a uniquely exciting experience, unfortunately denied to men. But although in the present state of medical technology women are uniquely capable of *bearing* children, nothing in the present state of expert knowledge suggest that they are uniquely capable of *rearing* them. Once emerged from the birth canal—certainly once moved from breast to bottle—the baby can be as capably nurtured by the father as the mother. The recipe for successful parenting is not written in any one genital arrangment. . . .

Rewarding as child rearing can be, it simply is not enough to fulfill the *person* needs of a reasonably intelligent adult, male or female. Who would suggest that a man ought to find sufficient fulfillment in being a good husband and father?

In a work-oriented society personal identity and sense of self are linked inextricably to occupation. A man *is* what he *does*; and what someone does is generally understood to mean what his gainful employment is. . . .

The social value of housewifery is indicated by the fact that when a woman is asked if she works, it is understood that the question means work outside the home, for pay. Thus the housewife's labor in the home and even her volunteer activities outside the home are not significant enough to be comprehended by the term "work" as it is commonly used. The housewife has accepted this valuation. When asked if she works, she typically replies that she is only a housewife—only a housewife, whose services are not included in the Gross National Product.

Imagine asking a man between the ages of twenty-five and sixty if he works. Even if one asked a man of seventy about gainful employment, the question would be "Do you still work?" rather than "Do you work?" Males are expected to work in this society, from young adulthood to retirement age; it is unacceptable for them to be willfully unemployed. In sharp contrast, there is no such expectation of women, especially if they are married and their husband's income sufficient.

Both my husband and I have doctorates from Berkeley, but the community has different expectations of us. Despite the fact that society has put many resources into my education, I could elect to sit in my house without a job for the rest of my days and my suburban neighbors would not think less of me. My husband, however, does not have this privilege. If he left teaching and research, took up househusbandry full time, and began to make the rounds of ladies' morning coffee klatches, he could scarcely expect to escape social stigmatization.

In an achievement-centered culture, with achievement defined largely in occupational terms, economic equality will produce as many career-oriented women as men. . . .

They include women who see gainful employment as a unique means of using talents, expressing creativity, fulfilling internal need, and achieving recognition. And if women want to be equal, they must achieve equality within whatever economic context exists at the time, even though they may simultaneously work to change that context.

Americans are too striving, too acquisitive. Work-styles and life-styles would be more attractive if competition were softened and the "rat race" decelerated. Nevertheless, the pressures society imposes

on men to "make it" should be borne equally by women. . . .

The issue of economic equality cannot be engaged adequately without discussing economic power. There are two crucial kinds of economic power: collective power exercised through ad hoc groupings to pursue a specific collective purpose, and individual power exercised on a continuing basis by virtue of institutional position.

It is deplorable that women, given the role they have traditionally been assigned as family purchasing agent, do not use their collective consumer power effectively. Why are there so few campaigns and protests and boycotts against price gouging, shoddy workmanship, unsafe products, and goods whose production unnecessarily pollutes the environment? A collective refusal to buy will scare any seller.

The second kind of economic power entails participating in such decisions as what goods to produce, how much capital to invest, and how to distribute income. This power is exercised by individuals and small groups in executive suites and corporate boardrooms.

In the past women have shied away from power. But America is not an economic democracy; thus if women are to share in the decision making which shapes the economic destiny of our nation, they will have to fight their way into an almost exclusively male establishment. Making this fight will require the same career concentration men practice. There is no other way.

What is being discussed here—a world in which women enjoy full economic rights and opportunities and accept commensurate economic responsibilities —is the most revolutionary idea in the history of human relations. It requires profound changes in family roles, in the organization of work, in all social intercourse.

Many women are frightened by this concept. Polls show that the ERA is supported by a higher percentage of men than women. In declining to ratify the amendment, for example, legislators in Georgia were influenced by the number of females who came forward and declared publicly that they did not wish to be equal.

It is not my purpose here to tell women that they ought to want equality, but rather to describe what equality looks like and what it requires of them. Equal division of opportunities and responsibilities between males and females is liberating to both. This equality, however, is not achievable without some male and female identity crises. . . . Meanwhile, liberated women can take steps to rearrange their personal lives while waiting for society to catch up to them.

Although the individual female finds herself largely at the mercy of fate, chance, and social institutions, there is one decision she can control. A person picks his mate. If a woman bonds with a man, she can choose an equalitarian male; the liberated woman must settle for nothing less. If she wants to avoid the traditional trap, she must pick a mate who is sufficiently secure in his sense of self-worth and self-achievement that he will look on her accomplishments with pride, rather than seeing in them a threat to his fragile ego. And if she has children, she must socialize them—boys and girls alike—for equalitarian roles.

The equalitarian prize is rich in opportunity, but its price is high in obligation. This fact must not be overlooked in reflecting on the stunning defeat of state ERAs in New York and New Jersey, or on polls which show men to be more favorable than women to the central purpose of the ERA.

Attempts to explain these phenomena have made much of Phyllis Schlafly's nonsense about coeducational locker rooms and of feminist leaders who, in defiance of the pluralist tradition, insist on linking women's rights to lesbian rights and anticapitalist politics. These explanations must not be taken lightly. But it is also useful to ask how many women are truly ready for the full responsibilities of equalitarianism.

Other women who try to enter the labor market do so, not out of economic necessity, but because of "the problem that has no name."[31] They are subject to the boredom, tension and anxiety accompanying the performance of similar, unchallenging tasks on a daily basis. Yet few outlets in or out of the world of work have been provided for females to express their creativity and satisfy their ambitions. The resurgence of the women's movement in the 1970s is largely an outgrowth of the realization that women can make their lives more meaningful through an active participation in all aspects of the world around them.

Race, Ethnic, and Sex Inequality Today

Is our society moving toward tolerance and accommodation and away from prejudice and discrimination? Or is it sinking more deeply into institutional racism and divisiveness?

Current social conditions indicate the scope of the problems resulting from prejudice and discrimination. The minority groups experiencing the worst discrimination—the black population, American Indians, Mexican-Americans, and Puerto Ricans—usually are forced to live in isolation from the rest of society. Segregation into internal colonies has been most apparent among the American Indians, cut off from the rest of American society on reservations for more than a century, and the Mexican-Americans, scattered in remote rural poverty throughout the Southwest. Recently Mexican-Americans and Indians have been moving to the cities, where they join other minority immigrants in urban segregation.

Although one out of every ten people in the United States is black, and in many cities blacks form a third or more of the population, the environments of the black and white population are so separate that the two races seem to live in different countries, unable to cross borders, known to each other mainly through stereotypes created by the communications media. A 1978 poll reveals that 49 percent of white Americans still agree with the statement that "blacks tend to have less ambition than whites."[32] While this figure represents a 21 percent decrease from a 1967 poll asking the same question, it demonstrates the strength of racial stereotypes.

Although court rulings and other forms of social change have broken down some barriers to full equality for blacks, significant obstacles still remain in major social institutions and in the racist attitudes of a portion of the population. One discouraging sign for the prospect of improved race relations is the recent reemergence of attempts to link intelligence to race. Arthur Jensen touched off an enormous controversy in the early 1970s when he published findings that intelligence (as measured by IQ tests) is genetically transmitted.[33] Actually, Jensen's data establish no clear link between race and IQ, and the fact that such a relationship was reported is an example of the imposition of an individual scientist's interpretations onto equivocal findings. Although he points to the inadequacies of studies focusing only on environmental factors, Jensen ignores important evidence demonstrating the impact of environment on intelligence. Moreover, the inadequacy of using pencil-and-paper tests to measure the quality called intelligence has been well documented. Such tests measure only certain concrete performances and are permeated by class and value biases. At present, there is no widely accepted scientific evidence linking race to differences in intelligence or personality characteristics.

Serious dangers arise when attempts are made to use such findings as a basis for social policy. Some have interpreted Jensen's work as evidence that black academic performance cannot be improved by altering social factors such as educational arrangements or economic status. Accordingly, it has been advocated that compensatory education programs, such as Head Start, designed to provide better educational opportunities for blacks be abandoned.[34]

When problems come to be defined as being genetic rather than social in nature, social programs will give way to genetic ones. Such solutions not only pose serious moral and ethical problems but could also have grave political implications. It is difficult to see how reintroducing these old and abandoned ideas can have other than a detrimental effect on race relations.

For more than a decade plans have been proposed and implemented to bring about greater equality in the areas of education and occupations. One such plan, affirmative action, has come under considerable criticism on the basis that it encourages reverse discrimination. There are many issues to consider in determining whether members of minority groups merit special consideration in achieving goals that have traditionally been denied them. Not the least of these issues is whether past wrongs can be undone by putting members of contemporary majority groups at a disadvantage for actions committed by their ancestors. Affording special treatment to minority groups need not imply rewarding incompetence or lesser competence, however. For example, lower scores on standardized admission tests do not necessarily mean lower ability to perform certain tasks.

Just as the person who has a graduate degree in chemistry may be better qualified to fulfill the medical school's goal of producing a certain number of doctors to do medical research, just as a woman may be better qualified to become a sensitive and effective gynecologist, so is the person who has experienced a lifetime of racial discrimination better qualified to understand and solve the problems of people in similar circumstances.[35]

The recent Supreme Court decision on the Allan Bakke case gave neither the advocates of affirmative action or its opponents a total victory. The Court decided that race could be considered as a factor in determining admissions policies, but strict numerical quotas are unacceptable. Since the decision applied only to racial factors in medical school admissions, it is not known at this time whether it will have any impact on race as a factor in employment or on ethnic or sex discrimination.

Violence

The most basic right in a society is the right to life. Systematic violence directed against members of minority groups, often engaged in directly or tacitly supported by legal authorities, has infringed on even this right throughout our history. Physical attack and murder, extreme manifestations of majority group domination of minority groups, have taken many lives and left a heritage of violence in American majority-minority relationships. The number of Indians massacred during the expansion of the frontier may never be known. In this century more than a thousand black people had been lynched by the time of World War I. In Tennessee a crowd of 3000 once came to watch a black person be burned alive.[36] So much violence against minorities has encouraged violence in return; in 1967 alone, racial disorders involving blacks and police occurred in 56 cities and resulted in 84 deaths, more than 9000 arrests, and millions of dollars in property damage.[37]

The violence created by discrimination has afflicted many and varied minority groups in America. An anti-Catholic mob burned a convent in Massachusetts in 1831; anti-Greek riots in the early part of this century took place from Boise, Idaho, to Roanoke, Virginia (in one such riot in 1909 a mob caused $250,000 in damages and drove a thousand people out of town).[38] A Jewish man was lynched in Georgia in 1915, and picture postcards of his hanging were sold in Georgia drugstores.[39] A mob of whites invaded a Chinese community in Wyoming in 1885, killed 16 people, and burned their homes to the ground.[40] Susan Brownmiller has pointed out the degree to which women have been attacked and abused in various wars. Organized violence against black females by the Ku Klux Klan was common during Reconstruction.[41]

Violence against minority groups continues today in seemingly more isolated instances but with the same effects. In South Dakota in 1973, Raymond Yellow Thunder, an Indian, was beaten by a white gang, thrown into an American Legion dance hall half-naked, and found dead the next day.[42] His death preceded Indian demonstrations at Wounded Knee.

Violence against minority groups is often of an institutional type—police brutality and unjust enforcement of the law, for instance. The 1968 Kerner report analyzing civil disorders documented minority complaints against police. In the area of a riot in Denver, 82 percent of the people believed that there was police brutality; in the Watts area of Los Angeles, 74 percent of the black men believed the police were disrespectful or directed insulting language at blacks.[43] In cases like these, members of the police force are seen not as members of the community who help maintain order within the neighborhood but rather as outsiders who help maintain majority group domination over minorities.

In response to these problems, some representatives of minority groups have demanded that citizen review boards be established to investigate complaints of police brutality. Others have formed their own self-defense units, or, in rare cases, engaged in guerrilla warfare attacks on the police. Such attacks on law enforcement officials (or on white people in general) seem to follow the same general pattern as attacks by majority group members on minority people; usually a police officer is not known as an individual but is attacked because of affiliation with a group—in this instance, the police. Many of the ghetto uprisings of the 1960s were precipitated by a confrontation between an individual on the police force and a black citizen. A major issue in the black movement of the 1970s has thus become community control of the police.

Besides institutional violence, there is another kind of violence caused by severe discrimination: destruction of the quality of life. Black legislator Julian Bond has described this kind of violence:

Four out of every five Americans are more affluent than any other people in history. They have reached that affluence by degrading the fifth person, the poor Black and Brown Americans and others who have neither the power nor the resources to significantly improve their lot. . . . we need to discover who is and who isn't violent in America. Violence is black children going to school for twelve years and receiving five years of education. Violence is 30 million hungry stomachs in the most affluent

A policeman attempts to keep a black counter-demonstrator away from marching members of the Ku Klux Klan. As organizations like the Klan become less acceptable to all Americans, confrontations between hate groups and minorities will be less frequent.

nation on earth. Violence is having Black people represent a disproportionate share of inductees and casualties in Vietnam. Violence is an economy that believes in socialism for the rich and capitalism for the poor. Violence is spending $900 per second to stifle the Vietnamese, but only $77 a year to feed a hungry person at home. Violence is J. Edgar Hoover listening to your telephone conversation. Violence is an assistant attorney general proposing concentration camps for white and black militants.[44]

Crime

The oppression and discrimination that force minorities into urban ghettos create a climate of violence that leads to crime among members of minority groups. As long ago as 1870, gangs of young people prowled the urban poor neighborhoods. Police were unable to maintain order as thousands of poor European immigrants were entering the slums. Today crime in America has reached such proportions that there is one murder every half hour in the United States and one violent crime, such as rape, robbery, or murder, every minute.[45] This increase in crime particularly affects minority groups who live under conditions that make crime more likely. The chances of a black person's being robbed, raped, or violently assaulted are more than two and a half times those for a white person.[46]

When members of minority groups are victimized, they are likely to be treated more harshly by the agents of the criminal justice system. For example, rape victims are frequently subject to demeaning interrogations and much suspicion when they report their victimization. In addition, differential administration of the law makes the minority person more likely to be arrested and convicted and even more likely to be sentenced to a longer term in prison than a member of the majority group.

At every stage in the law enforcement process, from arrest to parole or execution, a greater proportion of the defendants or prisoners is black than at the previous stage. Such a situation is an inevitable consequence of a system designed to enforce laws made by whites and operating through a structure created and staffed by whites. The cultural myopia of a white society permeates our judicial system, making it inherently incapable of delivering justice to people of color.[47]

The sense that society is unjust, that force is often used in an illegitimate manner, and that the representatives of the law are oppressors contributes to disrespect for the legal system. "The unequal dispensation of justice is a result both of the origin of legal institutions and their present operation by white citizens who do not recognize the worth of non-white cultures."[48] For many blacks, Mexican-Americans, Indians, and women law means white male oppression.

Blocked Opportunity

The problems of Spanish-speaking people in the United States serve to illustrate the inequality of opportunity in our society, as would those of any group that suffers discrimination. Of more than 11 million people of Spanish background in the United States today, more than 6.5 million are Mexican-American, the second largest minority group; only blacks outnumber them. More than 23 percent of families with heads of households who are of

Spanish origin are living in poverty. The problem is particularly critical among Puerto Rican families, of whom 39 percent of all families are in poverty.[49]

The despair caused by such difficulties in our society is reflected in statistics on drug addiction, mental illness, and suicide. In New York City, where about half of all the addicts in the country live, 46 percent of the people reported to the narcotics register were black and 23 percent were Puerto Rican. The rate of drug addiction in central Harlem was reported to be seven times higher than in the rest of the city.[50]

The living conditions in the ghettos and the lack of adequate psychiatric help available to the poor, along with the frustrations and fears of a difficult existence, probably contribute to the high rate of mental illness among the black and Puerto Rican populations.[51] According to Manuel Maldonado-Denis, a Puerto Rican sociologist, the problems of alienation and identity inherent in Puerto Rico's colonial situation lead to an uncertainty among immigrant Puerto Ricans about who and what they are. Second generation Puerto Ricans on the mainland are rejected by American society and in Puerto Rico as well, if they return. This problem of identity, in the view of Maldonado-Denis, is related directly or indirectly to the abnormally high rate of mental illness among Puerto Ricans.[52]

The frustrations of discrimination are also apparent among American Indians. At the Pine Ridge Reservation in South Dakota, a recent analysis indicated a high rate of suicide attempts, alcoholism, broken family structures, and feelings of futility and inferiority. There, where "abandoned, rusted cars cluster around tumble-down shacks and litter the prairie hills, the best acres of which are grazed by white man's cattle,"[53] the school dropout rate is 81 percent by the twelfth grade. More than half the families receive welfare, and unemployment reaches 70 percent in the winter.[54]

In 1975, the death rate for alcohol cirrhosis was 6.1 per 100,000 for the general population in contrast to a rate of 27.3 per 100,000 for American Indians.[55]

The inflexibility of stereotyped sex roles has also prevented women from making much progress in their struggle for equality. The common assumption that chores such as child care and housework are women's work limits the opportunity of females to partake of much meaningful social activity. In addition, women in the United States are generally not treated as legally equal to men in seeking credit, buying land, or pursuing certain careers. Despite recent advances in some of these areas, the dominant social roles assigned to women are more restrictive than those assigned to men.

As with other minority groups discussed previously, women suffer from a disproportionate number of problems. Women suffer from a higher rate of both physical and mental health problems than do men.[56] Not only do women have higher rates of physical problems, but their problems are usually of longer duration than are men's. While men may have higher rates of certain types of mental disorders, rates of manic depressive psychosis and neuroses have been shown to be consistently higher among women.[57] Explanations for these phenomena vary, but one which is being recognized with greater frequency is the importance of restrictive sex roles. Typical women's roles are confining and boring, and this lack of stimulation and challenge in the lives of females leave many susceptible to both mental and physical disorders.[58]

Resistance to Inequality and Discrimination

The movements against prejudice and discrimination grew out of the experiences of idealists like W. E. B. DuBois, who tells how as a child in New England the first realization of prejudice swept across him like a shadow when he went to school. In a happy exchange of cards with the other children, one child peremptorily refused his. "Then it dawned upon me with a certain suddenness that I was different from the others . . . shut out from their world by a vast veil."[59] Rather than desiring to tear down that veil, his reaction was contempt for everything beyond the veil. Such self-protective psychological mechanisms are common among the victims of discrimination. As time went by, DuBois's contempt for whites began to fade, for he saw that the dazzling opportunities were theirs, not his. He decided to get some of the white world's rewards—by reading law, or healing, or telling the tales in his head.

With other black boys the strife was not so fiercely sunny; their youth shrunk into tasteless sycophancy, or into silent hatred of the pale world about them and mocking distrust of everything white; or wasted itself in a bitter cry. Why did God make me an outcast and a stranger in mine own house? The shades of the prisonhouse closed round about us all.[60]

And what of the white world which tried to be gracious when he reached sophisticated levels as a writer and intellectual of his day?

They approach me in a half-hesitant sort of way, eye me curiously or compassionately, and then, instead of saying directly, How does it feel to be a problem? They say, I know an excellent colored man in my town; or, I fought at Mechanicsville; or, Do not these Southern outrages make your blood boil? At these I smile, or am interested, or reduce the boiling to a simmer as the occasion may require. To the real question, How does it feel to be a problem? I answer seldom a word.

And yet, being a problem is a strange experience—peculiar even for one who has never been anything else, save perhaps in babyhood and in Europe.[61]

DuBois was writing at the turn of the century, but his experiences have been repeated countless times since then. For many, the effects of prejudice led to a bitter rage. For some, like DuBois, the sense of injustice also led to movements for human dignity. He and other young blacks demanded aggressive action for human brotherhood in the Niagara Movement of 1906; by 1910 the young radicals had joined with educators and social workers in forming the National Association for the Advancement of Colored People (NAACP). Although, as John Hope Franklin has written, "the presence of Dr. DuBois on the staff branded the organization as radical from the beginning,"[62] the radicalism at this stage was more rhetorical than real.

While the NAACP worked to end segregation and gain the right to vote for all black people, another group, the National Urban League, was formed in 1911 to help blacks who were moving into urban centers and to gain new opportunities for blacks in industry. The gains made by these groups formed a necessary prelude to the long marches for civil rights of the 1950s.

In 1954 the Supreme Court held that segregation in the public schools was unconstitutional and must be ended. The separation of races in the schools had become fully effective in the South in the 1890s; its overthrow by the Court was a major inroad on the systems of institutional racism. Inroads on other institutionalized discriminatory practices were soon forced. The Montgomery bus boycott, perhaps the beginning of the modern civil-rights movement, led by Martin Luther King, Jr., began after a black woman was arrested in December 1955 for refusing to give up her seat to a white man in the "colored" section of a bus. It ended when the Supreme Court ruled against segregation on Montgomery buses.

As the movement grew, white resistance increased. Attempts to desegregate schools—from the 1956 effort at the University of Alabama to those at elementary and secondary schools in many cities—occasioned mob violence against blacks and required the use of National Guard troops to protect black students. When in 1957 whites resisted nine black students trying to enter Central High School in Little Rock, Arkansas, President Eisenhower ordered troops to the city, the first use of federal troops in defense of black people's rights in the South since Reconstruction.

The "sit-in" movement began in 1960 when black college students at a segregated lunch counter in North Carolina were refused service and stayed in their places. Soon tens of thousands of black and white people were joining together in sit-in protests around the country. Many were arrested. Black college students then organized the Student Nonviolent Coordinating Committee (SNCC), and nonviolent demonstrations spread to segregated beaches and churches. Others joined in "freedom rides," a deliberate flaunting of segregated seating and accommodations, to protest segregated buses. Their efforts led to an order by the Interstate Commerce Commission against segregation on buses and in terminals. Another important step in the civil-rights struggle was the voter registration drive which was directed against unlawful practices, such as sham literacy tests and poll taxes, that had deprived a large portion of the black citizenry of their right to vote.

In the summer of 1963, efforts to end discrimination on the one hand and resistance to these efforts on the other resulted in demonstrations, bombings, and the arrests of thousands. Some 250,000 people joined to march into Washington that August, in the largest gathering in history to demonstrate for civil rights.

The next year Congress passed the Civil Rights Act of 1964, which had many provisions against segregation, such as those outlawing segregation in public places and in programs receiving federal aid. The act established a sixth-grade education as sufficient proof of literacy for voting and gave the attorney general authority to act in desegregation and equal protection cases.

Attempts to register black voters sometimes resulted in white retaliation, including arrest by antiblack law enforcement officers. Three volunteers were murdered in the 1964 Mississippi Summer Project of voter registration, and a thousand people were arrested. Three also died as a result of the march from Selma to Montgomery in the campaign for the right to vote. The march—which contributed to passage of the Voting Rights Act of 1965, greatly facilitating the registration and vote for southern blacks—also proved to be the final large demonstration in the civil-rights movement, in which black and white people had worked together to end legal discrimination in many areas of American life.

Black Power

By 1965 the fight against inequality and discrimination had moved to the northern cities, where large numbers of rural blacks had migrated. Many were unable to find jobs or join unions and lacked the training to deal with modern technology. Families were crowded into slums and relocated in impersonal housing projects; children failed to learn in schools that were not geared to deal with their educational needs. As Martin Luther King had represented the resentments of southern blacks, Malcolm X voiced the frustrations of urban blacks. Turning away from the goal of integration, Malcolm X sought racial solidarity—cooperation with the black people of Africa in a struggle for basic rights in political, social, and economic spheres. He urged positive identification, pride in being black.

Black power first emerged as a concept in a speech to a crowd of poor people in Mississippi by Stokely Carmichael, chairman of SNCC. Later he and Charles Hamilton explained the concept in their book *Black Power*.[63] Rejecting the dominant society's values and institutions, black power, as described by Carmichael and Hamilton, is "a call for black people in this country to unite, to recognize their heritage, to build a sense of community."[64] "It is a call for black people to begin to define their own goals, to lead their own organizations and to support those organizations."[65]

Pointing out that ethnic groups traditionally have found social and political strength by setting up their own institutions to represent their needs within the society, Carmichael and Hamilton set the theme of ethnic self-determination and a rejection of old ideas of assimilation. Underlying this new movement was the fundamental premise: *Before a group can enter the open society, it must first close ranks.*

In the racial violence of the 1960s, Martin Luther King, Malcolm X, and many others were killed; groups like the Black Panthers developed a more militant position; and white society became more apprehensive. Despite its tendencies to violent action, black power appeared to be a promising indication of the vitality of the black community. The drive for economic, political, and social power gained momentum; pride in blackness led to new confidence; and black solidarity began to have significant effects in the larger society.

Self-Determination among Other Groups

Other minorities seeking establishment of their rights have since followed the example of blacks. Political, social, and economic development among Mexican-Americans took place in the 1960s through the efforts of the Chicano movement.[66] Beginning with the Delano grape strike in 1965, Cesar Chavez emerged as an advocate of unionization and other reforms for Chicano agricultural workers working under intolerable conditions. The efforts resulted in a contract signed with growers of about 50 percent of the table grapes from California in 1970, the first time Chicano farm workers had any control over their working conditions. On another front, Fries Lopez Tijerina tried to reclaim the New Mexico lands once owned by the Hispanic-Mexican peoples, now owned by Anglo-American ranchers and the American government. In Denver, Colorado, "Corky" Gonzales led another Mexican-American group toward such goals as better housing and education in a new Chicano society. Jose Angel Gutierrez, working in Crystal City, Texas, started La Raza Unida to gain political, economic, and social control of areas of south Texas. Not surprisingly, there has been a recent movement in some parts of the country for a coalition between Chicano and black groups to form in their common struggle for equality.

Puerto Rican groups have also translated cultural pride and self-determination into a positive force. Striving for improved educational opportunities for young Puerto Ricans, Puerto Rican educators established bilingual programs for schoolchildren, while mobile street theaters and dance groups worked to build cultural identity. On American college campuses, Puerto Rican and Afro-American groups have sometimes joined efforts in third world (non-Caucasian) coalitions.

Indians, too, began to organize as new leaders worked for greater self-determination. The American Indian Movement (AIM), which began in 1968 in Minneapolis, has led demonstrations in various places. In one case AIM members led a lengthy seige of a portion of the Wounded Knee, South Dakota, reservation to dramatize Indian grievances. Although eventually they were ousted by federal authorities, this event served to focus public opinion on the plight of native Americans. Other Indian groups are attempting to

Positively proud: The sixties inspired minority groups with a new attitude of positive group identification and an emphasis on self-determination.

regain tribal lands or to receive adequate compensation for property taken from them through the years. They are also seeking community control over their schools and other institutions.

Movements which began as a reaction to inequality and discrimination have evolved into a new social and political force. People from various ethnic groups have begun to emphasize their cultural heritage and question previous ideas of assimilation. It remains to be seen, however, whether the new vitality of the minority groups will lead to more divisiveness or to improved relations among all members of the society.

The Women's Movement

Contrary to the belief of many, the struggle of women for equality and dignity did not begin in the 1960s and 1970s. The resurgence of interest in women's rights represents only the latest effort by women in a struggle that dates back well over 100 years. The first public meeting on women's rights took place in 1848 and drew up a Declaration of Sentiments, which declared that "all men and women were created equal." From 1848 until the beginning of the Civil War, women's rights' conventions were held almost every year in cities across the country.[67]

The passage of the 19th Amendment on August 26, 1920, giving women the right to vote was the culmination of a long, hard struggle that began shortly after the Civil War. For several years thereafter, women's groups sought suffrage through petitioning, writing newspaper and magazine articles, and holding public meetings. It was not until the movement resorted to mass demonstrations and hunger strikes that federal action was taken to ensure women the right to vote.

After some four decades of relative calm, a renewed outburst of feminist agitation in the late 1960s sent shock waves throughout the nation as women found that they continued to play a second-class role in society. Fed by the fires lighted by other liberal reform movements such as the War on Poverty and civil-rights and Vietnam War protests, women came to the realization that a change of status was possible.

At the outset, the women's movement consisted of two major strains, which have since merged in some respects while dividing numerous times in others.[68] Among younger, more educated women, activity in the movement took the form of rap groups and consciousness-raising sessions. Women gathered to discuss and help each other comprehend their common oppression and to explore methods of overcoming the limitations placed on them by society. Among other housewives and professional women, the movement took the form of organizations seeking legal reform. The National Organization of Women (NOW) was formed in 1966 for the purpose of instigating legal reform.

The women's movement today consists of persons with diverse ideologies and perspectives. Some groups struggle to solve the problems of sex inequality, while others believe that equality can only be achieved by abolishing the current patriarchal structures and rebuilding society from the ground up. The range of issues to which these groups give attention covers a wide span of social problems. Some members of the movement claim that all social problems are women's problems since women comprise more than

Mr. Voter:

VOTE NO
ON WOMAN SUFFRAGE
NOVEMBER 6

The Ballot will secure a Woman
no Right that she Needs and
does not Possess

WOMAN'S ANTI SUFFRAGE ASSOCIATION
280 MADISON AVENUE
NEW YORK

National Women's Conference 1977

half the population. But the more strictly feminist issues about which women are concerned include the demand for complete equality under the law, particularly in the areas of education, jobs, wages and property ownership. Many of these reforms are included in the proposed Equal Rights Amendment (ERA) to the Constitution. Although adopted by Congress, it must now be ratified by the requisite number of states before becoming the law of the land.

Feminist groups are also proposing a restructuring of work schedules to take into consideration the special needs of women. For example, more part-time jobs, more flexible time schedules and more comprehensive day-care centers are viewed as factors that would allow women greater freedom. Some groups demand the right of complete control over their bodies through unrestricted access to birth control and safe, legal abortions. Others attack the male-dominated medical establishment and propose the institutionalization of women's medical clinics.

Whatever the accomplishments of the women's movement to date, it has established itself as a vital social and political force in society. It has brought to the attention of the entire population the many injustices to which women have been subject over the centuries.

Although women have come a long way politically and socially since they were granted the vote in 1920, many forms of discrimination remain. Fighting for an equal role in society demands political action, and women have once again organized to achieve their objectives.

No longer can thousands of lynchings take place without arousing the disgust and anger of the general population; fortunately, that period of racial violence is over. Legalized discrimination has been virtually ended by the civil-rights movement. But less blatant forms of oppression of minority groups continue: discrimination by custom, as in housing, and by institutions, as in education. These intentional and unintentional discriminatory practices still result in unequal opportunities for members of minority groups and in the perpetuation of stereotypes, thereby slowing further progress.

Progress in Education

The area of education illustrates particularly well the complexity of problems stemming from inequality, discrimination, and hostility in majority-minority relations. Despite the 20 years of political and social change that followed from the Supreme Court's landmark 1954 decision that segregation in the schools could not be tolerated, much de facto segregation remains in both northern and southern regions.

Satisfactory answers have not yet been found to remedy the situation, although it seems clear that no simple solution will work. For a time, decentralization of the educational system was urged to restore educational power to local communities and to begin to correct inequities. But decentralization easily leads to power battles between hostile racial groups, while the essential goal—improved education for children—is lost in the antagonisms. Busing has been considered an answer by some, but again, hostile reactions divert attention from the goal of improved education. The merging of suburban and city school systems also has an uncertain future in the face of legal and parental opposition. (See Chapter 3 for discussion in greater detail of educational developments relating to integration and educational quality.)

Nonetheless, there are some promising developments. One is the growth of private and public schools that stress quality education and cultural pride for minority children. Schools like Harlem Prep, the Rough Rock Demonstration School (on a Navajo reservation in Arizona), and the bilingual schools for Puerto Rican and Mexican-American children build learning achievement through pride in ethnic identities. Other hopeful trends are the growth of open admission plans, which broaden opportunities for minority students to enter college, and the development of community colleges in urban neighborhoods. These colleges address themselves to the needs of people of many ages within minority communities and often are staffed by educators from minority backgrounds. Within a center-city neighborhood, such colleges can be focal points for cultural and community development.

Analyses of recent trends in educational attainment indicate significant gains among blacks as well as the continuing presence of a sizable gap between black and white attainment. In the postwar period there were large differences in the proportions of whites and blacks graduating from high school. From 1960 to 1970, however, the percentage of black males finishing high school jumped from 36 to 54 percent; among black women the figure rose from 41 to 61 percent.[69] The attainment gap has continued to narrow in the 1970s, and among those in their late twenties today, 85 percent of whites as compared to 74 percent of blacks have completed high school.[70] At the college level, the disparity between black and white enrollment remains high; 25 percent of blacks, aged 18–29, as compared with 37 percent of whites of the same age enrolled in college at the beginning of the Fall 1977 term.[71] Thirty-six percent of the female population of the same age were in colleges in 1977 as compared to 35 percent of the male population.[72] The gap in higher education is not as severe as it once was. While such statistics do not take into account the difference in the quality or subject matter of education provided for majority and minority students, they do indicate significant changes.

Economic Progress

The economic gaps between minority populations and the majority remain large. Median family income is the most widely used statistic to indicate economic position of various groups in our society. Table 8.1 presents comparative data on the median family income of whites and nonwhites from 1947 to 1977. The median income of nonwhites peaked during the early 1970s at 65 percent of that of whites. This ratio has begun to decline somewhat since then. With the severe economic recession and the absence of strong civil-rights pressure in the 1970s, the gains of the 1960s among nonwhites are in danger of elimination.

While there is some evidence that blacks are now able to get better jobs than they were in the 1960s,[73] it is clear that they still do not earn as much money as whites for the same jobs. For example, in 1975 black male professionals earned only 78 percent of the income of their white counterparts. Black female professionals earned only 56 percent of the income made by white female professionals.[74]

Historically, unemployment among nonwhites has exceeded that of

	White and Nonwhite Family Income Trends, 1947–1977		**Table 8.1**
	Median Family Income in Current Dollars		Nonwhite Median Income as Percent of Whites
Year	Whites	Nonwhites	
1947	$ 3,157	$ 1,614	51
1950	3,445	1,869	54
1955	4,613	2,544	55
1960	5,835	3,230	55
1965	7,251	3,993	55
1970	10,236	6,516	63
1975	14,268	9,321	65
1977	16,740	10,142	60

Source: U.S. Bureau of the Census, *Current Population Reports, Consumer Income, Money Income and Poverty Status of Families and Persons in the United States: 1977 (Advance Report),* Series P-60, No. 116 (Washington, D.C.: Government Printing Office: July 1978), p. 9.

whites by a ratio of about two to one. Unemployment has traditionally been a chronic problem among young nonwhite males; the rate has not been below 15 percent since the Korean War, and it reached a staggering recession level of 29 percent in April 1975.[75]

Although the number of unemployed whites has dropped by 28 percent between the first half of 1975 and the first half of 1978, the number of blacks who were unemployed during these two periods remained unchanged.[76]

Females employed in every occupational group earn significantly less than their male counterparts. On the average, male white-collar workers earn $7000 more than white-collar females. In the blue-collar occupations, males earn over $5000 more than females. Table 8.2 demonstrates the comparative figures for males and females for eight occupational categories.

Political Progress

In 1973 in Los Angeles, a city where blacks make up less than a fifth of the total population, Thomas Bradley, a black, was elected mayor with 56 percent of the vote. A black mayor of the third largest city in the country is one indication of black political gains in the early 1970s.

The trend toward political consolidation of city and suburban areas (which reduces the percentage of black people within the new governmental unit), however, would appear to threaten continued political progress for blacks. In Jacksonville, Florida, as the whites moved to suburban areas and the number of blacks living in the city proper approached 50 percent of the population, a metrogovernment consolidation of Jacksonville and the suburban area was proposed. One analysis of the Jacksonville consolidation indicates that what happened there is an old story; when blacks seemed to be moving toward their share of political power, "the rules of the game were changed."[77] Such consolidation can have important practical advantages; it provides more revenue and a stronger economic basis for city services, as well as a potential for greater governmental efficiency. But it strips power from the urban black majority and encourages neglect of black needs.

When individual members of minority groups do gain political power,

Table 8.2	Median Annual Earnings of Workers, by Sex and Occupation, 1976		
Occupation Group		Male	Female
White-collar workers		$15,852	$ 8,853
Professional, technical and kindred workers		16,939	11,072
Managers, administrators (except farm)		16,674	9,804
Sale workers		14,586	6,272
Clerical, kindred workers		12,843	8,128
Blue-collar workers		12,469	6,808
Craft, kindred workers		13,638	7,765
Operatives		11,688	6,649
Laborers (except farm)		10,104	7,613
Service workers		10,030	5,674

Source: U.S. Bureau of the Census, *Statistical Abstract of the United States, 1977* (Washington, D.C.: Government Printing Office, 1977), p. 411.

commensurate economic gains for the entire group are not necessarily achieved. Robert Curvin, who organized the black and Puerto Rican coalition at the convention that nominated Kenneth Gibson for mayor of Newark, New Jersey, discussed results after Gibson's first year in office and found that "black power in city hall will not necessarily deliver solutions to the problems faced by black people in urban areas."[78] As in most cities, not only are there two racial Newarks, there are also two economic Newarks. One is mostly black and without economic power; the other is the thriving white business community.

The 1979 election of Jane Byrne as mayor of Chicago marks the first successful attempt by a woman to achieve the highest office of one of the nation's largest cities. The mayors of San Francisco, San Jose and Cincinnati are also female. Ella Grasso, the governor of Connecticut is the only woman to hold such a post.

At the national level after the 1978 election, only 17 of the 435 members of the House of Representatives were black and there were no black senators. Female membership in the two federal bodies number 16 and 1, respectively.[79]

Assimilation, Pluralism, or Separatism?

In the past, immigrants were expected to shed their own cultures and fit into American life and culture as quickly and as completely as possible. According to the melting-pot theory, the pasts of many people merged and in so doing contributed to a newer, better product—the American way of life. Yet, in spite of this "contributions" theory, the individual immigrant families were expected to sing a few ethnic songs, cook a few ethnic dishes, and give up their ethnic life-styles, aiming at assimilation into the American cultural mainstream by the third generation. Now, however, sociologists are beginning to question whether the ethnic background of immigrants has truly been erased. Some have suggested that, in fact, ethnic background remains a continuing basis for identity and social conflict in America.[80] And in recent years, rather than stressing homogeneity resulting from a process of assimilation, more emphasis has been placed on the need to preserve the distinct cultures in America and to understand how they function for the individual and society.

Minorities such as blacks and Chicanos have become increasingly disillusioned with the idea of assimilation; they have begun to advocate that minority people take pride in the uniqueness of their own group identity and their distinctive cultural heritage. This call for cultural pluralism involves a rejection of older notions of integration. Members of minority groups who advocate pluralism do not wish to assimilate; instead they demand justice and equality and the accompanying right to live their lives as they desire while retaining their own cultural identity and unique customers.[81]

Since cultural pluralism remains a goal rather than a concrete reality, its full ramifications cannot yet be assessed. Pluralism and its emphasis on group identity may exacerbate problems in majority-minority relations by defining more clearly the boundaries and differences between groups. On the other hand, it may improve relations by focusing attention on the positive and distinctive aspects of the cultures of minority groups, resulting in tolerance and mutual respect between groups. Whitney M. Young, Jr., stated the ideal another way: "In the context of positive pluralism, black people would enter the dominant white society with a sense of roots," he wrote. "By now, we ought to see the fatal flaws of the old melting-pot theory, which sought to strip people of culture and traditions in order to transform everyone into middle-class, white Anglo-Saxons."[82]

Sociologist Andrew Greeley has also rejected the notion that groups must be assimilated into American culture. He has argued, instead, for an American culture that understands its diversity. Citing the conclusion of French anthropologist Claude Levi-Strauss that diversity is necessary for human society, Greeley finds that although differences between peoples are the focus of social conflict, the differences are not likely to be eliminated. "The critical question is how to use these tensions and diversities to create a richer, fuller human society instead of a narrow, frightened and suspicious society."[83]

Some would maintain that the differences are so sharp that the only resolution is separation. This has been the practical outcome of the white retreat into the suburbs. The farther members of the white majority have fled from the minority communities, however, the more strained the American social fabric has become. Separatism has also been proposed by blacks, among them the late Marcus Garvey, whose back-to-Africa movement once involved thousands of people. Separatism will always have some appeal, but it can never lead to the conditions necessary for a harmonious society because it avoids confronting the diverse issues.

Many feminists claim that women will never be assimilated completely into American society as it exists today since the institutional structure is itself sexist. Those institutions must be altered dramatically to provide women with the mechanisms necessary to achieve success. The women's movement has begun the process through which these changes may occur, but the sexist ideas and actions developed over hundreds of years will be difficult to change rapidly.

Prejudice and discrimination feed upon an insecurity that fears diversity. Psychological, economic, and social disorder combine in hostility and discrimination directed at minority groups. Yet the categories that make people objects of prejudice are not immutable; they change, and some years later the violence earlier directed against one such group may hardly seem comprehensible to society at large.

Summary

Prejudice and discrimination endanger American society by damaging the community of belief and action that enables that society to function. Prejudice is a preconceived, hostile attitude toward certain people based on their membership in a group. Discrimination is the favorable or unfavorable treatment of individuals on the basis of their membership in a group rather than on the basis of their qualities as individuals. The most prevalent kind of discrimination practiced in America is the denial of certain kinds of jobs, housing, education, and other benefits of society to members of specific racial, ethnic, and sex groups.

Psychological factors (such as fear of change), socioeconomic factors (such as competition for job opportunities), and sociological factors (such as the desire for social prestige and power) combine to perpetuate prejudice in American society.

The Europeans who colonized America brought inequality with them. Unable to appreciate the different "pagan" cultures they found, they took little care to respect America's native inhabitants, who remained outside their community of belief. As American society developed, the prejudice which permitted such actions persisted. Black slaves were considered property rather than human beings; Indians and Mexican-Americans were conquered and then exploited. None of the members of these cultural groups was ever recognized as having a claim to the kind of treatment received by members of the dominant European groups. Females of any group were seldom accorded the same legal and social rights as males. Although slavery was abolished, social custom and law continued to discriminate against blacks. These sanctions were accompanied by an ideology of white superiority, fully developed by the turn of the twentieth century, which we have come to recognize as racism.

Discrimination against other groups—Puerto Ricans, Mexican-Americans, Orientals, and American Indians—has also been practiced by the larger society. Procedures of the majority group in our country for dealing with these groups parallel those used in keeping blacks from full participation in American life.

Women have been dealt with in similar fashion. When they are useful to society, such as during wars, they are permitted jobs in many support areas. But they are quickly excluded from these same positions when these crises pass.

Inequities and discrimination are responsible for the segregation of minority groups in urban ghettos or on federal reservations. The effect of such segregation is often to increase the difficulties of living for the minority involved. Crime, disease, and disorder in minority group life can in large part be ascribed to segregation. Discrimination in hiring limits job opportunities for minorities. Poor education limits opportunities still further.

Discrimination is so deeply rooted in American society that to reverse it to any degree has required radical action. Black attempts to combat it began early in this century and culminated in the civil-rights movement of the 1950s and 1960s. The 1954 Supreme Court decision against segregation in the public schools gave the movement impetus. A later development was the drive for black power, both political and economic, and a search for African cultural roots. Blacks and other minorities subject to discrimination have in general followed the nonviolent confrontation methods advocated by Martin Luther King, Jr., although a few groups, such as the Black Panthers, have advocated violent resistance to the oppression of prejudice and discrimination.

Minorities have made some progress against discrimination in educational, economic, and political fields. The federal government has been an active agent in changing discriminatory practices in education and employment. Most institutions are now prohibited from discriminating on the basis of race, creed, ethnic origin, or sex. In politics, an increasing number of minority candidates are winning elections not only in minority areas but even in such places as Los Angeles, which is predominantly white.

Minority resistance to prejudice and discrimination has revived the ethnic identity of national groups once thought to have been assimilated into American society. Although such a revival has often served to counter black and other minority demands, it has stimulated discussion of pluralism, rather than assimilation, as a goal for American society. Conflicts between groups have in some instances become sharper than they were before, but American society may nonetheless be moving toward a recognition of diversity in individual and group relations.

Notes

[1]Norman R. Yetman and C. Hoy Steele, eds., *Majority and Minority* (Boston: Allyn and Bacon, 1971). p. 4.

[2]*Report of the National Advisory Commission on Civil Disorders* (New York: Bantam Books, 1968), p. 220.

[3]Robert Blauner, *Racial Oppression in America* (New York: Harper & Row, 1972), p. 22.

[4]L. Paul Metzger, "American Sociology and Black Assimilation: Conflicting Perspectives," *Race Relations,* ed. Edgar C. Epps (Cambridge, Mass.: Winthrop Publishing, 1973), p. 2.

[5]Gordon W. Allport, *The Nature of Prejudice* (Reading, Mass.: Addison-Wesley, 1954), p. 7.

[6]Ibid., pp. 14–16.

[7]Ibid., p. 396.

[8]T. W. Adorno et al., *The Authoritarian Personality* (New York: Harper & Row, 1950).

[9]Milton Rokeach, *The Open and Closed Mind* (New York: Basic Books, 1960).

[10]Matt S. Meier and Feliciano Rivera, *The Chicanos* (New York: Hill & Wang, 1972), pp. 74–84.

[11]See John Higham, *Strangers in the Land: Patterns of American Nativism 1860–1925* (New Brunswick, N.J.: Rutgers University Press, 1955); and Gustavus Myers, *History of Bigotry in the United States* (New York: Random House, 1943).

[12]Alphonso Pinkney, *Black Americans* (Englewood Cliffs, N.J.: Prentice-Hall, 1969), pp. 1–2.

[13]C. Vann Woodward, *The Strange Career of Jim Crow* (New York: Oxford University Press, 1966), p. 74.

[14]William E. B. DuBois, *The Souls of Black Folk* (Chicago: McClurg, 1903), introduction.

[15]Murray L. Wax, *Indian Americans* (Englewood Cliffs, N.J.: Prentice-Hall, 1971), p. 32.

[16]John Collier, "The United States Indian," *Understanding Minority Groups,* ed. Joseph B. Gittler (New York: Wiley, 1956), p. 34.

[17]Wax, *Indian Americans,* pp. 88–132.

[18]Thomas F. Gossett, *Race: The History of an Idea in America* (New York: Schocken Books, 1965), pp. 232–233.

[19]John Kifner, "At Wounded Knee, Two Worlds Collide," *New York Times,* 24 March 1973, p. 14.

[20]Wax, *Indian Americans,* pp. 64–65.

[21]Ibid., p. 65.

[22]Howell Raines, "American Indians: Struggling for Power and Identity." *The New York Times Magazine,* 11 February 1979, p. 21.

[23]Bureau of Indian Affairs, "American Indian Tribes of Montana and Wyoming," Report No. 262 (Washington, D.C.: Government Printing Office, October 1978), p. 113.

[24]Meier and Rivera, *The Chicanos.*

[25]Stan Steiner, *LaRaza: The Mexican Americans* (New York: Harper & Row, 1970), p. 24.

[26]Salvatore J. LaGumina and Frank J. Cavaioli, *The Ethnic Dimension in American Society* (Boston: Allyn and Bacon Holbrook Press, 1974), p. 230.

[27]Kathleen Gough, "The Origin of the Family," *Toward an Anthropology of Women,* ed. Rayna Reiter (New York: Monthly Review Press, 1972), p. 70.

[28]Karen Socks, "Engels Revisited: Women, the Organization of Production, and Private Property," *Toward an Anthropology of Women* ed. Rayna Reiter (New York: Monthly Review Press, 1975), p. 240.

[29]Barbara Ehrenreich and Deidre English, "The Manufacture of Housework," *Capitalism and the Family* (San Francisco: Agenda Publishing Company, 1976), pp. 7–42.

[30]Cynthia Fuchs Epstein, "Sex Roles," *Contemporary Social Problems,* 4th ed., ed. Robert K. Merton and Robert Nisbet (New York: Harcourt, 1976), p. 430.

[31]Betty Friedan, *The Feminine Mystique* (New York: Dell, 1974), pp. 24–25.

[32]Dennis Williams with Jerry Buckley and Mary Lord, "A New Racial Poll," *Newsweek,* 26 February 1979, p. 48.

[33]Arthur R. Jensen, "How Much Can We Boost IQ and Scholastic Achievement?" *Harvard Educational Review* 39 (Winter 1969), 1–123.

[34]Ibid.

[35]Charles Lawrence, "Are Racial Quotas Defensible?," *Current* 198 (December 1977), p. 9.

[36]John Hope Franklin, *From Slavery to Freedom: A History of Negro Americans,* 3rd ed. (New York: Knopf, 1967), p. 439.

[37]Pinkney, *Black Americans,* pp. 205–206.

[38]Oscar Handlin, *A Pictorial History of Immigration* (New York: Crown Publishers, 1972), p. 250.

[39]Lenora E. Berson, *The Negroes and the Jews* (New York: Random House, 1971), p. 30.

[40]Alphonso Pinkney, *The American Way of Violence* (New York: Random House, Vintage Books, 1972), p. 73.

[41]Susan Brownmiller, *Against Our Will* (New York: Simon and Schuster, 1975), pp. 126–129.

[42]Kifner, "At Wounded Knee," p. 14.

[43]*Report of the National Advisory Commission on Civil Disorders,* p. 302.

[44]Julian Bond, "Foreword," *Black Business Enterprise: Historical and Contemporary Perspectives,* ed. Ronald W. Bailey (New York: Basic Books, 1971), pp. viii–ix.

[45]Pinkney, *American Way of Violence,* p. 6.

[46]Ben J. Wattenberg and Richard M. Scammon, "Black Progress and Liberal Rhetoric," *Commentary* 55 (April 1973), 40.

[47]Louis L. Knowles and Kenneth Prewitt, eds., *Institutional Racism in America* (Englewood Cliffs, N.J.: Prentice-Hall, 1969), pp. 58–59.

[48]Ibid., pp. 76–77.

[49]U.S. Bureau of the Census, *Current Population Reports, Persons of Spanish Origin in the United States: March 1977,* Series P-20, No. 329 (Washington, D.C.: Government Printing Office, 1978), p. 15.

[50]Pinkney, *Black Americans,* p. 134; Joseph P. Fitzpatrick, *Puerto Rican Americans: The Meaning of Migration to the Mainland* (Englewood Cliffs, N.J.: Prentice-Hall, 1971); Kenneth Clark, *Youth in the Ghetto* (New York: Harlem Youth Opportunities Unlimited, 1964), pp. 144–145.

[51]U.S. Office of Management and Budget, *Social Indicators, 1973* (Washington, D.C.: Government Printing Office, 1973), p. 13.

[52]Manuel Maldonado-Denis, *Puerto Rico: A Socio-Historic Interpretation,* trans. Elena Vialo (New York: Random House, 1972), pp. 320–321.

[53]Kifner, "At Wounded Knee," p. 14.

[54]Ibid.

[55]Associated Press, "High Alcoholism of U.S. Indians," *San Francisco Chronicle,* 7 September 1978, p. 38.

[56]C. A. Nathanson, "Illness and the Feminine Role: A Theoretical Review," *Social Science and Medicine* 9 (February 1975), p. 57.

[57]Bruce Dohrenwend, "Problems in Defining and Sampling the Relevant Population of Stressful Life Events," *Stressful Life Events: Their Nature and Effects,* ed. B. S. Dohrenwend and B. P. Dohrenwend (New York: Wiley, 1974), p. 369.

[58]R. Seidenberg, "The Trauma of Eventlessness," *Psychoanalytic Review* 59 (Spring 1972), 95–109.

[59]DuBois, *Souls of Black Folk,* p. 1.

[60]Ibid., p. 2.

[61]Ibid., p. 3.

[62]Franklin, *From Slavery to Freedom,* p. 447.

[63]Stokely Carmichael and Charles V. Hamilton, *Black Power: The Politics of Liberation in America* (New York: Random House, 1967).

[64]Ibid., p. 37.

[65]Ibid., p. 44.

[66]Meier and Rivera, *The Chicanos,* pp. 250–276.

[67]Judith Hole and Ellen Levine, "The First Feminists," *Radical Feminism,* ed. Ann Koedt, Ellen Levine, and Anita Rapone (New York: Quadrangle/New York Times Book Company, 1973), p. 9.

[68]Ibid., pp. 9–10.

[69]Wattenberg and Scammon, "Black Progress and Liberal Rhetoric," pp. 35–44.

[70]U.S. Bureau of the Census, *Statistical Abstract of the United States, 1977* (Washington, D.C.: Government Printing Office, 1977), p. 136.

[71]U.S. Bureau of the Census, *Current Population Reports, School Enrollment-Social and Economic Characteristics of Students: October 1977 (Advance Report)*, Series P-20, No. 321 (Washington, D.C.: Government Printing Office, March 1978), pp. 3–4.

[72]Ibid.

[73]Wattenberg and Scammon, "Black Progress and Liberal Rhetoric," pp. 37–38.

[74]Robert B. Hill, *The Illusion of Black Progress*, (Washington, D.C.: National Urban League, 1978), p. 35.

[75]Reynolds Farley, "The Economic Status of Blacks: Have the Gains of the 1960s Disappeared in the 1970s?" unpublished paper read at the annual meeting of the American Sociological Association, San Francisco, 25–29 August 1975, p. 14.

[76]Hill, *The Illusion of Black Progress*, p. 4.

[77]Lee Sloan and Robert M. French, "Black Rule in the Urban South?" *Transaction* 9 (November/December 1971), 29–34.

[78]Robert Curvin, "Black Power in City Hall," *Society* 10 (September/October 1972), 55–58.

[79]*The World Almanac and Book of Facts, 1979* (New York: Newspaper Enterprise Association, 1979), pp. 38–40.

[80]Nathan Glazer and Daniel P. Moynihan, *Beyond the Melting Pot* (Cambridge, Mass.: MIT Press, 1963), pp. 13–24.

[81]Metzer, "American Sociology and Black Assimilation," p. 10.

[82]Whitney M. Young, Jr., *Beyond Racism: Building an Open Society* (New York: McGraw-Hill, 1969), p. 152.

[83]Andrew M. Greeley, *Why Can't They Be Like Us?* (New York: Dutton, 1971), pp. 15–16.

Health Care

9

Problems of Progress

Our Ailing System of Medical Care

Health Care: Right or Privilege?

The Cost of Good Health

Improving Delivery of Health Care

Summary

Notes

The impact of social change on American life is nowhere more apparent than in the deep-seated problems now confronting the nation in the area of health care. At first glance the situation seems a paradox. The scientific competence of our medical profession and the technological sophistication of our medical facilities are unsurpassed. The capacity of medicine to prolong life and enhance human functioning continues to expand with new advances in the understanding and treatment of disease. The United States invests more money in health care than any other nation in the world.[1] Yet providers and consumers of health services, public officials, and scholarly authorities all agree that we are in the midst of a health care crisis of mounting proportions.

Although few would argue that good health care is not a primary national goal, agreement on the means for achieving such a goal is missing. Physicians, administrators, insurance companies, and consumers all claim the right and the ability to determine the organization of health care services in America. Traditional privileges as well as recent social and technological changes have served to enlarge their differences, causing health care delivery to become disorganized, and major portions of the population to be systematically excluded from adequate care. Because of the rapid growth in technical knowledge, the size of investments needed to build and equip modern medical centers, physician specialization, and even rank profiteering in medicine, health care has become extremely expensive and thus inaccessible to many Americans. The unemployed, who are not covered by health insurance, and the aged, who have fixed incomes and high rates of utilization, are particularly affected by the resulting social disorganization. Other groups, the poor and the rural dwellers, are also excluded from adequate medical care because of unequal distribution of income and the lack of physicians who are available to treat them.

Diagnoses of the problem as well as remedies for dealing with it may vary, but the symptoms are hardly in dispute. The major issues have grown in prominence concurrently with the growth of medical expertise and the accompanying increase in national expenditures and health consciousness. They include low levels on international vital health indexes, where other countries, expending smaller proportions of their Gross National Product on health services, surpass us in the results achieved. Our international ranking on infant mortality, for instance, has declined steadily since 1950, until we now find ourselves in twentieth place. Our infant mortality rate was 15.1 per thousand live births in 1976, compared to Norway's 11.1 and Sweden's 8.7.[2]

It is easy enough to locate the immediate causes of these serious shortcomings. They originate not in the deterioration of American medicine but in its enormously improved technical proficiency—which has produced exorbitant costs, rising expectations, and a bureaucratic reorganization of the medical enterprise. At the same time, private practice has remained locked in an unrealistic entrepreneurial approach that treats health care as a marketplace commodity and makes impossible the equitable distribution of its enhanced capacities.

There remains, however, another aspect of the health care crisis, perhaps more crucial than any other. A high assessment of health and prolonged life and a belief in the equal worth of all individuals, the efficacy of science, and the power of human beings to control their destiny through rational action are articles of faith entrenched in American attitudes. Commitment to these values constitutes the underlying source of our dissatisfaction with the medical care system in this country. The ultimate origin of the health crisis lies in our belief that health and therefore access to medical care are basic human rights.

The application of equalitarian ideals in the realm of health, however, is in direct conflict with other deeply embedded American values. If the state of good health as a basic human right is a goal, with which few would quarrel, the right of access to medical care is not. Organized medicine has long maintained that health care is a privilege to be dispensed in exchange for payment or as an act of deliberate charity. To treat it otherwise, according to this ideology, entails an infringement on the right of medical practitioners to operate as autonomous professionals as well as an intrusion on the doctor-patient relationship.

In the view of some authorities, the continuing strength of this privilege concept of medical care is directly responsible for the current health services crisis:

Even when we have taken steps to improve medical care for the poor, as under Medicaid, or for the self-supporting, as under voluntary health insurance plans, we have used a systematized flow of money simply to purchase the services of physicians or hospitals in the open market. We have not organized the provision or "delivery" of health services in the way that other services deemed essential to society have been organized, such as education or protection against fire.[3]

By assessing our former attitudes toward health care and by outlining the systematic changes that have led to our present situation, it may be possible to gain some perspective on the solutions now being offered.

Problems of Progress

Of all the changes accompanying the economic and social revolutions of the late eighteenth century, none were more profound than the transformation it effected in the most basic aspects of the human conditions—the impact of disease and the duration of life itself. The average life span increased by 20 to 30 years, and age-old scourges lost their power to kill. Other related changes followed. New disease patterns and new problems of disease control emerged. Expectations for health and longevity escalated with succeeding medical breakthroughs and are undoubtedly the most important factors in an ever-mounting demand for medical services. The alteration in the nature of medical care and the organization of the medical profession has become more and more prominent with increasing technological complexity.

Although major credit for the dramatic health gains of the past hundred or more years must be assigned to scientific discoveries, these cannot be isolated from the economic, intellectual, and social milieu that produced them. Similar improvements in mortality indexes have occurred in other countries experiencing industrialization; gains in health seem to be closely associated with advances in nutrition, sanitation, and education that accompany rising levels of economic production.

The striking contrast between the mortality and disease patterns of peasant societies in underdeveloped areas and those of industrial societies give some indication of the extent to which modern problems of health care have been generated by medical and social progress. In preindustrial societies, astronomical infant mortality rates are due mostly to nutritional disorders and infections; and major causes of death are epidemic diseases, such as typhoid, typhus, cholera, and plague, or endemic killers, such as malaria, tuberculosis, and syphilis. Chronic noninfectious diseases are responsible for only a minor proportion of total deaths.

The solution of these earlier problems, however, has brought new ones into prominence. The leading causes of death and the major health hazards in most industrial societies including the United States are the degenerative diseases associated with the aging process. The disease pattern characteristic of an industrial society centers around the chronic disorders that increase markedly at middle age, often require continuing care, and so far have no ready solution (see Figure 9.1).

In addition, medicine is now expected to concern itself with new classes of behavior as well, including alcoholism, obesity, modes of sexual intercourse, pregnancy, and child development. The conditions of modern life are held responsible for the emergence of new epidemic diseases such as lung cancer, coronary heart disease, and peptic ulcer. Ironically, medical advances have themselves produced health hazards. Wherever other physical disorders threatened preindustrial man, penicillin poisoning was not among them. Hospital care itself has proved to be a health hazard. It has

Ten Leading Causes of Death, 1900, 1940, and 1976 (Depicted as Death Rate per 100,000 Population)

Figure 9.1

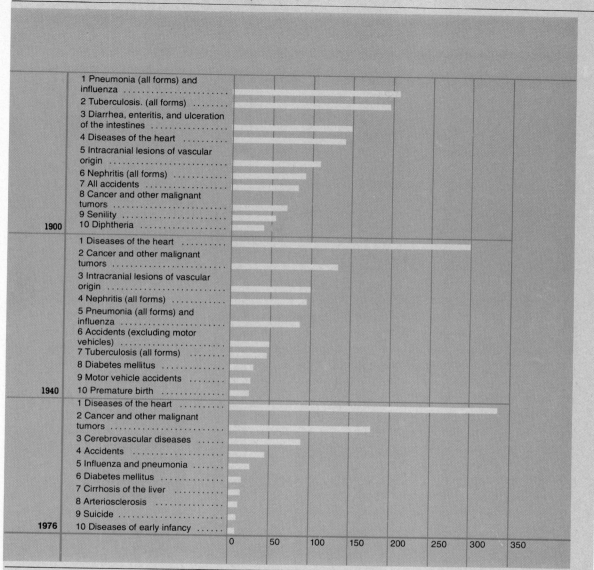

1900
1. Pneumonia (all forms) and influenza
2. Tuberculosis. (all forms)
3. Diarrhea, enteritis, and ulceration of the intestines
4. Diseases of the heart
5. Intracranial lesions of vascular origin
6. Nephritis (all forms)
7. All accidents
8. Cancer and other malignant tumors
9. Senility
10. Diphtheria

1940
1. Diseases of the heart
2. Cancer and other malignant tumors
3. Intracranial lesions of vascular origin
4. Nephritis (all forms)
5. Pneumonia (all forms) and influenza
6. Accidents (excluding motor vehicles)
7. Tuberculosis (all forms)
8. Diabetes mellitus
9. Motor vehicle accidents
10. Premature birth

1976
1. Diseases of the heart
2. Cancer and other malignant tumors
3. Cerebrovascular diseases
4. Accidents
5. Influenza and pneumonia
6. Diabetes mellitus
7. Cirrhosis of the liver
8. Arteriosclerosis
9. Suicide
10. Diseases of early infancy

0   50   100   150   200   250   300   350

Source: Leon Bouvier and Everett Lee, "The Health of Americans," *Population Profiles* (Washington, Ct.: Center for Information on America, 1976), p. 5; U.S. Bureau of the Census, *Statistical Abstract of the United States, 1978* (Washington, D.C. Government Printing Office, 1978), p. 75. Reprinted by permission of the Center for Information on America, Washington, Ct. 06793.

HEALTH CARE CRISIS

Advances in science and technology have wrought miracles in medicine—meaningless miracles for many, however, since access to the growing multitude of expensive specialists is limited and family physicians are in short supply. A thing of the past, the house call of the family doctor has been replaced by treatment in clinics, public health departments, and emergency rooms, or no treatment at all. Clearly, health care in the U.S. is in critical condition. *Clockwise from top left:* A time gone by, when the doctor came to the house to treat the sick; modern dental equipment, far removed from the pliers of the past; a machine now diagnoses mineral deficiencies and endocrine problems; patients having their blood cleansed by kidney dialysis machines; waiting interminably for treatment; techniques not even dreamed of in the early part of this century are common practice in modern heart surgery.

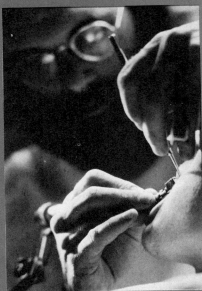

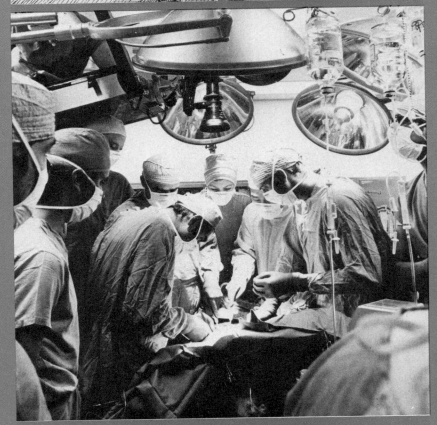

been estimated that 1.5 million of the 33 million Americans hospitalized each year contract infections during their stays. Despite precautions of hospital staffs, 36 percent of all patients who spend time in intensive care units develop infections resulting from the care they receive.[4]

Rising Expectations and Growing Demand

The health care crisis in the United States does not, however, stem from the occasional failures of medical science but rather from its great accomplishments. Particularly over the past 40 years, these accomplishments have stimulated an unprecedented demand for medical care. A new health consciousness that has developed has made medical care a top priority and resulted in a rush on health services. People now seek preventive care and treatment for relatively minor conditions. The value of regular checkups and early attention to symptoms has been publicized for many years, but there has recently been discussion and concern over what is being called "overutilization." As an example, the admission rate to general hospitals rose from about 60 per thousand population in the early 1930s[5] to 110 per thousand in 1950 and reached 168 per thousand in 1976.[6]

Large as the growing demands for health services have been, there are good indications that they would rise much higher if financial and social barriers limiting access to medical care were removed. The health care consumer explosion produced by the passage of Medicare and Medicaid, which for the first time made available to the poor both medical purchasing power and the dignity of private medical service, has clearly indicated that the new health consciousness crosses socioeconomic and ethnic lines.

From GP to Specialist: A Loss of Access

Our medical care system has a built-in incapacity for satisfying the steadily mounting demands for health services. The very scientific advances largely responsible for rising expectations have also entailed fundamental alterations in the institutional organization of medicine and the procedures involved in the delivery of medical services. Among other changes, there has been a shift to the practice of limited specialties rather than all-encompassing personalized care and to reliance on costly hospital technology for treatment as well as diagnosis.

Nonetheless, the free enterprise ideology of organized medicine has consistently stood in the way of innovations designed to modify the traditional system controlling access to the new modes of care. An idealized model of the doctor-patient relationship supports this ideology. The physician is seen as a family doctor who, functioning alone, is able to provide excellent primary care to patients in their homes as well as in the private office. Motivated by altruistic concern and possessing high technical expertise, the physician not only is available for house visits and night calls but bestows services on all who need them, whether rich or poor and regardless of race or creed. This benevolence and conscientious concern are dictated by the ethical requirements of the medical profession as well as by the physician's own sense of dedication and compassion. In sum, they are not merely personal attributes but firm obligations.[7] In this idealized model, the autonomy and absence of regulation of the doctor is counterbalanced by the patient's unrestricted choice of doctors.

If dissatisfied, [the patient] could always choose another physician. Because of this, the physician tried very hard to please his patient. He charged on a fee-for-service basis, discriminating only in accordance with the patient's income. Thus, he charged the poor little or nothing, and gave much free service in the hospital. The doctor made up for this in Robin Hood fashion by "soaking the rich."[8]

From a contemporary perspective, the preeminence of the individual physician as the all-authoritative source of health care seems rooted in tradition. It was not until the reform of medical education after 1910, however, that medical knowledge and technique advanced sufficiently to establish the general physician's monopoly on healing. "The nostalgic and sentimental image of the old-fashioned family doctor who was all things to all men is based upon the fleeting period in history when folk practice had declined but medical specialization was still in an incipient state."[9]

The high point of the concentration of medical authority in the independent general practitioners occurred in the generation just prior to World War II. Specialists and hospital resources provided an important but secondary backup to their expertise. Even then, however, the expanding base of medical knowledge was placing increasing emphasis on the role of the specialist; the growing complexity of diagnostic procedures and treatment was making the use of hospital facilities both more important and more expensive. In addition, by the early 1930s the problem of hospital care had already forced the institution of a limited form of voluntary health insurance, a first departure from the principle of direct payment by the consumer for services rendered.

The High Price of Technology

After World War II the knowledge base and technological capacities of medical science advanced with a quantum leap, forcing a drastic and apparently irreversible reorganization of medicine's professional structure, prestige hierarchy, and treatment procedures. The hospital with its indispensable and costly equipment, technicians, and consultants, now became the center of the medical system, replacing the home and physician's office as the locus for treatment and nursing care. As medical care grew vastly more specialized and dependent on technology, the generalist lost prestige and popularity, and solo practice began to be an anachronism.

Clearly, with the rise of modern medicine, it became difficult to practice alone and, what is more positively unrealistic, to attempt to handle the whole range of human ills. Over the past fifty years, general practice has declined and practice limited to particular organs, specific illnesses, or special procedures has increased remarkably. In 1923, for example, only 11 percent of all physicians were engaged in limited practice. By 1967, however, the proportion of all active physicians engaged in giving patient care in some speciality had risen to 71 percent.[10]

Through the 1950s and 1960s these trends accelerated and intensified, leading to further emphasis on the science rather than the art of medicine and on the role of scientific expertise developed and concentrated in large institutions with little public accountability. New medical schools and the major teaching hospitals affiliated with them became the bases of great research-oriented medical centers.—"medical empires," they have been called—which replaced the individual hospital as the basic unit of the medical system. Bolstered by massive federal funding, these institutions trained a new medical elite geared to specialized practice and research. The results have been pioneering medical discoveries, elaborate treatment and diagnostic equipment, a need for more technicians and other hospital personnel, and, in addition, skyrocketing costs and an increasing movement of medical staff away from primary noncrisis medicine and comprehensive care.

A Third-Party Payment Plan

Throughout the period during which these profound alterations were taking place, the fee-for-service, laissez-faire philosophy continued to define medical care as a privilege and preclude any interference with the autonomy of the medical profession or the individual professional. Control of the system for the provision of personal health services remained firmly in their hands. Compulsory health insurance, expansion of the number of physicians and medical technologists, prepaid group practice, and other innovations designed to widen the scope and availability of health services did not become viable possibilities until the health care crisis of the mid-1960s made reassessment unavoidable. A 1932 statement by the American Medical Association (AMA) attacking a proposal for medical reform has become a classic position statement, characterized by many as reactionary:

> The alignment is clear—on the one side the forces representing the great foundations, public health officialdom, social theory—even socialism and communism—inciting to revolution; on the other side, the organized medical profession of this country urging an orderly evaluation guided by controlled experimentation which will observe the principles that have been found through the centuries to be necessary to the sound practice of medicine.[11]

Organized medicine did give its approval to voluntary health insurance as a means of providing service benefits for hospital care without destroying personal relationships and patient's free choice of physician and hospital. In 1932 the American Hospital Association not only endorsed but helped organize the Blue Cross system of voluntary hospital insurance as "one of the most effective ways to offset the increasing demand for more radical and potentially dangerous forms of national or state medicine."[12] A major impetus behind this move was the serious financial situation of voluntary hospitals during the early days of the Great Depression, when philanthropic contributions had dwindled and patients were unable to meet what were already considerable bills for hospital care. Blue Cross thus became a third-party agent between consumer and provider of health services in the payment of fees for services rendered. Blue Shield, a prepayment plan to cover in-hospital surgical and medical care, followed shortly thereafter. Although a number of commerical insurance companies now offer a variety of coverage plans, all have been criticized for their high costs.

Our Ailing System of Medical Care

No society can survive unless its members enjoy a minimal life span and state of health sufficient at least to ensure the continuity of generations and the effective performance of essential tasks. All societies develop mechanisms for meeting this need, and the American system of medical care serves the same fundamental functions in this respect as that of any other social collective. Compared to preindustrial societies, or even to the situation existing within this society in the fairly recent past, however, our medical care system occupies a much more strategic place within the large institutional structure. Not only does it serve the economy by helping to maintain a high level of worker productivity, but it is itself a major component of the economy, accounting for almost 9 percent of the Gross National Product.[13] Not only does it support the family and religious institutions in their care and solace of the sick, but it has taken on the major role in performing that function.

With most serious contagious and parasitic diseases under control, medicine's assignment is not simply to alleviate illness but to prevent it and, even further, to produce an optimum condition of health. The magnitude of this last assignment is indicated by the statement of the United Nations World Health Organization, often quoted in this connection, which defines health as a "state of complete physical, mental and social well-being and not merely the absence of disease and infirmity."[14] In addition, the social control and supportive functions assigned to the medical care system have expanded. Our present system of medical care charged with this enhanced and complex role is, however, marked by a lack of coordination among its components, which have developed without reference to any overall, rational plan consistent with social realities. Some persons have suggested that health care is organized in such a haphazard fashion that it is stretching the point even to refer to it as a system.[15]

The problems now facing the "ailing" system are attributed by many critics to this fact as well as to failures within the components themselves.

The Doctor Deficit

According to 1976 figures, of 318,400 physicians engaged in patient care, only 17 percent were in general medicine, with the other 83 percent divided among various specialties.[16] Significantly, more then 30 percent of these were in surgical specialties.

Another way of considering the professional distribution of physicians is in terms of the administration of primary care. It is estimated that the United States needs 133 general practitioners per 100,000 population to ensure quality care, but the national average is only 59 per 100,000.[17]

Private practice tends to be concentrated in middle-class urban and suburban areas, especially in the vicinity of the great medical centers, which have available a wealth of treatment resources and medical expertise. The dependence of the modern physician on colleagues and hospitals for consultation and treatment facilities is probably more responsible for the geographical maldistribution of doctors than prestige and financial inducements, however.[18] The pressures of modern medical practice force the conscientious physician out of professional isolation. The proportion of doctors who practice alone is steadily decreasing.[19] In fact, true solo practice is actually a rarity; private practice is typically marked by informal but well-integrated cooperative arrangements with a network of colleagues and a reliance on hospital ties.

In a further departure from the solo practice ideal, physicians are now joining forces in legal partnerships and group practices which explicitly involve an interdependent team relationship among three or more full-time doctors. Besides the advantages that group practice offers the physician with respect to expenses, equipment, consultations, and patient referrals, it has been strongly advocated as a means of counteracting the fragmentation of medical care. Although still a minor feature of the medical scene, group practice is growing steadily and now involves about 24 percent of the nation's physicians.[20]

The professional orientation of the nation's physicians must be viewed against the background of their training. Those who have received their training since World War II are the products of a medical education that has stressed federally supported biomedical research and specialized knowledge. During this period, interest in effective means of delivering health care has taken second place to interest in effective ways of treating disease, the clinician has taken second place to the research scientist, and the provider of primary care has taken second place to the specialist. It is only in the past few years that medical schools and their affiliated hospitals have begun to emphasize training in family medicine and community-based outpatient care. Pressures both from society and from the more recent crop of medical students are held responsible for this move.

Closely linked with the dynamics of the doctor shortage are problems of the quality of care. The lack of continuity, the impersonal nature of care, and the fragmentation widely noted and criticized in the delivery of health services can be attributed as much to the dearth of primary-care physicians as to the emphasis on restricted speciality practice. In addition, the scarcity of practitioners oriented to comprehensive care makes it increasingly difficult for patients to find a point of entry into the system, a problem that obviously becomes crucial in an emergency and hinders early detection and treatment of disease.

Sociologically, the doctor shortage can be viewed as the manifestation of an intrinsic contradiction between the self-defined interests of two opposed groups within an institutional system. Patient expectations and professional intentions have grown increasingly incompatible under the pressure of social change. The expectations, ironically, derive much of their force and legitimacy from the ideal doctor-patient model traditionally promoted by organized medicine and from the enhanced potentialities of medical science. Doctors, on the other hand, are now confronted with the imperatives of a vastly altered professional milieu that no longer bestows rewards on the basis of the old norms and role definitions.

The AMA: Monopolistic Manipulations

The origins of the numerical doctor shortage are clear. Acting in the classic pattern of an economic monopoly the organized medical profession undertook and succeeded in sharply limiting the number of new entrants into its ranks. Late in the nineteenth century, the American Medical Association persuaded state legislatures to set up procedures for licensing the practice of medicine. Then it conducted a successful legislative campaign to force medical schools of poor quality out of business. With this accomplished, standards of medical training were raised and admissions curtailed.

For several decades the ratio of physicians to the population continued to decline; then in the 1940s and 1950s it stabilized at a comparatively low level. During this time, despite greatly expanded demand, the AMA contin-

Barbara Ehrenreich and John Ehrenreich
The American Medical System: Profits, Research, Teaching

The most obvious function of the American medical system, other than patient care, is profit-making. When it comes to making money, the health industry is an extraordinarily well-organized and efficient machine. The most profitable small business around is the private practice of medicine, with aggregate profits running into the billions. The most profitable big business in America is the manufacture and sale of drugs. Rivaling the drug industry for Wall Street attention is the burgeoning hospital supply and equipment industry, with products ranging from chicken soup to catheters and heart-lung machines. The fledgling nursing home (for profit) industry was a speculator's dream in 1968 and 1969, and even the stolid insurance companies gross over ten billion dollars a year in health insurance premiums. In fact, the health business is so profitable that even the "nonprofit" hospitals make profits. All that "nonprofit" means is that the hospital's profit, i.e., the difference between its income and its expenditures, is not distributed to shareholders. These nonprofits are used to finance the expansion of medical empires—to buy real estate, stocks, plush new buildings, and expensively salaried professional employees. The medical system may not be doing too well at fighting disease, but, as any broker will testify, it's one of the healthiest businesses around.

Next in the medical system's list of priorities is research. Again, if this undertaking is measured in terms of its dividends for patient care, it comes out looking pretty unsystematic and disorganized. Although the vast federal appropriations for biomedical research are primarily motivated by the hope of improving health care, only a small fraction (much smaller than need be) of the work done in the name of medical research leaks out to the general public as improved medical care. But medical research has a *raison d'être* wholly independent of the delivery of health services, as an indispensable part of the nation's giant research and development enterprise. Since the Second World War, the United States has developed a vast machinery for R.&D. in all areas—physics, electronics, aerospace as well as biomedical sciences—financed largely by the government and carried out in universities and private industry. It has generated military and aerospace technology, and all the many little innovations which fuel the expansion of private industry.

For the purposes of this growing R.&D. effort, the medical system is important because it happens to be the place where R.&D. in general comes in contact with human material. Medical research is the link. The nation's major biomedical research institutes are affiliated to hospitals to a significant extent because they require human material to carry out their own, usually abstract, investigations. For instance, a sophisticated (and possibly patentable) technique for investigating protein structure was recently developed through the use of the blood of several dozen victims of a rare and fatal bone marrow disease. Even the research carried out inside hospitals has implications for the entire R.&D. enterprise. Investigations of the pulmonary disorders of patients in Harlem Hospital may provide insights for designing space suits, or may contribute to the technology of aerosol dissemination of nerve gas. Or, of course, it may simply lead to yet another investigation.

Human bodies are not all that the medical care system offers up to R.&D. The sociological and psychological research carried out in hospitals and ghetto health centers may have pay-offs in the form of new counterinsurgency techniques for use at home and abroad. And who knows what sinister—or benignly academic—ends are met by the routine neurological and drug research carried out on the nation's millions of mental hospital inmates?

Finally, an important function of the medical care system is the reproduction of its key personnel—physicians. Here, again, there seems to be no system if patient care is the ultimate goal. The medical schools graduate each year just a few more doctors than are needed to replace the ones who retire, and far too few doctors to keep up with the growth of population. Of those who graduate, a growing proportion go straight into academic government, or industrial biomedical research, and never see a patient. The rest, according to some dissatisfied medical students, aren't trained to take care of patients anyway

—having been educated chiefly in academic medicine (a mixture of basic sciences and "interesting" pathology). But all this is not as irrational as it seems. The limited size of medical school classes has been maintained through the diligent, and entirely systematic, efforts of the A.M.A. Too many—or even enough—doctors would mean lower profits for those already in practice. And the research orientation of medical education simply reflects the medical schools' own consuming preoccupation with research.

Profits, research and teaching, then, are independent functions of the medical system, not just adjuncts to patient care. But they do not go on along separate tracks, removed from patient care. Patients are the indispensable ingredient of medical profit-making, research, and education. In order that the medical industry serve these functions, patient care must be twisted to meet the needs of these other "medical" enterprises.

Excerpted from *The American Health Empire: Power, Profits, and Politics*, prepared by Barbara Ehrenreich and John Ehrenreich. Copyright © 1970 by Health Policy Advisory Center, Inc. Reprinted by permission of Random House, Inc.

ued to press its opposition to any increase in the output of doctors by insisting that quantity would reduce quality. The first cautious shift in this position came in 1958, but it was not until the early 1960s that the AMA admitted the existence of a doctor shortage.[21]

During the past decade efforts have been made to augment the nation's supply of physicians. The scope of these efforts remains limited, however; and results still lag so far behind need that graduates of foreign medical schools, many of them Americans denied admission to schools in the United States, are now welcomed as additions to the nation's pool of physicians. These physicians educated abroad presently comprise about 36 percent of new medical licentiates each year.[22]

Hospital Boom

Today's medical care system centers around the short-term general hospitals. These are largely nonprofit institutions controlled by private citizens and sectarian groups, the most prestigious of which are affiliated with medical schools as teaching hospitals. These so-called voluntary hospitals are to be distinguished from proprietary hospitals, which are operated for profit.

Of the 7082 hospitals in the United States, 5956 are of the short-term type.[23] This figure includes a comparatively minor proportion of proprietary and nonfederal governmental facilities. The short-term general hospital, whether voluntary or proprietary, provides treatment for patients with acute conditions that involve a stay of less than 30 days. It is the key factor in the organization and financing of personal health services and has been the component of the medical care system that has changed most in the past 40 years. The growth of the general hospital for inpatient care has been dramatic and rapid. Much of the complex technology now taken for granted was nonexistent only a few years ago. Among such innovations are cardiac care units, therapeutic radiation services, advanced laboratory tests of body fluids, computerized consultation services, and kidney dialysis units.

Voluntary hospital personnel, in a development linked with technological advance, grew in number from less than 500,000 in 1950 to more than 1 million in 1965 and almost 1.8 million in 1976. Financial assets of voluntary hospitals have increased almost fivefold since 1960. Current expenses have multiplied by 20 since 1950, when they were approximately 1.5 billion dollars.[24] Costs to the patient have, of course, greatly increased in a snowball-

At Beth Israel Hospital the administration demands that its staff minister to the human concerns of the patients as well as their physical ailments. A warm atmosphere in a waiting room, the replacement of a lumpy mattress or a burned out light bulb, or detailed explanations of treatments—all are recognized as rights of patients.

The Smiling Hospital

Entering Boston's Beth Israel Hospital for surgery, Carol Wein, 22, of Brookline, Mass., wondered at first if she had come to the wrong place. Instead of the usual sterile hospital lobby, she found a large, warmly decorated room with brightly colored window hangings and a garden of potted palms and dracaenas off to the side. In the second-floor admissions area, she was interviewed, not at a crowded public desk but in a small, tastefully decorated private office. Corridors were carpeted and traditional hospital smells and white walls were conspicuously absent. After Wein settled into her stylishly furnished, pastel-colored private room ($180 a day), the head nurse entered and cheerfully announced: "Carol, you have rights in this hospital and I want to explain them to you."

Carol's pleasant welcome reminded her of an episode from TV's *Medical Center.* But Beth Israel, a major teaching facility of Harvard Medical School, is a real-life institution. Opened only a few weeks ago at a cost of $16 million, Beth Israel's posh 176-bed Feldberg Building has already won a reputation among patients as the hotel with nurses and operating rooms. It is far more than that. More than a decade in the planning, the wing caps a long campaign by Beth Israel's innovative director, Dr. Mitchell Rabkin, 45, to ensure patients a "full bill of rights," which he feels is long overdue. As the Harvard-educated endocrinologist puts it: "We have reached the point where doctors and hospitals can really tyrannize patients."

Full Explanation. That tyranny has been ended at Beth Israel. Soon after patients enter the hospital, they are given a little blue and white brochure. It tells them, among other things, what they are guaranteed: the best possible care regardless of the form of payment; a full explanation of their illness and treatment; knowledge of who is in charge of their care; and the privilege of leaving the hospital at any time, even over a doctor's objections.

One of Rabkin's favorite innovations is what he calls "a telephone hot line for patients," which enables them to call direct from their rooms to the hospital service manager if a bulb burns out or the kitchen is late in delivering dinners ordered from one of the seven different room-service menus. Says Rabkin: "I have seen a lumpy mattress replaced within 20 minutes of the hotline call."

The director periodically reviews the log of calls—and the responses to them —to keep the staff on its toes. He may also take other action; even his fellow doctors are not spared Rabkin's criticism. After he discovered that a patient had been left unattended in a corridor, he rebuked the physician responsible (without naming him) in his weekly "Dear Doctor" memo to the staff. Explains Rabkin: "A patient's rights brochure is not worth the paper it is printed on if it does not reflect an institutional commitment." At Beth Israel, whose bright new wing is attracting many patients, the commitment is apparently real. As Trustee Eliot Snider explains: "We want this to be a smiling hospital."
TIME, JULY 26, 1976

ing process involving indirect payment procedures, operating expenses, and expanded use.

In terms of the delivery of medical care, the most relevant aspect of all this growth is the great increase in hospitalization it signifies. (See Figure 9.2 for a breakdown of health care expenses in the United States.) Whereas 1 out of every 10 persons in the population was admitted to a hospital for inpatient care in 1946, the figure had risen to 1 out of every 6.5 persons by 1976.[25] From 1950 to 1976 there was a 52 percent increase in admission rates, from 110 admissions per thousand population in 1950 to a rate of 168 in 1976.[26]

More recently a number of other trends seem to indicate a new develop-

Figure 9.2   Health Expenditures in the U.S., 1977

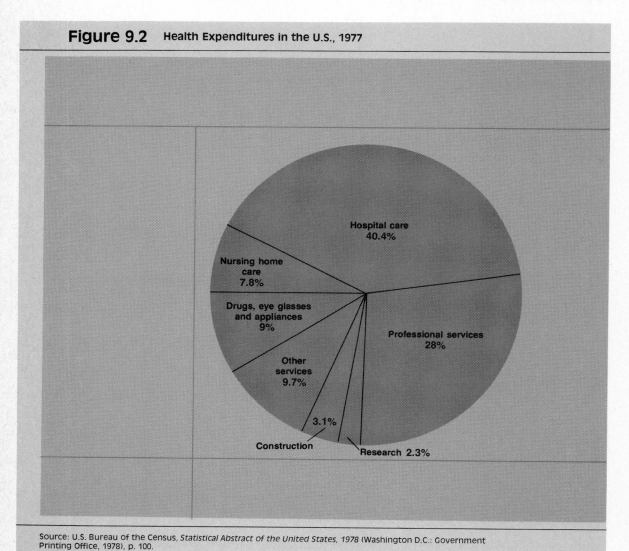

Source: U.S. Bureau of the Census, *Statistical Abstract of the United States, 1978* (Washington D.C.: Government Printing Office, 1978), p. 100.

ment in the hospital's role. One has been the increased use of outpatient facilities as clinics. From 1970 to 1976 the rate of outpatient visits in the United States increased by 41 percent,[27] a change that may be tied to the short supply of primary-care physicians. Another trend is the growth of programs for providing health care on a walk-in basis to surrounding neighborhoods. Although many of these "outreach" operations are still experimental, they reflect a greater commitment by voluntary hospitals, especially those affiliated with medical schools, to community medicine. To a large extent, this new commitment is emerging in response to vociferous consumer demands for realistic attention to health needs and for representation on the decision-making bodies of community hospitals.

Health Care: A Right or a Privilege?

One of the differences between the poor and nonpoor is their respective levels of health. Key indexes leave no doubt that poverty is associated with significantly lower levels of health, especially when paired with minority racial status. Another difference is in health care. The poor not only receive less of it, but what they do receive is inferior in kind, being largely outside the mainstream of private medicine. Economic barriers clearly impose effective limitations on access to services, which is scarcely surprising in a system that dispenses these services as market commodities. Differentials in levels of health and receipt of services are indisputable. What is a matter of debate, however, is the degree to which there is a cause-and-effect relationship between them.

Two arguments call such a relationship into question. One holds that the conditions of life experienced by the poor may be more accountable for health deficiencies than inadequate medical care. Housing, sanitation, nutrition, and recreational resources are among the factors cited in this connection. The other holds that noneconomic cultural factors are also crucial in shaping patterns of behavior relevant to health apart from access to medical care. These include norms regarding illegitimacy and child-rearing practices, as well as attitudes toward sickness that influence people to seek medical care.

Nonetheless, the force of these arguments is diminished by the size of the poverty-linked differentials in both health levels and health services. In one evaluation of factors responsible for the wide discrepancy between white and nonwhite mortality rates in the 25-to-44 age range, where the nonwhite rate is more than two and a half times greater than the white, it was noted that "the differential is probably too great to be explained by social conditions and undoubtedly reflects an actual difference in available care."[28]

Social class differences in health care are, of course, not unique to the United States. The effect of social class in modern industrial society is nowhere more evident than in the distribution of health and disease, showing up most strongly in infant mortality rates, stillbirth rates, and death rates of

Class Determines Care

men from respiratory tuberculosis, rheumatic heart disease, pneumonia, and bronchitis.[29]

What is unique to the United States is the extent of the differences when analysis focuses on racial comparisons. The 1976 estimates of life expectancy for white males, for instance, is 69.7 years, whereas for nonwhite males it drops to 64.1 years (see Table 9.1).[30] The dramatic contrast between white and nonwhite infant mortality rates has often been noted, as has the phenomenally high nonwhite maternal mortality rate. In 1976 the infant mortality rate was 13.3 per thousand live births for white mothers and 23.5 for nonwhite mothers.[31] Nonwhite infant mortality rates, although they have improved over the past two decades, are largely responsible for the poor standing of the United States relative to many other countries.

Inequality based on income and race dominates participation in our medical care system, whether judged by frequency of use or by quality of service. When average number of physician contacts is estimated, for instance, a strong pattern of economic differentials emerges.[32] Significantly, poor people—and especially nonwhites—are admitted to hospitals less frequently than those more favored economically and socially, but when admitted they remain for longer periods. It seems probable that they have developed more serious conditions and require more extended treatment because their illnesses were not treated earlier.

With the exception of the elderly now subsidized by Medicare, low-income people remain outside the mainstream of private health care. The sources of their medical care are hospital outpatient and emergency departments and health department clinics. Hospital emergency departments are, in fact, the only or primary source of care for many inner-city households. Yet they provide only episodic treatment seldom geared to a comprehensive approach. According to one study, health services for the poor suffer more than others from depersonalization, disorganization, and inadequate em-

Table 9.1	Life Expectancy and Percent of Population Reaching Age 65 in the United States, by Race and Sex					
Life Table Value and Year	Number of Years	White		Nonwhite	
		Men	Women	Men	Women
Expectancy from birth: 1976	72.8	69.7	77.3	64.1	72.6
1974	71.9	68.9	76.6	62.9	71.3
1972	71.1	68.3	75.9	61.5	69.9
1970	70.9	68.0	75.6	61.3	69.4
1960	69.7	67.4	74.1	61.1	66.3
1900	47.3	46.6	48.7	32.5	33.5
Expectancy from age 20:					
1976	54.6	51.6	58.7	46.8	34.9
1900–1902	42.8	42.2	43.8	35.1	36.9
Percent reaching age 65:					
1976	75.1	70.1	83.5	55.0	72.1
1900–1902	40.9	39.2	43.8	19.0	22.0

Source: U.S. Department of Health, Education and Welfare, National Center for Health Statistics. *Vital Statistics of the United States, 1976*, vol. 2, sec. 5 (Hyattsville, Md.: Public Health Service, 1977), p. 5-4; and U.S. Bureau of the Census, *Statistical Abstract of the United States, 1978* (Washington, D.C.: Government Printing Office, 1979), p. 69.

phasis on health counseling.[33] This situation can be attributed to the continuance of charity attitudes in the conduct of clinic services. One solution advocated is providing sufficient financial support for everyone to be a "paying patient," able to choose among health services.

So far, government efforts to open up access to medical care for the low-income population have been somewhat limited. Since 1967 a number of neighborhood health centers originally funded through the Office of Economic Opportunity have been set up to offer comprehensive care in poverty areas. They have reached only small numbers at a high cost, however.[34] The federal government also disburses grants to states, localities, and private sector institutions for a variety of specific purposes, including maternal and child health services, services for crippled children, and infant care. In addition, the Medicaid program, established by Congress in 1965, provides benefits to those defined as needy under widely differing state formulas through a system of matching state and federal funds. The benefits can be applied to private treatment. The program has been criticized for the low eligibility levels and elaborate red tape characterizing the separate state plans, as well as the inflated medical fees and fraud it has produced.

As the fiscal crisis of many states worsened, during the 1970s, there have been forced cutbacks in some Medicaid programs and others have not been able to increase payments to keep up with inflation. In New York State, for example, Medicaid reimbursement rates for stays in hospitals have maintained an almost constant dollar amount from 1976 to 1977 while hospital costs have risen 10 percent.[35]

The most far-reaching attempt to reduce economic barriers to health care is the Medicare program for people 65 and older. It pays up to 80 percent of "reasonable charges" over the first 160 dollars in each calendar year. Medicare does not involve a means test. For the first time, it makes medical benefits available as a right to a major segment of the population, excluding only those not covered by social security. However, due to the seriousness of the health problem among the aged, the financial burden remains great despite government assistance. In 1977, Medicare payments covered only 44 percent of the personal health care expenditures of the aged.[36]

The Cost of Good Health

Health care costs have risen dramatically over the past few decades (see Figure 9.3). From 1970 to 1978 the total cost of health care has increased threefold, to the point where an estimated $200 billion was spent in 1978. Health care has become the nation's third leading industry, behind food and construction.[37] From 1970 to May 1978 medical costs increased at a rate more than double that of inflation for consumer goods. During this period the consumer price average rose 66 percent, whereas physicians' fees rose 160 percent and hospital daily service charges were up 400 percent.[38] By 1978 the average cost of a day in the hospital was $200.[39] Hospital charges, rising at a rate of 12 percent a year, are now nearly out of reach of even the

Figure 9.3 Indexes of Medical Care Prices: 1960 to 1977

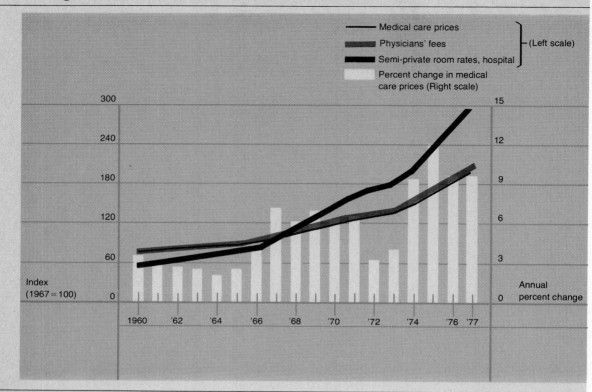

Source: U.S. Bureau of the Census, *Statistical Abstract of the United States, 1978* (Washington, D.C.: Government Printing Office, 1978), p. 96.

affluent unless they have hospitalization insurance, which itself is becoming increasingly expensive and restrictive.

Depending on one's viewpoint, the financing of personal health care in the United States can be described as either pluralistic or chaotic. It is marked by diversity in the sources and procedures of payment, as well as by considerable controversy over the appropriate rationale for financing arrangements. Chief features of the situation at present are the increasing proportion of government funds as opposed to private funds as the source of payment, the dominance of voluntary insurance rather than direct payment for meeting hospital expenses, and the importance of hospital care as an item of expense. With few exceptions the principle that shapes the system of financing remains the fee-for-service approach.

Alternative approaches are receiving new attention because of the health care crisis, but they are still of minor significance in the overall picture. One method reimburses the physician with a fixed salary. Another provides payment on a "capitation" basis, under which the physician receives a stated fee for each patient for whatever services are required over a set period of time. With a growth in prepaid group health plans, these systems of payment should become more widespread. The fee-for-service principle still predominates, however, whether in the form of direct payment by consumers or indirect payment through voluntary or public insurance. Whatever the source of funds or the procedures used for their transmission, they are disbursed for specific services rendered. This applies to expenditures made under the government's Medicare and Medicaid programs as well as to private payments.

The difference between Medicare and Medicaid lies in the onus of responsibility for making the payments and reflects a new approach to financing health care. The great breakthrough made by Medicare, and the reason for the intense controversy surrounding it, was the assumption of government responsibility for financing the health needs of the aged regardless of their ability to pay. Medical care for 10 percent of the total United States population thus came to be considered not a privilege but a right.

The key characteristic of our present pluralistic financing system is the high proportion of expenditures channeled to the providers of health care through third parties. This represents a considerable shift from the past. Whereas more than 59 percent of all health payments in 1950 came directly from the consumer at the time of service, in 1977 the proportion of payments made in this way had dropped to 30 percent.[40]

Health Insurance

The focal point of organized health care financing, then, is voluntary health insurance geared to hospital expenses, just as the focal point for the organization of health services is the voluntary general hospital. Voluntary health insurance is, in fact, almost wholly limited to inpatient surgical and medical care. It does not cover such nonhospital connected services as preventive health examinations, outpatient care, or extended home care. Approximately 78 percent of the population under age 65 is now covered by voluntary hospital insurance and 78 percent by insurance for surgeons' fees.[41] About two-fifths of the coverage is under the AMA-sponsored Blue Cross and Blue Shield plans; the rest is divided among industrial and union programs, independent plans, and commerical insurance companies.[42] The national network of nonprofit Blue Cross and Blue Shield plans, largely controlled by hospital administrators and physicians, is, however, a dominant force in the voluntary insurance field.

A number of additional facts about voluntary health insurance are relevant to current health care problems. Voluntary health insurance is primarily group insurance covering all members of an identifiable group, such as employees of a certain company. Nonaffiliated or lone subscribers are penalized by high premiums and less extensive coverage, a situation that discriminates against the disadvantaged. Unitl recently, insurance payments have been made to hospitals on the basis of "reasonable" costs, without regard to efficiency in hospital administration—a method charged with rewarding inefficiency and contributing to runaway costs. Close to three-quarters of the cost of group health insurance is contributed by employers as a fringe benefit that is now a standard item in collective bargaining negotiations. This makes rising insurance costs a matter of increasing concern to both management and labor.

The problem of rising medical care prices is primarily the problem of rising hospital costs. According to a widely held view, a major factor responsible for hospital costs is the third-party system of funding, which in its present fee-for-service form encourages excessive use of inpatient care, unnecessary treatment, irresponsible investment in elaborate technology with limited application that often duplicates facilities already available, and inefficient hospital management. Voluntary health insurance benefits, since they are almost wholly limited to inpatient care and hospital-related expenses, exert pressure on both patients and doctors to use hospital facilities. In contrast, prepaid group plans, where physicians work on salary and patients are covered for all kinds of services, show a 20 percent lower rate of hospital utilization than under the fee-for-service third-party system.[43]

In addition, extensive hospitalization is held responsible for a great deal of unnecessary treatment, especially surgery. Estimates indicate that there are twice as many operations among Blue Shield participants who pay surgeons on a fee-for-service basis than among members enrolled in a prepaid group practice plan where surgeons draw flat salaries.[44] For both doctors and hospitals, surgery produces higher revenues than other forms of treatment. In England which has a national insurance plan that does not pay per operation, the rate of operations is one-half the American rate.[45]

Hospital Procedures

An even more basic question has been raised regarding the value of the complex medical equipment associated with rising hospital costs. The expensive procedures involved are helpful to comparatively few patients; yet the cost of maintaining them must be shared by all. Furthermore, it is argued, the new facilities are often used unnecessarily:

A hypothetical serum analysis might show chemical imbalance indicative of specific pathological conditions for which "cures" exist. The analysis may be expensive but may also be routinized—results back in 12 hours or less. This laboratory analysis "saves lives," but whether it will help a given patient is uncertain. A small minority of patients are known to benefit from the laboratory procedure. But the medical practice in the modern hospital is to order this analysis for a majority of the patients *each day*. Ten years ago these tests were not available (i.e., routinized in hospitals or private laboratories); at that time related but more laborious analyses were rarely prescribed. Now the tests are available and are frequently used, increasing the cost of medical care.[46]

Finally, the fee-for-service third party system of financing is also capable of boosting hospital costs by promoting a number of serious and costly inefficiencies. The fact that funds have been transmitted by third-party agents, both governmental and private, with scant regard for cost control or accountability has in effect invited fiscal irresponsibility. The rapid infusion of Medicare and Medicaid funds has exacerbated these inflationary trends even further. Third-party pressures have recently moved hospitals to develop record-keeping systems that permit an accurate cost-benefit analysis. Interestingly enough, when this attempt has been made, hospitals have discovered in many cases that they literally did not know what various services cost; nor did they know how to evaluate alternative methods of providing the same service. Computerized systems and techniques are now being called on to cope with the problem, an undertaking that in itself involves considerable expense.

Apart from the inflationary effects of third-party funding, medical advances have undoubtedly made a large contribution to rising costs by the increasingly sophisticated methods of treatment they involve. These call for both costly equipment and an expanded and expert staff. The fact that hospital payroll expenses rose 147 percent during the period between 1960 and 1969 is attributed to the new personnel needs accompanying medical progress as well as to wage boosts for hospital staff at all levels.[47]

Malpractice

The rising cost of health care has also been influenced recently by the increase in medical malpractice suits and the price physicians must now pay for malpractice insurance. Premiums for this type of insurance have risen 1000 percent in the past decade.[48] Hospitals, facing similar suits and sharp increases in their insurance premiums, are raising their daily rates, sometimes as much as 12 dollars a bed, in order to cover the cost of this additional expense.[49] In addition to increasing costs, the threat of such suits may also intimidate medical personnel, who then may not wish to perform especially risky operations and procedures.

Although physicians are considered professionals exhibiting perhaps the greatest service orientation in their work and have traditionally been accorded much deference and prestige, the recent popularity of malpractice suits seems to indicate that the public is beginning to question their privileged status. There are several possible grounds for the increasing frequency of client revolts against medical and other professions as well: expertise is considered inadequate, claims to altruism are thought to be

---

Berlin's Victory

An Illinois doctor last week won the most significant victory yet in the medical profession's counterattack on harassing malpractice suits. In Chicago, a circuit court jury awarded Radiologist Leonard Berlin $8,000 in his countersuit against a patient who had named him in a $250,000 malpractice suit.

The patient, Harriett Nathan, had come to the suburban Skokie Valley Community Hospital in October 1973 for treatment of a finger that she had injured while playing tennis. An X ray, taken under Dr. Berlin's supervision, failed to disclose a small fracture that was later located by another X ray. This prompted Nathan to file her quarter-million-dollar suit against Dr. Berlin, the hospital and the orthopedic surgeon who had treated her.

Berlin promptly countersued both Nathan and her lawyer husband, who helped her to bring the malpractice suit against him "without reasonable cause," and also sued her lawyers for filing the suit without proper investigation. When she subsequently dropped her suit, Berlin decided to press on. He admitted that the fracture had not shown up in the first X ray, but demonstrated that the treatment Nathan received was the same as that normally given for a fracture. That was enough to convince the jury, which deliberated only 15 minutes before giving Dr. Berlin $2,000 in compensatory and $6,000 in punitive damages. The award was directed not only against Nathan and her husband but also against her two attorneys.

Berlin's victory may well help to stem both the rising number of malpractice cases and the increasingly large awards, which have driven malpractice insurance costs beyond the reach of many doctors (TIME, March 24, 1975). The verdict, says Dr. Max Parrott, president of the American Medical Association, should "discourage the filing of frivolous, nonmeritorious cases against doctors" and "puts lawyers on notice that they are placing themselves in jeopardy if they do not adequately investigate a case before filing suit."

TIME, June 14, 1976

Suit against suit: Confronting the malpractice fad.

unfounded, the organization of the delivery system supporting their authority is inadequate, and the system exceeds the appropriate limits of its power.[50] To this list one might add the high costs of health care, the relative wealth of physicians, and the generally impersonal nature of modern medical practice. Almost any of these grounds could, to some extent, be considered legitimate. That they are any more true now than in the past, however, is doubtful.

The increase in client revolts is more probably related to changes in clients themselves and changes in other agencies outside the medical profession. For one, clients are becoming both more educated and more organized. As such, they are better able to judge the quality of services they receive and better able to communicate their dissatisfactions. The crusades led by consumer advocate Ralph Nader and the following he has gathered are indicative of this point.

Another important change facilitating client revolts is the number of lawyers who are willing to take such cases. Because there is wide stratification and differentiation within the legal community, conflicting positions on numerous issues have emerged among its members. Although lawyers in prestigious law firms affiliated with large corporations are against client revolts, those in less prestigious and more independent positions tend to support them.[51] Without the interest and investments of this group of lawyers, many malpractice suits would never get off the ground.

Medical Fraud and Abuse

Another factor contributing to the increase in medical costs is the level of illegal activities engaged in by doctors, pharmacists, patients, operators of hospitals and nursing homes, laboratories, and clinics. One federal government estimate claims that one billion dollars of total Medicaid expenditures alone have been lost due to fraud and abuse.[52] Doctors bill Medicaid programs for services never rendered or double-bill for services performed only once. Pharmacists charge Medicaid or Medicare for more expensive brand-name drugs while supplying the patient with a generic drug. Patients have also falsified their income levels in order to gain federal or state support for medical care.

In addition, federal authorities have uncovered serious abuses in the operation of clinical laboratories and nursing homes. Laboratories may "rent" office space from community clinics in return for a contract to do all of the clinic's testing. To compensate for the "rent" the labs then charge the clinics rates that are twice as high as the rates for private physicians. The exorbitant rates are then billed to Medicaid. Pharmacists have also been implicated in schemes in which nursing home operators are given a percentage of the Medicaid or Medicare funds for prescriptions filled for residents of the homes. Some of the more flagrant cases of abuse result from Medicaid's practice of paying nursing home operators a flat per diem rate for needy patients. When Medicaid had been unable to raise the daily rate on the request of home operators, patients sometimes find services being cut, heat being turned down, uneaten food being recycled, and general conditions deteriorating.[53]

Public disclosure by the media of such frauds and abuses has pushed Congress and law enforcement officials into action. The financial costs and human suffering deriving from such activities is great. But, perhaps more important, as some politicians have pointed out, the inability of authorities to prevent such actions in Medicare and Medicaid programs raises the question of the government's ability to run a smooth, efficient national health care system.

Improving Delivery of Health Care

It must be kept in mind that the problems of health and those of health care are not necessarily identical. It is probable that changes in life-styles and living conditions as well as public health measures are at least as important as personal medical care for improving health today. The failure of mortality rates to decline further in this country during the past 15 years despite advances in medical science is attributed by many experts to the determining influence of cultural and environmental factors.[54]

If optimum health rather than health care is the objective, then cultural and societal areas requiring attention should include, among other things, nutrition and diet; exercise; the misuse of alcohol, drugs, and tobacco; environmental pollution control; unemployment; housing and urban renewal; accident prevention; and recreation. Some of these are matters to which a medical care system can address itself directly. Others belong in the domain of economic and social policy and programs. Still others are rooted in cultural patterns that are highly resistant to planned change.

The widespread perception of health as a social problem, however, focuses on the failure of the medical care system to match the delivery of health services with its potential. Remedies for that failure range from the cautious to the visionary, covering a spectrum from slight modifications of the status quo to a complete restructuring of the present system into some variety of national health service. On a practical level, proposals for change have three principal targets—financing, the organization of practice, and the size of the medical work force.

Rising costs have created a climate receptive to the idea of federally financed health insurance. This development is clearly related to the wide diversity of groups whose interests are now affected—industry and labor, hospitals and insurance companies, and consumers at all levels. In recent years many bills designed to initiate some form of national health insurance have been presented in Congress, and it seems inevitable that a national health insurance program of some kind will be enacted in the near future. Sponsors of the bills run the gamut from organized labor to organized medicine, the insurance industry, and leading Republican and Democratic senators.

Proponents of the more comprehensive plans begin with the assumption that "the current nonsystem of medical care is a failure"[55] that has helped drive up inflation while creating thousands of human tragedies. Their plans are designed to provide comprehensive health services, including mental health and preventive services, for all Americans regardless of age or social

Meeting the Cost Crisis— National Insurance

Richard J. Margolis
National Health Insurance—The Dream Whose Time Has Come?

During the next four years, Jimmy Carter and the Congress will probably decide whether universal national health insurance—a dream so long deferred that scholars call it "the lost reform"—shall at last be deemed an idea whose time has come, or whether it shall remain an idea that is merely long overdue. Something more than our health appears to be at stake: as with other tough dilemmas (segregation, for example), this one raises questions about the resources and capacities of our political institutions. In particular, it tests our abilities to overcome the great weight of health-care inertia, a weight that seems to be composed in roughly equal parts of history, bureaucracy, and avarice.

The opinion polls suggest that a sizable majority of Americans is now ready for fundamental changes in health care, and the President appears publicly committed to such changes. The 1976 Democratic platform, largely a Carter creation, calls for "a comprehensive national health-insurance system with universal and mandatory coverage"—meaning a program that goes about as far as it can go: all of the people insured all of the time for all of their care.

Nothing could be simpler; nor, if the past turns out to be prologue, more difficult to achieve. The fact is, we have been here before. The history of national health insurance in this country is strewn with predictions about its imminent arrival.

Part of the trouble may arise from the complexity of our burgeoning medical system, which defies instant rehabilitation, and from the apparently high price we must pay for its reform. Many of the recently tried solutions, notably Medicare and Medicaid, have themselves become part of the problem, encouraging waste and driving up costs. Thus far, at least, reform has played handmaiden to inflation. Nowadays, we spend 8.6 percent of our gross national product on health care, about double the portion two decades ago.

The new Congress and the new President will have to confront this general paradox of social progress, in which measures designed to lighten the burden of some may end by increasing the burden of all. As regards the medical-care paradox, it is not as if there have not been efforts ro resolve it. Ever since that A.M.A. Journal editor 62 years ago urged doctors to quit "the eternal struggle for advantage over one's neighbor," reformers have been plumping for national health insurance (without, however, any further encouragement from the A.M.A., which soon changed both its mind and its leadership). Franklin D. Roosevelt came within an ace of combining health insurance with Social Security in 1935, only to be dissuaded by the A.M.A., notably by Dr. Harvey Cushing, author, brain surgeon and father-in-law of young James Roosevelt.

Whatever recommendations FDR might decide to make, Cushing wrote to the President, "no legislation can be effective without the good will of the American Medical Association, which has the organization to put it to work." In the politics of health reform, Cushing's comment remains the heart of the matter; and nowadays politicians must seek the cooperation not only of the A.M.A. but also of other health interest groups that have grown up in the interim. Over the decades our health-care system has invented a potpourri of patchwork schemes as substitutes for "the lost reform," and each new expedient, Blue Cross, for example, in the 30s and 40s—has given rise to a new organization in Washington. Like all newcomers, these organizations have become instantly suspicious of change and broadly committed to things as they are. If Cushing were alive today, he could cite at least four other groups whose goodwill may now be required: the "Blues," the private insurance industry, the hospitals and the medical schools.

The battle did not end with the New Deal. Harry S Truman took up the cudgels, to secure passage of the Murray-Wagner-Dingell bill, a measure the A.M.A. dismissed as "Marxist medicine." It never reached the floor of Congress, but it has since seen several reincarnations.

Considering the discouraging record, it wasn't any wonder that John F. Kennedy and Lyndon B. Johnson chose to fight on narrower ground. Each came to the White House prepared to settle for something less than "the lost reform." With the passage of Medicare and Medicaid in 1965, the Congress conferred the blessings of free or low-cost medical care upon both the elderly and the poor. The new programs enlarged the public's sense of possibilities. If we are closer now to the Promised Land, it is because the events of 1965 showed us a way out of the wilderness.

No sooner, it seemed, had the bills been signed

into law than news of yet another "health care crisis" —it was really the same old one—spread throughout the land. LBJ called on Congress to do something about "the soaring cost of medical care," and also about "the inexcusably high rate of infant mortality in the United States." (Seventeen countries still have rates below ours.) A few years later Richard M. Nixon sounded the familiar alarm: "We face a massive crisis in health care, and unless action is taken . . . we will have a breakdown in our medical care system."

The Congress began to consider new measures, a fresh generation of legislative proposals that would extend the protection of health insurance to some or all of the remaining population. Such proposals have grown more numerous of late. In the last Congress, the 94th, no less than 18 different bills were submitted, each alleging to offer the most practical solutions. These plans are Jimmy Carter's health reform legacy.

If the titles sound maddeningly alike, their contents exhibit some real differences. By and large, they reflect the contradictory hopes of people and organizations who have something to gain or lose from the redistribution of health care in America—doctors, hospitals, insurers, medical schools and patients. As consumers and taxpayers, one can try to test the merits of the proposals by keeping close to two familiar touchstones: the benefits offered and the costs incurred. In addition, one can examine any bill for its reform potential, meaning the extent to which it can be expected to reorganize health care along lines that make sense.

Of the 18 now before Congress a half-dozen perhaps can be considered "major," either because of the power and celebrity of their Congressional sponsors or because of the influence of their outside backers. Like the lobbies that support them, these six are a mixed bag. All but one would make health insurance compulsory. They range from a modest proposal that would extend benefits to citizens who have incurred unusually high medical costs—the so-called "Catastrophic Health Insurance and Medical Assistance Reform Act," introduced by Democratic Senators Russell Long of Louisiana and Abraham Ribicoff of Connecticut—to the sweeping "Health Security" measure that Senator Edward M. Kennedy has been promoting since 1969.

Taken together, the six proposals offer a fair sampling of what the experts are thinking, what the health care industry is demanding as ransom and what the public is wishing. What we see is what we may get. Before we pursue this pharmacopeia—an all-Democratic drugstore, no less—it may be well to glance at one object of great attention, what commentators are pleased to call "the national health-care delivery system." In truth, it is less a system than a collection of medical sins and services, a network that appears to be ever-expanding and evermore remote from the patient. Most of us have sensed the new remoteness, both in the reckonings we get and in the services we do not.

We are the world's only industrialized nation without a universal health-insurance program; yet no country on earth spends as much per capita as do we on health care. In a single generation, the total price has soared from $12 billion (in 1950) to $133 billion (in fiscal 1976), making health care America's third largest industry, just behind agriculture and construction. Some of the increase reflects genuine improvements in medicine, and some can be attributed to a wider distribution of services; but much of it must be chalked up to medical inflation pure and simple. Hospital charges, for instance, have risen four times as fast during the past decade as the Consumer Price Index itself.

Health care inflation is not a new problem; it has long been a fixture on the medical landscape. "Everywhere," lamented the health demographer Louis I. Dublin in 1927, "there is a feeling that something is wrong with the economics of medicine. Large numbers of middle-class families . . . chafe under what they generally consider the unjustifiably heavy cost." With the passage of Medicare and Medicaid, however, inflation took a quantum leap: Costs more than tripled, while annual per capita expenditures shot up 250 percent. In 1965, the average American spent $198 for health care; last fiscal year the sum was more than $500. The alarming spiral seems to have a life of its own; it has proved confoundedly resistant to voluntary self-controls and to Congressional tinkering, like the introduction two years ago of "peer review" for all treatments paid for by the federal government.

The dismal history of the medical dollar has made many wary of starting another round of reform. Yet there seems nothing mysterious or inevitable about medical inflation; in theory, at least, it can be controlled. Richard Nixon came close to doing just that with his 1971–74 price freeze, when health-care prices climbed at about one-third their usual rate. What seems chiefly at fault is Medicare's and Medicaid's peculiar method of reimbursement, whereby they pay whatever the doctor or the hospital claims to be "reasonable" and "customary." In effect, the Congress has handed a blank check to the health care industry, with predictable results. Not only has the industry jacked up prices for unimproved services, in many instances it has submitted bills for services never rendered. Fraud begets inflation.

It is true that only about one-third of the national health care bill is charged directly to consumers. The rest is paid for by the Federal Government, the states and the private insurance companies. But the citizen ultimately pays those bills, too, in higher taxes and stiffer premiums. Medicare premiums have been hiked a half dozen times since the program's inception; during the same period, Blue Cross rates in some areas have risen fourfold.

Although four-fifths of the population is covered by some kind of health insurance, the protection afforded is often skimpy and unreliable. In last year's recession an estimated 27 million workers and their families were deprived of coverage because of lay-offs. Many of the policies still in force, moreover, fail to protect patients against the costs of home care or visits to the doctor's office. Close to half the people who file pleas for bankruptcies each year do so because of medical debts.

Americans might bear these medical burdens more cheerfully were they getting their money's worth; but if the price of health care isn't right, neither is the product. As nearly everyone knows by now, the medical network suffers from several strains of maldistribution, both professional and geographic, Chief among these is a surplus of specialists, particularly of surgeons, and a shortage of primary care physicians—internists, pediatricians and general practitioners. . . .

The desperate shortage of health care personnel in some areas works to strengthen local medical oligopolies, inviting its practitioners to profit at the paitent's expense. I came across an instance of how this can occur, and the misery it can cause, when I interviewed a woman who lives in the hills of eastern Kentucky. One day, she told me, her 4-year-old son, Danny, complained of a pain in his stomach.

"I didn't have much money, but Danny was in awful pain, so I paid somebody to ride me into Prestonsburg. The doctor, he looked at Danny. He said the boy had to be operated before his appendix ruptured, but first I had to work things out with the hospital director. Me and Danny went to the director. He told me it would cost $350 and I would have to give a $100 down payment. I said I didn't have no $100. He said, 'Well, when you get it come back, and we'll fix your boy up.' My Danny was vomiting right there in the director's office. He was real sick. I went and borrowed the money from a cousin, and I came back with the money. The director, he says, 'you have to show you got an income so as you can pay the debt.' I said all I ever get is a check every month from the Veterans for $57. He said that would be just fine. Then he made me sign a paper promising to turn over the check to him each month till the bill was paid. I couldn't fight him. My Danny had to be operated."

One story does not make a pattern, but the hearing rooms of Congress over the past few years have resonated with hundreds of such tales. The impression one gets overall is that something has gone sour in American health care and that money has had a lot to do with it—which may be why more patients are writing their Congressmen nowadays.

Overlaid upon all these headaches is the increasingly widespread suspicion that the health care network, having run amok, is now beyond political reach and therefore beyond redemption. Its phenomenal growth in recent years has been unruly and unplanned, and that is a major part of the problem. But in the political arena the industry, for all its disunity and competing claims, has presented a single face to the public. It is the face of an institution that does not suffer reform gladly. . . .

Excerpts from "National Health Insurance—The Dream Whose Time Has Come," *New York Times Magazine,* January 9, 1977. © 1977 by the New York Times Company. Reprinted by permission.

class. Limits on the number of hospital days or physician visits would be abolished so that costs of catastrophic illnesses would be fully covered.

A necessary ingredient of all plans is the protection against runaway health care costs. Hence, limits would be set on the revenues of hospitals and physician services. Such limits would result from annual negotiations involving representatives of hospitals and doctors, private insurers, public authorities and other health personnel. Federal authorities would be responsible for assuring compliance with the established limits.

It is felt by its proponents that the costs of a comprehensive national health insurance would be significantly lower than those of the current "nonsystem." The costs would be borne through a combination of employer-employee contributions and federal general revenues. Premiums for employers would be based on a percentage of the total payroll, and employees would pay a given percentage of their wages and salaries. The costs of benefits to the unemployed and aged would be provided by the federal government through a revision of the current Medicare system.

Opponents of such comprehensive plans point to the serious problems facing the British government in running its National Health Service (NHS). As Britain's largest single employer, NHS costs $12 billion a year.[56] In recent years, this system has reached a crisis point due to escalating health costs, the growing bureaucratic structure, and the general stagnation of the British economy. In 1968 there was one administrator for every 9.5 hospital beds. In 1978 the rate declined to one administrator for every 4.8 beds. Long waiting lists have formed for those seeking noncritical surgery. Yet even the British critics of the NHS admit that for many working-class and lower-middle-class persons, the system works better than any private system.[57]

The American proposals for a comprehensive plan vary significantly from the British system. Ownership of the hospitals in the U.S. would remain in private hands. Physicians would not be paid by the government but rather through prepaid premiums of employers and employees and by tax revenues. Perhaps the most significant difference between the British system and the proposed American program lies in the philosophy supporting the initiatives. In Britain health care is viewed as one of the basic rights deriving from citizenship. In the United States, although there is a general consensus concerning the need to improve the health care of various groups, equal access to health services has not been defined as a civil right.[58]

After a long uphill fight for acceptance, increasing numbers of prepaid group health plans are being established with the help of federal grants and foundation subsidies by medical schools, hospitals, labor unions, community groups, and insurance organizations, frequently in cooperation with each other. Almost all the major proposals for national health insurance contain some provisions for encouraging prepaid plans, or health maintenance organizations as they are currently called, as an alternative method of paying for health services. The one exception is the AMA proposal. After years of fierce opposition, however, organized medicine now seems prepared to permit, if not promote, what has been described as a basic revolution in the relationship between patients and those who treat them.

Prepaid group health plans are advocated on the grounds of quality and economy. Evidence from ongoing programs shows lower hospitalization rates and consumer costs. Even more impressive, they have at the same time delivered continuous comprehensive services stressing preventive medicine and primary care. The fact that members of HIP (Health Insurance Plan of Greater New York—one prepaid group practice organization)

Prepaid Group Practice

have 25 percent fewer hospital admissions than comparable Blue Cross members is, for instance, attributed to the effective preventive care they have received.[59]

Prepaid programs vary in size and organizational details, but all involve the elimination of fee-for-service payment and solo practice. Instead, in return for a fixed annual fee, the services of a group of salaried doctors, specialists as well as general practitioners, are made available to the consumer. Most plans cover virtually all health needs, including hospital and home care, diagnostic and laboratory procedures, and even drugs. An important innovation marking many of them has been consumer participation in policy decisions and management. Most frequently cited as a successful model of prepaid group practice is the Kaiser Permanente organization, with three million members, 2000 doctors, and a network of hospitals and outpatient clinics in California, Oregon, and Hawaii.

Although prepaid group practice is being hailed as the hope of the future, organizations operating along these lines presently make up only a tiny proportion of the medical care scene. Although most Americans still pay for their medical care through the familiar fee-for-service system, more than 6 percent are now utilizing prepaid plans.[60] Spurred by federal support since 1973, health maintenance organizations increased in number from 42 in 1973 to 165 in 1977.[61] Significant increases are not likely to occur overnight, but the process has begun and the success to date will likely breed further increases.

Solving the Doctor Shortage

Opening the door to medical care through national health insurance cannot help but make the doctor shortage even more severe. Without positive steps to alter the present situation, prospects for reducing this shortage seem dim. The remedies proposed so far, however, appear to be inadequate.

The most obvious approach, training more doctors, has been taken to a limited degree. Since the 1950s there has been a continuing expansion in medical education promoted largely through government grants. In 1960 some 7500 students graduated from the 91 medical and osteopathic schools. In 1976, there were 14,300 graduates from the 123 existing schools.[62] Unfortunately, the scale of this increase hardly begins to match the magnitude of present and impending needs, particularly with the dominant emphasis on specialization. A number of schools have therefore begun to experiment with ways of speeding up medical education by consolidating graduate and undergraduate training and by conducting year-round classes. Meanwhile, efforts to add to the number of new medical schools and students continue.

A more innovative and, according to many authorities, a more promising approach is to develop midlevel professionals who can replace the physician for certain tasks. New kinds of medical personnel are now being trained along these lines to work both on their own and under the direct supervision of a doctor. These include physicians' assistants, nurse practitioners, and child health practitioners. Some programs are building on the skills of former members of the medical corps in the armed services, who are trained to take over routine work in clinics and physicians' offices. Other programs provide nurses with training that equips them to function on their own or in teams, with the backup of supervising physicians.

The problem of geographical distribution of physicians remains one of the most difficult and controversial. Despite attempts by the federal government to lure new physicians into under-served areas, 90 percent of medical school graduates between 1967 and 1971 chose to work in metropolitan areas where only 75 percent of the population lives.[63]

Yet, past experience indicates that whenever direct action is proposed, knotty issues arise. Medical educators, for instance, expressed strong opposition to a recent New York State bill requiring that state medical schools reserve vacancies for students who agree to practice in communities without an adequate number of doctors.[64] Despite their avowed support for its goals, opponents argued that the bill would reduce the caliber of medical students, increase already tight competition among superior applicants (who presumably would not agree to the terms), and create two classes of students. There would seem, then, to be a basic conflict between the norms and values dominating professional medicine and the felt needs of the larger public.

Interesting evidence of ambivalance on this score is to be found even within organized medicine. One example is the published reaction to a recent proposal of the AMA president for subsidized medical education as part of a campaign to solve the maldistribution of doctors. The graduating doctors whose education had been financed would in return spend three years in areas short of medical services, receiving a limited license that would permit them to practice only where they were assigned. The article reporting this plan in the publication of the Medical Society of the County of New York made the following comment:

Some 20, 10, or even 5 years ago such a suggestion by the President of the AMA might have been unthinkable—indeed impeachable—but times have changed. . . . Thus Dr. Hoffman's ideas are today tolerable, if not yet wholly acceptable. . . . As Dr. Hoffman states, his plan would be a most radical concept for most of the medical profession, but it is one that might be tried to see how it works. Somehow the unequal distribution of physicians must be overcome.[65]

As to the lopsided balance between specialists and primary-care physicians in the medical care system, various small-scale programs for dealing with it are undergoing trial runs. As noted earlier, medical schools have initiated specialists in family medicine, for instance, and training in community-based ambulatory care. A more drastic reorganization of medical education has been urged to produce increased numbers of primary-care physicians. The medical mainstream, however, is apparently still headed in the opposite direction.

Summary

Because of the rapid growth in technical knowledge and the size of all medical facilities, health care in the United States has become disorganized and consequently inaccessible to major social groupings. Present institutional structures, which are survivals of a time when medical practice was a simple, small-scale endeavor, no longer provide adequate guidelines for the utilization of health facilities to their full potential.

The United States spends more of its national income on health care than any other nation; yet some industrial nations with a much smaller investment, such as Sweden and England, achieve better health care results. Exorbitant costs, discrimination in service, and lack of quality treatment characteristic of the present American health care system are conditions that have developed while American medicine has been making its most dazzling technical advances. The promise of better health today has also meant that more people want more types of care, at a time when there are neither enough doctors nor adequate health facilities to go around. Americans have come to view health care as a right, but physicians' services and care facilities are still organized on a fee-for-service basis, which treats it instead as a marketable service.

Modern medicine has become largely a matter of specialist treatment in technologically sophisticated facilities. The personalized doctor-patient relationship, though touted by organized medicine in support of its free enterprise medical ideology, has largely disappeared from the scene. More hospital care has meant more and higher medical costs, which in turn have forced Americans to rely on third-party medical insurance concerns to help pay medical fees. Some observers see the third-party fee-for-service funding system as responsible for encouraging excessive use of facilities, unnecessary treatment, and irresponsible investment.

The poor, especially minorities, are less healthy than the nonpoor; they live in areas where doctors and hospital facilities are scarce or too expensive. The little health care they do receive is inferior. Federal aid in the form of Medicare and Medicaid has alleviated this situation somewhat for older citizens. Nevertheless, the aged have a number of unique health problems that demand attention. As the economic picture worsens and pressure for tax cuts and reduced spending increases, government programs are finding it more difficult to provide adequate financial support.

The shortage of doctors and other medical personnel is not only a shortage in numbers but is related to geographical distribution and distribution among the medical specialties. The shortage is most critical in rural and inner-city locations and in the area of primary care.

Numerous proposals for national insurance programs have been put forth and it has become increasingly more likely that some form will be passed by Congress in the near future. Since any national health program is likely to cause the demand for medical care to mushroom, some form of cost control and better management of available resources will be necessary to hold prices in check and to avoid declining quality of care in the future. A reorganization of the systems of payment has also been proposed, with physicians being paid fixed salaries or stated fees for each patient for whatever services are required over a fixed period of time.

Notes

[1]David Kotelchuck, "The Health Status of Americans," *Prognosis Negative,* ed. David Kotelchuck (New York: Random House), reprinted in Cary Kart (ed.) *Exploring Social Problems* (Sherman Oaks, Calif.: Alfred Publishing Company, 1978), pp. 203–215.

[2]*Reader's Digest 1979 Almanac and Yearbook* (Pleasantville, N.Y.: Reader's Digest Association, 1979), pp. 475–478.

[3]Milton I. Roemer, "Nationalized Medicine for America," *Transaction* 8 (September 1971), 31.

[4]Matt Clark with Stryker McGuire and Elsie Washington, "Battling Hospital Bugs," *Newsweek,* 19 June 1978, p. 82.

[5]Odin W. Anderson, *Health Care: Can There Be Equity?* (New York: Wiley, 1972), p. 129.

[6]U.S. Bureau of the Census, *Statistical Abstract of the United States, 1978* (Washington, D.C.: Government Printing Office, 1978), p. 110.

[7]Monroe Lerner, "Health as a Social Problem," *Handbook on the Study of Social Problems,* ed. Erwin O. Smigel (Chicago: Rand-McNally, 1971), pp. 291–330.

[8]Ibid., p. 301

[9]Eliot Friedson, "The Organization of Medical Practice," *Handbook of Medical Sociology,* ed. Howard E. Freemen, Sol Levine, and Leo G. Reeder (Englewood Cliffs, N.J.: Prentice-Hall, 1972), p. 344.

[10]Ibid., p. 345.

[11]Anderson, *Health Care,* p. 68.

[12]Ibid., p. 69.

[13]U.S. Bureau of the Census, *Statistical Abstract of the United States, 1978,* p. 99.

[14]This definition appears on page 1 of the Constitution of the World Health Organization; it can be found in E. L. Sullivan, *The World Health Organization: A Functional Approach to the Politics of Health* (Ann Arbor, Mich.: University Microfilm, 1969), appendix A.

[15]Edward Kennedy, "New National Health Insurance Program," *Congressional Record,* vol. 124, No. 157, 2 October 1978.

[16]U.S. Bureau of the Census, *Statistical Abstract of the United States, 1978,* p. 106.

[17]National Council of Organizations for Children and Youth, *America's Children* (Washington, D.C.: NCOCY, 1976), p. 42.

[18]Eliot Freidson, *Profession of Medicine* (New York: Harper & Row, 1970), pp. 87–136.

[19]Barbara Ehrenreich and John Ehrenreich, *The American Health Empire: Power, Profits, and Politics* (New York: Random House/Vintage Books, 1971), pp. 29–39.

[20]Louis Goodman, Edward Bennett and Richard Odem, "Current Status of Group Medical Practice in the United States," *Public Health Reports* 92:5 (September–October, 1977), p. 433.

[21]Anderson, *Health Care,* p. 95.

[22]U.S. Bureau of the Census, *Statistical Abstract of the United States, 1978,* p. 104.

[23]Ibid., p. 109.

[24]Ibid., p. 110; and U.S. Bureau of the Census, *Statistical Abstract of the United States, 1975* (Washington, D.C.: Government Printing Office, 1975), p. 79.

[25]U.S. Bureau of the Census, *Statistical Abstract of the United States, 1978,* p. 110

[26]Ibid., p. 110.

[27]Ibid., p. 110.

[28]Anderson, *Health Care,* p. 151.

[29]Mervyn W. Susser and W. Watson, *Sociology in Medicine,* (New York: Oxford University Press, 1971), p. 111.

[30]U.S. Bureau of the Census, *Statistical Abstract of the United States, 1978,* p. 69.

[31]Ibid., p. 74.

[32]Lerner, "Health as a Social Problem," p. 305.

[33]Mary Herman, "The Poor, Their Medical Needs and the Health Services Available to Them," *Annals of the American Academy of Political and Social Science,* January 1972, p. 21.

[34]Roemer, "Nationalized Medicine for America," p. 33.

[35]Ronald Sullivan, "New York's Cutbacks on Medicaid Backed," *New York Times,* 5 April 1977, p. 36.

[36]Robert M. Gibson and Charles R. Fisher, "Age Differences in Health Care Spending, Fiscal Year 1977," *Social Security Bulletin* 42:1 (January 1979), p. 11.

[37]Philip Shabecoff, "Soaring Price of Medical Care Puts a Serious Strain on Economy," *New York Times,* 1 May 1978, p. 1.

[38]U.S. Bureau of the Census, *Statistical Abstract of the United States, 1978,* pp. 99, 490.

[39]Shabecoff, "Soaring Price of Medical Care," p. 1.

[40]Gibson and Fisher, "Age Differences in Health Care Spending, Fiscal Year 1977," p. 11; and U.S. Bureau of the Census, *Statistical Abstract of the United States, 1975,* p. 70.

[41]U.S. Bureau of the Census, *Statistical Abstract of the United States, 1978,* p. 103.

[42]Paul B. Horton and Gerald R. Leslie, *The Sociology of Social Problems,* 4th ed. (New York: Appleton, 1970) p. 550.

[43]Odin W. Anderson and Ronald M. Andersen, "Patterns of Use of Health Services," *Handbook of Medical Sociology,* p. 400.

[44]Matt Clark with Marianna Gosnell, Dan Shapiro, Mary Lord, and Frank Meier, "Too Much Surgery," *Newsweek,* 10 April 1978, p. 65.

[45]Ibid., p. 65.

[46]Leonard L. Magnani, "Health Institutions: A Brief Introduction," *American Social Institutions,* ed. Dorothy Flapan (New York: Behavioral Publications, 1972), p. 284.

[47]Sydney H. Croog and Donna F. Ver Steez, "The Hospital as a Social System," *Handbook of Medical Sociology,* p. 277.

[48]Gary Bellow, "Malpractice: Patients Pay the Bill," *Working Papers for a New Society* 6 (January/February, 1978), p. 10.

[49]"Malpractice Nightmare," *Time,* 24 March 1975, p. 62.

[50]Marie Haug and Marvin B. Sussman, "Professional Autonomy and the Revolt of the Client," *Social Problems* 17 (Fall 1969), 153.

[51]Kenneth Reichstein, "Ambulance Chasing: A Case Study of Deviation and Control within the Legal Profession," *Social Problems* 13 (Summer 1965), 3–17.

[52]Peter Bonventre with Nicolas Horrock and Elaine Shannon, "℞ for Medifraud," *Newsweek,* 9 May 1977, p. 92.

[53]Dan Thomasson and Carl West, "Our Multibillion-Dollar Medicaid Scandal," *Reader's Digest,* May 1977, pp. 87–91.

[54]Ibid., p. 89.

[55]Edward Kennedy, "New National Health Insurance Program".

[56]R. W. Apple, Jr., "Britain's 30-Year Health Service: Hope Gives Way to Resignation," *New York Times,* 6 July 1978, p. 1.

[57]Ibid.

[58]Anderson, *Health Care,* p. 191.

[59]Horton and Leslie, *Sociology of Social Problems,* p. 553.

[60]Ronald Sullivan, "Health Maintenance Groups Take Growing Role as Resistance Eases," *New York Times,* 21 May 1978, p. 1.

[61]Ibid.

[62]U.S. Bureau of the Census, *Statistical Abstract of the United States, 1978, p.* 104.

[63]Ellen K. Coughlin, "$430-Million in Federal Funds Fail to Draw Doctors to Under-Served Areas," *The Chronical of Higher Education,* 16 October 1978, p. 12.

[64]M.A. Farber, "Study Will Explore State Doctor Shortage," *New York Times,* 13 June 1973, p. 39.

[65]"Solving the Maldistribution of MD's," *New York Medicine,* February 1973, pp. 56–60.

Aging

10

Social Nature of Aging

Stages of Life

Neither Young nor Old: Mid-Life

Americans Are Growing Older

Overcoming the Problems

Summary

Notes

Americans have always been oriented toward youth. Ours is a young nation and our population has, for at least the last century, been youth-oriented. "Tomorrow's leaders" and "the hope of the future," are only two of the many phrases that illustrate the value placed on youth in our society. Think for a moment about the television commercials you saw last night. What age group was most frequently portrayed? To what audiences were most of them addressed? What life styles were most often pictured? The chances are that the answer to all these questions is the same—youth. Maybe there were some commercials showing middle-aged or older persons. Think again. What were these people doing? The chances are that they were shown dyeing their hair, covering facial wrinkles, taking vitamins, or buying new sports cars, all for one purpose: to look, to feel, to be young again. Youth in American culture has come to be seen as all that is beautiful, happy, intelligent, vigorous, and useful. It has even come to be synonymous with life itself.

Where does this cultural orientation leave the middle-aged or older persons in society? Generally, they are on the outside looking in, often times wanting to recapture their youth but finding it impossible to do so and resigned to growing old in a society with seemingly little understanding or sympathy for their problems. It is not uncommon to hear the aged agree with one writer's statement that "America is one of the worst countries in the world in which to grow old."[1] But perhaps not for long. An important shift is occurring in our population that may ultimately change this. Our society is growing older. There are more older people in America than ever before, both in terms of actual numbers and in proportion to the rest of the

Problems of Human and Physical Resources

population. The baby boom of the 1940s and early 1950s means that by the mid-1980s there will be a swelling of people in the middle-age categories. And, provided that there is not another baby boom in the immediate future, the 35–44 age group may become the single largest age group in the country by 1980. This honor will remain with this cohort as its members enter their older years.

The change in the composition of the population suggests that value conflicts may arise. With the increase in nonyouthful populations, it is unlikely that a youth-oriented culture can long remain dominant. Senior citizens have already begun to demand their right for a share in the political arena. Traditional age roles are being rejected by older Americans who refuse politely to bow out of society at age 65 or 70. They are seeking to live out their lives in a meaningful way while making positive contributions to the society in which they live.

While older persons are realizing that they are assigned few meaningful roles by society, middle-aged persons are also questioning what their roles are. Neither group can easily adjust to the expectations assigned to them, and few alternative structures have been institutionalized to help solve this problem. The present social structure is not adequately meeting the needs of these groups, and social disorganization is the end product.

Current demographic trends imply that unless society can adjust to meet the demands of the changing population, problems associated with aging will become more widespread. To date, society has done little to alleviate the problems. The lag between changes in population composition and alterations in social service programs provides one illustration. The increasing proportion of older persons in society today, and the consequent decreasing proportion of younger populations, suggests that there should be an increase in social service programs and aid for the elderly and a corresponding decrease for young people. Instead of expanded university facilities, innovative retirement complexes may be required.

The questions that must be answered immediately include: Who will care for the elderly? How can the elderly remain active participants in society? How can midlife career changes be facilitated? To analyze the problems of an aging population, both the social disorganization and value conflict approaches are useful and necessary. This chapter will examine the inability of the present social structure to deal adequately with the problems associated with aging as well as the consequences of the refusal of the aging to conform to the roles assigned to them.

Social Nature of Aging

Aging is not a social problem. The fact that all 215 million Americans wake up each morning of the year one day older than they were the preceding day does not constitute a social problem. This is not to say, however, that social problems do not arise in certain age groups or are not associated with certain age statuses. In fact, social scientists have gone so far as to label one of our major social problems after a particular age grouping. Juvenile delinquency has long been recognized as an issue of major importance by sociologists, psychologists, and criminal justice practitioners. What is important to realize for our discussion is that juvenile delinquency is not "caused" by individuals' turning 13 years old. Juvenile delinquency results from a series of interrelated factors, some particular to the juvenile age status and others more general but equally influential in determining youthful lawbreaking.

So, too, the problems dealt with in this chapter are not the result of an individual, or a large group of individuals, turning age 40 or 50 or 65. The situations accompanying such events for large groups of people are what constitute the social problem, and the roots of the problem must be traced through the new biological, psychological, and social states in which these groups find themselves. While the maxim, "you're only as old as you think you are," may be a valid one, it is clear that the particular problems discussed in this chapter are relevant for persons at specific stages of their life careers, regardless of how old they feel mentally or physically.

The Middle Years

Setting boundaries around "middle age" is more difficult than around other age categories. The terms "adolescence" or "old age" are usually clearly defined by legal or economic criteria. But middle age provides no such easy demarcation. To a grade school student, an adult neighbor who is no longer youthful might be considered middle-aged. Teenagers, on the other hand, might believe that being over a specific age, say 30, is the criterion necessary to be labeled middle-aged. College students, being more sophisticated, are likely to determine middle age by a number of criteria, including age (over 30), marital and family status (married with or without children), and life-style (a 9-to-5 job and little outside activity). The same college student might change the criteria for a 32-year-old parent if the life-style included partaking of night life or physical or athletic endeavors. However, any 30- or 32-year-old person, regardless of life-style or marital and family status, would probably be horrified if it were realized that the term "middle-aged" was being applied to him or her.

The difficulty of establishing strict chronological limits around the category of middle age will be seen later in the discussion of life course transitions. For now, the category will be described by the major issue or question relevant to individuals. Whereas, the problems of young adulthood focus around the concern of moving into the adult world and establishing a career, the problems of the middle-aged in America center around the questions people have about the life they have moved into. "What have I done with my life?" becomes a major source of tension, stress and doubt! For some, the question leads to disillusionment and dissatisfaction with career choices. Some attempt to reject choices they made previously by changing careers or changing spouses. Still others turn to alcohol and drugs to help them cope with the present or help them forget the past. These problems are not unique to the middle years, but their recognized existence in the proportions that are present constitutes a basis of concern for all of society.

The Older Years

Who are the old? Many definitions have been offered. Some are more useful than others. It is clear that sociologists cannot work with the definition of old age given by statesman Bernard Baruch when he said, "old age is always my age—plus ten." More acceptable, although perhaps just as arbitrary, is the lower boundary for the old-age category, long established and widely accepted as 65. No upper "limit" has been set, since death is usually considered the final point for this category. The choice of a chronological lower limit rests on the assumption that age 65 represents a turning point in the life cycle for most individuals, that is, this is the time when people have traditionally retired. In fact, the choice of 65 as the age marker allowing individuals the right to receive old-age benefits was the result of a congressional decision made in the 1930s. Yet many persons today are retiring as early as age 55, while others may now decide to work up until age 70 or beyond. Even though some people continue working until the day they die, age 65 is the consensual lower limit of the old-age category.

The problems associated with old age are many. They range from biological to psychological to sociological. It is clear, however, that at the core of many of the problems is a socioeconomic root. At the very time when biological processes determine that individuals must take special care of their bodies, many of the aged cannot afford the medical or nutritional aids necessary. As failing health and even senility prevent the aged from caring for themselves, they frequently find themselves widowed, separated from their children, and alone. To compound their difficulties, the income of older Americans is frequently not sufficient to allow for adequate housing, since pensions are frequently frozen while taxes and rents increase.

But not all of the problems of the older years are physical or financial in nature. One of the major concerns of the aged is maintaining productive, useful roles in society. This, however, is difficult.

Having completed the child-rearing stage, older persons find themselves stripped of their parental roles. Once they are also forced out of the labor market, older persons find their productive roles strictly limited. The aged, once looked upon as the most respected group in society, are now shunned by a society that has come to emphasize the value of youth.

Process of Aging

In the past two decades, there have been thousands of articles, both in scholarly and popular journals, concerned with racial and sex discrimination. Less attention has been focused on age discrimination. But like racism and sexism, "ageism" is a widespread social phenomenon affecting millions of Americans. Ageism is discrimination based solely on a person's age. As we shall see, ageism affects all age groups but it is particularly relevant to middle-aged and older populations.

It does not take a sociologist to point out that age stratification, age inequalities and age segregation take place. In fact, it is possibly the first basis of stratification that a child recognizes. Long before a child realized that his or her color or sex are the bases of differential treatment, age inequalities are recognized. How many children cry and complain when older brothers and sisters can stay up later at night than they can? The 5-year, 11-month-old boy who cannot play on the Little League because he happened to be born one month too late probably understands the patterns of age segregation as well as anyone. Although such forms of age-related inequalities can, to a degree, be legitimized by biological factors, other forms cannot be dismissed as easily, and it is these forms which we shall discuss here.

Age inequalities may be based upon membership in age strata or age co-

We're never too old to learn, as thousands of senior citizens are proving in college classrooms all over the country. These two coeds, sharing their thoughts about a course assignment, can learn and grow together despite a difference in age.

horts.[2] Inequalities based on age strata are those similar to the would-be Little Leaguer who is unable to play simply because of the stage of the life cycle he is in. Twenty-year-olds in some states complain that they are being treated unequally because they are not allowed to consume alcoholic beverages. Some groups are excluded from certain occupations simply because of age constraints. For example, no one under 35 years of age may be elected president of the United States. Many cities and states have regulations prohibiting the hiring of persons under 21 as policemen or firemen. Behavior considered criminal among adult populations may be thought of differently for young people. Few policemen would want to handcuff and arrest a 3-year-old who is parading nude down a beach. However, adults would be responsible for their conduct under public decency statutes.

At the other end of the spectrum, an employer is legally guilty if he fires an employee simply because the person is 62 years old. Under current regulations, however, anyone over 70 years of age can be automatically fired. Discrimination based on age strata also takes place in hiring. Although the number of employment advertisements calling for "young creative minds" or "young energetic workers" has declined because of federal laws forbidding discrimination on the basis of age alone, such discrimination continues. More subtle means are now being utilized. How many 60-year-olds would be able to answer an ad which called for someone with "1 to 3 years' experience"? As with racial and sexist job discrimination, ageism is a fact of life in many sectors of society.

Age segregation is also widespread today. The solution to many of the housing problems of the elderly has been to erect multistory modern apartment complexes for senior citizens. The growth of senior citizen communities, especially in Florida and Arizona, and the recent emergence of apartment buildings that do not allow families with children to rent units, are other examples of segregation based on membership in age groups.

Inequalities due to membership in a specific age cohort refer to those that arise from the experiences shared by persons born during the same, relatively short time span. For example, of persons born in the United States in the period from 1890 to 1900, less than 12 percent would have received one or more years of college training. Educational opportunities changed so drastically and swiftly that of the cohort of persons born in the 1940s, more than 35 percent received one or more years of college.[3] Today, many types of employment require training that has been available only in the past two decades. Persons receiving their schooling before that time are, in effect, being discriminated against when applying for that position. In this case, it is societal dynamics, or the nature of the society at the time individuals pass through life cycle stages, that lead to the discrimination. As we shall see, the problems that are discussed in later sections of the chapter represent inequalities based upon both age strata and age cohorts, and in some circumstances a combination of the two.

Stages of Life

From the moment a fetus is conceived in the womb, the aging process has begun. For some people, it is a process that lasts for a century. For all, it is a process that continues until the last dying breath. In this sense, aging is synonymous with living, yet aging has great effects on our living. As we age, our lives change. Children are different from infants, adolescents are different from children, young adults are different from adolescents, and so on. It is necessary to see life as a process, as something that is always changing. Every day we are slightly different people than we were the day before, or will be the day after. We do not always notice the change over a period of days, weeks, or months, but it is still there.

This phenomenon of constant change makes it difficult for scientists when they want to be able to study change in individuals or groups. Conceivably, they could make up a name for every day of a person's life and study what happens to the person on each day. But this is impractical. Rather, they have chosen to group together a number of days into periods or stages in an individual's life cycle. The choice of the number of stages is arbitrary. The simplest might consist of three stages: youth, adulthood, and old age. Yet each of these stages can be subdivided into smaller categories. Infancy, childhood, and adolescence are traditionally subdivisions of youth. Early, middle, and late adulthood have been used to subdivide the middle years, and recently some authors have distinguished a young old (65–75) from an old old (75+) age category. The number of categories depends largely on what is being studied. In our discussion, we shall divide the life cycle into four stages: childhood, adolescence, adulthood, and old age. In keeping with our view of aging as a process, we shall discuss not only the roles played by persons in the various age groups but also the problems that arise when people give up roles associated with one age category and move into another. The roles and transitions occurring within and around the adult years of life will, of course, be our primary focus.

Roles are the sets of expectations held by society for persons in specific social positions. Many social positions and roles are directly related to specific age categories. The role of playmate is associated with childhood. The role of spouse in our society is connected with adulthood. The grandparent role necessitates middle or later stages of the life cycle. Other roles clearly transcend age categories. The roles we play as brother or sister may be carried through from childhood to old age. Many of us attempt to play the role of athlete during various stages of our life cycle. Neighbor roles are another that stretch over the span of years. This section will deal with problems of two sorts. The first are problems experienced by persons within certain stages of the life cycle.

One way of viewing the life cycle was described by Erik Erikson who suggested that psychosocial stages and physiological stages are roughly coterminous.[4] He chose to analyze the life cycle on the basis of eight psychosocial stages. These stages will be incorporated into the discussion of our four age-related categories.

Although Erikson was trained as a Freudian psychoanalyst, he rejected Freud's emphasis on sexual repression and concluded instead that many emotional problems were caused by problems of identity. That is, at various points in the life cycle, people experience personal crises that are intimately related to the social environment. Persons suffering from identity problems lose sight of their goals in life; they are confused about who they are and what they stand for. In each stage of the life cycle, individuals must rediscover and redefine themselves and their environment in order to build the basis for a healthy transition to the next stage.

Childhood

Erikson's first psychosocial stage encompasses the first year of life. During this period, the dominant psychosocial factor involves the trust or mistrust developed by the infant. If the infant's needs are met in terms of care, affection and attention, the infant will likely develop a trusting view of the world as she or he matures. If the infant's needs are not met, such trust will be absent.

Between the ages of 2 and 3, children begin to learn the basic rules of the game of life. They begin by seeing and imitating. Erikson claims that at this age the individual must deal with the second psychosocial issue, which involves the sense of autonomy or doubt. Children attempt to perform actions for themselves and thus develop a sense of personal autonomy. If they are reprimanded too often or have everything done for them, they may develop doubts about their own abilities.

The third stage of the life cycle involves the child's attempt to initiate, rather than imitate or follow, particular activities or conversations. If the endless questions about why the sky is blue or the grass green are ridiculed, the child may develop feelings of guilt about self-initiated activities. If the initiatives are encouraged, the likelihood is greater that the child will develop a sense of confidence that will encourage further independence. Typically this stage takes place around ages 4 or 5.

Beginning at about age 6 children enter Erikson's fourth stage of development, which he calls industry versus inferiority. It is during this stage that children are active and industrious, making attempts at new and creative projects and ideas. For those who are encouraged or rewarded, industry is enhanced. For those who are not, feelings of inferiority may develop. During this stage the importance of the parents as socializers diminishes, and teachers, friends and peers begin to play an increasingly important role. This period in the life cycle goes on to approximately age 11.

A somewhat similar view of childhood has been taken by sociologist George Herbert Mead, who envisioned three stages of development that all children experience.[5] The preparatory stage of human development takes place up to age 3 or so. During this period, children come to distinguish between self and others. They begin to imitate the behavior of those closely associated with themselves. However, there is no understanding of why certain activities are engaged in. Nor is there any consistency of action. This is the reason why a 2-year-old girl may cuddle her doll one moment, imitating maternal behavior, but the next moment fend off her older brother by whacking him over the head with it. In the second stage, the play stage, children begin to have some understanding of the reasons for their behavior, but switch their roles rather erratically. The young boy may be a policeman one minute, a baseball player the next, and later a mailman. Although they are only pretending to take the roles of others, this is important play because it allows them to learn to see ideas and events as others might see them.

While it was once common for a child to grow up in a home with at least one grandparent present, today it is much less so. The modern nuclear family of parents and children has no room, physically or emotionally, for the aged.

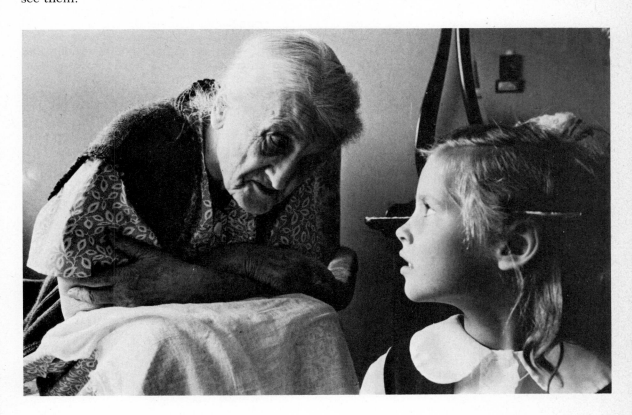

The final stage of Mead's scheme is referred to as the game stage. Role behavior becomes more consistent and the child is able to sense the roles of others. To play a game, the child must know the rules; that is, she or he must know what actions to perform and what actions everyone else in the game will perform. Children in this stage can sense the interaction that their behavior will elicit from others. A batter who hits the ball to an infielder knows that it is the job of the infielder to throw the ball to first base before the batter can get there. The child also knows that certain behaviors are expected of him or her by others. When the ability to recognize the expectations, or rules, of organized games is expanded to include the recognition of rules governing other social settings, the child is said to have internalized the concept of the "generalized other." The concept can be equated to the standards and values of the general community.

Such a realization allows children to adapt more easily to roles and expectations associated with their age. Whether it is performing tasks around the home or learning to cope with the role of student, being able to take the roles, perspectives, and expectations of others into account is the mark of a socialized person.

Adolescence

Although there is no consensus as to the boundaries around the period of adolescence, one common marker for the lower boundary is the transition from elementary to junior high school. The upper boundary is usually at entry into one or more of the adult roles. These may include marriage, financial independence, full-time employment or parenthood.[6]

Part of the lack of consensus may be due to the fact that adolescence is a relatively new category in the life cycle. Prior to the modernization of the twentieth century, it was common for children to move directly into adult roles. There was no period of adolescence. Before the period of extensive division of labor and the consequent need for widespread growth in secondary education, the concept of adolescence was largely unknown and unnecessary.[7]

According to Erikson, the central task of the adolescent period is the establishment of a consistent identity. The adolescent attempts to fit his or her many roles into a unified, coherent whole. The individual makes strides in the direction of increasing autonomy by making more and more decisions, independent of other family members.

However, the adolescents' roles are not clearly defined for them. Many of the roles assigned to them in our society are marginal at best. No longer children, but not yet adults, adolescents are put in a holding pattern for a number of years. They are required by law to stay in school until 16 and are encouraged by a tight labor market to remain there even longer. Adolescence is the period when society, primarily through the family and school system, makes its final attempt to bring the person into line with adult standards. Yet, even for those who conform perfectly, the privileges of adulthood are denied.[8] Adolescents are barred from the economic sector by the inability to find full-time employment. They are barred from the political sector by the inability to vote. They are barred from the sexual sector by a society that frowns on such relationships among people their age. Although they are banned from engaging in many of the activities of the adult world, adolescents are expected to be able to present a rough draft of what they want their adult life to look like.[9]

The process of "pulling up roots" and establishing a life relatively independent of parents can be a long, drawn-out one. Some people enter this period at 17 and do not exit until 22 or later. Others do not even begin until 21 or 22. In all cases, however, the problems of the transition are similar. They revolve around the issues of locating oneself in a peer group role, a sex role, an anticipated occupation, and an ideology or world view.[10]

Adulthood

During the transitional period to adulthood, individuals are frequently overcome with the sense that the lives they have been leading are not part of the real world. They feel that their families have shielded them from participating in this world, so they try to forget past associations. Some choose to join strict authoritarian groups that command the individual to break off all ties with the past. Others are content with less drastic measures. Moving away from the parents' home for short periods of time, to college or to the army, is a more common form of escaping the parents' influence. Such steps can be seen as preliminary inquiries into life in the adult world that allow the adolescent the opportunity to examine possible career lines and life-styles.[11]

Although most young adults struggle to establish a firm identity for themselves, most accomplish this without undergoing a major personal crisis. According to Erikson's scheme, they must face the issue of establishing close, intimate relationships (sharing oneself with another person) or of remaining somewhat isolated (incapable of such intimacy). In dealing with the issues of identity and intimacy, young adults fall into one of four broad categories. Persons in the "moratorium" group are unsure of the identity and level of intimacy that they desire. Yet they struggle to find the right combination. They delay finding solutions but feel that delaying is only making matters worse. Persons in the "identity-diffused" group are also unsure of what values or identity to attach themselves to, but they do not attempt to define or confront these issues. Either because of attitudes of inferiority, alienation, or fatalism, people in this group allow things to pass as they are and do not see themselves in any major crisis. The "identity-foreclosed" group includes those who have passively accepted the identity designed for them by their parents. There is no struggle or crisis for this group either. Finally, the "identity-achieved" group has endured a crisis and succeeded in obtaining a clear identity, value system, and philosphy of life. It is possible for individuals to be members of all of these groups at some time or other during the young adult stage, and even to belong to one group at two different times. However, unless an individual experiences some crisis, it is unlikely that any strong identity will be established.[12]

As adults approach the mid-twenties, they are frequently confronted with two contradictory tasks. The first is to keep career options open and maintain a sense of adventure. The second involves the creation of a more stable life structure.[13] The working out of a solution may involve many false starts. Commitments may be made in some areas but not in others. But by the age of 28 or so, most key decisions concerning occupation and marriage will have been made.

The situation is complicated by the belief that whatever decisions are made are irrevocable. It is assumed that the career choice made during this period is something that cannot be changed.[14] Marriages that take place during the "trying twenties" are often a series of ups and downs. The romantic illusions about crisis-free, wedded bliss come tumbling down when both parties realize that the equal growth and development plans are easier to conceptualize than implement.

The transition to age 30 actually begins around age 28 and continues to age 33. Some persons make only minor changes in their lives in order to enrich certain aspects. Most men experience a moderate or serious crisis when they realize that it is "now or never" if they are going to establish new career lines. If women have been staying home as housewives and mothers, there may be a desire to move out and expand their horizons. Couples married during the "trying twenties" reevaluate their commitment. It is not until the early thirties that many individuals begin to settle down.

During the period from 32 to 40 most men seek to secure two major objectives. The first is to "establish a niche" in society. Roots planted in the early years are watered and take hold. The second task is to work at "making it." This involves the setting up of a series of career goals and progressing towards them. Whether the goals are material success or the respect of colleagues, the rules of the game are studied and followed. Toward the end of this period, this task becomes one of "becoming one's own man." The man attempts to establish himself as independent and self-sufficient while simultaneously desiring respect from others.[15]

In setting his goals on the climb up the ladder, a man's relationships with relatives, friends, and co-workers may become strained. He may feel that relatives are using him or depriving him from his goals. Bosses may be seen as tyrannical, and co-workers as jealous.

For both men and women, the realization that life is half over creates both a sense of fear and of doubt. They question whether the goals they set for themselves will be reached. They wonder what will happen when the children are gone. It takes the death of only one friend to reemphasize the closeness of death. For housewives and career women, for corporate executives and laborers, the question will arise, "Is this all there is?" Achieved roles seem confining. The loss of physical prowess is symbolic of the loss of youth and the idealism that goes with it.[16]

Levinson found that 80 percent of his male subjects experienced a crisis in which they "question virtually every aspect of their lifes and are horrified by what they find."[17] To try to change his present situation, a man in mid-life would be working against everything that he had spent his last 20 years achieving. His spouse, boss, and friends are likely to try to dissuade any serious changes.

Frequently these concerns are made worse by the fact that the wives of these middle-aged men are now being freed from child-care activities and are starting out on new careers. "She is ready to strike out, go back to school, get a job, kick up her heels, just as he is drawing back, gasping for breath, feeling futile about where he has been. . . ."[18]

Erikson's characterization of the psychosocial task for this period pits the forces of generativity and concern for others against self-absorption. Parents realize that children are taking their first steps toward independence and that this will leave more time for their own interests. Generativity refers to the use of this time for serving others. Self-absorption implies a serving of one's own interests. The suggested therapy for males confronting the crisis of middle age is to turn outward to begin serving others. However, the problem for females, who have often been serving others for their whole adult lives, is different. This is the time that women realize that the opportunity to fulfill their dreams and cultivate abandoned talents is present. Although menopause may cause severe psychological crises, it has also been shown to unleash a new creativity in women. Women frequently come to feel that they are in the prime of life.[19]

Since six of Erikson's eight stages of the life cycle are concerned with what are basically youthful phases of development, some social scientists have sought to provide a more comprehensive analysis of the middle and late years. Peck has derived four issues that must be solved by persons in the middle to late middle years of life.[20] First, valuing wisdom over valuing physical prowess is the result of slow loss of physical strength and health. Second, finding a new balance between socializing and sexualizing refers to the necessity of redefining relationships with men and women as a result of social and biological factors. Third, cathectic flexibility versus cathectic impoverishment refers to the emotional states acquired by persons as familial ties are broken and old interests give way to new ideas. Finally, the issue of mental flexibility and mental rigidity focuses on the willingness of persons to accept new ideas that are contrary to the patterns followed for several decades. Healthy adjustment to the aging that takes place in adulthood is dependent upon one's being able to adapt to changing social and biological conditions.

After one has managed to escape or live through the mid-life crisis of the forties, a period of renewal may follow. Secondary interests are frequently cultivated that can be carried into retirement. To people in their fifties, the prospect of retirement is not far off. This necessitates their beginning to redefine their attitudes about many issues. Financial security often becomes a dominant concern for the late middle-aged, who are fearful of being burdens of their children. Facing the prospect of loneliness and death, many turn back to religions which they had left behind in the midst of earlier concerns with the material world. Persons between 50 and 60 must begin making many of the adjustments that will in large measure determine the manner in which they will live out the rest of their years.[21]

Old Age

Erikson's final psychosocial stage views the major theme of old age as being one of integrity versus despair. Individuals look back over their whole lives and decide whether they are satisfied with it or not. If their lives are viewed as meaningful, if they feel that they have accomplished something positive, they experience a sense of integrity. Those who feel that they made too many wrong choices or missed too many opportunities will have a sense of despair. This review of one's life is a characteristic of almost every older person.[22]

The solution to the problems of the transition to this stage is not made any easier by the way the old are treated in our society. Although we will analyze many of their problems in a later section of this chapter, it is clear that the lives of the aged in our society are often difficult. Separated from family members, frequently widowed, and usually unable to work, the aged tend to become social isolates. Others may maintain social contact but feel guilty because they perceive themselves as burdens.

A study of personality changes from middle to old age has shown that a transition from an active perception of one's role in society to a more passive one takes place.[23] Many middle-aged persons may feel that the world is there for their taking, whereas older persons often see the world as an over-powering force. The old often adopt fatalistic attitudes about the world around them and accept the idea that change is impossible.

Studies of attitudes toward death demonstrate that most people do not think about dying as a result of the aging process but more frequently see death coming in the form of an outside force, as the result of an accident or deliberate act.[24] But, as the aging process continues, death begins to loom more certain and finally is seen as inevitable. Most people hope that their death will not be a long, drawn-out process. The right to a "good death" is increasingly on the minds of older persons today. The advances of modern medical technology have made it possible to prolong human life much more than ever before. These same advances have raised questions that never had reason to arise before. What is death? When does it occur? Should medical practice overrule natural processes? To what extent should artificial means be used to maintain life? What are the "rights" of the patient to choose or refuse medical care? What are the rights of families of dying patients? Of the doctors?

None of these questions has a clear-cut answer. Some people argue that life should be maintained as long as possible because any form of life is

Old age does not mean a Florida retirement community for everyone. Many cannot afford to retire and others would have nothing else to do if they stopped working. Ideally, older people should be able to choose what life-style is most rewarding to them.

Problems of Human and Physical Resources

worth saving. Others suggest that while patients are living off machines, a cure may be found for their malady. On the other side, though, are persons who argue that artificial methods are demeaning to human life and that patients have a right to choose to die a good death. Many older persons, and even some young ones, have chosen to sign "living wills" that request that they be allowed to die, rather than undergo heroic artificial measures if the need ever arises (see Figure 10.1).

Neither Young nor Old: Mid-Life

As mentioned earlier, the number of persons in the middle years of life will grow significantly by the mid-1980s. Depicting the typical middle-aged person is not easy. Middle-aged persons today will likely be quite different from the middle-aged of the late 1980s. Today's middle-aged are those who were

"A Living Will" **Figure 10.1**

TO MY FAMILY, MY PHYSICIAN, MY LAWYER, MY CLERGYMAN
TO ANY MEDICAL FACILITY IN WHOSE CARE I HAPPEN TO BE
TO ANY INDIVIDUAL WHO MAY BECOME RESPONSIBLE FOR MY HEALTH, WELFARE OR AFFAIRS

Death is as much a reality as birth, growth, maturity and old age—it is the one certainty of life. If the time comes when I, _____ can no longer take part in decisions for my own future, let this statement stand as an expression of my wishes, while I am still of sound mind.

If the situation should arise in which there is no reasonable expectation of my recovery from physical or mental disabilities, I request that I be allowed to die and not be kept alive by artificial means or "heroic measures". I do not fear death itself as much as the indignities of deterioration, dependence and hopeless pain. I, therefore, ask that medication be mercifully administered to me to alleviate suffering even though this may hasten the moment of death.

This request is made after careful consideration. I hope you who care for me will feel morally bound to follow its mandate. I recognize that this appears to place a heavy responsibility upon you, but it is with the intention of relieving you of such responsibility and of placing it upon myself in accordance with my strong convictions, that this statement is made.

Signed _____

Date _____

Witness _____

Witness _____

Copies of this request have been given to _____

_____

_____

_____

Source: Reprinted with permission of the Concern for Dying, 250 West 57th Street, New York, N.Y. 10019.

born into a world of the 1930s and 1940s, a world vastly different from the one into which later generations were born. The initial childhood experiences of the current generation of middle-aged were influenced by the Great Depression and the associated poverty, unemployment, and corresponding economic and mental insecurity. Most were also affected early in life by World War II. Some lost a parent early in life who was killed in the war, while many experienced a few years without a father at home. Frequently, when fathers were gone and mothers were working for the war effort, the children were left with relatives or friends. Hence, for many of today's middle-aged, childhood was a period of uncertainty and insecurity, but a time when they were taught to aspire to those life goals that would bring them those qualities their own early lives lacked.

Economic stability and prosperity began to emerge as this generation was entering the labor force. New career opportunities were emerging and jobs were opening up. The period of the 1950s and 1960s saw this generation beginning the climb up the ladder. By the time of the social unrest of the 1960s, this group was implanted in the economic and political structures, albeit on the lower rungs. It seems fair to say that this generation of middle-aged is an in-between generation, too young for participation in the war movement of the 1940s and too old for the antiwar movement of the 1960s.

Many of the problems associated with the middle-aged today do not seem to be unique to this generation. The problems they are experiencing may be the same ones that past generations have undergone and future generations will undergo. Many of the problems are already widespread. Others are showing signs of increasing. With more people moving into this period of the life cycle, it is important to understand what the problems are and what their sources are. This section will deal with these issues.

Illusions Come Tumbling Down

By the time we reach our mid- to late twenties most people have laid out a plan for the rest of their lives. We set goals that we want to achieve in life. Some of these goals may deal with the type of occupational position we want. Others may deal with the type of family situation we want to be part of. Additional goals probably focus on the type of person, personality, or philosophy that we want to achieve.

Frequently, the picture we paint is one of where we will be when we reach age 40 or 45. Whatever the occupation, whatever the life-style, whatever the person we are at age 45, the probability is great that there will be a gap between what we envisioned for ourselves and what we have actually accomplished. "No matter how close a person comes to achieving his dream, it will not fulfill all his wishes. The loss of magic that he feels—that everyone feels to some degree in mid-life—is the loss of magical hopes attached to the dream when it originally took shape."[25]

A part of the many dreams of young adults is the "gratification fantasy," which suggests that once we make it to where we want to be, we will be respected, admired, and deferred to by others. A second part of the dream usually centers on autonomy. In varying degrees this fantasy suggests that, once we make it, we will be free from the influence of others and that we can decide for ourselves how our lives will be run.[26] Yet, there is no one, whatever social class or political position, who is answerable only to himself

Daniel J. Levinson

The Mid-Life Transition: A Period in Adult Psychosocial Development

Within a given life structure certain components are *central:* they occupy most time and energy, provide the basis on which other components are chosen, and have the greatest significance for the self. Occupation and family are usually most central in a man's life; other important components include ethnicity-religion, peer relations, and leisure. The *peripheral* components are more detachable and changeable; they involve less investment of the self and are less crucial to the fabric of one's life.

In this view, adult development is the *evolution of the life structure.* The life structure does not remain static, nor does it change capriciously. Rather, it goes through a sequence of alternating stable periods and transitional periods. The stable periods ordinarily last some 6–8 years, the transitional periods 4–5 years.

The primary developmental task of a *stable period* is to make certain crucial choices, build a life structure around them, and seek to attain particular goals and values within this structure. Each stable period also has its own distinctive tasks, which reflect the requirements of that time in the life cycle. Many changes may occur during a stable period, but the basic life structure remains relatively intact.

The primary developmental task of a *transitional period* is to terminate the existing structure and to work toward the initiation of a new structure. This requires a man to reappraise the existing life structure, to explore various possibilities for change in the world and in the self, and to move toward the crucial choices that will form the basis for a new life structure in the ensuring stable period. Each transitional period also has its own distinctive tasks reflecting its place in the life cycle. . . .

The Mid-life Transition serves as a developmental link between two eras in the life cycle: early adulthood and middle adulthood. . . . Each era contains a series of developmental periods (see below), but it also has an overall character of its own. It must suffice merely to identify the eras and their approximate age spans:

Pre-adulthood: Age 0–22
Early Adulthood: Age 17–45
Middle Adulthood: Age 40–65
Late Adulthood: Age 60–85
Late Late Adulthood: Age 80+

The shift from one era to the next is a massive developmental step and requires a transitional period of several years. Every transition is both an ending and a beginning, a departure and arrival, a death and rebirth, a meeting of past and future. The basic task of a cross-era transition is to terminate the era just ending and to create a basis for the next. . . .

During the 30s, a man's primary developmental task is to build a satisfactory life structure. Within it, he tries to establish his place in society, to pursue his youthful aspirations, and to live out important aspects of the self. The late 30s mark the culmination of early adulthood. The Mid-life Transition, which lasts from roughly 40 to 45, provides a bridge from early to middle adulthood.

The start of the Mid-life Transition brings a new set of developmental tasks. Now the life structure itself comes into question and cannot be taken for granted. It becomes important to ask: What have I done with my life? What do I really get from and give to my wife, children, friends, work, community—and self? What is it I truly want for myself and others? What are my real values and how are they reflected in my life? What are my greatest talents and how am I using—or wasting—them? What have I done with my early dreams and what do I want with them now? Can I live in a way that best combines my current desires, values, talents, and aspirations?

Some men—but very few, according to our study—do very little questioning or searching during the Mid-life Transition. They are apparently untroubled by difficult questions regarding the meaning, value, and direction of their lives. They may be working on these questions in implicit or unconscious ways that will become evident later. If not, they will pay the price in a later developmental crisis or a life structure minimally connected to the self. Other men, again not a large number, realize that the character of their lives is changing, but the process is not a painful one. They are, so to say, in a manageable transition without crisis.

For the great majority—about 80% of our subjects—this period evokes tumultuous struggles within the self and with the external world. Their Mid-life Transition is a time of moderate or severe crisis. They question virtually every aspect of their lives and are horrified by what they find. They cannot go on as before, but it will take several years to form a new path or to modify the old one.

Because a man in this crisis is often somewhat irrational, others may regard him as "upset" or "sick." It is therefore important to recognize that he is working on a normal mid-life task and that the desire to question and enrich his life stems from the most healthy part of the self. The doubting and searching are "normal"; the real question is how best to make use of them. The difficulty is compounded by the fact that the process of reappraisal activates neurotic problems (the unconscious baggage carried forward from hard times in the past) which hinder the effort to change. The pathology is not in the desire to improve one's life but in the inner obstacles to pursuing this aim. The pathological anxiety and guilt, the ancient dependencies, animosities, and vanities of earlier years, keep one from examining the real issues at mid-life. They make it difficult for a man to free himself from an oppressive life structure.

A profound reappraisal of this kind cannot be a cool, intellectual process. It must also involve emotional turmoil, despair, the sense of not knowing where to turn or of being stagnant and unable to move at all. A man in this state often makes false starts. He tentatively tests a variety of new choices, not only out of confusion or impulsiveness but also out of a need to explore, to learn how it feels to engage in a particular love relationship, occupation, or solitary pursuit. Every genuine reappraisal must be agonizing, because it challenges the assumptions, illusions, and vested interests on which the existing structure is based.

The life structure of the 30s was initiated and stabilized by powerful forces within the person and in his environment. These forces continue to make their claim for preserving the status quo. The man who attempts a radical critique of his life at 40 will be up against the parts of himself that have a strong investment in the present structure. He will often be opposed by other persons and institutions—his wife, children, boss, parents, colleagues, the organization and the broader occupational system in which he works, the implicit web of social conformity—that

seek to maintain order and prevent change. With luck, he will also find support in himself and others for the effort to examine and improve his life. . . .

In the Mid-life Transition a man is more able to look at himself and to deal with illusions about himself. . . .

As the Mid-life Transition nears its end in the middle 40s, a man has to make new choices or recommit himself on different terms to old choices. . . .

The life structure that emerges in the middle 40s varies greatly in its satisfactoriness, that is, in its suitability for the self and its viability in the world. Some men have suffered such irreparable defeats in childhood or early adulthood, and have been able to work so little on the tasks of their Mid-life Transition, that they lack the inner and outer resources for creating a minimally adequate structure. They face a middle adulthood of constriction and decline. Other men form a life structure that is reasonably viable in their world. They keep busy, perform their social roles, and do their bit for themselves and others. However, this structure is poorly connected to the self, and their lives are lacking in inner excitement.

Still other men have made a start toward a middle adulthood that will have its won special satisfactions and fulfillments as well as burdens. For these men, middle adulthood is often the fullest and most creative season in the life cycle. They are less tyrannized by the ambitions, instinctual drives, and illusions of youth. They can be more deeply attached to others and yet more separate, more centered in the self. For them, the season passes in its proper rhythm.

The Mid-life Transition is not the last opportunity for change and growth. Work on our developmental tasks can continue through middle adulthood and beyond, and there are later transitional periods to facilitate the process. As long as life continues, no period marks the end of the opportunities, and the burdens, of further development. . . .

Exerpts from "The Mid-life Transition: A Period in Adult Psychosocial Development" reprinted by permission from *Psychiatry*, Vol. 40, May 1977, pp. 99—112. Copyright © 1977 by The William Alanson White Psychiatric Foundation, Inc. Reprinted by special permission of The William Alanson White Psychiatric Foundation, Inc.

or herself, and there will always be someone to disagree or criticize the things that we feel are our most outstanding achievements. Upon reaching middle age, persons often begin to sense that "this is it." They believe that whatever they do or whatever happens to them will not have any significant impact on them or their lives.

Yet changes do occur in males and females as they enter and leave the mid-life stage. Earlier we saw what some of these changes are. In addition, important mid-life changes are also likely to occur in levels of life and work satisfaction, family happiness, and physical well-being. A recent study illustrated this by examining the perceptions of general well-being of four age groups.[27] The four groups were comprised of high school seniors, newlyweds, middle-aged persons, and people in the preretirement years. Overall, middle-aged men and women in the survey were found to be less satisfied than newlyweds and preretirement persons, but slightly more satisfied than the high school seniors. A more detailed analysis of the data focused on specific positive and negative factors that comprised the overall index of well-being. Positive emotional states were assumed when individuals experienced feelings "of being on top of the world," were excited or interested in something, were pleased about having accomplished something, and had pride because someone complimented them on something they did. On the feeling of pride the middle-aged population was about even with the preretirement population, but on all other indicators the middle-aged scored lower than the three other categories. Study participants were also queried about the four components making up the negative factors of the life satisfaction index. The four indicators were loneliness, boredom, depression, and restlessness. In all cases, the middle-aged reported significantly fewer negative feelings than the two younger age groups. The middle-aged, however, tended to have slightly more negative feelings than did the older, preretirement group.[28]

With the exception of the high school seniors, the middle-aged had the smallest range of positive to negative responses. This implies that the middle-aged persons were less likely to report emotional experiences of any sort, either positive or negative. Although the research did not gather detailed information on the causes of this "dulling" effect on the middle-aged, it is likely that personality factors such as indifference combine with structural factors such as a lack of opportunity to alter careers to produce the effect. However, middle-aged men did report that their sense of coming to a standstill in promotions and salaries did have an impact on their decreasing life satisfaction.[29] The level of job satisfaction among the middle-aged, so important in a work-oriented society such as our own, appears to play a particularly important role in determining one's sense of personal worth and emotional well-being.

Job Dissatisfaction

Although the question of job dissatisfaction was considered in more detail in Chapter 4, the issue takes on new significance in discussing the problems of the middle-aged. By the time a person reaches age 40 or so, it is probable that she or he has been in a particular job for at least ten years. Frequently, these people have been performing the same tasks for this entire period. Many have reached positions where their responsibilities begin to grow. For many, the monotony of the work becomes a source of boredom and tension.

One begins to ask if this is all that she or he was meant to do. In a book entitled *Where Have All the Robots Gone?*, Harold Sheppard and Neal Herrick report that 51 percent of the male blue-collar workers between the ages 40 and 49 whom they surveyed had considered making a career change because of dissatisfaction with their current jobs.[30]

This phenomenon appears to be as true for some professionals as for blue-collar workers. Seymour Sarason's discussion of physicians in the midlife period points out that they, too, must face a confrontation between myth and reality. According to one doctor to whom many other doctors went for medical advice:

Ninety percent of what I deal with is depression. In some instances their children are causing them all kinds of worry, and it really affects the satisfactions they get from their work. Or there are marital problems which they feel are destroying them . . . it exacerbates their feeling that medicine is like being on a treadmill, but you can't stop it, and you don't know who is at the controls. . . . the majority wanted to be healers, not only to understand how the body works, but to contribute to that understanding in some way. . . . But that is maladaptive today because of scads of patients, more and more specialization and most important of all the economics of becoming a doctor and becoming a prisoner of a high standard of living. Medicine has become a business and business has become the tail that wags the dog.[31]

On-the-job pressure also increases as the individual advances through the job hierarchy. Watching over a number of subordinates may initially be a source of pride, but one soon learns that it is the supervisor whom management holds at least partially responsible when things go wrong. This pressure on the individual may raise the question of whether the responsibility is worth the extra money and status.

The same study that investigated life satisfaction asked the respondents about the sources of stress that they were experiencing. Forty-five percent of the men the middle-aged and preretirement stages listed work as a source of stress. No other aspect of their lives, including finances, death, health, or family was viewed as stressful by more than 18 percent of the males. For females, health and family were the major sources of stress, with 38 percent and 26 percent of the respondents listing them, respectively. Work was recognized as a cause of stress by 21 percent of the women in the middle-aged and preretirement stages.[32]

Family Problems

Perhaps because of job dissatisfaction and work-related stress, a growing proportion of middle-aged persons appears to be looking outside of work for their enjoyment and satisfaction, as well as for their source of meaningfulness. In this time of personal uncertainty, the middle-aged man often turns toward the family. "More and more he thinks less and less of himself and what his work means. He needs to know he matters to the children. . . . he's feeling that all his past absences have to be made up for. . . ."[33]

But at the very same time that men turn back to their families to find satisfaction, the families that they expected to find are usually not there. The years that the middle-aged man has spent devotedly establishing himself in his career have seen his family change considerably. When, at age 40 or 45, he turns to help his growing children, his help and advice may be rejected by them as they try to establish their independence.

The experience of coming to the end of child rearing for mothers is a bittersweet one. For years many of them have devoted themselves solely to the raising of their children. Many mothers see this as an enjoyable, rewarding task but one that inhibits the development of other aspects of their being. As the adolescent's assertion of autonomy turns against the motherly hand, it allows the mother the opportunity to build new interests or rekindle those left behind with motherhood. Ironically, the wife's perspective on life begins to turn outward from the family at the same time that the husband's is turning back to the family.[34]

Strain is a natural phenomenon under these circumstances. Compounding this strain is that placed on middle-aged families by other consequences of personal change. Both husband and wife entered into the marriage some numerous years earlier at least partially because of similar or compatible interests. But interests change over time, and there are a number of reasons why the middle-aged husband and wife may have developed new interests that are no longer similar or compatible. In our society, husbands have traditionally gone off to work while wives take care of the children. If the wives are fortunate enough to be able to maintain some career of their own, they are not likely to be in the same occupations or positions as their husbands. Under such situations, it is understandable that the interests and world views of middle-aged husbands and wives may have grown farther apart over the years. And indeed, the strain created by divergent interests that seem to materialize in the middle-aged period appears to be influencing the divorce rate for this age group. As Table 10.1 shows, since 1970, the rate of divorce for once-married males and females between the ages of 35 and 54 has risen rather sharply. Although the official data do not indicate it, at least one commentator has asserted that rather than divorce, middle-aged couples are more likely to separate in order to stimulate individual growth.[35]

Physical Changes

Interacting with and possibly contributing to the problems of the middle-aged are the physical changes taking place within their bodies. Research has shown that most people reach their maximum strength between the ages 25 and 30. After this peak, there is a slow but steady decline throughout adult life. By the time most people reach middle age, sustained muscular effort is difficult. The eyes begin their decline during infancy, the ears after age 20, smell after 40, sensitivity to touch after 45, taste after age 50. Sexual capacity begins declining for males after age 18 and frequently presents psychological problems for males in mid-life. Females reach their fullest sexual capacity at ages 30 or 31 after completing the usual baby-bearing.[36]

As men and women enter mid-life, their social problems are complicated by the changes in their physical structure. Middle-aged men may be moved from hard physical labor jobs to less demanding positions, which may not pay as much. Middle-age women may be discriminated against as the result of a male employer's conceptions of the physical changes that accompany menopause. Whatever physical changes that occur to all of us as we grow old, they determine how we view ourselves and others, for as we are all taught in childhood and adolescence: youth is beautiful and strong; all else is not.

Table 10.1 Percent of Ever-Married Persons 35–54 Years Old Who Were Divorced or Separated: 1970 and 1976

Age and Sex	Percent Divorced			Percent Separated		
	Total	White	Black	Total	White	Black
1970						
Male						
35–44	3.0	2.6	5.8	2.1	1.1	11.6
45–54	3.9	3.7	6.7	1.9	1.0	11.7
Female						
35–44	5.6	5.3	8.8	3.1	1.6	16.3
45–54	5.1	4.9	7.6	3.1	1.9	14.9
1976						
Male						
35–44	5.8	5.4	10.0	2.5	1.5	11.7
45–54	5.5	4.9	11.6	2.5	1.3	14.2
Female						
35–44	9.0	8.5	14.0	4.5	3.0	17.0
45–54	7.4	7.0	11.8	3.2	1.9	15.3

Source: U.S. Bureau of the Census, *Statistical Abstract of the United States, 1977* (Washington, D.C.: Government Printing Office, 1977), p. 75.

Americans Are Growing Older

That Americans are growing older does not appear to be a very startling revelation, since people of all nationalities age every day. What is important about the statement is that Americans are living longer today than they ever did. Life expectancy at birth has risen from 47.3 years in 1900[37] to 72.5 years in 1975.[38] In 1880 only 3.4 percent of the population was over 65,[39] whereas in 1976 it was reported that about 10.7 percent of the population had reached 65.[40] This total is expected to climb even further; by the year 2000, 12.2 percent of the population will be 65 or over. Estimates beyond 2000 begin to diverge due to the impossibility of predicting precise fertility rates. Based on demographers' estimates of the course of fertility rates, the Bureau of the Census states that the proportion of the population aged 65 or over in the year 2020 may be as low as 13 percent or as high as 17.5 percent.[41] The variation in estimates for this group as well as for the 75 and over, and the 85 and over, can be seen in Figure 10.2.

There are now more than 23 million Americans over 65 years of age. But who are these older Americans? Where did they come from? What forces have helped to shape their lives? Answering these questions may help us understand the problems faced by this group today.

Older Americans in 1979 include those people born prior to 1914. Many were immigrants from Europe who sailed to the United States just before World War I. This generation was born at a time when life expectancy was under 50 years. This was due in large part to the ever-present spread of communicable diseases. Tuberculosis and typhus epidemics were not uncommon, and many deaths from pneumonia, malaria, influenza, and syphilis were reported. As this generation reached their late teens and early adulthood, the Great Depression brought on severe economic hardship. A few years later these men and women experienced World War II, either abroad as active participants or at home in the production lines of the nation's factories. By the time of the Korean War, the cold war, and the McCarthy era of the early 1950s, this generation had lived through one of the most turbulent and dynamic half centuries in the history of civilization. They had given their skills and their labor to making America the richest, most powerful nation on earth. And, in general, they had benefited, too, with a high standard of living and physical comfort, upward mobility, and political and economic security.

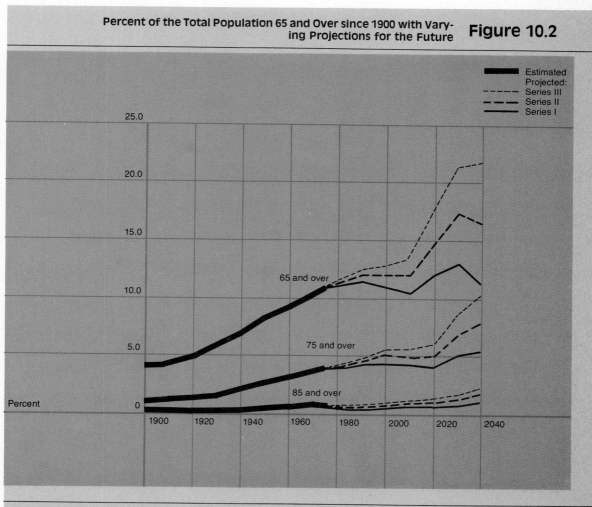

Percent of the Total Population 65 and Over since 1900 with Varying Projections for the Future   **Figure 10.2**

Source: Current Population Reports: Special Studies, *Demographic Aspects of Aging and the Older Population in the U. S.* (Washington, D. C.: Bureau of the Census, January 1978), p. 4.

AGING

Often the elderly are abandoned to face impending death alone, without purpose, means, or mobility. Recently they have begun to struggle against the role of aimless inactivity society imposes on them, uniting to aid one another. *This page, clockwise from top left:* Destitution—psychological, physical, economic; senility is an aspect of aging that is easier to ignore and avoid than to accommodate; isolation, even within the family, is perhaps the most overwhelming aspect of aging; the elderly rich seem to have fewer problems than the elderly poor; being together means happiness even to those living in a nursing home. *Opposite page, clockwise from top left:* Retirement villages, where they can be with others who share their interests, are the answer for some; this leathercraft worker has found a useful retirement role teaching his hobby in the VISTA program; four generations are represented in this family photograph. If one must grow old, it is easier in an environment characterized by love, respect, acceptance, and the feeling of being needed; quilting is the way these senior citizens raise money to help others in their community

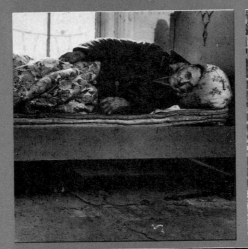

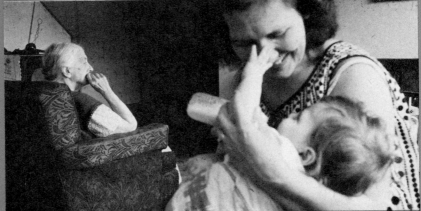

But, since then, things have begun to change for this generation of Americans. In the 1960s and 1970s, as the number of elderly people grew larger, their sense of security diminished. Confused by social and political unrest, frightened by new dangers in their old neighborhoods, dissatisfied by the lack of concern from social institutions in which they had always believed, and, now, caught in the grueling inflation of the 1970s, elderly Americans often feel that they are in a battle for their very survival.

It is little wonder that many senior citizens now find themselves feeling helpless, alone, alienated, and fearful. The reasons are many, but all lie rooted in a society that has not responded to the needs of a large segment of its citizens. Although the fights against racism and sexism have already been launched on a scale large enough to bring about significant gains, the fight against ageism is relatively new. It is up against ingrained cultural values and social arrangements that have heretofore not had to accommodate large numbers of aged persons. For the elderly, the consequences of contemporary social life include poverty, inadequate medical care and housing, and, possibly more humiliating, an infringement of the rights of an increasingly large segment of society to lead fruitful and productive lives.

Alex Comfort writes that there are two types of aging. The first, physical aging, is a normal and universal process that manifests itself over time by physical changes such as graying hair, skin wrinkling, and sometimes ill health. He estimates that 25 percent of the current American image of aging is accounted for by this form of aging. The other 75 percent is accounted for by sociogenic aging. This type has no physical basis but is the role that our "folklore, prejudices, and misconceptions about age impose on 'the old.'" Comfort continues:

The fact that many, if not most older people obstinately fail to be as we describe them is beside the point. As they are well known to be unemployable, we don't let them work, as they are known to be asexual, and it is embarrassing if they are not, we can herd them into institutions which deny them elementary privacy. As they are known to be liable to go crazy, symptoms due to infection or overmedication, or simple exasperation with a society which demeans the senior citizen, are interpreted as senility.[42]

Retirement

On April 6, 1978, President Carter signed into law a bill that raised the mandatory retirement age in the private sector of the economy from 65 to 70 years old. At the same time, federal employees were freed from any type of mandatory retirement regulations. This change was directed at solving many of the basic problems associated with old age as well as ameliorating the impending fiscal crisis within the social security program.

The latter problem has resulted from the growing number of retirees. In 1945, the social security system had 35 workers paying into the fund for every one recipient of funds. By 1977 the rates of wage earners to recipients was already down to 3.2 to 1, with expectations that the situation would get worse before it got better. Changing the mandatory retirement age was one way of delaying the problem.[43]

The change was also intended to allow those people who were still capable of performing productive work, and desired to do so, the opportunity to maintain their positions and consequently their income. Contrary to the belief of many, this is not a novel idea. Rather, the very concept of retirement is a fairly recent one for most societies. Prior to the development of the modern industrial era, persons did not leave the labor force at a particular age but remained as long as their bodies allowed them to engage in work activity. In the United States, as late as 1900, more than 68 percent of all males over 65 were still in the labor force.[44] By 1976, 81 percent of all males over 65 were *not* in the labor force. It is predicted that by 1990, this figure will climb to 84 percent.[45]

In recent years there has also been a pattern of persons retiring before the age of 65. Labor unions have recently succeeded in obtaining in many contracts clauses that allow employees to retire with full benefits after 25 or 30 years with the same company. Other contracts allow workers to retire at age 60 or 62 with full or fractional parts of pensions. Unions argue for these policies to enable older workers a greater period of leisure time and to allow for more jobs for their younger union members.

Retirement is one of the most crucial changes in life and demands a major adjustment on the part of the older person. It is a change that many people do not choose voluntarily. A 1975 poll by Louis Harris and Associates revealed that 45 percent of all retired and unemployed persons 65 and over did not look forward to stopping work.[46] It appears that there are two key factors that affect a person's decision to retire or remain in the work force: the individual's financial situation and health status. Research conducted by A. William Pollman indicates that 47 percent of a sample of retired males stated that possession of an adequate retirement income was the primary reason for their retiring before the mandatory age; 24 percent of the sample listed poor health; 19 percent suggested the desire for greater leisure time as the primary reasons; and only 9 per cent recognized job dissatisfaction or dislike of the boss or fellow employees as the crucial factor.[47]

Once retired, however, many people experience difficulty adjusting to the new life-style. Others discover that their fixed pensions and their social security incomes are not sufficient to meet their expenses during a period of rapid inflation. Both the adjustment and financial problems in turn lead to various other concerns for the elderly.

Role Changes

When an individual retires from work, many aspects of his or her life are affected. No longer does the person have a determined place to be for eight hours a day doing a specific task according to a boss's expectations. The amount of time that is a person's own increases by 50 percent. Patterns of interaction that have been exercised daily for many years with work associates are suddenly destroyed.

Yet there is frequently little to fill the void. Often the retired person has few precise norms to follow. This has led some sociologists to refer to the state of retirement as the "roleless role."[48] What expectations there are for retired persons are vague and ambiguous. It is expected that more time will be spent with the family and friends and, of course, that leisure activities will become more prominent. But, none of these expectations is sufficient to fill the void left by retirement from a role from which an individual has been deriving an identity for a considerable period of time.

As a consequence, the retired person experiences a situation in which much of his or her social identity is denied. The respect derived from the traditional work ethic is withdrawn; at least it is perceived so by the retiree.

The research findings of Back and Guptill indicate a change in the self-concept of the retired men they studied.

Without the job around which their life had been built for some forty or fifty years, these retired men were unable to avoid feeling less useful, less effective and less busy than the men who were still employed.[49]

From the few studies done of retirement of female workers, it appears that an even sharper increase in feelings of uselessness is found among women than among their male counterparts.[50]

However devasting retirement may be in this respect, it does not change all social-psychological states of the individual. Nor do the changes brought about by retirement affect all persons in the same way. The same two variables that affect a person's voluntary decision to retire—health and economic status—are important in determining one's adjustment to retirement.[51] Poor health severely limits the ability of a retired person to seek other sources of enjoyment. And, to those who have few financial resources, retirement can be a traumatic, restrictive experience.

Loneliness and Dependency

When the possible loss of self-esteem due to retirement is joined with the consequences of other age-related phenomena, the effect on older persons increases. By the time parents reach the age of 65, their children have usually moved away to establish their own families. In these cases, the death of a spouse can leave the remaining partner alone. The support given to widows and widowers immediately after the loss of a spouse is helpful, but too often it disappears before the person is fully recovered from his or her grief. This loss of support can have devastating consequences, often manifesting itself in more intense feelings of unhappiness and a higher rate of suicide and death experienced by widows and widowers than married persons of the same age.[52]

The fear of becoming dependent, either physically or financially, is one of the most dreaded changes accompanying old age. Older persons do not want to burden their families or friends, nor do they want to be dependent on social service agencies. The aged have lived in a culture that has instilled in them the ideals of independence and mastery of oneself and one's environment. Thus, to be dependent on others indicates a weakness, a vulnerability, an inability to control one's destiny.[53]

Yet, older persons frequently suffer from debilitating illnesses that prevent them from taking care of themselves. At other times, financial resources are exhausted and older persons must rely on their children or the government for support.

Income Deprivation

For the elderly, like many other minority groups, obtaining an adequate income is a difficult and worrisome task. No longer is income tied directly to what a person can produce on the job. Instead, income is now derived from the pension plans and social security benefits that workers have been contributing into during their working years. For most of the elderly, this income, along with whatever assets they have been able to accumulate over the years, represents the total sum of money available to them for the expenses of day-to-day life.

Assets, in the form of savings accounts, stocks, and so forth, tend to be highly correlated with income earned when in the labor force. This means that persons who earned the lowest incomes are also likely to have the lowest assets when they retire. Of all the elderly who reach retirement without having owned a home during their lifetime, more than half have assets of less than $1000.[54] And these assets, of course, are ideally to be spread over the number of years from retirement to death. Since, on the average, the person who reaches age 65 today can be expected to live another 15.6 years, the assets spendable per year for a large portion of the aged could be less than $100.

In 1974, the median income of a family with a head 65 years or older was $7298, compared to a median of $12,836 for all families. Although the ratio has risen since 1965, families with heads 65 and over still have a median income less than three-fifths that of all families. This ratio is actually lower than it was in 1950, and, over the past three decades, has hovered in the range of 49 to 57 percent.[55]

In 1976, 15 percent of all persons over 65 years of age were living below the government-established poverty line. Almost 18 percent of all females over age 65 were below this line, and 10.8 percent of all such males were classified as below the poverty line. Race must also enter the picture. Although 13.2 percent of all white persons over age 65 were living in poverty, the corresponding figure for blacks was 34.8. When the three factors of age, race, and sex work against the group, the situation is even worse. Of all black females over 65 years of age living in the United States, 39.6 percent are living below the poverty line.[56]

Health

One measure of the health of older populations in general is the number of years that one can expect to live after she or he reaches age 65. Figure 10.3 shows the figures for the years 1900–1902, 1929–1931, 1949–1951, and 1974. The average remaining lifetime has shown a gradual increase over these years. However, this paints only one side of the picture.

Although persons are living longer today than ever before, this does not mean that they go through life free from health problems. All age groups experience illnesses, but many of the problems of the elderly are unique to that age group. In fact, along some measures, the elderly are more healthy than younger groups. The elderly are less likely than many younger age groups to be afflicted with conditions classified as acute, such as colds and infectious diseases.[57] However, with regard to chronic conditions, the elderly are not as fortunate. Four out of five of all older persons suffer from at least one chronic condition, and more than one in four suffers limitations in their activities due to the condition. The most common chronic conditions to

Figure 10.3 Average Remaining Lifetime at Birth and at Age 65 and Age 75: 1900–02, 1929–31, 1949–51, and 1974

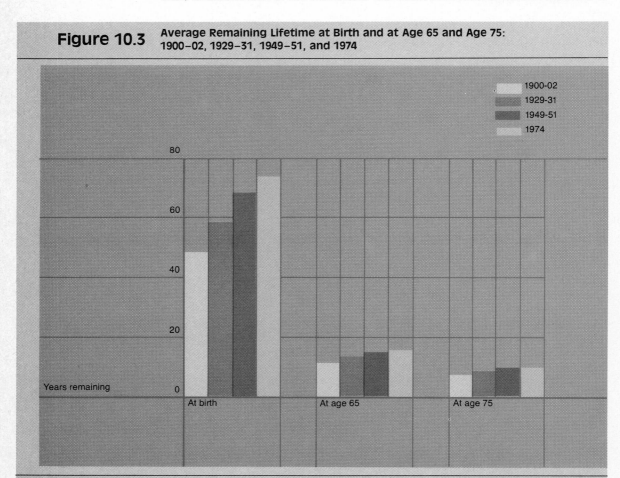

Source: Current Population Reports: Special Studies, *Demographic Aspects of Aging and the Older Population in the U.S.* (Washington, D.C.: Bureau of the Census, January 1978), p. 27.

which the elderly are particularly susceptible are arthritis, rheumatism, heart disease, and high blood pressure.

The duration of these conditions also increases with age. The proportion of long-term disabilities is significantly higher than in any other age category. Fourteen percent of all persons aged 65 to 74 suffer from some long-term disabling condition, as compared to 5 percent of persons in the 45–64 age group.[58] In addition, the rate of institutionalized disabilities is roughly double that of the next younger age group. This problem is considerably worse for those persons over 75.

Long-term institutional care is a worry of many senior citizens but an actual problem for only a small percentage. Giving up one's residence, abandoning or being abandoned by one's family, the loss of independence, and the belief that institutionalization is the final step before death all work together to give the elderly a rather bleak picture of institutions.

Most long-term care facilities are privately owned. Unfortunately, many owners have been more concerned with profits than with patients. The structure and organization of such facilities are often such that patients are dehumanized. Senator Charles Percy, who has long been an advocate of nursing home reform, investigated a nursing home in one eastern state. Among other conditions he found:

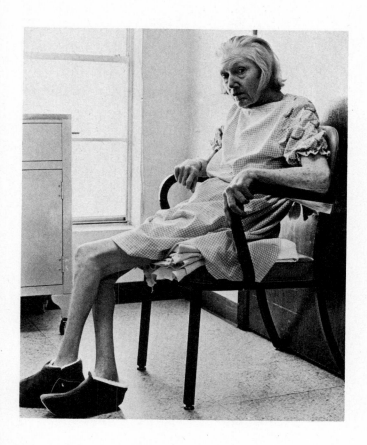

Unable to care for themselves and with no family to care for them, many elderly persons must spend their last years in nursing homes. This nursing home resident, tied to her chair to keep her from falling or wandering away, must sometimes question the values of a society that relegates its old to human junk heaps.

1. aides, nurses, and orderlies ignoring patients' calls;
2. heavy doses of sedatives given to patients who cause trouble for the staff;
3. clothes being distributed from a common pile into which deceased patients' clothes are thrown;
4. lack of sufficient linens and diapers for patients who are incontinent, so that rags or shower curtains are used;
5. total lack of privacy when patients are undressed and bathed in front of everyone else;
6. staff members using derogatory nicknames when addressing patients;
7. patients being tied to their beds for hours at a time; and
8. a house doctor who visited once a month to check all 60 residents in two hours.[59]

Recently, after a number of exposes by journalists and congressional investigators, some steps have been taken to improve the situation, and most facilities are now safer, and better-staffed than they were previously. Yet since it is these better institutions that charge high fees, the poor elderly may again find themselves left out.

Figure 10.4 **Percent Distribution of the Male and Female Population 65 Years Old and Over by Living Arrangements: 1975**

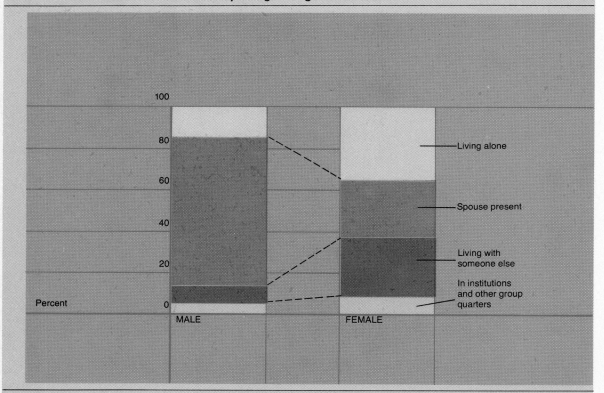

Source: Current Population Reports: Special Studies, *Demographic Aspects of Aging and the Older Population in the U.S.* (Washington, D.C.: Bureau of the Census, January 1978), p. 45.

Recent research has indicated that 70 percent of all heads of households who are over 65 years of age own their own home.[60] Such information may appear to indicate that housing for the elderly is not a severe problem. But this statistic is misleading since many older persons are not heads of households. Also, the type of housing owned by the elderly demonstrated the existence of a housing problem. A high proportion of their homes are old and dilapidated; many are in high crime areas of the city; after property taxes, little money is left for upkeep of the house; and, the elderly often feel trapped in these houses because there are no adequate alternatives.

Although financial constraints prevent some older persons from moving, many simply do not want to move. They have lived in these houses for considerable lengths of time and any move, either voluntary or involuntary, is a physical and social-psychological separation from their heritage and friends.[61]

There are significant differences in the living arrangements of older men and women, as illustrated in Figure 10.4. Three quarters of all elderly males live in a household with their spouse, while another 7 percent live with someone else. Females 65 and over are living with their husbands in only 36 percent of all cases, and are with someone else 23 percent of the time. Figure 10.4 also shows that 35 percent of women and 14 percent of men are living alone.

The principal factor contributing to this discrepancy is the higher mortality rates for married men relative to the rates for married women. This is caused by the joint effect of higher mortality rates for men in general and the fact that husbands in this generation are typically older than their wives.

Overcoming the Problems

The problems of the middle- and older-aged populations would not be considered problems if they were unsolvable. If there were no possible way by which these problems could be ameliorated, humankind, the adaptable creatures that we are, would most likely adjust or come to accept the problems as "facts." Yet, some solutions are available already and new ones are constantly being discussed, planned, and implemented. Some of these possibilities will be presented here.

It is likely that, short of a change in age and sex role stereotypes, many of the problems of mid-life will be dealt with through counselors and therapists. Some companies have initiated counseling programs for their workers, thus providing an opportunity for the employees to seek professional help in order to work out problems with which they may be having trouble. However, such solutions deal with only the cure and not the prevention of the problem. To handle social problems adequately, social, not psychological, solutions are required. Unfortunately, few of these exist for the problems of mid-life.

Mid-Life Crisis

Gordon F. Streib and Ruth B. Streib
Communes and the Aging

Amana is the third oldest among the few "successful" utopian communities formed in the nineteenth century—having survived over one hundred years. Amana seems to approach the ideal of what has been recommended by contemporary experts in aging as a totally supportive and benign environment for older people.

The first Amana colony in Iowa was founded in 1854 by the Society of True Inspirationists, a group of about 800 people who had emigrated from Germany a decade earlier to escape persecution and to follow their way of life without interference. The colony's 26,000 acres of rich farmland and forests, still owned by the society, afforded the young colony a stable economic base. Its 7 villages were laid out in a centralized European pattern with the residents living together in towns and going out to the fields to work. From the very onset, Amana created a diversified economic base, including small industries, and some of these—a woolen mill, furniture factory, meat smoking plant, bakeries and wineries—have survived for a century.

Originally Amana was a communal society. All property was held in common, and there were communal kitchens, with women assigned to gardening and food preparation. In 1932, by a vote of the people, the community was reorganized into a proprietary stock corporation with a one-share-one-vote stock arrangement. The economic enterprises were controlled by the company whose stock was owned by the colony members, with a manager guiding the day-to-day operations. In addition, the Amana Church Society was organized to preserve the religious, cultural, and social traditions of the colony.

A brief account of the situation of the elderly in the colony today demonstrates how the community has met the needs of its older citizens.

(1) *Economic needs.* When Amana was a communally organized society, all members were guaranteed lifetime subsistence—food, shelter, clothing, medical and dental care, and whatever cash they needed.

After the reorganization, all adult members of the society continued to receive medical, dental, and burial services, but the day-to-day subsistence became a private matter. Most of the members continued working in the colony farming enterprises and small factories. However, they received wages which they could spend as they pleased instead of being given coupons for their needs.

Although older Amana residents today, like most other Americans, suffer a decline in income after retirement, there are a number of factors which help to cushion the reduction in income. The society has a modest retirement plan. In addition, residents are eligible for social security benefits, as are other Americans who have been gainfully employed. When the typical Amana male retires, he has many opportunities within the community for part-time work. Because many economic enterprises are controlled by the society, and because agriculture is still the most important economic enterprise, there is flexibility as to hours of work and conditions of employment. In addition, the growth of a substantial tourist industry, with restaurants, gift shops, and the like, offers a variety of part-time employment for many retirees.

(2) *Health.* Members are provided with lifetime medical and dental care. This is a tremendous economic advantage for the aged and also affords considerable psychic security, which is relatively rare in American society. The older Anamites' medical needs are met by the doctor, who has taken care of their illnesses all of their lives.

The provision of lifetime medical services is a *right* which is an integral part of the socioeconomic structure of Amana and does not have the connotations of a "government handout" which characterize some of the medical services provided for other older Americans.

(3) *Housing.* Many families live in large nineteenth-century houses, which means that their housing arrangements can be retracted or expanded. In earlier times, families lived in separate apartments in the same large house. As a new young family needed more space, the parents would be assigned to a smaller apartment in the house. This move was decided by the Elders, so that the problem of conflict within the family because of the displacement of the older couple by the younger family was minimized. As long as the older couple could remain living by themselves, they were permitted to do so. This flexibility meant that older people could live near their

children and grandchildren, yet retain their privacy. Thus, the elderly are not cut off from persons in other stages of the life cycle, as in most contemporary retirement communities.

(4) *Social contacts.* Because the Amana villages are laid out in a centralized pattern rather than in separate homesteads typical of rural America, older people can enjoy the benefits of sociability more easily than most elderly people in farming communities. There is not the same need for transportation services. In most villages older residents can walk to church services, which are an important part of their weekly activities.

(5) *Feelings of usefulness.* The long tradition of handicrafts in the colony has great psychological and economic benefits. Almost all Amana men and women have some arts and crafts skills such as knitting and quilting or wood whittling and leather or metal work. With the contemporary interest in handicrafted products, their handiwork finds an eager market in the tourist shops. To have their work admired by people from the outside gives older persons a feeling of pride and self-worth. The regular quilting sessions provide many old women with important social contacts and feelings of "belonging."

The heritage of vegetable and flower gardening is another important aspect of Amana life which benefits older people, providing nutritious food, extra income, physical exercise, and feelings of usefulness. Visitors to Amana are struck by the variety and beauty of the gardens which surround every house. To see the pleasure which their gardening gives to visitors enhances older people's pride in their community.

(6) *Philosophy of life and religious beliefs.* Perhaps the most important factor which integrates the life of the elderly and gives coherence to every facet of daily life is their commitment to their religious beliefs. The ethical bedrock of the community is indicated in the high priority given to the treatment of the aged. . . .

The Kibbutzim or collective settlements in Israel must be studied carefully by the advocates and opponents of intentional communities for older persons, for they were established with the explicit goal of creating a new kind of social structure. Rooted in an ideology of nationalism, egalitarianism, and collective membership, rather than in religious commitment, the Kibbutz is a significant example of communal living that bears on the condition of old people.

Many of the basic problems of aging have been solved in the Kibbutz, for there is full economic security, health care, gradual retirement, social integration with other age groups, and provision of functions to compensate for loss of roles in the occupational sphere. However, growing old in the Kibbutz is not always a smooth process, for old persons are under cross pressures in a youth-centered society with a future orientation. They sometimes have special feelings of guilt when they are no longer productive and cannot share in the ongoing work of the community.

One finds two kinds of elderly persons in the contemporary Kibbutzim—those who have lived in collective settlements for most of their adult lives, and those who moved to the commune after retirement to be near their adult children. Although family ties in the Kibbutz were originally deemphasized, the membership of some settlements have gradually made adaptations to the needs of the traditional family, most importantly by permitting old parents to move to the Kibbutz. It is necessary to differentiate between two types of retirees, because, according to Talmon, their adjustment is difficult: the lifelong members have greater difficulty in coping with the problems of aging—health, feelings of uselessness, and lower morale. The newcomers appear to adapt more favorably because they do not have a loss of role and decline of prestige in the community where they have always lived. Instead, they can build an entirely new role, which includes the new experience of living with their children and grandchildren.

In considering the relevance of such settlements for the United States, one should note that the Kibbutzim are an integral part of Israeli society and have been a prime source of political, bureaucratic, and military leadership there. This is unlike the situation in the United States where communes are not considered a training ground for national leadership and are not accepted by the power structure. . . .

This excerpt from "Communes and the Aging: Utopian Dream and Gerontological Reality," by Gordon F. Streib and Ruth B. Streib, is reprinted from *American Behavioral Scientist*, Vol. 19, No. 2 (Nov./Dec. 1975), pp. 178–183 by permission of the publisher, Sage Publications, Inc.

Given the fact that peoples' interests change over time, the idea of one 40-year career may not fit the needs of many workers. This is based on the assumption that individuals should be able to derive something from the work experience other than wages. Alienation from work is not something that affects only the assembly line or clerical worker, however. The problem has reached the level of many white-collar and executive positions. Seventy percent of the middle managers surveyed by the American Management Association in 1973 reported that they wanted to make a career change in the foreseeable future. The reason most frequently given was not dissatisfaction with their present positions but rather a desire to search after jobs that would provide for their new interests.[62] Yet, in all likelihood, many of these people will never move. The small chance of finding another company that would pay them the salary they are currently earning is usually sufficient to lock them in. The Age Discrimination in Employment Act of 1967 was passed by the federal government to protect workers between 40 and 65 from being fired, passed over in promotions, or not hired because of their age. Although most newspapers no longer carry advertisements for "young, creative minds" or "young, dependable workers," more subtle methods of discrimination have come about. "The average man, however, lives in a land where 'older persons need not apply' advertisements have only recently been ruled illegal, but where age discrimination continues unabated, and remains socially if not legally sanctioned."[63]

In order to allow persons to enrich certain aspects of their lives, time off from work is now being provided by some employers. The issuance of sabbaticals or leaves of absence is one way that some middle-aged persons may refresh their enthusiasm for work in particular and life in general. However, this too may be seen as more of a stopgap measure, since it does not attack the source of the problem, which often lies in the nature of the job itself.

Federal Assistance

Dealing with the problems of older Americans requires more organized and comprehensive action. As we have seen, their needs range from income and housing to more clear-cut roles and norms. Some attempts to solve their problems have been instituted, but they remain largely of a patchwork nature. For example, a number of cities have instituted policies reducing public transportation fares for the elderly, and many pharmacists now grant discounts to the elderly on the purchase of prescriptions. Although beneficial for some, such programs are uncoordinated, random, and of only marginal long-range significance. Even though some comprehensive programs have been started, such as social security and Medicare, the patchwork variety still dominates.

Much of the government's financial aid to the elderly comes in the form of social security. Nine out of ten American workers are now in occupations covered by social security. Payments given to the elderly upon retirement are based on their average earnings over the past 10 or 20 years. In 1975 the average payment given to a single ex-worker was $164 a month, or less than $2000 a year. If older persons try to supplement their income by obtaining jobs, they may be penalized $1 for every $2 they earn in excess of $3000. The argument may be made that social security is only meant to supplement private pension plans. Yet, only about one-fourth of all persons who receive social security payments also receive money from private pension programs.[64] As we saw earlier, more than one out of every six American older persons are considered impoverished by government standards. Recent attempts by the Carter administration to increase social security taxes deducted from employee paychecks in order to raise the benefits are aimed at alleviating part of this problem.

The provision of Medicare is the second major program of the federal government that attempts to provide financial assistance to the elderly who are in need of medical care and treatment. When Medicare legislation was passed in 1966, the United States became the last major industrialized nation to provide some form of national health insurance, and that for only its elderly citizens.[65] Medicare is divided into two key parts. Basic hospitalization insurance is provided to all who qualify for social security benefits or pensions from railroad companies. In some circumstances it also applies to their dependents. In 1979, coverage under this plan began after the recipient paid the first $160. Included under this coverage is regular nursing care, inpatient drugs and equipment for up to 60 days. From the 61st through the 90th day, patients are required to pay $40 a day. A second part of Medicare is available on a voluntary basis at a supplemental fee that is deducted from social security payments. This service provides, after an annual deductible is paid, doctor's fees, drugs and supplies, emergency room services, 100 house calls and ambulance fees, among other items. When all these fees (the premiums, the deductibles, and expenses) are totaled, the average annual medical bill for persons over 65 amounts to a sum which is three times higher than that paid by the remainder of the adult population.[66] This fact, in conjunction with what we know about the income of older Americans, paints a sad picture of old age in our society today.

With the increasing proportion of the elderly in the United States, more attention will have to be paid to both the age-related illnesses of the elderly and their ability to gain access to adequate care. Recently, the number of physicians specializing in geriatric care has risen. In 1950 there were 352 members in the American Geriatric Society. By 1977 this number had climbed to more than 7000. Medical schools are also beginning to emphasize care of the elderly in their programs.[67]

Many programs have now been initiated that are designed to keep the elderly integrated in their social and physical environments. The raising of the mandatory retirement age to 70 is one that we have already discussed. Yet even this move does not alter the fact that many physically and mentally capable people are forced to change their lives involuntarily. As we have seen, this sudden change in life and life-style is the source of many problems for the elderly. A more humane approach that could be adopted in the United States might be one which incorporated parts of the Swedish system. In Sweden, provision is made for gradual retirements. The slow reduction in the number of hours that a person works allows for an easier adjustment to the retired state.

The federal government has sponsored a series of programs aimed at keeping older citizens active. The Retired Senior Volunteers Program (RSVP), the Service Corps of Retired Executives (SCORE), Foster Grandparents and Senior Companions are ways through which older people can

Keeping Active

remain involved. Many other local programs complement these activities. Yet most participation in social life by the aged is probably through membership in church, fraternal, and social organizations. Estimates of the proportion of the elderly involved in any of these voluntary organizations range from 20 percent to 48 percent. However, for every three organization memberships that older citizens retain, they are likely to drop two.[68] The functions served by these memberships go beyond simply allowing older persons to find something to do with their time. They permit older persons to feel useful and to engage in interaction that would otherwise be absent. They also serve as a means of consciousness raising by which members come to the realization that they are not alone in their problems.

Providing Care

Many changes are also being made to make the physical environment more conducive to the needs of senior citizens. The growth of retirement villages and centers is one response to the perceived needs of the elderly. Here group activities may be organized for the elderly and the necessary physical equipment can be supplied. The concept of public housing projects for the elderly that was popular in the 1960s and 1970s was another attempt to satisfy the housing needs of older Americans. Research on the response of older people to efforts of this type have shown that the majority would prefer greater financial assistance instead so that they may choose their own place of residence voluntarily.[69] Apparently, age segregation is not something that is desired by many older people.

The neighborhood may also provide difficulties for the elderly. Although older people have some control over facilities in their homes, they have little to say about what the neighborhood will look like. The location of public transportation, retail stores, and social service agencies are determined largely in the political realm, where older citizens, until recently, have not a significant voice. Recently, though, techniques of social science have been used to identify the needs of the elderly and to make suggestions for public policy. One example of such a technique is called cognitive mapping. This technique calls for a number of senior citizens to outline on a large-scale map the areas they utilize most frequently. This would include marking off the places they have to visit, (e.g. physicians' offices, stores, and so forth). Each respondent's answers are then combined onto one map so that a consensual view of a neighborhood and most needed areas can be developed.[70] The results of this process can be used to make recommendations on rerouting bus lines and selecting sites for social service agencies and other needed services.

The problems of finances are particularly acute for those people who are in need of long-term care. Institutionalization is necessary when the needs of a patient are such that constant 24-hour care is required. It has been pointed out, however, that 17 to 25 percent of the persons currently in long-term care facilities do not require such treatment.[71] The only reason they are there is because there are no alternative care arrangements available to them. Recent studies funded by the federal government have shown that home health programs, day-care, and day hospitalization programs are viable alternatives to long-term facilities.[72] The development of hospice programs is another alternative. Hospice programs stress the importance of home care in order to allow terminally ill patients to continue living their usual life-style patterns for as long as possible. The Department of Health, Education, and Welfare is currently making a major effort to deinstitutionalize many of the elderly who are not in desperate need of such facilities.[73]

As we mentioned earlier, the change toward an older population is likely to alter the present youth orientation of the American culture. But numbers alone will not effect change. Women are a majority in the United States, but they still suffer many disadvantages relative to men. And, like blacks and females before them, the elderly are now organizing to insist that their rights be upheld. The Gray Panthers are probably the best-known group working for the rights of the elderly. This organization now has local chapters in many cities and has formed an alliance with youth groups to publicize the extent of ageism in America. Other goals of the Panthers include an attack on the dehumanization of the health care system, an attempt at consciousness raising among the elderly, and calling the attention of the rest of society to the plight of the elderly.

Summary

In a society dominated by a youth culture, everything comes to be analyzed by its role relative to the role of youth. The productiveness of the middle- and old-aged is measured relative to the productiveness of youth. The accomplishments of the middle- and old-aged are measured by their consonance with the ideals of youth. The inevitability of the middle-age and old-age groups failing to "keep up" with youth leads to social problems of enormous proportions. The source of these problems lies in the stereotypical views that society has of older populations and in the inability of the social structure to intervene effectively to solve the problems.

Middle-aged persons can feel trapped by their social environment. By the time most people reach their late thirties and early forties, they begin to realize that the goals they set for themselves as idealistic young adults are unattainable. Jobs once viewed as exciting and creative have grown monotonous and boring. Children who once openly displayed their love and dependence now assert their independence from parents. Yet few outlets have been devised to ease the process of experimenting with new ideas or careers.

The conception of the old held by many members of society is one of weakness, frailty, and uselessness. Apparently, individuals awaken on their 65th birthday to find their strength gone weak, their health gone ill, and their mental alertness gone senile. If such were not the case, why would people be forced to retire, to give up an important source of identity they have been carrying for years? Or why would we force people into institutions when they don't need them, as is done today? The older populations realize that they can remain active and useful but their voices go unheard in the thick of political struggles.

As greater proportions of Americans move into these age categories, society will be called upon to respond to their needs. Legislation has already been passed to prevent age discrimination for those between 40 and 65, and President Carter has recently signed a bill extending the age of mandatory retirement to 70. These two actions are designed to facilitate mid-life career changes and to allow the aging to maintain useful, self-fulfilling roles in society.

A number of federal programs have been initiated to provide monetary assistance for the elderly in need. It is generally recognized that current social security payments alone cannot provide sufficient incomes to the elderly, but the Carter administration hopes to be able to raise benefits in the near future. Medicare was established to help the elderly overcome the hardships connected with their failing health and, particularly, the chronic health problems to which they often fall victim.

As more and more people reach middle and old age in our society, the entire conception of aging is likely to change. The problem facing society today is to meet the needs of these populations while anticipating programs for the future.

Notes

[1] Vivian Gornick, "For the Rest of Our Days, Things Can Only Get Worse." *The Village Voice*, 24 May 1976, p. 32.

[2] Matilda White Riley and Joan Waring, "Age and Aging," *Contemporary Social Problems*, ed. R. Merton and R. Nisbet (New York: Harcourt, 1976), p. 358.

[3] U.S. Bureau of the Census, "Educational Attainment in the United States: March 1973 and 1974." *Current Population Reports*, Series P-20, No. 274 (Washington. D.C.; Government Printing Office, 1974).

[4] For a complete development of the psychological stages, see Erik Erikson, *Childhood and Society* (New York: Norton, 1963).

[5] George Herbert Mead, *Mind, Self, and Society* (Chicago: University of Chicago Press, 1934.)

[6] Glen Elder, "Adolescent in the Life Cycle: An Introduction," *Adolescence in the Life Cycle: Psychological Change and Social Context*, ed. Sigmund Dragestin and Glen Elder (New York: Wiley, 1975), p. 3.

[7] Ibid, p. 9.

[8] Norman Goodman and Kenneth Feldman, "Expectations, Ideals and Reality: Youth Enters College," *Adolescence in the Life Cycle*, ed. Sigmund Dragestin and Glen Elder.

[9] Glen Elder, *Adolescent Socialization and Personality Development* (Chicago: Rand-McNally, 1968), p. 26.

[10] Gail Sheehy, *Passages: Predictable Crises of Adult Life* (New York: Dutton, 1974), p. 38.

[11] Ibid., p. 40.

[12] Ibid., pp. 57–58.

[13] Daniel J. Levinson, "The Mid-Life Transition: A Period In Adult Psychological Development," *Psychiatry* 40 (May 1977), p. 103.

[14] Sheehy, *Passages*, p. 88.

[15] Levinson, "The Mid-Life Transition," p. 104.

[16] Sheehy, *Passages*, p. 246.

[17] Levinson, "The Mid-Life Transition," p. 107.

[18] Sheehy, *Passages*, p. 290.

[19] B. L. Neugarten, "The Awareness of Middle Age," *Middle Age and Aging*, ed. B. L. Neugarten (Chicago: University of Chicago Press, 1968).

[20] R. Peck, "Psychological Developments in the Second Half of Life," *Middle Age and Aging*, ed. B. L. Neugarten.

[21] R. Peck and H. Berkowitz, "Personality and Adjustment in Middle Age," *Personality in Middle and Late Life: Empirical Studies*, ed. B. L. Neugarten (New York: Atherton, 1964).

[22] R. Butler, "Age: The Life Review." *Psychology Today*, December 1971, pp. 49–51.

[23] D. Gutman, "An Exploration of Ego Configurations in Middle and Later Life," *Personality in Middle and Late Life*, ed. B. L. Neugarten.

[24]E. Kubler-Ross, *On Death and Dying* (New York: Macmillan, 1969).

[25]Sheehy, *Passages,* p. 278.

[26]Ibid., p. 279.

[27]Marjorie Fiske Lowenthal, Majda Thurnher, David Chirisoge, and associates, *Four Stages of Life: A Comparative Study of Women and Men Facing Transitions* (San Francisco: Jossey-Bass, 1975).

[28]Ibid., chap. 5.

[29]Ibid., p. 173.

[30]Harold Sheppard and Neal Herrick, *Where Have All the Robots Gone?* (New York: Free Press, 1972), p. 156.

[31]Seymour B. Sarason, *Work, Aging, and Social Change* (New York: Free Press, 1977), pp. 101–102.

[32]Lowenthal, et al., *Four Stages of Life,* p. 167.

[33]Sheehy, *Passages,* p. 292.

[34]Ibid., p. 293.

[35]Ibid., p. 302.

[36]Lillian Troll, *Early and Middle Adulthood* (Monterey, Calif.: Brooks/Cole, 1975), chap. 2.

[37]U.S. Public Health Service, National Center for Health Statistics, *Vital Statistics of the United States 1970,* Vol. II—*Mortality* (Washington, D.C.: Government Printing Office, 1977), p. 65.

[38]U.S. Bureau of the Census, *Statistical Abstract of the United States, 1977* (Washington, D.C.: Government Printing Office, 1977), p. 65.

[39]U.S. Bureau of the Census, *Census of the Population,* Vol. I: Characteristics of the Population (Washington, D.C.: Government Printing Office, 1973).

[40]U.S. Bureau of the Census, *Statistical Abstract of the United States, 1977,* p. 327.

[41]U.S. Bureau of the Census, *Current Population Reports: Special Studies, Demographic Aspects of the Aging and the Older Population in the U.S.* (Washington, D.C.: Government Printing Office, 1978), p. 4.

[42]Alexander Comfort, "Age Prejudice in America". *Social Policy,* November/December 1976, pp. 3–8.

[43]"The Graying of America," *Newsweek,* 28 February 1977, p. 52.

[44]Riley and Waring, "Age and Aging," p. 367.

[45]U.S. Bureau of the Censor, *Statistical Abstract of the United States, 1977,* p. 387.

[46]National Council on the Aging, Inc., *The Myth and Reality of Aging in America* (Washington, D.C.: National Council on the Aging, 1975), p. 217.

[47]A. William Pollman, "Early Retirement: A Comparison of Poor Health and Other Retirement Factors." *Journal of Gerontology* 26 (1971), pp. 41–45.

[48]Ernest Burgess, "Aging in Western Culture," *Aging in Western Societies,* ed. E. W. Burgess (Chicago: University of Chicago Press, 1960), p. 20.

[49]Robert Atchley, *The Social Forces in Later Life: An Introduction to Social Gerontology* (Belmont, Calif.: Wadsworth, 1975), p. 168.

[50]Gordon Streid and Clement Schneider, *Retirement in American Society: Impact and Process* (Ithaca: Cornell University Press, 1971) p. 161.

[51]G. Maddox, "Retirement as a Social Event in the United States," *Middle Age and Aging,* ed. B. L. Neugarten.

[52]Riley and Waring, "Age and Aging," p. 391.

[53]Richard A. Kalish, *Late Adulthood: Perspectives on Human Development* (Monterey, Calif.: Brooks/Cole, 1975), p. 85.

[54]Atchley, *The Social Forces in Later Life,* p. 145.

[55]U.S. Bureau of the Census, *Demographic Aspects of the Aging and the Older Population in the U.S.,* pp. 52–54.

[56]U.S. Bureau of the Census, *Current Population Reports: Consumer Income Characteristics of the Population Below the Poverty Level: 1976* (Washington, D.C.: Government Printing Office, 1978), pp. 21–22.

[57]Atchley, *The Social Forces in Later Life,* p. 115.

[58]Riley and Waring, "Age and Aging," p. 363.

[59]Charles Percy, *Growing Old in the Country of the Young* (New York: McGraw-Hill, 1974), pp. 86–92.

[60]H. B. Brotman, *Facts and Figures on Older Americans* (5, An Overview, 1971). (Washington, D.C.: Department of Health, Education, and Welfare, 1972).

[61]M. Fried, "Grieving for a lost Home," *People and Buildings,* ed. R. Guttman (New York: Basic Books, 1972).

[62]Quoted in Sheehy, *Passages,* p. 282.

[63]Peter C. Haw, *The Inner World of the Middle-Aged Man* (New York: Macmillan, 1976), p. 149.

[64]Jon Hendricks and G. David Hendricks, *Aging in Mass Society: Myths and Realities* (Cambridge, Mass.: Winthrop Publishers, 1977), p. 246.

[65]R. Harris, *The Sacred Trust* (New York: New American Library, 1966).

[66]Hendricks and Hendricks, *Aging in Mass Society,* pp. 201–202.

[67]*Newsweek,* "The Graying of America," p. 64.

[68]Hendricks and Hendricks, *Aging In Mass Society,* p. 300.

[69]Victor Regnier, "Neighborhood Planning for the Elderly," *Aging: Scientific Perspectives and Social Issues,* ed. Diana Woodruff and James Birren (New York: Van Nostrand, 1975), p. 296.

[70]Ibid., p. 304.

[71]Faye Abdellah, "Long Term Care Policy Issues: Alternatives to Institutional Care," *Annals,* July 1978, p. 31.

[72]Ibid., p. 31.

[73]Ibid., p. 35.

Population and Environmental Crises

Population Planning

Crisis—Belief and Disbelief

Summary

Notes

Ten thousand years ago, when human beings survived by exploiting the earth's resources through hunting, food gathering, farming, and herding, the entire population of the earth was only about 5.3 million—less than the number of people who now live in New York City alone. Today the earth's population stands at about 4.0 billion,[1] and it is increasing more rapidly than at any other time in history. This vast population is a comparatively recent phenomenon. As late as 1850 the earth's population was only 1 billion. The fact that so many people now depend on the limited resources of the earth for sustenance is a sobering one, as is the knowledge that, unless some effective means of population control is employed, the earth's present population will double by the year 2012.[2]

Only a third of the world's present population lives in the economically developed countries of North America, Europe, the Soviet Union, and Japan, where advanced technology has permitted a higher standard of living than ever before in the world's history. To maintain this standard, these countries consume a disproportionate amount of the world's limited resources. Two-thirds of the world's population live in the economically underdeveloped countries of the world—predominantly in Africa, Asia, and Latin America. The technological and social influences of the developed world have begun to penetrate into these countries, and living standards there have risen, at least for some segments of the population. But expectations have risen faster than living standards. Populations in underdeveloped countries continue to swell out of proportion to economic advance, and rigid social structures funnel much of the wealth into a few hands.

Surpluses in the developed countries have often been sent to relieve shortages—especially of food—in the underdeveloped countries. Yet such moves would not be necessary if an adequate base for technological advance could be constructed in the underdeveloped world. Short of catastrophes such as war or famine, the means available for controlling the press of population on the world's resources are closely connected with social and attitudinal changes within *all* societies of the world.

World population growth has changed basic conditions of social life. Because of the growth in population size and density, values and institutions that functioned effectively in the past no longer provide useful guidelines for action. The religious, economic, and political systems typically a part of agrarian and industrializing social orders, for example, often distribute authority and wealth in ways that foster and encourage population increase and place strains on natural resources. The systems may even encourage population growth when its probable consequences are unemployment, famine, and disease. This failure of social institutions to adapt to changing conditions—social disorganization, in other words—has thus become pervasive in much of the world.

Economic development and population control are two strategies for relieving the strain on natural resources caused by overpopulation. Though perhaps often complementary, they have frequently formed the basis for conflicting perspectives on the solution to population problems, representing the discrepant positions of many elements of the world. In many underdeveloped countries plagued by poverty and high birthrates, economic development is often seen as the ideal way of solving all social problems. Yet in advanced industrial nations, most of which have low birthrates already, population control is seen as the most fruitful method.

While the industrial nations have benefited greatly from technological advances, they have also experienced an accompanying environmental dilemma. The huge increases in air, water, and land pollution of the past quarter century due to unregulated use of our natural resources now poses problems of health and welfare for a large portion of the population. A threatened environment, like a weak house close to crumbling, puts us in a precarious position. The more we produce goods that do not fit into nature's cycle (DDT, for example), the more we pollute and thus undermine our own health and well-being.

The damage to our environment and the harm it can bring to human and animal life resulting from injudicious alteration of the ecosystem that took billions of years to evolve is obvious. Areas devastated by one or more problems (Los Angeles with its smog, West Virginia with its strip mining) are trying to correct the problem; other areas not yet polluted are taking measures to ensure that the quality of their water, air, and land is not degraded. Yet often it has taken either government or representatives of private interests to point out the dangers; many communities were unaware of the threat until the late 1960s, when in a number of cases the problem had already become nearly irremediable.

Problems of population growth and environment and resource depletion are best understood by combining the social disorganization and value conflict perspectives. Both population and environmental problems have been brought about by growth and rapid social change. Industrialization, expanding population, higher living standards, and rising expectations have worked together to force change on the natural environment in a radical way without proper regard for the consequences. The traditional means and goals of most societies no longer appear appropriate in the face of potential population and ecological disasters sufficient to cause us to question our very future.

Population Processes

Before sociologists can analyze the clustering of people in cities, study the causes of rapid population growth, or make recommendations for the control of population, they must accurately measure a population and its changes. Changes in the size of a population result from changes in the numbers of births and deaths and the movements of people in or out of an area. These three processes—fertility, mortality, and migration—are the essential subjects of demography.

Fertility

For the purposes of demographic analysis, fertility is defined as the actual number of births to women of childbearing age. A woman is capable of bearing children from approximately age 15 to age 49. Theoretically, one woman can give birth to as many as 15 or 20 children. This biological capacity for childbearing is called fecundity, and social factors produce a large differential between fertility and fecundity—that is, between the actual number of births to women of childbearing age and their biological capacity for childbearing.

The cultural regulation of sexual conduct is universal, although sexual mores vary widely in detail. Each society has different practices, attitudes, and values that influence the number of children a couple may have. The social variables affecting fertility may be classified by the three stages of the reproductive process: exposure to intercourse, exposure to conception, and exposure to gestation and birth.[3] The frequency and occasion of a woman's exposure to intercourse reflect the social norms of her group. In India girls are expected to marry in their early teens; in Ireland marriages may be delayed until a woman is in her late twenties. In some societies premarital and extramarital intercourse are proscribed, and widows are forbidden to remarry. In such societies, fertility is negatively affected. Certain occupations, particularly those related to religion, may require celibacy and enforce it institutionally.

Cultural attitudes to childbearing and child rearing also affect the process of conception. While in India failure to conceive a child is considered a grave misfortune, in modern industrialized societies, even voluntary refusal to conceive a child is increasingly accepted behavior. Some societies provide easy access to contraceptives, and some do not; the Catholic Church condemns their use altogether. After conception, social norms—often embodied in the law—determine whether the prospective mother has access to, and is willing to undergo, a voluntary abortion.

Mortality

The incidence of death is, by and large, influenced by economic rather than social factors. Thus explanations of mortality differentials are concerned with differences in the standard of living. Factors that affect longevity—public health facilities, sanitation conditions, housing, nutritional standards, medical knowledge—are all variables related to the material wealth of a society and how it is distributed.

The infant mortality rate may well be the most sensitive quantitative indicator of social welfare that we possess, since a baby is most vulnerable to adverse living conditions. In fact, there is an almost one-to-one relationship between infant mortality rates and living standards, both between countries and between different groups living within a country.

Migration

The movement of people from one geographic area to another affects the size and particularly the age and sex distribution of a population. Movement into a country is called immigration; movement out is called emigration. Similarly, movement into an area within a country is called in-migration, while movement out of an area is termed out-migration. Typically, those who immigrate are young and, in the early stages of population movement, male. This affects the age and sex distribution of the population left behind. Those who move also tend to be poor and from rural areas. In the cities where they settle, they provide cheap labor.

The nineteenth century and first three decades of the twentieth century witnessed the most extensive mass movements in recorded history. Probably a total of 60 million people left Europe in the nineteenth century, and perhaps three-fourths of these did not return.[4] The migration out of Europe during this time is an instance of people freely leaving to enter a new area, but migration between countries is seldom totally free any more. In 1922 the United States passed the first national quota law, which limited the total number of people admitted and specified the proportion to be admitted from each geographical area, discriminating against all except those from northern and western Europe. Few countries invite immigration today. Those that do are predisposed to welcome those who are young, white, and skilled or professionally trained. Some countries, particularly the Soviet Union and some Eastern European nations, control emigration as well as immigration.

Migrations may also be forced, as when Africans were brought to this country as slaves. For both religious and political reasons, India and Pakistan were forced to exchange populations after achieving their independence from Great Britain in 1947. Religious persecution was the major reason for the earliest immigration to the United States, and religious and political persecutions were important in forcing many people to migrate from areas under Nazi control during World War II.

In more recent history, the major reason for people to pull up stakes and move has been economic—the hope of a better life for themselves and their children. Migration, then, tends to be the demographic process most determined by social rather than biological factors, and it has an effect on size and growth of population that is more complex than may be immediately surmised. The age, class, sex, and race of those both entering and leaving a country and of those moving within a country have a profound impact on the birth and death rates as well as the age/sex composition, which together determine the size and rate of growth of a population.

Measuring Population

All industrialized countries collect data on their populations. They keep on-going records of births and deaths and periodically make a total count of their people in the form of a census. The U.S. Constitution requires a census every ten years to determine the number of representatives from each state to Congress. The United Nations publishes demographic statistics for all the countries of the world. Accurate population statistics are still unavailable in many of the underdeveloped countries, however, because census taking is such an expensive enterprise.

The most familiar population statistics, crude rates of birth and death, are calculated, respectively, by dividing the number of births and deaths in one year by the population count in the middle of the year. This number is then multiplied by a thousand to yield the figure per thousand people.[5] For example, the crude birthrate in India from July 1971 to July 1972 was 42 per thousand; the crude death rate was 17 per thousand. The difference between the two, 25 people a year per thousand, is the crude rate of population change (also expressed as 2.5 percent). Similarly, the difference between immigration and emigration gives the crude rate of net migration. The rates are called crude because they are gross figures and do not reflect either the sex or age of the population. Sex and age, of course, are factors that must be determined in order to arrive at the fertility rate.

The sex and age distribution within a population gives a clearer picture of population trends and potential growth. It is normally shown by means of population pyramids. The distribution of the two sexes of a population in various age groups determines the pattern of the pyramid. The largest segment of India's population is in the age groups under 15. The number of Indians in these groups is almost equal to the number in the groups between 15 and 45, the childbearing ages. Given this set of statistics, it is quite clear that 15 years from now the number of Indians of childbearing age will have drastically increased. Thus even a substantial reduction in the number of births per female will not immediately reduce the rate of population growth.

The age structure in the United States is in sharp contrast to India's; population is more or less evenly distributed through age groups up to 55. At 55 it tapers off gradually. The number of Americans in the age groups under 15 is slightly more than half the number between 15 and 45. After 15 years, the number of Americans of childbearing age will have increased only minimally, and any reduction in the birthrate would actually reduce the rate of growth of the United States population.

The World's Expanding Population

Until very recently the world's population increased almost imperceptibly. By about the beginning of the Christian era, the earth may have supported 250 million people, but another 1650 years were required for the population

INDIA

Present estimates indicate the world's population will double within forty years. With the massive populations of underdeveloped nations already draining not only their own resources but those of the entire world, zero population growth has become a policy the world cannot do without. Indeed, unless population growth is limited, the physical, social, and political well-being of all humanity is endangered. In India, family planning efforts are being made on a large scale. *Clockwise from top left:* hunger and disease exist everywhere, but are most prevalent in the newly developing nations of the world. This mother knows the heartache of hearing her baby cry for food; a survey is made for Bombay's family planning program; advertisements even on village walls in India extoll the benefits of family planning; Peace Corps representatives distribute contraceptive information in India; densely populated Indian refugee camp could be a vision of the future for the rest of the world; Indian railroad station sign advocating sterilization.

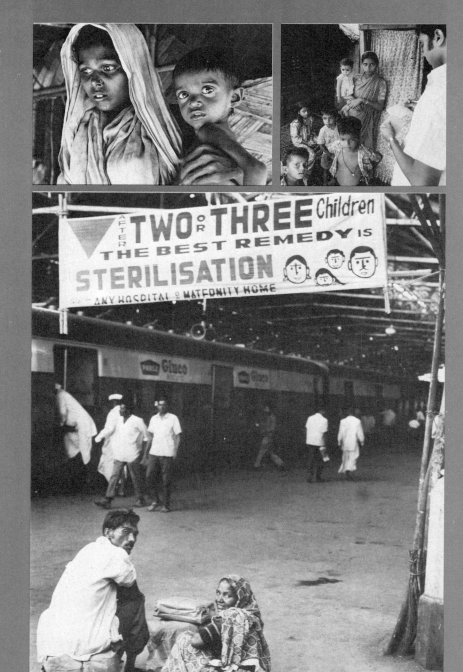

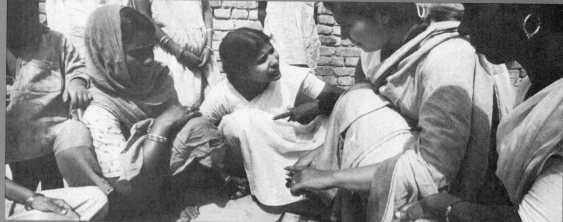

to reach an estimated half billion. It took only 200 years more to double that figure, however, and only 80 years more to double it again and reach 2 billion, the earth's population in 1930. That figure has doubled in less than 50 years and the present total of about 4 billion may be doubled in only 37 years, according to recent United Nations' estimates.[7]

Population growth has been neither a gradual nor an orderly process. Increases in the size and density of the population have followed technological advances as people have achieved greater control over their physical environment. According to one theory, there have been three major revolutions in human history—agricultural, urban, and industrial—and each has been accompanied by a marked increase in population.[8]

Agricultural and Urban Revolutions

The earliest humans were nomadic hunters and food gatherers, few in number and scattered. The first great population surge occurred about 8000 B.C. with the agricultural revolution. The domestication of plants and animals and the invention of agricultural tools helped bring about permanent food supplies, a more stable pattern of settlement, and a great increase in population.

The building of cities marked another great revolution in humanity's development. Cities brought centralized control of soil and water resources and the organization of great irrigation systems; they gave rise to long-distance trade and supported dense populations, with specialized work roles and complex social systems.

The first great cities arose about 3500 B.C. in Mesopotamia, along the Tigris and Euphrates rivers. Other cities followed in Egypt, Crete, and India, and later in China and parts of Central America. After the urban revolution, population rose steadily but very slowly through the growth of the Roman Empire, the European Middle Ages and the Renaissance. Although many technological developments during this period encouraged population growth, mortality rates were still high. Lack of medical knowledge left human beings helpless in the face of serious illness or injury. In 1347 bubonic plague—the Black Death—one of the most terrible epidemics in history, erupted in Europe. Conservative estimates indicate that at least one-fourth of Europe's total population died in this epidemic. Most of the population increase from the mid-seventeenth century on can be traced to the decline in mortality effected by better diets and expanding medical knowledge.

The Industrial Revolution

The eighteenth and nineteenth centuries witnessed a revolution in technology comparable to the earlier agricultural and urban revolutions. New manufacturing techniques, the fruit of flourishing science and engineering skills, brought about vast increases in the efficient production and distribution of goods in the West. Medical knowledge grew, and new cities were built with improved sanitation and safe water supplies. The result was a wholesale change in the physical and social world of the European countries and North America—and a pronounced increase of births over deaths.

As a result, at the turn of the nineteenth century, manipulation of the fertility process came into play. The manipulation was of two types. One, involving the development of birth control methods, might be called technological. The other, sociocultural in nature, was related to the social processes within the industrial society and the consequent change in attitudes toward family size.

By the 1870s the birthrate in the developing countries began to decline, a trend that continued until the "baby boom" of the 1940s and 1950s. New social conditions had begun to make large families impractical, and people began to realize that their place in the new order of things might relate rather directly to the ways in which they controlled their rate of reproduction. On farms large families provided the necessary labor; but in the industrialized cities, where housing, food, and other basic needs were expensive and education was the key to success, the small family was more practical. One sociologist termed this sociocultural phenomenon "social capillarity": just as a column of water must be thin to rise by capillary action, so must a family be small to rise in the social scale of the industrial society.[9]

So it is that in developed countries, despite short-term surges such as the baby boom mentioned above, the birthrate has generally continued to decline. Widespread birth control, lessening religious influences, greater educational and employment opportunities for women, and the certainty that most children born will grow to majority have contributed to a lower fertility level in recent years, just as improved diet and medical knowledge contributed to a lower mortality level 200 years earlier.

Prior to World War II, the nations of Africa, Latin America, and Asia (with the exception of Japan) had death rates equivalent to those of Europe during the Middle Ages.[10] After the war, international agencies such as the World Health Organization (WHO), Pan American Health Organization, and the United Nations International Children's Education Fund (UNICEF) brought the benefits of twentieth-century medicine to underdeveloped nations. Insecticides, antibiotics, preventive public programs, and modern medical techniques were all introduced. And the current population explosion in these nations can be attributed to the resultant sudden decline in death rates.

In Ceylon, for example, the death rate dropped by 40 percent in a three-year period (1945–1948) as a result of malaria control achieved with DDT.[11] Imposed from the outside, the drop in mortality was not an organic part of the technological and social development of the Ceylonese. As birthrates outstripped death rates, underdeveloped nations like Ceylon found that their technological resources could not hope to support their rapidly growing populations. In addition, their social systems were not sufficiently evolved to cope with the societal problems engendered by their growing masses.

The values of these countries, which had long been adapted to conditions of subsistence agriculture and high mortality rates, were not easy to change. In India, for instance, large families were the norm because only a few of the children born could be expected to survive beyond childhood. The parents depended on the few children who survived to help them provide for the family or village unit and to care for them in their old age. Today, however, most of the children live. A change in technology is much more rapid than a change in custom; in spite of the reduced mortality rates, large families are still common in India, as in other developing nations.

The Underdeveloped Nations: Population Explosion

The combination of sharply reduced mortality and continued high fertility has given rise to abnormally young populations whose reproductive potential poses an unprecedented threat to the economic development of these nations. (See Table 11.1 for average annual rates of population growth between 1965 and 1976.) Not only are these large numbers of dependent children a threat to the future economy, but they are also a significant drain on current resources. Their education and training demands economic resources that might more profitably be employed elsewhere, especially considering the fact that many of those trained cannot be absorbed into the underdeveloped economies of these countries. Indeed, with no promise of employment, and detached from the mainstream of society, many of these youths eventually turn to antisocial behavior, causing problems of order and control.

A Revolution of Rising Expectations

The smaller a nation's population, the fewer people there are to divide its national income. The fewer people to divide the national income, the greater the amount of money available to be spent on food, clothing, and shelter for each.

Industrially developed nations such as the United States have kept their populations at a reasonably low level, and there is abundant material wealth to be converted to a high standard of living for most of the population. Most people have enough food to eat, adequate clothing to wear, and decent housing to live in. In the United States, the issue of population growth as viewed by the middle class is normally related to questions about the distribution of wealth, the social priorities involved in its use, and the quality of life. How does overcrowding in cities affect the way people live? How does traffic congestion affect the emotional and mental stability of the city dweller or bumper-to-bumper commuter? How can enormous wealth, symbolized by concrete and steel skyscrapers, exist minutes away by subway from stultifying ghetto tenements?

Most underdeveloped countries are too involved with achieving sustenance levels for their people to consider population growth as anything but an economic problem. They are constantly engaged in trying to raise their people's standard of living, and uncontrolled population growth prevents

Table 11.1	Average Annual Rate of Population Increase between 1965 and 1976	
		Percent
Africa		2.7
North America		1.0
Latin America		2.7
East Asia (China, Japan, etc.)		1.6
South Asia (India, Pakistan, etc.)		2.6
Europe		.6
Oceania (Australia, New Zealand, etc.)		2.0
USSR-URSS		1.0

Source: *Demographic Yearbook, 1977* (New York: United Nations, 1977) p. 115. Copyright, United Nations, 1977. Reproduced by permission.

them from significantly doing so. Most economists believe that a nation with a stable population must invest 3 to 5 percent of its annual income in new income-producing development in order to raise the standard of living of its people. Many underdeveloped countries have a population growth rate of close to 3 percent. For such countries to raise the standard of living of their people requires an investment as high as 20 percent.[12] Poor nations can rarely afford this. They are forced by mushrooming population growth to spend most of their national income on imports of food and other staples. Even when they can afford it, population growth spreads the benefits so thin as to make them barely recognizable.

Capital investment is essential to the expansion of an economy. So is a large and skilled labor force. In countries with a huge population growth rate, large numbers of the people are too young to work. Those who must care for children are likewise economically unproductive. Quality education is scarce in underdeveloped countries, and the incentive to get an education is low, because jobs are rarely available even for the educated. The labor force remains proportionately small and unskilled. Remedying this situation calls for large injections of capital investment.

The world's poor are becoming more politically aware, however. They no longer accept poverty as fate or the will of God, and they are seeking better economic conditions. However, increased population growth prevents attainment of better economic conditions, as do the rigid and often exploitative governments and social systems in many of the underdeveloped countries. Both block the aspirations of the poor and can lead only to political upheaval in the future. Many sociologists have pointed out that people are satisfied with their lot in life, however hard, so long as it is all they expect; but when expectations change, dissatisfaction grows. We are on the verge of a revolution of rising expectations.

The Scope of the Population Problem

In technologically advanced countries, where social norms and economic priorities have the potential for controlling population growth, the population problem is primarily a problem of the quality of life. Advanced technology helps solve many human problems, but it causes others—congested cities, a depopulated and economically depressed countryside, and environmental pollution. High-level technologies consume resources at so fast a rate that industrial nations are beginning to face the problem of scarcity. In highly developed countries there is also a gap between population change and social change, for the proportion of the aged within the population has increased, resulting in new strains within the social structure.

In underdeveloped countries population growth remains so rapid that the first priority is the development of means by which the survival of these populations can be guaranteed, while at the same time the struggle for social progress and technological and industrial advancement continues. In ancient civilizations, large supplies of manpower were regarded as sources of strength in a society. Even in modern history, excess labor has been used in the construction of public works—as, for example, in the United States during the depression. Both India and the People's Republic of China have utilized labor-intensive means for just this purpose. If left unsolved, however, the problems of food distribution and social services undermine even this tactic.

The gap between the developed and underdeveloped countries is constantly widening in terms of population growth, industrial and political organization, and international power to influence the use and distribution of the world's resources. Population growth and movement are intimately bound up with the use of natural resources, and beneficial management of them for the world's peoples is to a great extent conditioned by how the population problem itself is resolved.

Let us consider now the comparative growth rates in the developed and underdeveloped countries and the variables that affect population makeup and movement. We will then consider the social, political, and ecological consequences of these changes.

Growth Rates in Industrialized Nations

Low, relatively stable rates of birth and death now characterize technologically advanced countries. The United States, with a population of 216.8 million, seems to be headed for zero population growth (the situation which results when the increase in population through births and immigration is equal to population loss through deaths and emigration). In the United States, the trend toward smaller families is gaining ground quickly. In 1977 there was an average of 1.8 children per family.[13] On the strength of these developing patterns, the U.S. Bureau of the Census projects that there will be 250 to 300 million Americans by the year 2000, 25 to 50 percent more than at present, yet 20 million less than previous forecasts indicated.[14]

It is not at all certain, however, that the United States will reach zero population growth. The rapid growth following World War II has given the American age structure a large number of young adults who, to bring the growth rate to a halt in the near future, would have to limit themselves to one child per couple. Unless they and their children continue a commitment to replacement levels of childbearing, the United States will still be faced with the consequences of growing population.

Europe's growth rate declined following World War I, with France not even able to replace her population during the depression; and, although Europe too experienced a post–World War II baby boom, its birthrate soon began a decline, which accelerated in the mid-sixties. Growth rates in the highly industrialized western and northern countries of Europe have declined faster than growth rates in southern and eastern countries.[15]

The people of West Germany (with a growth rate of 0.2 percent), England and Wales (0.2 percent), and Sweden (0.4 percent) have rapidly adopted contraceptive practices. Slightly higher growth rates in Italy (0.8 percent) and Spain (1.1 percent) may be partly due to religious opposition to birth control. In eastern Europe growth rates are also declining (Poland, 0.9 percent; Czechoslovakia, 0.7 percent; Hungary, 0.4 percent).[16] The use of contraceptives is widespread in eastern European nations, and the practice of abortion is publicly advocated by many governments.

Population growth rates in the Soviet Union have declined almost 50 percent over the past decade. In western areas of the country birthrates have declined sharply, partly because of a gap in the age structure caused by loss of life in World War II and partly because of Europeanized life-styles. Although birthrates are still high in the Asiatic regions of the Soviet Union, the overall decline in population has caused some official concern, since Soviet plans for agricultural, mineral, and industrial developments in the sparsely inhabited lands of the north and east require large labor forces.[17]

Japan's present rate of growth is less than half the Asian average. The most advanced industrial nation in Asia, Japan reacted to a postwar growth spurt with a campaign for control that produced "the swiftest drop in reproduction that has ever occurred in an entire nation."[18] As a small island nation with a limited supply of arable land and industrial resources, Japan depends largely on imports to maintain its industrial capacity and high standard of living. Without population control, Japan would become unbearably crowded and living standards would decline sharply. Even with control, parts of Japan are very densely populated. A strong tradition of social control has enabled the Japanese to curb population growth and endure very crowded living conditions, but there is still much to be done to further limit growth and control density.

Growth Rates in Underdeveloped Countries

The highest growth rates are found in the economically underdeveloped nations, which can least afford to support growing populations.[19] Illiteracy, ignorance of contraceptive methods, and cultural resistance to smaller families impede efforts to control population. Unfortunately, population growth and economic underdevelopment are closely linked, since much of the wealth and resources of underdeveloped nations that might otherwise be spent on developing new industries and raising living standards has to be spent on food imports to support the growing population.

Asia is the area of the world that most clearly characterizes overpopulation. In most Asian countries, from Turkey to Hong Kong, populations will double in 30 years or less. India, for example, exhibits a crude birthrate of approximately 43 live births per thousand persons.[20] As a whole, the population of South Asia has been growing at an annual rate of 2.6 percent per year, adding an estimated 313 million persons between 1965 and 1974 to its already expansive population (compare these figures with figures in Table 11.1). And much of this growth is of the type noted earlier, which places more and more of the population in a younger age category, thereby guaranteeing high growth rates for years to come unless drastic measures are taken.

Although South Asia has the largest numerical increase in population of any area in the world, in some ways the figures are misleading. If one looks at only the numerical increase in population size, rates of birth and growth are disproportionately represented because of the already large populations in this area. For example, while South Asia showed a population increase of 313 million persons between 1965 and 1976, Africa showed an increase of only 103 million and Latin America only 86 million. Actually, the African continent has the highest growth rate (2.7 percent). Nations such as Morocco, Nigeria, Ethiopia, Zaire, and South Africa show birthrates of almost 50 per thousand, close to three times those of the developed nations.[21] Such countries will double in population over the next two decades. Even now growth is straining the ability of their limited arable lands to produce enough food. A number of African countries have achieved a small industrial base that allows them to engage in some international trade and thus to acquire food, supplies, and technical advice for development from outside. Swift population growth takes up any slack that develops, however.

Latin America, another area of burgeoning populations, shows a birthrate of 38 per thousand and a growth rate similar to that of Africa, 2.7 percent. Evidence of transition to the patterns prevalent in developed nations can be found, however, in the growth rates of countries such as Cuba (1.8), Argentina (1.3), and Uruguay (1.2). Most other Latin American nations have a growth rate of around 3 percent and double their populations approximately every 25 years. Mexico, for instance, is expected to double its population in 21 years.[22]

Sociological Interpretations: Malthus to Marx

A variety of social maladies related to population size and the resources needed to support it are classified as population problems. From the social disorganization perspective, many such problems appear to result from the failure of social institutions to adapt to conditions created by rapid population growth. Religious systems in many parts of the world, for example, continue to promote large families, which, though functional in previous societies with high mortality rates, are dysfunctional for most modern societies. Similarly, many economic, political, and kinship institutions throughout the world no longer provide adequate guidelines for behavior that influences population size. To a large extent these institutions seem to perpetuate population growth while intensifying the problems it creates.

Overpopulation: A Cancer

Concern with population problems formally originated in 1798 with *An Essay on the Principle of Population*, by philosopher Thomas Malthus, who hypothesized that while technological improvements in productive capacity increase only arithmetically, population size increases geometrically. As a result, he theorized, populations will always tend to outstrip their means of support, until checked in growth by war, famine, unemployment, or the like.[23] Malthus's ideas bolstered the ascending bourgeoisie in eighteenth-century England by legitimating the obviation of social welfare measures customarily provided by the landed aristocracy for peasant farmers. These welfare measures allowed peasants to remain in the country during bad times rather than move into the city and become part of the industrial labor force. Against welfare, Malthus argued that it only served to perpetuate population growth, which would inevitably drag the whole society into destitution. If the peasants did not go where they could find work to support themselves, they should be left to starve.

With notable modifications, Malthusian ideas have survived to form the ideology of many powerful world planning and development organizations, including the International Planned Parenthood Federation, Ford Foundation, Rockefeller Foundation, Population Council, and World Bank.[24] Maintaining that without population control the consequences of population growth for the world order could be disastrous, these agencies advocate the dispensation of social welfare *only* where contraception and family planning programs have been instituted.[25] As reflected in a similar neo-Malthusian view known as Gregg's law, this policy intimates that overpopulation is a cancer, to be excised rather than fed.[26]

Other theorists contend that, at least in some cases, technological innovation and economic development will outstrip population growth. Kingsley Davis, for example, believes that for Europe and most of the Western world, economic development surpassed population growth during industrialization, raising the general standard of living.[27] Although the size of the populations in these areas increased during this period, the rate of increase declined. Moreover, this decline was not due solely to contraception or family planning but also to social and cultural systems that positively sanctioned small families while negatively sanctioning large ones. In addition, during much of the nineteenth century, an outlet existed for surplus populations that does not exist today—emigration.

On the other hand, population growth in non-Western and nonindustrialized nations has increased at high rates while economic development has faltered. According to Davis, the high rates of increase are due to declining mortality rather than rising fertility. In Davis's view, contraception and family planning are ineffective means for limiting population growth; and ultimately, some change in the collective attitude to family size, similar to that in the West, will have to take place.[28]

While nonindustrialized countries must contend with the dangers of overpopulation, industrial societies are threatened by the consequences of large-scale economic development. Pollution and the depletion of limited resources are two such consequences that affect the welfare of industrialized nations. The Club of Rome, an organization of approximately 100 top international businessmen, scientists, and scholars, warned in 1972 that there are definite limits to economic growth and that if population growth were not curbed, disaster would inevitably befall the world.[29] In light of the international recession of the 1970s and a strong environmental movement, the Club of Rome has since revised its recommendations. Instead of advocating no economic growth, it now indicates that growth must be selective, oriented toward equalizing the distribution of the world's wealth across all nations.[30] This amounts to economic planning and severe restriction of the world's "free" market economy.

Economic Inequities

More recent theorists have disagreed with the Malthusian contention that population problems are due almost solely to the consequences of population growth and have attributed population problems largely to the irrational organization of economic institutions. For example, according to Karl Marx, the tendency of the capitalistic economic system to pursue maximum profits inherently will lead to the introduction of automation in place of human labor to increase productivity. Since the worker's only source of income under this economic system is the wages earned by his labor, any movement toward mechanization creates additional financial strain on the disadvantaged segments of the population.[31] Further economic crises occurs when industry produces goods in excess of market demand and are forced to sell their products at reduced prices. This phenomenon, which

Marx called the "falling rate of profit," will eventually cause marginal businesses to close, a decrease in the buying power of the general public, and ultimately lead to the collapse of the capitalistic economic system.[32]

The Marxist orientation believes that capitalist economic development tends to create a society where wealth is concentrated in the hands of an elite group. From this position of power, the elites control the economy and dictate which economic policies will be established. In advanced nations this income inequality does not necessarily result in poverty for the remainder of the population since the economy is relatively stable and can support a large labor force. In less advanced or unstable economies, however, income inequality does create a condition of deprivation in which large elements of the population are unable to satisfy basic human and social needs.

Marx observed that the problems of economic systems are not limited by national boundaries. Because industrialized nations consume at tremendous rates, they use up a disproportionate amount of the world's resources. Marx and his followers charge that the industrialized nations, in their pursuit of needed resources, have unscrupulously procured materials from underdeveloped countries through neocolonialism and exploitation.

Proponents of this perspective advocate the implementation of socialism as a solution to these problems. Unemployment, poverty, and related issues are understood as problems to be solved by social reform and economic development, and not necessarily by controlling population growth. That these views are being modified, however, is evidenced by the fact that some socialist nations, including Cuba, belong to the International Planned Parenthood Federation. Also, the People's Republic of China has attempted to lower its fertility rate by raising the minimum legal age for marriage, legalizing abortion, and making information on contraception and contraceptive devices available.[33]

To the poor and underdeveloped nations, the dangers of limited resources and pollution seem of little consequence compared to their immediate problems of poverty and misery. Economic development, through revolutionary means if necessary, appears to be the more relevant task. Also, population control often violates strong religious and cultural mores that some nations have inherited from feudal-agrarian orders in their not-too-distant past. On the other hand, in industrialized nations where social and cultural systems already support a low birthrate, further economic development seems undesirable. Thus value conflicts concerning solutions to national and international population problems are evident and must ultimately be reckoned with. Perhaps by analyzing such problems we can better understand their dynamics, and thus the viability of different solutions can be made more apparent.

Consequences of Growth

Expanding populations increase the demand on food, energy, and mineral resources. In recent years, the dramatic ecological consequences of the population explosion—vanishing fisheries, costlier fuels and mineral ores, con-

Garrett Hardin
Tragedy of the Commons

We can make little progress in working toward optimum population size until we explicitly exorcize the spirit of Adam Smith in the field of practical demography. In economic affairs, *The Wealth of Nations* (1776) popularized the "invisible hand," the idea that an individual who "intends only his own gain," is, as it were, "led by an invisible hand to promote . . . the public interest." Adam Smith did not assert that this was invariably true, and perhaps neither did any of his followers. But he contributed to a dominant tendency of thought that has ever since interfered with positive action based on rational analysis, namely, the tendency to assume that decisions reached individually will, in fact, be the best decisions for an entire society. If this assumption is correct it justifies the continuance of our present policy of laissez-faire in reproduction. If it is correct we can assume that men will control their individual fecundity so as to produce the optimum population. If the assumption is not correct, we need to reexamine our individual freedoms to see which ones are defensible.

The rebuttal to the invisible hand in population control is to be found in a scenario first sketched in a little-known pamphlet in 1833 by a mathematical amateur named William Forster Lloyd (1794–1852). We may call it "the tragedy of the commons," using the word "tragedy" as the philosopher Whitehead used it: "The essence of dramatic tragedy is not unhappiness. It resides in the solemnity of the remorseless working of things." He then goes on to say, "This inevitableness of destiny can only be illustrated in terms of human life by incidents which in fact involve unhappiness. For it is only by them that the futility of escape can be made evident in the drama."

The tragedy of the commons develops in this way. Picture a pasture open to all. It is to be expected that each herdsman will try to keep as many cattle as possible on the commons. Such an arrangement may work reasonably satisfactorily for centuries because tribal wars, poaching, and disease keep the numbers of both man and beast well below the carrying capacity of the land. Finally, however, comes the day of reckoning, that is, the day when the long-desired goal of social stability becomes a reality. At this point, the inherent logic of the commons remorselessly generates tragedy.

As a rational being, each herdsman seeks to maximize his gain. Explicitly or implicitly, more or less consciously, he asks, "What is the utility to me of adding one more animal to my herd?" This utility has one negative and one positive component.

1) The positive component is a function of the increment of one animal. Since the herdsman receives all the proceeds from the sale of the additional animal, the positive utility is nearly +1.

2) The negative component is a function of the additional overgrazing created by one more animal. Since, however, the effects of overgrazing are shared by all the herdsmen, the negative utility for any particular decisionmaking herdsman is only a fraction of −1.

Adding together the component partial utilities, the rational herdsman concludes that the only sensible course for him to pursue is to add another animal to his herd. And another; and another. . . . But this is the conclusion reached by each and every rational herdsman sharing a commons. Therein is the tragedy. Each man is locked up into a system that compels him to increase his herd without limit—in a world that is limited. Ruin is the destination toward which all men rush, each pursuing his own best interest in a society that believes in the freedom of the commons. Freedom in a commons brings ruin to all.

Some would say that this is a platitude. Would that it were! In a sense, it was learned thousands of years ago, but natural selection favors the forces of psychological denial. The individual benefits as an individual from his ability to deny the truth even though society as a whole, of which he is a part, suffers. Education can counteract the natural tendency to do the wrong thing, but the inexorable succession of generations requires that the basis for this knowledge be constantly refreshed.

taminated air and water—have aroused worldwide concern. The immediate consequences differ from nation to nation, but the long-range consequences concern every human being on earth.

Feeding the World: Surplus to Famine

With large areas of arable land and highly efficient agricultural techniques, the United States would not seem to have any urgent concerns about food supplies. There are signs, however, that American agricultural abundance is not inexhaustible. In 1972 the U.S. Commission on Population Growth and the American Future reported that faster population growth would soon require the farming of marginal lands, a costly process. The commission members warned that three-child reproduction averages (admittedly higher than present patterns) could lead to 40 to 50 percent increases in farm food prices.[34]

Most advanced industrial nations now either maintain their populations in line with domestic food production or depend on food imports to meet some of their needs. At the present time the United States, Canada, Australia, and Argentina are able to produce large quantities of food for export. If however, population growth creates increased demands for food within those countries, there may be no food left to export.

In the underdeveloped nations, agriculture is typically at the subsistence level, barely keeping pace with population growth at an inadequate level of nutrition. (See Figure 11.1 for a comparison of population density and average per capita calorie intake around the world.) Experts estimate that two-

Politics and profit, two factors that adversely affect the distribution of food to the world's starving populations: In 1974 members of the National Farmers Organization shot more than 650 calves to protest low prices of meat and dairy products, while in other parts of the world children were dying of malnutrition.

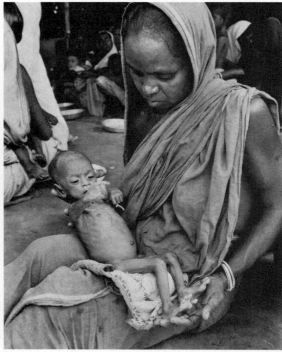

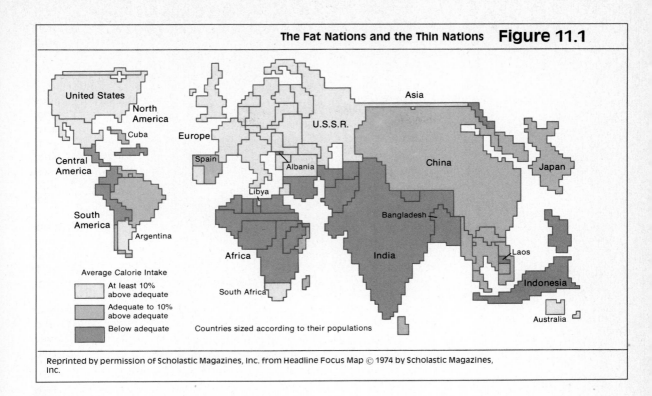

The Fat Nations and the Thin Nations **Figure 11.1**

United States
North America
Cuba
Central America
South America
Argentina
Europe
Spain
Albania
Libya
Africa
South Africa
Asia
U.S.S.R.
China
Japan
Bangladesh
India
Laos
Indonesia
Australia

Average Calorie Intake

At least 10% above adequate

Adequate to 10% above adequate

Below adequate

Countries sized according to their populations

thirds of the 800 million children of Africa, Asia, and Latin America now suffer from malnutrition. Natural disasters that affect agriculture can turn subsistence nutritional levels into outright famine. In 1972 crop failures brought on by drought conditions caused severe food shortages in India and Central America, and in Africa there was a tragic migration in search of food by millions of nomads across a 2000-mile belt of the south Sahara. The agriculture of underdeveloped nations is clearly inadequate, but not even the most advanced agricultural technology can feed a chronically expanding population.

An equally serious consequence of growth is the rapid consumption of the world's nonrenewable natural resources. Worldwide usage rates are increasing faster than population, so there are more people consuming at the same time that average consumption is rising. The most liberal estimates of reserves indicates that continued consumption at this level will lead to severe scarcities and higher costs in the years ahead. Within a century, some minerals may be totally exhausted.

Energy is essential for all production. Our industries and power plants have long relied on fossil fuels to generate power. But the energy crisis the world faces now is due to the very fact that these fuels are nonrenewable and quickly running out. Once they have been used up, we will have to depend on new types of energy.

Dwindling Energy

Ravaging the land for oil: Miles and miles of valuable land have been sacrificed to the Alaskan pipeline for stopgap energy production.

The need for oil is increasing; yet we have depleted most of our oil deposits. Since 1970, U.S. oil exploration has doubled, from 1014 drilling rigs operating in the continental United States in 1970 to 2240 in 1978. But the amount of oil produced by this increased effort has actually declined during this period.[35] Confronted with the prospect of rationing fuel, we now seek offshore oil, but to date have had little success. Despite the hazards it poses for the environment, we proceeded with the Alaskan pipeline, and in 1978 began to receive oil from this previously untapped supply.

The decline in domestic oil production has forced us to rely heavily on foreign producers of oil—in particular, those in the Middle East. The Organization of Petroleum Exporting Countries (OPEC) plays an increasingly significant role in international affairs since the demand for OPEC oil gives the cartel tremendous leverage to influence the foreign policies of the United States and other major powers. Since 1970, OPEC has raised the price of oil per barrel from less than 5 dollars to an average of more than 18 dollars per barrel in 1979.[36]

The growing crisis in fuel production has caused many to turn prematurely to nuclear energy before enough was learned about controlling dangerous radioactive elements.

The environmental consequences of [using nuclear fuels] are that we shall be exchanging some of our current problems, particularly in air pollution, for the problems of managing radioactive wastes. The former are mostly health and aesthetic threats while the latter are hazards to human health and genetics.[37]

The safety of nuclear reactors themselves has also been questioned. Some have asserted that while earthquakes, fires, and sabotage can create emergency conditions for nuclear power plants, there is no way in which these plants can quickly shut down in response to such emergencies. This point was demonstrated when officials at Three Mile Island in Pennsylvania experienced difficulty in cooling off a reactor when problems arose in 1979. Although actuaries estimate the chance of a person being killed in a nuclear accident as 5 billion to 1, these odds become meaningful for social policy only when combined with the other environmental dangers of radioactive wastes and interpreted in the light of some scheme of social and economic values.[38]

In a context of declining oil reserves and the cartelization of their production, refinement, and marketing, nuclear energy appeals as a cheap and efficient way to maintain our life-style of high energy use while also preserving our economic independence from other oil-producing countries. It is claimed, for example, that in 1975 nuclear reactors saved the United States about 2 billion dollars in fuel costs, which is equivalent to about 170 billion barrels of oil from overseas.[39] Whether these economic benefits offset the dangers of nuclear power, however, is not so clear.

Other new technologies, while providing hope for solutions to energy problems, are not yet feasible and may also have detrimental effects on the environment. Recent advances in the conversion of oil shale, solar energy, geothermal energy, and solid wastes have received favorable publicity as energy alternatives, although current projections indicate that all of the above could fill only 13 percent of the energy demands in America by the year 2000.[40] Solar energy, though clean in operation, causes some pollution in the production of necessary supporting facilities. Geothermal energy is problematical in that it involves sulfide emissions into the air and leaves behind a brine that must be disposed of—a potential soil and water pollutant. Oil shale development has an impact on the environment; it produces dust, sulfur dioxide, and nitrogen oxide, and requires extensive mining operations. And residues from the conversion of solid wastes into energy resources may include mercury, ash deposits, and waste waters.[41]

The cones of Three Mile Island—symbols of our energy salvation or of future catastrophe? Nuclear energy will continue to be controversial since the possibility of an accident will always be present. Are the benefits worth the risk?

Poisons in the Air

Air pollution is not only ugly and uncomfortable for the eyes and lungs, it is harmful to living things. Pollutants from automobiles, homes, industries, and power plants permeate the air from Maine to California; it is estimated that more than 200 million tons of contaminants are released every year.[42] New Jersey's oil refineries cast a dark cloud over New York City; Detroit's pollutants contaminate the Canadian woods; vast mists of polluted air encircle the entire earth daily. Although Americans are probably the leading air polluters, the task of cleaning up the air is really an international one.

Over one-third of the pollutants released into the air come from the exhaust pipes of automobiles. The major chemical component of this exhaust is carbon monoxide, known to be highly toxic. Also found in exhaust fumes are nitrogen oxides, which give the air a brown tinge. The action of sunlight causes these oxides to combine with waste hydrocarbons also emitted from exhausts, forming peroxyacetyl nitrate, a chemical that causes eyes to smart and water and may also damage the lungs.

Automobiles, however, are not the only culprits. Electric utilities using low-grade fossil fuels give off troublesome sulfur oxides; about 30 million tons are released by all American industries each year. When mixed with other chemicals normally present in the air, the sulfur oxides turn into sulfuric acid. Recent rains over Chesapeake Bay were found to contain large amounts of sulfuric acid.

The problems of air pollution are worsened by occasional air inversions, in which the layer of air over low-lying cities is trapped by a layer of warmer air in the upper atmosphere. All pollutants are thus held firmly in place over the city, creating a smog and causing the issuance of an air quality alert.

What damage does air pollution do? It is known to kill plants; more than a million trees have died from California's smogs, and crop losses due to air pollution are thought to be high. It erodes buildings and public monuments made of stone; it causes house paint to deteriorate and clothes to need fre-

Industrial gas chambers: For years industries have emitted poisonous gases and harmful substances into the air, slowly suffocating the nearby communities.

quent washings. Air pollution also appears to be hazardous to human health. Medical researchers have found that it greatly affects the bronchitis death rate. And although pollutants may not be the cause of many illnesses, significant relationships have been established between air pollution and lung cancer, stomach cancer, heart disease, emphysema, and infant mortality. Indeed, analysis indicates that cleaning the air everywhere to the level enjoyed by the area with the best air would reduce the death rate for bronchitis alone by 40 to 70 percent.[43] The air we breathe, as vital as it is to our well-being, is so often taken for granted that we tend to forget about the long-term effects of air pollution.

How do we solve the problem? Certainly some progress has been made in limiting industrial pollutants and auto emissions, but a workable and permanent solution is still decades away. Because of the close interconnection of the animate and inanimate in the ecosystem, cleaning up one part of the environment or one area of the country is not enough; the whole system must be treated in order to combat the problem successfully.

Purifying the Atmosphere

The Clean Air Act of 1970 established rather stringent requirements on the auto industry, electric utilities, pulp and paper industries, and steel mills, as well as other major polluters.[44] Federal and local authorities have set standards in most areas, but the equipment necessary to greatly reduce pollutants has not yet been manufactured or perfected. When these devices are working, perhaps by the mid-1980s, the air will be appreciably freer of major polluting gases.

Ameliorating the air pollution caused by the electric utilities has given rise to another environmental problem. The utilities are major polluters because until recently their production depended on low-grade (high-sulfur) coal as the chief source of power. The Environmental Protection Agency (EPA) and local agencies banned the use of "dirty" coal in most regions (on the Eastern Seaboard since the late 1960s) and mandated that only "clean" fuel could be burned after 1976, although different areas continue to have different standards of cleanness. The problem of obtaining low-sulfur coal is twofold. To get this fuel, strip-mining is usually employed, and this leads to destruction of land resources. In addition, low-sulfur coal is most abundant in the Northwest—Montana, Wyoming, and other adjacent states. Transporting it from this area to other parts of the country is thus almost prohibitively expensive, and the cost of electricity and power could rise drastically. And it is unfortunate, but nonetheless the case, that the quest for clean fuels, whether clean coal or gas or oil, leads directly to other environmental problems.

One feature of all suggested solutions to the problem of air pollution is that they cost money. It costs a great deal to convert old engines or develop new nonpolluting ones; therefore, the public will end up paying the bill. Yet economists point out that we already pay many hidden costs of air pollution. Polluted air causes so much damage to people, plants, and buildings that American economists generally agree it will be cheaper in the long run simply to lay out the billions of dollars necessary to clean it up.[45] Certainly, when we take into account the hundreds of thousands of people who are ill and hospitalized because of respiratory disease partially caused or severely

VISIBLE POLLUTION

Not all pollution is visible. But the pollution we can see is symptomatic of a disease infecting our society and our world—a lethal disease that now appears to spell the doom of our air, our land, our water, and our future generations, if it cannot be cured. *Clockwise from top left*: Inoperative oil field—land exploited and deserted; enduring eyesore —junk decomposes slowly, if at all; strip mining plays havoc with the land; this pile of pesticide containers is trash the soil cannot readily absorb; Las Vegas— aesthetically abominations, these signs use quantities of vital electricity to promote private profit; abandoned automobile —monument to the ills of affluence.

aggravated by air pollution, the staggering crop losses each year due in part to dirty air, and the damage being done to private homes and public buildings, we must affirm that the costs of air pollution are very high indeed.

Contaminated Water

Like the air we breathe, water is essential for human and plant life. It is estimated that the average person uses between 50 and 100 gallons of water a day for such things as bathing, flushing toilets, drinking, cooking, and washing.[46] Yet, like the air, much of the water we use is polluted.

The nation's rivers and lakes have long been the dumping grounds for many industries. Major industries—paper, steel, automobile, chemical—depend on the water for cooling and production as well. They take water from the rivers and return it polluted and heated, thus doubly affecting aquatic life. Pollutants that industries discharge into rivers and oceans are many and various: solid wastes, sewage, nondegradable by-products, synthetic materials, toxic chemicals, even radioactive substances. Add to this the sewage systems of towns and large cities, detergents, boat and ship spills, oil spills, pesticide runoff from agricultural areas, and acid run-

Thor Heyerdahl
Polluting the Ocean: Can Man Survive a Dead Ocean?

Since the ancient Greeks maintained that the earth was round and great navigators like Columbus and Magellan demonstrated that this assertion was true, no geographical discovery has been more important than what we all are beginning to understand today: that our planet has exceedingly restricted dimensions. There is a limit to all resources. . . .

Because of the population explosion, land of any nature has long been in such demand that nations have intruded upon each other's territory with armed forces in order to conquer more space for overcrowded communities. During the last few years, the United Nations has convened special meetings in Stockholm, Caracas, and Geneva in a dramatic attempt to create a "Law of the Sea" designed to divide vast sections of the global ocean space into national waters. The fact that no agreement has been reached illustrates that in our ever-shriveling world there is not even ocean space enough to satisfy everybody.

And only one generation ago, the ocean was considered so vast that no one nation would bother to lay claim to more of it than the three-mile limit which represented the length of a gun shot from the shore.

It will probably take still another generation before mankind as a whole begins to realize fully that the ocean is but another big lake, landlocked on all sides. Indeed, it is essential to understand this concept for the survival of coming generations. For we of the 20th century still treat the ocean as the endless, bottomless pit it was considered to be in medieval times. Expressions like "the bottomless sea" and "the boundless ocean" are still in common use, and although we all know better, they reflect the mental image we still have of this, the largest body of water on earth. Perhaps one of the reasons why we subconsciously consider the ocean a sort of bottomless abyss is the fact that all the rain and all the rivers of the world keep pouring constantly into it and yet its water level always remains unchanged. Nothing affects the ocean, not even the Amazon, the Nile, or the Ganges. We know, of course, that this imperviousness is no indicator of size, because the sum total of all the rivers is nothing but the return to its own source of the water evaporated from the sea and carried ashore by drifting clouds. . . .

Only when we fully perceive that there is no fundamental difference between the various bodies of water on our planet, beyond the fact that the ocean is the largest of all lakes, can we begin to realize that the ocean has something else in common with all other bodies of water: it is vulnerable. In the long run the ocean can be affected by the continued discharge of all modern man's toxic waste. One generation ago no one would have thought that the giant lakes of America could be polluted. Today they are, like the largest lakes of Europe. A few years ago the public was amazed to learn that industrial and urban refuse had killed the fish in Lake Erie. The enormous lake was dead. It was polluted from shore to shore in spite of the fact that it has a constant outlet through Niagara Falls, which carries pollutants away into the ocean in a never-ending flow. The ocean receiving all this pollution has no outlet but represents a dead end, because only pure water evaporates to return into the clouds. The ocean is big; yet if 10 Lake Eries were taken and placed end to end, they would span the entire Atlantic from Africa to South America. And the St. Lawrence River is by no means the only conveyor of pullutants into the ocean. Today hardly a creek or a river in the world reaches the ocean without carrying a constant flow of non-degradable chemicals from industrial, urban, or agricultural areas. Directly by sewers or indirectly by way of streams and other waterways, almost every big city in the world, whether coastal or inland, makes use of the ocean as mankind's common sink. We treat the ocean as if we believed that it is not part of our own planet—as if the blue waters curved into space somewhere beyond the horizon where our pollutants would fall off the edge, as ships were believed to do before the days of Christopher Columbus. We build sewers so far into the sea that we pipe the harmful refuse away from public beaches. Beyond that is no man's concern. What we consider too dangerous to be stored under technical control ashore we dump forever out of sight at sea, whether toxic chemicals or nuclear waste. Our only excuse is the still-surviving image of the ocean as a bottomless pit.

It is time to ask: is the ocean vulnerable? And if so, can man survive on a planet with a dead ocean? Both questions can be answered, and they are worthy of our attention.

First, the degree of vulnerability of any body of water would of course depend on two factors: the volume of the water and the nature of the pollutants. We know the volume of the ocean, its surface measure, and its average depth. We know that it covers 71 percent of the surface of our planet, and we are impressed, with good reason, when all these measurements are given in almost astronomical figures.

If we resort to a more visual image, however, the dimensions lose their magic. The average depth of all oceans is only 1,700 meters. The Empire State Building is 448 meters high. If stretched out horizontally instead of vertically, the average ocean depth would only slightly exceed the 1,500 meters that an Olympic runner can cover by foot in 3 minutes and 35 seconds. The average depth of the North Sea, however, is not 1,700 meters, but only 80 meters, and many of the buildings in downtown New York would emerge high above water level if they were built on the bottom of this sea. During the Stone Age most of the North Sea was dry land where roaming archers hunted deer and other game. In this shallow water, until only recently, all the industrial nations of Western Europe have conducted year-round routine dumping of hundreds of thousands of tons of their most toxic industrial refuse. All the world's sewers and most of its waste are dumped into waters as shallow as, or shallower than, the North Sea. An attempt was made at a recent ocean exhibition to illustrate graphically and in correct proportion the depths of the Atlantic, the Pacific, and the Indian oceans in relation to a cross section of the planet earth. The project had to be abandoned, for although the earth was painted with a diameter twice the height of a man, the depths of the world oceans painted in proportion became so insignificant that they could not be seen except as a very thin pencil line. . . .

When viewed in full, from great heights, the ocean's surface is seen to have definite, confining limits. But at sea level, the ocean seems to extend outward indefinitely, to the horizon and on into blue space. The astronauts have come back from space literally disturbed upon seeing a full view of our planet. They have seen at first hand how cramped together the nations are in a limited space and how the "endless" oceans are tightly enclosed within cramped quarters by surrounding land masses. But one need not be an astronaut to lose the sensation of a boundless ocean. It is enough to embark on some floating logs tied together, as we did with the *Kon-Tiki* in the Pacific, or on some bundles of papyrus reeds, as we did with the *Ra* in the Atlantic. With no effort and no motor we were pushed by the winds and currents from one continent to another in a few weeks.

After we abandon the outworn image of infinite space in the ocean, we are still left with many wrong or useless notions about biological life and vulnerability. Marine life is concentrated in about four percent of the ocean's total body of water, whereas roughly

96 percent is just about as poor in life as is a desert ashore. . . .

What is worse is the fact that life is not evenly distributed throughout the thin surface layer. Ninety percent of all marine species are concentrated above the continental shelves next to land. . . . This concentration of marine life in shallow waters next to the coasts happens to coincide with the area of concentrated dumping and the outlet of all sewers and polluted river mouths, not to mention silt from chemically treated farmland. The bulk of some 20,000 known species of fish, some 30,000 species of mullusks, and nearly all the main crustaceans lives in the most exposed waters around the littoral areas. . . .

When we speak of farmable land in any country, we do not include deserts or sterile rock in our calculations. Why then shall we deceive ourselves by the total size of the ocean when we know that not even one percent of its water volume is fertile for the fisherman?

Much has been written for or against the activities of some nations that have dumped vast quantities of nuclear waste and obsolete war gases in the sea and excused their actions on the grounds that it was all sealed in special containers. In such shallow waters as the Irish Sea, the English Channel, and the North Sea there are already enough examples of similar "foolproof" containers moving about with bottom currents until they are totally displaced and even crack open with the result that millions of fish are killed or mutilated. In the Baltic Sea, which is shallower than many lakes and which—except for the thin surface layer—has already been killed by pollution, 7,000 tons of arsenic were dumped in cement containers some 40 years ago. These containers have now started to leak. Their combined contents are three times more than is needed to kill the entire population of the earth today.

Fortunately, in certain regions modern laws have impeded the danger of dumpings; yet a major threat to marine life remains—the less spectacular but more effective ocean pollution through continuous discharge from sewers and seepage. Except in the Arctic, there is today hardly a creek or a river in the world from which it is safe to drink at the outlet. The more technically advanced the country, the more devastating the threat to the ocean. A few examples picked at random will illustrate the pollution input from the civilized world.

French rivers carry 18 billion cubic meters of liquid pollution annually into the sea. The city of Paris alone discharges almost 1.2 million cubic meters of untreated effluent into the Seine every day.

The volume of liquid waste from the Federal Republic of Germany is estimated at over nine billion cubic meters per year, or 25.4 million cubic meters per day, not counting cooling water, which daily amounts to 33.6 million cubic meters. Into the Rhine alone 50,000 tons of waste are discharged daily, including 30,000 tons of sodium chloride from industrial plants.

A report from the UN Economic and Social Council, issued prior to the Stockholm Conference on the Law of the Sea four years ago, states that the world had then dumped an estimated billion pounds of DDT into our environment and was adding an estimated 100 million more pounds per year. The total world production of pesticides was estimated at more than 1.3 billion pounds annually, and the United States alone exports more than 400 million pounds per year. Most of this ultimately finds its way into the ocean with winds, rain, or silt from land. A certain type of DDT sprayed on crops in East Africa a few years ago was found and identified a few months later in the Bay of Bengal, a good 4,000 miles away.

The misconception of a boundless ocean makes the man in the street more concerned about city smog than about the risk of killing the ocean. Yet the tallest chimney in the world does not suffice to send the noxious smoke away into space; it gradually sinks down, and nearly all descends, mixed with rain, snow, and silt, into the ocean. Industrial and urban areas are expanding with the population explosion all over the world, and in the United States alone, waste products in the form of smoke and noxious fumes amount to a total of 390,000 tons of pollutants every day, or 142 million tons every year. . . .

The world was upset when the *Torrey Canyon* unintentionally spilled 100,000 tons of oil into the English Channel some years ago; yet this is only a small fraction of the intentional discharge of crude oil sludge through less spectacular, routine tank cleaning. Every year more than *Torrey Canyon's* spill of a 100,000 tons of oil is intentionally pumped into the Mediterranean alone, and a survey of the sea south of Italy yielded 500 liters of solidified oil for every square kilometer of surface. Both the Americans and the Russians were alarmed by our observations of Atlantic pollution in 1970 and sent out specially equipped oceanographic research vessels to the area. American scientists from Harvard University working with the Bermuda Biological Station for Research found more solidified oil than seaweed per surface unit in the Sargasso Sea and had to give up their plankton catch because their nets were completely plugged up by oil sludge. They estimated, however, a floating stock of 86,000 metric tons of tar in the Northwest Altantic alone. The Russians, in a report read by the representative of the Soviet Academy of Sciences at a recent pollution conference in Prague, found that pollution in the coastal areas of the Atlantic had already surpassed their tentative limit for what had been considered tolerable, and that a new scale of tolerability would have to be postulated.

The problem of oil pollution is in itself a complex one. Various types of crude oil are toxic in different degrees. But they all have one property in common: they attract other chemicals and absorb them like blotting paper, notably the various kinds of pesticides. DDT and other chlorinated hydrocarbons do not dissolve in water, nor do they sink: just as they are absorbed by plankton and other surface organisms, so are they drawn into oil slicks and oil clots, where in some cases they have been rediscovered in stronger concentrations than when originally mixed with dissolvents in the spraying bottles. Oil clots, used as floating support for barnacles, marine worms, and pelagic crabs, were often seen by us from the *Ra*, and these riders are attractive bait for filter-feeding fish and whales, which cannot avoid getting gills and baleens cluttered up by the tarlike oil. Even sharks with their rows of teeth plastered with black oil clots are now reported from the Caribbean Sea. Yet the oil spills, and dumping of waste from ships represent a very modest contribution compared with the urban and industrial refuse released from land.

That the ocean, given time, will cope with it all, is a common expression of wishful thinking. The ocean has always been a self-purifying filter that has taken care of all global pollution for millions of years. Man is not the first polluter. Since the morning of time nature itself has been a giant workshop, experimenting, inventing, decomposing, and throwing away waste: the incalculable billions of tons of rotting forest products, decomposing flesh, mud, silt, and excrement. If this waste had not been recycled, the ocean would long since have become a compact soup after millions of years of death and decay, volcanic eruptions, and global erosion. Man is not the first large-scale producer, so why should he become the first disastrous polluter?

Man has imitated nature by manipulating atoms, taking them apart and grouping them together in dif-ferent compositions. Nature turned fish into birds and beasts into man. It found a way to make fruits out of soil and sunshine. It invented radar for bats and whales, and shortwave transceivers for beetles and butterflies. Jet propulsion was installed on squids, and unsurpassed computers were made as brains for mankind. Marine bacteria and plankton transformed the dead generations into new life. The life cycle of spaceship earth is the closest one can ever get to the greatest of all inventions, *perpetuum mobile*—the perpetual-motion machine. And the secret is that nothing was composed by nature that could not be recomposed, recycled, and brought back into service again in another form as another useful wheel in the smoothly running global machinery.

This is where man has sidetracked nature. We put atoms together into molecules of types nature had carefully avoided. We invent to our delight immediately useful materials like plastics, pesticides, detergents, and other chemical products hitherto unavailable on planet earth. We rejoice because we can get our laundry whiter than the snow we pollute and because we can exterminate every trace of insect life. We spray bugs and bees, worms and butterflies. We wash and flush the detergents down the drain out to the oysters and fish. Most of our new chemical products are not only toxic: they are in fact created to sterilize and kill. And they keep on displaying these same inherent abilities wherever they end up. Through sewers and seepage they all head for the ocean, where they remain to accumulate as undesired nuts and bolts in between the cogwheels of a so far smoothly running machine. If it had not been for the present generation, man could have gone on polluting the ocean forever with the degradable waste he produced. But with ever-increasing speed and intensity we now produce and discharge into the sea hundreds of thousands of chemicals and other products. They do not evaporate nor do they recycle, but they grow in numbers and quantity and threaten all marine life.

We have long known that our modern pesticides have begun to enter the flesh of penguins in the Antarctic and the brains of polar bears and the blubber of whales in the Arctic, all subsisting on plankton and plankton-eating crustaceans and fish in areas far from cities and farmland. We all know that marine pollution has reached global extent in a few decades. We also know that very little or nothing is being done to stop it. Yet there are persons who tell us that there is no reason to worry, that the ocean is so big and surely science must have everything under control. City smog is being fought through intelligent legislation. Certain lakes and rivers have been improved by leading the sewers down to the sea. But where, may we ask, is the global problem of ocean pollution under control?

No breathing species could live on this planet until the surface layer of the ocean was filled with phytoplankton, as our planet in the beginning was only surrounded by sterile gases. These minute plant species manufactured so much oxygen that it rose above the surface to help form the atmosphere we have today. All life on earth depended upon this marine plankton for its evolution and continued subsistence. Today, more than ever before, mankind depends on the welfare of this marine plankton for his future survival as a species. With the population explosion we need to harvest even more protein from the sea. Without plankton there will be no fish. With our rapid expansion of urban and industrial areas and the continuous disappearance of jungle and forest, we shall be ever more dependent on the plankton for the very air we breathe. Neither man nor any other terrestrial beast could have bred had plankton not preceded them. Take away this indispensable life in the shallow surface areas of the sea, and life ashore will be unfit for coming generations. A dead ocean means a dead planet.

Excerpts from "How To Kill an Ocean," *Saturday Review*, November 29, 1975, Vol. 3, No. 5, pp. 12—18. © Saturday Review 1975. Reprinted by permission.

off from strip-mined land, and the enormity of the problem is even clearer. The fact that the Cuyahoga River, which runs through Cleveland, recently caught fire dramatizes the situation's severity.

Phosphates from fertilizers and detergents are among the most troublesome pollutants of lakes and rivers. These chemicals "fertilize" the algae in the water, which then experience a population explosion. Food supplies run short, the algae die, and bacteria begin to live on the remains. The increased bacteria use up all the oxygen dissolved in the water, making it uninhabitable for other living things. The result is an ugly, smelly, useless body of water.

The Refuse Act of 1899 outlaws the discharge of pollutants other than municipal sewage into navigable waters without a permit from the Army Corps of Engineers.[47] How, then, have so many private industries been able to go on polluting our public waters? The answer is, as usual, an economic and political one. Industries that help keep the economy growing have generally had little trouble from government authorities about polluting the environment. Only recently, and only because of public awareness and outrage, has the government started fining major polluters. There are thousands of examples of this "look-the-other-way" attitude. Even more disturbing is the fact that when federal and local authorities do fine a major polluter, that industry usually continues its polluting activities; it is often cheaper to pay the fine than to stop polluting.

One of the most publicized enforcement actions has been against the Reserve Mining Company of Minnesota.[48] Since 1955, this company has deposited more than 190 million long tons of taconite tailings from its iron ore processing into Lake Superior, and it adds another 60,000 tons each day. EPA finally gave Reserve 180 days to find other ways of disposing of these wastes. EPA consultants suggested five alternatives; all were rejected by Reserve. The case then went to the Justice Department in 1972, and it is still under litigation. All the while, Reserve continues to pump 60,000 tons of tailings into the lake every day.

This type of noncompliance with laws is not infrequent. Even though

one or two large companies can seriously pollute a body of water that thousands of people use, these private interests have so far maintained the right to do so with little opposition.

The major problem in pollution control is the vast economic and political power of large polluters. Water pollution exists, in large part, because polluters have more influence over government than do those they "pollute." So long as this disproportionate influence persists, so will the pollution. It is a mistake to suppose that new laws with higher clean-up requirements and tougher penalties will ultimately succeed in eliminating environmental contamination; unless new laws also tip the scales of influence over government in favor of the public, the requirements they set will be consistently violated and the penalties rarely used.[49]

The oceans are another problem, and the amount of pollutants spewed into them daily is incalculable. Oil spills from ships and offshore wells can ruin hundreds of miles of shoreline and endanger aquatic life. Mercury poisoning in fish has also been on the increase. Like inland rivers and lakes,

The polluted Potomac: A serious health hazard and a bane on recreation.

the oceans are our dumping grounds. Unless our waters and the waters of the world are protected from industrial pollutants, people everywhere will be faced with the possibility of drinking contaminated water, the devastation of water-oriented recreation areas, and a loss of many species of fish.

Wastelands

Pollution of our land takes many forms—destruction of forests, strip-mining, buildup of pesticides and herbicides in our soil, neglect, even the paving of highways and roads. Our dumps for waste materials, and especially our habit of littering the landscape with all kinds of trash from bottles to automobiles, make land pollution the most visible—and aesthetically disgusting—environmental menace.

Although they dramatically increase crop yields, chemical fertilizers have unfortunate side effects on our land; they diminish the land's natural capacity to produce its own nitrates. Nitrates from chemical fertilizers can cause an often fatal disease in infants, called methemoglobinemia. Many cases of the disease have been reported in the agricultural regions of the Midwest.

The accumulation of pesticides in the soil is another threat to our health, since they contaminate the plants and animals that are consumed by human beings. Many of these pesticides, like DDT, are cumulative poisons that increase at each level of the food chain. Fears of the effects of high concentrations of DDT have led to a ban on its use, but there is evidence that many of its replacements may be just as harmful. The extensive use of pesticides has already threatened many species of wildlife, such as the bald eagle and brown pelican, with extinction.

Each of these problems carries serious repercussions for all parts of the ecosystem, the intricate web of relationships between all living things and the physical environment they share. Animal life disappears, trees and other plant life die, the ability of the soil to retain water is diminished, and erosion takes place. Flooding becomes more frequent, and finally we have a barren, useless land. The disastrous Dust Bowl situation in the midwestern and western states during the 1930s was largely caused by unchecked deforestation and overuse of the farmlands.[50] After a series of prolonged droughts and dust storms, once highly productive farmland became devoid of top soil and agriculturally unproductive. We had blindly neglected the very soil from which we get our wealth, food, and shelter.

The problems we face in the future are similar. Although some land is being set aside by both federal and local governments as wilderness areas or national parks, far more will have to be allotted in the coming decades. To meet the demands of our growing population, our farmlands must be expanded and used for more diverse crops—without being depleted or over-dosed with nitrate fertilizers and other forms of destructive chemicals. Solid waste will also multiply, and we must find new ways of recycling our goods before a large portion of our land becomes a garbage heap. Our need for fos-

America the beautiful? A society which produces so much waste must consider what to do with it. So far, we have relied heavily on simply dumping it—anywhere.

sil fuels and other resources will continue to skyrocket, yet strip mining is not the ecological answer to our energy needs. Cities and suburbs continue to sprawl, destroying more land. Without care, planning, and an eye toward ecological balance, what we now call land may be called wasteland by future generations.

Although technology may provide many solutions, it was technology in response to population growth that caused most of the environmental problems with which we are now contending. Technological solutions represent the belief that science can save us, that continued domination of the environment by the human race is necessary, although it must be done in a more environmentally safe and economically efficient way. Other solutions reflecting alternative value orientations prescribe the limitation of population growth, energy consumption, and technological innovation and involve an attempt to accommodate human activities to the demands of the environment. A consideration of current responses to population and environmental problems can index for us the value orientations that are now directing trends in policy formation.

Population Planning

In times of drought and famine, the Bushmen of the Kalahari Desert abstain from sexual intercourse. This is the only form of birth control they know, and they do not wish to bring children into the world at a time when they would not survive and their birth would put a strain on other members of the group. Most of the world's people would rather not adopt the Bushman method of family planning, but until the twentieth century it was the only absolutely reliable method. Today there are several; the problem is to make the knowledge and means of these methods of birth control available on a worldwide scale and to change whatever social attitudes hinder their adoption.

Contraception

In 1833 an Englishman named Francis Place published a treatise on contraception entitled *To the Married of Both Sexes of the Working Class.*[51] To overcome the strain of postponed marriage, Place advocated early marriage and the use of a contraceptive, namely a sponge. Other nineteenth century advocates of birth control suggested coitus interruptus and an astringent douche as effective contraceptives. Whatever the methods advocated, interest in birth control grew during the latter part of the nineteenth century, particularly in western Europe. In 1913 an American, Margaret Sanger, toured western Europe to gather information about contraceptive methods that could be used in the United States. She not only initiated the birth control movement in the United States but also helped start movements in Hawaii, Japan, and China.

Some of the more popular birth control methods today include spermicidal agents, the condom, and the diaphragm; none of these methods is completely reliable, and the diaphragm must be fitted individually by a doctor. The rhythm method (in which the couple refrain from intercourse during the woman's fertile period) requires careful attention to the calendar and is highly unreliable. The various contraceptive pills on the market require strict adherence to instructions, and their effect on women's health is still being debated. The intrauterine device (IUD) requires installation by a doctor, is not totally reliable, and can cause internal bleeding. Surgical sterilization is completely effective, but it is usually irreversible.

In some countries abortion, though prohibited by law, is the only means available to avoid unwanted children. In 1937 a French doctor estimated that there were at least 120 illegal abortions for every 100 live births, and in 1961 the estimates ran to a total of 800,000 abortions—equal to the number of live births—occurring in France each year.[52] In Chile one out of every three pregnancies ends in illegal abortion. In Colombia the need for medical care after illegal abortion constitutes the second largest cause of hospital admissions.[53]

Family Planning in the United States

Up to the present, the major effort to control population in the United States has been through programs of voluntary family planning. Such programs have been effective for the most part, despite the religious views and sometimes the political views of some groups within society.

A family planning program not only helps a couple avoid children they do not want; it also helps them have the children they do want. Such a program normally features qualified medical personnel to recommend and assist with various contraceptive devices. Advice is given with particular concern for the good of the family. What will be best for the health of both mother and child? How many children can the family support? Will there be enough money to educate the children properly when they are grown? This economically oriented approach has proved successful with middle-class American couples.

The most common criticism of family planning is that the number of children a couple want to have is often more than they ought to have. Some observers also feel that not enough people avail themselves of the services, either because they are unaware of the facilities or because family planning takes place in clinics, which tend to frighten people away. Other criticisms are that family planning often deals only with married couples, ignoring pregnancies among unmarried women and girls; that in underdeveloped countries medical personnel are often unavailable to implement the programs; and that the programs' support of the family as a social institution can only encourage increasing birthrates.

Controlling population growth depends on successfully disseminating contraceptive information.

The most decisive statement concerning family planning and population growth in the United States is contained in the report of the U.S. Commission on Population Growth and the American Future. The result of a two-year study, the report offers sweeping recommendations aimed at improving both the quality and quantity of family planning services currently available in the United States. Among the commission's recommendations are:

1. The nation should welcome and plan for a stabilized population.
2. States should make contraceptive services and information available to everyone, including minors; responsible sex education courses should be widely available.
3. All restrictions to voluntary sterilization should be eliminated so the decision can be made solely between patient and doctor.
4. States should liberalize abortion laws along the lines of the New York State statute; all levels of government should provide funds for abortion services; abortion should be included in comprehensive health insurance benefits.[54]

Although there are still many controversies in the courts concerning the availability of contraceptive devices and conditions under which birth control information can be provided to the public, and although Catholic groups and others have been active in efforts to reinstate and maintain laws against abortion, there seems to have been a general realization across the country that legal provision should be made for many of the commission's recommendations. The women's liberation movement has been in the forefront of the fight for more liberalized abortion laws, arguing that a woman should have the right of control over her own body. As noted in Chapter 2, the Supreme Court recently issued a decision that made abortion legal during the first 12 weeks of pregnancy and allowed the state to regulate the provision of abortion only after that period.

Nevertheless, there are people who object to the increasingly visible public programs to limit population as a way of improving the quality of life in the United States. Some black groups, for example, have protested that population control is a program to limit the strength and political power of blacks by controlling their numbers. Throughout the world, whether in advanced or underdeveloped nations, it is the poor who have most of the children. As families ascend the social and economic scale, whether in Japan or Mexico, they tend to have fewer children. And the poor in most countries have neither the knowledge about birth control methods nor the means for implementing them.

As might be expected, countries such as India actively encourage birth control. Family planning clinics have been established in a large number of Indian urban and rural areas, although they are not always effective because of traditional attitudes favoring large families. In some cases, the government has made payments to men who undergo voluntary sterilization after the birth of their second child. Other Asian nations, such as Pakistan and the Republic of Korea, have programs similar to India's. Japan has had an

Worldwide Family Planning

effective birth control program for years, and China, the world's most populous nation, has made considerable progress in population control.

Countries such as Great Britain, Sweden, Finland, and Denmark put great stress on personal welfare and individual choice. In most of these countries contraceptives are readily available, sex education is a regular part of the school curriculum, and abortion is essentially legal.

Most international efforts to control population have been carried out through the United Nations. The UN established its Population Commission in 1946, but it was not until 1962 that the General Assembly recognized that "economic and social development and population policies are closely interrelated."[55] In 1965 the Economic and Social Control (ECOSOC) requested that advisory and training services for population programs be provided to governments that want them. With the creation of the Population Trust Fund in 1967, all UN agencies with a potential role in the solution of population problems were mobilized, including the World Health Organization, UNICEF, the International Labor Organization, and numerous others.

In 1965 the United States Agency for International Development (AID), which is primarily responsible for foreign aid, announced its intention to provide interested governments with assistance in developing family planning programs. Although only $2 million was earmarked for this program, the policy was a radical departure from the government's earlier position that family planning was not a suitable area for government interference. Since then, AID assistance in the field has grown rapidly.[56]

Beyond Planning

Population planner Bernard Berelson has discussed the nature of proposals that go beyond the family planning concept.[57] Some of them involve measures (such as involuntary fertility control) that would be labeled totalitarian by many in the United States. He rates the proposals by several criteria of acceptability. Berelson is not alone in thinking that more efforts than family planning will be needed to solve the world's population problem. Politically, it is difficult to advocate anything more than family planning; yet the very acceptability of the family planning concept, with its voluntary decisions about family size, makes it ineffective for population control. Kingsley Davis has suggested that wide-ranging social and cultural change, involving national population policy rather than national family planning policy, is what is needed. Included among these are measures that would positively sanction small families while negatively sanctioning large ones —equal employment opportunities for women, a requirement of proof of economic viability before a marriage license is granted, and tax incentives.[58]

The population problem is a social problem, but in some countries it is a major political and economic problem as well. In systems where a small business class or a class of large landowners controls the political apparatus or where neocolonial powers are entrenched in the political and economic system, needed social reforms are scarce. And certainly the inequities and insecurities created by unstable economic systems contribute to the ill effects of rapid population growth. In those countries that have not yet attained a reasonable standard of living for the majority, population planning coupled with economic reform is probably the only alternative to revolution.

The scope of the related environmental problems confronting us has been well established. The question is: What can individual citizens do to ease the burden on the environment? Action groups have been formed in many communities to ensure passage of environmental legislation; ecology courses are given at many levels of the education system; and even the regulation of energy consumption, air, oil, and water pollution, and recycling on an individual basis is a beginning. But these and other measures assume a knowledge that the ecosystem is in danger. Certainly not everyone knows or agrees with this. General acceptance that there is a problem, combined with real concern, is essential before society can make a commitment to the costs and efforts of the cleanup ahead. The minority cannot achieve a clean, healthy world; it will take a vast majority of the population to make that world a reality.

Changing Values: Ecology versus GNP

In many ways, the underlying competitive, commercial ethic of the United States hinders the reordering of our national priorities. Although in the past we have worked together as a country to defeat similar problems, we have not yet realized as a nation that we must start to cooperate in the task of cleaning up the environment. During World War II, recycling of goods was necessary and popular. No one thought twice about saving materials, returning bottles for reuse, or rationing gasoline. But now, because the problem either is not recognized or seems too remote to matter, we produce millions of throwaway bottles, cans, and plastic containers and pretend they will just disappear after we have discarded them. Any real change in the situation will have to involve an accompanying change in our values.

It is clear that the value of consumption conflicts in many ways with the goal of a clean and safe environment. Attaining a healthy environment will therefore require modification or replacement of this value. Currently we tend to measure the state of the nation in terms of its output. Gains in the Gross National Product (GNP) are viewed as a sign of social health and prosperity. But a factory that produces ten million dollars worth of paper may also produce tons of waste that enter nearby streams; as the GNP rises through increased production at such factories, so does the waste output. Both economists and sociologists have suggested that we pay less attention to the GNP and more to increases or decreases in real social welfare. A new statistical measure might distinguish between the production of goods and the production of amenities. Thus the small firm that produces a limited output while improving its environment might be rated more highly than one that produces a large volume while it degrades the environment.

There are signs that some change is taking place in values that call for more and more production, to be followed by more and more consumption, in an ever-expanding economy. As this reevaluation takes place, our ability to solve environmental problems will increase.

Waste not, want not? Although environmentally oriented groups have undertaken recycling projects to reduce pollution, such efforts will have small effect until the entire population participates.

Taking Action

To curb its pollution, an industry must either cut back production or incur the increased costs of pollution control devices. This leads to financial problems. How our society's industries can clean themselves up and still remain in operation is a difficult question to answer at this time, although much exploration of alternative measures is currently in progress.

If industries are compelled to spend a large portion of their profit margin in fines, penalties, or taxes because of their pollution, most will find a way to remedy the problem. If laws are strict enough, polluters will have to measure up to the regulations and stop dragging their feet. In the case of automobile manufacturers, the 1970 Clean Air Act made it clear that by the late 1970s auto emissions would have to be cut. This will be achieved with new equipment, modification of the internal combustion engine, and other add-on parts such as the catalytic converter. The consumer, of course, will probably pay the cost of such improvements.

Most of us have trouble understanding a problem until it directly affects us. Air pollution seems to many people just a discomfort, but when the fact was publicized that New York City air was so bad that a resident there, just by standing on a street corner, breathed enough pollutants to equal the harmful effect of smoking two packs of cigarettes a day, people began to understand. Or when a man in Tokyo was able to develop a photograph in the city's river because the water was contaminated with chemical wastes, people again took notice. And when the "energy crisis" hit America in 1973 and people could not buy enough gas to take a short trip, citizens began to feel the effects of our environmental problems firsthand. This growing awareness of society's previous and present disrespect for nature and its resources causes individuals and communities to reorder their priorities for action in the future.

Environmental problems, by their very nature, cannot readily be solved by individual action; they require the concerted action of government intervention. Such intervention has been increasingly frequent, and its effects are beginning to be seen. Recent studies show that the air quality in Los Angeles, New York, Chicago, Pittsburgh, and other cities has improved since the 1960s.[59] The nation's rivers are not receiving as much sewage or as many industrial pollutants as in previous decades, because laws now prohibit this mode of disposal. DDT has been outlawed by Congress, thus halting the deadly cycle that proved fatal to many segments of the ecosphere.

Strip mining is being watched carefully, and in some parts of the country, state governments are ruling against huge mining operations because of the eventual depletion of resources and ruin of the land. Federal measures to regulate strip mining have been caught in the crossfire between business and environmental interests. The Ford administration, claiming that strict laws could reduce coal production anywhere from 48 to 141 million tons a year, made extensive amendments to a bill introduced into the Congress to control strip mining.[60] Finally in 1977, the Surface Mining Control and Reclamation Act was passed requiring the Department of the Interior to establish uniform environment standards for strip-mining, but as late as 1979 the Carter administration has delayed the enactment of these statutes at the request of industry.[61]

New laws and regulations, such as the 1970 Clean Air Act and 1972 Water Quality Act, are steps toward a solution. Effectively policing these laws is difficult, but the EPA is committed to settling disputes and ensuring that the laws are enforced. Nonetheless, problems of conflicting priorities still rise. When Detroit auto makers appealed for a one-year extension on meeting the law for auto emissions, the EPA was forced to grant it because of the prospect of unemployment in Detroit; economic needs seemed more immediate than environmental ones in this case. A difficult choice had to be made—the sacrifice of a thousand jobs (or so the auto industry claimed) or continued harmful pollution. The decision was made on a short-term basis, as is often the case. This kind of issue-ducking and law reversal does not bode well for the long-term prospects for the environment; and even though there are numerous laws on the books, environmentalists continue to worry because these laws are so often disregarded, flagrantly violated, or simply rewritten to suit the economic producers in the country.

Government Steps In

The problem is not confined to our country alone. In the past several years the United Nations has become increasingly concerned with the fate of the environment. A UN conference held in Sweden in 1972 laid some groundwork for international cooperation on ecology. The United States and Canada have committed themselves to cleaning up the Great Lakes, and the Soviet Union and the United States are planning to trade vital information on controlling pollution of all kinds. Scientists are making progress in the battle against pollution, but the various governments and their constituents must be knowledgeable and willing to follow their lead.

Summary

To comprehend the worldwide problems posed by population growth, it is necessary to study the intimate relationship between sophisticated ways of counting people, cultural and behavioral patterns in the societies of the world, and analyses of the limits and stratification of the world's natural resources. Many countries with underdeveloped economies and high birthrates desire economic development while discounting the relevance of population control. Alternatively, industrial nations are beginning to balk at the specter of further economic development and espouse population control as the most desirable solution.

Demography, the science of counting people, involves a study of the processes that cause changes in a given population: fertility, mortality, and migration. The study of fertility involves analysis of social practices, attitudes, and values, as well as biological capacities for childbearing. The study of mortality involves a knowledge of public health facilities, sanitation conditions, housing, nutrition, and medical care in a given area. Migration is the study of population movements.

Technological advances give people greater control over their physical environment. This control permits sharp increases in population size and density. In developed countries, however, advanced birth control methods and a socially conditioned preference for smaller families have led to declines in population growth rates. In underdeveloped countries, on the other hand, technology has cut mortality rates, but customs and ignorance have kept birthrates high. This combination has led to young populations with high growth rates in countries that can least afford rapid growth.

Expanding populations increase demands on food, energy, and mineral resources. Some advanced nations maintain their populations in line with domestic food production. Others depend on food imports to meet their needs. In underdeveloped countries, however, malnutrition is prevalent; agriculture is typically at the subsistence level, and these nations are too poor to import needed supplies. While the population explosion continues in the underdeveloped world, the developed countries demand more and more of the world's resources to keep their own high standard of living.

In our pursuit of these needed resources, society has carelessly abused the environment. As a consequence of this action, America now faces severe environmental problems, four of the major ones being the depletion of scarce natural resources and air, water, and land pollution.

All our development has been based on the free availability of resources, but these resources—oil, for instance—are now running out, and they are not renewable. The environmental risks of drilling for offshore oil or importing it by tanker from the Middle East or by pipeline from Alaska are great. Yet to cut back on consumption means, among other things, doing without the transportation systems that depend on fossil fuels.

Air pollution—the product of chemical emissions from automobiles and industries—damages crops, destroys property, and is hazardous to human health. Control devices that limit automobile emissions and the use of higher-grade coal for industrial production may reduce air pollution; but the price of such devices will inevitably be passed on to the consumer, and high-grade coal can be obtained only by the destructive technique of strip-mining. Any solution will cost a great deal of money; yet the social costs are so high that some move to clean up the air must be made.

Water is essential for human and plant life. Supplies of pure water for the large American population are endangered by pollutants dumped into the nation's rivers and lakes. Industrial pollution and human waste also kill aquatic life and thus throw a major portion of the ecosystem out of balance. Although laws for preventing water pollution have been in force since 1899, the government has tended to be indulgent when industrial polluters important to the economic life of the nation are involved. Small fines are levied only after tortuous litigation, and the companies meanwhile continue polluting. Even the oceans have been affected by waste dumped into them from ships, by oil spills, and the like.

Land pollution takes many forms, from the destruction of forests and strip-mining to the litter and trash that disfigure the landscape. Chemical fertilizers, while they increase crop yields, lower the capacity of the land to replenish its own natural elements. Pesticides kill insects but also build up to toxic levels in the tissues of other forms of life. Despite the amount of land set aside for national parks, the recreational, food, and production needs of our growing population continue to put pressure on available land.

A major problem in population control is making the knowledge and means of birth control available. Family planning programs sponsored by national governments and by international agencies are operating today around the world. These programs are much more successful in countries where the social preference is for small families than in countries where religious and social norms encourage large families.

Most of the programs have been operated on a voluntary basis. Some commentators on the issues, however, view population control as so vital that they have proposed programs which limit birth by law, by enforced sterilization, and so on. At present, the social and political implications of these plans have made them unacceptable. Neither control of population growth worldwide nor control of the strain it places on the world's resources has yet been achieved.

To combat environmental problems, there must first be public acceptance that they exist. Growth and increased consumption are currently primary social values. Ecology requires that they be replaced by values emphasizing greater regard for public, rather than individual, welfare. Legal changes embodying these revised values have begun to be implemented, as has government regulation of industry in areas relating to environmental pollution, although the necessity for safeguarding the economy has prevented rapid progress.

Notes

[1] UN Statistical Office, *Demographic Yearbook, 1976* (New York: United Nations, 1977), p. 115.

[2] United Nations, *World Population Prospects, 1970–2000, as Assessed in 1973* (New York: United Nations, 10 March 1975).

[3] Kingsley Davis and Judith Blake, "Social Structure and Fertility: An Analytic Framework," *Economic Development and Cultural Change*, vol. 1, ed. Bert F. Hoselitz (Chicago: University of Chicago Press, 1952), pp. 211–235.

[4] Dennis H. Wrong, *Population and Society*, 3rd ed. (New York: Random House, 1967), p. 73.

[5] Quentin H. Stanford, ed., *The World's Population* (New York: Oxford University Press, 1972), pp. 7–8.

[6] Ibid., pp. 8–13.

[7] United Nations, *World Population Prospects*, p. 12.

[8] V. Gordon Childe, *Man Makes Himself* (New York: New American Library, Mentor Books, 1951), p. 19.

[9] United Nations, "Factors Affecting Fertility," *The World's Population*, ed. Quentin H. Stanford, p. 110.

[10] Philip M. Hauser, ed., *The Population Dilemma*, 2d ed. (Englewood Cliffs, N.J.: Prentice-Hall, 1969), p. 16.

[11] Kingsley Davis, "The World's Population Crisis," *Contemporary Social Problems*, 4th ed., ed. Robert K. Merton and Robert Nisbet (New York: Harcourt, 1976), p. 272.

[12] Kingsley Davis, "The World's Population Crisis," *Contemporary Social Problems*, 2d ed., ed. Robert K. Merton and Robert Nisbet (New York: Harcourt, 1966), p. 382.

[13] George E. Delury, ed., *The World Almanac and Book of Facts* (New York: Newspaper Enterprise Association, Inc., 1978), p. 205.

[14] U.S. Bureau of the Census, *Statistical Abstract of the United States, 1977* (Washington, D.C.: Government Printing Office, 1977), p. 26.

[15] UN Statistical Office, *Demographic Yearbook* (New York: United Nations, 1976), p. 115.

[16] Ibid., p. 123.

[17] Alfred Sauvy, "Population Problems in Europe and the Soviet Union," *International Aspects of Overpopulation*, ed. John Barratt and Michael Louw (London: Macmillan, 1972), pp. 185–193.

[18] Kingsley Davis, "Fertility and Mortality in the Developed and Underdeveloped Countries," *World's Population*, p. 58.

[19] L. Jay Atkinson, *World Population Growth: Analysis and New Projections of the United Nations*, Economic Research Service, U.S. Department of Agriculture, Foreign Agricultural Economic Report No. 129 (February 1977), pp. 4–6.

[20] UN Statistical Office, *Demographic Yearbook, 1976*, pp. 115–120.

[21] Robert C. Cook, "World Population Projects 1965–2000," *World's Population*, ed. Quentin H. Stanford, pp. 24–31.

[22] UN Statistical Office, *Demographic Yearbook, 1976*, pp. 115–120.

[23] Thomas Robert Malthus, *Population: The First Essay*, paperback ed. (Ann Arbor: University of Michigan Press, 1959), p. 8.

[24] José Hernandez, *People, Power, and Policy* (Palo Alto, Calif.: National Press Books, 1975), p. 153.

[25] Ibid., p. 154.

[26] Garrett Hardin, "Gregg's Law," *BioScience* 25 (July 1975), p. 415.

[27] Davis, "World's Population Crisis," *Contemporary Social Problems*, 4th ed., pp. 273–280.

[28] Ibid., pp. 292–302.

[29] "Club of Rome Revisited," *Time*, 26 April 1976, p. 56.

[30]Ibid.

[31]Ernest Mandel, *An Introduction to Marxist Economic Theory* (New York: Pathfinder Press, 1971), p. 51.

[32]Richard P. Appelbaum, "Marx's Theory of the Falling Rate of Profit," *American Sociological Review* 43 (February 1978), p. 67.

[33]Hernandez, *People, Power, and Policy,* p. 161.

[34]U.S. Commission on Population Growth and the American Future, *Population and the American Future* (Washington, D.C.: Government Printing Office, 1972), p. 28.

[35]"Oil Problem: How to Cut Consumption and Inflation," *New York Times,* 7 January 1979, sec. 12, p. 43.

[36]Ibid., p. 43.

[37]Brubaker, *To Live on Earth,* p. 153.

[38]"How Safe Is Nuclear Power?" *Newsweek,* 12 April 1976, pp. 70–75.

[39]Ibid., p. 73.

[40]U.S. Environmental Protection Agency, *Control of Environmental Impacts from Advanced Energy Sources* (Washington, D.C.: Government Printing Office, 1974), p. 14.

[41]Ibid.

[42]Kenneth Auchincloss, "The Ravaged Environment," *Newsweek,* 26 January 1970, pp. 30–32.

[43]Sterling Brubaker, *To Live on Earth* (New York: New American Library, 1972), p. 153.

[44]James Rathlesberger, ed., *Nixon and the Environment* (New York: Village Voice, 1972).

[45]U.S. Council on Environmental Quality, *Environmental Quality: The Third Annual Report of the Council on Environmental Quality* (Washington, D.C.: Government Printing Office, August 1972).

[46]David Zwick and Marcy Benstock, *Water Wasteland* (New York: Grossman Publishers, 1971), p. 32.

[47]U.S. Council on Environmental Quality, *Environmental Quality,* p. 119.

[48]Barry Commoner, *The Closing Circle* (New York: Knopf, 1972), p. 128.

[49]Zwick and Benstock, *Water Wasteland,* p. 395.

[50]Paul R. Ehrlich and Anne H. Ehrlich, *Population Resources, Environment* (San Francisco: Freeman, 1970).

[51]Garratt Hardin, *Population, Evolution and Birth Control* (San Francisco: Freeman, 1969), pp. 197–199.

[52]Tadd Fischer, *Our Overcrowded World* (New York: Parent Magazine Press, 1969), p. 72.

[53]Ibid., p. 169.

[54]U.S. Commission on Population Growth and the American Future, *Population and the American Future,* pp. 168–171, 177, 191.

[55]Philander P. Claxton, Jr., "The Development of Institutions to Meet the World Population Crisis," *U. S. Department of State Bulletin,* 16 August 1971, p. 169.

[56]Clyde Sanger, "Family Planning in Columbia: A Case Study," *The World's Population,* ed. Quentin H. Stanford, p. 231.

[57]Bernard Berelson, "Beyond Family Planning," *Ekistics* 27 (May 1969), 288–291.

[58]Davis, "World's Population Crisis," *Contemporary Social Problems,* 4th ed., pp. 299–300.

[59]Lawrence G. Hines, *Environmental Issues* (New York: Norton, 1973), p. 278.

[60]Eliot Marshall, "Ford's Rewrite of the Scuttled Coal Bill," *New Republic,* 8 March 1975, pp. 8–10.

[61]"Curbs on Strip Mining Put Off After Industry Enlists Aides to Carter," *New York Times,* 7 January 1979, p. 1.

Problems of Deviant Behavior

Social norms are created over a period of time through the interaction of individuals and collectivities. When a norm is well established with a society it acts as a guide for individual conduct, prescribing appropriate forms of behavior and proscribing other forms considered inappropriate. A certain amount of nonconformity to normative standards is usually tolerated by most members of a society. Persons may drink to excess on occasion or violate norms concerning extramarital sexual relations without having their behavior defined as deviant. However, more serious violations—those that offend cherished values or break important social rules—are considered by most people to be deviant behavior and to represent a problem for the larger society.

Older views interpreting such deviations as the result of individual defects or inadequacies have now largely been rejected by sociologists. One current sociological theory proposes that factors such as social change and restricted social opportunities weaken the influence of normative standards on the behavior of some individuals. When standards of expected conduct are not strong enough to regulate individual behavior effectively, there is an increased likelihood that persons who find themselves in situations of stress will engage in rule-breaking activities, or deviant behavior.

Some forms of conduct defined as deviant have also been interpreted as the result of social conflict. Many normative standards are not consensual products of all members of society. Various groups within the society have different values and interests, but those with the greatest social power have a disproportionate ability to incorporate their own values and interests into the standards that define acceptable versus deviant behavior. For example, marijuana and other drugs preferred by youth and other relatively powerless groups are subject to strong legal sanctions, but alcohol, the preference of many middle-class adults, is not. Indeed, behavior considered deviant may merely be behavior that conflicts with the values of the dominant groups. From this social conflict perspective, it appears that the problem lies in certain of the rules themselves more than in the fact that some people at some times fail to follow the rules.

Recent developments in deviance theory emphasize the notion that acts are not inherently deviant; deviance is a social product intimately tied up with processes of social interaction, subjective assessments of particular acts, and the situation in which those acts occur. The act of taking another's life, for example, is generally considered abhorrent. Still, during wartime this same act may be expected conduct and may even be considered heroic. The behavior of a man screaming hysterically outside his home may appear deviant and be taken as indicative of mental illness, but this same behavior is likely to be viewed differently if it is learned that a tragedy has just occurred. This interpretation, known as the labeling or social reaction perspective, holds that since public responses to deviance are centrally important phenomena, deviance must be analyzed from the point of view of those who define and react to various behaviors as deviant.

On the basis of their objectionable behavior, individuals are defined and typed as being deviant not only in specific ways but in their general character as well. They are treated in special ways by others during social encounters—with contempt, avoidance, ostracism, or hostility. Moreover, they tend to be excluded from certain social roles (for example, persons defined as mentally ill may be excluded from many responsible occupational roles). As a consequence of having been assigned a deviant social identity, an individual is likely to develop a deviant self-concept. Subsequently, the individual will begin to behave in accord with this emerging and deviant definition of self.

The processes described here are operable in a number of areas of human interaction in defining behavior as deviant and people as deviates. In this section of the book we shall examine a number of behaviors typically thought of as deviant.

Mental Illness

12

In spite of sustained research in both the physical and social sciences, mental illness remains an incompletely understood phenomenon. In the traditional medical approach to understanding mental disorders, attention is focused on factors within the individual that are believed to result in such illness, in much the same way that a virus or bacteria is sought as the cause of a physical ailment. Behavioral abnormalities are viewed as symptoms of an underlying disorder within the individual personality, perhaps traceable to genetic or biological factors, or even to childhood experiences. Critics of this medical model argue that it fails to take into account social and situational factors that are related to the development of mental disorders.

Recently some theorists have formulated an alternative perspective that interprets mental illness as a form of social deviance. Emphasis is placed on the role of social processes in the emergence and stabilization of behavior patterns that are socially defined as indicative of mental illness. Any behavior that violates the routine expectations of others may be labeled deviant, and the person engaging in that behavior may be treated as being "different" from others in some important way. Social deviance, then, is a product not only of the nature of a particular behavior but also of how other people define and react to that behavior. For example, in some social contexts, marijuana smoking may be treated as an instance of deviant behavior (or even as an indication of mental illness), whereas in other contexts it is treated as normal and acceptable behavior. The crucial point in this approach is that the application of a deviant label such as "mentally ill" and the differential social treatment that typically follows such labeling is very likely to have significant consequences for the future behavior of the individual thus labeled.

From a sociological viewpoint, the interest is not so much in the original causes of episodes of abnormal behavior as in the social processes that result when the person who has engaged in such behavior is defined by others as mentally ill. The processes of labeling and differential treatment may set off a chain of events by which the episodes of aberrant behavior become stabilized or amplified. In other words, the acquisition of deviant status may function to shape an individual's life-style and interaction with others to the extent of an entire career of deviance. Underlying this approach is the theory that an individual's self-appraisal is a reflection of how that person is viewed by others. When someone is consistently and widely defined as mentally ill, this labeling may have "so overwhelming an impact that the deviating individual may find himself unable to sustain any alternative definition of himself."[1] An individual's acceptance of the label of mentally ill frequently results in behavior more and more like that expected of mentally ill persons in general.

There is a universal human tendency to classify and categorize objects in the environment, out of which arise both the general process of social typing and the application of particular deviant labels to others. Categorization of others serves the very important purpose of rendering social interaction predictable, of simplifying and organizing huge volumes of information pertaining to others. Instead of having to assess the unique qualities and characteristics of others, people can treat each new individual they confront as an instance of a more general type of person. Both expectations of how others will act and behavior toward others are structured and shaped by this process of social typing. Deviant categories tend to dominate all other categories of which a person is a member. That is, people who are typed as mentally ill will be treated by others as if this were their most important characteristic.

The reactions of others to persons with mental disorders—in the form of fear, avoidance, and rejection—are as important to a sociological understanding of mental illness as are the original causes of the abnormal behavior. Being labeled mentally ill in our society carries with it a powerful and enduring social stigma. The stigma of mental illness frequently prevents an individual from securing employment and participating in other aspects of community life. Relations with friends, relatives, and others may be impaired, and family life may be temporarily or permanently disrupted. Indeed, it is this breaking of normal or routine patterns of interaction coupled with the social and economic liabilities incurred by persons who are viewed as mentally ill that constitute the basis for treating it as a social problem.

Definitions of Mental Illness

Definitions of mental illness vary according to their orientation and frame of reference. Before considering the ways in which they differ, it is worth noting that they do share a common viewpoint: all characterize the problem in relative rather than absolute terms, and none can define in any absolute sense the difference between a "sick" and a "normal" person.

Clinical Definition

Because the mentally ill are often treated by physicians, it is not surprising that one of the earliest clinical or pathological definitions grew out of the medical tradition. According to the medical model, mental disorders involve aberrant behaviors that result from a diseased or disordered state within the individual. This state is evidenced and diagnosed on the basis of "symptoms" observed in a clinical setting—such as the twitching of facial muscles or perhaps the confused use of language.

Although the clinical definition relies on objective observation, it is not entirely free of social judgments. Two observers might concur on the existence of a facial twitch; but, given different backgrounds, they might meaningfully disagree on what constitutes confused language or inappropriate laughter.

Statistical Definition

A second definition, along statistical lines, is purely descriptive and devoid of social judgment. In this approach, whatever strays far from the normal is, quite simply, abnormal. The definition is based on the bell-shaped curve of normal distribution, which graphically portrays the relative frequency of a given trait in the general population. The traits of most people tend to cluster around the high middle of the curve, and the statistical viewpoint maintains that these are in the majority and can therefore be considered average or normal. Traits outside the average or normal range are considered statistically deviant.

There are several difficulties in using the statistical approach to define mental illness. First, it is more dependable when simple, tangible traits (such as age, sex, height, and weight) are described than when psychological factors are assessed. After all, it is more difficult to measure intelligence, aggressiveness, or jealousy. Second, the definition is not applicable to a large number of traits and behaviors, for we have come to accept statistical divergencies without question. We do not conclude that people who are left-handed are abnormal or mentally ill just because the average person is right-handed. Third, that which is most frequent is not necessarily most "normal." If practically everyone in our society were to come down with the measles, we would not rush to the conclusion that this is a normal state of affairs.

Social Definition

The social definition of mental illness is based not on the actual frequency of occurrence of traits or behaviors within the general population but rather on the behavioral norms that a society approves and upholds. Thus many behaviors and attitudes that are not generally approved by the members of society, and over which the individual apparently has little or no control, are considered manifestations of abnormality or mental illness. Although this is the most arbitrary of definitions, it is not applied to the same extent as in the past. Today, for example, we do not resort to burning witches at the stake. Nevertheless, we do still use this definition; we do not hesitate to say that any parent who repeatedly beats a child is abnormal or sick, for we think child beating indicates inability to control aggressive impulses. There are many such behaviors that people in American society implicitly agree are abnormal as well as some that are more controversial.

Practical Definition

Still another definition of mental illness derives from purely practical criteria: Can the person function at home or on a job? A person who cannot function is more likely to be labeled mentally ill than one who displays many of the same symptoms but has nonetheless managed to maintain a position in society. People who behave strangely, talking to themselves or to passersby in public, are apt to be called "crazy," especially if they are unemployed, without means, and alone. But if such an individual happens to be an artist or scientist, with a regular income and a respectable social position, that individual may well be thought a genius.

Mental Health— What Is It?

All definitions of mental illness presuppose some understanding of positive mental health. However, there is no generally accepted definition of what constitutes good mental health. Many of the theories on mental health that have emerged over the years suffer from an overdependence on specific cultures or periods and are therefore limited in their validity.

One useful definition, developed in the early 1950s by A. H. Maslow and B. Mittlemann, postulated ten criteria for a personality possessed of mental health. The Maslow-Mittlemann list was subsequently modified by other authorities, but its basic tenets still suggest the consensus on mental normalcy: (1) an adequate feeling of security, (2) a realistic self-evaluation, (3) attainable life goals based on realistic self-evaluation, (4) adequate contact with the everyday world of reality, (5) self-consistency, (6) the ability to profit from experience, (7) a judicious degree of spontaneity, (8) emotionality appropriate to the occasion, (9) a judicious balance between in-group cooperativeness and maintenance of individuality, and (10) appropriate physical desires gratified in appropriate ways.[2] Of course, not all these qualities are present to an equal degree in all mentally healthy persons at all times. It is the general profile that has practical significance.

Another useful definition of mental health that preceded the one offered by Maslow and Mittlemann was proposed by a commission of the 1948 International Congress on Mental Health. This commission defined mental health as a quality that operates at both the individual and societal levels:

1. Mental health is a condition which permits the optimal development, physical, intellectual and emotional, of the individual, so far as this is compatible with that of other individuals.
2. A good society is one that allows this development to its members while at the same time ensuring its own development and being tolerant toward other societies.[3]

As common as any of these definitions is the notion that mental health is equivalent to happiness. Even if this were so, it would not be helpful from the standpoint of definition, for happiness, like mental health, is a quality often conspicuous by its absence. Probably happiness on a long-range basis is not possible without mental health, but mental health can certainly exist separately from feelings of happiness.

Types of Disorders

For more than 4000 years, we have been observing and classifying disturbed behaviors and attitudes that have come to be called mental illness. Not surprisingly, the disturbances that accompany the aging process were among the first to be noted, as were alcoholic disorders. The ancient Greeks studied and described a number of physical ailments that seemed to spring from mental disturbances. Their descriptions, though somewhat simplistic, helped to lay the ground for the medical orientation toward mental illness that predominated for many centuries.

In some periods, for example in the Middle Ages, the medical model was supplanted by a belief in supernatural causes. The disturbed person was thought to be obsessed by an external devil or possessed by one within and was regarded less as a patient than as a sinner. Progress to a more scientific consideration of mental illness occurred during the eighteenth and nine-

Popularly known as Bedlam, the Bethlem Royal Hospital in England is one of the oldest institutions in Europe for the care of the mentally ill. This eighteenth century engraving by Hogarth pictures Bedlam some three centuries after its founding.

teenth centuries, when asylums first brought large numbers of the mentally ill under the systematic observation of doctors.[4] From the 1840s on, under the early leadership of Dorothea Dix, Americans began to build asylums to care for the mentally ill. In France, Philippe Pinel initiated the practice of taking case histories and keeping records on patients. He formulated a simple classification system on the basis of his observations. Similar work was undertaken in the United States by Benjamin Rush, "Father of American Psychiatry" and author of this country's first treatise on mental illness.

With the advent of the first psychological laboratory in Leipzig, Germany took the lead in psychiatric and psychological inquiry. Emil Kraepelin, the man responsible for the first modern classification system, emerged out of this background in the second half of the nineteenth century. His work, like Pinel's, was based on studies of the people housed in asylums. A major contribution was his observation that the symptoms of the mentally disturbed usually form clusters, or syndromes. He regarded these as symptomatic of specific mental conditions, and on this basis he worked out the first modern classification. With the development of more sophisticated research and clinical techniques, further refinements in diagnosis became possible.

The first statistically based nomenclature was set up in 1917 by the organization that subsequently became the American Psychiatric Association. Naturally, the nomenclature has been periodically revised in accordance with new research. Some of the most important categories will be briefly described here.[5] It should be kept in mind, however, that this classification derives from a psychiatric perspective of mental disorders. These categories are not universally accepted as valid by social scientists, who often employ alternative perspectives.

Psychoses

The most debilitating of the mental disorders are the psychoses, including schizophrenia, paranoid psychoses, manic-depressive psychoses, involutional melancholia, and a number of related disorders. All are characterized by unusual behavior, gross distortion of reality, and an inability to function adequately either all or part of the time. Psychotic patients are more likely than others to be institutionalized. Usually they are committed because they threaten harm to themselves or others, because they are unable or unwilling to attend to their basic needs, or because their behaviors have become intolerable to family and friends. If they are afraid of self-destruction, they may admit themselves voluntarily. It is not unusual for patients who are diagnosed as psychotic—particularly if they are old or impoverished—to be permanently institutionalized. Nevertheless, it is estimated that at any given time there are as many psychotics in the community at large as in the institutionalized population.[6]

Among the psychoses, a further distinction is drawn between organic brain syndromes and functional psychoses. The former have clearly defined organic causes such as a specific malfunction or structural change in the nervous system stemming from a brain tumor or a mechanical injury. Mental disorders associated with old age, such as senile dementia or psychosis with cerebral arteriosclerosis, typically have an organic basis. The functional psychoses, on the other hand, do not originate in neurological impairment; rather, they are believed to be psychological in origin and related to personality conflicts or environmental stress. In Western culture, the functional psychoses are far more prevalent, and the bulk of research and therapeutic efforts focus on these disorders.

Schizophrenia. The most prevalent of the psychoses, schizophrenia accounts for more than 50 percent of all chronic mental hospital cases. Its principal symptoms include delusions, hallucinations (especially "inner voices"), bizarre responses, and withdrawal from personal relationships. Schizophrenics often have only limited understanding of their own behavior, but during periods of lucidity they may appear perceptive and normally intelligent.

Persons experiencing symptoms of schizophrenia find the real world too painful and so proceed to develop a variety of delusions about it; gradually, they construct an "unreal" self to deal with others. If elements of paranoia are present, they may believe that hostile forces influence external occurrences, such as the weather, political events, or the deaths of famous people. Despite episodes of seemingly bizarre behavior, the actions of an individual suffering from schizophrenia are frequently understandable in rational terms. It is not difficult, for example, to understand why an institutionalized patient who receives no letters or visits from a family that professes to love him may accuse the nurses of an elaborate plot to steal his mail and refuse entrance to his visitors.

Inasmuch as schizophrenic behavior appears to be a rational attempt to escape an unbearable family or social environment, there is much to be gained from a psychological-sociological approach to studying it that concentrates on the environment, its meaning to the patient, and its effect in precipitating and sustaining the illness. For example, studies have noted the presence of distinctive interaction characteristics in families with schizophrenic members.[7] Children who are socialized in these families appear to have a greater likelihood of experiencing mental disorders than children in "normal" families.

Catatonic schizophrenics are characterized by drastic changes in attitude and mood, ranging from frenzied violence to mute rigidity.

Although the transmission of schizophrenia through the family is a complex and incompletely understood phenomenon, several general findings have emerged. The family milieu tends to be filled with inconsistencies, contradictory meanings, and factual distortions. Verbal communication of the parents to the child tends to conflict radically with concrete parental behavior. Such interaction patterns, whereby the child is continually subjected to conflicting messages or demands on different levels, are referred to as double bind situations:

The child, in seeking to gain approval or to avoid punishment, is damned if he does and damned if he doesn't—and is cognitively and emotionally torn apart by the conflicting messages. Sometimes one parent sets the bind and in other situations the child cannot meet the conflicting and irreconcilable demands and needs of the two parents.[8]

The result of these family patterns is that the child is taught distorted meanings and forms of reasoning and may subsequently encounter great difficulty in developing a stable identity, self-reliance, and an adequate conception of appropriate role behavior.

The problem of schizophrenia has also been investigated from a biological perspective. Studies of identical twins have attempted to separate genetic and environmental factors and, simultaneously, to trace their interdependence.[9] Biochemical work has concentrated on abnormalities of neuroregulatory agents and blood proteins, with inquiry into the related role of diet and nutrition; for example, the deficiency or malabsorption of vitamin B_{12} is a possible causative factor.[10] A research group recently isolated an enzyme, monoamine oxidase, that is a possible indicator of vulnerability to schizophrenia.[11] Although findings in this area are not yet definitive, there is some evidence that genetic vulnerability is involved in schizophrenia. That is not to say that heredity is a direct cause of this disorder but rather that individuals with a certain genetic makeup are more likely to display schizophrenic symptoms under conditions of environmental stress, family problems, or other situational factors.

Paranoia.   In paranoid reactions, the dominant diagnostic feature is suspicion, and the degree varies in accordance with the extent of personality disorganization. This disorganization is mild to moderate in paranoia and the paranoid states, but it is severe in paranoid schizophrenia. Central to paranoid reactions is an internally consistent system of delusions based on feelings of persecution or grandiosity. No hallucinations or impairment of intelligence are involved.

No definite cause has been established for paranoid reactions, although a number of theories attempt to explain their dynamics.[12] Freud's formulation, for instance, postulates a defense mechanism—projection—that is present in all individuals but excessively so in neurotics and psychotics. Traits unacceptable in oneself are projected onto another person or persons.

A sociologically more significant theory argues that the individual's suspiciousness may be a realistic, rather than delusional, response to a situation that is itself misunderstood by the patient.[13] Suppose, for example, that members of the disturbed person's family have noticed increasing oddities of behavior. Their reaction is to accelerate their watchfulness. They may compare observations among themselves and fall silent whenever that individual appears. The disturbed person, unaware of the family's concern, notices only the secret watching and the furtive conversations, and, based on these correct observations, makes the incorrect but logical assumption that he or she is the victim of a conspiracy. This formulation calls for the investigation of the paranoid reaction as a function of the environment in which it occurs. Significant in terms of this theory is the fact that paranoid patients often come from changing inner-city neighborhoods that offer much material for paranoid delusion.

Manic Depression and Involutional Melancholia. In addition to schizophrenia and paranoid reactions, two other disorders are classified as functional psychoses. Both involve excessive or inappropriate affective states, in the direction of either depression or excitement and elation.

Manic-depressive psychosis is the diagnosis given by psychiatrists where states of high excitement and elation alternate with severe depression and melancholia. The illness is characterized by rapid mood swings of sudden onset and equally sudden disappearance. It tends to recur at intervals, sometimes as long as several years, and approximately five people per thousand are affected. Patients, most of them in their middle years, may exhibit either depressive or manic (elated) reactions, with some manifesting both stages on a cyclical basis.

Involutional melancholia is characterized by a constant state of depression in the patient. It almost always appears during or after middle age and without previous history of depression or violent mood alterations. This diagnosis is applied more often to women, especially to those who are near menopause. Since the symptoms of this disorder overlap with those of depressive reactions in manic-depressive psychosis, physicians often apply differing diagnoses to the same set of symptoms. Because of the complexity and ambiguity of many of the symptoms of the functional psychoses, the diagnosis often depends as much on the doctor as on the symptoms.

Neuroses

In contrast to the psychoses, neurotic disorders do not entail the same high degree of impaired functioning of the individual. The neurotic person is in touch with reality but may experience such high levels of anxiety and emotional discomfort that normal interaction, family life, and occupational performance are disrupted. Although there are many differing manifestations of neurosis, common to most of them are inflexibility, anxiety over change (no matter how small), and unrealistically high or low aspirations, with consequent discrepancy between the neurotic's self-image and actual role in the world. When anxieties become too great, the neurotic may have a so-called nervous breakdown and require hospitalization.

It is now generally believed that neuroses are related to a person's efforts to cope with anxiety, and the kinds of symptoms exhibited depend largely on the manner in which the individual deals with it. Neurotic symptoms may take the form of specific fears, unreasonable ideas, compulsive behavior, or hysteria. The behavioral manifestations may be similar to those of psychotic disorders but in a less extreme and narrower form.

On the other hand, the anxiety that all of us experience at one time or another may reach a level where it produces headaches, loss of appetite, hypertension, or other physiological symptoms. The body responds to stressful mental states in many ways, and in recent years the number of physiological disorders labeled psychosomatic—related to mental distress—has been steadily growing. Current research suggests that the development of psychosomatic disease may be more complex than formerly believed. It now appears that widely differing conditions, from viral infections to stomach ulcers, may be at least partly due to the interaction of early life experience and current environmental stress.[14]

Stress may act nonspecifically and may lead to widely differing pathological results. As early as 1947, Margaret Mead stated her conviction that culture is a vital component in the development of sickness. The disease-producing responses of individuals are not separable from the stresses to which society subjects them.[15]

The Prevalence of Mental Illness in the United States

Until fairly recently the extent of mental illness was extremely difficult to determine with any accuracy because of the imprecision of definitions and the confusion in nomenclature and classification. Beginning in the 1950s, a number of studies were undertaken to provide more dependable estimates of the relative prevalence of various debilitating mental conditions. One such study was Benjamin Pasamanick's 1961 survey of mental disorders in the population of Baltimore, Maryland, which was later applied to American urban populations in general.[16]

Rates of Affliction

Pasamanick's study confirmed some figures suggested by earlier surveys. Considering all forms of mental disturbance together, it appears that approximately 12.5 percent (one of every eight persons) of the total urban population of the United States suffer from some form of mental or emotional affliction. The affliction rate among the rural population is believed to be slightly lower. Of this total, between 7 and 8 percent are acutely psychotic, and over 75 percent are neurotic. On the basis of these data, Pasamanick has concluded that "the group of diseases under the heading of psychiatric disorders is probably as frequent and far more disabling and costly than any other comparable group of diseases."[17]

Another study, the results of which are illustrated in Figure 12.1, lends further support to this conclusion. In a survey of 1660 people chosen to represent the residents of midtown Manhattan, a team of researchers concluded that 23.4 percent were impaired in psychological functioning, ranging from those whose symptoms were not severe but interfered in their life adjustment to those whose symptoms were incapacitating.[18] Another 58.1 percent exhibited mild to moderate symptom formation but with no apparent interference in life adjustment. Only 18.5 percent of the sample showed no significant symptom formation.

Two key concepts in the study of disease, whether mental or physical,

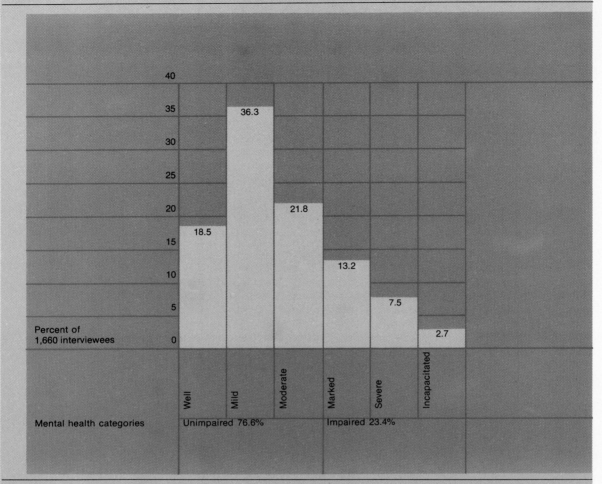

Figure 12.1   Prevalence of Psychological Inpairment, Midtown Manhattan Study

Source: Data from Leo Srole et al. *Mental Health in the Metropolis The Midtown Manhattan Study* (New York: New York University Press, 1978, p. 197.

are prevalence and incidence. Prevalence denotes the percentage of cases of an illness existing within a population at a given point in time. Incidence refers to the proportion of new cases that occur within a population during a given period. Thus, prevalence indicates how widespread the problem is, and incidence reveals how quickly the problem is growing or disappearing. After estimates on prevalence and incidence are established, the figures are broken down in terms of several variables in order to make them more meaningful. In research on mental illness, the most important variables have been found to be social class, occupation, age, sex, race, and ethnic background.

Recent studies have been undertaken jointly by sociologists and psychiatrists to determine the prevalence of certain mental illnesses in various socioeconomic classes and in different settings (such as hospitals, outpatient facilities, and private facilities). These studies have demonstrated a clear relationship between type of illness and socioeconomic status as well as between social status and form of treatment administered.[19]

Socioeconomic Status.   Schizophrenia was found to be more prevalent in the lowest socioeconomic groups. Treatment for all types of mental illness in these groups was usually administered in a hospital or clinic setting, often utilizing electroshock or chemotherapy (the least costly and most easily administered forms of treatment). Patients of higher socioeconomic standing were much more likely to be treated privately with some form of supportive or reconstructive psychotherapy. The outlook of the patient and the patient's family for eventual recovery differed markedly from class to class, with disadvantaged patients displaying far more pessimism and negativism toward psychiatric intervention than those who were more affluent.[20]

One of the earliest and most significant studies was made by A. B. Hollingshead and F. C. Redlich in New Haven, Connecticut, in 1950 and 1951.[21] The investigators considered all persons receiving any type of psychiatric treatment during a five-month period. They divided this population into five social classes: Class I, the community's business and professional leaders; Class II, the managerial people; Class III, those in administrative or clerical jobs; Class IV, members of the skilled working class; Class V, semiskilled and unskilled laborers with no more than an elementary school education.

The results indicated a higher prevalence of psychoses, especially schizophrenia, in Classes IV and V, whereas the prevalence of neuroses was greatest in Class I. However, these findings were not regarded as conclusive, since the authors also found a marked tendency for patients from a disadvantaged background to be kept longer in those mental institutions where psychotic, rather than neurotic, disorders are common. Thus, the rate for psychoses among those on the lower-income scale may be higher than it would be were patients of all socioeconomic classes treated in like manner.

Treatment According to Class.   Unfortunately, the social class patients belong to makes a great difference in the way they are treated. Hollingshead and Redlich found that persons in Classes I and II were more likely than others to be seen by private psychiatrists who use the most sophisticated and up-to-date methods. Such patients were institutionalized mainly in private hospitals. Those in Classes III, IV, and V, however, were likely to be cared for in public institutions.

The quality of treatment varied correspondingly. While nearly all the Class I patients saw a therapist for the standard 50-minute session, less than half the Class V patients were so fortunate; many saw a therapist for less than 30 minutes at a time, and virtually none received continuous treatment for a significant period of time. Still, in spite of this apparent relationship between social class and the types of mental disorders diagnosed

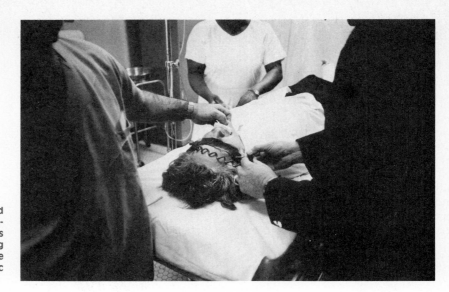

Electroshock therapy, used to combat severe depression and schizophrenia, is commonly used in treating mental illness among the lower socioeconomic classes.

and kinds of treatments prescribed, it has not been established that socio-cultural factors are the essential causes of mental distress.[22] That is, just because so many Class V patients diagnosed as psychotic are found in mental hospitals, we cannot conclude that poverty is invariably the cause of psychoses.

A follow-up of the New Haven study was conducted ten years after the original research and was successful in locating 99 percent of the study population.[23] This detailed study amassed considerable evidence in support of the proposition that social class is an important determinant of the type of treatment received and the patient's adjustment in the community subsequent to treatment. It was found that lower-class patients were more likely to be hospitalized in the follow-up period, irrespective of whether they had previously been outpatients or had been committed to an institution. Among the original noninstitutionalized patients, those of higher social class were more likely to have received treatment in the follow-up period either from a private physician or at an outpatient clinic without being hospitalized.

In addition, the researchers investigated the community adjustment of the former patients in terms of mental impairment, adequacy in the performance of occupational roles, and participation in other aspects of community life. A somewhat unexpected finding emerged from this analysis. Among those who had previously been hospitalized, patients from the upper and middle classes showed greater psychological impairment than their lower-class counterparts. This finding suggests that environmental stress may not necessarily be greater and more harmful for those in the lower socioeconomic strata.

Occupational Status. The Hollingshead-Redlich study also provided much related information on the education, occupation, and income of mental patients, findings substantiated by later studies. It is now well documented that there is a higher rate of first admissions to mental hospitals among patients from lower occupational categories. This seems to hold true for all mental illnesses. The higher the occupational status, the less likely is the prospect of hospitalization.

Occupational status, or the lack of it, also seems to be related to the kind of illness involved. The unemployed and those in unskilled and semiskilled occupations show a greater tendency toward schizophrenia than toward other psychoses. Manic-depressive psychosis, on the other hand, is more common among the professional and business groups. One interesting study has suggested that there is a high incidence of schizophrenia among persons who experience a discrepancy between their educational background and occupational status.[24]

Age. Some general correlations also exist between age and type of mental illness. Patients under 18 are most often admitted as a result of acute, temporary reactions to stressful situations, whereas for those past the age of 65 the most probable diagnosis is chronic brain syndrome. Except for mental retardation, a few major disorders appear during the childhood years; the psychoses seldom manifest themselves before late adolescence.[25] From that period to early middle age, the incidence rises steadily and most likely diagnosis is schizophrenia. During the ensuing 20 years the psychoses of middle age—manic-depressive psychosis and involutional melancholia—are most common.

The neuroses also seem to appear most frequently during the middle years. The trend begins to manifest itself among those between 18 and 24 years of age; for them neuroses and personality disorders constitute the most frequent admission diagnosis in outpatient facilities. These disorders predominate to about age 60 or 65, until the onset age for senile disturbances and other syndromes of advanced age.

Sex. What about sexual differences? Generally speaking, only minor trends appear in the statistics, for example, a slightly higher hospitalization rate for psychoses among men, probably connected with the greater frequency among men of mental conditions related to alcoholism and syphilis.[26] However, this trend is partly offset by the greater frequency of depressive disorders and psychoneurosis among women.

In the under-18 age group, differences between the sexes are somewhat more marked. Data for outpatient psychiatric services reveal that among males of that age group, more than 25 percent of the cases were classified as hyperkinetic reaction (abnormal restlessness) and 29 percent as unsocialized aggressive reaction.[27] No such trend appeared among female patients. Their diagnoses were rather evenly divided among the subcategories of childhood behavior disorders, except for an exceptionally low incidence of hyperkinetic reactions.

Other Factors. Both outpatient and inpatient admission rates in institutions for the mentally disturbed show a preponderance of admissions for nonwhite races. This correlates with the finding that the psychoses predom-

D. L. Rosenhan
On Being Sane in Insane Places

Eight sane people gained secret admission to 12 different [psychiatric] hospitals. . . .

The eight pseudopatients were a varied group. One was a psychology graduate student in his 20's. The remaining seven were older and "established." Among them were three psychologists, a pediatrician, a psychiatrist, a painter, and a housewife. Three pseudopatients were women, five were men. . . .

After calling the hospital for an appointment, the pseudopatient arrived at the admissions office complaining that he had been hearing voices. Asked what the voices said, he replied that they were often unclear, but as far as he could tell they said "empty," "hollow," and "thud." The voices were unfamiliar and were of the same sex as the pseudopatient. The choice of these symptoms was occasioned by their apparent similarity to existential symptoms. Such symptoms are alleged to arise from painful concerns about the perceived meaninglessness of one's life. It is as if the hallucinating person were saying, "My life is empty and hollow." The choice of these symptoms was also determined by the *absence* of a single report of existential psychoses in the literature.

Beyond alleging the symptoms and falsifying name, vocation, and employment, no further alterations of person, history, or circumstances were made. The significant events of the pseudopatient's life history were presented as they had actually occurred. . . .

Immediately upon admission to the psychiatric ward, the pseudopatient ceased simulating *any* symptoms of abnormality. . . .

Despite their public "show" of sanity, the pseudopatients were never detected. Admitted, except in one case, with a diagnosis of schizophrenia, each was discharged with a diagnosis of schizophrenia "in remission." . . .

. . . it cannot be said that the failure to recognize the pseudopatients' sanity was due to the fact that they were not behaving sanely. While there was clearly some tension present in all of them, their daily visitors could detect no serious behavioral conse-

quences—nor, indeed, could other patients. It was quite common for the patients to "detect" the pseudopatients' sanity. During the first three hospitalizations, when accurate counts were kept, 35 of a total of 118 patients on the admissions ward voiced their suspicions, some vigorously. "You're not crazy. You're a journalist, or a professor [referring to the continual note-taking]. You're checking up on the hospital." . . . The fact that the patients often recognized normality when staff did not raises important questions. . . .

All pseudopatients took extensive notes publicly. Under ordinary circumstances, such behavior would have raised questions in the minds of observers, as, in fact, it did among patients. . . . The closest any staff member came to questioning these notes occurred when one pseudopatient asked his physician what kind of medication he was receiving and began to write down the response. "You needn't write it," he was told gently. "If you have trouble remembering, just ask me again."

If no questions were asked of the pseudopatients, how was their writing interpreted? Nursing records for three patients indicate that the writing was seen as an aspect of their pathological behavior. "Patient engages in writing behavior" was the daily nursing comment on one of the pseudopatients who was never questioned about this writing. . . .

There is by now a host of evidence that attitudes toward the mentally ill are characterized by fear, hostility, aloofness, suspicion, and dread. The mentally ill are society's lepers.

That such attitudes infect the general population is perhaps not surprising, only upsetting. But that they affect the professionals—attendants, nurses, physicians, psychologists, and social workers—who treat and deal with the mentally ill is more disconcerting, both because such attitudes are self-evidently pernicious and because they are unwitting. . . .

Consider the structure of the typical psychiatric hospital. Staff and patients are strictly segregated. Staff have their own living space, including their dining facilities, bathrooms, and assembly places. The glassed quarters that contain the professional staff, which the pseudopatients came to call "the cage," sit out on every dayroom. The staff emerge primarily for caretaking purposes—to give medication, to conduct a therapy or group meeting, to instruct or reprimand a patient. Otherwise, staff keep to themselves, almost as if the disorder that afflicts their charges is somehow catching. . . .

Eye contact and verbal contact reflect concern and individuation; their absence, avoidance and depersonalization. The data . . . do not do justice to the rich daily encounters that grew up around matters of depersonalization and avoidance. I have records of patients who were beaten by staff for the sin of having initiated contact. During my own experience, for example, one patient was beaten in the presence of other patients for having approached an attendant and told him, "I like you." Occasionally, punishment meted out to patients for misdemeanors seemed so excessive that it could not be justified by the most radical interpretations of psychiatric canon. Nevertheless, they appeared to go unquestioned. Tempers were often short. A patient who had not heard a call for medication would be roundly excoriated, and the morning attendants would often wake patients with, "Come on, you m-----f-----s, out of bed!" . .

Powerlessness was evident everywhere. The patient is deprived of many of his legal rights by dint of his psychiatric commitment. He is shorn by credibility by virtue of his psychiatric label. His freedom of movement is restricted. He cannot initiate contact with the staff, but may only respond to such overtures as they make. Personal privacy is minimal. Patient quarters and possessions can be entered and examined by any staff member, for whatever reason. His personal history and anguish is available to any staff member (often including the "grey lady" and "candy striper" volunteer) who chooses to read his folder, regardless of their therapeutic relationship to him. His personal hygiene and waste evacuation are often monitored. The water closets may have no doors.

At times, depersonalization reached such proportions that pseudopatients had the sense that they were invisible, or at least unworthy of account. . . .

A nurse unbuttoned her uniform to adjust her brassiere in the presence of an entire ward of viewing men. One did not have the sense that she was being seductive. Rather, she didn't notice us. A group of staff persons might point to a patient in the dayroom and discuss him animatedly, as if he were not there. . . .

Whenever the ratio of what is known to what needs to be known approaches zero, we tend to invent "knowledge" and assume that we understand more than we actually do. We seem unable to acknowledge that we simply don't know. The needs for diagnosis and remediation of behavioral and emotional problems are enormous. But rather than acknowledge that we are just embarking on understanding, we continue to label patients "schizophrenic," "manic-depressive," and "insane," as if in those words we had captured the essence of understanding. The facts of the matter are that we have known for a long time that diagnoses are often not useful or reliable, but we have nevertheless continued to use them. We now know that we cannot distinguish insanity from sanity. It is depressing to consider how that information will be used.

Not merely depressing, but frightening. How many people, one wonders, are sane but not recognized as such in our psychiatric institutions? How many have been needlessly stripped of their priviledges of citizenship, from the right to vote and drive to that of handling their own account? How many have feigned insanity in order to avoid the criminal consequences of their behavior, and, conversely, how many would rather stand trial than live interminably in a psychiatric hospital—but are wrongly thought to be mentally ill? How many have been stigmatized by well-intentioned, but nevertheless erroneous, diagnoses? On the last point, . . .a "type 2 error" in psychiatric diagnosis does not have the same consequences it does in medical diagnosis. A diagnosis of cancer that has been found to be in error is cause for celebration. But psychiatric diagnoses are rarely found to be in error. The label sticks, a mark of inadequacy forever.

Finally, how many patients might be "sane" outside the psychiatric hospital but seem insane in it—not because craziness resides in them, as it were, but because they are responding to a bizarre setting, one that may be unique to institutions which harbor nether people? . . .

Excerpts from D. L. Rosenhan, "On Being Sane in Insane Places," *Science* 179 (1973), 250–258, not including footnotes. Copyright 1973 by the American Association for the Advancement of Science. Reprinted by permission.

inate in the lower-income groups, of which nonwhite people form a large percentage. Nonwhite admission rates to state and county mental hospitals in 1975 was double the rate for white patients.[28] Another trend that has been noted is that Jews have a lower overall rate of first admission than other whites, mostly due to the low incidence of organic mental disorders. But the incidence of other mental disorders among Jews is higher than the incidence among other whites.[29]

Institutionalized Populations

A foremost critic of mental institutions is sociologist Erving Goffman, who has characterized these and similar settings such as prisons, monasteries, and army boot camps as total institutions. A total institution is

a place of residence and work where a large number of like-situated individuals, cut off from the wider society for an appreciable period of time, together lead an enclosed, formally administered round of life. Prisons serve as a clear example, providing we appreciate that what is prison-like about prisons is found in institutions whose members have broken no laws.[30]

Goffman has pointed out that when people are admitted into mental institutions, they are forced into self-mortification and the assumption of a "disidentifying role" in the daily life into which they have been thrust. Their privacy has been violated, their environment invaded; they are required to divulge facts and feelings about themselves to strangers whom they invariably regard as hostile. Constantly within sight and earshot of someone (if only fellow inmates), they are kept behind locked doors. They must adapt to collective sleeping arrangements and doorless toilets.[31]

Such conditions are likely to accentuate feelings of anxiety. In an effort to emerge from the prisonlike existence and remain physically and psychologically undamaged, inmates attempt to adjust to their alien environment. Eventually, mental patients may accept the hospital staff view of them and try to assume the role of the "perfect inmate." If they have been previously institutionalized in an orphanage, reformatory, jail, military compound, or religious retreat, Goffman believes their adjustment will not be so difficult; their previous experiences will enable them to learn adaptive techniques. Most inmates of mental hospitals feel that the time spent in such institutions has been wasted and that, in effect, they have been "exiled from living." Yet patients frequently become apprehenisve when they are about to be released and wonder if they can get along in the outside world.[32]

Mental patients can find themselves in a special bind. To get out of the hospital, or to ease their life within it, they must show acceptance of the place accorded them, and the place accorded them is to support the occupational role of those who appear to force this bargain. This self-alienating moral servitude, which perhaps helps to account for some inmates becoming mentally confused, is achieved by invoking the great tradition of the expert servicing relation, especially its medical variety. Mental patients can find themselves crushed by the weight of a service ideal that eases life for the rest of us.[33]

Statistically speaking, the great majority of institutionalized patients suffer from the more debilitating disturbances—psychoses, brain syndrome, and severe mental deficiency. Between the ages of 25 and 65, schizophrenia and alcoholic disorders together account for more than 60 percent of all patients admitted to state and county mental institutions. After age 65, organic brain syndrome predominates. As noted previously, those of the youngest population—patients under 18—are usually admitted for temporary disorders that occur as a result of stressful situations, such as a change in role and responsibility or a change in family structure (death of a parent or perhaps marriage of a close sibling).[34]

In evaluating these figures, we should remember that they refer only to institutionalized patients and that many disturbed persons, especially in rural areas, do not seek or receive treatment and therefore are not counted. Moreover, statistics based on admission diagnoses are not in themselves completely accurate. Even the present classification system leaves considerable room for clinical interpretation. Sometimes, too, the psychiatrist is motivated by nonclinical considerations. There may be a reluctance to stigmatize a bright middle-class girl with the label schizophrenic; on the other hand, the withdrawn older man, who has been admitted mainly because there is nowhere else to put him, may be routinely diagnosed as schizophrenic.

Statistics on admission and discharge of mental patients are probably less troublesome than those based on diagnosis. State mental hospitals, traditionally the primary facility for the care and treatment of mentally ill persons, have experienced a steady decline in their inpatient populations since 1955 (see Figure 12.2). A combination of medical, social, and economic factors has been responsible for this trend. Following the development of the major tranquilizing drugs in the mid-1950s, many patients were either released after shorter periods of institutionalization or treated as outpatients. Elderly patients have been increasingly referred to other types of facilities, such as geriatric hospitals or nursing homes. Perhaps most important, the rising costs of institutional care have resulted in deliberate decisions by state officials to reduce the resident populations in state mental hospitals.[35] At the same time, there has been a great increase in the number of persons treated in such outpatient facilities as community mental health centers, halfway houses, and psychiatric clinics in general hospitals, as Figure 12.2 illustrates. Two-thirds of all persons under care are now treated in some type of outpatient facility. The introduction of these community treatment centers has been a significant factor in altering the nature of psychiatric care available in the United States today.

Critics of the traditional custodial institution argue that a sizable percentage of institutionalized patients could be released or treated in other types of facilities without presenting a danger to the community. Several studies have provided support for this contention.[36] A 1966 study of state hospital patients in Texas found that one-fourth of the patients were judged suitable for release, nearly one-third could be transferred to other types of institutional care, and only 43 percent required continuing institutionalization in state mental hospitals. Similarly, a 1970 study of patients in St. Elizabeth's Hospital in Washington, D.C., found that more than 50 percent could be transferred to nursing or foster homes, and only 32 percent required further hospitalization.

MENTAL INSTITUTIONS

Discomfited by the odd behavior of the mentally ill, society has for centuries stashed them away in institutions, denied them individual identities, and either ignorantly or maliciously mistreated them. Only in recent decades have these unhappy people begun to be recognized as human beings with rights—particularly the right to treatment and the right to live at liberty if they constitute no danger to others. *This page:* Group therapy—learning how to live with others, emotionally and socially; the creativity of arts and crafts—a therapeutic and fulfilling expression of the self; learning to cook—a simple and sustaining skill with profound significance in establishing identity and self-esteem. *Opposite page:* Ill and enslaved, their lives swept away by society's misconceptions about mental illness, the institutionalized were seldom rehabilitated in decades past; unable to communicate, they are often starved of spiritual and emotional nourishment; the traditional mental hospital often creates so much despair and hopelessness that patients grow worse rather than better; purposely tracing the paths of their prison day after day, these mentally ill are locked out of life.

Figure 12.2 Patient Population by Type of Facility, 1955–1975

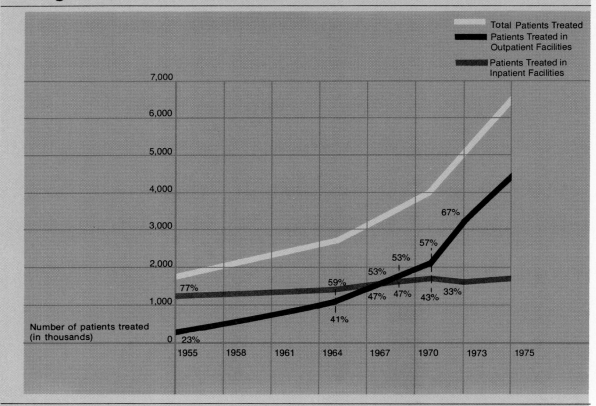

Source: U.S. Department of Health, Education and Welfare, National Institute of Mental Health, *State and County Hospitals*, United States, 1973—1974, Publication No. ADM 76-301 (Washington, D.C.: Government Printing Office, 1975), p. 7; and U.S. Bureau of Census, *Statistical Abstract of the United States, 1978* (Washington, D.C.: Government Printing Office, 1978), p. 115.

Sociological Explanations of Mental Illness

Sociological explanations of mental illness differ from organic and psychological explanations in that they stipulate the cause as external rather than as coming from within the individual. Focusing on aspects of the social environment thought to contribute to individual disorders, sociologists have identified conditions that are influential in the development of mental illness. These include social isolation, the improper perception or performance of social roles, and the differential social treatment of persons whose behavior is viewed as deviant.

Isolation from other people is an acknowledged factor in the development of emotional disturbance. Even well-adjusted persons may become more or less disturbed if they are forced to exist in seclusion for any length of time. Isolation has proved its effectiveness in breaking the resistance of prisoners of war; it is equally effective in breaking the spirits of the old and lonely; and it plays a role in the development of schizophrenia.[37]

Social isolation is a particularly important variable in the development of at least one schizophrenic type, the catatonic schizophrenic.[38] Studies have shown that these individuals experience isolation at a very early age. Anxiety and self-consciousness motivate them to stay close to home, and particularly to their mothers, and to shy away from social contacts with their peer group. Because these individuals so actively avoid company, the process of social isolation begins earlier and is more devastating than in other types of schizophrenia.

On the other hand, individuals displaying paranoid symptoms generally attempt social relationships. Because of their domineering or otherwise disturbing personalities, they are actively rejected by their peer group—but only after having been accepted. Once rejected, the need for an audience motivates them to seek new social contacts. Their sense of grandiosity allegedly makes rejection less painful. Although they may end up equally alone, their isolation usually does not begin as early as that of the catatonics, whose dread of leaving home largely precludes the initiation of social contacts in childhood and throughout life.

Isolation is clearly an important factor in the development of the schizophrenic syndrome. But although there is little question that social isolation tends to worsen schizophrenia, it does not suffice to explain it.

Role theory views individuals not only in the broad context of their interaction with the environment but in terms of the separate interpersonal relationships of which they are a part. Each of the roles a person plays supposes the existence of a separate social self. Thus, for instance, a man's role within the marriage unit demands quite another self than the role he assumes within the work unit (further divisible into his roles as superior, equal, and subordinate); still other male roles are father, son, and friend.

Social psychologists and psychiatrists sometimes use the levels of performance in each of these roles as indexes of mental health. One measure of such might be the degree to which role performance parallels social expectations of the role. Magazine quizzes—with titles such as "Are You a Model Working Woman, Wife, and Mother?"—are designed to measure the individual's fulfillment of social expectations.

On the other hand, one's level of competence in fulfilling a role may also be used as a measure of performance—for example, the success with which a family head is able to provide income for family support. Any income below that designated as a minimum performance level would indicate role failure. The inability to support one's family can lead to disruption of an individual's personal life and, in many cases, to a nervous breakdown or other manifestations of mental illness.

It has been suggested that for some people the stress involved in playing many, often conflicting, roles is great enough to cause a nervous breakdown or even manic-depressive psychosis.[39] Role conflict, as between one's occupational and family roles, may be resolved fairly readily in some settings or individual situations; in others, it presents chronic adjustment problems.

There is some reason to believe that the complex and competitive nature of modern society is responsible for the development of personal and interpersonal conflicts. Almost by definition, competitiveness involves hostility and resultant insecurity and may well contribute to the development of some neuroses.[40] In addition, recent studies—notably one comparing diagnosed schizophrenics and nonschizophrenics in the poorer sections of San Juan, Puerto Rico—indicate that escalating role and social conflicts may also play a significant part in the development of schizophrenia.[41]

Labeling Theory

Thomas Scheff has formulated an elaborate functional theory of serious and chronic mental illness.[42] In terms of the distinction presented earlier, the theory deals with psychoses rather than neurotic disorders and is concerned with explaining how behavioral abnormalities that may be relatively trivial at first become stabilized into a pattern of chronic mental illness. It holds that most chronic mental illness is at least in part a social role, and that labeling and stigmatization are the most important factors leading to entry into that role.

The labeling of an individual as mentally ill typically results from violations of residual rules—social norms other than those for which there are explicit deviant labels such as criminal or sinful. The expectations that one be in contact with reality and involved during social interaction are examples of residual rules. Violations of such rules would include extreme withdrawal, inappropriate conversation, or hearing voices that are not present. The violations arise from a variety of sources, including external stress, organic disorders, and psychological conflict. In fact, nearly everyone in today's world has moments of intense emotional stress that result in deviance from these residual rules. However, most such violations are denied and are not taken by others to be manifestations of mental illness. They are thus of only transitory significance. The denial process frequently takes the form of conversational disclaimers on the part of the deviating individual, such as "I'm just not with it today" or "I've been preoccupied with another problem." Typically, the denial is accepted by others, and the residual rule breaking has few, if any, social consequences.

However, if an individual's violations of residual rules are defined by others as symptomatic of an underlying mental disorder, then the individual may be labeled a disturbed person. The crucial sociological process is the differential social treatment and response to those so labeled. Once assigned this role and treated by others in terms of it, the individual may gradually come to accept that definition of self and begin to act the role of mentally ill. He or she then tends to be rewarded for acting in accord with stereotypic conceptions of the mentally ill; there is often pressure from psychiatrists and other treatment personnel to accept "the fact" of being sick.

On the other hand, the person assigned such a label is blocked or punished when attempting to return to a conventional role. Further, since residual rule breaking frequently occurs during some kind of crisis period, the individual is disoriented or under acute stress and is likely to be more open to the idea that the mentally ill role is indeed applicable. Scheff views labeling processes as the single most important factor in the continuation and stabilization of residual rule breaking and the emergence of an enduring deviant career centered about the fact of mental illness.

Conditions in our society facilitate the labeling of persons as deviant, both interpersonally and at the organizational level. The identification of individuals as deviant and the spreading of information that a particular individual belongs in a deviant category are crucially important labeling processes and are increasingly the work of those who might be termed imputational specialists.[43]

The growing army of social workers, psychologists, psychiatrists, police, etc., constitutes a stratum with a precise interest in ensuring a flow of persons defined as deviant. The training undergone by such specialists creates a stratum whose aim it is to discover "out there" in the empirical world those sorts of people they have been trained to see.[44]

Often these specialists, because of their authority or presumed expertise, are crucial in setting off escalating processes of labeling, differential treatment, and acceptance of the deviant identity.

The theory that labeling itself is responsible for much disturbed behavior is not particularly congenial to proponents of the medical model. Walter R. Gove feels that Scheff has exaggerated the effect of labeling (both inside and outside the mental hospital setting) as well as the degree to which former patients suffer from the stigma of having been confined for a mental disorder.[45] Gove and others focus on the rather important question of why a deviant commits the acts that invite undesirable labeling.

In addition, Gove has noted that the labeling process itself is not so rigorous. The family of mentally ill persons, far from imposing a label, may go to extraordinary lengths to deny the bizarre nature of the behavior of the disturbed. Even within the mental hospital setting, patients often are not regarded as mentally ill, either by themselves or by their associates. Moreover, an increasing proportion of patients admit themselves voluntarily, which may imply that they have labeled themselves as mentally ill before anyone else.

According to Gove, the evidence strongly suggests a cause-and-effect relationship opposite of that postulated by Scheff and others. Although he has conceded that in the long run the expectations of doctors, parents, and other key figures may be an important determinant of a person's behavior, in the short run it is the individual's behavior that determines the expectations of others.

Mental Illness as a Myth

Some medical and social scientists have posed the question of whether there really is such a condition as mental illness. In various forms, and from different vantage points, this provocative question has been asked with increasing urgency in recent years. Among the earliest and most controversial of the questioners is psychiatrist Thomas Szasz, who has answered with a resounding no.[46]

An opponent of the medical model, Szasz believes that mental deviations constitute not illnesses but rather disturbances due to faulty learning—disturbances that result in a distorted self-image and, finally, the assumption of the role of patient. According to Szasz, the very person whose function it is to correct this faulty view—the therapist—plays no small part in causing and reinforcing it. By placing disturbed individuals in the role of patient, the therapist encourages them to accept further distortions of their self-image.

In this view, the doctor-patient relationship is a tragic partnership in which each participant endlessly reinforces the faulty concept of the other. At best, these relationships are altruistically motivated; at worst, they represent psychological and financial exploitation on the part of the therapist of the most callous kind.

Szasz maintains that although there is nothing to heal, since no one is sick, there is much to learn. An individual with an information deficit must learn to adjust to the world. Since environment is a powerful teacher, the patient in the hospital does, indeed, proceed to learn, from the moment of admission, to be a mental patient. Other observers have emphasized this aspect of hospitalization,[47] as have the many mental patients who claim they are sick because they are in the hospital, rather than the reverse.[48]

It is too early for a comprehensive evaluation of Szasz's contribution, but his influence has already borne fruit in a number of areas, among them obtaining recognition of the rights of mental patients, whether institutionalized, noninstitutionalized, or in the process of changing from one status to the other. A gradual decline in infringements on these rights is making itself felt, together with a lessening of the authoritarian and often downright punitive aspects of confinement for mental problems. Apparently, many Americans are judged incompetent on insufficient grounds and are unnecessarily committed to mental institutions.[49] As a result, more stringent tests have now been developed to determine competency and to guard against unnecessary hospitalization. In addition, hospitalized patients, along with mental health associations, have brought charges against governmental agencies on the ground that their civil rights have been violated.

Two legal issues are presently at the center of the debate and controversy concerning mental patients' rights: the right of involuntarily confined patients to liberty and the right of such patients to treatment.[50] In June 1975 the Supreme Court handed down a decision in the much publicized Donaldson case. Kenneth Donaldson had been diagnosed as a paranoid schizophrenic and confined in a Florida state institution for almost 15 years, even though he had not been found to be dangerous to either himself or others. He successfully sued the hospital and its staff members, charging that he had been intentionally deprived of his constitutional right to liberty. In its landmark decision, the Court held that a simple diagnosis of mental illness is not sufficient for involuntary commitment in custodial confinement for an indefinite period of time.[51]

The Supreme Court refused to rule on the question of the involuntarily confined patient's right to treatment, and the issue thus remains unresolved legally. Certainly this question is not a simple one. In Alabama a right to treatment decision by the state courts was interpreted by state officials as presenting only two practical alternatives: either allocate more money for treatment in institutions or release patients for whom treatment could not be provided. Within a short time the hospitalized population had been reduced by more than a third.[52] Advocates of right to treatment laws argue that they are necessary to upgrade or to institute treatment programs in custodial institutions. Further, by making possible the release of many patients who are simply "warehoused," existing treatment resources could be focused and used more effectively. However, others have expressed reservations over the possibility that such a ruling might subject patients to forced treatment.

Responses to Mental Illness

For a problem so large and broad in scope as mental illness, many approaches are required to meet the needs of those affected and to attempt to lower the incidence of such disorders. As attitudes toward mental illness change, new ways to deal with the problems emerge.

Preventive Psychiatry

Intensive research into the causes of mental illness has suggested innumerable causative factors. Moreover, it has been shown that timely crisis intervention can often prevent mental disorder, even under stressful conditions.[53] The accumulation of so many promising insights has resulted in the development of preventive psychiatry. Its aims are threefold: (1) to reduce the incidence of mental disorder (primary prevention), (2) to shorten the duration of disorders that cannot be forestalled (secondary prevention), and (3) to reduce the degree of impairment that may result from mental disorders (tertiary prevention).

Preventive psychiatry focuses on the physical, psychosocial, and sociocultural "supplies" that people need in order to function adequately at various stages of their development.[54] In the psychological area, these supplies are roughly synonymous with the various aspects of life that provide satisfaction of interpersonal needs—the need for parental attention and peer group support in adolescence, for example. Preventive psychiatry seeks to provide or restore those supplies without which mental illness may occur. Of equal importance is an emphasis on personal crisis periods as stages in life when people may be actively helped in avoiding mental illness.

Preventive psychiatry presently encompasses teaching at the individual, familial, and broad social levels; consultation in contexts ranging from personal to governmental and international; research and development of diagnostic tools and treatment techniques; and, finally, community planning.

The Community Mental Health Movement

Strongly interrelated with preventive psychiatry are the community mental health services. Enthusiasm for these services is the result of a widespread reaction against the isolation of mental patients from their families and society at large. Many professionals agree that the mentally disturbed should, if at all possible, be treated in the community to which they belong. Recent research has shown that as many as three-fourths of those schizophrenics scheduled for hospitalization could function successfully at home when treated with drugs and receiving support from clinic personnel.[55] Availability of help within the local community also results in the earliest possible treatment for those who need it. In the event that they are institutionalized, treatment within the community context can ease the readjustment period following discharge.

While, ideally, public mental hospitals should operate within the framework of the local community mental health program, very few are so organized at this time; nor, for the most part, are there many equipped to provide the variety of services to which the community mental health movement is committed. These services include everything from outpatient psychiatric clinics to day centers (where outpatients may spend their days in various therapies) and halfway houses (which provide a bridge between the hospital and the community).

During the late 1970s, the community mental health movement began to meet opposition from several sources. Hospital employees became worried about its economic impact, while local residents of areas which receive the released patients expressed concern about property values and community safety. Although this opposition succeeded in slowing the movement in some areas, most planners and professionals continue to push for greater development of community centers. At present there are few studies indicating the effects of the community treatment movement on the patients from which generalization can be drawn; however, one survey did report that 75 percent of the released patients felt that they had benefited from community living arrangements.[56]

Therapies

If one subscribes to the view that mental disturbances are due to faulty learning, it follows that therapy must be a process of reeducation. Such is indeed the view of many therapists of widely different orientations, including, interestingly enough, a number of proponents of the medical model. The fact is that most therapeutic approaches contain a large educational component. Among the few that do not are psychosurgery (treating emotional problems with surgical techniques), electroshock treatment (the application of electric shocks to the brain), and drug therapy. Of these, drug therapy is by far the most widely used.

Drug Therapy. Since their development in the 1950s, the ataractic drugs, or major tranquilizers, have become the dominant form of treatment in mental institutions. This therapy is largely responsible for the fact that

Has the community mental health movement gone too far? Some claim yes, charging that countless patients in need are being released too early from mental hospitals or aren't being admitted at all. This advertisement charges that private agencies are providing inadequate community-based treatment for the mentally ill and retarded.

Peter Koenig
The Problem That Can't Be Tranquilized

If you live on Manhattan's West Side, or if you ever get over there, you may well have crossed paths with Gerard Kerrigan, the part-time delivery man at the Eat Shoppe, a dinette on Broadway between 95th and 96th Streets. Kerrigan spends a good portion of each day out on the street, and he's hard to miss. . . . He seems drunk. High on something. Noticing his tattered duffel coat and half-laced sneakers, strangers sidestep him on Broadway and hurry on by.

To his few acquaintances, Kerrigan looks like a prizefighter. They call him Rocky. Others, kidding him about his appetite, call him Eat 'Em Up. Those who know him and are at all articulate say he's obsessed with food, money and clothes. By current standards, there's little out of the ordinary in these obsessions, but the forms they take *are* queer. His fixation on clothes, for instance: Kerrigan has to have trousers with silver zippers. The trousers with gold-colored zippers that come his way—from the Salvation Army or Goodwill—get trash-canned. Except for the drain it places on Kerrigan's $3,000-a-year income, there's nothing sinister in this. Still, when Kerrigan examines his trousers on Broadway to reassure himself that his zipper is silver, it upsets Zabar's-bound shoppers, sets off disorderly alarms in orderly minds, and is one more of those incidents that make formerly hospitalized mental patients a political issue.

The shorthand term for this issue is dumping: the dumping of poor, chronically mentally ill patients out of state hospitals into dilapidated quarters in neighborhoods reluctant to accept them. The controversy does not concern the man or woman who simply checks into a mental hospital for depression, for example, responds to treatment, then checks out and goes home. Dumping is not new, nor is it exclusive to the Upper West Side, although that neighborhood's approximately 7,000 chronically mentally ill residents are among the greatest concentrations of deinstitutionalized mental patients in the United States.

Dumping dates back to the 50's, to the invention of tranquilizers and to the subsequent ascendance of a medical ideology rooted in the axiom that disturbed patients are better off close to home rather than locked away out of sight. Syncopate this with the civil-rights movement, which eventually extended its concern to the mentally ill, and Supreme Court rulings such as the one handed down in 1975 declaring that states cannot constitutionally detain without treatment "a nondangerous individual who is capable of surviving safely in freedom by himself or with the help of willing and responsible family members and friends," and one begins to understand how and why we are now dumping the mentally ill out of hospitals instead of into them. In 1955, there were 550,000 patients in state mental hospitals across the country; today there are 190,000. . . .

Gerard Kerrigan, 50 years old, wakes at 6:30 each morning in a 7- by 11-foot room in the Continental Hotel at 330 West 95th Street, one of approximately 145,000 souls in the five square miles bounded by 72d Street, the Hudson River, 110th Street and Central Park. He rises, dresses, shaves, does some laundry in his sink, and walks the two blocks to the Eat Shoppe, where he runs up a $100-a-month breakfast tab. After eggs and toast, he stations himself in an unlighted back booth and waits for customers to call in orders. "I go to gas stations, parking garages," he says. "I get a quarter tip. Come back. Go out. I get a quarter tip. . . . Once the regular delivery boy didn't come all day, and I made $5."

In comparison to many others among the 40,000 chronically mentally ill persons city officials estimate live in New York City, Kerrigan is fairly normal. For one thing, he takes tranquilizers and an antidepressant daily. The wild man staggering down Broadway in bare feet, hair in tangles, has probably stopped taking medication. For another thing, Kerrigan may be alarming when considered as an abstraction, but in the flesh he's meek. After the Eat Shoppe's regular delivery boy shows up at 9, he meanders over to the Salvation Army outlet on 96th Street to help unload trucks, or he takes a walk, or he browses for a new pair of trousers. Eventually, he heads back to the Continental.

The Continental is one of a string of hotels owned by landlord Hugo Wolff. Built in 1907, chopped up in the 40's, the place is said to have housed show people in the 50's after the middle class migrated to the suburbs but before the welfare populations had migrated to the West Side. Today it is one of nine single-room-occupancy (S.R.O.) hotels in the 94th-95th Street helix so notorious that the Welfare Department stopped referring clients to them last year, and recently resumed doing so on only a limited basis. At the moment, 92 of the 192 residents in the Continental are formerly hospitalized mental patients; the majority of them have been loosely diagnosed as chronic schizophrenics. . . .

The fixed star in Kerrigan's universe is Ken Quagenti, a social worker who runs an advice bureau in the Continental—one of 15 such programs in S.R.O.'s sponsored by the city's Human Resources Administration. After eight years at this job, Quagenti avoids psychological analysis when discussing his clients. "Mr. Kerrigan arrived at the Continental in 1974," he says. "He was having problems handling his money. I put him on a budget."

Quagenti takes Kerrigan's $238.65 monthly Supplemental Security Income check (welfare for the disabled—Federal rather than local), pays Kerrigan's $68 rent (a deal, since many Continental residents pay half again as much), settles his $100 tab at the Eat Shoppe, and gives him $2.50 a day in spending money.

Quagenti's office is perpetually hazy with tobacco smoke. Inside it, a woman rests against her walker and reads the paper. A second woman nods off in a folding chair, clutching a paper soup bowl from lunch. A man leans against a cabinet and picks at the plaster on his leg cast. Mr. Q, as the residents call Quagenti, a slight man concealed behind a melodramatic blond mustache, works up a report on an ancient typewriter. . . .

The rest of Kerrigan's day is just as grim, and each day is just about the same. Once a month he sees a therapist for 20 minutes. In the late afternoons he's out and about doing errands for quarter tips. . . .

For all the despair inside the Continental, the hotel seems most frightening from the sidewalk. Once you've seen their beds and bureaus, the former mental patients on Broadway seem less alien. But few outsiders venture into welfare hotels. Mothers picking up their children at P.S. 75 across the street steer clear of the hotel's entrance. Pedestrians pass hurriedly by.

The dumping issue becomes explosive when concentrations of middle-class voters and ex-patients live side by side. . . .

As street life deteriorates, West Siders become more frustrated, and, in their frustration, confuse their fear of crime with their fear of insanity. Some argue that former mental patients cause crime.

"That's not right," says Lieut. David Velez, until recently the administrative officer for the local 24th Precinct. "In most cases, the mentally disabled are victims of crime, not perpetrators, especially if they live in S.R.O.'s. You're throwing goldfish among the piranhas there."

In one recent five-month period, according to police, seven robberies, nine burglaries, four felonious assaults and one attempted murder occurred in the Continental—and these figures only hint at what actually goes on. . . .

Returning them to state institutions is not the answer, for if S.R.O.'s are hellholes, most state mental hospitals are more wretched. Dumping has improved conditions somewhat by reducing the strain of overcrowding, but lately the number of patients in state mental hospitals has begun to creep upward again as dumped patients whose condition has deteriorated on the street are readmitted.

Psychiatric outpatients living on the West Side who get worse instead of better end up in the West Side Unit of the Manhattan State Psychiatric Center on Ward's Island. On the wards there, bodies lie about like sandbags, dozing or unconscious. In the therapy rooms, patients sit around tables and clip colored paper or leaf through dogeared magazines—reality orientation, it's called. . . .

Looking through the barred windows down the East River toward Manhattan's skyline, an outsider fights back panic. Although some patients make progress in such a place, inmates are usually discharged as quickly as possible on humanitarian and clinical grounds as well as for budgetary and constitutional reasons. Psychiatrists call this "the revolving door syndrome." The chronically mentally ill are hospitalized, dumped, readmitted and dumped again. . . .

Excerpts from "The Problem That Can't Be Tranquilized," *New York Times Magazine,* May 21, 1978, p. 14. © 1978 by the New York Times Company. Reprinted by permission.

many such institutions now report more discharges than admissions in any given year as well as a marked decrease in length of hospital stay. Drug therapy has proved most beneficial in the treatment of the psychoses. A given dosage may make schizophrenic "voices" disappear and render the patient accessible to other forms of therapy. For the outpatient, drugs have the advantage of being self-administered and less expensive than other therapies. The actual therapeutic effects of the major tranquilizers have been questioned, however. One critic has even asserted that they may produce a kind of medicinal straitjacket, making the patient so stiff and sedated as to prevent any type of behavior, disturbed or otherwise.[57] If insight and self-understanding are important therapeutic processes, the dulling and confusing effects of such drugs may actually impede recovery.

Psychotherapy.   The psychotherapies attempt to treat mental illness in psychological terms rather than through purely medical means and, unlike the above-described treatments, generally attempt some form of reeducation. Freudian psychotherapy (called psychoanalysis) relies on intensive sessions between analyst and patient, generally extending over a three- to four-year period. During these sessions, patients become aware of early childhood experiences and conflicts that may be unconsciously affecting their present behavior. The analyst encourages patients to talk freely, without inhibition—that is, to free-associate—and guides them in the growing self-awareness that results from analysis of their thoughts and memories. Psychoanalysis is a costly therapy, requiring great commitment on the part of the patient as well as considerable verbal skill. It is a therapy that has been largely limited to the educated middle and upper classes.

Other forms of psychotherapy, less intensive than analysis, do not extend over such a long period. Generally, a non-Freudian therapist (a psychiatrist or clinical psychologist) will take the present behavior problem of the patient as a starting point, drawing on unconscious memories of early childhood less than the Freudian analyst does. Most psychotherapists guide the patient toward self-awareness and shun giving direct advice; non-Freudian psychotherapists are somewhat more directive than Freudian analysts, for they are more often in the position of helping the patient overcome an immediate stress or problem. There is an exceedingly wide variety in the techniques employed by psychotherapists today.

Behavior Modification.   A therapy that differs in approach from traditional psychotherapies is behavior modification. According to behavior modification theory, people are maladjusted when they have learned or been taught maladjusted behaviors. A therapist can teach them to substitute new responses for those that they have displayed to their own disadvantage in the past. The therapy more or less dismisses the unconscious and its motivations and addresses itself solely to current behavioral problems that can be objectively described. For example, the behavior modification therapist has no concern with the symbolic meaning of a patient's peculiar walk or the unconscious conflict it may portray. Effort is expended instead on changing the peculiar walk, by providing positive reinforcement for the patient whenever the desired gait and posture are attained.

Within a limited sphere, behavior modification has been very successful. Perhaps because it refuses to consider behavioral maladjustments as symptomatic of deeper problems, its success has so far been confined to the alleviation of very specific, concrete disorders, such as phobias and compulsions.

Group Therapy.   Group therapies have grown up around many different therapeutic orientations. From a sociological viewpoint, their most important feature lies less in the therapist's orientation than in the group's effects on the individual members. In group therapy, patients become members of an in-group and thus gain a sense of belonging. They learn how to respond to others and how others are likely to perceive and react to them—a long step toward healthy interpersonal relations in society at large. Finally, the group, though supportive, is less inclined than outsiders to tolerate interpersonal dishonesty or pretense. The maladjusted individual, who may have "turned off" people on countless occasions without knowing why, gets instant feedback from peers on a specific subject. This feedback may prove painful at first; however, as the individual learns to profit from it, such occasions become less frequent. Moreover, interpersonal relations with all groups in which the individual takes part become correspondingly healthier and more satisfying.

Summary

The behavior of mentally ill persons often violates commonly held social norms and thus may be viewed as a form of deviant behavior. Mental illness constitutes a social problem because it tends to fracture normal patterns of social interaction and disrupt family, occupational, and other spheres of life.

Definitions of mental illness vary. The clinical or medical definition holds mental illness to be a diseased state within an individual. Statistically, mental illness can be viewed as a deviation from the norm in any quality relating to mental functioning. Socially, mental illness is a quality sometimes ascribed to those whose behavior or attitudes are not approved by the larger society. A practical definition describes mental illness as a condition that causes difficulty in an individual's functioning at home or at work. Although there is no general agreement on a definition of mental health either, there is agreement about some characteristics a mentally healthy person should have, among them an adequate feeling of security and adequate contact with the real world.

Many varieties of mental illness are classified by psychiatrists according to their symptoms. Of the most debilitating psychoses, the most prevalent form is schizophrenia, which is characterized by delusions, hallucinations, and withdrawal from personal relations. Other psychoses are paranoia (characterized by suspicion) and manic-depressive conditions (characterized by rapid changes between high exuberance and deep depression). People with psychotic disorders are more likely than other mentally ill individuals to be hospitalized.

Less debilitating, but still seriously damaging, are the neuroses, which are compulsive behavior patterns that interfere with everyday functioning. Most mental disorders in the population are of this sort.

There appears to be a relationship between the incidence of specific types of mental illness and rank on the socioeconomic scale. Psychoses are more prevalent among the poor and minorities; neuroses are more prevalent among the middle class and those of higher socioeconomic status. The type of mental illness suffered may also be related to age or occupational status.

Mental hospitals, which for a century have provided the principal mode of treatment for mental disorders, have recently been heavily criticized. Sociologist Erving Goffman has argued that these institutions actually require the kind of behavior that leaves a person unable to get along anywhere except inside a mental institution. Some modifications of organization within mental hospitals have been made in response to such criticism. There are many more disturbed persons in the population who are not hospitalized, however. One study revealed that although one of every four people interviewed felt the need of professional help for a disturbed condition, only one out of seven sought it.

Sociological explanations of mental illness look for causative factors in conditions outside the individual. One factor is prolonged isolation from social contact. Role theory deals with mental illness caused by the strain of social roles too numerous or ambiguous to be played successfully. Labeling theory emphasizes the extent to which defining and treating someone as mentally ill actually contributes to that person's illness.

As ideas of what causes mental illness have changed, new ways of dealing with it have emerged. Preventive psychiatry acts on the causes of mental illness at an early stage. The community mental health movement attempts to treat people in their own environment. Various forms of therapy hold faulty learning during childhood responsible for mental illness and attempt a reeducation process as a cure.

Notes

[1]Edwin Schur, *Labeling Deviant Behavior: Its Sociological Implications* (New York: Harper & Row, 1971), p. 51.

[2]A. H. Maslow and B. Mittlemann, *Principles of Abnormal Psychology* (New York: Harper & Row, 1951), pp. 14–15.

[3]Rene Dubos, *Mirage of Health* (New York: Harper & Row, 1959), p. 71.

[4]A review of the development of techniques and facilities for treating the mentally ill can be found in Albert Deutsch, *The Mentally Ill in America* (New York: Columbia University Press, 1959); and David J. Rothman, *The Discovery of the Asylum* (Boston: Little, Brown, 1971).

[5]This section is based on classifications found in American Psychiatric Association, *Diagnostic and Statistical Manual of Mental Disorders* (Washington, D.C.: American Psychiatric Association, 1968).

[6]Benjamin Pasamanick, "A Survey of Mental Disease in an Urban Population," *Archives of General Psychiatry* 5 (1961), 151–155.

[7]David Hamburg, *Psychiatry as a Behavioral Science* (Englewood Cliffs, N.J.: Prentice-Hall, 1972), pp. 25–46.

[8]Theodore Lidz, "The Family, Language, and the Transmission of Schizophrenia," *The Transmission of Schizophrenia*, ed. David Rosenthal and Seymour G. Kety (Oxford, England: Pergamon, 1968), p. 179.

[9]"Genetic Studies," *Transmission of Schizophrenia,* pp. 15–126.

[10]H. L. Newbold, "The Use of Vitamin B-12-b in Psychiatric Practice," *Orthomolecular Psychiatry* 1 (First Quarter 1972), 27.

[11]"Schizophrenia Clue," *Behavior Today,* 19 March 1973, p. 3.

[12]Leonard P. Ullman and Leonard Krasner, *A Psychological Approach to Abnormal Behavior* (Englewood Cliffs, N.J.: Prentice-Hall, 1969), p. 437.

[13]Edwin M. Lemert, *Human Deviance, Social Problems, and Social Control* (Englewood Cliffs, N.J.: Prentice-Hall, 1967), pp. 197–211.

[14]Peter E. Nathan and Sandra L. Harris, *Psychopathology and Society* (New York: McGraw-Hill, 1975), pp. 415–433.

[15]Margaret Mead, "The Concept of Culture and the Psychosomatic Approach," *Psychiatry* 10 (February 1947), 57–76.

[16]Pasamanick, "A Survey of Mental Disease," pp. 151–155.

[17]Ibid., p. 155.

[18]Leo Srole et al., *Mental Health in the Metropolis* (New York: McGraw-Hill, 1962), p. 138.

[19]A. B. Hollingshead and F. C. Redlich, *Social Class and Mental Illness: A Community Study* (New York: Wiley, 1958).

[20]Jerome K. Myers and Lee L. Bean, *A Decade Later: A Follow-up of Social Class and Mental Illness* (New York: Wiley, 1967).

[21]Hollingshead and Redlich, *Social Class and Mental Illness.*

[22]Ibid., p. 360.

[23]Myers and Bean, *A Decade Later.*

[24]Jacob Tuckman and Robert J. Kleiner, "Discrepancy between Aspirations and Achievement as a Predictor of Schizophrenia," *Behavioral Science* 7 (1962), 443–447.

[25]Walter R. Gove, "Societal Reactions as an Explanation of Mental Illness: An Evaluation," *American Sociological Review* 35 (1970), 873–883.

[26]Carl A. Taube, "Admissions to Outpatient Psychiatric Services, 1969, by Age, Sex and Diagnosis," *Statistical Note 48,* National Institute of Mental Health (Washington, D.C.: Government Printing Office, 1971).

[27]Ibid.

[28]Darrel Rieger, "Trends in White Admissions and Admission of Other Races to Selected Mental Health Services, United States, 1971–1975," *Memorandum No. 39,* National Institute of Mental Health (Washington, D.C.: Government Printing Office, 1978).

[29]Benjamin Malzberg, "Mental Disorders in the United States," *The Encyclopedia of Mental Health,* ed. Albert Deutsch and Helen Fishman (New York: Grolier, Watts, 1963), pp. 1064–1065.

[30]Erving Goffman, "Introduction," *Asylums* (New York: Doubleday/Anchor Books, 1961).

[31]Ibid., pp. 22–25.

[32]Ibid., p. 70.

[33]Ibid., p. 386.

[34]U.S. Department of Health, Education, and Welfare, National Institute of Mental Health, *Additions and Resident Patients at End of Year State and County Mental Hospitals by Age and Diagnosis, by State, United States 1976* (Rockville, Md.: National Institute of Mental Health, 1978), p. 2.

[35]U.S. Department of Health, Education, and Welfare, National Institute of Mental Health, *State and County Hospitals, United States,* 1973–74, Publication No. ADM 76-361 (Washington, D.C.: Government Printing Office, 1975), p. 1.

[36]Ibid., pp. 1–2.

[37]R. E. L. Faris, "Cultural Isolation and the Schizophrenic Personality," *American Journal of Sociology* 39 (September 1934), 155–169.

[38]H. Warren Dunham, *Sociological Theory and Mental Disorder* (Detroit: Wayne State University Press, 1959).

[39]H. S. Sullivan, *The Interpersonal Theory of Psychiatry* (New York: Norton, 1953).

[40]Karen Horney, *The Neurotic Personality of Our Time,* rev. ed. (New York: Norton, 1937).

[41]Lloyd H. Rogler and August B. Hollingshead, *Trapped: Families and Schizophrenia* (New York: Wiley, 1965).

[42]Thomas J. Scheff, *Being Mentally Ill: A Sociological Theory* (Chicago: Aldine, 1966).

[43]John Lofland, *Deviance and Identity* (Englewood Cliffs, N.J.: Prentice-Hall, 1969), p. 136.

[44]Ibid.

[45]Gove, "Societal Reactions as an Explanation of Mental Illness," pp. 873–883.

[46]Thomas Szasz, *The Myth of Mental Illness* (New York: Harper & Row, Hoeber Medical Division, 1967).

[47]R. D. Laing, *The Politics of Experience* (New York: Pantheon, 1967); Goffman, *Asylums.*

[48]David L. Rosenhan, "On Being Sane in Insane Places," *Science* 179 (January 1973), 250–258.

[49]Daniel Oran, "Judges and Psychiatrists Lock Up Too Many People," *Psychology Today*, August 1973, p. 20; Thomas Scheff, "The Societal Reaction to Deviance: Ascriptive Elements in the Psychiatric Screening of Mental Patients in a Mid-Western State." *Social Problems* 11 (Spring 1964), 401–413.

[50]Barry E. Wolfe, "The Donaldson Decision," *Schizophrenia Bulletin*, National Institute of Mental Health, Summer 1975, pp. 4–6.

[51]Ibid.

[52]Ibid., p. 5.

[53]Eli M. Bower, "Primary Prevention of Mental and Emotional Disorders," *American Journal of Orthopsychiatry* 5 (October 1963), 832–848.

[54]Ibid,. pp. 837–844.

[55]Benjamin Pasamanick, Frank R. Scarpitti, and Simon Dinitz, *Schizophrenics in the Community* (New York: Appleton, 1967).

[56]Roger M. Williams, "From Bedlam to Chaos: Are They Closing the Mental Hospitals Too Soon?" *Psychology Today* 10 (May 1977), 124–127.

[57]J. O. Cole, "Behavioral Toxicity," *Drugs and Behavior*, ed. L. Uhr and J. G. Miller (New York: Wiley, 1960), pp. 100–183.

Crime and Justice

13

Page one of a big-city newspaper headlines the discovery of a third rape-murder victim in another city. Page three details some local news: three people have been robbed at knifepoint, a young boy has been shot and killed by "an unknown assailant," and a policeman is in critical condition after tangling with a killer. Page five tells the story of a bank robbery in which hostages were taken to ensure the safety of the bank robbers. Page seven quotes a police official saying that three recent murders are the result of a feud between rival drug traffickers. Page twenty reports that a prison riot has been suppressed in a distant state, and a feature article on page thirty-two advises ways of burglarproofing the home.

In the same newspaper are reports of other crimes that arouse no fears. A man is arrested for falsifying income tax returns. A financier flees the country after defrauding investors of many millions of dollars. A case is documented against local judges benevolent to organized crime figures who appear before them. An automobile manufacturer has knowingly ignored a defect in its cars that may cause thousands of highway accidents.

Americans fear crime on a selective basis. They are frightened and outraged by the crimes in the first category—crimes of violence and crimes against personal property. But the fleeing financier may be regarded by many as a clever rascal, and the cheating taxpayer who is caught may be perceived as unlucky. Our attitudes toward these different types of crime and criminal behavior reveal a certain amount of hypocrisy. The individuals who fear street crime and hate criminals may think nothing of taking some office supplies; yet, they do not think of themselves as criminals. Clearly, when citizens vote overwhelmingly for a politician who promises to get tough on crime by stricter law enforcement and harsher criminal penalties, they seldom expect such policies to affect price fixing or industrial espionage. The politician and the voters understand that what is wanted is a crackdown on crime in the streets, not crime in the executive suites.

Crime has traditionally been studied as a form of deviant behavior. The processes of rule creation, individual deviation from those rules, and social control (the application of sanctions to rule violators) are common to all social groups. Children's play groups, factory workers, and juvenile gangs alike establish certain rules and take action against those who violate the rules. Criminal and delinquent behaviors represent deviations from a very important set of social rules, namely those that have been codified in the criminal law. The law is used as a means to organize the ways in which a society reacts to rule violations, and it specifies sanctions to be applied to various offenses, ranging from fines to imprisonment to loss of life.

The great classical sociologist Emile Durkheim broke with previous thinking in arguing that crime is not a social pathology but rather a normal phenomenon, inextricably bound up with the fundamental conditions of all social life. In Durkheim's view, a society without crime is an impossibility, for the very organization of complex societies prevents total conformity to all social rules by all members.[1] Moreover, crime has positive consequences for a social system. The existence of crime strengthens collective sentiments as to what is right and proper; it serves to contrast the unacceptable from the acceptable. Collective solidarity is enhanced as conformers are united in emotional solidarity against deviators.

Those who engage in criminal behavior are not necessarily parasitic elements set apart from conventional society; they play a definite role in normal social life, and this role may even be a positive one. Durkheim used the example of Socrates to illustrate that crime may serve the valuable function of pointing to areas of the social system where change is necessary.

Many Americans look upon taking office supplies as part of what their employers owe them rather than as the crime of theft.

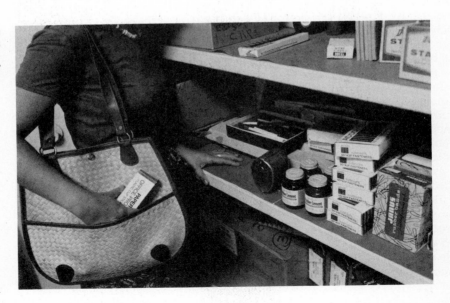

According to Athenian law, Socrates was a criminal, and his condemnation was no more than just. However, his crime, namely, the independence of his thought, rendered a service not only to humanity but to his country. It served to prepare a new mortality and faith which the Athenians needed, since the traditions by which they had lived until then were no longer in harmony with the current conditions of life.[2]

From one perspective, then, the existence of crime may be taken as an indication of a healthy flexibility necessary for a society to adapt to changing conditions. Crime may serve to enhance the process of adaptation by pointing to defects in societal organization.

Various mechanisms of social control exist within collectivities to deter or prevent deviant behavior. The most fundamental mechanism is the individual internalization of social norms, which is promoted by major institutions such as religion and the family. Indeed, the widespread acceptance and support of basic normative standards by members of society is the most effective force in suppressing deviant behavior. However, since conflict over the content and legitimacy of social rules nearly always exists, societies also establish formal mechanisms of control. Official agencies of the state enact legislation prohibiting certain types of behavior, and a formal enforcement apparatus is vested with the power to detect and punish violations of these rules.

The value conflict approach is particularly useful in understanding problems related to the formal mechanisms of social control, for it focuses attention on the criminal laws themselves—who makes them and what interests they serve—rather than entirely on those who break the laws. Powerful and influential groups have a disproportionate ability to establish rules that reflect their own interests and values. Whereas some parts of the criminal law —homicide laws, for example—reflect the values of the vast majority of the population, others conflict with the values and interests of certain groups to which they apply. The conflict and controversy surrounding current marijuana and sexual conduct laws are clear examples of situations in which certain groups do not support or approve of rules that those with political power have succeeded in having codified into law.

Current conflicts over the causes and prevention of crime are partly a reflection of old and new attitudes toward crime. Traditional interpretations involve the perception of criminals as an essentially separate class of people whose behavior can be explained in religious terms ("criminals are evil, possessed by the devil") or biological terms ("you can tell a criminal by the shape of his head," or "black people are just naturally inclined to crime") or social terms ("only lower-class people engage in crime"). Traditionally solutions to crime are simple and punitive: criminals should be locked up and punished; if punishments are harsh enough, criminals will be afraid to break the law. More recent attitudes involve an essentially sociological perspective, which locates the causes of criminal behavior in environmental factors such as poverty, overcrowding, frustration over racial discrimination, and cultural norms favoring violence and aggression. Viewed in this perspective, crime rates can be reduced only by changing the environmental conditions that influence criminal behavior.

Conflict exists not only with regard to the content of the criminal code and the cause of crime but also concerning the actions of the official agencies of social control. Various groups hold differing views as to the appropriate operation of the social control system and what is problematic in that system. Opinions diverge on issues such as the powers of police agencies, citizen committees to review police actions, and the rights of the individual versus the "handcuffing" of enforcement personnel charged with the investigation of crimes. Since the legal system is such a pivotal social institution, continuing conflict may be expected to permeate that system and contribute to the social problems arising from its operation. At the same time, however, conflict may be a forerunner of needed changes in the law and the legal system.

Characterizing Crime and Criminality

Crime can be defined legally in terms of a body of law that codifies a society's rules about proper and improper behavior. The American legal system includes both civil and criminal codes. The civil code defines certain kinds of behavior as civil wrongs and entitles those offended to compensation or redress; the civil courts act only as arbiters between private parties. Libel suits or suits demanding compensation for a work-related injury are examples of civil suits.

Criminal law governs behavior that is described as an offense aganist the state; essentially, criminals are considered threats to public order. Criminal law involves penal sanctions imposed by the state. Someone who breaks a criminal law can be arrested, brought to trial, and penalized. Criminal statutes are very specifically worded, outlining the exact nature of the offense, the different ways in which it can be committed, and the penalties attached. A felony is defined as a crime serious enough to warrant imprisonment for more than a year, whereas a misdemeanor is a lesser offense warranting a fine or imprisonment for less than a year. Simple assault is a misdemeanor, whereas assault with a deadly weapon, a more serious offense, is a felony.

Crime can be considered in a cultural or social context as well as a legal context. In our society bigamy is illegal; in a Moslem society a man can have as many as four wives. In some communist countries free enterprise is illegal; the free enterprise system is a solid tradition in the United States, and many American laws reinforce this system. What comes to be defined as crime varies from culture to culture depending upon the political ideology and values of the dominant class.

Rising Rates and Growing Fear

The major source of statistical information on crime in the United States is the set of *Uniform Crime Reports* published annually by the Federal Bureau of Investigation. To compile these figures, the FBI relies on statistics submitted by local police departments. A crime index is issued, based on seven offenses thought to serve as a weather vane for all crime: murder and nonnegligent manslaughter, forcible rape, aggravated assault, robbery, burglary, larceny, and auto theft. The first four offenses make up the category of violent crime or crime against persons, while the latter three are classified as property crimes. Property crimes usually account for about 90 percent of all crimes committed in the United States.[3]

The *Uniform Crime Reports* for 1977 reveal an increase over 1973, in all but one crime contributing to the index. The only crime that decreased during this period was murder. A comparison between the 1977 and 1968 indexes suggests a phenomenal growth in crime over the past decade, ranging from a 39 percent increase in the murder rate to a 99 percent rise in the rate of forcible rapes.[4] Since 1977, the number of crime index offenses and the rate of offenses per 100,000 residents of the United States have both increased more than seven times the overall population growth of the country (see Figure 13.1).

These figures seem to justify the growing fear of crime in this country. And there are indications that they do not even reflect a true picture of the extent of crime. Many crimes, for instance, are never reported to the police. Forcible rape is rarely reported, because the victims are unwilling to endure the painful processes of investigation and trial. Minority group victims may mistrust the police and be afraid to get involved in a police investigation. Many people fail to report crimes because they do not believe the police will find the offender.

Other facts can also distort the crime picture. Police departments do not necessarily record all the crimes reported to them or include them in statis-

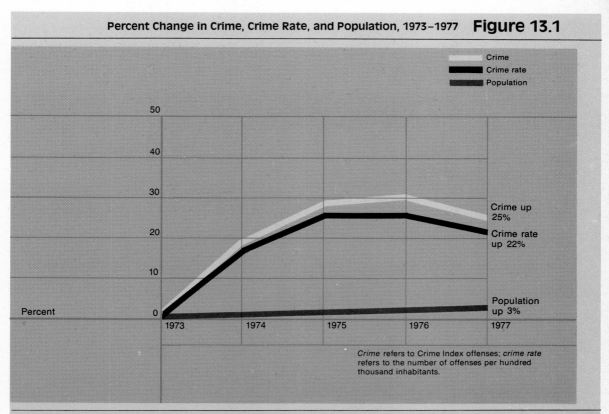

Percent Change in Crime, Crime Rate, and Population, 1973–1977　**Figure 13.1**

Crime up 25%

Crime rate up 22%

Population up 3%

Crime refers to Crime Index offenses; *crime rate* refers to the number of offenses per hundred thousand inhabitants.

Source: U.S. Federal Bureau of Investigation, *Uniform Crime Reports, 1977* (Washington, D.C.: Government Printing Office, 1978), p. 35.

tics sent to the FBI. In the past, some crimes committed in the ghetto, or by one minority group member against another, have not been considered important enough to be recorded or investigated by police. High crime rates have always been associated with the slums, but dramatic increases in crimes reported from these areas may represent changes in reporting rather than changes in actual crime rates. A rise in reported crime may also reflect increased police efficiency. A low crime rate may mean that many crimes are undetected and therefore unreported; higher rates may mean improved methods of detection and reporting rather than an increase in the true incidence of crime.

All these considerations indicate that the FBI's official records offer a somewhat misleading view of the extent of crime today and in the past. In a sense, it is impossible to obtain really accurate measures of the extent of crime, since an unknown quantity of crimes go completely undetected and unreported.

Despite such deficiencies in the official crime statistics, social scientists have been able to make certain generalizations about the distribution and trends of crime. One study, for example, has found that adult crime rates, particularly rates of property offenses, correlate directly with unemployment.[5] This suggests that a good deal of the recent increase in crime may be related to the economic recession in this country. If crime competes with legitimate occupations as a source of income for certain segments of the population, then as unemployment rises and legitimate opportunities are

Enforcing honesty: A large part of "the rising cost of doing business" is due to shoplifting, which costs business due to direct thievery and because additional personnel and technology are necessary to prevent losses.

reduced, property crimes may become an increasingly attractive alternative as a means of earning a living.

Statistically, most crimes occur in inner-city areas, and research suggests that residents of these areas are indeed worried about their personal safety. Yet the same research points out that residents of low-crime areas (such as wealthy suburbs) are even *more* fearful than residents of high-crime areas. The people who express the most fear about crime also report the most apprehension about changing social conditions—particularly racial integration.[6] In analyzing the "crime problem" in the United States, it may be more useful to examine who is arrested for crimes and how those crimes are perceived than to consider the actual extent of crime.

Who and Where Are the Criminals?

To the people who live in comfortable suburbs, it may seem obvious that crime is a city problem. To a policeman investigating gambling and prostitution, it may seem that organized crime is the heart of the problem. To residents of poor central-city neighborhoods, the police themselves may seem like criminals. Where does crime occur, and who are its perpetrators? Sociological studies of criminals often focus on five major demographic variables: sex, age, race and ethnicity, social class, and geographical location.

Sex

Males are far more likely to engage in criminal behavior than females. Statistics from 1977 show that male arrests outnumbered female arrests by a ratio of five to one. Males committed 91.9 percent of all auto thefts, 94.0 percent of all burglaries, and 92.6 percent of all robberies reported. The only serious crimes for which the percentage of female offenders is significant are murder (14.5 percent) and larceny (31.8 percent).[7]

There are some indications that the trend is shifting. FBI statistics from 1968 to 1977 show male arrests for major crimes increased 36 percent while female arrests increased 116 percent (see Table 13.1).[8] The greatest increases have been in property crimes such as larceny, but there are also many more female assaults and robberies. In a society that traditionally encourages active and aggressive behavior in males and passivity in females, the differences between the amount of criminal behavior among the two sexes are not surprising. And it is conceivable that the recent increase in female crimes may be partially due to the increased opportunity of women today in all areas of national life.

Age

Teenagers and young adults have sustained higher crime rates than other groups for as long as studies have been conducted. FBI statistics for 1977 indicate that persons under 15 comprised 8.8 percent of the total police arrests for that year. Persons under 18 constituted 24.0 percent of the total arrests made, and persons under 21 accounted for 40.3 percent of all arrests.[9] Although young people are seldom involved in sophisticated or career crimi-

Table 13.1 — Arrest Increases between 1968 and 1977, by Sex

	Arrest Increases	
	Men	Women
Violent crime	48.9	72.0
Murder and nonnegligent manslaughter	30.8	17.9
Forcible rape	57.2	—
Robbery	45.4	99.5
Aggravated assault	52.0	71.0
Property crime	33.7	121.3
Burglary—breaking or entering	31.0	90.6
Larceny—theft	52.7	128.8
Motor vehicle theft	18.6	36.3

source: U.S. Federal Bureau of Investigation, *Uniform Crime Reports 1977* (Washington, D.C.: Government Printing Office, 1978), p. 175.

nality, they are overrepresented in property crimes, vandalism, and the offenses that apply only to juveniles, such as truancy or running away. Of course, the number of arrests of young people for drug violations has increased sharply in recent years. In 1977, 51 percent of the arrests for narcotics drug law violations were of persons under 21.[10]

Race and Ethnicity

The ethnic differences in criminal behavior have been somewhat politicized in recent years, and the sociological evidence is often conflicting. Blacks, Mexicans, Puerto Ricans, and American Indians all maintain high crime rates, whereas the rates for both Jews and Orientals remain much below the average for all groups.[11] Yet these differences are subject to closer scrutiny.

The black crime rate is estimated to be two to five times as high as the black percentage of the population.[12] This could be a result of differential enforcement by legal agencies. At least one study has indicated that blacks are usually arrested, brought to trial, and convicted more often than whites. Once blacks are convicted, they are also less likely to receive probation or a suspended sentence or to be paroled.[13] More recent studies have produced conflicting findings.

The relationship between race and crime is an exceedingly complex one, and substantial methodological problems present themselves in interpreting this relationship. A recent analysis of studies that have found minimal discriminatory treatment of blacks suggests that the effect of race on case disposition may be masked by its complex relations with other factors and that discrimination may be operating in subtle and indirect ways.[14] Race and social class also tend to overlap; thus, black-white differences in crime rates may not be a result of race per se but rather of factors associated with low socioeconomic status.

Data on the criminal behavior of immigrant families seem to bear out a correlation between crime and low socioeconomic status. In the past, immigrants and the children of immigrants—who are usually very low on the socioeconomic scale—had very high crime rates.[15] In fact, the attitude of the middle class toward these new immigrants—the Irish, Italians, Greeks, and others—was very similar to the middle-class attitude toward blacks and Puerto Ricans today. As the children and grandchildren of immigrants moved up the economic scale, the high crime rates associated with those ethnic groups disappeared. Middle-class blacks and Puerto Ricans show the same relatively low crime rates as middle-class people from any other ethnic groups.

Social Class

As might be expected, most persons who commit the ordinary or index crimes come from low socioeconomic backgrounds. This is particularly true for younger offenders. Any number of studies of juvenile offenders have concluded that the vast majority of the subjects lived in low-income areas.[16] But there is another view, supported by self-report studies involving subjects of all socioeconomic groups, that lower-class people are simply more likely to be arrested and convicted, whereas middle- and upper-class offenders often manage to avoid arrest and particularly conviction.[17] Consider the staggering amount of white-collar crime in this country—an activity of members of higher socioeconomic classes than the blue-collar crimes of assault, robbery, and burglary—and this theory seems quite plausible. Even for their crimes, the poor pay more.

Many crimes of violence occur between friends, neighbors, and family members. Here, the police are available to prevent a crime. More often, they're not.

Geography

For a variety of reasons, cities seem to produce and nurture considerably more crime than rural areas. Suburban crime rates are higher than rural rates but still considerably below urban rates. One reason for the high urban rates is the presence of slum or ghetto areas with their poverty, unemployment, and overcrowding—all conditions associated with crime.[18] As the distance from the inner city increases, the crime rate tends to go down. Cities also attract people in search of anonymity; those who commit crimes often fall quite neatly into this group.

Caution must be used in interpreting these findings, however, because crime that is not too serious may be handled informally in rural and some suburban areas. A rural youth in trouble will probably be dealt with by police officials who know the family and are more likely to resolve the problem by talking it over with family members than by making an arrest. Consequently, the incident is never recorded in official crime statistics. Urban police seldom take such an individualized approach to criminal offenders.

Nonetheless, in recent years there has been a notable increase in reported crime in suburban and rural areas. The official statistics for the year 1977 indicate that while violent crime decreased 7.2 percent in cities with a population over 1,000,000 and 2.5 percent in cities larger than 250,000, it increased by 2 percent and 6 percent in both suburban and rural areas respectively.[19] This statistical increase in suburban relative to urban crime may be a reflection of greater police surveillance and effectiveness in such areas. Then, too, certain types of crime may be "safer" as well as more lucrative in nonurban areas, where police are less concentrated. Other factors affecting rising suburban crime rates are the growing urbanization of these areas and their linkage to the center cities by means of high speed transportation arteries. Superhighways make fast movement in and out of suburban areas possible. Further, a substantial portion of suburban crime is taking place in the large shopping centers located on or near major transportation arteries.

Urban-rural differences are the most significant factors in the geographic distribution of crime. For obvious reasons, states with large urban centers usually have higher crime rates than rural states. There are slight regional differences in types of crime committed, with western states supporting the highest property crime rates and the South particularly noted for homicide.[20]

Uncovering the Roots of Criminal Behavior

Clearly, there are no simple correlations between crime and sex, age, geography, race and ethnicity, or even social class. Hence, more elaborate theories of criminal behavior have been developed in an attempt to understand who becomes criminal and why.

Philosophers, theologians, and revolutionaries, as well as social scientists, have long pondered the question of why some individuals deviate from social rules. Theories of some psychological or biological factor that makes criminals different from noncriminals have difficulty in explaining the preponderance of conforming behavior in those who possess the suspected trait or characteristic. Theories constructed to explain habitual or sustained criminal activity have been found inadequate to explain episodic or isolated acts of crime.

Social scientists now look to several types of factors in explaining the wide variety of criminal behavior. Some of these factors relate to features of the social structure, such as restricted and unequal opportunities, and others relate to the unique experiences and life histories of the individual. Although the specific tenets of the various sociological theories differ, and no single theory is presently accepted as a comprehensive explanation of criminal behavior, it is generally agreed that most criminal conduct, like other forms of deviant action, is socially learned behavior.

From Medieval Demons to Environmental Evils

Crime has always been a part of Western culture, and the most popular explanations of crime have been those that somehow distinguish criminals from the rest of society.[21] After the Middle Ages, when criminals were believed to be evil by nature or possessed by demons, theological explanations became less popular, and theories of criminality based on class distinctions gained support. People with social position and property were responsible citizens; lower-class people were rough, ill-bred, and inclined toward crime. When an upper-class person committed a notorious crime, this was seen as an aberration of nature or the effect or a low-born ancestor somewhere in the past. Upper-class people used this idea to justify strong legal controls over the lower classes. Nineteenth-century debates on the extension of voting privileges revolved in part around the question of whether the lower classes, with their "criminal tendencies," could be trusted with voting power. Of course, many of the corrupt or harmful actions of members of the upper classes were not defined as crime by those in positions of legal authority.

During the late nineteenth century, theories based on psychological and mental abnormalities became popular. The Italian criminologist Cesare Lombroso originated this approach by making precise measurements of the skulls of criminals, on which he based his theory of the "born criminal."[22] Lombroso believed that criminals could be distinguished from noncriminals in terms of measurable physical differences. The presence of certain physical stigmata, such as a receding forehead, prominent eyebrows, and a twisted nose, was viewed as evidence of an "atavistic type" of human being with traits approximating those of primitive people and lower animals. Lombroso's work was heavily criticized on methodological grounds (including the failure to use control groups) and for being unable to explain occasional criminal behavior, and he subsequently modified his position to recognize the significance of environmental factors in shaping the criminal.

Other early attempts to explain crime were similarly based on the assumption that criminal individuals represent a special, different type of human being.[23] Physicians studied criminals to see whether physical illness had something to do with behavior. Biologists looked for hereditary differences between criminals and noncriminals. Freudian theorists viewed crime as still another unconscious effort to resolve psychic conflict. Recently a new twist has been added to this type of approach, as researchers have attempted to link male criminal behavior with the presence of an XYY chromosome imbalance.[24]

Underlying all these approaches is a fundamental belief that criminals are aberrant individuals, possessing some quirk of mind or body that is not present in the rest of us. Yet psychological theories of criminal behavior have proved inadequate, and the search for physical causes of criminal behavior has been even less successful. Certain brain tumors may cause violent and aggressive behavior, but this is a rare condition and does not really explain criminality.

Finally, sociologists began to investigate environmental factors as causes of criminal behavior; this approach has been the most successful so far in explaining the differences between criminals and noncriminals. Sociological theories assume that social variables, not individual differences, are responsible for criminal behavior. Early studies identified high crime rates with overcrowded inner-city poverty areas.[25] No matter what racial or ethnic groups established themselves in certain slums, crime rates continued to be high. People have always associated high crime rates with slum dwellers, but the sociologists had for the first time identified crime with the slum environment rather than with the particular people who lived there. This change in perspective was important because it implied that crime could be eliminated by changing factors in the environment that engendered criminal behavior. Today there are many sociological theories of the cause of crime; among the most widely accepted are those that attribute criminal behavior to social structure, delinquent subculture, differential association, and labeling.

Anomie: Social Structure Theory

Searching for an explanation of suicide rates in different cultures, Emile Durkheim developed the concept of anomie.[26] This French term translates roughly as normlessness, or a state of confusion produced by sudden or dramatic changes in the social structure. Robert Merton, a contemporary American sociologist, has taken the concept one step further in studying crime. He points out that although American society sets cultural goals that revolve around material success, it severely limits the opportunities for various social, ethnic, and racial groups to achieve this kind of success. Merton maintains that where a disjunction between cultural goals and institutionalized means for their achievement exists, a condition of anomie prevails.[27] When this happens, acute problems of crime and delinquency follow. Conversely, when a society provides fairly equal access for all to its material benefits, anomie and crime are not as prevalent. The Scandinavian countries, for instance, have largely homogeneous populations with no great extremes of poverty and wealth, and crime rates in these countries are far lower than in the United States.[28]

American culture does place great emphasis on material success. Advertisements present new products as seductively as possible and urge people to buy—a house, a car, new clothes, a swimming pool, an electric toothbrush. Most of us cannot afford all these luxuries, but we come to *want* them. So some people turn to crime: a little shoplifting, income tax evasion, or armed robbery. The poorest in our society are likely to be the most frustrated. The unemployed ghetto youth may hold up a liquor store, start selling drugs, or even engage in random violence and vandalism out of rage and frustration.

Although in agreement with Merton that juvenile crime usually emanates from lower-class neighborhoods, Albert Cohen feels that it represents a reaction to values imposed by middle-class social institutions, such as schools. Since lower-class youths are unprepared to measure up to middle-class standards of ambition, deferment of gratification, and control of aggression, they develop status anxiety. To cope with this anxiety, they subscribe to the norms of a delinquent subculture—a different set of standards, in which middle-class values are repudiated.[29] Other researchers have isolated three types of subcultures: the criminal (money-oriented), the conflict (gang-oriented), and the retreatist (drug-oriented). Criminal subcultures exist where illegal activities are condoned by community values. Conflict patterns occur where there are no effective controls on young people, and retreatist subcultures absorb those who cannot adapt to criminal activity or enter into a conflict pattern and seek simply to escape into drugs or alcohol.[30]

One difficulty with subculture theory is that it accounts for only lower-class males. Another is that delinquent youths, especially in gangs, may engage in activities that characterize all these subcultural types—crimes, gang fighting, and drugs. Finally, little importance is attributed to social variables such as the family, which may produce a great deal of the stress and frustration that drive the delinquent youth to criminal behavior.

Differential association theory explains a wider range of criminal behavior than the two theories already discussed. Its basic hypothesis is that criminal behavior is learned through interaction with a group that offers rewards to the learners and so helps them build criminal identities.[31] Specific tech-

Criminal Youth: Delinquent Subculture Theory

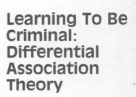

Learning To Be Criminal: Differential Association Theory

Viewing the policeman as a friend and helper is an important part of delinquency prevention. Often for just reasons, minority youths see the policeman as an enemy, the enforcer of a value system which oppresses and abuses them. Most police departments are now working hard to change that image.

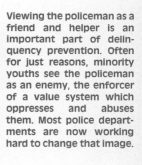

niques for committing crimes, as well as motives, drives, rationalization, and attitudes essential to criminality are all part of the learning process.

A new salesperson may be surprised to discover from others on the sales staff that cheating on expense accounts is *expected*. Since the company can count expense account payments as tax-deductible business expenses, company officials would rather have their employees "adjust" their expense accounts than ask for raises in salary. If the newcomer has any doubts, friendly company accountants provide reassurance and assistance in filling out the forms.

In the ghetto, a youth may learn early in life that certain criminal behaviors are not only condoned but encouraged by his peers. An older brother or a friend may instruct him in the fine arts of purse snatching or breaking and entering, lend him a gun or knife, and recruit him into a gang. Young people are particularly susceptible to social pressure from their peers; when the peer group is engaged in criminal behavior, a youth is unlikely to resist the pressure to conform.

In prison, convicts overwhelmingly identify with other convicts. Criminal behavior becomes the norm, and the first offender may leave prison with an increased commitment to crime and greater knowledge of criminal techniques—thanks to the encouragement and advice of more experienced criminals.

Living Up to a Reputation: Labeling Theories

Some criminologists argue that a person once labeled criminal will tend to live up to that reputation. Thus deviance (or criminality) is not a quality of behavior but a consequence of the way society treats an offender.[32] In other words, the nature and implications of criminal acts are determined by our social handling of them. The trial procedure is an example of a "status degradation" ceremony, in which a person's law-abiding status is taken away and a criminal status is substituted.[33] In response to the degraded status that the individual has been assigned and rejection by others who have maintained their law-abiding status, the individual may come to construct a new, criminal self-image and associate more frequently with persons or groups who support this new identity. Largely cut off from legitimate opportunities because of this criminal status, the individual's new social affiliations are likely to provide greater access to illegitimate opportunities. In this manner, "the stigmatization of the deviant and the isolation imposed on him often force him to seek out social circles which support him but also tend to perpetuate his deviancy."[34]

A study carried out by sociologists Richard Schwartz and Jerome Skolnick indicates the extent to which legitimate social opportunities may be reduced following the labeling of an individual as criminal.[35] Fictitious employment applications were prepared that were identical in all respects with the exception of the presence or absence of a criminal record for assault. These applications were submitted to prospective employers to test their reactions to a person with a criminal record and to assess the employment liabilities that accompany such a status. The results were striking. Of the applications that contained no criminal record, 36 percent received positive response from employers, whereas only 4 percent of the applications containing a record of a criminal conviction were given a favorable response.

Thus the labeling of a person as criminal is systematically related to a reduction in legitimate employment opportunities and may make participation in criminal activities appear an increasingly attractive alternative. "In effect, the original 'causes' of the deviation recede and give way to the central importance of the disapproving, degradational, and isolating reactions of society."[36] Stated in its simplest form, then, labeling theory holds that the nature of the societal reaction to criminal behavior may act to reinforce, cement, and even amplify the objectionable conduct.

There is no shortage of theories about criminal behavior, and each of the concepts discussed here offers some important insights. It is probably impossible to develop one major unifying theory of crime that would help us devise specific ways of attacking the problem. It is not enough to be aware that a delinquent subculture may exist in center-city neighborhoods, or that some people may use criminal behavior as a means to achieve material success. Crime in the United States involves a widely disparate group of lawbreakers who do not always behave according to our sociological explanations.

Cataloging Criminal Behavior

A full catalog of criminal activities would include violations ranging from adultery to abduction and from selling beer to a minor to skyjacking. Clearly, the diversity of criminal behavior makes a comprehensive list impossible. Our concern in this section is with law-violating behaviors reflecting patterned interaction or a purposeful social organization centered around criminal activities. These patterns are juvenile, professional, organized, and white-collar crime.

Juvenile Crime

The sheer growth of crime committed by persons under 18 troubles everyone concerned with criminology. FBI statistics show that from 1968 through 1977 arrests of juveniles for violent crimes increased by 59 percent, whereas arrests for all criminal violations increased only 50 percent. In 1977, 28 percent of all arrests for index offenses involved juveniles, whereas persons 10 to 17 years of age accounted for only about 15 percent of the total United States population.[37] Between 1968 and 1977 juvenile arrests for all index crimes, with the exception of motor vehicle theft, rose significantly. The most drastic increase was the 77 percent change in arrests of juveniles for aggravated assault.[38] Juveniles under the age of 15 accounted for 18 percent of all arrests for index property crimes and 6 percent of all violent crimes in 1977.[39]

Juvenile crime is usually termed *delinquency*. Different rules apply to offenses committed by juveniles, and these offenses are handled by separate juvenile courts. The violations for which minors can be arrested include not only the ones applicable to adults in the same jurisdiction but also a series of vague categories such as habitual vagrancy, sexual promiscuity, truancy, incorrigibility, and deportment endangering morals, health, or general welfare of the minor. The vagueness of many offenses is intentional; judges are expected to be flexible in judging young people and devising ways of rescuing them from lives of crime. The system has been abused, however, because many judges have provided differential justice to various categories of juvenile defendants. Some judges consistently sentence girls accused of sexual promiscuity to reform schools while dismissing cases of boys similarly accused. Others tend to release middle-class youngsters to the custody of their families while sentencing lower-class minority youths charged with the same offenses to correctional institutions.

Much delinquency involves behavior considered criminal for any age group. Auto theft and drug abuse are particularly prevalent now, and to an extent these offenses cut across social, regional, and racial distinctions. Teenage gangs still flourish in most major cities. Some have become more sophisticated, better organized, and thus more dangerous. Although most members are juveniles, the leaders are often men in their twenties. And while some gangs have been connected with drug traffic and gunrunning, others have been credited for positive activities, such as keeping neighborhoods free of drug pushers, alcoholics, and prostitutes.

Professional Approach to Crime

The attitudes and behavior of professional criminals distinguish them from others involved in crime. These people make their careers in larceny, forgery, robbery, confidence games, or some other illegal activity; they approach their work with the same sort of professional standards as do doctors and lawyers. They are usually skillful enough to make crime an economic livelihood and are seldom apprehended, because nothing illegal is attempted before either the police or the courts or both have been paid off to ensure safety.[40] Even in the more hazardous occupation of robbery, professional criminals are considerably more prudent than amateurs and are less likely to be caught.

Professional criminals also maintain a status system, which attaches the highest prestige to confidence schemes. These operations begin with the premise that most conventional citizens are basically out to earn a fast dollar. The "mark," or victim, is approached with some dishonest plan for making a great deal of money and is ultimately relieved of some of his own money by the confidence man. Unwilling to admit to being duped or engaged in some shady activity, the mark rarely reports losses to the police.

Because professional criminals take great pains to protect themselves, their social visibility is low and their total contribution to crime in the United States remains uncertain. It is believed, however, that there are not many professional criminals and that the number has been declining in recent years.[41]

Organized Crime

Some of the wealthiest American criminals lead quiet, respectable lives in exclusive suburbs. They are often good family men who attend church regularly and love their children. They are successful businessmen, but their business is crime and their business methods often include torture and murder. They are the leaders of organized crime. Organized crime is distinguished from other types of crime by its hierarchical structure, monopolistic control and influence, dependence upon violence for enforcement, immunity from the law through the corruption of police and judicial processes, and incredible financial success.[42]

Traditionally, organized crime has been seen as a "family" affair led by bosses of various ethnic traditions. Today, however, organized crime is increasingly viewed as activity, based on the same market processes as legal businesses, which provides services that cannot be supplied as efficiently or as cheaply by legitimate enterprises. It should be viewed, in other words, as the "extension of legitimate market activities into areas normally proscribed, for the pursuit of profit and in response to latent illicit demand."[43]

The activities of organized crime are threefold. One involves traditionally illicit services, such as gambling, narcotics, loan sharking, and prostitution. A second is the infiltration of legitimate businesses—from advertising to sales of surplus scrap. These businesses are bought and controlled through a number of procedures, by investing concealed income from illegal activities, extortion, or foreclosing on usurious loans, to name a few. The third major enterprise is racketeering—essentially the extortion of money from legitimate businesses on a regular basis.

Organized crime remains arrogantly resistant to all efforts to control or eliminate it. Witnesses are difficult to come by, people who are victims of the "services" seldom complain, and few law enforcement agencies are equipped to tackle such huge criminal conglomerates. Consequently, there is no indication that major gains toward eradicating or even diminishing its power will be made in the near future.

White-collar crime accounts for enough violations of law to dwarf burglary, larceny, and other conventional types of crime by comparison. Yet a strange principle applies here; people tend to tolerate it because they sometimes indulge in it themselves.[44] White-collar criminals are doctors, accountants, public officials, TV repairmen, corporate executives, and people who sell term papers to college students. In other words, they are the people responsible for determining and supporting the community standards that lawbreakers supposedly violate.

There are actually two kinds of white-collar crime: occupational and corporate. The occupational variety consists of violations committed in the course of one's work and offenses by employees against their employers. Employee thefts from retail stores, warehouses, and docks, and the trickier crime of embezzlement are all familiar examples of occupational white-collar crime.

Corporate white-collar crime differs somewhat: it consists of offenses committed by corporate executives for their corporation and offenses attributed to corporations themselves. A study of the 70 largest corporations in the United States found an average of eight court or commission rulings against each of these corporations over a period of eight years for false advertising, unfair labor practices, infringements of trademarks and patents, and illegal monopoly.[45] Since federal law recognizes the corporation as a legal entity, it is seldom that the officials of corporations, the people who make the actual decisions that result in law violations, are punished. More typically, the corporation itself is fined by a court or a commission, and its officials evade censure. Frequently, the fines are so small that they are accepted as a normal business expense.

The problems of prosecuting white-collar crimes are deeply embedded in our value system. Although we fear and hate street crime, we tend to view

White-Collar and Government Crime

white-collar crime as more comparable to traffic offenses than to larceny or burglary. An extension of these views can be found in the sympathy given to leading characters in the Watergate scandal.

In recent years, increased attention has been focused on governmental crime as institutional rather than individual activity. Revelations concerning the illegal covert activities of the Central Intelligence Agency both abroad and in the United States have led to attempts by Congress to curb its power. The prosecution of officials and agents of the agency has been hampered by the court's hesitance to hear cases in which evidence bordering on issues of national security must be given. The abuse of institutional power by governmental officials at federal, state and local levels and the ability to avoid prosecution because of their influential positions raises serious questions about the concepts of justice and equality in our society.

With Justice for All?

In a completely just society, the innocent would be protected and those guilty of a crime would be apprehended, separated from society if necessary, and reformed if at all possible. The American system of justice falls far short of this ideal vision. Hundreds of thousands of crimes—including violent crimes—go unsolved every year. (Figure 13.2 indicates the surprisingly low percentages of known crimes that result in arrest.) Justice is unevenly administered; convicted of the same crime, one person may receive a heavy prison sentence while another is released on probation. Prisons do not rehabilitate. The prison experience itself may turn a first offender into a life-time criminal. The three major elements of the American criminal justice system are the police, the courts, and the correctional or penal system. To understand why the system is not working, we must first understand how these institutions are supposed to function and why they are failing.

Problems of Police Protection

To the speeding motorist or the inner-city drug merchant, the police are The Law. Although they are themselves as soldiers in the front lines of a war against crime, individual members of the force are often betrayed, not only by their commanders, judges, and lawyers, but also by the people they are supposed to protect. The police are asked to prevent crime, protect innocent citizens and property, and apprehend criminals. In the course of duty they are also required to respect individual rights and use no unnecessary force.

In recent years judges have ruled that suspects cannot be coerced into confessing. They have a right to a lawyer's help even if they cannot afford it. They must be informed of their rights at the time of arrest. Finally, evidence obtained through illegal search and seizure cannot be used in court. These court decisions were based on documented evidence of police abuses, and most thoughtful citizens recognize the importance of protecting constitutional rights. But the average policeman feels that these rulings coddle criminals and handcuff the police and deeply resents the rules that keep changing.

The police have other reasons for resentment. For the most part, they are

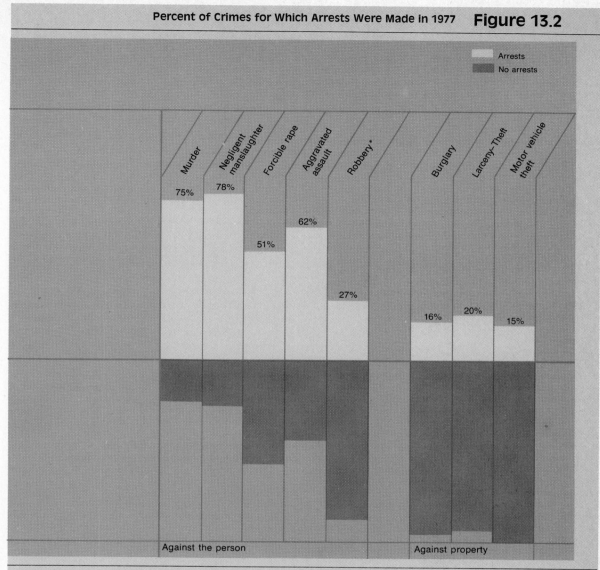

Arrests

No arrests

Murder — 75%

Negligent manslaughter — 78%

Forcible rape — 51%

Aggravated assault — 62%

Robbery* — 27%

Burglary — 16%

Larceny-Theft — 20%

Motor vehicle theft — 15%

Against the person

Against property

Source: U.S. Federal Bureau of Investigation, *Uniform Crime Reports, 1977* (Washington, D.C.: Government Printing Office, 1978), p. 161.

poorly paid and understaffed. In a society in which violence is common and guns are readily available, their jobs are dangerous. Between 1968 and 1977, a total of 1094 policemen were killed in the line of duty; 94 percent of those killed were killed by guns.[46] Although ordinary middle-class citizens loudly demand police protection against violent crime, they are often contemptuous of the individual police officer—particularly when charged with traffic violations. The police are also required to deal with victimless crimes

—drunkenness, drug abuse, gambling, and prostitution and other illegal sexual behavior. The fact that large segments of the population engage in or condone such behavior induces a certain cynicism in the average member of the force.

Middle-class citizens generally expect and get polite treatment from the police. People who live in inner-city slums invariably expect and sometimes get police treatment that is biased, brutal, and belligerent. In one study, researchers reported that police used abusive language in 14 percent of their contacts with victims, witnesses, and defendants in cases of suspected crime.[47] Members of the research team also observed a considerable amount of physical abuse. One can only wonder about the frequency of such abusive police behavior when observers are not present. New training programs to sensitize police to the needs of community members and police-community relations programs are indications that some effort is being made to correct this problem.

Recently a number of major cities have experienced scandalous revelations of police corruption. In New York City the Knapp Commission uncovered the involvement of hundreds of policemen—some of high rank—in criminal protection rackets involving gambling, drug trafficking, and prostitution. In Chicago widespread involvement in extortion and outright burglary was uncovered in certain police districts, and a small group of policemen were indicted for dealing in drugs and murdering several people to protect their activities. In its task force report *The Police,* the President's Commission on Law Enforcement and Administration of Justice reported that "a significant number of officers engaged in varying forms of criminal and unethical conduct."[48]

Most policemen start their careers with high ideals; many of those caught committing crimes claim that they gradually became disillusioned by the corruption they saw all around them among politicians, businessmen, and other policemen. Organized crime figures offer huge sums of money as bribes; the ill-paid policeman needs great strength of character to turn down such money when asked merely to look the other way. Once corrupt practices become entrenched in a police district or a whole department, they are difficult to root out. The honest newcomer in the department is under severe pressure to accept bribes or at least to keep quiet about the activities of colleagues. Since he is often not sure just how high up in the department such corrupt practices extend, he may be afraid to inform his superiors and jeopardize his career.

Many, perhaps most, policemen are honest, dedicated, and hardworking. They perform difficult tasks, hampered by inadequate resources and staff, archaic administrative procedures, and the ambiguous attitudes of many citizens toward law enforcement. The flaws in the justice system tend to harm the individual policeman as well as the accused criminal and members of society at large. Many of the flaws are found not in police operations but in the two other institutions of the justice system—the courts and the penal system.

The Court System on Trial

The primary function of the courts is to mete out justice to those who have been accused of a crime. Through the legal processes of the courts, the innocent are presumably acquitted and freed, and the guilty are fined, released provisionally, or imprisoned. Court processes involve an adversary system of prosecution versus defense and a system of determining guilt or innocence that may involve a judge alone or a judge and a jury of the accused's peers.

The American court system includes federal, state, and local courts. A person convicted in a lower state or federal court may appeal the conviction to a higher court until it reaches the Supreme Court, whose decision is final. With a few exceptions, such as kidnapping and bank robbery, most criminal activity falls under the jurisdiction of the state courts. Since each state enacts its own criminal code, an activity that is severely punished in one state may be only lightly punished in another. For instance, forcible rape can be punishable by the death sentence in several southern states, but in other states, such as Connecticut and Illinois, it can be punished by a fine of several hundred dollars or probation.

Embedded in our Constitution are a number of rights that pertain to persons accused of a crime—among them the right to a swift trial and due process of law. The President's Commission on Law Enforcement and Administration of Justice discovered that most accused persons could expect far less than this constitutional ideal.[49] A major problem is overcrowding. As they are now set up, the criminal courts cannot possibly handle the volume of defendants awaiting trial, and some defendants have to wait a long time before their cases are heard. The problem is especially acute for poor people, since those who cannot afford bail must usually remain in jail until their trials are scheduled. In some instances, people have spent several years in jail and then been acquitted. Those who cannot afford a lawyer are provided with the services of a public defender, but public defenders carry very heavy case loads and can spend only a little time on each client. Through sheer lack of time, the public defender may present a wholly inadequate defense for a client. Finally, the poor defendant may be persuaded to accept plea bargaining to resolve a case.

Plea bargaining allows defendants to plead guilty to a lesser crime—simple assault rather than assault with a deadly weapon, for instance—instead of waiting for a trial in which they may be found guilty of the more serious offense. Prosecutors and judges view the practice as a necessary one, for if all defendants were to exercise their right to demand a jury trial, the court systems would be literally inundated with cases. Yet it must be emphasized that plea bargaining is an expedient, not a procedure for achieving justice. An innocent person who has spent weeks or perhaps months in jail awaiting trial may choose plea bargaining out of desperation and hope that the sentence will not involve any additional time in prison. But on the other hand, a person who commits a violent crime may plead guilty to a lesser offense and receive a correspondingly lighter sentence—all in the name of expediency.

The structure and the day-to-day operating routines of the court system serve to support the practice of plea bargaining. Prosecutors are under pressure to obtain a high conviction rate and are generally quite willing to reduce charges in exchange for a plea of guilty. Judges, concerned with reducing the backlog of cases awaiting trial, seldom reject a negotiated plea of guilty. Defense attorneys often play the game because they wish to remain on good terms with judges and prosecutors with whom they interact every day. Further, career-oriented attorneys often move back and forth between the prosecutor's office and private practice, and some may have an eye on a judgeship in the future; it is quickly learned that a "don't rock the boat" attitude is most conducive to these personal goals. As a consequence, the adversary system of justice is undermined, if not negated. In the words of one defense attorney: "It's like a family. Me, the prosecutors, the judges, we're all friends. I drink with the prosecutors. I give the judge a Christmas present, he gives me a Christmas present."[50]

Plea bargaining is one important stage where inequality before the law manifests itself. Affluent or influential persons are able to secure the services of high-quality legal counsel with good contacts among prosecutors and judges, which helps in obtaining the most advantageous bargain. As an example, Spiro Agnew was permitted to plead no contest to a minor tax violation rather than be tried for the more serious offenses of receiving bribes and evading taxes on that income. But poor defendants are likely to be represented by an overworked public defender who has arranged "routine deals" with the prosecutor for different offenses in order to achieve a manageable case load.[51] Low-status defendants seldom have their cases decided before a jury of their peers; one public defender's office in a major urban area reports that 90 percent of its cases are resolved by plea bargaining.[52] As Figure 13.3 shows, in 1977 some 9.6 percent of those charged with violent crime and 4.1 percent of the persons charged with property crime were found guilty of a lesser charge.

The quality of American trial judges also has an effect on the judicial system. Judges alone often decide the innocence or guilt of a defendant, and in most states they determine the sentence. In jury trials, judges sum up the evidence and instruct the jury on the legal points they must decide. Unfortunately, judges are often political appointees; they do not necessarily have great knowledge of or experience with criminal law. Then, too, some judges are corrupt, narrow-minded, or unsympathetic to defendants from social and cultural backgrounds other than their own. Many judges do their best but are hampered by their middle-class cultural indoctrination or inexperience. The problem is compounded by the fact that there are no systematic training programs for judges. They are expected to know their jobs automatically upon appointment to the bench.

Judges, prosecutors, and other court officials are in the forefront of movements for court reforms. Throughtful officials realize that the processes with which they are involved affect defendants' lives in the most serious way possible, by either granting them freedom or sentencing them to a term of imprisonment and stigmatization for the rest of their lives.

Discretionary Justice of Juvenile Courts

Separate court systems for juveniles emerged in this country toward the end of the nineteenth century due to the efforts of reformers in what has been termed the "child-saving movement."[53] The reformers were concerned with removing juveniles from the often harsh machinery of adult criminal processing. By doing so and by providing special programs for delinquent children, they hoped to prevent juveniles from graduating to careers as adult criminals. Unlike the criminal courts, whose function was to mete out justice to those accused of violating the law, the philosophy of the juvenile court was to provide for the best interests of the child. The court's attitude toward its wards was to protect rather than punish them.

The statutes creating the juvenile courts were exceedingly broad and au-

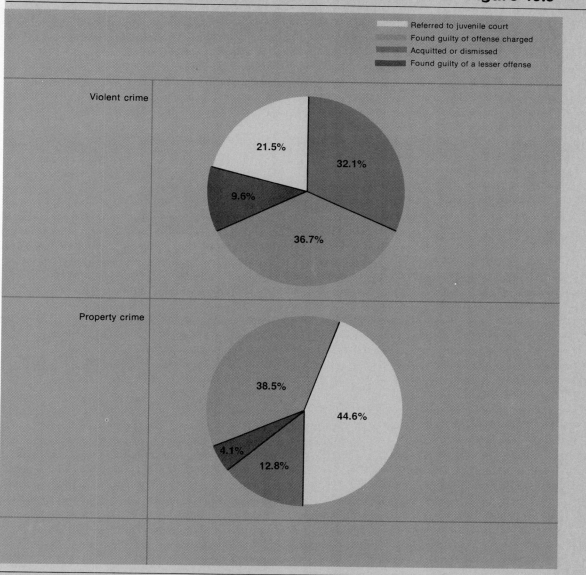

Source: U.S. Federal Bureau of Investigation, *Uniform Crime Reports, 1977* (Washington, D.C.: Government Printing Office, 1978), p. 216.

thorized judges to consider the needs, the character, and the social circumstances of the child, as well as the child's behavior. The jurisdiction of the new courts extended beyond criminal behavior to include vague categories such as incorrigibility and immoral behavior. Juvenile court procedures also differed in several important respects from those of adult courts.

Lance Morrow
On Crime and Much Harder Punishment

Everyone except the abnormally saintly or submissive possesses the retaliatory instinct. It lurks like a small black gland at the base of the brain, in the mind's nonreasoning regions. When a person's elemental sense of justice is offended, the retributive instinct flares and hops in outrage; it gesticulates like Mussolini; it demands satisfaction. The urge is deep and primitive. Some cannibals on Pacific islands used to eat convicted murderers for dinner—a practice that appeased both their hunger for food and their thirst for justice.

Over many months, the American retributive gland has grown more and more inflamed. A few weeks ago, Robert Jones, 36, stood before the bench in a Chicago courtroom, having just been sentenced to 100 to 300 years in prison for murdering two brothers in a robbery. A voice boomed: "I hope you die in prison!" It was not one of the victim's family or the prosecutor who cried out; it was the judge.

Across the country, the law-abiding are in a punitive mood. A Gallup poll last spring showed 62% of Americans in favor of the death penalty. The public sense of justice, of the simple fairness and fitness of things, is frayed. The nation's crime rate has risen 300% in the past 18 years, though a part of the increase merely reflects greater attention to reporting crimes. . . .

Many Americans harbor an unwholesome and even dangerous contempt for the justice system. Neither criminals nor victims have much faith in its workings: the one class does not fear it much, and the other does not trust it. A mugger leaves a victim crippled, life blighted, and bound to ruinous expenses for treatment. Through plea bargaining and parole indulgences, the attacker emerges from his "punishment" in a matter of months or less, to resume his career. The social contract gets badly tattered in its passage through such a system.

A hard, punitive glare has become respectable for liberals who in years past were all for the Warren Court's protections of the offender. One index of the respectability of the tougher line: Edward Kennedy, who owns the most liberal voting record in the Senate, is the co-author of the revised U.S. Criminal Code that would, among other things, abolish parole boards and indeterminate sentences. There is a certain wistfulness in such measures. Says L. Ray Patterson, dean of the Emory School of Law in Atlanta: "The concern of the public is not so much for vindictive retribution, but for *some* retribution."

The four classic purposes of imprisonment have been: 1) to deter others from committing crime, 2) to protect society from the criminal, 3) to rehabilitate the criminal, and 4) to give him his "just deserts." Today the first three are not persuasive. The prospect of jail does not seem to be a very forbidding deterrent. Society is obviously not safer but more dangerous these days, even though America's prisons and jails burst with a population of 500,000 inmates. Nearly all rehabilitation programs are well-meaning exercises in futility. That leaves reason No. 4, just deserts—punishment, social retribution, the community's retaliation against the criminal for having violated its rules.

Punishment raises some of the most difficult questions that the moral intelligence has ever confronted, and most of man's answers over the centuries have been neither very moral nor very intelligent. The principle of exact retaliation formulated in Mosaic law ("An eye for an eye, a tooth for a tooth") was actually a kind of early legal reform that placed precise limitations upon the extent of permissible revenge. When medieval kings began establishing strong central authority, and various offenses were perceived as crimes against the king's peace and his formal vanity, the older one-to-one system of compensation was abstracted into a legal machine of great brutality. After centuries of racks, gougings, hangmen and unspeakably inventive tortures, much of mankind adopted the lockup as its principal instrument of punishment, with occasional resort to the noose, guillotine and electric chair.

Now many citizens in the West have begun to detect what might be called the Fallacy of Progress. For a century or more, "progress" in penal thinking has signified increasingly human treatment for criminals, as if punishment were in itself a vestigial barbarity. But if progress implies a steady mitigation of punishment, then at some point "punishment" must logically lose its meaning, crossing over to become something else. Besides, not many people are pitilessly marched to jail today for stealing loaves of bread. Poverty may breed crime, but few thieves steal because they are starving in a society of food stamps and welfare.

The reformer's morality has always taught that the main objective of punishment is ulterior: to deter or rehabilitate. In this design, punishment should not do the one thing it says it will do—punish. It is not to make the criminal suffer, to make him feel the force of society's anger for his deed. It is surely not communal revenge.

But punishment *should* be punishment before it is anything else. If it does deter other potential criminals or rehabilitate the convicted, then that should be greeted as a pleasant surprise. The first business, without being bloodthirsty about it, is to keep society's contract with itself and punish a crime as it promised it would. Author C.S. Lewis has pointed out the totalitarian possibilities in treating criminals as sick people who need to be cured: "If crime and disease are to be regarded as the same thing, it follows that any state of mind which our masters choose to call 'disease' can be treated as crime; and compulsorily cured." The KGB understands the logic.

To be told the law, to be told the punishment, and to be punished if one breaks the law, is a sounder and more reliable system of justice than the confusing and ineffective process now operating. A society can be subverted by a system that appears to be not only inconsistent but almost whimsical in its workings. A huge sense of grievance festers. The injustice of the courts seems to mirror the injustice of the economic system. All the rules of society seem to have been changed. You work hard, but inflation destroys your gains; so much for the work ethic. You obey the law, but somehow you get hurt and criminals profit, unpunished.

If the law has meaning, it must carry predictable consequences. And the law for some years has not been certain whether it meant to be a guilt-ridden social worker or a hanging judge. The erratic justice that emerges from the badly overburdened system has been further complicated by the society's spasms of conscience. These arise from the larger unsolved questions of social justice in the U.S., principally poverty and racism. But those questions cannot be solved by a mindless leniency toward criminals in the courts. That policy invites contempt from the poor, who are much more likely than others to be the victims of criminals, and who, in fact, are more likely to favor the death penalty.

The Christian ethic counsels individuals to turn the other cheek, but it does not hold that a society should operate on the principle. Turning the other cheek is an ideal, says Roman Catholic Theologian Daniel Maguire, "like a horizon to turn to. It is not a practical guide for the police in The Bronx."

Although the punitive-minded want higher maximum sentences, much can be gained by a rigorous and consistent imposition of sentences already set. It is possible to argue endlessly about the two central questions surrounding the death penalty: 1) Does it deter? and 2) Is it moral? But the great importance of the issue is symbolic. The argument would tend to abate if the courts worked better at imposing noncapital penalties. On the other hand, restoring capital punishment would produce a moral mess. It would open the U.S. further to charges of racism and hypocrisy; every time a black man was executed in Alabama, the Soviets would feel further justified—by whatever false comparisons—in the conduct of their own Gulags. Not that they need such justification. More important than this propaganda effect would be the domestic divisions and bitterness in the U.S. The death penalty would be ethically shaming and emotionally exhausting. In the end, only a few criminals would be removed (permanently) from circulation. Blood vengeance is not what it is cracked up to be. Much better to concentrate on locking up the incorrigible for long terms.

The realities are more complicated than the rhetoric. Stiffer jail terms, without parole, would mean building a lot more jails. The people who call for tough retribution would be among the first to howl against the taxes that would be needed to finance new prisons and expanded courts. It would be self-defeating to turn into a society of police and wardens in order to restore confidence in the law's consequences. But confusion of judicial purpose, with lapses into wistful incompetence and the sociological sigh, is just as destructive to public morale. Within civilized limits, speed and certainty of punishment represent an approachable ideal.

Reprinted with deletion from "On Crime and Much Harder Punishment," *Time,* September 18, 1978, pp. 54, 59. Reprinted by permission from TIME, The Weekly Newsmagazine; copyright Time, Inc.

Judges were given wide discretion in handling individual cases, and they were expected to examine the motivation of a child's behavior and the child's moral reputation. Children were not formally accused of a crime; rather, a hearing was held in which the court offered guidance and assistance. Hearings tended to be informal, and records were not made public in an effort to avoid stigmatizing the child. Finally, and of great significance, the safeguards of due process did not apply to juvenile hearings, because these were defined by statute as civil proceedings.[54]

The structure and the philosophy of the present juvenile justice system remain quite similar to those at its inception. The major changes that have occurred in the system were brought about by a recent Supreme Court decision in which it was held that juveniles are entitled to many of the same legal rights as adults.[55] Under certain conditions, juvenile defendants now have the protection of due process, the right to legal counsel even if they cannot afford it, and other rights applicable to adult defendants. However, the policy of individualized treatment geared to helping the child remains the guiding philosophy of the juvenile courts.

The treatment of a juvenile offender, whether it takes the form of a verbal warning, probation, or confinement in a detention center or reformatory, is to be based more on the circumstances of the individual than on the type of offense committed. Out of this philosophy grew the practice of indeterminate sentencing, in which a juvenile's release from confinement is not determined by the sentencing judge but rather by correctional authorities who consider the juvenile's behavior, attitude, and progress toward rehabilitation while in the institution. While originally hailed as a progressive reform measure, this practice has recently come under heavy criticism by those concerned with juvenile rights and justice. The effect of indeterminate sentencing has been to make many juveniles serve lengthier sentences than adults for identical offenses. For example, a 14-year-old committed for larceny or even a status offense such as truancy or incorrigibility may be legally confined until the age of 18 if authorities consider it warranted. The wide discretion given to court and correctional officers concerning length of confinement creates a situation where bias and discrimination can enter the decisions.

Prisons: Punishment or Reform?

At various times and places crimes have been punished by hideous tortures and mutilations. In eighteenth-century England, a man or woman might be hanged for stealing a watch or a handkerchief. Although our Constitution forbids such cruel and unusual punishments, many people consider our present penal institutions barbarous and inhumane. Former U.S. Attorney General Ramsey Clark described the results of a 1966 investigation into two prison farms in Arkansas:

Discipline was basically maintained by prisoners themselves—trustees with shotguns—with only a handful of paid employees supervising. Allegations, at least partially verified and largely credible, included the murder of inmates, brutal beatings and shootings. Shallow graves with broken bodies were uncovered. Food unfit to eat was regularly served. Forced homosexuality was openly tolerated. Extortion of money by wardens and sexual favors from families of inmates to protect their helpless prisoner relatives from physical injury or death were alleged. Torture devices included such bizarre items as the "Tucker telephone," components of which were an old telephone, wiring and a heavy duty battery. After an inmate was stripped, one wire was fastened to his penis, the other to a wrist or ankle, and electric shocks were sent through his body until he was unconscious.[56]

Although this is an extreme example, the pattern of brutality is common in most prisons. Many prison administrations try very hard to prevent brutality on the part of guards or between prisoners. Yet even the best conventional prisons release prisoners who are hostile and embittered at the system and likely to commit further crimes. Typically, prisons do nothing to help inmates cope with the problems that led to their criminal behavior and provide few opportunities for the development of skills that would make them any better able to handle their life situations.

When a person enters prison, he or she loses all freedom of action, privacy, and many other rights that people in the outside world take for granted. Our society places great value on individuality and freedom of choice; yet the new prisoner is placed in a situation in which every move is dictated by rigid, and often arbitrary, prison rules.[57] Many prison customs are humiliating and degrading. The strip search, a security measure, means that a prisoner is ordered to strip naked and is then physically searched by a guard for weapons or other contraband. Incoming inmates in many prisons must submit to being sprayed from head to foot with a delousing solution. In our culture, a man who is humiliated and oppressed is expected to fight back, verbally or physically. But the prisoner who rebels is likely to find himself in solitary confinement, and continuous rebellion will destroy any chances for early parole.

Part of the underlying problem in the penal system is indecision on the part of society concerning the basic purpose of imprisonment. Is it to separate criminals from society, thereby protecting society from their antisocial behavior? Is it to punish them for their crime? Or is it to rehabilitate them, to change them into valued citizens? Criminologists and other experts would overwhelmingly choose the third goal, but many Americans seem to be concerned only with the first and second goals. Numerous surveys of penal institutions reveal that in most of the nation's prisons rehabilitation programs are woefully inadequate, sometimes even nonexistent.[58] Occupational training programs and psychological counseling and guidance are rare, and where vocational programs do exist, they rarely teach skills that are valuable in the outside world. Most Americans desperately want to reduce crime rates; however, by failing to demand massive prison reform they support a system that tends to reinforce criminal behavior and turn first offenders into hardened criminals.

Proposals for Reducing Crime

If we want to reduce the incidence of crime, there are certain obvious steps we can take. Some involve administrative reform and the investment of more resources; others, however, involve difficult changes in attitudes and customs. Unfortunately, most Americans do not see these reforms as obvious or necessary, and political leaders often respond by proposing only simplistic and short-sighted solutions to the problem of crime.

PRISON

Punishment has little effect in discouraging criminal behavior in contemporary society. Overcrowded prisons that deprive inmates of every vestige of privacy and human dignity only aggravate their frustrations and intensify their rebellion against societal norms. Until vocational and social rehabilitation, rather than abuse and degradation, characterize our treatment of convicted criminals, there is little hope that prisons will serve society in any way other than as expensive holding-pens. *This page:* A crowded prison with beds in hallway, an invitation for violence and sexual attacks; eating humble pie three times a day, every day, while dignity dies of starvation. *Opposite, clockwise from top:* The strip-search, a degrading way of looking for contraband; the structural trades training this prisoner is receiving is designed to prepare him for a useful life after release; only a few prisons provide the emotional and social therapy that make it possible for convicts to return successfully to life outside; coeducational cafeteria in rehabilitation-oriented prison, where prisoners are allowed to function in a near normal social setting at mealtimes; inmates in this self-governing rehabilitation unit make their own regulations and help each other stick to them in preparation for a law-abiding life.

James Q. Wilson
Death Penalty: Pro and Con

The death penalty can be defended or criticized on grounds of either justice or utility. By "justice" I mean considerations of fitness and fairness: Death either is or is not a fitting, appropriate, or necessary punishment for those who commit certain kinds of crimes, and such punishment either can or cannot be fairly administered. The Biblical injunction, "an eye for an eye," is an argument for death (or at least maiming) on grounds of justice; so also is the argument that the supreme penalty is the only appropriate response to the supreme crime, that we cheapen the value of human life if an innocent victim dies while his convicted murderer lives.

Appeals to justice can also be used to argue for the abolition of the death penalty. Human life is sacred and may never be taken deliberately, even by the state. Further, society ought not to encourage sentiments of vengeance or cater to morbid interest in ritual executions. Moreover, no penalty is acceptable if it is administered in ways that are grossly unfair; in this country, at least, certain disadvantaged groups have experienced a disproportionate number of executions.

The argument on grounds of justice is certainly the most profound and to me the most interesting. As I shall suggest in the course of this discussion, it may be the only proper basis for a decision. And at one time, discussion of capital punishment was often based entirely on considerations of justice and morality. The most striking aspect of contemporary discussions of this issue, however, is that, except for the fairness question, they almost never proceed along moral lines. And for opponents of capital punishment, the assertion that it is imposed unfairly seems their weakest argument, for it might be answered by making executions mandatory for those convicted of the relevant crimes. This was the case in England, for example, where, until hanging was abolished, the judge was required to sentence to death *any* person convicted of murder (all murder was the same, there being no distinction, as here, between first and second degree homicide).

Perhaps because we find it hard to argue about first principles, perhaps because our leaders and spokesmen are untrained in the discipline of philosophic discourse, perhaps because we are an increasingly secular and positivist society that has little confidence in its ethical premises, the capital punishment debate has been framed largely in utilitarian terms. Most of the literature, in short, does not explore the moral worth or evil of execution so much as the consequences of executions for other parties, or for society at large. The utility of capital punishment can depend on several considerations: Executions are cheaper than confinement in prison for long terms; an executed man cannot commit additional crimes, and executions deter others from committing certain crimes. The first two utilitarian reasons are rarely taken seriously: We usually assume that cost (within reason) should make no difference when a human life is at stake and that life imprisonment can prevent the convicted person from committing additional crimes as surely as execution. (In fact, of course, the alternative to execution is not often, or even usually, life imprisonment, but in many states a life *sentence* with eligibility for parole in 7, 10 or 15 years. Furthermore, prison may protect society against convicts, but it often does not protect convicts from each other.) . . .

Here it is interesting to note that in Great Britain, where judges had less discretion in imposing the death penalty than they do in the United States, the number of murderers found insane—and so spared the gallows—dropped sharply after the death penalty was abolished in 1965. It is hard to believe that there were fewer insane persons in Britain after abolition of the death penalty; what apparently happened was that the authorities no longer felt it as necessary to protect the accused from penalties when the penalty was no longer death. No one should assume that any judicial outcome can be made truly "mandatory" —discretion removed from one place in the criminal justice system tends to reappear elsewhere in it. . . .

If public opinion is to play a role in these matters, what can we expect of it? In 1964, the citizens of Oregon voted in a referendum to abolish the death penalty in that state, but in 1966, Colorado voters chose to retain its death penalty statute, as did the voters in Illinois in 1970. In a nonbinding referendum in 1968, Massachusetts voters expressed the view that they favored keeping capital punishment. These referenda were all broadly phrased, of course, and even if one accepts the results, they do not settle such issues as the circumstances under which death might be imposed.

Gallup polls taken over several years indicate that support for the death penalty declined from 68 per cent in 1963 to 42 per cent in 1966. In that year, a majority of those interviewed would have repealed the death penalty for murder. Perhaps because of the rise in crime rates during the late nineteen-sixties, support for capital punishment has gone up again slightly. In 1969, 51 percent said they favored it. Young persons are more opposed to death penalties than older ones and women more than men. Somewhat surprisingly, the better-educated and higher-income respondents are not much more opposed to it than those with less education or income. As Hugo Bedau put it, there is little evidence in the polls that the death penalty is more favored by the "hard hats" than by the professional classes.

Given the fact that blacks are disproportionately the victims of murder, one might suppose that they would favor the death penalty. But quite the opposite is the case. Hans Zeisel reports survey data indicating that only a third of black men, but over half of white men, favor capital punishment. Black women are even less inclined to support the death penalty.

People often adapt their views to support whatever state of affairs happens to exist, and attitudes toward the death penalty may be no exception. Until the Supreme Court decision, California had the death penalty, and almost two-thirds of those polled in that state said they favored its retention. Minnesota has not had the death penalty since the early part of this century, and two-thirds of those polled in that state said they opposed restoring it.

These changes in attitude have been accompanied over the years, by a trend to greater respect for human life and a tendency to regard execution as somehow barbaric, even if necessary. A hundred years ago a large crowd would turn out for a public hanging; today, public opinion only barely supports executions at all, and a large majority would probably condemn its being a public spectacle. A hundred and fifty years ago, a large number of offenses were punishable by death; today, scarcely anyone regards it as remarkable that in general only murder is considered a sufficiently grave crime to warrant the thought of capital punishment. One of the striking facts about the Supreme Court decision of last year is that, although only a bare five-man majority found the death penalty as administered to be unconstitutional, eight of the nine Justices indicated their personal opposition to it.

The main issue remains that of justice—the point is not whether capital punishment prevents future crimes, but whether it is a proper and fitting penalty for crimes that have occurred. That is probably as it should be, for such a question forces us to weigh the value we attach to human life against the horror in which we hold a heinous crime. Both that value and that horror change over time. In our modern culture we seem to be uncomfortable about considering these matters, and thus both proponents and opponents of execution fall back on "scientific" assertions about deterrence that are not only dubious but are likely to remain so. The quality of public debate would be substantially improved if all sides recognized this.

Excerpts from James Q. Wilson, "Death Penalty: Pro and Con Arguments," *New York Times Magazine*, October 28, 1973, p. 27. © 1973 The New York Times Company. Reprinted by permission.

Revising the Law

Most criminologists strongly recommend that we decriminalize certain categories of behavior that are now considered crimes. These include victimless crimes such as gambling and unconventional sexual behavior between consenting adults. Many experts also agree that alcoholism and narcotics addiction should be treated as medical, rather than criminal problems. In 1972 the National Commission on Marihuana and Drug Abuse recommended that marijuana use should no longer be subject to criminal penalties.[59] The decriminalization of these categories of behavior would enable police forces to devote more staff and resources to the investigation of crimes against people and property.

Such reform would eliminate the problem of selective enforcement for political reasons or because of bias and would constitute a significant step toward the reduction of police and judicial corruption. Most important of all, perhaps, these reforms would greatly reduce the income of organized crime, which revolves largely around popular but illegal vices. If heroin addicts could obtain sufficient doses of heroin or a substitute from a physician, they would not need to buy it at exorbitant prices from illicit dealers. They would also not have to resort to robbery or prostitution to support an expensive habit; this in itself would probably help reduce crime rates.

Agreement to these reforms is unlikely in the near future. The present attitudes of many are extremely unsympathetic to decriminalizing such behavior. And politicians, forced to cater to their constituents, are unlikely to take the lead in demanding such reforms, for they do not wish it to appear that they are in favor of vice.

Another legal reform that might greatly reduce crime rates is gun control legislation. FBI statistics for 1977 show that 63 percent of all murders were committed through the use of firearms (48 percent involved handguns), while 42 percent of all robberies involved the use of firearms by the perpetrator.[60]

Administrative Reforms

Both the police and the courts would benefit greatly from increased funding. The federal government has attempted to help by providing money through the Law Enforcement Assistance Administration. Increased funds can be used to enlarge a police force, and the presence of more police personnel may deter some crime, especially in crowded inner-city areas. Additional computers and other technological devices would improve record keeping and information retrieval systems. Reform of internal structure and jurisdictional overlap would also promote greater efficiency. For instance, many metropolitan areas include within their boundaries independent city, state, county, and township police forces; centralized control would provide better police service for the entire area.

But increased efficiency, however necessary, may have little effect on the *quality* of services provided by the police and court system. In this connection, experts have recommended reforming recruitment and training programs. Proposed police reforms include the raising of educational standards and the attraction of better-educated recruits through increases in the minimum and maximum salaries, more hiring of recruits from minority groups, and the use of tests and interviews to screen out people who are essentially unsuited to police work. It has been suggested that a member of any police force should have integrity, openness, flexibility, and a reluctance to use force except when it is unavoidable.[61] Present police training programs tend to be brief and concerned primarily with technical procedures at the expense of human relations aspects of police work. Suggested reforms include longer training programs with greater emphasis on the constitutional rights of suspects and police relations with all segments of society.

The selection of judges is now largely a political process, and the fate of the accused often depends solely on the discretion of the presiding judge. Many of the judges themselves are vitally interested in judicial reform. One goal of reformers is to reduce political influence in the selection of judges.

This might be accomplished by having local bar associations compile a list of candidates on the basis of merit, from which a judge or judges would be elected or appointed. Through research and consultation, judges and bar associations could draw up uniform codes to guide judges in setting bail, conducting a trial, and sentencing convicted criminals. Bar associations might also prepare guidelines to help judges determine which accused criminals can be safely released without bail when they cannot afford it; thus the prisoner who is a "safe risk" would not have to spend days, weeks, or months in jail awaiting trial.

One stage of the criminal justice system which desperately needs reform is sentencing. At present, judges determine sentence on the basis of limited information about the defendants and the crime committed. In addition, sentences vary from judge to judge, jurisdiction to jurisdiction, and case to case. In one study, 28 judges were asked to determine the sentences they would impose on a criminal in a hypothetical case. The judges were given information such as presentence reports which they normally use when sentencing an actual criminal. One judge refused to cooperate, ten said they would place the defendant on probation, and the other 17 said they would sentence him to a term of one year or more.[62]

Promoting Penal Reform

Even if radical reforms take place in legal codes and in police and judicial administration, there still remains the problem of the penal system. No area of the system of justice has a greater traumatic effect on the convicted criminal; to a great extent the nature of the prison experience will determine whether the released convict will resume criminal activities or go on to achieve a productive life.

A variety of reforms have been suggested to make the present penal structure more humane. Overt brutality and verbal abuse could be eliminated by more careful selection of guards and administrators, prison rules could be changed to allow more individuality and freedom of action, and the physical architecture of the prison could be improved. Psychologists have discovered that human beings have a basic need for a certain amount of space and privacy. Overcrowding and lack of privacy, conditions that are characteristic of modern prisons, often lead to increased tensions, hostility, riots, and violence. Thus physical redesign of prisons might prevent riots and lesser forms of violence. Greater educational opportunities and counseling services could also be provided, particularly to young inmates.

Many reformers now believe, however, that the essential nature of the correctional process must be changed if true rehabilitation is to take place. The principle behind the new reform idea is that rehabilitation cannot take place when the inmate is completely separated from the rest of society, since it is precisely the larger society to which the inmate must learn to adjust if further periods of incarceration are to be avoided. Clearly, some criminals, especially the mentally disturbed, must be separated from society until such time as they are no longer dangerous. But the goal in regard to most inmates is to return them as quickly as possible to an environment in which they can live and work as normal citizens.

Some propose housing offenders in homelike, perhaps coeducational, institutions where new skills and attitudes can be learned prior to release.[63] Work-release programs would provide freedom to go to school or work during the day, on the condition that the inmate return to the prison at night. Halfway houses, where inmates could live prior to complete release from prison, would grant them almost complete freedom under the loose supervision of a correctional official. Finally, a greater number of offenders might be released directly after conviction on a probational basis. This would increase the role of the probation officers, who presently often have difficulty just keeping track of probationers. Under the new system they would be expected to provide extensive and multifaceted counseling services. Success in implementing a greater use of probation, however, would be predicated upon expanding the system so that each supervising officer had a manageable case load.

These new proposals are in dramatic contrast to the traditional correctional approach. So far the techniques have been tried only on a limited basis with carefully selected inmates, but the results are encouraging.[64] There are, of course, many problems that must be solved in connection with the proposed new systems. Techniques that work well with essentially middle-class inmates may not work at all with inner-city youths or with older, hardened criminals. Most businesses are still highly reluctant to employ ex-convicts. The most serious problem of all is probably public reaction to such programs. The idea of releasing inmates under these circumstances is likely to cause an uproar among people who believe in a punitive correctional system. In fact, public opinion now seems to favor harsher treatment of criminals.

The new breed of penal reformer, however, believes that if people are treated like animals they will behave like animals, and if they are treated with dignity and respect they will behave like human beings. Crime is not a simple matter of "us against them." Every American is involved in the value system that makes some crimes more respectable than others and some people more likely to be arrested and convicted than others. Most Americans deplore violent crimes, but many of those same Americans are not willing to deal meaningfully with the root causes of crime—poverty, oppression, injustice, and overcrowded slums. Present judicial and penal systems have demonstrably failed to reduce crime; yet many Americans call for more of the same. Until some of the basic contradictions in American society are resolved, there is little chance of a real reduction in crime.

Summary

Crime is a form of deviant behavior that has become a major social problem in modern America. A certain amount of crime should be seen as a normal part of social life, with positive as well as negative consequences. The value conflict approach to crime and social control is useful because it focuses attention on such questions as who makes law and what interests are served rather than on offenders themselves. Conflict currently exists over the content of criminal codes, the cause of crime, and the actions of official agencies of social control.

Criminal and delinquent behavior represent deviations from social rules that have been codified in the criminal law. There are two kinds of law: civil and criminal. Criminal law differs from civil law in that it must be enacted by a duly constituted political body, it always imposes penal sanctions carried out by the state, and statutes are specific in nature.

There are two types of crime: felony and misdemeanor. A felony is a serious crime punishable by more than one year's imprisonment. A misdemeanor is a lesser offense usually punishable by a fine or local imprisonment for one year or less.

Since 1960 there has been a significant increase in the amount of crime in the United States. Although the reliability of official crime data is questionable, it would appear that the increase is in terms of actual numbers of offenses and in the rate of offenses. Males outnumber females as offenders in known crimes, but the rate of increase in crimes committed by females has been far greater than in those committed by males in recent years. Crime is also associated with age, since persons under 21 account for more than 40 percent of all arrests. The relationships between crime and race, social class, and residence all seem to point in the same direction: most crime is associated with the poor who live in urban areas.

Widely accepted sociological explanations of crime include: (1) social structure theory, which attributes crime to a state of confusion produced by sudden changes in social structure; (2) subculture theory, which attributes crime to the "status anxiety" prevalent in lower-class subcultures; (3) differential association theory, which attributes crime to behavior values and rationalizations learned in association with others; and (4) labeling theories, which attribute crime to the effects of the label of criminality on the personality and behavior of an individual.

Four types of crime that reflect patterned interaction are: juvenile crimes, committed by minors; professional crimes, committed by career criminals; organized crimes, committed by organizations with monopolistic control and influence, characterized by dependence on violence for enforcement, immunity from the law through corruption, and extraordinary financial success; and white-collar crimes, committed by employees and corporate executives in the course of their work and often in the name of the corporation.

The American criminal justice system consists of police, courts, and prisons. The system is not working well. Police are hampered by inadequate resources and staff, archaic administrative procedures, and ambiguous attitudes toward law enforcement. Courts are hampered by overcrowding, understaffing, and a lack of uniform sentencing codes. Prisons are hampered by violence and society's indecision as to the purpose of imprisonment.

Proposed legal reforms include decriminalizing certain victimless behaviors, treating alcoholism and narcotics addiction as medical problems, and passing gun control legislation. Proposed administrative reforms include increasing police and court funds, improving recruitment and training programs, and reducing political influence in judge selection. Proposed penal reforms include carefully selecting prison personnel, redesigning prisons, and maintaining closer ties between the convict and society.

Notes

[1] Emile Durkheim, *The Rules of Sociological Method,* trans. Sarah A. Solovay and John H. Mueller (New York: Free Press, 1966), pp. 64–76.

[2] Ibid., p. 71.

[3] U.S. Federal Bureau of Investigation, *Uniform Crime Reports, 1974* (Washington, D.C., Government Printing Office, 1977), p. 37.

[4] Ibid., p. 35.

[5] Daniel Glaser and Kent Rice, "Crime, Age and Unemployment," *American Sociological Review* 24 (October 1959), 685.

[6] Frank R. Furstenburg, "Public Reaction to Crime in the Streets," *American Scholar* 4 (Autumn 1971), 565–572.

[7] FBI, *Uniform Crime Reports, 1977,* p. 183.

[8] Ibid., p. 175.

[9] Ibid., p. 182.

[10] Ibid.

[11] Albert K. Cohen and James F. Short, Jr., "Crime and Juvenile Delinquency, " *Contemporary Social Problems,* 4th ed., ed. Robert K. Merton and Robert Nisbet (New York: Harcourt, 1976), pp. 62–63.

[12] Richard Quinney, *Criminology* (Boston: Little, Brown, 1975), p. 102.

[13] Sidney Axelrad, "Negro and White Male Institutionalized Delinquents," *American Journal of Sociology* 57 (May 1952), 569–574.

[14] Peter J. Burke and Austin T. Turk, "Factors Affecting Postarrest Dispositions: A Model for Analysis," *Social Problems* 22 (February 1975), 328.

[15] Edwin H. Sutherland and Donald R. Cressey, *Criminology,* 9th ed. (Philadelphia: Lippincott, 1974), pp. 132–149.

[16] For a summary of these findings, see Judith A. Wilks, "Ecological Correlates of Crime and Delinquency," *Task Force Report: Crime and Its Impact—An Assessment,* President's Commission on Law Enforcement and Administration (Washington, D.C.: Government Printing Office, 1967), pp. 138–156.

[17] Edwin H. Sutherland, *White Collar Crime* (Hinsdale, Ill.: Dryden Press, 1949), pp. 3–13.

[18] Robert H. Gordon, "Issues in the Ecological Study of Delinquency," *American Sociological Review* 36 (December 1967), 927–944.

[19] FBI, *Uniform Crime Reports, 1977,* pp. 147–148.

[20] Ibid., p. 36.

[21] Stephen Schafer, *Theories in Criminology* (New York: Random House, 1969), pp. 97–122.

[22] Cesare Lombroso, *Crime, Its Causes and Remedies,* trans, H. P. Horton (Boston: Little, Brown, 1912).

[23] Schafer, *Theories in Criminology,* pp. 183–202.

[24] R. W. Stock, "XYY and the Criminal," *New York Times Magazine,* 20 October 1968, p. 30.

[25] Clifford R. Shaw and Henry D. McKay, *Delinquency Areas* (Chicago: University of Chicago Press, 1929).

[26] Emile Durkheim, *Suicide,* trans, J. A. Spaulding and G. Simpson (New York: Free Press, 1951).

[27] Robert K. Merton, *Social Theory and Social Structure* (New York: Free Press, 1968), pp. 183–214.

[28] Compare with Walter C. Reckless, *The Crime Problem,* 3rd ed. (New York: Appleton, 1961), p. 3.

[29] Albert K. Cohen, *Delinquent Boys* (New York: Free Press, 1955), p. 121.

[30] Richard A. Cloward and Lloyd E. Ohlin, *Delinquency and Opportunity* (New York: Free Press, 1960).

[31] Edwin H. Sutherland, "Theory of Differential Association," *Juvenile Delinquency,* ed. Rose Giallombardo (New York: Wiley, 1972), pp. 81–83.

[32] Howard S. Becker, *The Outsiders* (New York: Free Press, 1963), p. 9.

[33] Harold Garfinkel, "Conditions of Successful Degradation Ceremonies," *American Journal of Sociology* 61 (March 1965), 420–424.

[34] Simon Dinitz, Russell Dynes, and Alfred Clarke, *Deviance: Studies in the Process of Stigmatization and Societal Reaction* (New York: Oxford University Press, 1969), p. 19.

[35]Richard Schwartz and Jerome Skolnick, "Two Studies of Legal Stigma," *Social Problems* 10 (Fall 1962), 133–142.

[36]Edwin Lemert, *Human Deviance, Social Problems and Social Control* (Englewood Cliffs, N.J.: Prentice-Hall, 1967), p. 17.

[37]FBI, *Uniform Crime Reports, 1974,* p. 160.

[38]Ibid., p. 174.

[39]Ibid., p. 180.

[40]Edwin H. Sutherland, *The Professional Thief* (Chicago: University of Chicago Press, 1937), pp. 197–215.

[41]Marchall B. Clinard, *Sociology of Deviant Behavior,* 4th ed. (New York: Holt, Rinehart and Winston, 1974), p. 340.

[42]Ibid., p. 328.

[43]Dwight C. Smith, Jr., "Organized Crime and Entrepreneurship," *International Journal of Criminology and Penology* 6 (1978), 161–177.

[44]Donald J. Newman, "Public Attitudes toward a Form of White Collar Crime," *Social Problems* 4 (January 1957), 228–232.

[45]Edwin H. Sutherland, "Is 'White Collar Crime' a Crime?" *The Sociology of Crime and Delinquency,* ed. Marvin E. Wolfgang (New York: Wiley, 1962), pp. 20–27.

[46]FBI, *Uniform Crime Report, 1977,* p. 293.

[47]Bruce J. Terris, "The Role of the Police," *Annals of the American Academy of Political and Social Science* 374 (November 1967), 58–69.

[48]President's Commission on Law Enforcement and Administration of Justice, *The Police: Task Force Report* (Washington, D.C.: Government Printing Office, 1967), p. 208.

[49]President's Commission on Law Enforcement and Administration of Justice, *Challenge of Crime in a Free Society,* p. 128.

[50]"The Defender: 'It's the Wild West,'" *Newsweek,* 9 March 1971, p. 29.

[51]David Sudnow, "Normal Crimes: Sociological Features of the Penal Code in a Public Defender Office," *Social Problems* 12 (Winter 1965), 255–276.

[52]"The Defender," p. 29.

[53] Anthony Platt, "The Rise of the Child Saving Movement: A Study in Social Policy and Correctional Reform," *Annals of the American Academy of Political and Social Science* 381 (January 1969), 21–38.

[54]Ibid., p. 28.

[55]The decision appears in the President's Commission on Law Enforcement and Administration of Justice, *Juvenile Delinquency* (Washington, D.C.: Government Printing Office, 1967), pp. 57–76.

[56]Ramsey Clark, *Crime in America* (New York: Simon and Schuster, 1971), pp. 193–194.

[57]Bruce R. Jacob, "Prison Discipline and Inmates' Rights," *Harvard Civil Liberties Law Review* 5 (April 1970), 227, 234–240.

[58]For a discussion of this point, see Jessica Mitford, *Kind and Usual Punishment: The Prison Business* (New York: Knopf, 1973), p. 97.

[59]National Commission on Marihuana and Drug Abuse, *Marihuana: A Signal of Misunderstanding* (Washington, D.C.: Government Printing Office, 1972).

[60]FBI, *Uniform Crime Reports, 1974,* pp. 10, 19.

[61]Arthur Niederhoffer, *Behind the Shield: The Police in Urban Society* (Garden City, N.Y.: Doubleday, 1967), pp. 11–32.

[62]"Test Presentence Report and Summary of Ballot," *Federal Rules Decision* 27 (June 1961), 383–388.

[63] A variety of community-based correctional programs are reviewed in Oliver J. Keller, Jr., and Benedict Alper, *Halfway Houses: Community-Centered Correction and Treatment* (Lexington, Mass.: Lexington Books, 1970).

[64]Bertram S. Griggs and Gary R. McCune, "Community Based Correctional Programs: A Survey and Analysis," *Federal Probation* 36 (June 1972), 7–13.

Violence

Every society known to us exhibits violence in one form or another. Although violence is by no means new to Americans, the war in Vietnam, rioting in black ghettos, unrest on the campuses, assassinations, and fears about crime in the streets in the 1960s caused many Americans to focus their attention on the problem of violence for the first time. In this chapter we will discuss the causes and forms of violence in contemporary American society.

In what sense are we justified in considering violence a social problem? First, a large number of people are affected by it every day. If the occurrence of violence were restricted to an occasional suicide or an infrequent homicide, we could perhaps leave it to psychologists to discover the reasons people sometimes harm themselves and others. Unfortunately, acts of violence are by no means so rare; indeed, few of us are lucky enough not to encounter some form of anger and hostility almost every day. These emotions may be blown into violent and sometimes earth-shaking proportions—criminal assault or even war, for example. Each of us is affected in countless ways by the climate of violence in American society.

Second, violence is a disruptive force within society. Every society creates institutions designed to achieve certain ends—elections are held to choose leaders, a court system is established to administer justice, and so on. Violence is a shortcut for normal institutional functions. Someone who murders in anger or frustration is ignoring the socially acceptable ways of resolving disputes and is expressing contempt for the normal legislative and judicial processes. Every act of violence, from assault to armed revolution, detracts to some degree from the authority normally vested in society.

Violent Groups, Violent Individuals

Human history is replete with examples of the brutal use of force by one group against another. Invading armies have time and time again pillaged and destroyed conquered towns, murdering and raping the inhabitants or capturing them to be used as slaves. In medieval times, the arbitrary and unchecked power of feudal lords gave them free license to execute any who defied their will. Punishment often included physical mutilation, and bodies were put on public display to impress upon others the consequences of incurring the wrath of the powers that be. During the Spanish Inquisition, heretics were publicly burned at the stake in the name of the Church.

When social groups come into conflict, violence is frequently used to advance and protect the interests and values of the group in power. Nowhere has that been demonstrated more vividly than in America. During the expansion of the western frontier, the goals of white settlers, merchants, and industrialists came into conflict with those of native Americans, and somewhere between 6 and 10 million of the latter were systematically exterminated. The Ku Klux Klan and other terrorist organizations in the South have threatened life and property in an effort to maintain white supremacy, often with the tacit or even direct support of law enforcement officials. The labor movement in the United States has sometimes resorted to violence to advance its interests, but just as often the violence has been perpetrated by management or by local or federal troops called in to support the industrialists.[1] As these examples suggest, violence is frequently the result of a clash of values and interests between groups. Moreover, in the past the use of violence against Indians, blacks, and labor organizers has typically been legitimized by influential segments of the American population in the belief that their interests were threatened by those groups.

History also provides many examples of individual acts of violence. The circumstances surrounding intergroup violence differ from those surrounding individual acts of violence, even though the same behaviors—homicide, assault, and robbery—may be involved in both cases. Individual acts of violence, while sometimes related to group value conflict, are more often the result of a substantially different constellation of norms and expectations. Child abuse, for example, violates the normally accepted standards of child treatment in our society; if detected, this act is likely to be subject to legal sanctions. An individual who commits a robbery may be pursuing the widely shared cultural goal of financial success but is employing means to achieve that goal that are defined as illegitimate and deviant.

The values that are internalized by an individual during socialization differ according to that individual's location in the social structure. In some social contexts "toughness" is a valued trait, whereas in other contexts much less emphasis is placed on the ability to respond aggressively to challenges or aggravating situations. Thus, interpersonal assault may be accepted in juvenile gangs or in some ethnic or class contexts as a "fair fight," a reasonable means of coping with a situation, but will be defined by the legal system as deviant behavior that violates acceptable standards of social conduct.

A central distinction between group or collective violence and individual violence involves the concept of legitimacy. Legitimacy refers to a belief by group members that an action is proper, justified, and appropriate to the circumstances. In the collective violence of group conflict, at least one group involved believes that its violent actions are a legitimate means to a certain goal. Violence is carried out in the name of the group and is intended to serve group purposes. Individual acts of violence, on the other hand, are typically not widely supported or legitimized by a larger collectivity. Thus, while individual violence may be explained in terms of deviant behavior, intergroup violence is most fruitfully studied from a value conflict perspective.

Legitimacy is a complex social product that often changes over time. In today's society, where a multitude of different social groups support their own distinctive norms and value standards, there is frequently disagreement over what are appropriate uses of violence. Violent protest against school busing, war, capital punishment, and euthanasia are all areas where different segments of the population disagree as to the legitimacy of the use of violent means. As the structure and value standards of society change, acts of violence once condoned by influential groups or a majority of the population may undergo a process of delegitimation. Corporal punishment in the public schools, physical assault by police as a method of interrogating suspects, and flogging of prison inmates are all acts of violence that have undergone delegitimation in recent times.[2]

Legitimation and Delegitimation

Causes of Violence

Who are the perpetrators of violence in American society? None of us is entirely untainted. Those who have witnessed or participated in ostensibly nonviolent peace rallies know that good intentions are, at best, an inadequate basis for the eradication of violence. A problem cannot be solved until it is thoroughly understood. Perhaps the first step in undermining violence is to work toward a fuller understanding of the roots and forms of violence in American society today.

Every society, from the simplest hunters and gatherers to the most complex industrial nations, has found it necessary to establish institutions to control and minimize acts of violence. Whether the tendency toward violence is a genetic inheritance is a question still open to debate. In this section we will consider some of the theories which have been offered to explain that tendency.

Are we compelled to perform violent acts by biological factors beyond our control? According to Konrad Lorenz, although many animals kill for food, only rats and humans kill their own kind in anger.[3] Although most animals are equipped with teeth and claws, they do not turn these potentially lethal weapons against others of their species. Lorenz has suggested that the inhibiting mechanisms that prevent a species from endangering its own survival seem to be poorly developed in *Homo sapiens*: "Human behav-

Biological Theories

ior. . . far from being determined by reason and cultural tradition alone, is still subject to all the laws prevailing in all phylogenetically adapted instinctive behavior."[4]

An interesting biological theory of human behavior has inspired the effort to establish a causal link between violent behavior in humans and a specific genetic anomaly. Although preliminary research has disclosed the presence of an extra sex chromosome among some criminals and mentally ill and retarded individuals, control data on the incidence of this anomaly in the general population have yet to be developed. Until more conclusive evidence can be produced, we must continue to assume that there are no "natural-born" violent individuals.[5]

Anthropological Theories

Recognizing that violence is present in some form in every known society, anthropologists have addressed themselves to examining some of the ways in which various societies maintain social order. In most societies, order is maintained not through the threat of force but rather through the establishment of norms accepted by the majority as proper standards of behavior. Unlike many societies, however, the United States is a nation of many different regional, ethnic, racial, religious, and economic subcultures, each with its own standards of acceptable behavior. The same regional differences that led to the Civil War over a century ago and later motivated northerners to support the civil-rights struggle in the South are still causing tension and internal conflicts today. It is frequently misleading to generalize the causes of violence in a society as complex and varied as that of the United States.

Subcultural differences within a region may involve exclusionary tactics of the dominant class; that is, the group with the greatest amount of power may segregate itself in restricted neighborhoods and private clubs while ethnic minorities live together in ghetto areas. In America, blacks, American Indians, Mexican-Americans, and other minority group members stigmatized because of ethnicity, race, or religion often find it difficult to find work for which they are qualified or homes in neighborhoods they can afford. Discriminatory practices resulting from cultural variation often create inequities that are long-lasting in their effects. When regional norms are not held in common by the society as a whole, the legitimacy of such inequities may be strongly questioned by the stigmatized groups. Eventually, these feelings of frustration and injustice usually lead to violence.

Psychological Theories

Psychologists have devoted a great deal of attention to the problem of the violent personality. Freud believed that violence is linked to a human impulse to return to the inorganic state known as the death instinct.[6] According to Freud, the death instinct is centered in the id (the unconscious reservoir of instinctual, biological drives) and must be controlled by the ego (the self) and the superego (that portion of the mind concerned with social norms). Although the Freudian hypothesis may serve to explain cases of individual deviance, it fails to take into consideration the social and environmental variables that are believed to elicit violent behavior.

In the theory of Erich Fromm, human aggression stems from the character of individual personalities, determined mainly by incidents in the individual's personal life history. Three potentially aggressive personality types are characterized in Fromm's theory: the *sadistic*, who compensates for real or imagined impotence by seeking absolute control over others; the *necrophiliac*, who is driven to destruction and annihilation by hatred for life; and the *bored*, who displays a lack of interest not only in other people and things but in himself as well.[7] Fromm's theory ascribes the cause of most contemporary aggression and violence to the bored personality and emphasizes the role of the parent in shaping the personality of the child. Seeds of violence are planted early in life.

In their analysis of violence, some psychologists have attempted to consider the influence of social factors on personality development. The frustration-aggression theory maintains that violent behavior results from the frustration of purposeful activity.[8] Factors that may turn frustration into aggression include ethnic discrimination, poverty, and emotional deprivation. Although this theory makes a valuable contribution to the study of violence, it ultimately fails to account for the fact that repeated frustration may produce violent behavior in one individual and not in another.

Social psychology is a field of inquiry that combines elements of both psychological and sociological approaches; it focuses on the creation of individual psychological content that directly results from the immediate social environment in which the individual is embedded. The frustration-aggression theory, with its emphasis on the social factors that produce frustration, was one of the earliest applications of a social psychological approach in the explanation of violent behavior. More recently, Albert Bandura and Richard Walters have formulated a social learning theory of aggression that focuses on the imitation, especially by children, of aggressive role models to which they are exposed.[9] The typical sequence by which children learn new behaviors is observation of role models, imitation of those roles, and practice in acting out the roles. In this view, extent to which the various models are aggressive or nonaggressive is of critical importance in determining whether the child learns aggressive behavior.

Both the modeling-imitation theory and the sociological theories discussed below stress that violent or aggressive behavior is essentially learned behavior. The social groups and significant individuals with whom we interact serve to shape our values, attitudes, and standards of conduct.The Bandura-Walters approach, however, emphasizes the learning of aggression takes place not only in interpersonal interaction but also in any other setting that may act as a learning experience. A great deal of the research supporting this interpretation has focused on the impact of televised violence on children's aggressive behavior. Findings of a large number of experiments strongly support the idea that children can readily learn aggressive behaviors from behavior models on television or in films, or from real-life persons. Certainly, abundant models for learning violent behavior are available to an individual growing up in America. Parental aggression, the portrayal of violence in media, and the various forms of violence ensuing from racial prejudice are all significant elements in the development of the violent personality in America.

Sociological Theories

The phenomenon of violence as it occurs within the context of the ordered society has been an enduring subject of sociological investigation. Weber argued that the legitimate use of violence is restricted to the state.[10] Durkheim maintained that some degree of punishment is necessary to integrate and to promote solidarity among the conforming members of society by defining the limits of acceptable behavior.[11] But when large numbers within a society adopt violence as a means of achieving their ends, the bonds that normally hold that society together begin to disintegrate. Excessive violence may be evidence of the need to restructure some social institutions.

Sociologists warn against accepting as satisfactory those institutions that are contributing to social disruption. In dealing with civil violence, generalized abstractions rarely offer adequate solutions to real social problems. Ascribing violence to tension or strain does nothing to explain the specific injustices against which civil disorders might be directed, "nor does it help illuminate the historical patterns of domination and subordination to which the riot is one of many possible responses."[12]

Specific injustices, for example, can be pinpointed within the administration of our systems of law and justice. Plea bargaining is a pretrial negotiation that puts the accused in the position of *negotiating* the seriousness of his or her offense. The failure to prosecute white-collar crime is another instance of the inconsistent administration of justice. Such contradictory and discriminatory application of social norms may contribute significantly to the frustration of those victimized by it. Clearly, inconsistency of this sort can subvert the shared norms and values that sustain social control. Disorder and violence may be the result.

In attempt to define in concrete terms the underlying causes of the alienation of lower-class youth from social norms, sociologists have devoted a great deal of attention to the phenomenon of the juvenile gang. A delinquent subculture in revolt against middle-class values and behavioral standards, the gang is a social microcosm that exposes its own life-style, traditions, and focal concerns. Members of lower-class gangs apparently adhere to the social goals of wealth and upward mobility but find access to them blocked by racial and class discrimination.[13] The delinquent gang provides an alternative route to success by offering an opportunity to prepare for a rewarding career outside the law. A crucial part of this training is an education in the use of violence. Status is generally gained through the judicious use of violence—to be tough, to live by one's wits, and to hustle for survival are the norms that determine social conformity among these youthful groups of the urban poor.[14]

While gang violence thus can be understood as a reaction to discrimination within our society, violence can result from other types of social conflict and may reflect group struggle to modify or maintain existing social relationships. Those who feel unjustly deprived of social benefits under current arrangements may use violent means to alter those arrangements. On the other hand, police and other representatives of the established order may use violence to control opposing forces and protect vested interests. The civil-rights movement of the sixties and police reaction against demonstrators exemplify such a clash of interests.

A great deal of the violence in our society is related to fundamental and deep-seated value conflicts. For example, those who profess humanitarian values may condemn police brutality in the apprehension and interrogation of suspects, while advocates of a tough law-and-order stance may argue that such practices are justifiable if they lead to more efficient apprehension of law violators. Still, the very ambiguity of society's attitude toward violence may lead to violence. In condoning violent repression by the military and police establishments, society may unwittingly encourage individuals or groups of individuals to adopt violent tactics as legitimate means of achieving their goals.

From a sociological viewpoint, violence is the outcome of many variables encountered by an individual during the socialization process and complicated by the conflicting values of society. In dealing with the problem of human aggression, acts of violence—whether committed by individuals or by groups—must be viewed within the specific contexts in which they occur. The casual repression of violence is a poor substitute for the study of its underlying causes. To control violence without discovering and treating its sources is ultimately to invite more violence.

Forms of Violence

So far, we have spoken of violence as if it were a single, isolated social phenomenon. In actuality, violence may assume many different forms, ranging from individual violence directed against the self to the violence of one society against another. Let us now consider some of these forms and examine their relevance to the problem of violence in American society.

Perhaps the most elementary form of violence is the taking of one's own life. In the United States, more than 27,000 persons are definitely known to have taken their lives in 1975.[15] Suicides are grossly underreported, however, because of the social and religious stigma attached to self-destruction. Doubt about the circumstances of death or pressure from relatives may lead doctors or coroners to list the cause of death as accidental or unknown.[16] One estimate places the number of attempted suicides at over 200,000 each year.[17] In fact, statistics place the suicide rate consistently well above the homicide rate (see Figure 14.1).

In his classic study, *Suicide*, Emile Durkheim observed that "so long as society remains unchanged the number of suicides remains the same."[18] That is, the suicide rate of a given society seems to vary directly with the integration of the structure and fabric of that society. In describing fundamental categories of suicide, Durkheim stressed that each has causes attributable to society rather than to the individual.

Egoistic suicide is personally motivated and is an indication of a lack of group unity and identification. This type of suicide is most common when interpersonal relations do not bind a person to others. *Altruistic suicide* involves the sacrifice of one's life for the sake of some higher cause or power. Such suicides usually involve religious, political, or military allegiances. *Anomic suicide* results from the failure of society to properly regulate the individual. Economic changes that cause previously accepted norms to be inoperative maximize conditions for anomic suicide. Sudden wealth or poverty sometimes act as catalysts for suicide when individuals are unable to cope with their precipitously altered status. Divorce is another major factor in anomic suicides. With the removal of the regulatory mechanisms of

Suicide

VIOLENCE

Those who have been its victims may dispute the positive power of violence. Yet, as a society we condone and legitimate much violent action simply because it enforces our ethical and moral standards, supports our economy, or provides us with relief from monotony. Still, violence is a learned behavior, and the proliferation of legitimate models of violence may well lead to a corresponding proliferation of unacceptable violent acts. *This page:* Warfare is legitimated violence between nations that introduces thousands into the cult of killing; National Guardsmen in gas masks show their anger and frustration by almost tearing apart a civil rights demonstrator. *Opposite page clockwise from top left:* A violent means to an end, the electric chair has often been used to underline society's moral code of conduct; these Iranian women are prepared to use guns and death to achieve their political objectives; the sport of killing; football—violence for viewing pleasure.

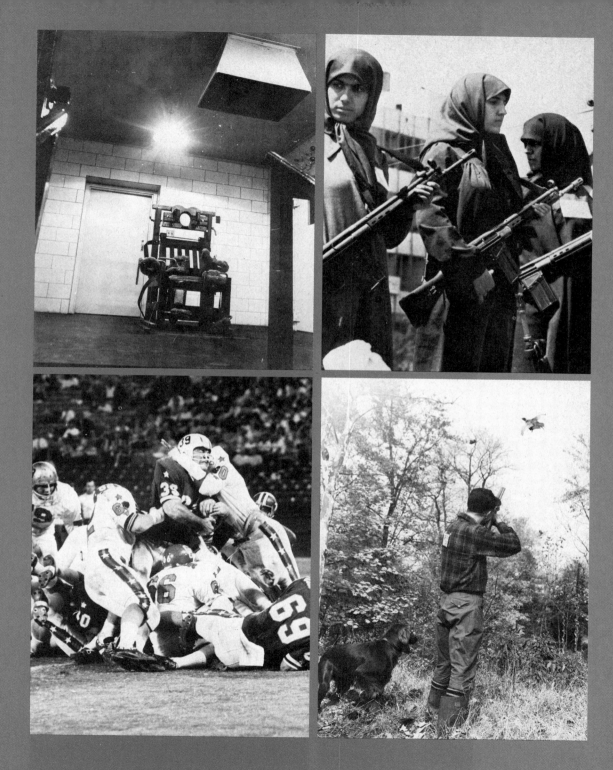

Figure 14.1   Homicide and Suicide Rates, 1930–1975

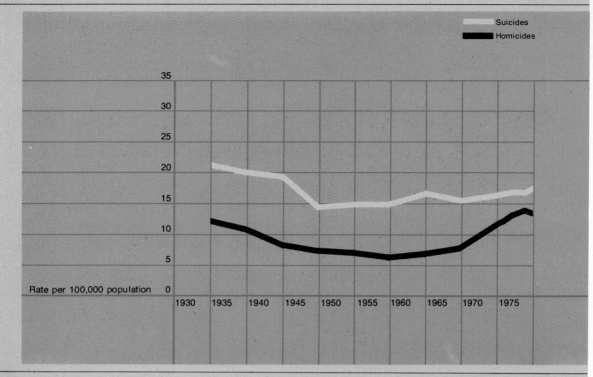

From U.S. Bureau of the Census, *Statistical Abstract of the United States* (Washington, D.C.: Government Printing Office, various years)

marriage, an individual may feel lost and alone. Suicide rates among divorced men and women are considerably higher than among married ones.

Rather than confining his study to indivdual psychological circumstances, Durkheim directed his attention to suicide rates, which he correlated with other social phenomena. Although the factors of changing norms and societal integration discussed by Durkheim do not entirely explain available suicide statistics, they do offer valuable insights. In keeping with Durkheim's theories, the suicide rate in the United States rises sharply with advancing age and is twice as high for men as for women. On the other hand, there seems to be no significant variation in the suicide rate between urban and nonurban areas. Furthermore, white Americans are statistically more prone to commit suicide than nonwhites.[19] Despite this national tendency, a study of suicides in New York City indicates that "among blacks of both sexes between the ages of twenty and thirty-five, suicide is decidely more of a problem than it is in the white population of the same age."[20] Recalling Durkheim's definition of anomic suicide, it seems likely that what has been called the revolution or rising expectations may account for the disproportionately high suicide rate among young urban blacks. The social structure has failed them; it does not offer them the minimum economic, emotional, and psychological support needed to integrate them into productive roles in society.

Recent work on suicide has buttressed Durkheim's theory that suicide is largely a function of social integration and social cohesion. Since in today's society occupations are central mechanisms by which individuals are integrated into the larger social structure, many recent studies have focused on the relationship between employment or satisfaction with occupational roles and suicide. It has been found that problems related to downward mobility—to a loss of social status stemming from unemployment or other work-related difficulties—increase the likelihood of suicide.[21]

The economic recession of the early and mid-1970s placed a substantial number of persons in positions of downward mobility, creating a serious conflict between their expectations and the reality of their current circumstances. An informal survey of suicide prevention centers in 1975 found that both the number of suicides and the number of suicide attempts were on the rise, with much of the increase attributed to financial pressures and unemployment. Noting the sharp increase in suicidal acts since 1973, a counselor at one prevention center stated that in recent years more of the callers have been "people who are not able to meet their monthly bills, who are losing their jobs for the first time, and are panicked because for the first time economic failure is staring them in the face."[22]

Statistics indicate that children constitute a relatively small number of known suicides compared with other age groups in the population, but that fact is somewhat misleading since the frequency of suicide threats and attempts is highest among children. Although a great deal is not known about suicide among children, some believe that it may be influenced by the child's distorted conception of death. One study which involved researchers questioning a number of 6- to 11-year-olds about death showed that 50 percent of them described death as a reversible event, going to sleep and eventually waking up again.[23] Adolescent suicides, on the other hand, have increased dramatically in the past 20 years. Psychologists generally attribute this to the social and emotional pressures experienced by adolescents, considered greater at this time than at any other period of human development. One of the segments of the youthful population hit hardest by these pressures are college students, who are bombarded by not only the problems of adolescence but also by the stresses of competition and achievement present in the college environment. Suicidal behavior on the campus has been labeled a major health problem and ranks among the leading causes of death for this age group.[24] Suicide at any age is a tragic event, but this sadness is accentuated when it is a young person who takes his or her own life.

Criminal Violence

Although crimes against property, such as theft and embezzlement, are statistically more common than crimes of violence, it is the increase in violent crime that has been most distressing to the American public in recent years. Between 1969 and 1977, the national rates of criminal homicide, aggravated assault, and forcible rape all increased (see Figure 14.2).[25] Although a change in police reporting procedures may play some small part in the increased rate of reported crimes, there is nonetheless considerable evidence to suggest that the incidence of violent crime in America has risen substantially over the last several years.

Susan Griffin
Rape: The All-American Crime

Though the theory that rapists are insane is a popular one, this belief has no basis in fact. According to Professor Menachem Amir's study of 646 rape cases in Philadelphia, *Patterns in Forcible Rape,* men who rape are not abnormal. Amir writes, "Studies indicate that sex offenders do not constitute a unique or psychopathological type; nor are they as a group invariably more disturbed than the control groups to which they are compared." Alan Taylor, a parole officer who has worked with rapists in the prison facilities at San Luis Obispo, California, stated the question in plainer language, "Those men were the most normal men there. They had a lot of hang-ups, but they were the same hang-ups as men walking out on the street."

Another canon in the apologetics of rape is that, if it were not for learned social controls, all men would rape. Rape is held to be natural behavior, and not to have to be learned. But in truth rape is not universal to the human species. Moreover, studies of rape in our culture reveal that, far from being impulsive behavior, most rape is planned. Professor Amir's study reveals that in cases of group rape (the "gangbang" of masculine slang) 90 percent of the rapes were planned; in pair rapes, 83 percent of the rapes were planned; and in single rapes, 58 percent were planned. These figures should significantly discredit the image of the rapist as a man who is suddenly overcome by sexual needs society does not allow him to fulfill.

Far from the social control of rape being learned, comparisons with other cultures lead one to suspect that, in our society, it is rape itself that is learned. (The fact that rape is against the law should not be considered proof that rape is not in fact encouraged as part of our culture.)

This culture's concept of rape as an illegal, but still understandable, form of behavior is not a universal one. In her study *Sex and Temperament,* Margaret Mead describes a society that does not share our views. The Arapesh do not ". . . have any conception of the male nature that might make rape understandable to them." Indeed our interpretation of rape is a product of our conception of the nature of male sexuality. A common retort to the question, why don't women rape men, is the myth that men have greater sexual needs, that their sexuality is more urgent than

women's. And it is the nature of human beings to want to live up to what is expected of them.

And this same culture which expects aggression from the male expects passivity from the female. Conveniently, the companion myth about the nature of female sexuality is that all women secretly want to be raped. . . .

The theory that women like being raped extends itself by deduction into the proposition that most or much of rape is provoked by the victim. But this too is only myth. Though provocation, considered a mitigating factor in a court of law, may consist of only "a gesture," according to the Federal Commission on Crimes of Violence, only 4 percent of reported rapes involved any precipitative behavior by the women.

The notion that rape is enjoyed by the victim is also convenient for the man who, though he would not commit forcible rape, enjoys the idea of its existence, as if rape confirms that enormous sexual potency which he secretly knows to be his own. . . .

And in the spectrum of male behavior, rape, the perfect combination of sex and violence, is the penultimate act. Erotic pleasure cannot be separated from culture, and in our culture male eroticism is wedded to power. Not only should a man be taller and stronger than a female in the perfect love-match, but he must also demonstrate his superior stength in gestures of dominance which are perceived as amorous. Though the law attempts to make a clear division between rape and sexual intercourse, in fact the courts find it difficult to distinguish between a case where the decision to copulate was mutual and one where a man forced himself upon his partner.

The scenario is even further complicated by the expectation that, not only does a woman mean "yes" when she says "no," but that a really decent woman ought to begin by saying "no," and then be led down the primrose path to acquiescence. . . .

That the basic elements of rape are involved in all heterosexual relationships may explain why men often identify with the offender in this crime. But to regard the rapist as the victim, a man driven by his inherent sexual needs to take what will not be given him, reveals a basic ignorance of sexual politics. For in our culture heterosexual love finds an erotic expression through male dominance and female submission. A man who derives pleasure from raping a woman clearly must enjoy force and dominance as much or more than the simple pleasures of the flesh. Coitus cannot be experienced in isolation. The weather, the state of the nation, the level of sugar in the blood—all will affect a man's ability to achieve orgasm. If a man can achieve sexual pleasure after terrorizing and humiliating the object of his passion, and in fact while inflicting pain upon her, one must assume he derives pleasure directly from terrorizing, humiliating and harming a woman. According to Amir's study of forcible rape, on a statistical average the man who has been convicted of rape was found to have a normal sexual personality, tending to be different from the normal, well-adjusted male only in having a greater tendency to express violence and rage. . . .

The assumption that a woman who does not respect the double standard deserves whatever she gets (or at the very least "asks for it") operates in the courts today. While in some states a man's previous rape convictions are not considered admissible evidence, the sexual reputation of the rape victim is considered a crucial element of the facts upon which the court must decide innocence or guilt. . . .

According to the double standard a woman who has had sexual intercourse out of wedlock cannot be raped. Rape is not only a crime of aggression against the body; it is a transgression against chastity as defined by men. When a woman is forced into a sexual relationship, she has, according to the male ethos, been violated. But she is also defiled if she does not behave according to the double standard, by maintaining her chastity, or confining her sexual activities to a monogamous relationship.

One should not assume, however, that a woman can avoid the possibility of rape by behaving. Though myth would have it that mainly "bad girls" are raped, this theory has no basis in fact. Available statistics would lead one to believe that a safer course is promiscuity. In a study of rape done in the District of Columbia, it was found that 82 percent of the rape victims had a "good reputation." Even the Police Inspector's advice to stay off the streets is rather useless, for almost half of reported rapes occurred in the home of the victim and are committed by a man she had never before seen. Like indiscriminate terrorism, rape can happen to any women, and few women are ever without this knowledge.

But the courts and the police, both dominated by white males, continue to suspect the rape victim, *sui generis*, of provoking or asking for her own assault. According to Amir's study, the police tend to believe that a woman without a good reputation cannot be raped. The rape victim is usually submitted to countless questions about her own sexual mores and behavior by the police investigator. This preoccupation is partially justified by the legal requirements for prosecution in a rape case. The rape victim must have been penetrated, and she must have made it clear to her assailant that she did not want penetration (unless of course she is unconscious). A refusal to accompany a man to some isolated place to allow him to touch her does not, in the eyes of the court, constitute rape. She must have said "no" at the crucial genital moment. And the rape victim, to qualify as such, must also have put up a physical struggle—unless she can prove that to do so would have been to endanger her life. . . .

An article in the 1952–53 *Yale Law Journal* describes the legal rationale behind laws against rape: "In our society sexual taboos, often enacted into law, buttress a system of monogamy based upon the law of 'free bargaining' of the potential spouses. Within this process the woman's power to withhold or grant sexual access is an important bargaining weapon." Presumably then, laws against rape are intended to protect the right of a woman, not for physical self-determination, but for physical "bargaining." The article goes on to explain explicitly why the preservation of the bodies of women is important to men:

The consent standard in our society does more than protect a significant item of social currency for women; it fosters, and is in turn bolstered by, a masculine pride in the exclusive possession of a sexual object. The consent of a woman to sexual intercourse awards the man a privilege of bodily access, a personal "prize" whose value is enhanced by sole ownership. An additional reason for the man's condemnation of rape may be found in the threat to his status from a decrease in the "value" of his sexual possession which would result from forcible violation.

The passage concludes by making clear whose interest the law is designed to protect. "The man responds to this undercutting of his status as *possessor* of the girl with hostility toward the rapist; no other restitution device is available. The law of rape provides an orderly outlet for his vengeance." Presumably the female victim in any case will have been sufficiently socialized so as not to consciously feel any strong need for vengeance. If she does feel this need, society does not speak to it. . . .

Excerpts from Susan Griffin, "Rape: The All-American Crime," *Ramparts,* September 1971, pp. 26–35. Published in *Women: A Feminist Perspective,* edited by Jo Freeman (Mayfield Publishing Company, 1975). Reprinted by permission of the author.

Figure 14.2 Crimes of Violence, 1969–1977

Violent crime

Rate

+60
+50
+40
+30
+20
+10

Percent change over 1969 0

1969 1970 1971 1972 1973 1974 1975 1976 1977

Violent crime up 53%

Rate up 42%

*Limited to murder, forcible rape, robbery and aggravated assault

From U.S. Federal Bureau of Investigation, *Uniform Crime Reports—1977* (Washington, D.C.: Government Printing Office, 1977), p. 37.

Rape is the most underreported of all crimes for several reasons. Many women are reluctant to file a report with the police due to embarrassment and social pressures, especially in cases where the rapist is a relative or friend. Furthermore, women who report rape are frequently subject to the harassment of male police and justice officials, who may prefer to believe that the rape victim actually provoked the rape. Finally, the requirement in most states that the victim produce corroborative evidence of the crime makes conviction on a rape charge close to impossible.

Although most violent crime in America takes place in large cities, the occurrence of such crimes is not evenly distributed throughout each city. Rates of violent crime are disproportionately higher in black ghettos; and urban arrest rates for homicide, rape, and robbery are higher for blacks than for whites. In a study of 17 cities, a victim-offender survey found that 90 percent of urban homicides, assaults, and rapes involve victims and of-fenders of the same race and that most victims and offenders are males, poor persons, blacks, and youths.[26] The survey further indicated that most homicides and assaults occur between relatives and friends, often provoked by family quarrels, disputes over money, jealousy, or other personal matters.

Young males at the bottom of the socioeconomic scale are the most frequent perpetrators of violent crime. In 1977 the rate of arrests for violent crimes was nearly nine times higher for males than for females, with 58 percent of the offenders under 25 years of age.[27] Although arrests for rape, robbery, and assault are concentrated among those who are 15 to 24 years old, there has been a marked increase in the arrest rate of youths from 10 to 14 years of age. Local studies indicate that the poor and the uneducated are most likely to commit crimes of violence. Philadelphia police data indicate that unemployed skilled and unskilled laborers constitute 90 to 95 percent of the criminal homicide offenders, 90 percent of the rape offenders, and 92 to 97 percent of the robbery offenders.[28]

Clearly, the crowded conditions, high unemployment, substandard housing, and low educational level that characterize the urban slums are related to the large percentage of violent crimes that occur there. The gap in crime rates between middle-class whites and ghetto blacks cannot be explained on the basis of race. It is without doubt the inequality of opportunity that makes for this type of inequality in social behavior. Violent crime is almost invariably the result of desperation.

Family Violence

A great deal of violence in America occurs within the home. Members of a family are normally bound by the exchange of love, respect, and personal services. But when one member begins to feel that her or his contribution to the family outweighs the benefits derived from the other members, quarrels may arise. When both parties to a quarrel feel they are already giving more than they are receiving, it may be difficult for either of them to conceive of a resolution of the argument. Because the emotional investments both in a family relationship and in an argument of the moment are too great and the costs of leaving too high, it may become difficult for quarreling family members to terminate a dispute. Ultimately, because intimates cannot retreat behind the polite masks they wear for the rest of society, family members may be unable to find any suitable alternative to physical violence.

The idea that considerable violence occurs within the family setting is foreign to our idealized conception of the family as based on love. But a series of studies concerning both historical and contemporary family relations in America indicates that there is a significant discrepancy between idealized notions and the realities of family life. The institution of the family is intimately interwoven with the larger social fabric, and, as has been indicated previously, the larger value system in American society is by no means nonviolent. In the early periods of American history, male dominance in the family and norms governing family relations were such that "it was considered quite appropriate for a husband to physically punish an erring wife."[29] Nor has this pattern of violence between husbands and wives disappeared in more recent times. A 1970 survey conducted by the National Commission on the Causes and Prevention of Violence found that one out of five husbands approved of slapping a wife's face under appropriate conditions. In light of these and other research findings, we are led to the unsettling conclusion that violence is a fundamental part of American family life.[30]

The most common estimate is that 50 percent of all American couples engage in some form of physical abuse.[31] This figure was supported by a re-

The battered wife: The organization Women's Aid has set up offices like this throughout Great Britain to help women who suffer repeated beatings by their husbands.

cent national survey that estimates that approximately 13 million couples have experienced physical violence and about one and three-quarter million individuals have been confronted by a spouse wielding a knife or gun.[32]

The magnitude of this problem is concealed by the fact that only about one out of 270 wife-beating incidents are reported to the authorities.[33] Contrary to popular belief, the wife is not always the victim of familial aggression. Often the male partner is the recipient of physical punishment. The degree of underreporting of this phenomenon is equal if not greater than that for wife beatings, primarily because of the reluctance of the male to admit the physical dominance of the female in the marital relationship. In general, there is little difference between husbands and wives in their usage of physically violent acts to resolve marital conflicts.[34]

Violence within the family is not a simple matter of aggression by one party against an innocent second party. Rather, because of the complex and highly emotional relationship between spouses, violent behavior is frequently the result of an escalating process of conflict in which the victim plays an active role in precipitating the assault. This element of victim precipitation is typically present regardless of whether the husband or the wife initiates the violence.

Only recently, however, has there been a growing recognition that family violence constitutes a social problem of substantial magnitude. This recognition has come about, in part, due to detailed analysis of patterns of interpersonal violence in our society. One recent study found that in 29 percent of all homicides in the United States both the offender and the victim were members of the same family.[35] Comparable figures have been found in several other studies. Further evidence of the magnitude of the problem is contained in a study that indicates that the number of police calls involving family conflict is greater than the number of calls for all other criminal incidents.[36]

Battered Children

Violence against children has occurred throughout human history, often in the most atrocious and unthinkable forms; yet, like marital conflict, it has been largely ignored or neglected until recent times because it is so incongruent with our idealized notions of family life. In early America, the violent treatment of children was a customary part of their education and family training. The use of the birch stick by school teachers was socially approved as an acceptable means of teaching discipline and obedience. Early childrearing practices were intimately tied up with harsh religious beliefs, and the Biblical dictum "spare the rod and spoil the child" found expression in the regular beatings of both children and infants.[37]

An extreme manifestation of the prevailing attitude toward children in colonial times was the passage of the "stubborn child law," which prescribed the death penalty for children whose parents declared them to be utterly unmanageable and sinful.[38] Although there is no evidence that a child was ever executed under this statute, there is little doubt that the prevailing standards of child rearing were brutal and sanctioned the use of corporal punishment not as a last resort but as the first measure to be taken against a child's infractions.

Supported as they were by religious and governmental institutions, these harsh child-rearing standards became an integral part of American culture. In 1871 the Society for the Prevention of Cruelty to Children was founded to draw attention to the fact that such methods of inculcating discipline sometimes exceeded civilized standards and resulted in brutal mistreatment. But the extent of physical injuries to children resulting from parental violence was unknown. Injured children were typically sheltered from the public view, and when medical attention was required, parents generally attributed injuries to accidental causes. Only with the development of X rays did it become evident that a sizable percentage of children's injuries treated by physicians were not accidental. Medical personnel were in the forefront in drawing public attention to the problem, and at a special symposium conducted by the American Academy of Pediatrics in 1961, the term *battered-child syndrome* was coined to describe the medical conditions of severely abused children. The information presented at this symposium, detailing fatalities and cases of permanent brain damage and skeletal deformities, marked the beginning of the present-day concern with child abuse.[39]

Violence aginst children today is still much higher than might be com-

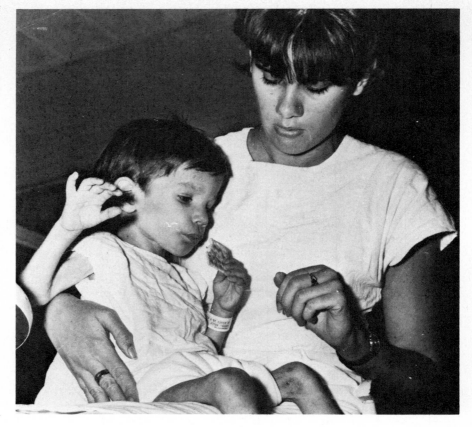

This four-year-old is one of the known victims of child abuse. Found imprisoned in a homemade cage and weighing less than 15 pounds, this child will bear more than physical scars from his parental "love and care."

monly thought, although official statistics on child abuse are notoriously difficult to interpret because so many cases go unreported. Indeed, reliable figures on the true incidence of abuse are probably unobtainable. Many cases of children who are not injured seriously enough to require medical attention never enter the official records. Family physicians may not report cases among their private patients because of possible legal sanctions and the social stigma that now attaches to child-abusing parents. Moreover, physicians may not even recognize a large number of cases because the parents concoct stories describing accidents from which injuries could have resulted. Thus, only the most severe and crippling cases are reported in the official figures. One expert on child abuse estimates that approximately two million cases of abuse of varying degrees of severity occur each year.[40]

Social scientists have typically explained child abuse as a consequence of mental illness in the parents or as a product of a lower-class "culture of violence." Taken alone, both explanations are inadequate. Although some parents who abuse their children unquestionably suffer from mental disorders, recent studies indicate that the majority do not. Researchers are beginning to reject the view that individual psychopathology is the cause of child abuse; rather, child maltreatment is coming to be viewed as a form of deviant behavior that is produced by a constellation of social factors as well as factors within the personalities of parents.[41] Although it is well documented that child abuse occurs disproportionately in the lower and working classes, the class differences may be attributed to the fact that social factors that produce the stress and frustration leading to child abuse impinge more frequently and more directly on members of these classes.

Recent studies have identified several sources of parental stress and frustration that may be expressed in the mistreatment of children. Unemployment and dissatisfaction with occupational roles place great strain on family relationships. Marital conflict stemming from any number of factors increases the likelihood that either spouse will vent hostilities on a child. Abused children are frequently the result of an unwanted pregnancy where the added responsibility and economic burden of the new child creates a situation that parents are unable to cope with adequately. This is of particular importance in accounting for the fact that infants and children under the age of 3 are the typical victims of child abuse. Moreover, since the burden of responsibility for child care falls on women in our society and the addition of a new child may restrict the mother's freedom or disrupt her occupational plans, the mother-child relationship produces a particular pattern of stress and frustration that makes mothers more prone to child abuse than fathers.[42]

Factors that produce the kinds of stress and frustration discussed above may trigger or directly precipitate violence against children, but other factors must also be taken into account. Many parents experience high levels of frustration in their daily lives. Why do some react by striking out violently against their children while others do not? Study after study has found that abusive parents were themselves abused as children. A parent who grew up in a violent household where physical force was used to train children has learned a particular type of parental role, a role that centers around the use of force and violence as a means of family problem solving.[43] In their relationships with their own children, people reenact the behavior they have learned from their parents. When social stresses become intolerable, the parental response imitates that of the previous generation. In this way, generation after generation of battered children have grown up and battered their own children in turn.

Since child abuse is neither a behavior limited to "sick" parents nor a product of a lower-class culture of violence, but is rather a phenomenon related to the very structure of society, the issue of appropriate remedial action is a complex one. Laws requiring hospitals, physicians, and school personnel to report suspected incidents of child abuse to the proper authorities have been adopted in all 50 states. Court convictions are very difficult to obtain, however, because abuse is nearly always hidden from public view and because young children are not considered competent to provide testimony in a court of law. Where evidence of mistreatment is found, courts are empowered to remove the child from the home or order protective surveillance by a child welfare or protective agency.

Family counseling services and self-help groups such as Parents Anonymous are available, and sometimes highly effective, for parents who voluntarily seek help. It is unrealistic, however, to suggest that social work agencies alone, which are typically understaffed and inadequately funded, can have more than a minor impact on the problem of family violence. These agencies, valuable as they may be, can treat only the symptoms of the problem. What is needed is a more fundamental approach that acknowledges that family behavior is directly related to the way society functions:

> The poverty and frustration which the structure of society creates for millions of families must be reduced if there is to be any substantial reduction in the level of intra-family violence. The models of violent behavior presented on television and the models embodied in the actions of public figures who "retaliate" by saturation bombing of cities and towns cannot continue if we are to have less violence in family relationships.[44]

Family violence is inextricably tied up with our cultural value system and the current structure of our political, economic, and social institutions, as well as the related problems of poverty, unemployment, education, and inequality. To speak of meaningfully reducing the level of family violence is to speak of changes in major social institutions, in rigid and restrictive sex roles, and in the often excessive demands made on children that are characteristic of our culture.

Adolescent Aggression

Violent behavior of juveniles as a means of achieving status within the subculture of the gang has already been discussed in this chapter. While gang violence is a very real problem, it is possible that the media have exaggerated the intensity of this type of delinquent behavior:

> Gangs are not primarily assaultive or violent in their delinquent behavior and, what is more, the greatest part of their time is spent in non-delinquent activity. . . . Assaults are more often minor than major, gang fighting seldom involves massive confrontations between warring hordes; robbery often means purse snatching or veiled threats accompanying theft; . . . gang vandalism often means writing gang names on playground walls or throwing stones at the windows of condemned tenements.[45]

At least one observer believes that "the gang more commonly does nothing so much as wonder what to do."[46]

Nonetheless, violence in the school systems, though not exclusively or even predominantly a gang problem per se, manifests the extent to which youthful segments of the population are willing to engage in destructive or violent behavior. A Senate subcommitte on juvenile delinquency released a report in 1974 based on a detailed study of a sample of school districts that enrolled about half of the nation's schoolchildren. In these districts alone 100 children were murdered on school grounds in 1973.[47] Between 1970 and 1973 the nationwide figures for assaults on teachers rose by 77 percent to a total for 1973 of more than 70,000 serious assaults. During this same time period, the number of assaults on students increased 85 percent, and the number of weapons confiscated in the schools rose 54 percent.[48] Vandalism in public schools now costs more than the total sum of money spent on textbooks. Terms such as *guerrilla warfare* and *anarchy* are increasingly being used to characterize the situation in many public schools.

National Education Association Vice-President Willard McGuire argues that all parties involved—students, teachers, principals, school board members, and the community—prefer to avoid the problem or place responsibility with one of the other parties. In consequence, teachers, principals, and parents as well are now on the verge of losing control of the schools.[49] In many center-city high schools, armed guards presently patrol the hallways because of the climate of fear that hangs over students and teachers alike.

McGuire has suggested a number of specific proposals intended to combat the problem of school violence. The responsibilities of teachers and the range of problems they can reasonably be expected to deal with must be more clearly defined; beyond this range, appropriate community agencies must be brought in to work more closely with the schools in areas such as drug rehabilitation. Violence against students as a teaching technique or control device needs to be eliminated in both its overt and its more subtle forms. To accomplish this, there is a need for improved teacher training and the establishment of in-service courses on how to deal with aggressive and disruptive behavior. Finally, greater effort should be put into the design and implementation of experimental programs and alternative approaches to educating students who are not motivated by traditional instruction.[50] To avoid becoming battlegrounds and educational ruins, our schools must institute greater flexibility in the types of programs and training offered and begin to adapt their curricula more closely to the needs of all students.

Assassination

In a study of 84 countries over a 20 year period (1948–1967), the United States ranked fifth in frequency of political assassinations.[51] Studies indicate that assassination—politically motivated homicide—is closely linked to internal political violence, systemic frustration, external aggression, minority tension, and high homicide rates.[52] The high level of tension among ethnic, racial, linguistic, and religious groups in the United States may be a significant factor in explaining the incidence of political violence.

The presidency, a highly visible center of both symbolic and actual power, is a prime target for those who would express their resentment of authority through assassination. A survey of the personalities of the assassins of Lincoln, Garfield, McKinley, and Kennedy, as well as the would-be assassins of Jackson, Theodore Roosevelt, Franklin Roosevelt, and Truman, reveals a number of striking similarities.[53] All were men who had difficulty making friends and developing satisfactory relationships with women. Most came from broken homes in which at least one parent was either dead or unresponsive to their needs as children. All had been unable to work steadily for at least a year prior to the assassination or attempt, and most were aligned with some political or religious cause although not members of any organized movement. All but Oswald—Kennedy's alleged assassin—used a handgun, and nearly all assassinations and attempts occurred while the president was appearing in a crowd. The psychological profile which emerges is that of individuals alienated from fellow human beings and from society—failures who feel compelled to perform a public deed of great significance in order to assert their own value as human beings.

Although the assassin is usually a highly disturbed personality, the act of assassination carries grave political implications. The frequent performance of antisocial acts by disturbed individuals may indicate a significant level of social and political unrest within society. The act of assassination frequently sets off a chain of events in which other individuals, inspired by the assassin, may resort to violence to redress their greivances—sometimes legitimate, sometimes not—against society.

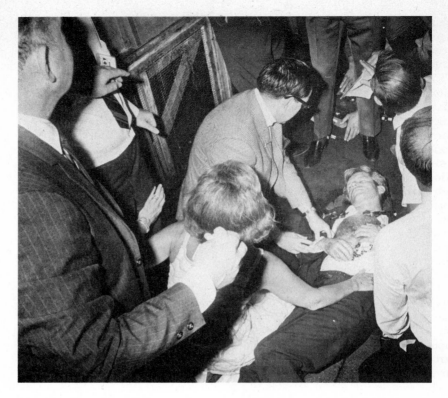

Political violence: Senator Robert F. Kennedy lies mortally wounded by an assassin's bullet—California, 1968.

Terrorism

Terrorism, the collective mode of politically oriented violence, has become a serious preoccupation of Western society in recent years, as the number of such incidents has increased dramatically. Public concern over these events results from terrorism's being one of the most widely publicized phenomena of our time, with bombings, kidnappings, mass murders and hijackings providing the media with tales of terror and excitement, guaranteed to capture the viewing audience. Because of such extensive exposure, it is popularly believed that political terrorism is of recent origin, unique to contemporary society. Such is not the case, for this form of violence is documented in numerous civilizations throughout recorded history. It has been employed in many ways—by governments and against governments; by one ethnic group against another (Arabs vs. Israelis); among members of the same nation (Irish); and equally by the radical left, the extreme right, and anarchists. It is because of this diversity that sociologists have found it extremely difficult to develop a comprehensive theory to explain this social behavior.[54]

Terrorists have employed many techniques in securing their objectives, but the most noted form utilized has been hijacking of commercial aircraft. Between 1960 and 1976 there were 473 hijackings of American and foreign aircraft, only 299 of which were successful.[55] From an average of five hijackings per year between 1960 and 1967, the number increased to 35 in 1968 and spiraled to 89 in 1969. Between 1970 and 1973 there was an average of 72 hijackings per year. As official efforts to assure public welfare intensified with the introduction of surveillance and protection devices, such as metal detectors at airport terminals, the average dropped to 24 per year between 1973 and 1976. The motive behind each hijacking varies from individual greed to revolutionary commitment.

The public's perception of the terrorist is generally an individual associated with a revolutionary cause, such as the Symbionese Liberation Army (SLA), the Irish Republican Army (IRA), or the Palestine Liberation Organization (PLO). Tactics employed by the various groups may differ greatly. Many direct their activities exclusively toward individuals they believe responsible for conditions of society they find objectionable. They may strike at such people through kidnapping or assassinations—for example, Italy's Aldo More. Other organizations strike out at the agents or representatives of their alleged oppressor; for example, the IRA attacks on British soldiers in Northern Ireland or the attack on the Israeli Olympic team in 1972 by members of the PLO. In addition, there are those revolutionary terrorists who do not discriminate when they perform their acts of aggression. The PLO's random attacks on the civilian population of Israel or the assaults of other groups on international travelers are acts not intended to eliminate the immediate victims, but are valued for the general intimidation they produce.

Terrorism is not always politically motivated. In fact, many acts of terror apparently have little logical explanation. The members of the Charles Manson cult killed without reason or direction in their effort to begin a race war. In other cases, terrorists have made demands which were virtually impossible to meet. For example, the Symbionese Liberation Army utilized terrorism in an effort to end what they perceived to be gross inequalities in our social system. Their most notorious crimes include the assassination of Oakland Superintendent of Schools Marcus Foster in 1973 and their abduction of Patricia Hearst in February 1974. Their demands for the release of their "prisoner" Miss Hearst included a food program for the urban poor to be financed by the Hearst family, which if actualized would have cost an estimated 239 million dollars. In the following months, the SLA provided the media with a series of sensational stories including the conversion of Patty Hearst to their ranks and the subsequent final shoot-out in Los Angeles witnessed across America via television.

The criminal element of society has also entered into the business of terrorism for their own reasons, mainly profits. In Italy, kidnapping has become a growing but deadly business, with approximately one abduction occurring per week. In the majority of cases, authorities have been unable to apprehend these offenders and therefore substantial ransoms have been paid to the criminals. Wealthy businessmen throughout the world have initiated their own programs to deter would-be assailants. Bulletproof cars, chauffeurs trained in evasive driving, and armed bodyguards are just a few of the numerous measures being taken to avoid possible incidents. In the strictest sense of the word, these criminals are not terrorists but are simply opportunists utilizing the tactics of the terrorist for their own interests and do not represent a threat to the political system.

In response to the problem of political terrorism, international conferences have been held to discuss techniques to curtail such activity. Cooperation between nations has successfully reduced the numerous skyjackings in recent years through increased utilization of airport security and by refusing to allow such terrorists to land in foreign nations. Other types of terrorism have proved more difficult to control, primarily because the random nature of the occurrences makes it impossible to predict when and where terrorist attacks will occur. Undoubtedly, terroristic acts will continue to threaten our society and unfortunately such acts of violence will continue to be glorified by mass media coverage.

Fighting for Civil Rights

A critical period in the history of American violence stems, ironically, from the nonviolent boycotts, marches, and sit-ins led by Martin Luther King, Jr., and other advocates of civil-rights legislation in the 1960s.[56] With the death of King, the move toward militancy grew as the black cause was more closely identified with the struggles of the revolutionary activities of all oppressed peoples. As it became more apparent that riots in the ghetto were a means of achieving quick, albeit transitory, results, the use of militant violence as a revolutionary tactic became the main thrust of the new movement.

By the close of the 1960s, "self-defense and the rejection of nonviolence; cultural autonomy and the rejection of white values; and political autonomy and community control" had replaced peaceful integration as the dominant theme of the black movement.[57] These new values, represented in different degrees by various organizations and individuals, reflected certain common goals in the black community. Through violence, militant blacks were struggling for "a measure of safety, power, and dignity in a society that has denied them all three."[58]

The ghetto riots which followed King's death served two principal functions. While providing an outlet for the repressed anger of the black community, they also called attention to the injustice of widespread discrimination against blacks. In some cases, middle-class blacks have benefited from the ghetto riots in better employment, higher pay scales, and readier access to a college education. For the most part, however, black militancy and the violence accompanying it has had the effect of polarizing attitudes of both blacks and whites. The liberal support of the black cause, inspired in part by the pacifism of King, has been replaced in many instances by fear and suspicion. Law and order has become a euphemism for the old repressive tactics used against members of the black community in the past. In too many cases, civil violence has been met by still greater violence on the part of the law enforcement establishment.

War: Violence between Nations

The most devastating form of violence known to humanity is the institution of war. Although few societies in the world have not experienced war at some point in their history, the ultimate causes of war have yet to be fully understood. It is believed by some that the waging of war is an integral feature of human society. Between the twelfth and twentieth centuries, there has been a general increase in the amount of warring activity.[59] Within a more recent time span, that covering the 150 years between 1816 and 1965, an international war was occuring in 126 of those years.[60] Compared to wars in earlier periods of history, the modern war is characterized by an increase in the size of armies, a decrease in duration and a tendency to involve wider areas and more countries.[61]

The United States ranks seventh among the nations of the world in terms of frequency of involvement in wars over the last two centuries. The six wars in which America has fought since 1860 have resulted in the battle deaths of almost 600,000 Americans. Another 1.6 million Americans have been injured in these wars.[62] These figures measure only the physical harm done to those directly involved. Other, less quantifiable consequences of war include the social-psychological problems that arise among participants, the devastation of environments, and the loss of money and energy that could be spent otherwise on many domestic problems.

To a large degree, war in modern industrial societies may be understood in terms of political and economic factors. Without war, the manufacturers of war goods and the military establishment would find themselves out of business. Politically and economically motivated competition for power and influence in the exploration of underdeveloped lands may bring about war, as was the case in Vietnam. Many Americans did not know the underlying causes of U.S. involvement in Southeast Asia. Indeed, modern warfare often involves a conflict between the governments rather than the people of nations. Governments, in fact, may use war as a political device to unite people or distract them from internal problems. As long as there is economic or political profit to be made from institutionalized violence, war will continue as a part of the American way of life.

War performs a number of secondary functions. By socializing the young men of a warring nation into the mystique of killing, war contributes to a climate of violence that may linger long after hostilities have ended. At the same time, it may serve to unite people by providing them with a common enemy. Londoners who survived the German bombardment of 1940 recall the event as a time when people helped each other and pulled together in their common cause. Class barriers collapsed, and people talked to each other as equals. Studies show that crime and suicide rates go down in time of war. It may well be that war provides a sense of belonging and purpose to soldiers and civilians alike.

American involvement in the Vietnam War was somewhat of an anomaly in this respect. Rather than uniting the American population behind a common cause, it brought about great divisions. These divisions were manifest in the halls of Congress and in the streets of cities across the country. Politicians were divided between the "hawks," supporters of American involvement, and the "doves," those who strove for faster, broader avenues to peace. The antiwar movement of the late 1960s and early 1970s involved the participation of hundreds of thousands and perhaps the sympathy of millions of others, but did not represent the views of all Americans. The size of the "silent majority," to which President Nixon turned for support of his war efforts is not clear, although he managed to win the 1972 election by one of the largest landslides in American history. The extent to which the divisiveness of the 1960s and 1970s caused by the war is likely to be overcome in the 1980s cannot be assessed at this time.

The Media Commitment to Violence

The entire spectrum of American media, from television and movies to newspapers and comic books, has consistently fed the public a heavy diet of violence. The reasons for this are complex and deeply embedded in our culture and the structure of our society. Advertisers, sponsors, and producers often demand that a certain amount of violence be contained in programs because they feel that it will increase audience size and thus the financial success of the program. The financial success of recent ultraviolent movies and the high ratings of action-adventure programs on television would seem to bear out this view. The American public appears fascinated by and attracted to violence in the entertainment media, whether in the form of sporting events or children's cartoons. Since the mass media in contemporary society play a significant role in shaping public opinions and attitudes, content and manner of presentation of violent subject matter are of considerable concern.

Earlier in this chapter we learned that aggressive behavior is apparently neither innate to the human species nor the result of individual pathologies; rather it is socially learned in the same manner as are more benign patterns of behavior. During the course of socialization children are equally capable of learning constructive or destructive responses to situations that confront them. The values to which children are exposed in the family and from other sources, the types of role models available to them, and the social sanctions associated with various patterns of behavior all influence the character of the behavior patterns a child learns. A series of recent government-sponsored studies, stimulated by growing concern over the amount of violence on television in particular, indicate that television viewing has become an important component in the socialization experiences of American children. The final report of the Surgeon General's Advisory Committee on Television and Social Behavior notes the significance of children's observation of violence on television:

For a child discovering his inner and outer world and learning to respond to each, television may be an important source of models which demonstrate when, why, and how aggression can be appropriate. . . . It also provides a setting in which a young person might learn the strategies, tactics, and techniques of aggression.[63]

The committee report cites figures detailing the average amount of television viewing and the frequency with which violent episodes are portrayed. In 96 percent of all American homes there are one or more television sets, and the typical home set is turned on for more than six hours per day. Frequent television viewing generally begins at about the age of 3 and remains relatively high until the age of 12.[64] Children under 5 years old watch an average of 23.5 hours of TV a week, an alarming statistic when one considers that psychologists generally maintain that by the time a person has reached the age of 5 he or she has undergone as much intellectual growth as will occur over the following 13 years.[65]

Violent episodes are portrayed in all types of programming at a rate of approximately eight per hour. Of particular significance is the fact that children's cartoons are the single most violent type of program on television; between 94 and 97 percent of all cartoons in a two-year period were found to contain some violence.[66] Network researchers state that the number of violent incidents portrayed on TV has declined by 24 percent since 1975.[67] Since its inception, television has been saturated with violent content, and many social scientists now contend that the television medium is the primary vehicle through which the majority of Americans are exposed to violence.

Researchers who have investigated the impact of televised violence distinguish two separate effects: imitation and instigation. *Imitation* refers to the direct copying or mimicking of observed behavior. Frequent imitation, especially by children, of behaviors observed on television is a well-documented finding: "There is little doubt that, by displaying forms of aggression or modes of criminal and violent behavior, the media are 'teaching' and people are 'learning.'"[68]

Instigation, on the other hand, refers to an increase in general aggressiveness following exposure to televised violence. Subsequent to watching violent behavior, certain children are more likely to engage in a wide variety of aggressive acts, some of which will be quite different from the specific act they observed. Children who are easily frustrated may learn from the media that aggression is one rather quick and easy means of problem solving, and consequently they tend to employ aggressive measures in coping with trying situations. Since many children and adults are continually and repeatedly exposed to televised violence, there is a very real possibility that a substantial portion of the violence in our society may be media-instigated.

Although it is difficult to disentangle the separate effects of exposure to media violence from other possible causes of violent behavior, there do seem to be concrete instances where media portrayals have been directly reenacted in the real world. The surge of airline hijackings discussed earlier in the 1960s and 1970s could well have been related to the media coverage given to such events. Prior to 1961, no airline hijackings were reported in the United States. Following a series of Havana to Miami hijackings between 1957 and 1960 that received heavy news coverage, the first hijacking in America occurred.[69] Throughout the 1960s the media continued to provide heavy coverage of airline hijackings, and the number of such incidents continued to increase. A similar relationship has been noted following the broadcast of a film in which a bomb threat was made against an airborne passenger plane; by the end of the week following the broadcast, airline officials had received twice as many bomb threats as they had during the entire preceding month.

Other theorists dispute the impact of television and media violence on the viewing audience. The proponents of the "no effect" argument have often criticized the research confirming this TV-violence relationship on methodological grounds, stating that it had been sloppily conducted or has been based on samples of insufficient size. Numerous experiments have produced evidence for this "no effect" position. One analysis rejecting the association between TV violence and aggression concluded there was no difference in the aggressive content of dreams between adolescent boys who had been exposed to videotapes of either violent or nonviolent television programs.[70] In another field experiment, preschool children were randomly assigned to watch either nonviolent or violent programs every day over a four-week period. The researchers observed no significant difference in aggression between groups in their play activities.[71] While these studies and others disagree with the association between media violence and aggression, the general scientific community continues to stress the detrimental effect of such programming on impressionable children and adults.

Partially in response to the findings of the Surgeon General's Committee concerning the impact of televised violence on children, some steps have been taken in an effort to reduce the amount of violence to which impressionable young children are exposed. The motion picture industry has instituted a system of ratings intended to serve as guidelines of a film's fitness for various audiences. More recently, a television family hour has been set aside exclusively for nonviolent programming. Other proposals have suggested that since television content in general is such a blend of fantasy and reality, the clear labeling of violence in children's programming as fiction might act to reduce media-instigated violence.

A Climate of Violence

So far we have examined some of the causes and forms of violence. What is it about American society that encourages these manifestations of violence to thrive and grow? What must be done to turn the tide? Where shall we look to put an end to the climate of violence in America? As we have seen, perhaps the most significant factor in shaping the American consciousness is the public communications media. Although representations of violence in books, newspapers, and films are of undeniable influence, the most significant contribution to media violence has been made by television. While warning against the type of facile judgment that would brand it as the scapegoat for widespread domestic violence, we must conclude that the violent world of television fiction has come to serve as a warped mirror of reality for much of the American public.

The He-Man Fallacy

Also contributing to the climate of violence in America is the misguided encouragement of sexual stereotypes. Violence is inevitable in a society that equates femininity with gentleness and masculinity with physical strength and brutality. In such a society, the occurrence of rape and the organizing of gangs as an expression of masculine power should not be surprising.

Compulsive masculinity is prevalent in urban homes in which boys grow up without the presence of a father figure as a model. A perverted notion of masculinity may contribute to the development of a violent personality. Superior strength and readiness become the norms of the violent subculture "concentrated in segments of the American population having little opportunity to wield symbolic power—among adolescents rather than adults, in the working class rather than the middle class, among deprived minority groups rather than among white Protestant Anglo-Saxons."[72] When accepted masculine roles cannot be played out, alienated individuals may choose violence as a convenient alternative.

A Right To Bear Arms?

A controversial aspect of American violence is the question of gun control. One out of every two households in the United States is armed; there are an estimated 90 million firearms in private hands. Although the majority of sportsmen and collectors are careful and responsible individuals, the general availability of cheap handguns may be seen as a significant factor in

Ramsey Clark
The Need for Gun Control

Two million firearms are manufactured in the United States annually for private ownership—70 per cent are rifles and shotguns. Of 1,200,000 guns imported annually, 60 per cent are handguns. America is the chief world market for pistols, which have little utility except to shoot people. Most of the pistols imported are inexpensive and so poorly constructed that they are dangerous to the user as well as anyone in the general direction they may be pointed. . . .

Murder and other crimes committed with firearms occur more frequently where guns are most plentiful and gun control laws least stringent. Surveys indicate 34 per cent of the households in the Eastern part of the United States contain guns, compared to 53 per cent in the West, 55 per cent in the Midwest and 64 per cent in the South. Not only is the percentage of murders committed by firearms higher in areas where there are more guns and weaker laws—the overall murder rate is higher, too. Rhode Island, New York and Massachusetts have strong gun control laws. Arizona, Texas and Mississippi have more guns per capita and very weak gun control laws. . . .

Until 1968 there was no federal law with effective sanctions to control interstate mail-order purchases of high-powered rifles or concealable pistols by persons the shipper could not identify. Anyone with the price could obtain the most deadly weapon anonymously. Lee Harvey Oswald, living in Dallas, Texas, purchased the rifle with which he assassinated President Kennedy from Klein's Sporting Goods Co., a Chicago mail-order house. On a coupon clipped from an advertisement in the February 1963 issue of the *American Rifleman* magazine, with a money order for $21.45 attached, Oswald wrote in his own hand the post office address and fictitious name to which the Manchester-Carcano 6.5-millimeter rifle was mailed—A. Hidell, P.O. Box 2915, Dallas, Texas. That was all it took to arm Lee Harvey Oswald and to change the course of history. No federal registration or licensing was required. Most states and cities had no effective gun controls; Illinois and Chicago were among them.

Despite the clear connection between the uncontrolled private ownership of guns and the enormity of the violence they cause, millions of Americans are ardently opposed to any restraints on their possession of firearms. . . .

Perhaps the major argument of those who oppose control is that people, not guns, are responsible for the murders, assaults, suicides, robberies and accidental deaths—and that guns are only the instrument. If guns were not available, it is argued, other methods of committing the same crime would be found. This position ignores human nature and the deadliness of guns.

Of course it is people—and not guns—that commit crime. But what enables people to commit crime? If you wanted to rob a bank and had only a knife, you might hesitate. A gun emboldens you. Suppose your victim is bigger than you. Guns more than equalize. With a gun you are eight feet tall. Many armed robberies are inspired by the sheer sense of power arising from the possession of a pistol. No other weapon has such an effect. A pistol can be concealed, directed accurately and used with sudden, terrifying and deadly effect. Surveys indicate one person in five who is assaulted with a gun dies, compared to one in twenty where a knife is the weapon.

Murder is a crime of passion. Few murders are premeditated. The tragedy is that the rifle was standing there in the closet when the son was seized by fury and shot his father, or the pistol was by the bed during a drunken argument and the husband shot his wife.

Suicide, too, occurs more frequently when firearms are readily available. Many kill themselves with guns who could not find the courage to use another way. Guns are easy, quick, sure—a split second and it is all over.

Several thousand die from the accidental discharge of guns each year. The accidental death rate in the United States is forty times the rate in the Netherlands, fourteen times Japan's, four times Italy's. The mere presence of so many guns insures a continuation of a high death rate caused by their accidental discharge.

In England, where police still function without carrying firearms, few officers die in the line of duty by assault. In America, between 1960 and 1968, 475 law enforcement officers were slain in the performance of their duty. Four hundred and fifty-five, or 96 per cent, died from gunfire. Handguns were the murder weapon in 350 cases. Shotguns were used fifty-eight times, and rifles forty-seven. By comparison, four officers were murdered with knives over the eight-year period. Only in desperation or madness will a person attack a policemen with a knife.

Two defensive arguments are found supporting the unfettered ownership of firearms. The first says that perhaps it would be best if there were no guns, but there are guns, criminals have them and there is no way of keeping them from their murderous hands. We should fight crime, not guns—indeed, we should fight crime with guns. We cannot disarm the good people and leave them at the mercy of the criminal.

It doesn't work that way. Crime is not a rational, calculated activity. A decrease in the availability of guns decreases the commission of crime with guns. The uniform experience in nations and states that have controlled guns has been a lower rate of crime committed with guns. The most rational criminal prefers to play the game of crime without guns because his risk is much higher when guns are used. For every law enforcement officer murdered in the line of duty, police kill fifty persons under color of law. But the criminal mind is rarely so logical. When guns are available, they are used. If guns are not at hand, the criminal will not find them. If he does, his possession of a gun should be treated as a crime for which he can be arrested before he commits a more serious one.

Finally, some protest the bother of gun control. They are angry that, as wholesome hunters, sportsmen, public defenders in the old tradition, they—the good folk—should be subjected to the inconvenience and indignity of registration or licensing. All that is at stake is a few thousand murders, a few more suicides and perhaps several hundred thousand robberies, assaults and accidental deaths and injuries. Is it too much trouble for a people who register wives, automobiles, dogs and many other conveniences and necessities that they should have to register their guns? . . .

After a major legislative battle, and the ardent urging of President Johnson, Congress—as a part of the Omnibus Crime Control Act of 1968—finally gave the federal executive departments some opportunity to control the mail-order purchase of handguns. Under the new Act, only federally licensed dealers could buy, sell or ship handguns in interstate commerce. Licenses were to be carefully regulated with strict qualifications imposed, careful record keeping on every gun required and regular inspections made. . . .

The new law provided a small beginning. Some progress toward effective control of handguns was possible, but it was far from the protection so desperately needed.

Even following passage of the Omnibus Crime Control Act with the first new federal firearms control provisions in thirty years, more comprehensive controls were sought. Proposals were advanced to extend the mail-order ban to rifles, shotguns and ammunition. In addition, some sought what must come if there is ever to be effective control: federal registration and licensing. In August, Congress extended the earlier prohibition of unlicensed shipment of handguns to include the interstate mail-order sale of long guns—rifles and shotguns—and, importantly, of ammunition. It failed to require federal registration or licensing of all firearms. The National Rifle Association, the major factor in the nation's failure to control firearms, had prevailed. . . .

No one should be permitted to have a gun in his possession unless he is licensed to possess it. Only then can we begin to control the use of firearms to commit crime. If this mass gathering of data proves expensive, we can afford it; what we can no longer afford is the violence caused by guns. . . .

Exerpts from Ramsey Clark, *Crime in America* (New York: Pocket Books, 1971), pp. 85–95. Copyright © 1970 by Ramsey Clark. Reprinted by permission of Simon and Schuster, a division of Gulf & Western Corporation.

our climate of violence. Homicide often seems to differ from assault only in the offender's choice of weapon—not in intent. Assaults generally involve knives, while homicides usually involve handguns.[73] (See Figure 14.3 for statistics on the kinds of weapons used to commit murder.) The skyrocketing of gun sales after major ghetto riots, instigated in part by white and black extremist groups, is evidence of this contention.

Opposition to the regulation of gun ownership is led by the National Rifle Association. It is difficult to dispute the NRA's position that the right to bear

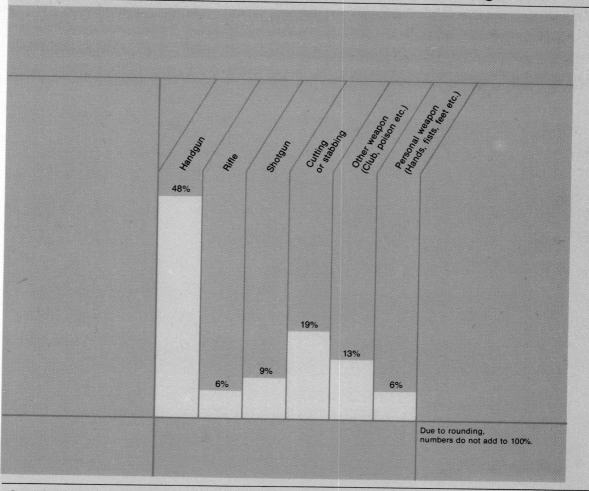

Handgun 48%
Rifle 6%
Shotgun 9%
Cutting or stabbing 19%
Other weapon (Club, poison etc.) 13%
Personal weapon (Hands, fists, feet etc.) 6%

Due to rounding, numbers do not add to 100%.

From U.S. Federal Bureau of Investigation, *Uniform Crime Reports—1977* (Washington, D.C.: Government Print-ing Office, 1977), p. 10.

arms is clearly guaranteed by the Constitution. Nevertheless, the abuse of this right has resulted in intolerable acts of violence and death. The United Nations World Health Organization reports that the United States leads all industrialized nations in all categories of deaths due to firearms, including accidents, suicides, and homicides.[74]

Having noted some underlying causes of violence in America, we are left with the difficult question of determining what, if anything, can be done about them. Out of the presidential commissions on civil disorders and vio-lence have come many recommendations for legal and social reform. In 1970 the National Commission on Violence advocated expansion of the

A pitch for putting a deadly weapon out of circulation.

THE SATURDAY NIGHT SPECIAL.

a major cause of heartburn.

That 10,340 people were killed by handguns in 1973 is unsettling enough. But the number has increased to 11,124 in 1974. Nothing is done.

Over 70% of these handgun murders are committed by previously law abiding citizens against people they know. So if you own a handgun to protect yourself against a criminal, the odds are far greater you will kill someone you know, or even love. Yet nothing is done.

Over 200,000 more people a year are injured, robbed, or raped at the business end of a handgun. Again nothing is done.

Before the end of 1976, almost 3 million new handguns will be added to the 40 million already in circulation. Still nothing is done.

But when 77% of the public want handgun control legislation, as the 1975 Harris Poll states, something must be done.

We need your help to bring handgun facts to the public.

Control Handguns

Send your tax deductible contributions to: THE COMMITTEE FOR THE STUDY OF HANDGUN MISUSE, INC., 23rd Floor, 111 East Wacker Drive, Chicago, IL 60601.

An affiliate of the Committee for Hand Gun Control, Inc.

1968 Gun Control Act's curb on the importing of "junk" guns to include domestic production and sale, as well as state and local registration of handguns and long guns. The commission further recommended the drastic overhaul of law enforcement and judicial procedures to ensure the equitable administration of justice.[75] Although little action has been taken on these recommendations to date, several of the commission's other suggestions have been implemented. The commission also expressed the belief that the integration of youth into the American political process might significantly reduce the incidence of unrest and violence. Although the voting age has now been lowered to 18, it is too early to draw any substantial conclusions as to the validity of that theory.

It was also the strong recommendation of the Commission on Violence that aggrieved groups be granted their constitutional right to protest and that institutional flexibility be ensured to promptly correct injustices that have been perpetrated. Schools, the Commission found, should "emphasize in American history and social studies classes the complexitites and subtleties of the democratic process; shun the myths by which we have traditionally made supermen of Presidents, 'founding fathers,' and other prominent persons; and restore to history books a full and frank picture of violence and unrest in America's past, in the hope that children can be educated to repudiate violence and recognize its futility."[76]

Can violence ever be eradicated from American society? Anthropologist Margaret Mead expressed the belief that peace can be established by "reducing the strength of all mutually exclusive loyalties, whether of nation, race, class, religion, or ideology and constructing some quite different form of organization in which the memory of these loyalties and organizational residues . . . cannot threaten the total structure."[77] Ultimately, the end of violence may depend on our ability to structure a society based not on competition and power but on human equality and mutual respect.

Summary

After the civil disorders and rising rates of violent crime in the 1960s, the violence of American history began to seem more characteristic of the country than its periods of social peace. The social disorder spawned by violence and the large number of persons affected by it—from suicide on the one hand to war on the other—warranted its emergence into the public consciousness as a social problem of importance.

Violence occurs in almost every human society. Various theories have arisen to explain its persistence. Biological theories of violence stipulate that human violence is instinctive—as is the violent behavior of animals—or that it is caused by genetic irregularities. The frustration-aggression theory posed by psychologists traces violence to the frustration of purposeful activity. Psychological character, made up both of inborn and learned elements, is also held to explain the violence of certain individuals. Anthropologists account for violence by stressing the different cultural norms which govern the functioning of one group within society as against another. Although sociologists draw on many of these theories in explaining violence, they focus primarily on the social environment as the cause of violent behavior, seeing in friction between classes, discrimination, and other social factors the keys to violent behavior.

Both the value conflict and deviant behavior perspectives are useful in understanding the roots of violence and the forms in which violence is expressed. Conflict between groups with differing values often results in the use of violence as one group attempts to advance and another to defend its vested interests. Nearly every society legitimizes some violence against perceived internal or external threats. Social power is a crucial factor in the ability to define acts of violence as legitimate or not; the legitimacy of particular uses of violence, such as in certain law enforcement practices, is sometimes contested.

Over the course of their socialization experiences, some individuals learn and accept patterns of behavior that are at variance with established social standards. When faced with stressful, challenging, or frustrating situations, the individual may respond in ways that are considered deviant or unacceptable by legal authorities and other members of the community. The same standards of acceptable conduct may not be shared by all members of society, but those standards used by the legal establishment are the most consequential in determining whether a given act constitutes deviant behavior.

Suicide in the United States has not increased markedly in recent years, although regional differentials may indicate that it is more characteristic of areas with fewer traditional social bonds of family and community (supporting Durkheim's characterization of some suicide resulting from lack of integration within a society).

The rates of violent crime—rape, robbery, aggravated assault, and homicide—have recently risen alarmingly. For psychological, social, and legal reasons, rape is probably significantly underreported. Violent crime occurs most often in large cities; yet again there are regional differences. There is a significantly higher rate of homicide in the South, for instance, than in other regions. Most violent crimes in cities are committed by poor and uneducated young men and are centered in ghetto areas. Accordingly, arrest rates for blacks are considerably higher than for whites. Studies have shown that the racial and other characteristics of most victims are similar to those of their attackers.

Family violence is also widespread in American society. The close ties of a family sometimes makes its members unwilling or unable either to escape or to submit during an argument, and violence results. Child abuse seems to have much to do with the way parents were treated when they themselves were children. Parents who were abused abuse their children. Changing attitudes toward parental authority over children have increased awareness of child abuse as a social problem.

The group violence of juvenile gangs is primarily an urban, lower-class phenomenon. Gang organization appears to compensate for social disadvantages by providing opportunities for adolescent achievement of self-esteem, self-expression, and status.

Political assassination, although it has significantly altered our history over the last century, seems in America most often to be the work of disturbed individuals rather than a feature of the American political system. Collective acts of terrorism have become a major international problem in recent years. Hijacking, kidnapping, bombings, mass murders and other similar activities are considered everyday phenomena, primarily due to extensive media coverage of such events. International efforts to curtail terrorism have been generally unsuccessful because the random nature of these actions have made it difficult to predict when and where the terrorist will strike next.

The civil violence of ghetto riots, however, has been viewed as an explosion of black rage against victimization by a white-controlled social and political system. In some instances the violence of such demonstrations has been perpetrated by police, who possess society's authority to commit violence in pursuit of public order.

Violence by legally constituted authority, including war—the most institutionalized mode of violence—has dominated recent history and, indirectly, American society. The imperatives of a society at war, which sometimes contribute to social cohesion, had the opposite effect in the 1960s.

Mass media broadcasts of violence, both in news-related and entertainment programming, may have resulted in the desensitization of many Americans to the effects of violence, thus creating more tolerance for violent behavior when it occurs but is not personally felt.

Social conventions that connect violence and manliness may also contribute to indifference to violence. Alienated from society's mainstream, denied the accepted masculine role characterized by physical prowess or material success, many chose violence as a means of proving masculinity.

The large-scale American commitment to individual ownership of firearms is based partly on an interpretation of the Constitution and partly on a tradition of individualism and self-defense. Private ownership of guns, unregulated by the law, has recently been criticized by many as promoting violence.

Notes

[1] Hugh Davis Graham, "The Paradox of American Violence," *Collective Violence,* ed. James F. Short, Jr., and Marvin Wolfgang (Chicago: Aldine-Atherton, 1972), p. 203.

[2] Sandra Ball-Rokeach, "The Legitimation of Violence," *Collective Violence,* p. 106.

[3] Konrad Lorenz, *On Aggression* (New York: Bantam Books, 1971), p. 229.

[4] Ibid.

[5] Donald J. Mulvihill and Melvin M. Tumin, eds., *Crimes of Violence: Staff Report Submitted to the National Commission on the Causes and Prevention of Violence* (Washington, D. C.: Government Printing Office, 1969), pp. 419–424.

[6] Sigmund Freud, *Civilization and Its Discontents* (New York: Doubleday/Anchor, 1956).

[7] Erich Fromm, "The Erich Fromm Theory of Aggression," *New York Times Magazine,* 27 February 1972, p. 14.

[8] John Dollard et al., *Frustration and Aggression* (New Haven: Yale University Press, 1939).

[9] Albert Bandura and Richard H. Walters, *Social Learning and Personality Development* (New York: Holt, Rinehart and Winston, 1963).

[10] Julien Freund, *The Rules of Sociological Method* (New York: Free Press, 1956).

[11] Emile Durkheim, *The Rules of Sociological Method* (New York: Free Press, 1956).

[12] Jerome H. Skolnick, *The Politics of Protest* (New York: Ballantine Books, 1969), p. 338.

[13] Richard Cloward and Lloyd E. Ohlin, *Delinquency and Opportunity* (New York: Free Press, 1961).

[14] Albert Cohen, *Delinquent Boys: The Culture of the Gang* (New York: Free Press, 1955).

[15] U.S. Bureau of the Census, *Statistical Abstract of the United States,1977* (Washington, D.C.: Government Printing Office, 1977), p. 173.

[16] Jack D. Douglas, *The Social Meaning of Suicide* (Princeton, N.J.: Princeton University Press, 1967).

[17] Ronald W. Maris, *Social Forces in Urban Suicide* (Homewood, Ill.: Dorsey, 1969), pp. 5–6.

[18] Emile Durkheim, *Suicide,* trans. John A. Spaulding and George Simpson (New York: Free Press, 1951), p. 304.

[19] Mulvihill and Tumin, *Crimes of Violence,* p. 104.

[20] Ibid., p. 102.

[21]John Newman, Kenneth Whittemore, and Helen Newman, "Women in the Labor Force and Suicide," *Social Problems* 21 (1973), 221.

[22]Berkeley Rice, "The Rising Cries of Suicide," *Psychology Today*, August 1975, p. 76.

[23]C. Hatten, S. Valente, and A. Rink, *Suicide: Assessment and Intervention* (New York, N.Y.: Appleton, 1977) pp. 160–161.

[24]Ibid., p. 165.

[25]U.S. Federal Bureau of Investigation, *Uniform Crime Reports, 1974* (Washington, D.C.: Government Printing Office, 1975), p. 37.

[26]National Commission on the Causes and Prevention of Violence, *To Establish Justice, to Insure Domestic Tranquility* (New York: Bantam Books, 1970), p. 21.

[27]U.S. Federal Bureau of Investigation, *Uniform Crime Reports, 1977,* (Washington, D.C.: Government Printing Office, 1977), pp. 177, 181.

[27]U.S. Federal Bureau of Investigation, *Uniform Crime Reports, 1977* (Washington, D.C.: Government Printing Office, 1969), p. 20.

[29]Suzanne K. Steinmetz and Murray A. Straus, eds., *Violence in the Family* (New York: Dodd, Mead, 1974), p. 6.

[30]Ibid.

[31]Suzanne K. Steinmetz, "The Battered Spouse: Dimensions of the Problem," *Resource Booklet for Battered Spouses* (Wilmington:Delaware Humanities Forum and Delaware Council for Women, 1977), p. 4.

[32]M. Straus, R. Gelles, and S. Steinmetz, *Theories, Methods and Controversies in the Study of Violence Between Family Members.* Paper presented at annual meetings of the American Sociological Association, New York, 1977.

[33]Steinmetz, "The Battered Spouse," p. 5.

[34]Ibid., p. 8.

[35]Stuart Palmer, "Family Members as Murder Victims," *Violence in the Family,* pp. 91–97.

[36]Raymond Parnas, "The Police Response to the Domestic Disturbance," *Wisconsin Law Review,* Fall 1967, pp. 914–960.

[37]Samuel X. Radbill, "A History of Child Abuse and Infanticide," *Violence in the Family,* pp. 173–179.

[38]Steinmetz and Straus, *Violence in the Family,* p. 141.

[39]Radbill, "History of Child Abuse and Infanticide," p. 179.

[40]David G. Gil, *Violence against Children* (Cambridge: Harvard University Press, 1970).

[41]Richard J. Gelles, "Child Abuse as Psychopathology: A Sociological Critique and Reformulation," *Violence in the Family,* pp. 190–204.

[42]Ibid., p. 196.

[43]Ibid., p. 199.

[44]Steinmetz and Straus, *Violence in the Family,* p. 20.

[45]Malcolm W. Klein, "Violence in American Juvenile Gangs," *Crimes of Violence,* pp. 1444–1445.

[46]Ibid., p. 1444.

[47]Willard McGuire, "What Can We Do about Violence?" *Today's Education,* November–December 1975, pp. 22–23.

[48]John DeCecco and Arlene Richards, "Civil War in the High Schools," *Psychology Today,* November 1975, p. 51.

[49]McGuire, "What Can We Do about Violence?" p. 23.

[50]Ibid.

[51]James F. Kirkham, Sheldon G. Levy, and William J. Crotty, eds., *Assassination and Political Violence: Staff Report Submitted to the National Commission on the Causes and Prevention of Violence* (Washington, D.C.: Government Printing Office, 1969), pp. 163–166.

[52]Ibid.

[53] Ibid.

[54]Walter Laqueur, "In Dubious Battle," *Times Literary Supplement,* 1 August 1975.

[55]Alona E. Evans and John F. Murphy, eds., *Legal Aspects of International Terrorism* (Lexington, Mass.: Heath, 1978), pp. 4–5.

[56]J. Bowyer Bell, *A Time of Terror* (New York: Basic Books, 1978), p. 40.

[57]Skolnick, *Politics of Protest,* p. 150.

[58]Ibid.

[59]Pitirim Sorokin, Social and Cultural Dynamics, vol. 3. *Fluctuation of Social Relationships, War and Revolution* (New York: American Book, 1937).

[60]J. David Singer and Melvin Small, *The Wages of War, 1816–1965* (New York: Wiley, 1972), p. 178.

[61]Quincy Wright, *A Study of War*, 2nd ed. (Chicago: University of Chicago Press, 1965), pp. 51–58.

[62]Singer and Small, *Wages of War*, p. 287.

[63]U.S. Department of Health, Education, and Welfare, Surgeon General's Scientific Advisory Committee on Television and Social Behavior, *Television and Growing Up: The Impact of Televised Violence* (Washington, D.C.: Government Printing Office, 1971), pp. 24–25.

[64]Ibid., pp. 1–2.

[65]"What TV Does to Kids," *Newsweek*, 21 February 1977, p. 63.

[66]Dept. of HEW, p. 3.

[67]"What TV Does to Kids," p. 69.

[68]W. Weiss, "Effects of the Mass Media of Communication," *Handbook of Social Psychology*, 2nd ed., ed. G. L. Lindzey and E. Aronson (Reading, Mass.: Addison-Wesley, 1969), p. 89.

[69]Albert Bandura, "Social Learning Theory of Aggression," *Control of Aggression: Implications from Basic Research*, ed. J. F. Knutson (Chicago: Aldine-Atherton, 1971), p. 49.

[70]D. Gaulkes, E. Belvedere, and T. Brubaker, "Televised Violence and Dream Content," *Television and Social Behavior*, eds. J. P. Murray, E. A. Rubinstein, and G. A. Comstock, (Washington, D.C.: U. S. Government Printing Office, 1972), vol. 5.

[71]R. M. Kaplan and R. D. Singer, "Television Violence and Viewer Aggression: A Reexamination of the Evidence," *Journal of Social Issues* 32, (4, 1976), 59.

[72]Jackson Toby, "Violence and the Masculine Ideal: Some Qualitative Data," *Annals of the American Academy of Political and Social Science* 364 (March 1966), 22.

[73]National Commission on the Causes and Prevention of Violence, *To Establish Justice*, p. 21.

[74]*Associated Press Almanac* (New York: Almanac Publishing, 1973), p. 147.

[75]National Commission on the Causes and Prevention of Violence, *To Establish Justice*, pp. 229–237.

[76]Ibid., pp. 231–232.

[77]Margaret Mead, "Alternatives to War," *War: The Anthropology of Armed Conflict and Aggression*, ed. Morton H. Fried (New York: Natural History Press, 1968), p. 224.

Variant Sexuality

15

540

In dealing with social conduct, sociologists speak of norms, meaning types of behavior not only approved of and legally sanctioned but presumably practiced by the vast majority of the society. However, in the realm of sexual behavior, every teenager growing up in America becomes aware that practice varies widely from precept. By way of illustrating this, it is necessary to cite only one primary "norm" of Western society: that sexual intercourse take place only between a female and a male legally married to one another. The number of deviants from this norm, or individuals engaging in nonconforming sexual behavior at one time or another in their lives, probably constitutes a majority of the population.

This may indeed have always been the case in our country; but certainly in the years since World War II our society has become increasingly engaged in a discussion and reassessment of its sexual norms. Sexuality has been accepted as a suitable topic for debate from the pulpit and podium, in the popular press and the mass media. The new outlook has been guided and directed by a steadily swelling stream of scientific investigations into sexual conduct and its motivations.

The new tolerance, which has permitted organized attempts by groups involved in the gay liberation movement to win social and legal recognition, reflects important changes in society itself. In the twentieth century, individuals are less subject to the pressures of conformity that have historically been enforced in small-town communities. The rising literacy level has similarly led to a greater degree of open-mindedness and understanding; two world wars have contributed to the breakdown of traditional values; and the changes in social structure wrought by industrialization and greater affluence have lessened blind adherence to established codes. Widespread acceptance of Freudian psychology, with its concept of sexual desire as normal and natural, has also led to less guilt, shame, and embarassment in the discussion and expression of that desire. Because of these recent developments, it is crucial that we reexamine the norms that have guided sexual conduct; in many instances, current legal restrictions seem out of step with social attitudes.

Nonconformity with certain social norms is more or less accepted by most members of society. The norms pertaining to extramarital sex, for example, are rather flexible and weak and are not routinely enforced by strong sanctions. Individuals who deviate from these norms are typically not stigmatized or excluded from full social participation to a significant degree. But other sexual inclinations and behaviors, such as homosexuality and prostitution, are not so widely accepted. There are stronger norms proscribing these types of behavior and more powerful sanctions attached to their violation. Accordingly, persons who engage in such forms of sexual behavior tend to be socially defined, labeled, and treated as deviant individuals.

It is crucial to note that individuals who are assigned a deviant label such as prostitute or homosexual are not only considered aberrant with respect to their sexual behavior but are viewed as essentially different from the majority in a basic and negative way. Since individuals who engage in homosexuality or prostitution tend to be stigmatized and ostracized in the wider society, they may attempt to conceal their deviance (a situation in which considerable anxiety is generated) or may enter a subculture, such as a gay community, for example, where social support and acceptance are available. Sexual deviance is considered a social problem because normal patterns of interaction are disrupted and a segment of the population incurs significant occupational and social liabilities.

American Attitudes toward Sex

The twentieth century has rebelled against the Victorian ideal of sexual love only within marriage. The Victorians have been criticized not so much for this ideal but for the double standard and hypocrisy it entailed. While "good" women were considered virtuous and free from physical cravings, men were expected to have strong and not necessarily licit desires. Hence, in order to protect the good women and the sanctity of the home, prostitution was tolerated and condoned in Europe, Great Britain, and the United States.

Then, too, Victorian morality was essentially a middle-class phenomenon and not necessarily expected of members of the lower class. And although an unbesmirched reputation was essential for any girl who wished to attain a position in the lower middle class, mill girls in factory towns were often forced to prostitute themselves to their employers if they wished to keep their jobs.[1]

The greater mobility and freedom of frontier society in America provided some alternatives to established morality. Although prostitutes in eastern cities with red-light districts were looked down upon and socially ostracized, the "bad" women of the West sometimes enjoyed unprecedented prestige. Between 1860 and 1875 in Virginia City, Nevada, the great silver boom town, ladies of easy virtue were the only women in town. They assumed integral roles in community life, nursing the sick, doing charity work, and organizing picnics and parades. Only after the arrival of wives and schoolteachers in the late 1870s were informal pressures exerted to drive these early pioneer women out of community affairs.[2]

Certain nineteenth-century religious communities also sought to channel or restrict the sex drive. The Shakers practiced celibacy, with males and females segregated in separate dormitories.[3] "Free" love in the Oneida community of John Humphrey Noyes was actually a strictly regulated form of intercourse between unmarried members of the community.[4] Polygamy, legalized by the Mormons who settled Salt Lake City, had to be abolished in order for Utah to become a state.

During the nineteenth century, pornography, like prostitution, was technically illegal—and flourished. Although not widely documented, homosexuality apparently existed in the early years of our country—partly because in frontier societies so few women were around. Homosexuality, in fact, was known to exist not only throughout Europe but also, according to travelers' memoirs, in the Near East, Far East, and primitive societies. The laws in Western Europe and America condemning it were essentially carryovers from the medieval canon law, which has condemned not only sodomy but every other so-called crime against nature, including masturbation.

Modern Mores

The social and technological upheavals in the years after World War I exerted a liberalizing force on sexual behavior. Women became emancipated, seeking jobs outside the home, cutting their hair, smoking and drinking like men, and demanding an end to the double standard. The introduction of the automobile provided for the first time an all-weather living room, secure from the prying eyes of parents and neighbors. Cheap and effective contraceptives for both men and women became widely available. Yet, for all the talk of emancipation, it was hard to tell how many men and women no longer adhered to traditional patterns of sexual behavior.

The uninhibited atmosphere of the 1920s was in part a by-product of its affluence, and with the coming of the Great Depression, something of a reaction set in. With many men unemployed and their wives forced to take menial jobs to support the family, traditional sex roles were often reversed. Nevertheless, books and movies of the period eulogized romantic, conjugal love. During World War II, a comparable situation prevailed. The reality was, however, that families were parted, servicemen overseas engaged in casual affairs, and prostitution near army bases increased. All the same, national interest dictated that popular literature and movies celebrate hearth, home, and the undying fidelity of men and woman alike.

The postwar era saw the publication of Alfred Kinsey's studies on sexual behavior of the male (1948) and female (1953). For the first time, Americans were given a statistical picture of the activities they actually engaged in—and the statistics were startling. Regardless of the moral and legal strictures against such practices, Kinsey's data indicated that nearly half of American females had engaged in premarital coitus,[5] fully 37 percent of the men had experienced homosexual contact to orgasm,[6] and 69 percent of the men had patronized prostitutes.[7]

Kinsey's studies were greeted with a barrage of criticism, most of it purely emotional but some of it based on legitimate scientific arguments. It had been difficult for him and his colleagues at the Institute for Sex Research in Indiana to find subjects to interview. In order to get a cross section of the population he approached leaders of community organizations and persuaded them to enlist the cooperation of their memberships. Thus, as sociologist Ira Reiss has pointed out, in the upper-class level, Kinsey's samplings are heavily weighted with the kind of people who join voluntary organizations. Their attitudes toward sex may be somewhat more conservative than the attitudes of nonjoiners in the same social class. For lower-class samplings, on the other hand, Kinsey was forced to rely heavily on prison populations—a segment well known to be more sexually permissive.[8]

Kinsey's findings therefore may not represent a totally accurate picture. Nonetheless, considering the problems he encountered, it is remarkable that his studies were as comprehensive and informative as they were. Since their publication, behavorial scientists and sociologists attempting to improve on Kinsey's methods have produced new data.[9]

The most comprehensive study of sexual behavior since Kinsey's works was conducted by Morton Hunt.[10] According to Hunt's findings, nonconforming sexual activity appears to have increased drastically, while other activities have shown no change or have actually declined in frequency. The percentage of adult females and males who have engaged in premarital intercourse has risen sharply to 67 and 97 percent, respectively. Extramarital sex, on the other hand, does not appear to be any more prevalent now than during Kinsey's time, with about 40 to 50 percent of men and about 20 percent of women engaging in this activity at least once during their marriage. Hunt estimates that 20 to 25 percent of all males have had an overt homosexual experience as an adult while about 10 percent of married women and 20 percent of single women have had such experiences. Only about 2 percent of men and slightly less than 1 percent of women are exclusively homosexual, however. Finally, the use of prostitutes appears less common, with only 19 percent of men under age 35 with at least some college education ever having had premarital intercourse with prostitutes. The corresponding figure for men over 35 is 52 percent.

Whatever the specific figures, it seems quite clear that the debate over just what constitutes permissible nonconforming sexual behavior has heated up. At the same time there appears to be increased ambivalence over personal values concerning sexual conduct and tolerance. These trends are likely to continue in the 1980s as old perspectives gradually give way to new and generational differences in expectations create tension and anxiety among both the young and old.

A Revolution of Permissiveness?

The most common form of nonconforming sexual behavior is intercourse between a male and female not married to one another. Reading the popular magazines of the day, one might conclude that—especially among young, unmarried people—everybody is engaged in this particular form of deviance. Yet, how recent and widespread is this so-called sexual revolution?

The idea of chastity before marriage has always been accorded more deference in principle than in practice. In folk societies, especially in northern Europe, older people frequently overlooked or even encouraged the engaged couple who consummated their relationship before the church ceremony; a pregnant bride was looked upon as a sign that the marriage would be fruitful. As long as the man was ready and able to marry his pregnant girl friend, premarital permissiveness did not interfere with the social goal of creating homes for rearing the young.

The twentieth century's development of contraceptives and the acceptance of the Freudian theory that sexual expression is desirable in itself have seemingly broadened the opportunities and incentives for premarital sex. However, the traditional belief in sex only with or as a prelude to marriage is deeply ingrained, not only in the law but also in religious codes. It is allied to the Judeo-Christian, and more especially Puritan, belief that only sexual experience between two people in love is important or socially valuable.

A Statistical Picture

Statistical surveys vary widely in their assessment of the situation. Kinsey found that nearly 50 percent of American women had engaged in premarital coitus. Robert Sorenson, in a 1973 study, found that 72 percent of the boys and 57 percent of the girls between the ages of 16 and 19 whom he interviewed said they were not virgins.[11] In 1968 sociologists Harold T. Christensen and Christina F. Gregg found a broad divergence in patterns of sexual behavior in their interviews of students at three colleges: a conservative Mormon college in the western United States, a moderately liberal midwestern college, and a liberal college in Denmark, where the society is known for permissiveness. In the western college, they found that only 37 percent of the males and 32 percent of the females had premarital coital experience. In the midwestern college, 50 percent of the males and 34 percent of the females had such experience. In Denmark, the figures were 95 percent and 97 percent.[12]

Several explanations for the wide discrepancies in the statistics can be advanced; most of them center on the variance in conduct and attitudes of different segments of the population. Ira Reiss has correlated attitudes on sexual conduct with other characteristics and related attitudes on conduct in general. Rather than a parallel between social class and sexual permissiveness, he found that persons who were divorced, infrequent churchgoers, or Jewish, living in towns of 100,000 or more, low on romantic beliefs, living in New England or the Middle Atlantic region, and believing that their standards did not apply to others were more likely to have liberal sexual attitudes regardless of their level of education.[13]

Obviously, the trend toward city living and the decline in religious influence have to some extent been related to the overall increase in permissiveness. Although statistics may vary on the actual extent of premarital sexual activity, they agree on the direction of the trend. Kinsey found that of the females in his sampling, fewer than half as many born before 1900 had had premarital coitus as those born in any subsequent decade.[14] Christensen and Gregg, whose 1968 survey was preceded by a similar study in 1958 at the same three colleges, found that the percentage of males with premarital sexual experience remained stable across that span of years. However, the percentage of females with such experiences had tripled at the western college, nearly doubled in the midwestern college, and even in Denmark increased by 50 percent.[15] Thus it appears that the first wave of "emancipation" did in fact occur with the generation of women who came to maturity after World War I. The second wave appears to have occured in the 1960s.

More tolerant attitudes on the part of parents have also contributed to some extent to the overall change in sexual behavior, although not all parents are equally permissive. The surprisingly broad extent of experience revealed by the Sorensen study, for example, may be somewhat weighted by the fact that out of his initial selection of 839 adolescents, only 508 sets of parents gave consent to have their children interviewed.[16] It can be argued that the parents who refused were probably less permissive in their attitudes—and their children correspondingly less experienced.

Other factors play a role in the changing situation. Seeking to combat the decline in church attendance, progressive members of the clergy are beginning to take a less restrictive attitude toward nontraditional sexual behavior. Another important development has been the introduction of the birth control pill. And yet another consideration is the growing rejection of conventional middle-class values by many members of the younger generation, who believe that love can be expressed in a free union, or even that sex itself can be undertaken without a need for permanent commitment or deep emotional engagement. As E. R. Mahoney has demonstrated using a national random sample, there has been a significant increase in permissive attitudes among all social class groups (see Table 15.1) toward premarital intercourse between the years 1972 and 1975.[17]

Table 15.1	Attitudes toward Premarital Coitus by Social Class and Year							
	Highly Restrictive		Moderately Restrictive		Moderately Permissive		Highly Permissive	
Social Class	N	%	N	%	N	%	N	%
Low								
1972	119	49.2	27	11.2	50	20.7	46	19.0
1975	102	36.6	38	13.6	64	22.9	75	26.9
Difference[a] (%)	−12.6		+2.4		+2.2		+7.9	
Middle								
1972	234	35.8	89	13.6	180	27.6	150	23.0
1975	194	31.9	74	12.2	152	25.0	189	31.0
Difference (%)	−3.9		−1.4		−2.6		+8.0	
High								
1972	90	34.4	32	12.2	69	26.3	71	27.1
1975	59	22.9	33	12.8	70	27.1	96	37.2
Difference (%)	−11.5		+0.6		+0.8		+10.1	

[a] + = 1975 > 1972; − = 1975 < 1972.
Source: E. R. Mahoney, "Gender and Social Class Differences in Changes in Attitudes toward Premarital Coitus," *Sociology and Social Research* 62 (January 1978), 282.

The statistics do indicate a trend toward greater sexual freedom, and much experimentation characterizes contemporary sexual relationships, particularly among the young. Communes, where unmarried groups of males and females live together, and the "swinging singles" complexes of apartment houses in some parts of the country have come into vogue. Coeducational dormitories are a recent innovation on college campuses, although this does not mean that all college students actually share beds or rooms with members of the opposite sex. Many young adults in cities have also begun to share apartments with roommates of either sex.

Sexually explicit movies, best-selling sex manuals, and even advertisements that portray sexual situations with increasing candor have all served to encourage these new experiments. The increase in divorce rates, together with the greater sexual freedom permitted divorced persons by society, have also contributed to an atmosphere of sexual freedom. In addition, the past decade has seen the development—or at any rate the mass media's discovery—of adulterous behavior sanctioned by marital partners and engaged in by both husbands and wives. These alternate patterns of more or less accepted conduct represent an attempt to incorporate the new approval of the need for sexual satisfaction into a society still organized around the nuclear family.

In theory, the practice of *swinging*—consensual exchange of marital partners for sexual purposes—affords husbands and wives a chance to find other sexual partners yet still maintain the economic stability and social prestige of a household. In practice, swinging may not represent a radical departure from established norms. Extramarital experience by husbands, like premarital sex between engaged couples, has long been tacitly accepted by society as a way of ensuring the continuance of households. What is new in swinging is that wives are expected to join their husbands, on the assumption that women need sexual satisfaction or variety as much as men

Savoring the New Freedom

Pornography for the public—the giant screen of a drive-in movie theater looms over Kansas City.

do. The assumption may not always be founded in fact. In a study of Toronto swingers by the Canadian sociologist Anne-Marie Henschel, 68 percent of the husbands had made the initial suggestion to swing.[18]

Brian Gilmartin and Dave Kusisto compared the attitudes and values of 100 swinger couples with those of 100 nonswinger couples who were matched by neighborhood, age, income, education, and number of children. In terms of personal and marital happiness, anomie, boredom or drinking habits, the two sets were very similar. Where the differences arose, as might be expected, were in attitudes toward abortion reform, legalization of marijuana and premarital sex for their children, with the swingers generally professing more permissive values. Swingers were also less likely than nonswingers to join neighborhood or religious organizations, to have relatives living in the area or to know many of their neighbors. The researchers claim that such autonomy allows swingers to ignore the possibility of relatives or friends discovering and disapproving of their activities.[19]

By and large, the twentieth century, especially the sixties and seventies, has seen an increase in extramarital sexual activity, expressed in various ways. For some sections of the population it has meant greater freedom to explore personal relations and to reconcile the relationship between love and sex. But not everyone has adopted the new life-styles, totally or even in part. Every year, millions of young couples still fall in love, go steady, and get married in a fashion not far removed from the tradition of their parents and grandparents.

Infectious Freedom: VD

The increased sexual freedom of the 1960s and 1970s broke down many traditional barriers to sexual expressiveness, but it was also accompanied by an enormous increase in venereal disease. For the years 1950 and 1960 the reported cases of gonorrhea were 287,000 and 259,000, respectively; in 1970 the figure reached 600,000, and by 1976 it had climbed to one million.[20] It is believed that these figures undercount the true incidence of venereal disease because private physicians are often hesitant to report cases to public health authorities, even though they are legally required to do so. A leading medical expert on venereal disease, after noting the small decrease in the number of cases during the 1950s, emphasizes that the recent trend is that of a classic epidemic completely out of control.[21] Gonorrhea now ranks as the most prevalent of these infectious diseases, with syphillis the fourth most prevalent.[22] Compounding the problem is the fact that new strains of the disease-producing organisms have evolved that are resistant to penicillin and other antibiotics.

VD rates are highest in urban areas, among populations whose access to medical services is most limited, and especially among young people. In many areas free treatment centers have been established where teenagers can be treated without revealing to their parents that they have a venereal disease. These centers are part of a nationwide campaign to educate the public concerning the severity of VD. It has now been established that VD is a prominent cause of sterility, and it may cause blindness in newborn infants if the mother is infected. Symptoms of venereal disease are varied, and some are difficult to detect, especially among carriers. If symptoms are not detected and properly treated, its advanced stages may be fatal.

This mobile VD clinic is trying to educate the public about one of our most rapidly spreading diseases. Venereal diseases of all types are amenable to treatment once they are discovered and cared for.

Pornography

One of the greatest controversies in the area of sexual permissiveness has concerned obscenity and pornography, the publication or public display or sexually explicit books, magazines, plays, and films. From prehistoric times, people have sought to depict and comment upon human sexuality, whether in the form of paleolithic fertility images, the *Kama Sutra,* or ribald comedies like those of the Ancient Greek playwright Aristophanes. Throughout most of human history, such activity has been more or less unchecked by legal authorities. Even the ecclesiastical censorship of the Roman Catholic Church before and during the Reformation was concerned primarily with the suppression of sacrilegious and anticlerical expressions of sentiment.

Only toward the early part of the nineteenth century did the common law of England evolve to the stage where it began to be applied in some cases to prohibit purely sexual works that did not attack or libel religious institu-

**Outlawing
the Obscene**

tions. Obscenity legislation was first enacted in England as part of the Vagrancy Act of 1824, which outlawed exposing an obscene book or print in public places.[23] In America, which derives its common law from the English law, no legislation was enacted before the nineteenth century except in Massachusetts in 1711. There were no prosecutions under this statute until 1821, when the publisher of *Fanny Hill* was found guilty of disobeying it.[24]

The nineteenth century, with its Victorian crusaders active in such organizations as the Committee for the Suppression of Vice, witnessed the growth of legal prohibitions in the United States as well as in England. Federal laws enacted during the 1800s prohibited both the importation of obscene publications and their dissemination through the mails. By the end of the century, some 30 states had their own obscenity statutes. In all cases, the definition of *obscene* was based on an 1868 English ruling, in which a magistrate named Hicklin determined that material is obscene when it exhibits a tendency "to deprave and corrupt those whose minds are open to such immoral influences, and into whose hands a publication of this sort may fall."[25]

A Changing Definition

In the twentieth century, United States judges began redefining *obscenity* and broadening the range of permissible literature. Judicial opinions began to require that literary quality be viewed as a counterbalancing value when obscenity was being determined. Significant new guidelines were the result of a 1933 decision by U.S. District Court Judge John Woolsey that permitted the publication of James Joyce's *Ulysses*. In rejecting the Hicklin concept that the effect on persons susceptible to moral corruption should be the criterion for judgment, Woolsey became the first to argue that the objective effect of a work should be determined by its effect on "the average person": "In 'Ulysses,' in spite of its unusual frankness, I do not detect anywhere the leer of the sensualist. I hold, therefore, that it is not pornographic."[26] In 1957 the United States Supreme Court issued the first broad guidelines concerning obscenity. Material was actionable if "to the average person, applying contemporary community standards, the dominant theme of the material taken as a whole appeals to prurient interest . . . [and is] utterly without redeeming social importance."[27]

In the decade that followed, further rulings limited the definition of obscenity still more rigidly. In 1964 the Court faced the question of defining *contemporary community standards*. The state of Ohio had prohibited the showing of *Les Amants*, a French picture that had been widely exhibited and acclaimed elsewhere. The Court held that national, not local, standards were applicable and the picture could be shown. And at long last permitting the publication of *Fanny Hill* in 1966, the Court ruled that to be considered obscene, material must be not only prurient but also "patently offensive."[28]

Given the increased liberality of the Court and the widening measure of public acceptance, books, magazines, Broadway plays, and movies sought to portray nudity and sexual behavior more explicitly than ever before. Local citizens' groups complained of the swelling volume of hard-core pornographic magazines and sex exploitation films. Such forms of erotica customarily avoided the possibilities of legal action by including texts or sound tracks of "educational" value. This enabled their owners and promoters to claim material had redeeming social importance.

The Case for Pornography

In 1967, declaring the traffic in obscenity and pornography to be "a matter of national concern," Congress established the Commission on Obscenity and Pornography to investigate "the gravity of the situation and determine whether more effective methods should be devised to control the transmission of such materials."[29] When the commission rendered its report in 1970, its findings must have come as a surprise to many members of Congress. Far from recommending more effective methods of control, it advocated fewer and less stringent ones. It based its case on one of the first genuinely thorough and scientific studies of pornography's social and psychological effects.

The commission found that, despite legal prohibitions, the vast majority of United States citizens had access to sexually explicit material—with no apparent harm to themselves or to society at large. Approximately 85 percent of adult men and 70 percent of adult women, the commission reported, had been exposed at one time or another to pornography. From one-fifth to one-quarter of the adult male population had had somewhat regular experiences with materials as explicit as the depiction of heterosexual intercourse.[30]

There was ambivalence over what those interviewed considered to be the results of such exposure. Both moral breakdown and improved sexual relations between married couples were believed to be possible effects. However, individuals were more likely to report having personally experienced desirable rather than undesirable effects.[31] Surveys of psychiatrists, psychologists, sex educators, social workers, counselors, and similar professionals revealed that large majorities of these groups felt that sexual materials were not harmful to either adults or adolescents. On the other hand, a survey of police chiefs found that 58 percent believed that obscene books played a significant role in causing juvenile delinquency.[32]

The evidence did not support this latter belief, however. In Denmark, where laws regarding the sale of pornography had been greatly liberalized, analysis of Copenhagen police records showed a dramatic decrease in reported sex crimes.[33] Statistical analysis of such records for the United States provided a more complex picture. During the period when there had been a marked increase in the availability of erotic materials, rates of arrest for certain sex crimes had increased and those for others had declined. In sum, the commission concluded: "The massive overall increase in sex crimes that have been alleged do not seem to have occurred."[34]

In examining the reasons for the popularity of pornography, the commission found that a large majority of sex counselors and educators felt that adolescents turned to such material out of a perfectly healthy curiosity. If sex education programs in schools, homes, and churches provided more adequate information, the interest in pornography would be reduced. Accordingly, it was recommended that a massive sex education effort be launched and that "federal, state and local legislation prohibiting the sale, exhibition of distribution of sexual materials to consenting adults should be repealed."[35] Continued restrictions prohibiting sales to young people and protecting adults against undesired solicitation through advertising mailers were advised.

Congress did not act upon the recommendations of the commission, and in 1973 the Supreme Court, in a series of five decisions, offered broader definitions of obscenity rather than narrower ones. Reversing the 1964 ruling on *Les Amants*, the Supreme Court held that *community standards* could indeed refer to the local community in which books are sold or movies shown. The way was thus opened for state and local authorities to challenge nationally distributed publications and films.

It is still too early to tell to what extent the promulgation of explicit sexual materials will be limited by the Court's 1973 decisions. Although many people originally feared that these decisions would form the base for repressive action across the nation, this situation has not occurred. Public opinion obviously remains divided on the issue, but sexually explicit material continues to be available in most places for those who desire it.

Prostitution

Prostitution continues to flourish even in an era of sexual freedom and permissiveness. For the purposes of this discussion, a prostitute is defined as a woman who accepts money in return for granting a man sexual favors. Although male prostitutes, who sell themselves to women, have likewise existed, they have been rare by comparison with female prostitutes. That in itself is an indication that the sociological phenomenon of prostitution is intimately related to the status of women in society.

Keeping a Rein on Sex Businesses

Because one person's spice is another person's porn, who can tell just how much commerical sex your town—or any town—will put up with?

On occasion this problem has left the U.S. Supreme Court muttering obscurely about "community standards," led perfectly respectable public figures to defend the publisher of the egregiously vulgar *Hustler* magazine and caused the mayor of Cleveland to seek community consensus through questionnaires circulated by city garbage collectors.

One point is clear, however. Sex in various marketable forms—peep shows, nudie cabarets, porn shops, "adult" movie houses, massage parlors—is one of this decade's growth industries. Virtually every area has some kind of sex business. In some places it is neighborhood convenience stores openly displaying journals of copulative mechanics. Elsewhere it is a declining motel that takes to endlessly unreeling X-rated film over closed-circuit TV. In a good many places sex-oriented establishments proliferate so abundantly that once-proud citizens wonder whether they really are living in Porn City.

Plenty of people would be happy to see the sex trades prohibited, flat outlawed. In a police state that might be feasible, but not in a free nation where, under law, the state may not bar any person from reading what he chooses to read or viewing what he elects to view, even though others regard his choices as vulgar, obscene, immoral or perverse.

Even the Supreme Court has remarked, however,

that popular attachment to constitutional freedoms for the purveyors and patrons of porn is not exactly fervent: ". . . few of us would march our sons and daughters off to war to preserve the citizen's right to see [sexually explicit motion pictures] exhibited in the theaters of our choice." Nevertheless, porn and the most elevated public discourse enjoy the same well-established constitutional protections, and abridging those protections to abate sex businesses would be a cure worse than the disease.

Then must this commerce be permitted to flourish untrammeled? Must nonparticipants in the sex trades—a category that surely includes most people most of the time—simply avert their eyes and silently endure the damage such enterprises do to their communities?

The answer is no. In commercial sex as in all else, liberty has its limits. The porn operator has no more right to go his way unrestrained than an automobile driver has to drive across your lawn. The motorist, be it noted, is not only subject to laws that safeguard others but is also licensed to drive, hence subject to having his license withdrawn. Similarly, many communities have sought to use licensing to restrain the spread of sex trades.

These and other control devices are analyzed by William Toner, a Chicago planning consultant, in his recently published study, *Regulating Sex Businesses* (American Society of Planning Officials, 1313 E. 60th St., Chicago, Ill. 60637. Price: $6). Most licensing laws, Toner reports, govern who may operate such a business, many specific details of how the business is to be run and often where it may be located.

In Royal Oak, Mich., for example, an adult bookstore may not operate within 1,000 feet of any residential dwelling or rooming unit. Knoxville, Tenn., forbids massage parlors within 1,000 feet of any "public or private building or premises likely to be utilized by persons under the age of 18 years." There may be special taxes and fees, too. The Falls Church, Va., massage parlor ordinance includes a special $5,000 tax. Applicants for a nude entertainment permit in Santa Maria, Cal., must make a $500 advance deposit "to pay the cost of providing extra policemen and vehicles."

The typical massage parlor license ordinance also demands extensive information on employes, including their health histories and any criminal records, and requires photographing and fingerprinting. In addition, there are detailed regulations on the facilities to be provided by the establishment and a long list of specific operational dos and don'ts.

"When reading a truly restrictive ordinance," Toner observes, "someone might get the idea that the purpose of the licensing procedure was to discourage the applicant. In a number of cases that is precisely the purpose. According to local officials sometimes it works and sometimes it doesn't."

One common difficulty is that the restrictive provisions of these new laws often have uncertain standing before the courts. Toner cites the "opposite sex standard" found in many message parlor ordinances as a case in point. It provides that no male person shall administer a massage to a female patron and vice versa. A Colorado court rejected this provision as "based on stereotyping and guilt by association" and for failure to provide due process by its "conclusive presumption that all who massage persons of the opposite sex would engage in improper conduct. . . ." A California court, on the other hand, found that this "barrier erected . . . against immoral acts likely to result from too intimate familiarity of the sexes is no more than a reasonable regulation."

Common as licensing laws have become, city planners and law officers have misgivings about them. For one thing, the laws apply to specific businesses and don't control any new types of sex businesses that might appear. Licensing strip joints, for instance, won't keep massage parlors from cropping up. Furthermore, licensing becomes a screening process that puts the emphasis on who is involved in the regulated activity rather than on the activity itself. Finally, some laws are so punitive and put such restraints on the content of what is marketed—the material in the books an adult bookstore sells, the acts portrayed in the films an adult movie theater shows—that the laws are left open to attack as forms of unconstitutional censorship.

A better approach, some suggest, would be to make zoning the tool for controlling sex enterprises. Basically, zoning marks out geographical areas and decrees what kind of developments or uses will be permitted in each zone. A salvage yard, for instance, would be defined as an industrial use. Therefore it could locate in an industrial zone but not in a residential or commercial zone, where industrial uses would be forbidden.

Zoning has certain obvious advantages for regulating the sex trades. It avoids any need to make moral or censorious judgments about individual businesses or entrepreneurs; businesses are allowed or zoned out by category, not by individual applicant. In addition, zoning provides definite, predetermined geographical limits to how far permitted sex businesses may spread.

Two dramatic examples of how sex businesses can be zoned are at hand. The two take diametrically opposed tacks—one aims to disperse the sex trades, the other to concentrate them—and both experiments are being closely watched.

Probably the better known of the two is Boston's widely reported experiment with concentrating its sex-oriented bookshops, peep shows, movie houses and strip joints in a small district popularly known as the "combat zone" and officially zoned as an "adult entertainment zone," the only such zone in the city.

Actually, a concentration of pornographic trades existed there before the zoning did. What the zoning accomplished was to restrict these sex-related businesses to the specified area and prevent their spread. The city has also refurbished the district, which was old and badly deteriorated, by repairing streets and sidewalks, installing new lighting and otherwise sprucing up.

The results seemed promising, at least at first. The area is less seedy than before, the businesses there operate with an enhanced aura of legitimacy, the city's administrative costs for policing and traffic control are more clearly identified, patrons know where to find the type of entertainment they seek, and citizens elsewhere consider their own neighborhoods safer from contamination.

But there have been disappointments, too. Providing a legal site for these commercial sex establishments has not eliminated two frequent objectionable by-products, crime and prostitution. Meanwhile, the porn businesses seem to be elbowing out the few conventional businesses remaining in the district.

The Detroit idea is to prevent the very concentration of sex establishments that Boston fosters. Detroit's concern dates back more than 15 years and initially had nothing to do with restricting the sex trades. What bothered Detroit at first was the development of new skid rows in the city. Alarmed officials noted that the phenomenon was usually characterized by an increasing concentration of certain kinds of businesses, principally bars, pawnshops and public lodging houses. In 1962 an anti-skid-row zoning ordinance was adopted to keep these kinds of establishments spread apart, to scatter them through the commercial and industrial zones and keep them out of the residential zones so that skid rows would not spring up.

Ten years later, after adult bookshops and adult theaters began to appear, these and other sex businesses simply were added to the dispersion list.

Where ordinances elsewhere were sometimes vague about just what it was that was being restricted, Detroit's aimed to be specific. It continued a list of "specified sexual activities" ("fondling or other erotic touching . . .") and "specified anatomical areas" ("less than completely and opaquely covered female breast below a point immediately above the top of the areola . . ."). And it made subject to restriction businesses whose stock in trade was "distinguished or characterized" by an emphasis on matter depicting, describing, or relating to those specified sexual activities or anatomical areas.

The key provisions for dispersal provided that no business so distinguished or characterized would be permitted within 500 feet of a residentially zoned area and, second, that no such use would be permitted within 1,000 feet of any two other regulated uses.

It was not long before the ordinance faced a court test. An abandoned gas station was converted into an adult minitheater, the Pussy Cat, and an existing theater, the Nortown, began showing X-rated films. Both violated the distance rules, both were denied permits to operate and both sued. Their lawyers charged the law was invalid on First Amendment grounds and also ran counter to both the due process and equal protection clauses of the Fourteenth Amendment.

A district court upheld the ordinance, it was reversed by the appellate court, and the case then went to the U.S. Supreme Court, which ruled in support of the ordinance in 1976. The majority opinion declared: "The record discloses a factual basis for the [Detroit city council's] conclusion that this kind of restriction will have the desired effect."

Since then, more and more communities have attempted to find legal means of controlling their local sex businesses. Of those that have chosen zoning as their instrument, most have followed the Detroit pattern, opting for dispersal and against concentration, for a very pragmatic reason. Many officials would gladly disperse their local sex trades into the next county, if they had legal means to do so, but few if any would care to be the first advocate of establishing a sexual shopping center where none exists already.

Thus an uneasy equilibrium prevails, with indignant citizens and porn operators eying each other warily and public officials in between doing as much as they feel they can to keep a lid on a steamy traffic that won't go away.

All the while there is this discomforting truth that somehow has to be included in the reckoning: It isn't timid public officials or lax laws that keep the porn trades alive. Those businesses' hold on survival is tenuous. The only thing that keeps any of them going is the customers.

Reprinted from "Keeping a Rein on Sex Businesses," *Changing Times*, January 1978, pp. 21–23. Reprinted with permission from Changing Times Magazine, © Kiplinger Washington Editors, Inc., January 1978.

Condoned and Condemned: Historical Perspectives

In the nineteenth century, prostitution was condoned because single men had no outlet for their sexual drives with woman of their own social standing. Married men might respect their wives and yet be unable to find sexual satisfaction with them. But today, in this period of relative sexual freedom, single man should be able to have sex with women of their own class; and frustrated married men presumably have several options—counseling, swinging, or divorce. Perhaps the fact that millions of American men still feel the need or desire to pay women for sexual favors illustrates that the so-called sexual revolution has not yet touched large segments of the population.

Certain aspects of prostitution, to be sure, have changed very markedly. There are, and always have been, two classes of prostitutes: the lowly streetwalker, or brothel inmate, who accepts a "trick" at a time, and the more elevated courtesan or mistress. In preindustrial societies, where a woman's means of finding a legitimate occupation outside of marriage or of engaging in social or intellectual activities were limited, it was possible for courtesans to enjoy relatively high social status. The *hetairae* of ancient Athens were among the best-educated woman of Greece; they maintained salons distinguished for wit and intellectual inquiry to which philosophers and statesmen flocked. The mistresses of Louis XIV and Louis XV held official positions at the French Court, counseled their lovers in affairs of state, and were fawned over by courtiers eager for political advancement.

Often the "fallen woman's" only way of supporting herself, and legal in many countries and eras, prostitution has frequently been outlawed since the nineteenth century. In France and Italy, pressure exerted by newly enfranchised women voters, who consider the profession demeaning and offensive, had this effect. With women more able to find other jobs and ways of achieving prominence in the arts and professions, both the economic incentives to engage in prostitution and the glamor of being a courtesan have diminished. Although the occasional high-class call girl like Xaviera Hollander continues to make headlines, prostitutes are now more likely to be studied by psychologists and sociologists as deviant individuals. Research is directed toward finding out how and why they continue to constitute a sizable subsection of the community.

In 1945 it was estimated that there were perhaps 600,000 women in the United States engaged in prostitution as a full-time occupation, with another 600,000 who could be categorized as occasional prostitutes.[36] Although this number was probably exaggerated in wartime, the number of prostitutes still appears to have decreased in the ensuing years. Recent estimates place between 100,000 and 500,000 women in the business.[37] These

In spite of society's more liberal attitudes toward free love, sex is still profitably for sale in many places.

numbers are consistent with the findings of studies indicating that men use prostitutes less now then in earlier years.

Kinsey found that the frequency of premarital sexual relations with prostitutes was more or less constantly lower in the younger generations he studied, at all education levels. In most cases, the average frequencies of intercourse with prostitutes were down to two-thirds or even one-half of what they had been in previous generations.[38] Kinsey attributed this decline to the extensive educational campaigns linking prostitution with venereal disease, plus the fact that police vigilance had eliminated many organized houses of prostitution.

Author Vance Packard conducted a survey of 200 sexually experienced males at one university in 1966. Comparing his findings with Kinsey's

1940s figures, he found that the percentage of college-educated men who had patronized a prostitute by the age of 21 had decreased from 22 percent to 4 percent.[39] Another study found that between the 1950s and 1960s the number of male students having their first sexual experience with a prostitute decreased from 25 to 7 percent.[40]

Prostitutes and Prostitution Today

Who are the prostitutes? A study conducted at three correctional institutions in Minnesota found that 16 of the 17 white prostitutes studied and 8 of the 12 blacks had a history of familial instability.[41] Such instability included a drunken, violent, or absentee parent (usually the father), extreme poverty, or families larger than the parent could cope with. More than half the informants had spent one year or more of their childhood in foster homes, living with relatives, or in other separations from the nuclear family.

Prostitutes characteristically drift into "the life" in their early teens, having first engaged in a series of casual sexual experiences in which money was not a consideration. Frequently, they are initiated into prostitution by a boyfriend who wants to live off their earnings. Although many prostitutes live with their pimps and turn over a substantial portion of their earnings to him, lesbian relationships with women are also common. The lesbian prostitute finds her sexual relations with men are depersonalized or exploitative and sometimes turns to women for affection and tenderness.[42]

Several different forms of prostitution are evident in American society today. The streetwalker solicits clients in public places, charges the least for her services, and is the most visible target for police crackdowns. Financial considerations are often crucial in the motivation to enter prostitution, and streetwalkers may earn many times what they could in legitimate occupations. Of somewhat higher status among prostitutes are the women who work in a brothel or an organized house of prostitution. Public solicitation is not required here, and the activities are less visible to the citzenry and police. Recently, some massage parlors have been used as fronts for what are actually houses of prostitution.[43] In both cases the prostitute pays a percentage of her fees to the house in exchange for secure working arrangements and a steady supply of customers. The highest status and the greatest earnings go to the third type of prostitute—the call girl. Typically, the call girl has a set of regular customers who make contact by telephone and whom she meets in her own apartment or in a private residence. Call girls are frequently patronized by wealthy or influential figures, and it is not rare for such a girl to make $100,000 a year or more during the prime of her relatively short career.

Since prostitution is illegal in the United States, except in Nevada, prostitutes are subject to frequent police harassment and arrest. (By contrast, patrons of prostitutes, or "johns," are seldom liable.) For protection, prostitutes have traditionally relied on bribes to the police or turned to organized crime for support. The evidence, however, does not suggest that at present big-league criminal organizations, such as organized crime, are affiliated with most prostitutes. The profits are too meager, and the competition from amateurs is too great.

If prostitution is less widespread than it used to be, at the same time it has—in the permissive atmosphere of the past two decades—become increasingly evident. Streetwalkers in Manhattan can be observed plying their trade on Park Avenue, and at conventions in most large cities it is not too difficult to make arrangements with "party girls." Many still find prostitution immoral and offensive and encourage police to crack down on it. On the other hand, a sizable number of lawyers and criminologists argue that it is a "crime without victims."[44] Since it endangers neither property nor life, police might well be more constructively occupied in combatting serious crime. Criminologist Norval Morris has suggested that the United States would do well to follow the English example.[45] In England, street solicitation is illegal, but prostitutes are legally available to those who want them.

Homosexuality

Another form of sexual deviance that has received extensive publicity within the last decade is homosexuality. A homosexual can be defined as a person who is erotically attracted to others of the same sex; homosexual desires can also be experienced by a person whose primary orientation is heterosexual. The degree to which individuals act out these desires or allow them to influence their life-style varies widely.

Although Kinsey found that 37 percent of the males in his sampling had at some point in their lives had homosexual experience, the vast majority of these men practiced predominantly heterosexual behavior. Only 4 percent of white males were exclusively homosexual throughout their lives.[46] Morton Hunt has similarly estimated the extent of genuine inversion in the United States at 2 percent of the male population.[47]

Female homosexuality, known as lesbianism, is thought to be only half as frequent as male homosexuality. Males also have more frequent homosexual experiences than females and continue their activities over a greater number of years.[48]

Since the Middle Ages, homosexuality has been regarded as a sin. American laws against fellatio, anal intercourse, cunnilingus, and mutual masturbation (all included in the general category of "crimes against nature") are carry-overs from religious law. In theory, they apply to heterosexual relations as well, even between married persons. The Judeo-Christian opposition to these types of sexual activity stems from the principle that sex ought to occur only in the family context, for the purpose of begetting children.

The conventional nineteenth-century Victorian looked down upon homosexuality with fear, disgust, and anger. The psychological literature of the early twentieth century treated the homosexual as emotionally crippled. In recent years, more sympathetic studies have attempted to analyze the extent to which individual homosexuals are deviant only in their sexual behavior—the assumption being that other aspects of their lives conform to social norms.[49]

In addition to statutes specifically directed against deviant sexual practices in force in most states, homosexuals are liable to prosecution in all states for offenses such as lewdness, solicitation for unnatural copulation, vagrancy, loitering near a public toilet, procuring, and prostitution (of a male by another male). Known homosexuals may be fired from their jobs and ostracized in small communities. The degree of acceptance is higher in large communities and sophisticated intellectual circles, where individuality of any sort is respected. Accordingly, since the mid-nineteenth century, cosmopolitan centers in both Europe and America have had certain quarters and meeting places—bars, pubs, restaurants, and nightclubs—where homosexuals can congregate and live in the gay life.

Popular opinion has held to a stereotype of the male homosexual: a mincing, flamboyantly dressed person with "artistic" predilections. Scholarly research, however, indicates that not all homosexuals conform to the stereotype. Either for reasons of personal preference or for fear of social castigation, most dress and act much like other men. Sociologists Maurice Leznoff and William A. Westley studied 60 homosexuals in a large Canadian city. On the basis of their findings they were able to describe the characteristics of both secret and overt homosexuals in the area:

The mode of adaptation is largely dependent upon the extent to which identification of the individual as a homosexual is a status threat. . . . Thus, there are many occupations, of which the professions are an obvious example, where homosexuals are not tolerated. In other areas, the particular occupation may have traditionally accepted homosexual linkages in the popular image or be of such low rank as to permit homosexuals to function on the job. The artist, the interior decorator, and the hairdresser exemplify the former type; such positions as a counter-man or a bellhop, the latter. Thus we find a rough relationship between form of evasion and occupation. The overt homosexual tends to fit into an occupation of low status rank; the secret homosexual into an occupation with a relatively high status rank.[50]

The Wrong Role: Why?

What makes a homosexual? There is little evidence that genetics is the cause.[51] Prenatal factors, either genetic, gonadal, or hormonal, can cause individuals to be born with imperfectly formed sex organs (for example, a genetic female can possess both ovaries and testicles). However, such a child identified by the parents at birth as a girl will grow up thinking and acting like a normal woman. Among transsexuals—the few individuals who undergo operations to achieve a change in sex—the male who opts to become a female is almost always physically normal but since early in life has had a strong feeling of being female and has developed a belief that he is, in fact, a woman.[52]

By contrast, the male homosexual is reared in a family where he is thought of as a boy, although his parents commonly suffer from emotional problems. George Henry's study, Sex Variants, chronicled the case histories of eight homosexuals, half of them male, half of them female. In the case of both sexes, the parents had ignored or implicitly rejected sexual education; mothers were often found to be stiff, unhappy, and reserved—yet also domineering and overprotective; and fathers were angry and destructive, or else negative, withdrawn ciphers. Both parents usually fought each other to win the affection of the child.[53] Not all children growing up in such circumstances, however, become homosexuals, and many changes in social attitude have occurred since Henry's study. Further research is needed to find specific factors that lead a child to identify more strongly with the parent of the opposite sex than his own.

William Simon and John H. Gagnon
Homosexuality: A Sociological Perspective

In addition to the fact that sexual contact with persons of the same sex, even if over the age of consent, is against the law in 49 of the 50 states, the homosexual labors under another burden that is commonly the lot of the deviant in any society. The process of labeling and stigmatizing behavior not only facilitates the work of legal agencies in creating a bounded category of deviant actors such as the "normal burglar" and the "normal child molester,". . .but it also creates an image of large classes of deviant actors all operating from the same motivations and for the same etiological reasons. The homosexual, like most significantly labeled persons (whether the label be positive or negative), has *all* of his acts interpreted through the framework of his homosexuality. . . .

It is this nearly obsessive concern with the ultimate causes of adult conditions that has played a major role in structuring our concerns about beliefs and attitudes toward the homosexual. . . .

Even with the relatively recent shift in the normative framework available for considering homosexuality—that is, from a rhetoric of sin to a rhetoric of mental health—the preponderance of the sexual factor is evident. The change itself may have major significance in the way homosexual persons are dealt with; at the same time, however, the mental health rhetoric seems equally wide of the mark in understanding homosexuality. . . . Accompanying this trend toward a reconceptualization of mental health has been a scaling-down of the goals set for men; instead of exceedingly vague and somewhat utopian goals, we tend to ask more pragmatic questions: Is the individual self-supporting? Does he manage to conduct his affairs without the intervention of the police or the growing number of mental health authorities? Does he have adequate sources of social support? A positively-balanced and adequately-developed repertoire for gratification? Has he learned to accept himself? These are questions we are learning to ask of nearly all men, but among the exceptions is found the homosexual. In practically all cases, the presence of homosexuality is seen as prima facie evidence of major psychopathology. When the heterosexual meets these minimal definitions of mental health, he is exculpated; the homosexual—no matter how good his adjustment in nonsexual areas of life— remains suspect.

Recent tabulations drawn from a group of 550 white males with extensive histories of homosexuality, interviewed outside institutions by Kinsey and his associates, suggest that most homosexuals cope fairly well, and even particularly well, when we consider the stigmatized and in fact criminal nature of their sexual interests. . . .

Like the heterosexual, the homosexual must come to terms with the problems that are attendant upon being a member of society: he must find a place to work, learn to live with or without his family, be involved or apathetic in political life, find a group of friends to talk to and live with, fill his leisure time usefully or frivolously, handle all of the common and uncommon problems of impulse control and personal gratification, and in some manner socialize his sexual interests.

There is a seldom-noticed diversity to be found in the life cycle of the homosexual, both in terms of solving general human problems and in terms of the particular characteristics of the life cycle itself. Not only are there as many ways of being homosexual as there are of being heterosexual, but the individual homosexual, in the course of his every-day life, encounters as many choices and as many crises as the heterosexual. . . .

An example of this is in the phase of homosexuality called "coming out," which is that point in time when there is self-recognition by the individual of his identity as a homosexual and the first major exploration of the homosexual community. At this point in time the removal of inhibiting doubts frequently releases a great deal of sexual energy. Sexual contacts during this period are often pursued nearly indiscriminately and with greater vigor than caution. This is very close to that period in the life of the heterosexual called the "honeymoon," when coitus is legitimate and is pursued with a substantial amount of energy. . . .

Another life cycle crisis that the homosexual shares with the heterosexual in this youth-oriented society is the crisis of aging. While American society places an inordinate positive emphasis on youth, the homosexual community, by and large, places a still greater emphasis on this fleeting characteristic. . . . Here, as with "coming out," it is important to note that most homosexuals, even with fewer resources than their heterosexual counterparts, manage to weather the period with relative success.

A central concern underlying these options and the management of a homosexual career is the presence and complexity of a homosexual community, which serves most simply for some persons as a sexual market place, but for others as the locus of friendships, opportunities, recreation, and expansion of the base of social life. . . .

It should be pointed out that in contrast to ethnic and occupational subcultures the homosexual community, as well as other deviant subcommunities, has very limited content. This derives from the fact that the community members often have only their sexual commitment in common. Thus, while the community may reduce the problems of access to sexual partners and reduce guilt by providing a structure of shared values, often the shared values structure is far too narrow to transcend other areas of value disagreement. . . .

Earlier we briefly listed some of the general problems that the homosexual—in common with the heterosexual—must face; these included earning a living, maintaining a residence, relations with family, and so on. At this point we might consider some of these in greater detail.

First there is the most basic problem of all: earning a living. Initially, the variables that apply to all labor force participants generally apply to homosexuals also. In addition there are the special conditions imposed by the deviant definition of the homosexual commitment. What is important is that the occupational activity of homosexuals represents a fairly broad range.

A second series of questions could deal with the effects of a deviant sexual commitment upon occupational activity itself. In some cases the effect may be extremely negative, since the pursuit of homosexual interests may generate irresponsibility and irregularity. . . . On the other hand, several positive effects can be observed. Detachment from the demands of domestic life not only frees one for greater dedication to the pursuit of sexual goals, but also for greater dedication to work. Also, the ability of some jobs to facilitate homosexual activity—such as certain marginal, low-paying, white-collar jobs—serves as compensation for low pay or limited opportunity for advancement. . . .

Similarly, just as most homosexuals have to earn a living, so must they come to terms with their immediate families. There is no substantial evidence to suggest that the proportion of homosexuals for whom relatives are significant persons differs from that of heterosexuals. The important differences rest in the way the relationships are managed and, again, the consequences they have for other aspects of life. . . .

This order of discussion could be extended into a large number of areas. Let us consider just one more: religion. As a variable, religion (as both an identification and a quality of religiosity) manifests no indication that it plays an important role in the generation of homosexual commitments. However, it clearly does, or can, play a significant role in the management of that commitment. . . . more than asking about the homosexual's religious orientation and how it expresses his homosexuality, we must also learn to ask how his homosexuality expresses his commitment to the religious.

The aims, then, of a sociological approach to homosexuality are to begin to define the factors—both individual and situational—that predispose a homosexual to follow one homosexual path as against others; to spell out the contingencies that will shape the career that has been embarked upon; and to trace out the patterns of living in both their pedestrian and their seemingly exotic aspects. Only then will we begin to understand the homosexual. . . .

Excerpts from William Simon and John H. Gagnon, "Homosexuality: The Formulation of a Sociological Perspective," *Journal of Health and Social Behavior* 8 (September 1967), 177–185, not including footnotes. Reprinted by permission.

Coming Out

It is increasingly thought that social as well as psychological factors are important to the appearance of homosexuality. The male homosexual characteristically discovers his erotic direction in puberty or adolescence. In a study of 55 admitted homosexuals, it was found that there was on the average a six-year interval between the time of first sexual feelings toward a person of the same sex and the decision for homosexual behavior. This decision is known as "coming out."[54] Of the subjects studied, 50 percent came out while associating with other homosexuals—in bars, at private parties, or in single-sex situations that provided convenient locales for homosexual activities, such as prisons, mental institutions, the military, or public men's rooms. Another 15 percent discovered their true identity while reading about homosexuality.[55]

It is during the period of coming out that sociocultural factors, as opposed to psychological ones, play a key role in the development of some homosexuals. This is apt to be the time when "many homosexuals go through a crisis of femininity; that is, they 'act out' in public places in a somewhat effeminate manner; and some, in a transitory fashion, wear female clothing, known in the homosexual argot as 'going in drag.'"[56] Also during this period, usually when the homosexual is between the ages of 16 and 30, he is most likely to become a member of the homosexual community. This organization of his life around homosexual behavior is a type of secondary deviance—"a special class of socially defined responses, which people make to problems created by the societal reactions to their deviance."[57]

Although most Americans place a high premium on youth, the homosexual undergoes a crisis of aging at an even earlier age than the heterosexual. Homosexuals over 40 are often derisively known as "aunties" and have difficulties in finding partners. Moreover, as they move up the social ladder,

A transsexual success story: Dr. Richard Raskind became Dr. Renee Richards and played in the women's singles competition of the U.S. open tennis tournament in 1976.

Problems of Deviant Behavior

homosexuals are apt to become progressively more conservative about revealing their deviance. They are most apt to prefer the atmosphere of private parties to that of the gay bar and are more likely to refuse to recognize overtly homosexual friends they meet on the street.

In these respects the case of the homosexual tranvestites parallels that of other homosexuals. As described by anthropologist Esther Newton in *Mother Camp*, transvestites fall into two classes: amateur "street fairies," who are usually young and wear effeminate garb in public, and professional female impersonators.[58] The latter, frequently older men, wear "full drag" only while doing their acts in gay bars or nightclubs. Offstage, they dress in casual sport clothes and avoid being seen with obviously effeminate men.

Lesbian Love

If many male homosexuals fail to capture the public eye, lesbianism is even less conspicuous. Although some female homosexuals affect the role of "butch" or "bull-dyke," with mannish clothes and straight, short hair, the vast majority prefer the role of "femme," dressing and acting like typical women. Lesbians partonize their own gay bars, but to a lesser extent than male homosexuals patronize theirs. Rather than seeking a variety of casual sexual encounters, they are more apt to fall in love with another woman and set up a more or less stable home.

Only in Spain, Austria, and the state of Georgia is there specific legislation against lesbian activities, and lesbians are not prosecuted to the same extent as men. This tendency has been variously interpreted. Some authorities see it as a sign that male homosexuality, with its rejection of the dominant, aggressive personality generally associated with the male sex constitutes more of a threat to established modes of social behavior. Others, however, say it is simply evidence that society is in general less concerned with protecting or defining the status of women.

For both males and females, homosexuality tends to be more prevalent in institutional settings. Studies of women's prisons, for example, place the number of inmates who are involved in a homosexual relationship during the period of their confinement at approximately half the prison population.[59] The figure is believed to be lower for male prison inmates. The vast majority of female inmates who enter into homosexual relationships are "jailhouse turnouts"—individuals who were heterosexual prior to their imprisonment and who return to heterosexual relationships upon their release. This high incidence of prison homosexuality is generally understood as a response to the deprivations and depersonalization of institutional life.

The overriding need of a majority of female prisoners is to establish an affectional relationship which brings in prison, as it does in the community, love, interpersonal support, security, and social status. This need promotes homosexuality as the predominant compensatory response to the pains of imprisonment.[60]

Current Attitudes toward Variant Sexuality

Responses to deviance, besides their intended outcomes, often have unintended consequences that are useful for society. The very act of sanctioning deviant behavior often serves the latent function of reestablishing the

DEVIANT SEXUALITY

For generations society has considered sex permissible only within the confines of marriage. While a bit of husbandly philandering or unrestrained premarital passion might be generously overlooked, any other divergence from norms for sexual behavior was viewed as deviant. In this century, however, sex has managed to escape the conjugal yoke so often and so openly that our society may well be forced to redefine deviant sexuality. *Clockwise from top left:* Hip padding—part and parcel of the female role this transvestite plays; love between men; a lesbian affair; happy to be gay; "coming out" looking like a lady; acting out feelings of femininity in full drag; adult bookstore, open for business 24 hours a day.

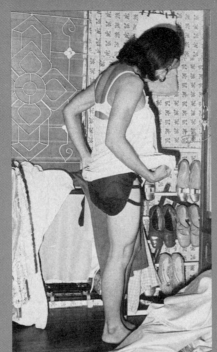

mores in question. This characteristic of responses to deviant behavior is especially pronounced where sexuality is concerned because of the central position sexual customs occupy in the social order. The negative sanctions imposed against the homosexual, for example, not only punish him for his violation of expected behavior but also indicate to others what is considered proper sexual behavior. In this way, commitment to conforming norms is reinforced and strengthened.

Society carefully chooses for stigmatization as sexual deviants those who are relatively powerless, disaffiliated, and unable to resist. In the words of Jean-Paul Sartre: "They must be bad by birth without hope of change. That is why one chooses men with whom the decent members of the community have no reciprocal relationship; so that these bad people cannot take into their heads to pay us back in kind and start thinking of us what we think of them."[61]

Although rejecting and stigmatizing the sexual deviant has been common practice in the past and still is to a large extent, many of those so treated have now organized to repel the label of deviant. Most notably, homosexuals in many parts of the country have become actively involved in movements to establish their claim on civil rights. Indeed, the twentieth century as a whole and the postwar years in particular have witnessed both the growth of literature depicting the homosexual condition sympathetically and organized attempts to gain legal and social respectability for homosexuals. The most publicized protest has been created by homosexuals themselves, through such organizations as the Mattachine Society, the Gay Activists Alliance, and the Daughters of Bilitis.

Although the organized efforts of homosexuals to claim their rights and change their image have increased, results have been slow in coming. In

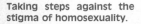

Taking steps against the stigma of homosexuality.

1962 the American Law Institute drafted a model penal code meant to serve as a guideline for legislation to update state criminal law. With respect to sex offenses, the code was significant in that it omitted prohibitions against any kind of sexual behavior among consenting adults in private.[62] Although legal sanctions against variations of heterosexual behavior have been liberalized in many states to coincide with the code, this has not been true for homosexual behavior. In 1967 Britain's Parliament, by an overwhelming majority, repealed the ancient statute making homosexuality between consenting adults a criminal offense. The decision was based in large measure upon the recommendations of the Wolfenden Commission's 1957 report, which argued that crime was not the same as sin. Britain's laws were thus brought into conformity with those of other European countries regarding this issue.

Presently, in America, homosexuality between consenting adults has been decriminalized in 18 states, while in some others it is punishable by as much as a five-year prison sentence. Many cities and counties have passed ordinances that prohibit discrimination in employment and housing based on a person's affectional or sexual preference. City officials in San Francisco, which has a large gay population, have revised the family-life curriculum in schools to acknowledge homosexual life-styles and have now begun to recruit gay personnel for the police department.

Yet these advances have brought about a countermovement by groups that claim that homosexuality is immoral and poses a threat to the very fiber of the family and the country. Led by singer Anita Bryant, the anti-gay-rights movement dwells heavily on the alleged homosexual threat to schoolchildren. These forces have succeeded in defeating or repealing antidiscrimination legislation in several cities and counties across the country. In spite of concerned action by gay rights organizations and the general trend toward greater tolerance of nonheterosexual orientations, older entrenched attitudes concerning homosexuality are slow to change, as Table 15.2 illustrates. Even though no polls have been taken, we can be assured that public attitudes toward other aberrant sex behaviors are even more disapproving. The efforts of the gay community have brought some issues to public attention, however. Today, movies, magazines, and novels have adopted homosexuality as a major theme.

On the basis of new knowledge, new laws, and new social movements, the treatment of sexual deviance is going through a period of change and enlightenment. Because treatment for problems of sexual deviance has fallen primarily within the domain of psychiatry, homosexuals and prostitutes especially have reacted negatively to the characterization by that discipline of their behavior as illness. As a result and despite dissension within the ranks of the psychiatric community, the American Psychiatric Association recently decided to remove homosexuality from its list of psychiatric disorders.[63]

The concept of sexual health is also being expanded to include sexual problems throughout the life cycle. Through sex education in the public schools and some church schools, young people and adults alike are now learning to deal constructively with problems that were once ignored until they manifested themselves in obtrusive ways. Among these are problems ranging from masturbation, homosexuality, pedophilia, and voyeurism to family planning, marriage counseling, and sexual adaptations of the aged.[64]

Table 15.2 Attitudes toward Sex and toward Homosexuality (Based on 3018 Interviews)

	What is your opinion if a married person has sexual intercourse with someone other than the marriage partner?	If a teenager (boy/girl) 16–19 has sexual intercourse with a (girl/boy) without love?	If an unmarried adult (man/woman) has sexual intercourse with a (woman/man) when they love each other?	What is your opinion of sex acts between two persons of the same sex when they have no special affection for each other?	When they love each other?
Always wrong	72.7%	51.7%	31.5%	77.7%	70.2%
Almost always wrong	14.3	19.4	14.0	8.4	8.4
Wrong only sometimes	10.7	19.6	22.2	6.3	7.2
Not wrong at all	2.1	5.0	28.7	5.6	11.4
Don't know	0.4	4.0	3.5	1.6	2.2
No answer	0.1	0.1	—	0.1	0.3
	99.8	99.8	99.9	99.7	99.7

Source: Eugene E. Levitt and Albert D. Klassen, Jr., "Public Attitudes toward Homosexuality: Part of the 1970 National Survey by the Institute for Sex Research," *Journal of Homosexuality* 1 (Fall 1974), 31.

The practice of sex therapy has also developed in recent years to treat those with such problems. As yet, however, the organization and professionalization of sex counseling services other than by psychiatrists is incomplete. Although some states license and certify psychologists or marriage counselors, none license sex counselors.[65] This means that standards for training and practice are undefined and opportunities for quackery plentiful. One indication of a move toward the accreditation of the practices of sex counseling, however, is the recent organization of the Council of Sex Therapists of Eastern Medical Schools.[66]

Summary

Social norms governing sexual behavior have been called into serious question in the twentieth century. The double standard of the Victorian era, when official morality insisted on the sanctity of the home but prostitution and other varieties of nonconforming sexual behavior flourished outside it, came under serious attack near the end of the nineteenth century. This was due partly to the studies of Freud and others who saw it as contributing both to private suffering and social disorganization. Increased communications, new technology—especially the automobile—and changed social conditions worked together to loosen both sexual habits and the social attitudes of Americans toward sexual behavior.

The extent and variety of American sexual behavior, as revealed by the Kinsey reports of 1948 and 1953, astonished many, however; and Kinsey's methods and findings came under attack. Attitude changes in the years since the reports were published is evidence that the findings of his study, as well as later research on sexual behavior, have been widely accepted. Changes in sexual norms have definitely occurred in America as evidenced by Hunt's research, although there is still much disagreement about the effects of such changes.

The most drastic increase in nonconforming sexual behavior has occurred in premarital intercourse between adults of the opposite sex. Premarital intercourse has always been accepted to a certain extent, provided couples were married by the time a child was born. In the twentieth century, contraceptives and a belief that sexual expression is desirable in itself have broadened the opportunities and incentives for premarital sex. Increased city living, a decline in religious influence, the post–World War I "emancipation" of women, and candid portrayals of sexual situations in films and books are other contributing factors. Emerging sexual permissiveness within marriage, involving the exchange of marital partners, is a more recent development.

Throughout most of human history sexuality has been written about, depicted, and commented on without legal restraint. In the nineteenth century however, legal restraints on the distribution of such work grew, especially in the United States and England. Until recently, twentieth-century judicial decisions were narrowing the definitions of obscenity and broadening the range of permissible literature. Recent Supreme Court decisions have reversed this trend, however, removing "redeeming social importance" as a protection for pornographic literature and allowing local communities to decide for themselves what is obscene. The findings of a recent national commission on pornography that most pornography is relatively innocuous have thus been rejected by the courts, as they had earlier been rejected by other government officials.

Despite greater permissiveness, prostitution continues to flourish, although there is a slight decline in activity from earlier decades. Prostitution remains illegal in most states, but it is more out in the open in today's permissive society. Prostitutes are frequently harassed and arrested, however, and turn to bribery and organized crime for protection and support.

Of all nonconforming sexual behavior, homosexuality has received the most public discussion over the past decade. It is estimated—following Hunt—that perhaps 1 to 2 percent of American men are homosexual, although many more have had homosexual experience. Female homosexuality is thought to be about half as prevalent. Until recently, male homosexuality was strongly condemned for religious reasons and because it was thought to undermine the institution of the family. Only male homosexuality has been extensively legislated against.

There are numerous psychological theories about the causes of homosexuality. Most center on the family situation in which a child is raised. During the period in which homosexuals characteristically realize their deviance, however, sociocultural factors shape their development. Attempts are currently being made to legalize homosexual behavior and to prevent the stigmatization of individuals because of their homosexuality.

Although sexual deviants, particularly homosexuals, have long been rejected and stigmatized, they have recently begun to organize groups to protect their rights and change their public image. Nevertheless, public attitudes and official reactions are slow to change. New treatment specialists and various types of sex therapies are being developed to help those engaging in deviant sexuality. And direct public education about sexual development and sexual problems that occur throughout the life cycle may help liberalize public opinion as well.

Notes

[1] Arno Karlen, *Sexuality and Homosexuality* (New York: Norton, 1971), pp. 161–174.

[2] Marion Goldman, "Prostitution and Virtue in Nevada," *Society,* November/December 1972, pp. 32–58.

[3] Rosabeth Moss Kanter, *Commitment and Community: Communes and Utopias in Sociological Perspective* (Cambridge, Mass.: Harvard University Press, 1972), p. 91.

[4] Ibid., p. 88.

[5] Alfred C. Kinsey et al., *Sexual Behavior in the Human Female* (Philadelphia: Saunders, 1953), p. 286.

[6] Alfred C. Kinsey, Wardell B. Pomeroy, and Clyde E. Martin, *Sexual Behavior in the Human Male* (Philadelphia: Saunders, 1948), p. 650.

[7] Ibid., p. 597.

[8] Ira L. Reiss, *The Social Context of Premarital Sexual Permissiveness* (New York: Holt, Rinehart and Winston, 1967), pp. 66–67.

[9] A review of Kinsey's major findings and a summary of recent surveys of sexual behavior can be found in Karlen, *Sexuality and Homosexuality,* pp. 438–455.

[10] Morton Hunt, *Sexual Behavior in the 1970s* (Chicago: Playboy Press, 1974).

[11] Robert C. Sorensen, *Adolescent Sexuality in Contemporary America: Personal Values and Sexual Behavior, Ages 13–19* (New York: World Publishing, 1972), p. 441.

[12] Harold T. Christensen and Christina F. Gregg, "Changing Sex Norms in America and Scandinavia," *Journal of Marriage and the Family* 32 (November 1970), 621.

[13] Reiss, *Social Context of Premarital Sexual Permissiveness,* pp. 61–63.

[14] Kinsey et al., *Sexual Behavior in the Human Female,* p. 298.

[15] Christensen and Gregg, "Changing Sex Norms," p. 621.

[16] Sorensen, *Adolescent Sexuality in Contemporary America,* p. 464.

[17] E. R. Mahoney, "Gender and Social Class Differences in Changes in Attitudes Toward Premarital Coitus," *Sociology and Social Research* 62 (January 1978), 279–286.

[18] Anne-Marie Henschel, "Swinging: A Study of Decision-Making in Marriage," *Changing Women in a Changing Society,* ed. Joan Huber (Chicago: University of Chicago Press, 1973), p. 126.

[19] Brian Gilmartin and Dave Kusisto, "Some Personal and Social Characteristics of Mate-Sharing Swingers," *Renovating Marriage: Toward New Sexual Lifestyles,* eds. R. Libby and R. Whitehead (San Francisco: Consensus Publishers, 1973), pp. 150–153.

[20] U.S. Bureau of the Census, *Statistical Abstract of the United States, 1978* (Washington, D.C.: Government Printing Office, 1975), p. 121.

[21] J. D. Millar, "The National Venereal Disease Problem," *Epidemic: Venereal Disease,* Proceedings of the 2nd International Venereal Disease Symposium (New York: Pfizer, 1973), p. 10.

[22] Ibid.

[23] *Report of the Commission on Obscenity and Pornography* (New York: Bantam Books, 1970), p. 351.

[24] Ibid., p. 352.

[25] Ibid., p. 363.

[26] Marc Schnall, "The United States Supreme Court: Definitions of Obscenity," *Crime and Delinquency,* January 1972, p. 61.

[27] Ibid., p. 62.

[28] *The Obscenity Report: The Report of the Task Force on Pornography and Obscenity* (New York: Stein & Day, 1970), pp. 84–85.

[29] *Report of the Commission on Obscenity and Pornography,* p. 1.

[30] Ibid., p. 27.

[31] Ibid.

[32] Ibid.

[33] Ibid., p. 31.

[34]Ibid.

[35]Ibid., p. 57.

[36]*Encyclopedia Americana*, 1945 ed., s.v. "Regulation of Vice."

[37]Marshall B. Clinard, *Sociology of Deviant Behavior* (New York: Holt, Rinehart and Winston, 1974), p. 507.

[38]Kinsey, Pomeroy, and Martin, *Sexual Behavior in the Human Male*, p. 411.

[39]Vance Packard, *The Sexual Wilderness* (New York: McKay, 1968), pp. 163–164.

[40]Kingsley Davis, "Sexual Behavior," *Contemporary Social Problems*, ed. Robert K. Merton and Robert Nisbet (New York: Harcourt, 1976), p. 251.

[41]Nanette J. Davis, "The Prostitute: Developing a Deviant Identity," *Studies in the Sociology of Sex*, ed. James M. Henslin (New York: Appleton, 1971), p. 303.

[42]Karlen, *Sexuality and Homosexuality*, p. 558.

[43]Albert J. Velarde and Mark Warlick, "Massage Parlors: The Sensuality Business," *Society* 11 (November/December 1973), 63–70.

[44]*Wolfden Report,* report of the Committee on Homosexual Offenses and Prostitution (New York: Lancer Books, 1964), p. 132.

[45]Norval Morris, "Crimes without Victims: The Law Is a Busybody," *New York Times Magazine,* 1 April 1973, p. 61.

[46]Kinsey, Pomeroy, and Martin, *Sexual Behavior in the Human Male,* p. 651.

[47]Hunt, *Sexual Behavior in the 1970s,* p. 313.

[48]Ibid., pp. 311–315.

[49]Edward Sazarin offers a review of a number of recent works on homosexuality in "The Good Guys, the Bad Guys and the Gay Guys," *Contemporary Sociology* 2 (January 1973), 3–13.

[50]Maurice Leznoff and William A. Westley, "The Homosexual Community," *The Problem of Homosexuality in Modern Society,* p. 328.

[51]Karlen, *Sexuality and Homosexuality,* p. 337.

[52]Ibid., p. 372.

[53]George W. Henry, *Sex Variants* (New York: Hoeber, 1948) pp. 1023–1029.

[54]Barry M. Dank, "Coming Out in the Gay World," *Psychiatry* 34 (May 1971), 182.

[55]Ibid., pp. 183–184.

[56]William Simon and John A. Gagnon, "Homosexuality: The Formulation of a Sociological Perspective," *Journal of Health and Social Behavior* 8 (September 1967), 345.

[57]Edwin Lemert, *Human Deviance, Social Problems and Social Control* (Englewood Cliffs, N.J.: Prentice-Hall, 1972), p. 73.

[58]Esther Newton, *Mother Camp: Female Impersonators in America* (Englewood Cliffs, N.J.: Prentice-Hall, 1972), pp. 7–19.

[59]David A. Ward and Gene G. Kasselbaum, *Women's Prison: Sex and Social Structure* (Chicago: Aldine, 1965), p. 92.

[60]Ibid., p. 76.

[61]Jean-Paul Sartre, *Saint Genet, Actor and Martyr,* trans. Bernard Frechtman (New York: Braziller, 1963), p. 30.

[62]Richard A. Myren, "Sex: The Law and the Citizen," *SIECUS Report* 13 (March 1975), 4.

[63]"Homosexual Legal Rights," *Editorial Research Reports,* 8 March 1974, p. 194.

[64]Harold J. Lief, "Sexual Health Services: Training and Treatment," *SIECUS Report* 11 (November 1973).

[65]Ibid., p. 19.

[66]Ibid.

Substance Abuse

16

The existence of any social problem, including that of alcohol and drug use, depends to a great extent on certain social definitions held within a given society at a given time. These definitions in turn depend on current and past social attitudes and behavioral norms, which are reflected in and reinforced by law and government regulations. Currently, considerable conflict exists within American society concerning the appropriate use of drugs, and this conflict is manifested in a lack of consensus about the nature of the drug problem.

Part of the disagreement over the appropriate use of drugs and alcohol is a reflection of our social attitudes and values. Americans ingest chemicals in quantity. We smoke, drink, and take pills at an ever-increasing rate, often only to induce pleasant physical or psychic states. Yet, studies have shown that a large majority of the population disapproves of the use of drugs for nonmedical purposes. In response to a survey conducted recently in New York, 90.3 percent of the people interviewed disagreed with the statement that "everyone should try drugs at least once to find out what they are like." And nearly 76 percent disagreed with the statement, "People can find out more about themselves through drugs."[1] Public attitudes concerning appropriate drug use, then, appear to be related to how a drug is obtained and the purpose for which it is used rather than to its effects.

The public definition of appropriate use is also a function of the type of people who use drugs. In the past, when the majority of illegal drug users belonged to outcast groups such as criminals, prostitutes, nonwhites, and the urban poor, the drug laws reflected and reinforced public attitudes that illegal drug use undermines moral restraints and leads to crime, violence, and other forms of deviance. In the last 1960s, however, illegal drug use spread to the middle and upper classes, particularly to the youth of these classes. Not only was there a startling increase in awareness and alarm concerning the new "drug problem," but the new users also elicited some changes in social attitudes and definitions. For many people, appropriate drug use has been redefined and extended to include the use of marijuana and has resulted in a call for changes in the drug laws. Yet others have consigned the young from respectable classes who use drugs to the stigmatized groups formerly associated with drug use.

Similar shifts in public mood concerning drugs have in the past taken place with regard to alcohol. Once illegal, alcohol is now legally and generally available to any adult. Alcohol consumption is not necessarily harmful either to individuals or to the social system. However, excessive drinking and alcoholism involve significant social costs in lost employment, family breakup, and social disorder.

Both the deviant behavior and value conflict approaches are useful in understanding the problems related to the use and abuse of drugs. The illicit use of certain psychoactive drugs and the abuse of alcohol (which is also properly classified as a drug) are viewed as forms of deviant behavior by many members of society. Patterns of behavior commonly associated with heroin addiction or alcoholism are defined by most people as violations of important social rules and values; drug-dependent individuals are often felt to be dishonest and irresponsible. Irrespective of whether any particular drug abusers actually possess these characteristics, it is likely that others will type or label them addicts or alcoholics and treat them as if they did in fact possess the qualities thought to be typical of such persons. Thus, individuals may come to accept and internalize the identity of alcoholic or addict that others assign them.

This process of acceptance of a deviant identity generally represents the beginning of what is referred to as secondary deviance. In response to the rejection, ostracism, and hostility of nondeviant co-workers, former friends, and acquaintances, the individual may seek out the company of like-situated others for acceptance and social support. As the individual becomes more involved in such deviant collectivities and begins to take on the attitudes, values, and beliefs of the group, there is likely to be a heightened involvement in deviant activity. The deviant subcultures of the many Skid Rows throughout the country, as well as the loose collectivities formed by persons addicted to heroin, represent situations where group affiliations serve to support and perpetuate individual involvement in deviance.

These social processes do not seem to operate in the same degree with regard to the use of nonaddictive drugs, such as marijuana or moderate amounts of alcohol. In American culture the use of alcohol for purposes of recreation or relaxation is now widely accepted and is not considered deviant behavior unless or until the stage of abusive drinking is reached. There appears to be less public consensus in viewing the use of other nonaddictive drugs as deviant behavior, less intense societal reaction toward their users, and less likelihood that these users will enter deviant collectivities or subcultures.

The value conflict perspective focuses attention on the wide public disagreement concerning the effects and consequences of the use of various types of drugs and on the issue of which drugs should be subject to criminal sanctions. The furor over what many persons viewed as a growing drug problem in the mid-1960s was at least in part a clash of values and interests between different groups, in which certain influential groups attempted to impose their own values on others. Concern with the problem of the "rising drug epidemic," then, was partially due to the fact that most users were members of the so-called counterculture, whose values and life-styles were offensive and even threatening to members of the middle class. Respectable businessmen who were alcoholics were not generally viewed as part of the drug problem. The 1973 report of the National Commission on Marijuana and Drug Abuse emphasizes the degree to which conflict is involved in determining what is acceptable drug use:

[The acceptability of drug use] is defined by the source and type of substance taken as well as by certain characteristics of the individual, such as age and socio-economic status. This society is not opposed to all drug taking but only to certain forms of drug use by certain persons. Self-medication by a housewife or a businessman with amphetamines or tranquilizers, for example is generally viewed as a personal judgment of little concern to the larger community. On the other hand, use of such drugs by a college student or other young person . . . is ordinarily considered a matter of intense community concern extending even to legal intervention.[2]

At various times in our history, legislation prohibiting the use of alcohol and other types of drugs has been enacted under pressure from influential groups. Each legislative ban, from Prohibition to contemporary marijuana laws, has generated tremendous controversy and conflict. Presently, legislators and members of other influential groups freely consume alcohol but continue to support legal prohibitions on the use of other drugs, some of which medical authorities consider less dangerous than alcohol. Thus, the implementation of legal sanctions for various types of drug use is not so much a result of the intrinsic qualities or effects of specific drugs as it is of the manner in which powerful social groups perceive and define different types of drug use and drug users. From the point of view of many young people today, the use of marijuana does not constitute a social problem; rather the problem lies in the laws that make marijuana use a criminal behavior.

Defining Drugs and Drug-Related Problems

Nowhere is the conflict of values and attitudes that surrounds the subject of drug and alcohol use more apparent than in the way terms are defined. What, for example, is a drug? For our present purposes, a drug can be defined as any chemical agent that produces an effect on a person's behavior by modifying thought processes, emotional states, or states of consciousness. This includes coffee, alcohol, and cigarettes, which are pharmacologically, but not socially, defined as drugs. The term *drug abuse* is also variously defined. Law enforcement officials consider it any illegal use of drugs, but most physicians view it as any nonmedical drug use.

Dependence and Addiction

Describing and defining the phenomenon of drug dependence is problematic for the medical sciences. In the 1950s the World Health Organization (WHO) drew a distinction between addiction and habituation.[3] Thus, *addiction* meant compulsive use, a tendency to increase dosage, psychological and physical dependence, and detrimental effects to the individual and society. *Habituation* meant a desire for the drug, no tendency to increase dosage, no dependence, and only personal detriment. Then, in 1969, WHO abandoned this distinction, suggesting that the term *addiction* be dropped in favor of the more specific term *physical and psychological dependence*.[4]

Yet the term *addiction* is still used and has been defined by researcher Jerome Jaffe as "a behavioral pattern of compulsive drug use characterized by overwhelming involvement with the use of a drug, the securing of its supply and a high tendency to relapse after withdrawal."[5] Jaffe believes that one cannot state precisely when compulsive use becomes addiction, and that it is possible to be physically dependent without being addicted and to be addicted without being physically dependent.

Physical dependence can be deducted from definite clinical indexes, and its deduction is an objective judgment. The clinical signs of physical dependence are the occurrence of withdrawal symptoms once the concentration of the drug in the blood has decreased. Psychological dependence must be inferred from the user's mental or emotional states and behavior patterns and involves a judgment on the part of the observer.

The devastation of drugs: Alcoholic oblivion (*left*) is only a degree above death from heroin sniffing (*right*)

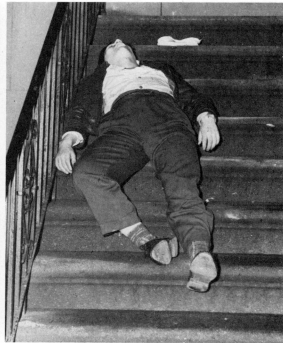

Alcoholism, like drug addiction, is also variously defined. E. M. Jellinek, who began his studies in the early 1940s, has described many different patterns, or kinds, of alcoholism, two of which he considers diseases. In both these disease patterns, the user is alcohol-dependent. But in one pattern, the user cannot control the amount of drinking; in the other, the user cannot abstain from drinking.[6]

An important publication of the Rutgers Center of Alcohol Studies stresses Jellinek's concept of the user's loss of control, defining the alcoholic as "one who is unable consistently to choose whether he shall drink or not, and who, if he drinks, is unable consistently to choose whether he shall stop or not."[7] Still another definition is preferred by sociologist Robert Straus, who holds that alcoholism is "the use of alcoholic beverages to the extent that it repeatedly exceeds customary dietary use or ordinary compliance with the social drinking of the community, and interferes with the drinker's health, interpersonal relations or economic functioning."[8] Alcoholism has also been defined in terms of degree of dependence, complications connected with nutritional deficiencies, or quantity of alcohol consumed.

Social Attitudes and Efforts at Control

The Food and Drug Administration (FDA), a federal agency, tests all drugs intended for sale in the United States. Its evaluation is made not solely in terms of safety but also on the basis of value in the treatment of health conditions. In addition, the FDA determines which drugs can be sold over the counter and which can be obtained only with a doctor's prescription. State and federal laws make illegal the nonprescription use of certain narcotics and barbiturates, amphetamines, tranquilizers, and other drugs classified as dangerous. It is presently illegal to sell, possess, or use heroin, opium, cocaine, and the various hallucinogens. These drugs cannot even be prescribed, although physicians with government permission can use hallucinogens in carefully controlled research and cocaine as a local anesthetic. Certain narcotic drugs such as morphine, codeine, meperidine, the barbiturates, and some amphetamines can be obtained legally with a doctor's prescription. Marijuana use has been decriminalized in several states and localities, but it remains illegal in the vast majority of jurisdictions.

Although the potential danger of alcohol and tobacco is well documented, their sale and consumption are subject to minimal control. Cigarettes cannot be sold to anyone under 18, but since they are freely available in vending machines, this prohibition is unenforceable. The sale of liquor to adults is legal in all states, although local governments are empowered to restrict such sales. Now that the voting age has been lowered, some states are lowering the age at which persons can buy or be served liquor from 21 to 18; however, there has been a recent countermovement in some places. Liquor and cigarettes do benefit society in one respect—they are heavily taxed and provide considerable revenue to all levels of government.

DRUG ABUSE

Differences of opinion over what constitutes criminal drug abuse have plagued our legal system. Typically, legal efforts to diminish the use of drugs have focused on laws prohibiting possession and sale, thus making users criminals as well as victims of addiction. Instead of more stringent legal restrictions, perhaps the solution is to decriminalize drug use and recognize addiction as a medical rather than legal problem. *This page:* Heroin addict injecting the illegal drug so expensive and so vital to his well-being; early opium den–source of delight and addiction. *Opposite page, clockwise from top left.* In behalf of pot–pitting facts against prejudice; alcoholic debauchery of this sort led reformers to work for the prohibition of liquor and the elimination of its effects on the human race; rolling up a relaxing break– marijuana smokers advocate social smoking instead of social drinking; revenue agents' raid–a common occurrence during Prohibition; poster for 1930s anti-marijuana movie "Marijuana: Weed with Roots in Hell."

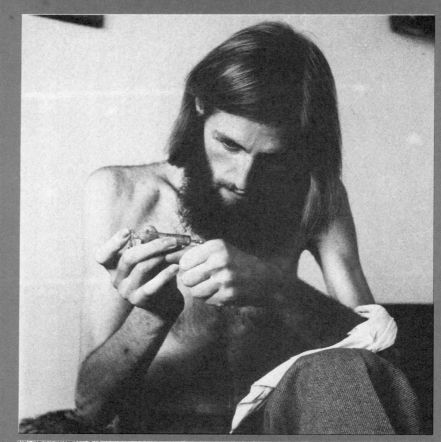

Eradicating the Evils of Alcohol— Prohibition

In the early days of America's history, people drank primarily wine and beer, although distilled alcohol in the form of rum was popular with the colonists. Drinking at that time was subject to strict family, community, and religious control. However, as new westward frontiers opened, as immigrants with different drinking habits swelled the population, and as the cities grew in size, American drinking patterns changed. By the mid-nineteenth century, drinking in the United States had surfaced as a social problem.

Concern about the problem prompted the reform movement of the early nineteenth century, the main mission of which was the elimination of drinking and its associated evils. Founded in 1826, the American Temperance Union distributed vast quantities of antiliquor propaganda in its attempt to persuade people to reform. Until the mid-1840s, religious organizations and local temperance societies continued to urge moral reform. When this proved generally unsuccessful, they turned to political action with better effect. By the time of the Civil War, 11 states had passed antiliquor laws.

The crusading Women's Christian Temperance Union regarded the use of alcohol not only as sinful but as the root cause of all social ills. Mainly rural, upper class, and Protestant, its members believed it their calling to teach the new immigrants the evils of drink. In 1870 the Anti-Saloon League began a political movement against alcohol. This new reform movement culminated in 1919 in the passage of the Eighteenth Amendment, the Prohibition amendment to the Constitution. Although this new amendment had no effect on decreasing the consumption of alcohol, the demand it produced for illegal alcohol fostered organized crime on a scale hitherto unknown in the United States. By the time of the repeal of Prohibition in 1933, attitudes toward liquor had changed. The affluent classes no longer considered drinking an evil, and without their support antiliquor laws proved unenforceable.

Turning On and Dropping Out

The use of drugs for inducing changed mental states is not confined to any particular society or historical age. For centuries, American Indians used peyote, a type of cactus that grows in the Southwest and Mexico, in their tribal religious ceremonies. Peyote was considered the most powerful and sacred of the various hallucinogenic plants in common use among the tribes for healing, prophecy, and divination.

Opium was used in Asian countries for centuries and became a serious problem in China in the early 1800s. Although many Chinese immigrants brought the use of the drug with them to the United States, opium was not unknown in America. It was the major ingredient in many nineteenth century patent medicines. Morphine, an opium derivative that was not at first thought to be addictive and was considered a miracle drug when introduced as a pain reliever in the early 1800s, was widely used during the Civil War in the medical treatment of wounded soldiers.

Prior to World War I, there were an estimated 200,000 to 500,000 drug addicts in the United States,[9] many of whom had become addicted through the use of patent medicines containing morphine. These medicines were widely advertised and available over the counter in any drug store for the cure of "female troubles" and many other diseases. A large proportion of the user population was white, middle class, and female. *Long Day's Journey into Night,* an autobiographical play by Eugene O'Neill, dramatizes his mother's addiction and the family's heartbreaking attempts to deal with it.[10] The users of laudanum, as morphine was called, were often not aware that it was addictive nor that they were addicts. Narcotic drugs and addiction were not yet viewed as a personal or social problem.

New addicts in the 1920s and 1930s were largely white males who frequented areas where illegal drugs could be purchased—the disorganized areas of the largest cities, characterized by overcrowding, crime, and other social problems.[11] In fact, narcotics use may actually have declined during the period between the two world wars. But by the early 1950s new population groups, primarily blacks and Puerto Ricans, were taking up residence in the slum areas where illicit drugs had long been available. Adolescents and young adults thus had access to drugs in their home neighborhoods. By 1960, in some neighborhoods as many as 10 percent of all males 16 to 20 years of age were officially recorded as drug users.[12] In recent years nearly three-fourths of all addicts recorded on the register of the Bureau of Narcotics have been black, Puerto Rican, or Mexican-American.

A major change in drug use patterns occurred in the mid-1960s, when young people, particularly white middle-class students, began smoking marijuana and taking nonnarcotic drugs such as barbiturates, tranquilizers, amphetamines, and hallucinogens for their euphoric effects. The boom in psychedelic drugs began as early as 1954 with the publication of Aldous Huxley's *The Doors of Perception*, in which he described his visions and insights under the influence of mescaline.[13] "Beat" writers—Allen Ginsberg, William Burroughs, and Ken Kesey—began writing about their drug experiences. At Harvard University in 1960 Professors Richard Alpert and Timothy Leary began using mescaline, psylocybin, and LSD in a research project, for which they were later dismissed from the university. Leary established a psychedelic cult, declaring it was time to "tune in, turn on, and drop out." By the late 1960s and 1970s, in addition to the increased use of nonnarcotic drugs, the consumption of heroin and cocaine had risen, including very high use in the armed services, particularly among troops in Vietnam.

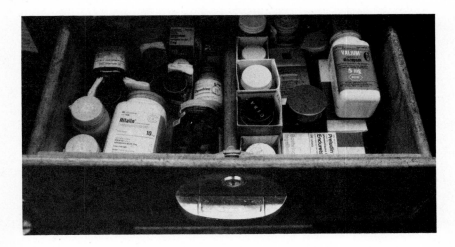

Legal drug abuse by middle-class white Americans.

During the late 1970s increased attention has focused on the abuse of legal, prescriptive drugs. The reason for this is clear. In a recent study, the drug most often mentioned by patients seeking emergency room treatment during the period May 1977 to April 1978 was not heroin, cocaine, or LSD. Rather, it was the tranquilizer, diazepam, usually obtained by the patient through a prescription from a doctor. Sixty-seven percent of those reporting diazepam as the problem drug were females. In all, tranquilizer abuse accounted for almost one-quarter of all emergency room visits for drug problems during the study period.[14]

The Drug Experience

Attitudes toward drugs have changed; the patterns of use among different segments of the population have varied over the years. An understanding of the phenomenon of drug and alcohol use calls for examination from a variety of perspectives, including the pharmacological properties of drugs and their effects on the physical functioning, emotional state, and behavior of the user. Each of these factors is influenced by the particular user's perception of drug use.

Properties and Effects of Drugs

Psychoactive drugs—sedatives, stimulants, narcotics, hallucinogens, and marijuana—affect the central nervous system (the brain, brain stem, and spinal cord) in such a way that physical functions, emotional states, and consciousness are altered. Physiologically, alterations occur because molecules of the drug penetrate cells or cell membranes and cause certain chemical changes.[15] This is called the *action* of the drug. The action triggers a series of biochemical and physiological reactions that are called the *effects* of the drug. The primary effects of the psychoactive drugs are either depression or excitation of the level of activity in the brain.

Statements about specific drug actions are always partly theoretical, because very little is known about the cellular biochemistry and physiology of the central nervous system. Medical researchers have long thought that brain cells have certain chemical structures or receptors into which the drug molecule fits.[16] Drugs are classified according to similarity of chemical structure and, more generally, similarity of effects. Table 16.1 shows the classification of drugs and many of their characteristics.

The effects of drugs on the physical and mental states of the user cannot be predicted with complete accuracy. In general, the size of the dose and the consequent level of drug concentration in the blood are the major determinants of effect. With small doses, many other factors may also come into play. These include individual sensitivity, which varies according to body temperature, inherited blood or enzyme deficiencies, sex, and age; the rate at which the drug is absorbed, broken down into chemically inert substances, and eliminated by the body; the presence of other drugs in the body; body weight; and the route of administration. Drugs are absorbed quickly if they are injected into a vein, more slowly if injected under the skin or inhaled, and still more slowly if swallowed and absorbed through the intestinal tract. Factors such as personality, mood, previous experience with the drug, expectations of drug effects, and the circumstances under which a drug is taken also influence effects. Such factors are particularly important with the hallucinogens.

In the wake of widespread public concern over the rising use of illegal drugs during the 1960s, it came as a considerable surprise to many Americans when the National Commission on Marijuana and Drug Abuse reported in 1973 that "alcohol dependence is without question the most serious drug problem in this country today."[17] A consideration of alcohol-related problems thus serves to place other types of drug use and abuse in perspective.

Alcohol, like the other substances discussed in this chapter, is a psychoactive drug. It is distinguished from the other drugs considered here only in that its moderate use is both legal and socially acceptable to the majority of the population. Beer, wine, hard liquors, and other alcoholic beverages have essentially the same effect on the human body, differing only in the amount of alcohol each contains. The primary effect of alcohol is its depressant or sedative action on the central nervous system. Although many people feel a stimulant effect from small amounts of alcohol, this action is produced only indirectly. Alcohol acts to depress those centers of the brain that are associated with judgment, self-control, and inhibition. When such depression has been effected, a person may feel stimulated or even euphoric because of this release from normal inhibitions.[18]

The attainment of a desired psychological state is the primary reason people drink, but alcohol also produces distinct psychological and physiological effects other than mild euphoria. A person's senses are progressively impaired as alcohol intake increases; the coordination required for tasks such as driving an automobile is correspondingly diminished. Alcohol intoxication impairs memory, decreases learning ability, and reduces a person's problem-solving ability. When consumed in sufficient quantity over a sustained period of time it can cause permanent brain damage.[19] Further, alcohol has the effect of compounding the action of many other drugs. When alcohol is taken in combination with barbiturates, for example, the additive effects of the two drugs can produce an overdose even when separate amounts of the drugs are not consumed in dangerous quantities. This potentiating effect of alcohol also occurs with certain over-the-counter drugs, such as cold remedies, and may produce unforeseen drowsiness or other sensory impairment.

Because alcohol is so widely used in our culture and because it is at least potentially a dangerous drug, the problems related to alcohol abuse are of staggering dimensions. Recent estimates indicate that there are at least ten million problem drinkers in the United States and that the abuse of alcohol results in economic costs of at least 25 billion dollars annually.[20] This latter figure includes lost productivity where alcohol interferes with occupational performance, alcohol-related costs in the criminal justice system, and the costs of educational and rehabilitation programs, to mention just a few. Other social costs are not so easily measured in monetary terms, but alcohol

Table 16.1 Some Facts about Drugs and Their Use

Name	Classification	Medical Use	Effect Sought	Long-term Symptoms	Physical Dependence Potential	Mental Dependence Potential	Organic Damage Potential
Heroin	Narcotic	Pain relief	Euphoria, prevent withdrawal discomfort	Addiction, constipation, loss of appetite	Yes	Yes	No
Morphine	Narcotic	Pain relief	Euphoria, prevent withdrawal discomfort	Addiction, constipation, loss of appetite	Yes	Yes	No
Codeine	Narcotic	Ease pain and coughing	Euphoria, prevent withdrawal discomfort	Addiction, constipation, loss of appetite	Yes	Yes	No
Methadone	Narcotic	Pain relief	Prevent withdrawal discomfort	Addiction, constipation, loss of appetite	Yes	Yes	No
Cocaine	Stimulant, local anesthesia	Local anesthesia	Excitation, talkativeness	Depression, convulsions	No	Yes	Yes?
Marijuana	Relaxant, euphoriant; in high doses, hallucinogen	None in U.S.	Relaxation; increased euphoria, perceptions, sociability	Usually none	No	Yes?	No
Barbiturates	Sedative-hypnotic	Sedation, relief of high blood pressure, epilepsy, hyperthyroidism	Anxiety reduction, euphoria	Addiction with severe withdrawal symptoms, possible convulsions, toxic psychosis	Yes	Yes	Yes

Amphetamines	Sympatho-mimetic	Relief of mild depression, control of appetite and narcolepsy	Alertness, activeness	Loss of appetite, delusions, hallucinations, toxic psychosis	No?	Yes	Yes?
LSD	Hallucinogen	Experimental study of mental function, alcoholism	Insightful experiences, exhilaration, distortion of senses	May intensify existing psychosis, panic reactions	No	No?	No?
DMT	Hallucinogen	None	Insightful experiences, exhilaration, distortion of senses	?	No	No?	No?
Mescaline	Hallucinogen	None	Insightful experiences, exhilaration, distortion of senses	?	No	No?	No?
Psilocybin	Hallucinogen	None	Insightful experiences, exhilaration, distortion of senses	?	No	No?	No?
Alcohol	Sedative hypnotic	Solvent, antiseptic	Sense alteration, anxiety reduction, sociability	Cirrhosis, toxic psychosis, neurologic damage, addiction	Yes	Yes	Yes
Tobacco	Stimulant-sedative	Sedative, emetic (nicotine)	Calmness, sociability	Emphysema, lung cancer, mouth and throat cancer, cardiovascular damage, loss of appetite	Yes?	Yes	Yes

Question marks indicate conflict of opinion. It should be noted that illicit drugs are frequently adulterated and thus pose unknown hazards to the user. Also, persons who inject drugs run a high risk of contracting hepatitis, abscesses, or circulatory disorders.

Source: Adapted from "Facts about Drugs," *Today's Education: Journal of the National Education Association* 60 (February 1971), 34–35.

Reprinted by permission.

Max Gunther
Female Alcoholism: The Drinker in the Pantry

Today, alcoholism in women is much more common than most people realize. In fact, it always was. People just didn't talk about it. Marty Mann, founder of the National Council on Alcoholism (NCA), is an alcoholic who had her last drink in 1939. She recalls that year as the most miserable in her life. "I knew there was something desperately wrong with me," she says, "but nobody seemed to have a name for it. I went to eight psychiatrists that year. Not one saw that what I had was, plainly and simply, the disease of alcoholism. It wasn't considered a disease in those days. It was a moral problem, and it was twice as shameful in a woman as in a man."

Today that attitude has changed and is still changing. "Most medical people now think of alcoholism as a sickness, no more shameful than the flu," says Frank Seixas, M.D., medical director of NCA. "Undoubtedly this is one reason why more and more women are coming forward today and saying, openly, that they have the sickness. They are asking for help. This is gratifying to us, of course—but at the same time we're worried. We have a question: Are we seeing more women alcoholics just because more are coming out of hiding, or because there actually *are* more? Nobody knows for sure."

One thing is certain. The number of self-revealed women alcoholics has grown fast in recent years. Alcoholics Anonymous (AA), an organization of men and women who've banded together for mutual help, used to state, as a rule of thumb, that about one-fourth of its members were women. A survey completed in 1974 revealed that, of all new members coming into AA since 1970, roughly one-third have been women.

Marty Mann goes further and reasons that, "It's still not as easy for a woman to say publicly that she has a drinking problem. My guess is that if you added up all the problem drinkers in the country today, the hidden as well as the revealed, the sex ratio would be just about 50-50."

Of all people who ever start drinking socially, says Dr. Seixas, between 9 and 12 percent eventually become alcoholics. "As far as we know," he says, "that ratio holds for men and women alike. Alcohol doesn't discriminate between the sexes: Its effects are the same in both."

Just what is alcoholism? The American Medical Association's (AMA) definition focuses on the common thread among many variables. Alcoholism is, they say, "an illness characterized by preoccupation with alcohol and loss of control over its consumption . . . a type of drug dependence that can harm a person's health and interfere with his ability to work and get along with other people. *The key factor is loss of control and craving for the drug, alcohol.*"

What happens to these uncontrolled drinkers, estimated at about 9 million people, is that they progress from "social drinking" to uncontrolled, frequent, sometimes almost constant drunkenness. This progression may happen fast, leaving its victim a teenage alcoholic, or it may take 30 years or longer: The final state of the disease may not show up until the occurrence of some late-life crisis, such as retirement or widowhood. Most commonly, though, the process seems to take between 15 and 20 years.

Alcoholism is treatable at almost any stage, but the earlier it is caught, the easier it is to handle. And the only way to catch it is to know what to look for. . . . While there is no well-defined "alcoholic personality," there is a more or less recognizable pattern to the drinking of an alcoholic, one that can be spotted by either the alcoholic herself or someone close to the victim. Max Glatt, M.D., vice-chairman of the British Medical Council on Alcoholism, studied hundreds of middle-class women alcoholics' case histories and compiled a statistical composite that neatly outlines the average progression. American AA sources say that there is no reason to think women's experiences in this country are different in any important way.

According to Dr. Glatt, the average woman alcoholic tasted her first drink before the age of 20. The final "loss of control" happened at about age 42. In between, there was a slow deterioration from regular drinking "in moderation" to frequent drunkenness at parties, to secret drinking and prolonged bouts of intoxication. Sometime in her mid-forties, this composite woman found her life coming apart. . . .

Among professionals, AA's methods are considered the most effective form of treatment for alcoholics. In a nutshell, AA's major axioms are that (1) an alcoholic must face the fact that she can't drink normally and therefore shouldn't drink at all; (2) she is powerless to stop drinking by herself; so (3) she must seek a source of strength beyond herself. That source of strength is the support and companionship of other alcoholics who have won the battle against drink.

AA's record of success isn't perfect, of course. Statistical records indicate that the average member's first year of sobriety is the toughest and most telling. After the first year, the statistical likelihood is that 79 percent will stay in AA, sober, for at least another year, as compared to the 65 percent of new members who will go back to drinking. And of those who have been sober longer than five years, 91 percent will stand firm. . . .

According to the AMA, "There is no conclusive evidence as yet to confirm or refute" the possibility that alcoholism may be an inheritable tendency. They do find that, "Alcoholism may be communicable . . . in the sense that circumstances in the home of an alcoholic sometimes pave the way for his children to become alcoholics." Not everyone finds the lost child within him when he drinks. It may be that families consciously or unconsciously encourage the connection between alcohol and feeling safe, protected, and free by demonstrating this attitude verbally and behaviorally. Later on, their children may prove susceptible to alcoholism and never know why. Once they are hooked, it doesn't matter. Drunks are remarkably alike, regardless of their origin. . . .

Why does this dreaded sickness pick on some people but leave others alone? "This is a question we would love to answer if we could," says Morris E. Chafetz, M.D., director of the National Institute on Alcohol Abuse and Alcoholism (NIAAA), in Rockville, Maryland. "Here at the institute we are strongly committed to research on that very subject. But I've got to say I'm not optimistic about coming up with any surefire forecasting technique. I don't think we'll ever be able to go up to a teenage girl and say, 'Young lady, we've concluded that you'll become an alcoholic if you ever start drinking, so don't.' Alcoholism is too complicated. It may be partly a physical problem, partly psychological, partly sociocultural. A given person might be a problem drinker in one country but not another, might drink normally in one marital situation but not another."

Dr. Chafetz is optimistic, however, about NIAAA's current research program. "What we're trying to do

right now is draw a better, more detailed picture of what we mean by normal, responsible, controlled drinking in our culture. How does the responsible drinker behave, what does he feel and think, how do others respond to him? Once we have more knowledge of that, we'll study early deviations from the norm and see how important each one is in the drinker's later history."

Meanwhile, it is comforting to know that the sickness is treatable. All medical facilities and professional programs for the alcoholic are aimed at the common goals of physiological care, social and occupational rehabilitation, psychological counseling, and long-term practical support. And there is no lack of places to turn.

In addition to AA, the Salvation Army, state hospitals, and various mental health centers equipped to deal with alcoholism within their communities, there are national resources designed to educate the alcoholic and those concerned for him. The National Institute on Alcohol Abuse and Alcoholism is one such source of educational materials; another is the Alcohol and Drug Problems Association of North America, headquartered in Washington, D.C. Many areas have access to Alcoholism Information Centers that work to coordinate local services, and an increasing number of companies have alcoholism programs for their employees. Two groups associated with Alcoholics Anonymous—Al-Anon Family Groups, and Alateens—work with, respectively, family members and teenage children of alcoholics to enable them to deal with the stresses of home life.

According to the AMA, because alcoholism is an ongoing or chronic disease, control short of cure is an acceptable criterion for success in treatment. "Although total abstinence is a desirable aim, improvements in social or occupational adjustments may be far better guides in determining whether a treatment effort is succeeding or failing."

The body itself is a good indicator. Alcohol, a depressant, affects the brain and nervous system, impairing judgment, memory, learning ability, coordination, and sensitivity to pain. Combined with the inadequate diet so often associated with alcoholism, the drug can eventually destroy nerve tissue and brain cells. It affects the stomach and intestines, ranging in degree from nausea or diarrhea to ulceration and internal bleeding. It affects the heart, injuring the muscle irreparably. It constricts the arteries and changes the circulation of blood.

But the physical damage needn't be permanent—if you stop it early enough. The liver can recover from the effects of alcoholic cirrhosis, can regenerate itself along with the alcoholic's psyche. Says Marty Mann, "Most recovered alcoholics are as healthy as though they never had the sickness."

Ms. Mann herself is a walking advertisement for her own statement. She is an erect, strong-voiced woman in obvious good health. She estimates that she travels some 65,000 miles a year to speak on her topic, and she seldom looks tired. Her age is 71.

Excerpts from Max Gunther, "Female Alcoholism: The Drinker in the Pantry," *Today's Health,* June 1975, p. 15. Reprinted with permission, *Today's Health* Magazine © June 1975–all rights reserved.

misuse is considered an important contributing factor in divorce, child mistreatment, and other problems of family and community life.

Two of the most visible and serious problems related to the misuse of alcohol are crime and motor vehicle accidents. The release of inhibitions that accompanies intoxication is often a contributing factor in the commission of crimes, particularly offenses involving interpersonal conflict, such as assault. Recent figures indicate that about half of all arrests annually are related to the abuse of alcohol.[21] Significantly, these alcohol-related arrests are not limited to minor offenses such as disorderly conduct and public drunkenness; approximately 50 percent of the homicides in the United States are alcohol-related.[22]

Because alcohol acts to impair judgment and reduce coordination, the National Safety Council has cited it as a major cause of traffic accidents. Estimates place the number of alcohol-related accidents at approximately 700,000 per year; these account for about 24,000 fatalities annually, or roughly half the highway deaths each year.[23] Further, accidents where alcohol is involved tend to be more serious than those where it is not a factor. A driver's blood alcohol content is used to measure the degree of impairment of driving ability. A level of .05 percent (on average, the equivalent of two mixed drinks) is considered safe, while a level of .15 percent or more is considered evidence of intoxication in all states. Presently, safety authorities in many states consider this to be too high and are moving to have the level of legal intoxication reduced to .10 percent.

One particularly alarming trend concerns alcohol abuse by teenagers, which appears to have grown in recent years. Since alcohol is easily obtained and the penalties for its consumption are mild relative to those for other drugs, alcohol is considered a safer high and is the most popular drug among teenagers. Drinking among adolescents is strongly related to attitudes and drinking practices of peer groups and parents. If drinking is accepted and engaged in by parents and if it is practiced or even expected by members of peer groups, then the likelihood of alcohol use is greatly increased. There is reason for particular concern with teenage alcohol abuse, for if an adolescent learns to cope with stress by drinking, this may become established as a general pattern for coping with any kind of stressful situation in adult life. Recognizing the seriousness of adolescent alcohol abuse, all 50 states have enacted legislation requiring alcohol education programs in the public schools.

Narcotics, the only effective drugs for relieving severe physical pain, act as selective depressants on the central nervous system. Some, but not all, brain functions are slowed. The general effects of moderate doses are pain relief, drowsiness, euphoria, difficulty in concentration, apathy, decreased appetite, itching, and sometimes nausea and vomiting. Narcotics are poisonous, and if a tolerance is not built up or a dosage is too large, there is danger of respiratory failure.

Narcotics produce a rapid and strong tolerance and are strongly addictive. Narcotic withdrawal symptoms are similar to those of alcohol and barbiturate withdrawal: chills and trembling, sweating, abdominal cramps, diarrhea, and muscle spasms—the classic "cold turkey" syndrome. The intensity of withdrawal symptoms varies according to the quality and quantity of the drug that the user has become accustomed to taking. In addition, there is some evidence that the user's psychological expectations and the situation in which withdrawal is experienced (therapeutic community versus solitary withdrawal) influence the severity of the symptoms.[24]

Accurate figures on the number of persons addicted to narcotics in this country are extremely difficult to obtain, for the obvious reason that penalties for narcotics violations are severe and users wish to avoid detection. Most estimates in the past have been based on arrest records and the number of persons treated in rehabilitation and detoxification centers, but such figures represent an unknown percentage of the actual addict population. Figure 16.1 gives the results of a nationwide drug survey of young adults between 18 and 25. Interestingly, this survey showed a lower rate of use for heroin than for any of the other drugs considered.

It is generally thought that the vast majority of narcotics users are young males living in urban areas. At least one study, however, has found that the incidence of narcotic addiction among physicians is also quite high, owing to their ready access to the drug and their knowledge of its euphoric effects.[25] Further, it was found that in contrast to the harsh legal sanctions typically applied to "street" users, the high-status physician addicts were treated leniently, were sanctioned by licensing authorities rather than criminal courts, and were not publicly stigmatized for their addiction.

One of the most commonly abused narcotics is heroin. It accounts for an average of 30 deaths and 700 injuries per month, largely as a result of accidental overdoses.[26] The drug can be taken orally or inhaled through the nasal membranes, but it is most commonly injected, either under the skin or directly into a vein. Injection increases the chances of an accidental overdose and carries the risk of causing hepatitis (a liver disorder that may result in death) in the user. Since little attention is usually paid to sterilizing needles and syringes, hepatitis can be passed on from one user to another.

Persons addicted to heroin commonly attempt to cease using the drug from time to time, either on their own or through the help of a narcotics treatment center. A great many users, however, return to a pattern of addiction within a relatively short period of time after having attempted to stay off the drug.[27] A sociological explanation of these abstinence and relapse cycles has been formulated in terms of the differing attractiveness of an "abstainer" versus an "addict" identity at different stages in a narcotics user's career.[28] The abstinence process begins for users when they call into question their life-style as an addict and their addict identity; the process is

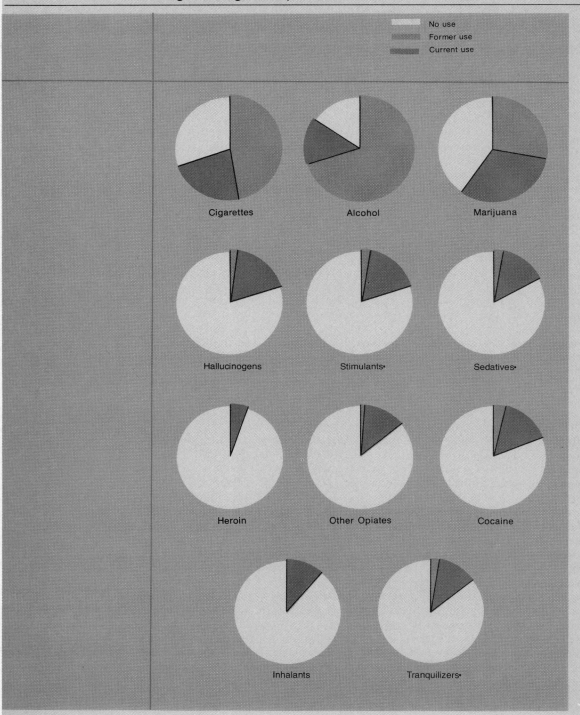

Use of Drugs among Nationwide Sample of Young Adults (age 18– 25), 1977			Figure 16.1
	Never Used	Current Use (past month)	Former Use
Cigarettes	30.3%	47.3%	20.3%
Alcohol	15.6%	70.0%	14.0%
Marijuana/Hashish	39.9%	27.7%	32.4%
Inhalants	88.8%	0	10.9%
Hallucinogens	80.1%	2.0%	17.9%
Cocaine	80.9%	3.7%	15.5%
Heroin	96.4%	0	3.3%
Other opiates	86.0%	1.0%	12.2%
Stimulants*	78.8%	2.5%	18.3%
Sedatives*	81.6%	2.8%	15.3%
Tranquilizers*	86.6%	2.4%	10.5%

* Nonmedical Use
Source: "National Survey on Drug Abuse: 1977" Volume 1 Main Findings, U.S. Department of Health, Education and Welfare (Washington: D.C.: Government Printing Office, 1977), p. 23.

completed when the addict identity and the values associated with it are rejected. Generally, one or more nonaddicts are crucial catalysts in the transition to abstinence. Relapse begins when abstainers feel their nonaddict identity is no longer viable and is completed when there is a redefinition of self as an addict. The critical phase in the abstainers' movement toward relapse involves the nature of their social experiences as nonaddicts.

When [the abstainer's] social expectations and the expectations of others with whom he interacts are not met, social stress develops and he is required to re-examine the meaningfulness of his experience in non-addict society and in doing so question his identity as an abstainer. This type of experience promotes a mental realignment with addict values and standards.[29]

Sedatives

The sedative drugs depress activity in the central nervous system and are often prescribed for their sleep-producing or calming effects. Barbiturates and tranquilizers are two common sedative drugs. Tranquilizers, sometimes called antipsychotic drugs, are also prescribed for anxiety and have been used widely in treating schizophrenics.

Sedatives are capable of depressing a wide range of functions. The progressive effects include conceptual disorganization, feelings of euphoria, release from anxiety, and a lessening of inhibitions. With high doses, the user loses control of speech articulation and coordination. Still higher doses depress body temperature and cause sleep. In massive doses of sedation, suppression of cardiovascular and respiratory control can cause coma and death.

Alcohol, the barbiturates, and the barbiturate-like tranquilizers, when taken in small doses, produce a tolerance—a resistance to the effects of the drug that may lead the user to increase the dose. These drugs all cause physical dependence, and when taken together or within a short time of one another, they are much more potent than when taken alone. Many accidental deaths as well as suicides have been attributed to the combination of alcohol and barbiturates.

Withdrawal symptoms reverse the effects of these sedatives. The symptoms range from a mild hangover through extreme agitation, insomnia, anxiety, nausea, vomiting, and delirium. Convulsions are common with barbiturate withdrawal, which is more severe and more often fatal than heroin withdrawal. When these drugs wear off, the user becomes more tense, anxious, or agitated than prior to taking the drug.

The tranquilizers, in contrast to other sedatives, are selective depressants. They do slow down responses to stimuli and decrease anxiety and tension, but they do not produce euphoria. Nor do they produce tolerance or physical dependence.[30]

Stimulants

Stimulants step up activity in the central nervous system. The general progressive effects include depression of appetite, a more rapid flow of thought, heightened sensitivity to sensory stimuli, a decrease in reaction time, an increase in motor activity, and the suppression of drowsiness or fatigue. The rate of the heartbeat and respiration are considerably increased, which, in the case of an overdose, can lead to convulsions, coma, cerebral hemorrhage, respiratory collapse, and death. Large doses of the common stimulants, cocaine and amphetamines, often produce a psychotic state accompanied by visual and auditory hallucinations. Users may have paranoid feelings of being persecuted or attacked, and because they also may feel abnormally powerful, they may constitute a danger to others.

Many users of stimulants, particularly the amphetamines, also use barbiturates to counteract the effect of coming down or "crashing." This cyclical drug use is extremely disorienting and harmful to the user, physically as well as psychically. With the exception of the milder antidepressants, stimulants produce a strong tolerance, and the dosage must be continually increased to attain the desired effect. It is difficult to know whether the depression and exhaustion that follow the use of these drugs are withdrawal symptoms or a natural result of loss of sleep.[31]

Hallucinogens

Hallucinogens produce changes in mood and perception and make users extremely sensitive to their emotional and physical environment. The intensity of the reactions depends on the dosage. But the reactions themselves are idiosyncratic and depend on the user's personality, emotional state, expections of effects, and immediate surroundings. The physiological effects include increased pulse rate, heartbeat, and blood pressure and irregular breathing, shivering, nausea, and loss of appetite—although these effects are usually mild enough to be insignificant for most users.

Moderate or large doses of hallucinogens cause distortion of the perceptual constants of space, time, solidity of objects, and body image. A minute may seem like hours, sound may be seen as colors, or colors heard as sound. Many users feel that their bodies are melting or that they no longer exist as physical beings. In some people this dissolution of ego boundaries produces a religious feeling of union with God, nature, or the cosmic consciousness. For others, the feeling can be extremely frightening, causing panic, depression, or periodic flashbacks of perceptual distortions.

There are no withdrawal symptoms with hallucinogens, and there is thus no physical dependence. Although LSD is by far the most potent of the hallucinogens, researchers have recently concluded that no evidence exists to show that normal doses of pure LSD cause chromosome damage or birth defects.[32] In 1966, however, the only recognized producers of LSD, in Switzerland, stopped shipment to the United States. It is assumed, therefore, that most of the LSD in this country comes from clandestine sources and may be mixed with other more harmful substances.

Marijuana

Marijuana and various preparations of it have been used since ancient times, for both medicinal and recreational purposes. Presently, the use of marijuana or hashish (the nearly pure resin of the hemp plant, several times more potent than regular marijuana) is as socially acceptable in many cultures as alcohol use is in our own. Researchers disagree on its pharmacological classification; it has been classed as a mild hallucinogen, as a sedative whose effects are similar to those of alcohol, and as a "mixed stimulant-depressant."[33]

Marijuana does not cause physical dependence; the effects of smoking it are extremely subtle and subjective and usually must be learned in order to be experienced. They are primarily emotional and perceptual; the user experiences feelings of elation and well-being, time and distance appear elastic, and sensory stimuli are intensified. Smoking marijuana increases the appetite and often induces a deep sleep. With larger doses, users usually become absorbed in their own experience of the drug. Some become sleepy; others become more active and talkative.

Psychiatrist Lester Grinspoon, in an exhaustive and careful examination of the pharmacology of marijuana and the major research studies concerning the effects of marijuana use, has pronounced it a relatively mild intoxicant with minimal harmful effects: "The use of cannabis products is generally less dangerous than the use of either tobacco or alcohol, and the use of marijuana, as it is commonly smoked in this country, is the least harmful of all."[34] Underlining the Grinspoon statement, a 1972 report of the National Commission on Marijuana and Drug Abuse recommended that possession of marijuana for personal use should no longer be a criminal offense, a recommendation similar to one made by study commissions in Canada and Scandinavia.[35]

Who Is High . . . or Low?

Although drugs of all kinds are being consumed by Americans in large amounts (Figure 16.1 shows the rate of nonmedical drug use for young adults), it is extremely difficult to determine the number of drug users and drug addicts in the United States. All users who come to the attention of the authorities in any way are reported to the Drug Enforcement Administration and officially listed. Nevertheless, the clandestine nature of illegal drug use makes such statistics difficult to compile and keep up to date. It is just as difficult to discover the number of alcoholics in the general population. Still, the available statistics suggest certain correlates of drug use.

Alcoholics Not Anonymous

A recent survey of American drinking practices examined a variety of factors such as age, sex, education, race, religion, socioeconomic class, region of residence, and size of community and correlated these variables with drinking.[36] The study concluded that persons most likely to be social drinkers are college graduates of high social and professional status, residents of eastern suburban cities and towns, and those whose fathers are foreign born. According to this survey, those most likely to be heavy drinkers are of a lower educational and occupational status and tend to reside in large cities in the East and in the Pacific states. Their marital status is single, divorced, or separated, and they are Protestants, Catholics, or without religious affiliation.

The authors of this survey classified 6 percent of the people interviewed as "heavy escape" drinkers—those who drink to escape "problems of everyday living." They differed from other heavy drinkers in being older, of lower social status and income, and more pessimistic and alienated. This group included an above average percentage of nonwhites.

The distinctions are not very clear-cut and thus illustrate that it is difficult to derive population characteristics for alcoholics. The literature of Alcoholics Anonymous stresses that alcoholism cuts across every social variable. "The investigation of any trait in alcoholics will show that they have either more or less of it . . . alcoholics are different in so many ways that it makes no difference."[37]

There has been some research on race or ethnic background variables in alcoholism. Studies of alcoholism in New York City have found the highest rates in ghetto areas and higher rates among blacks and Puerto Ricans than among whites.[38] In addition, there is some evidence that although rates of drinking are high for Jews, Irish, and Italian, the rates of alcoholism are very high for the Irish and very low for Jews and Italians. These variations are attributed to cultural differences in attitudes about drinking.[39]

Students, Housewives, Addicts

As with alcohol, drug use in general cuts across social variables. It appears, however, that certain groups of people are more likely to use certain drugs and to use drugs frequently. A 1967 Gallup poll of college students revealed that only 6 percent had ever used marijuana. By 1974, the estimate based on a poll taken for two national commissions had risen to 61 percent.[40] A 1977 national survey of high school students demonstrated that drugs are commonplace in high schools as well. Six out of every ten high school seniors reported using illicit drugs at some time in their lives. Fifty-six percent used marijuana at least once and 35 percent used it during the month preceding the survey. Contrasted with a 1975 survey in which 47 percent of the seniors reported some experience and 27 percent reported recent use, it is evident that use of various drugs is increasing in this group.[41]

Persons in the 18–25 age group are more likely to have used all types of "hard" drugs than persons in other age brackets.[42] White students are more inclined to use hallucinogens, whereas black students are twice as likely to use cocaine or heroin.[43]

A study of medical and illegal drug use in New York State based on interviews of householders over the age of 14 found a prevalence of use among white, middle-class women over 35 who rely on prescription drugs.[44] The findings of this study showed that of the 1 percent of people reporting heroin use, only .2 percent used it regularly. Of the regular users, race was not a significant variable; 50 percent were employed; and 15.6 percent belonged to the middle class. In the area of educational background, 34 percent were students, 50 percent had finished high school, and 15 percent had at least some college. None had dropped out of high school, and only 12.5 percent could not maintain employment. The study noted, however, that these findings are inconsistent with the findings of other studies of known addicts, which show that the majority of addicts come from the most disadvantaged slum areas and exhibit the social characteristics of typical slum residents.[45]

Where Does It All Begin?

Many hypotheses have been formed to explain why people use drugs. An individual may drift into the use of drugs or alcohol through the influence of peer groups. There may be easy access to a supply, as in the case of doctors or nurses. Or there may be psychological or physical factors that predispose an individual to alcohol or drug use. Explanations of how and why people start to use drugs or find themselves drinking to excess may be quite different from explanations of why they continue; all explanations depend on a complex combination of physical, social, environmental, and cultural processes.

Alcoholism— Loss of Control

The major theories of the causes of alcoholism propose transformations and combinations of the following factors: biochemical reactions to alcohol, low tolerance for stress and the consequent benefit of alcohol in reducing anxiety, cultural predisposition, and learned response to various stimuli.

Biochemical sensitivity to alcohol may well be a factor in the development of alcoholism in an individual, but so far a causal connection has not been proved. Such sensitivity does develop in some people with the high, continuous intake of alcohol, but it may be a product of the intake rather than a preexisting condition.[46]

A similar objection can be raised to the theory that alcoholism is the product of the "alcoholic personality," whose supposed qualities are low self-esteem, chronic anxiety, and emotional dependence. Studies have shown that this type of person does not inevitably or even usually become an alcoholic. Some alcoholics do show this repeated neurotic pattern of behavior, but it may be that the pattern is caused or increased by alcoholism rather than being the cause of alcoholism.[47]

Psychological and social factors working together appear to be important. Studies have consistently shown, for example, that the prevalence of drinking is greater and the incidence of alcoholism is less among Jews and Italians than among the Irish. One study of alcoholism among Irish-American males found a cultural pattern of dependence, intense frustration, hostility, and sexual prohibition for single men.[48] This was combined with social approval of frequent and excessive drinking by single men and a tendency to substitute alcohol for food. The drinking was further exacerbated by the anxiety caused by low economic status and a need to be independent. The study concluded that a combination of all these factors resulted in the high rate of alcoholism among Irish-American men.

On the basis of his studies, researcher E. M. Jellinek concluded that psychological and sociocultural factors account for the heavy drinking that paves the way to alcohol addiction.[49] However, he believed these could not explain the addictive process itself, which is characterized by what he found to be a loss-of-control phenomenon. He felt this could best be explained by biochemical factors and that researchers should study tissue metabolism and reactions to stress, as well as by possible inherited or developed abnormalities.

The concept of loss of control has been extended by researcher Mark Keller to include the consistent inability either to abstain from drinking or to control the amount consumed at a given time. Keller, who proposes this broader concept as the basis of alcoholism per se, attributes loss of control to conditioning. In his view, alcoholics respond to certain cues that, for them, have become strongly associated with drinking. Alcohol itself, or the particular blood alcohol level, may become the cue.[50]

Addiction— Refuge from an Alien Culture

Most researchers relate compulsive or addictive drug use to underlying psychological problems and environmental stress. Although a few believe that addiction is purely physiological and probably results from a metabolic deficiency, a direct causal relationship has not been proved, and this explanation is widely disputed.

According to one sociologist, it is not the pleasurable sensation of the drug that makes addicts continue its use but rather the fear of what would occur should they stop using it.[51] To become addicted, users must identify their withdrawal distress specifically with the drug and recognize that continued use will ward off withdrawal symptoms. This formulation helps explain the process of becoming "hooked" on drugs.

Another theory is that sustained drug use is the product of a learning process that takes place through a user's participation in a drug "culture" of other users.[52] In the process, the user first learns to experience the pleasurable effects (as defined by other members of the culture) of the drugs taken. Use is subsequently reinforced by the "specialness" of the experience; a new language relating to drugs is learned, as well as new behaviors that are part of the drug user's role. Once having learned to define the effects of the drug as enjoyable, continued use is likely, provided that the user retains a perception of the drug as capable of producing pleasure.

Most older theories about addiction focused on young heroin addicts in urban ghettos or in institutions. It was believed that the addict was either psychotic or neurotic and that drugs provided relief from anxiety and a means of withdrawing from the stress of daily existence in the ghetto. The portrait of addiction was that of passive adaptation to stress, in which drugs allowed the user to experience fulfillment and the satiation of physical and emotional needs. Early studies done in the ghettos tended to support this theory. It was concluded that ghetto youth who experienced double failure —who could not succeed in the gang subculture or in the legitimate larger culture—turned to drugs as a way of finding a place for themselves in society.[53]

More recent studies of drug use in urban settings have found that many different patterns of use exist. Many habitual users avoid addictive drugs or are weekend users. Because the street dose of heroin is relatively low in potency, many addicts are able to control their habits. They may work or attend school and must exhibit energy and resourcefulness in order to support their habits. Today, drug use is an integral part of the lives of many young urban residents who respond to the goals and beliefs of their drug subculture and in so doing gain status.

A study of New York street addicts has made the point that for some ghetto youths, the career of addict is much more rewarding and satisfying than any other they are likely to achieve. One research subject declared:

When I'm on the way home with the bag safely in my pocket, and I haven't been caught stealing all day, and I didn't get beat and the cops didn't get me—I feel like a working man coming home; he's worked hard, but he knows he done something, even though I know it's not true.[54]

This does not depict a psychologically disturbed addict unable to cope with the social environment.

Investigations of the more recent upsurge of drug use among middle-class youth have found that the majority tend to avoid hard drugs such as heroin and cocaine, generally come from stable homes, and are not psychologically disturbed. For these people, drug use appears to be a response to their environment, a way of dissenting from middle-class values and life-styles and of affirming their own values. A middle-class youth who is an illegal drug user may reject the values of society. This rejection may be either a result or a precondition of illegal drug use. But whether antiestablishment values encourage drug use or result from it, drug use probably reinforces these values.

One study of drug users in a southeastern university found that the strongest indicator of use was not found in social background characteristics or in feelings of alienation but in subcultural factors within the university environment. The more integrated students were into the student subculture, the more likely they were to use drugs.[55] Findings from a survey of junior and senior high school students revealed that the single best predictor of students' use of drugs was whether their friends used drugs.[56] These findings lend support to the more general differential association theory of deviance.

Drug Use: A Right or an Offense?

The current policy of making nonmedical drug possession and use a criminal offense is fairly recent. Prior to 1914, a person could purchase any available drug from a local pharmacy (usually part of a general store) or even from a mail-order supply house. With the passage of the Harrison Act in 1914, the sale or possession of opiates was prohibited except for legitimate medical purposes, and physicians were strongly discouraged from dispensing opiates to addicted patients. This act marked the beginning of a policy in which the regulation of drugs was to be treated as a legal rather than a medical matter. Since that time, the basic legal philosophy concerning illicit drug use has been to attempt to eliminate drug trafficking and to incarcerate drug sellers and users who are apprehended.

In 1937 marijuana was added to the list of controlled drugs under the Marijuana Tax Act. Since both this and the Harrison Act were framed as tax bills, enforcement powers were lodged in the Treasury Department of the federal government. Harry J. Anslinger, the zealous head of the Bureau of Narcotics within the Treasury Department, initiated a massive propaganda campaign against marijuana, proclaiming it a "killer weed" in spite of the fact that no objective evidence demonstrated any harmful effects from its use. It has been suggested that the motivation for this campaign, which was drastically out of proportion to the prevalence and the consequences of marijuana use, was related to the fact that the bureau's budget had been cut by 25 percent over the previous four years.[57] By creating a new drug menace in the public eye, Anslinger was able to regain large appropriations for the bureau and perpetuate its existence as a powerful federal agency.

During the 1960s, when drugs other than those controlled under previous statutes came into popular use, legislation was enacted that prohibited the possession of stimulant and depressant drugs without a prescription. The Federal Drug Administration was given the responsibility for determining which drugs, including existing and newly developed pharmaceuticals as well as new nonmedical drugs, should be placed on the controlled substances list. Under the provisions of this law, additional drugs with abuse potential could be made subject to legal controls without the passage of separate pieces of legislation. Since the enactment of this bill, the psychedelic drugs such as LSD, the new sedative-hypnotics such as quaalude, and other drugs have been added to the controlled substances list.

In the control of drug use, public policy continues to emphasize law enforcement. Currently, many government officials are pressing for more stringent drug laws, and at the federal level a reorganization of drug control programs has vested more power in the attorney general. Although federal government programs now include research, education, and treatment, the bulk of federal funds are allocated to law enforcement.

Ever since the failure of Prohibition, no real attempt has been made to limit the supply or possession of alcohol among adults. The legal drinking age varies between 18 and 21 in the different states, and movements are presently under way in several states with the higher drinking age to have it lowered.

Punishing a Bad Habit

Although in effect drugs cause crime, the causal relationship is not simple and direct. A user is not incited to criminal acts by the taking of a narcotic drug; in fact the reverse is the case. The narcotics, as their name implies, act to induce relaxation and contentment.

Treating drug abuse as a legal problem has produced a number of unintended consequences, including an increase in the overall crime rate. By legal definition, each time a connection is made between a dealer and a user, a crime is committed. This complicates enormously the problem of procuring drugs. Heroin is expensive. Addicts may have to generate from 50 to 100 dollars a day, every day, to support their habit. Some of this money may be earned legitimately, but sooner or later addicts are likely to turn to criminal behavior, either by dealing themselves or by stealing and selling stolen goods to others. For women, prostitution is a major means of obtaining cash for drugs. Various estimates put property loss due to drug-related crimes at well over a billion dollars a year.[58] Data from one study indicate that drug users account for more than 60 percent of all people arrested in six American cities, with robbery and other property crimes the most frequently committed offenses.[59]

This relationship between crime and drug abuse has led many to contend that government regulation of drugs should be abandoned—that drug distribution should be legalized and taken out of the hands of the pusher. By breaking the pusher's monopoly on drugs, prices would be lowered and the addicts' need to commit crime in order to obtain funds for drugs would be lessened. Psychiatrist Thomas Szasz strongly opposes the punitive approach to regulating drug usage, arguing that freedom of self-medication should be regarded as a fundamental right in a free society.[60] He proposes that the right of self-medication should not be an unqualified one, however; it should apply only to adults, and localities should retain the right to regulate drugs in the same way that counties now have the option of regulating alcohol use. The basis of Szasz's proposal is a philosophical argument concerning the rights of the individual vis-à-vis state power:

Every individual is capable of injuring or killing himself. This potentiality is a fundamental expression of human freedom. Self-destructive behavior may be regarded as sinful and penalized by means of informal sanctions. But it should not be regarded as crime or (mental) disease, justifying or warranting the use of the police powers of the state for its control.[61]

One can kill oneself just as surely with alcohol as with narcotics, so the potential for self-injury does not justify the prohibition of such drugs. Further, there are many instruments of destruction, from firearms to explosives, that are more dangerous than drugs but are not banned. The criminal penalties for drug use, according to Szasz, represent political and moral judgments and have no rational basis in science or law. To those who argue that such a proposal would lead to a breakdown in the social fabric, Szasz replies that the values of work and responsibility are strong and deeply ingrained in American society to a degree that would prevent this occurrence.

Breaking the Habit

Responses to problems of drug and alcohol abuse have involved educating the public by means of programs in the schools and churches, campaigns in the mass media, and social pressure among family and friends. Treatment of alcohol- and drug-dependent persons has varied in medical and penal institutions, depending upon attitudes toward the users. If such behavior is viewed as a moral failure, the user is treated punitively. If, on the other hand, it is seen as a behavior pattern for which the individual should not be held directly responsible, the treatment may be more humane. American

Donald B. Louria
The Future of the Drug Scene

The use of legal and illegal drugs, as a source of plea-sure and a means of escape from reality, may drasti-cally increase in the near future if present social trends and attitudes continue unchanged into the 1980s. To reduce drug abuse, society needs to offer other, more attractive ways to find pleasure, excite-ment, and escape from the fears and problems of re-ality.

It is astonishing to realize that the epidemic of il-licit drug use in the United States began only about a decade ago. Studies carried out between 1971 and 1976 by the National Institute on Drug Abuse indicate that the use of mind-altering drugs, which rose pre-cipitously during the late 1960s, has since leveled off. But the critical question is: "Where do we go from here?"

Although it has been receiving less attention lately, the drug scene has in no way disappeared. Mil-lions in the United States use marijuana at least once a week, there are several hundred thousand persons dependent on heroin, and roughly one high school student in every seven today has experimented with LSD-type drugs. These statistics may not seem to be cause for alarm in a society which has long tolerated the far greater damage caused by such legal drugs as alcohol and nicotine. Yet we must recognize that the present plateau in drug use is not necessarily perma-nent. . . .

The facile assumption that shutting off supplies and alerting young people to the dangers of drug abuse will be enough to eliminate or substantially re-duce the problem is not borne out by the evidence. In many ways, the efforts being made today to control the illegal shipment and sale of narcotics are more ef-fective than ever before. Yet drugs of every kind continue to be available. Worse yet, most anti-drug education programs have proven ineffective at turn-ing young people away from the drug scene. What then can be done to reduce the likelihood of a future upsurge in drug abuse?. . . .

By treating drug abuse as a symptom of other problems, it may be possible to choose policies and priorities for change that will enable us to head off a new epidemic of drug use before it starts.

The link between family breakdown and drug use has long been recognized and, if present trends continue, is likely to remain a major factor in influenc-ing the drug scene.

The stability of the family unit in the United States has deteriorated markedly during the 20th century. This is well illustrated by the dramatic figures on di-vorce. . . . More than one million divorces took place in 1975, a figure twice as high as that recorded only a decade earlier in 1965. Today, at least one U.S. marriage in every three ends in divorce.

Isadore Chein and his colleagues at New York Uni-versity, who conducted the first detailed medical analysis of heroin addiction in New York City in 1964, found that the vast majority of young heroin users came from broken homes. . . .

From the evidence of these and later studies, it seems clear that the nature of the family in American society in the 1980s will be a major factor in determin-ing the extent and severity of illicit drug use in the United States. . . .

At present, peer group influence already rivals that of the family in determining whether a young person will become involved with drugs. In our own studies, we found that peer group pressure outweighed all other factors as the single greatest contributor to il-licit drug use. . . .

Studies in Canada and the United States indicate that the drug use patterns of parents also have a great influence on the likelihood of their children be-coming involved with illicit drugs. If either parent smokes more than one pack of cigarettes a day, or uses stimulants or tranquilizers regularly, it was found, the children were two to seven times more likely to experiment with drugs themselves.

While the parents' use of alcohol, tobacco, or pills may not in itself lead to later drug use by the chil-dren. . . . frequent use of any drugs by parents tends to suggest a permissive and self-indulgent attitude toward *all* drugs—a message that is conveyed to chil-dren by what they see around them, in spite of what their parents or teachers *say*.

In the last 50 years Western civilization, led by the United States, has moved rapidly toward a hedonistic system of values that places physical pleasure above many long-held abstract values such as family loyalty, religious faith, dedication to "duty," or pride in crafts-manship. It is significant that among the approximately 20,000 junior and senior high school students interviewed in our New Jersey Medical School study, the search for pleasure was cited by the students themselves as the number one reason for drug experimentation. . . .

What does this portend for the future? If society continues to place a higher and higher value on personal pleasure and the avoidance of inconvenience or discomfort, then drug use will almost certainly increase. . . .

In a world beset by frustrations, heavy responsibilities, and troubles, all individuals need periodically to find some means of temporarily escaping from the demands of real life. Escapism of this kind is not irresponsibility, but actually a necessary component of responsible behavior because it provides for the mind what sleep provides for the body—a mechanism for renewing the strength needed to cope with the daily vicissitudes of life.

During the first half of the 20th century, the motion pictures served as a major mechanism for escaping from reality. . . . But movies today offer far less escape. In place of dreams, today's movie audiences are offered nightmares. And, for some reason, television fails to provide an adequate substitute. . . .

But as long as the pressures of daily life continue to mount, people will seek—and find—some means of temporary escape into happiness. If they cannot achieve flights of fantasy through public entertainment media, then there is every likelihood that they will tend in ever-greater numbers to seek relief from the rigors of daily life with a pill or a needle. In short, the future of popular entertainment will greatly influence the use of drugs in the years ahead.

Not least among the pressures being felt today is the threat of violence. . . . While the available evidence does not yet provide a conclusive answer, it does suggest that violence may contribute to increased drug use in two very different ways. First, there are informal data suggesting that many young persons in inner city ghettos react to the violence around them by turning to drugs to escape from the ugliness and fear in their environment. . . . It appears quite possible that many of these individuals will take tranquilizing drugs—including heroin—for the express purpose of controlling the urges toward violence they feel in themselves and cannot cope with by other means. . . .

There can be no doubt about the severity of the urban crisis in the United States. And it is in the decayed center city areas that family breakdown, violent crime and drug use are most prevalent. Up until the 1960s, the heroin problem in the United States was largely confined to the depressed inner cities. . . . Though the geographical distribution of heroin use has spread widely since 1950's, the central city is still the area most affected. . . .

If the life experience of inner city residents continues to follow its present pattern and drugs continue to be available, they will be used. Moreover, the evidence indicates that the spread of heroin abuse is primarily from user to user, not from seller to multiple clients. . . .

The United States is rapidly becoming a leisure-oriented society. Increasing automation and pressure for improved working conditions and fringe benefits from labor unions have acted to reduce working hours in nearly every field. Yet little thought has been given in many cases to the long-term consequences of a leisure/pleasure orientation for society as a whole. . . .

Few people are satisfied to remain completely idle for very long, and, unfortunately, the experience of recent years indicates that Americans—and perhaps people in other Western countries—have not developed the ability to utilize their growing leisure time constructively. Without this ability, excessive leisure almost inevitably leads to the dangerous malady known as boredom.

If people are bored, a certain percentage of them will devote their time to searching for excitement and physical pleasure. And, if mind-altering drugs are readily available, many will experiment with drugs. . . .

Any future that provides more leisure time without also offering opportunities—and even positive incentives—for using this "free time" constructively must almost certainly be a future of greater boredom and increasing resort to drugs.

At the present moment, the United States is still debating the status of marijuana and whether or not its use should be legalized. In modern times, Western society has "legitimized" the use of three mind-altering agents—alcohol, caffeine, and nicotine—for pleasure rather than for medical purposes. As the U.S. found during Prohibition, a society that has come to tolerate the use of a given intoxicant is likely to rebel if that intoxicant is suddenly proscribed. Thus there is good reason to be cautious about adding to the existing number of "licit" drugs. . . .

The nature and seriousness of drug abuse in the 1980s and 1990s will also reflect to a considerable extent the views that young people have regarding the future of Western society—and indeed their faith in the viability of planetary civilization as a whole. . . . If, at some time in the future, ours appears to be a doomed society, then it is likely that the drug scene will expand on a scale far greater than we have ever experienced. . . .

Consequently, it is essential that we maintain a climate of optimism as we confront our problems. . . . Young people must feel convinced that there *is* a future for themselves and for their children. . . .

If we are to avoid an upsurge in drug use by the 1980s and 1990s, we must begin now to consider viable alternatives to meet each of the different needs and desires that drugs are used to fill. Individuals, community groups, and government agencies must be willing to devote planning time, energy, and money to programs that can attack the *causes* of drug abuse.

Based on our studies, it would appear that a long-range program to control future drug use should incorporate efforts to:

• Strengthen family ties and reduce the influence of peer group pressure on individual behavior.

• Encourage the pursuit of goals other than immediate personal pleasure.

• Offer effective methods for "escaping from reality" without making these a substitute for living.

• Increase the attractiveness of the environment, particularly in the cities.

• Control acts of violence and reduce the threat and fear of violence at the community level and throughout the society.

• Provide opportunities for leisure activities that answer human needs for curiosity and excitement.

• Sharpen people's focus on the future. . . .

Excerpts from "The Future of the Drug Scene," *The Futurist,* June 1978, pp. 149–155. Reprinted by permission of *The Futurist,* published by the World Future Society, 4916 St. Elmo Avenue, Washington, D.C. 20014.

society has tended to treat the middle-class alcoholic in a medical or psychiatric setting and the lower-class user in the more punitive milieu of a penal or state mental institution.

AA and Other Programs

In recent years concerted efforts have been made by private and governmental institutions to prevent alcohol-related problems by educating the public about the potential effects and consequences of drinking. Alcohol education programs have been instituted in public schools throughout the country. Other efforts have been made to draw attention to the potential problems of the so-called social drinker and to publicize ways to recognize early signs of alcohol abuse. The National Safety Council has launched a vigorous advertising campaign that describes the degrees of driving impairment that result from the consumption of various amounts of alcohol.

Community detoxification centers have been established in many areas to provide short-term treatment for alcohol abusers who wish to "dry out." In some jurisdictions, drunkenness offenders may now be given the option of entering a detoxification center as an alternative to confinement in a local jail. Some alcohol abusers benefit from the brief but intensive counseling and medical treatment in these centers, but a general lack of adequate follow-up treatment limits their long-range effectiveness.

The organization that has demonstrated the greatest success in rehabilitating alcohol dependent persons is Alcoholics Anonymous. AA is a mutual aid organization that provides alcoholics with the opportunity to join together in an effort to break out of their destructive drinking patterns. During the regular meetings of the group, members share their own experiences and receive support and encouragement from the group for their abstinence. It is central to the AA philosophy that there is no such thing as a cure for alcoholism; abstinence requires a continuing personal commitment as well as sustained social support.

It was noted earlier in this chapter that applying the label *alcoholic* to a person typically has an impact on the individual's social identity and conception of self, and that the consequences of such labeling may be to perpetuate alcohol dependence. The operative principle behind the success of AA lies in the processes of first delabeling and then relabeling its members with a nondeviant social identity.[62]

Delabeling occurs by promoting an allergy concept of alcohol addiction; the AA belief system holds that individuals who become alcohol-dependent possess a physiological allergy to alcohol that is the root cause of their addiction. By defining alcoholism in this way, AA implies that factors beyond the control of the individual alcoholic have produced the disorder. Correspondingly, the individual's own responsibility for the development of the disorder is diminished, in the eyes of others and of the members themselves. Relabeling processes involve the former alcoholic's entry into a role of repentance, an accepted and valued role in the American cultural system. By defining former alcoholics who have participated in the AA program as persons who have helped themselves overcome their problems, members are enabled to assume a new, nondeviant role acceptable in the larger community.

Methadone Maintenance

As heroin addiction increased dramatically during the 1960s, several programs were developed to deal with various aspects of the problem. Methadone maintenance appears to have been developed as a means of dealing with the problem of street crime rather than with the underlying factors that result in an individual's addiction to drugs. Since methadone is a synthetic narcotic, it does not act to cure addiction; it simply substitutes one addiction for another. As one observer has written of the methadone maintenance approach:

It is now proposed that the federal government alone spend about $1 billion over the next three years [the period 1972–1975] in an effort to stem the tide of the urban drug crisis. Its major treatment approach will be the widespread use of methadone, a typically American answer to a large-scale American problem—the use of a synthetic chemical to cure a complex, socially rooted disease.[63]

Methadone is relatively inexpensive and easily administered at clinics, and it does serve to reduce a person's need to engage in criminal behavior to support a drug habit. Participation in methadone programs is often required under court sentences. Since persons must report to the clinic every day for their dose of the drug, this program facilitates supervision of a sizable portion of the addict population. Although some psychological and job counseling is provided at most clinics, these treatment services do not appear to be the major thrust of methadone maintenance.

The dosage level of the drug is varied over the course of participation in the program. Initially a "blocking dose" is administered, which is sufficiently high to eliminate any euphoric effects from the simultaneous use of heroin. The motivation to use heroin is thus reduced while the body's need for a narcotic to ward off withdrawal symptoms is satisfied. When urine tests indicate that the use of heroin has stopped, a reduction to a "maintenance dosage" is attempted, which is sufficient to prevent withdrawal but which does not narcotize the person to a point where employment or other functioning is impaired. Constant monitoring by chemical tests is performed, and if subsequent heroin use is detected, the dosage is again elevated to a blocking level.

Several unforeseen problems have developed in these programs. The drug is sometimes smuggled out of the clinic and sold on the streets, and it is not uncommon for some of the drug to be saved each day to be used in greater quantity than usual to achieve a high. More importantly, the methadone approach has not been highly successful in aiding people to kick their addiction permanently. A primary reason for this is that withdrawal from methadone is at least as severe as withdrawal from heroin, and perhaps more so.

Therapeutic Communities

The first therapeutic community, Synanon, was started in California in 1958 by a former alcoholic who applied the philosophy and techniques of Alcoholics Anonymous to a small group of addicted persons on a 24-hour-a-day live-in basis.[64] Since that time, programs modeled after Synanon have spread and have achieved considerable success in aiding persons to live addiction-free lives. Unlike methadone maintenance, therapeutic communities attempt to deal with the underlying problems that have led an individual to drug addiction. Since the program is composed entirely of former addicts and persons who are trying to kick the habit, the setting is one that promotes the discussion and resolution of problems common to members of the group as well as problems unique to any individual.

Synanon-type programs achieve their therapeutic effect through a combination of group support and group pressure and challenge. Members are encouraged to discuss frankly their reasons for using drugs and how they intend to go about staying off drugs in the future. Rationalizations or evasiveness are strongly discouraged by other members of the group. In this

Shiny symbolism: The shorn heads of these Synanon women testify to their acceptance of shared and equal responsibility with male Synanon members in the operation and management of their organization's rehabilitation programs for addicts.

way, members are induced to confront their problems and their life situation head-on. Important to the success of these programs is the fact that members assume the role of employee of the rehabilitative organization rather than the roles of inmate or prisoner.[65] Thus the member participates in the management and development of the program, identifies with its constructive goals, and is able to develop a sense of personal worth.

One major advantage of therapeutic communities is that withdrawal from narcotics appears to be less severe in these settings. Group support is critical during the withdrawal period, and persons who have experienced withdrawal themselves aid and encourage others who are doing so. The relative mildness of the symptoms experienced by residents (as compared to the more severe symptoms typically experienced in other settings) has been attributed to the fact that in a therapeutic community one's status is greatly enhanced by being drug free.[66] Nevertheless, the structure of these programs is rigorous and challenging, and for this reason they are unattractive to many addicted persons. Court commitments to therapeutic communities frequently result in failure. The greatest success appears to be achieved when there is a strong personal motivation to overcome addiction.

Summary

The recent shift in the use of drugs other than alcohol from the urban poor to portions of the middle class has created public concern over drug control and the social effects of drug abuse. Although this concern has focused on the use of substances other than alcohol, a national commission has concluded that alcohol dependence is America's most serious drug problem.

Both the deviant behavior and value conflict approaches are useful in understanding problems related to drug use and abuse. Users of drugs are likely to be labeled addicts or alcoholics and may come to accept and internalize the identities that others have of them. Accepting such identities may actually intensify their problems and increase their involvement with drug-supporting subcultures.

A drug can be medically defined as any chemical agent that affects living tissue. Drug abuse is therefore any nonmedical drug use, but law enforcement officials consider it any illegal use of drugs. Addiction is generally equated with physical and psychological dependence, although these are variously defined. Alcoholism can be the inability to abstain from drinking or to control the amount of drinking.

Government regulation of drugs and alcohol derives from differing social attitudes toward their use. In America, control of the use of alcohol became a social issue in the mid-nineteenth century, when new immigrants became the target of moral reform efforts. Political action against alcohol use culminated in 1919, with the passage of the Eighteenth Amendment, which prohibited its sale.

Demand for liquor during Prohibition led to the growth of an extensive criminal organization to supply it. This criminal element persisted even after the repeal of the Prohibition amendment in 1933. Although taxed and regulated, alcohol is now legally available to all adults in the population.

Most of the narcotic drugs derived from opium were put under strict control by the Harrison Act of 1914. At that time there were perhaps half a million narcotic addicts in the United States, most of them white middle-class women, who became addicted through patent medicines containing the drugs.

After World War II the use of illegal drugs became a phenomenon of urban slum areas, where the principal users were the poor, blacks, and Puerto Ricans. By the 1960s, however, many members of the military and middle-class white youth had begun to use marijuana and other drugs, a situation that prompted both stricter law enforcement and discussion of possible changes in drug laws.

The nature of the drug experience is a function of the properties of the chemical, its effects on the brain, dosage, and the characteristics individuals bring to it. Sedative drugs depress the activity of the central nervous system, can produce a physical dependence, and can build up a tolerance requiring increasing dosages. Narcotics, which are strongly addictive and produce high tolerances, are selective depressants used medically to minimize pain. Stimulants excite the nervous system; hallucinogenic drugs produce mood, sensory, emotional, and perceptual changes; marijuana is classified as a mild hallucinogen whose effects are similar to those of alcohol.

The extent of use of alcohol and other drugs in the United States is difficult to determine because no accurate statistics are available. Studies of the social variables involved in alcoholism have been inconclusive, although racial and ethnic backgrounds seem to have some significance. Middle-class drug usage seems to be primarily nonnarcotic; while black and other minority group members use "hard drugs" with greater frequency.

Theories that explain alcoholism and drug use in terms of psychological and social factors seem more persuasive than hypotheses concerning biochemical sensitivity to alcohol or the "alcoholic personality." In the case of drugs other than alcohol, self-definition and the positive aspects of involvement in a deviant subculture may be seen as adaptations to the stress and anxiety of ghetto life. Among middle-class youth, drug usage appears to be a mechanism of self-exploration, escape, and dissent from the dominant value norms.

Treating drug abuse as a criminal offense is a recent policy, although there are no current attempts to limit the supply or possession of alcohol among adults. By viewing drug abusers as criminals, society forces users into further crimes to support and maintain their habits. Psychiatrist Thomas Szasz argues that self-medication should be a fundamental right in a free society.

Solutions to the social problems of drug and alcohol abuse are in short supply. Although of uncertain success, the prevention of alcoholism and drug abuse through public education programs is subscribed to widely. While community detoxification centers provide some short-term programs, the most effective means of treating alcoholics has been through the self-help group Alcoholics Anonymous. Its primary success appears to lie in relabeling alcoholics with a nondeviant social identity. Methadone maintenance programs for narcotic users are popular but appear only to substitute one addiction for another. Therapeutic communities such as Synanon are successful when addicts are personally committed to overcoming their addiction.

[1]Carl D. Chambers, *Drug Use in New York State,* Special Report No. 2 (New York: New York State Narcotic Addiction Control Commission, June 1971), p. 3.

[2]*Drug Use in America: Problem in Perspective,* Second Report of the National Commission on Marijuana and Drug Abuse (Washington, D.C.: Government Printing Office, 1973), pp. 42–43.

[3]"Drug Addiction or Drug Habituation," *Chronicle of the World Health Organization* 11 (May 1957), 165.

[4]WHO Expert Committee on Drug Dependence, *World Health Organization Technical Report Series,* No. 407, Sixteenth Report (Geneva: World Health Organization, 1969).

[5]Jerome Jaffe, "Drug Addiction and Drug Abuse," *The Pharmacological Basis of Therapeutics,* ed. Louis S. Goodman and Alfred Gilman (New York: Macmillan, 1965), p. 286.

[6]Elvin M. Jellinek, *The Disease Concept of Alcoholism* (New Haven: Hillhouse Press, 1960), p. 35.

[7]Mark Keller and Mairi McCormick, *A Dictionary of Words about Alcohol* (New Brunswick, N.J.: Rutgers Center of Alcohol Studies, 1968), p. 12.

[8]Robert Straus, "Alcohol and Alcoholism," *Contemporary Social Problems,* 3rd ed., ed. Robert Merton and Robert Nisbet (New York: Harcourt, 1971), p. 181.

[9]John A. Clausen, "Drug Use," *Contemporary Social Problems,* 4th ed., ed. Robert K. Merton and Robert Nisbet (New York: Harcourt, 1976), p. 144.

[10]Eugene O'Neill, *Long Day's Journey into Night* (New Haven: Yale University Press, 1956).

[11]Charles Winick, "The Drug Addict and His Treatment," *Legal and Criminal Psychology,* ed. Hans Foch (New York: Holt, Rinehart and Winston, 1961), pp. 372–373.

[12]Marshall B. Clinard, *Sociology of Deviant Behavior* (New York: Holt, Rinehart and Winston, 1974), p. 416.

[13]Aldous Huxley, *The Doors of Perception* (New York: Harper & Row, 1954).

[14]*Drug Abuse Warning Network,* Phase VI Report, National Institute on Drug Abuse and the Drug Enforcement Administration (Ambler, Pa.: IMS, America, Ltd., 1978), pp. 19, 27.

[15]Leo G. Abood, "The Biochemistry of Psychoactive Drugs," *Drug Abuse,* ed. Brent Q. Hafen (Provo, Utah: Brigham Young University Press, 1973), pp. 32–38.

[16]Edward Fingl and Dixon M. Woodbury, "General Principles," in ed. L. S. Goodman and A. Gilman, *Pharmacological Basis of Therapeutics* (New York: Macmillan, 1970), p. 3.

[17]*Drug Use in America,* p. 143.

[18]Kenneth L. Jones, Louis W. Shainberg, and Curtis O. Byer, *Drugs and Alcohol* (New York: Harper & Row, 1969), p. 92.

[19]Ibid., p. 93.

[20]*Alcohol and Health: New Knowledge,* Second Special Report to the Congress from the Secretary of Health, Education, and Welfare (Washington, D.C.: Government Printing Office, 1974), pp. 49–59.

[21]Seldon Bacon, "The Problems of Alcoholism in American Society," *Social Disability,* ed. D. Maliken (New York: New York University Press, 1973), p. 8.

[22]*Drug Use in America,* p. 157.

[23]*Highway Safety, 1977,* United States Department of Transportation (Washington, D.C.: Government Printing Office, 1978), pp. 2, 5.

[24]Lewis Yablonsky, *The Tunnel Back: Synanon* (New York: Macmillan, 1965), pp. 196–199.

[25]Charles Winick, "Physician Narcotics Addicts," *Social Problems* 9 (Summer 1961), 174–186.

[26]Peter B. Bensinger, "Message from the Administrator," *Drug Enforcement* 6 (February 1979), p. 1.

[27]Clinard, *Sociology of Deviant Behavior,* pp. 423–424.

[28]Marsh B. Ray, "Abstinence Cycles and Heroin Addicts," *Deviance: The Interactionist Perspective,* ed. Earl Rubington and Martin S. Weinberg (New York: Macmillan, 1968), pp. 398–407.

[29]Ibid., p. 403.

[30]Fingl and Woodbury, "General Principles," pp. 24–26.

[31]Allen Geller and Maxwell Boas, *The Drug Beat* (New York: McGraw-Hill, 1969), pp. 248–255.

[32]Clausen, "Drug Use," p. 150.

[33]"Facts about Drugs," *Today's Education* 60 (February 1971), 34–35.

[34]Lester Grinspoon, *Marihuana Reconsidered* (Cambridge, Mass.: Harvard University Press, 1971), p. 368.

[35]Clinard, *Sociology of Deviant Behavior*, p. 434.

[36]Don Cahalan, Ira H. Cisin, and Helen M. Crosley, *American Drinking Practices* (New Brunswick, N.J.: Rutgers Center of Alcohol Studies, 1969), p. 189.

[37]Mark Keller, "The Oddities of Alcoholics," *Quarterly Journal of Studies on Alcohol* 33 (December 1972), 147.

[38]*New York City Alcoholism Study: A Program Analysis* (New York: Health Services Administration, 1972), pp. 6–16.

[39]Robert Freed Bales, "Cultural Differences in Rates of Alcoholism," *Quarterly Journal of Studies on Alcohol* 6 (March 1946), 480–499.

[40]Erich Goode, "Sociological Aspects of Marijuana Use," *Contemporary Drug Problems* (Winter 1975), p. 399.

[41]Lloyd Johnston, Jerald Backman and Patrick O'Malley, *Drug Use among American High School Students, 1975–1977,* (Rockville, Md.: National Institute on Drug Abuse, 1977), pp. 16, 18.

[42]Herbert Abelson, Patricia Fishburne and Ira Cisin, *National Survey on Drug Abuse, 1977* (Rockville, Md.: National Institute on Drug Abuse, 1977), pp. 18–25.

[43]Clausen, "Drug Use," p. 156.

[44]Carl D. Chambers, *Differential Drug Use within the New York State Labor Force* (New York: New York State Narcotic Addiction Control Commission, July 1971), p. 2.

[45]See as an example of such findings Isidor Chein et al., *The Road to H: Narcotics, Delinquency, and Social Policy* (New York: Basic Books, 1967), pp. 17–46.

[46]Straus, "Alcoholism and Problem Drinking," pp. 199–200.

[47]Ibid.

[48]Bales, "Cultural Differences in Rates of Alcoholism," pp. 480–499.

[49]Jellinek, *Disease Concept of Alcoholism,* pp. 154–155.

[50]Mark Keller, "On the Loss-of-Control Phenomenon in Alcoholism," *British Journal of Addiction* 67 (1972), 153–166.

[51]Alfred R. Lindesmith, *Opiate Addiction* (Bloomington, Ind.: Principia Press, 1947).

[52]Howard S. Becker, *Outsiders: Studies in the Sociology of Deviance* (New York: Free Press, 1963), chap. 3 and 4.

[53]Richard Cloward and Lloyd Ohlin, *Delinquency and Opportunity* (New York: Free Press, 1960), pp. 178–186.

[54]Edward Preble and John Casey, Jr., "Taking Care of Business—The Heroin User's Life on the Street," *International Journal of the Addictions* 4 (1969), 12.

[55] Charles Thomas, David Petersen, and Matthew Zingraff, "Student Drug Use: A Re-examination of the 'Hang-Loose Ethic' Hypothesis," *Journal of Health and Social Behavior* 16 (March 1975), 63–73.

[56]David Schulz and Robert Wilson, "Some Traditional Family Variables and Their Correlations with Drug Use Among High School Students," *Journal of Marriage and the Family* 35 (November 1973), 628–631.

[57]Donald Dickson, "Bureaucracy and Morality: An Organizational Perspective on a Moral Crusade," *Social Problems* 16 (Fall 1968), 146–156.

[58]Selma Muskin, "Politics and Economics of Government Response to Drug Abuse," *The Annals* 417 (January 1975), 30–31.

[59]Leroy C. Gould, "Crime and the Addict: Beyond Common Sense," *Drugs and the Criminal,* ed. James A. Inciardi and Carl D. Chambers (Beverly Hills, Calif.: Sage Publications, 1974), pp. 68–69.

[60]Thomas S. Szasz, "The Ethics of Addiction," *Harper's,* April 1972, pp. 74–79.

[61]Ibid., p. 74.

[62]Harrison M. Trice and Paul M. Roman, "Delabeling, Relabeling, and Alcoholics Anonymous," *Deviance: Action, Reaction, Interaction,* ed. Frank R. Scarpitti and Paul T. McFarlane (Reading, Mass.: Addison-Wesley, 1975), pp. 268–276.

[63]Florence Heyman, "Methadone Maintenance as Law and Order," *Society* 9 (June 1972), 15.

[64]Yablonsky, *The Tunnel Back.*

[65]John Lofland, *Deviance and Identity* (Englewood Cliffs, N.J.: Prentice-Hall, 1969), p. 215.

[66]Rita Volkman and Donald R. Cressey, "Differential Association and the Rehabilitation of Drug Addicts," *American Journal of Sociology* 69 (September 1963), 129–142.

Epilogue

Social problems, as opposed to personal troubles, are group conditions that are recognized as having significant detrimental consequences not only for individuals but for larger segments of the society as well. Three general perspectives have been employed in analyzing current social problems.

Social disorganization is a situation in which major institutional structures are not fulfilling their intended and necessary functions. Thus if the institution of the family fails to provide an adequate home environment and to socialize children according to certain values (e.g., respect for the rights of others), then a whole constellation of social problems may be generated.

The value conflict approach focuses on circumstances in which different groups within a society have divergent interests and values with respect to a given issue. In every society there are both common interests and values and conflicting ones. Problems arise when important social issues, such as the distribution of resources and rewards, become a source of widespread discontent and conflict.

Deviant behavior is the violation of norms that are important to most members of society or which are supported by powerful or influential groups. Deviance is problematic not only because it disrupts normal and routine social interaction but also because it tends to mobilize agencies of social control to take action against the deviant individual, often with personally damaging consequences.

As we have indicated, no single perspective affords a comprehensive understanding of social problems. Drug abuse, for example, is best analyzed both in terms of value conflict and deviance, whereas the problems of health care are best understood from the perspective of social disorganization. The interrelatedness of social problems should also be emphasized once again. Although many of the problems discussed in this book have been set forth in separate chapters for the sake of convenience and organization, their relationship to each other must not be overlooked. Poverty, a problem in its own right, also impinges upon the problems of the economy, government, family, crime, and drug use. For each social problem a similar list of interrelated problems could be presented.

Can we expect social problems to diminish or even disappear as we approach the society of tomorrow, or will disorganization, conflict, and deviance continue to present us with ever more serious problems in the future? Throughout this book we have asserted that social problems are not unique aberrations but are intimately tied up with fundamental social processes and the basic workings of a society. Recall, for example, the discussion at the beginning of the chapter on crime, which indicated that infractions of the criminal codes are expected and predictable social phenomena. Each era will define social conditions a bit differently, depending upon the attitudes and values which predominate at the time. Since certain social conditions will always have a detrimental impact upon some segment of society it must be concluded that, barring any unforeseen and dramatic transformation of our society into a utopia, social problems will be with us as far into the future as our sociological vision can see.

Perhaps our concern in the future will focus less on problems such as prostitution and drug use and more on large-scale, even global, problems. Within our own society, concern will most certainly be directed toward problems of inequality, the collective malaise that derives from feelings of individual powerlessness and ineffectiveness, and maintaining the expected quality of life in the face of painful changes that will inevitably occur in the decades ahead. On a wider scale, we will turn our attention increasingly to problems of overpopulation, the distribution of wealth, the proliferation of nuclear weaponry, and the consequences of resource depletion and environmental pollution on worldwide economic stability. In the next chapter, we shall examine some of these issues in more detail.

The Future
of Social Problems

17

Contemplating Coming Crises

Structural Crisis Tendencies /
Social Attitudes: Mass Malaise /
Changing Social Values: Tyranny by Technology /
Public Purpose versus the Planning System

Preparing for Future Problems: Simplistic and Realistic Remedies

Technological Utopianism / Equality

Challenge of the Future: Changing Our Values and Our Ways

Summary

Notes

Speculations about the future are the vogue today. Journalists are writing about it, scientists and philosophers are predicting it, institutes are planning for it, and ordinary citizens are wondering about it. To all, the future is a variety of mixed images, most of which border on the extremes of enthusiasm and despair. Futuristic themes of both utopia and catastrophe abound—the only certainty being that the future is likely to be different than the present. But how different and in what ways? Daniel Bell has defined the future as present expectations, on the grounds that "the world of the year 2000 has already arrived, for in decisions we make now, in the way we design our environment and sketch the lines of constraints, the future is committed."[1]

Nevertheless, there seems to be a growing feeling among those concerned with the future that civilization is entering a new period of crisis, that great troubles and immense social changes loom ahead for humanity. In what directions are the problems created by inflation, unemployment, and their effects on individual and family life leading? Will pollution and the destruction of the environment result in a situation where human habitation will be not only unpleasant but patently dangerous? Are centralization and the concentration of power in a small number of major institutions undermining democratic political structures? Will alienation and feelings of individual powerlessness bring about deterioration in the quality of life and decay in the fabric of society? Preconceived attitudes of naive optimism or gloomy pessimism are neither adequate nor appropriate for contemplating issues of this magnitude.

Contemplating Coming Crises

The preceding discussions of substantive social problems have all emphasized one common theme: such problems are inextricably bound up with the fundamental workings of society. They are rooted in dominant social institutions, particularly those in the economic and political spheres, as well as in the values that derive from the institutional structures. It is worth stressing again that social problems must not be viewed as isolated pathologies, within an otherwise smoothly functioning society, that can be remedied or ameliorated by piecemeal solutions that take into consideration only immediate and dramatic manifestations of problematic conditions. As Bell suggests, looking toward social problems of the future necessitates our retaining a focus on present institutional arrangements and value standards that will shape not only the nature and substance of future problems but also our ways of responding to them.

Examining the future is not always a pleasant prospect. The widely respected scientist Harrison Brown describes the scene as Americans look to the future.

But as we look down the road ahead, we see signs of impending trouble. A grave uneasiness is spreading over the land, shared in different ways by the poverty-striken of the slums of the central city and wealthy suburbanites with their swimming pools heated with once-abundant natural gas. Looking inward, many people are asking questions about both our poverty and our affluence, about unemployment and inflation, about crime, about strikes of public workers such as teachers, policemen, firemen, and bus drivers. They decry the ugliness of our cities, the noxious fumes in our air, and our wanton destruction of natural beauty. Looking outward they consider the nuclear umbrellas which can destroy us, the oil embargos, terrorism, and illegal immigration.[2]

The issues raised may not be comforting to contemplate, but to ignore them is to allow blind forces greater influence in determining our destiny than rational human efforts, values, and goals. Society will not remain static, and neither can our thinking. Most, if not all, spheres of social life will be touched by monumental changes within the next few generations. In order to deal intelligently with the future course of affairs, the pressing issues of our age must receive the attention and the resources of a public willing to step out of the complacency of everyday life and address difficult questions. To fail to do so condemns future generations to conditions of widespread unhappiness and chaos.

Structural Crisis Tendencies

A social system experiences certain tendencies toward crisis when the structure of that system does not permit sufficient possibilities for solving the problems that are threatening the system's existence.[3]

Knowledge of the crisis tendencies of any social structure is necessary as background for understanding particular social problems, since they are often manifestations of deep and basic structural strains. These tendencies may be the result of contradictions in the institutional arrangements of society.

Contradictions exist whenever the structure of society, or an institution within society, requires for its continued existence the achievement of incompatible goals.[4] The contradictions become manifest in conflicts occurring between elements of the structure itself. One example of contradiction centers around the economy and the use of modern technology. In attempting to increase profits and strengthen the economy, many industries utilize new technology without realizing the harmful effects it can have on workers and the environment. Almost 500,000 American workers die or fall ill every year as the result of exposure to dangerous substances on the job. Precautions taken to prevent such illnesses may be expensive in terms of the cost of insuring work places and in the delay in producing new, valuable (some even lifesaving) commodities. Thus, the system is faced with the problem of achieving what appear to be mutually contradictory goals: strengthening the economy and improving the quality of life for all Americans versus insuring the right of employees to safe, healthy work places.

In the past, alienation and cultural breakdown have been thought of as major crisis tendencies. For the future, at least one author has identified three categories of crisis tendencies: ecological balance, anthropological balance, and international balance.[5]

Ecological balance, the relationship between the human race and outer nature, was examined at some length in Chapter 11. Crises in the ecological balance stem from the constraints imposed on people by the limitations of the environment. The finiteness of natural resources and the levels at which pollutants can be absorbed are examples of these constraints. In the United States three institutional patterns seem to be pushing beyond the bounds that the environment can endure.

First, there has been an increasing application of energy resources toward raising the productivity of labor. As a result, severe strains are being placed on finite energy resources such as fuel, cultivable and inhabitable land, fresh water, and food. Although some claim, for example, that the oceans provide the potential for vast amounts of food in the future, it cannot be assured that such quantities will be available by the time the world's population needs them. The environment's ability to reabsorb heat and waste products is also limited. Since economically useful energy is ultimately released as heat, the continually increasing consumption of energy will eventually end in a rise in global temperature. At a minimum, such occurrence would drastically alter our ecological chain.

Second, consumption has become institutionalized as a source of status in American society. The desire to consume beyond what is useful, or even healthy, makes for a tremendous waste of natural resources. It is staggering to consider the resource savings the American nation would experience if each family were limited to only one automobile. The proliferation and increased reliance on the automobile has further resulted in a decline in more energy-conserving but less convenient forms of transportation, such as trains and buses.

A third strain on the environment comes from the bureaucratization of the economy and the consequent rationalization of the pursuit of profits. One such rational procedure is the attempt to increase profits by minimizing diminishing returns. In other words, as an economic market becomes satiated, the value of its commodity diminishes. The most profitable production is, therefore, for markets that are not easily satiated; and rational control has extended to the point of arbitrarily constructing such markets. The techniques for accomplishing this vary widely. Every year manufacturers spend millions of dollars advertising new "in" products. The new fads and fashions in clothes, cars, and appliances endure until the next year's models are created. Many items are designed to self-destruct after short periods of time. Some industries engage in expensive competition with an alleged communist enemy, reputed to be always on the verge of outdistancing us in the arms or space race. Other producers simply develop throwaway packaging and commodities. Although profits are kept up, this type of production is extremely demanding on finite resources. And the mountains of garbage left in the wake of the "throwaway revolution" create tremendous problems for disposal and reabsorption.

While ecological balance refers to limitations on the exploitation of outer nature, *anthropological balance* refers to limits on the exploitation of inner nature. In other words, to what extent can human beings be socialized? Dennis Wrong has answered this question with the charge that most social scientists have an "oversocialized" conception of people and that each individual has an inalienable private nature.[6] Yet there is a real tendency in modern society toward total institutions—institutions in which bureaucratic rationality attempts to dominate private identities. Sociologist Erving Goffman has noted that in such total institutions there develops an underlife, a coalition of those subject to public authority yet oriented toward maintaining private identities.[7]

As well as the limits to socialization imposed by "inner nature," there are also limits to the operation of certain techniques of socialization. As social organizations become larger and more complex, it becomes necessary for the steering or goal-setting mechanism of society to become independent of particularistic motives. This is accomplished through the production of generalized legitimacy schemes fashioned to elicit mass loyalty.[8] Present systems of socialization of identities and beliefs are produced through social interaction and participation. Inasmuch as the size and complexity of organizations tend to increase and to become increasingly formalized in the pursuit of efficiency, individual participation in decision making tends to decrease. The nonparticipative tendencies of large-scale organizations endanger their own legitimacy, that is, the people's ability to believe in and support large bureaucracies. The result tends to be a disenchantment of the masses and a resultant failure to conform to societal norms, as well as a proliferation of identity crises among individuals.

To prevent such crises, institutions often engage in symbolic actions designed to create the image of responsiveness to individual needs. Murray Edelman's analysis of regulatory agencies demonstrates the government's involvement in creating the image of responsiveness.[9] Through public statements and press releases citizens are convinced that actions are being taken to curtail the abuses of industry, when in fact the regulatory agencies are controlled by the industries. Increasingly, however, the real power sources are being revealed, and some groups are beginning to question the legitimacy of the agencies.

A surge of militarism in the United States (and in the USSR and other nations) has laid the groundwork for a crisis in *international balance*. Militarism is the "dominance of means over ends for the purpose of heightening the prestige and increasing the power of the military."[10] In this pursuit, the military has encouraged the routinization of arms production and the race to discover more sophisticated and more devastating weapons. But this race has not served the interests of the military alone. The desire of the business community for steady profits and government-subsidized innovative research has made it a willing partner in the proliferation of arms. And through default and moral apathy, politicians and the public have shared in this pursuit as well.

C. Wright Mills once claimed that the immediate cause of World War III will be the preparation for it.[11] And it is the astounding success of our past preparation that has put us in our present precarious position. Most identifiable among the symbols of this success is the thermonuclear bomb, a weapon that presents the possibility of total annihilation—of elite decision makers and top generals as well as citizens and soldiers.

This possibility for Armageddon is a qualitatively new factor in international relations, the implications of which are yet to be fully realized. Some patterns, however, are discernible.[12] First, it has forced the major powers to fight vicariously through brushfire wars between less powerful third parties. Second, it has redirected international tensions as forces for change from international warfare to attempts at internal revolution. It has also presented the possibility of military parity for small nations, allowing them a more equal footing in the world distribution of power.

But the redirection of international crisis tendencies is not their resolution. The institutional structures of militarism, war economies, and political insensibility that have created these crisis tendencies are still operative in nations throughout the world. Inasmuch as present commitments to these institutional patterns remain, expectations for future crises remain also.

Social Attitudes: Mass Malaise

In *An Inquiry into the Human Prospect*, economist Robert Heilbroner presents a detailed assessment of prominent themes in current social attitudes and their implications for the future.[13] The mood of our times, Heilbroner argues, is one of pervasive anxiety about the future course of events, who will control these events, and their effects on individual happiness and well-being. He identifies three distinct sources of present discontent and uneasiness, each of which calls into question the appropriateness of the values of Western industrial civilization for the society of the future.

First, several specific events during the past decade have thrust themselves into our daily lives, shaken our confidence, and produced a sense of unease and foreboding. The war in Vietnam and the Watergate episode have caused us to question some of the very foundations of our society. The belief that major institutions serve the public interest has been seriously undermined, and the view of our society as a bastion of morality and virtue has been shaken. Assassinations, unprecedented drug usage, and violence—both planned and random—have contributed to the feeling that all is not well. Behind the superficial amenities of contemporary life, there seems to be a recognition that civilization is not so advanced as we had thought.[14] Confidence in societal institutions apparently reached its lowest point in the mid-1970s. As the seventies came to an end there was a slight, but fairly consistent, increase in the percentage of the population expressing confidence in various institutions (see Table 17.1).

	Proportion of Population Expressing "Great Deal of Confidence" in Institutions				Table 17.1
	1966	1972	1976	1979	
Medicine	73	48	42	30	
Higher education	61	33	31	33	
Organized religion	41	30	24	20	
U.S. Supreme Court	50	28	22	28	
The military	61	35	23	29	
Major companies	55	27	16	18	
Executive branch of the federal government	41	27	11	17	
The press	29	18	20	28	
Congress	42	21[a]	9	18	
Organized labor	22	15	10	10	
Advertising agencies	21	—[b]	7	—[b]	

Source: Louis Harris, *The Harris Survey* (New York: Chicago Tribune–New York News Syndicate, 6 December 1973, 5 January 1978, 25 September 1978); Louis Harris, *The ABC News–Harris Survey* (New York: Chicago Tribune–New York News Syndicate, 5 March 1979). © by the Chicago Tribune–New York News Syndicate, Inc.
[a] Asked U.S. Senate in 1972
[b] Not reported in 1972 and 1979

Second, a series of general attitudinal changes has accompanied these specific events and reinforced the doubts growing out of them. Perhaps most important, Heilbroner argues, has been the loss of faith in "progress," in the belief that movement toward a better state of affairs is inevitable.[15] This can be seen most vividly in the actions of the antinuclear groups who view nuclear power as leading the country down the path to total annihilation. Faith in progress has sustained our culture and inspired confidence that by managing the direction of change even the most intractable problems can eventually be resolved. Recently, however, we have become aware of definite limitations on our ability to engineer social change and of the fact that many of our most pressing problems lie beyond our accustomed measures for bringing about change. Inflation, for example, seems to be as unmanageable as the forces that propel us into stockpiling an arsenal of obliterative weapons.

Moreover, the quality of life in our society seems to be on the verge of deteriorating. The so-called energy crisis—whether real or contrived—has generated the fear that continued economic growth cannot be sustained indefinitely. And the naive belief that material growth alone could solve the problems of poverty and related ills no longer seems plausible; the notion that growth is progress has exposed itself as a myth. Traditionally seen as contributing to the quality of life, economic growth now threatens massive environmental pollution and the depletion of nonrenewable resources.

Third, and more abstract, is a "civilizational malaise" in the current frame of mind, reflecting the "inability of a civilization directed to material improvement—higher incomes, better diets, miracles of medicine, triumphs of applied physics and chemistry—to satisfy the human spirit."[16] No longer is it easy to equate personal happiness with annual increments of new automobiles and color television sets. Further, a sense of direction, both in the personal life of the individual and for the society as a whole, seems to be lacking. The lack of confidence in the major institutions of society has been accompanied by a vague feeling that no one has command of the current situation or is equipped to deal with the critical problems of nuclear war, overpopulation, or unemployment. A central consequence of these broad changes in social attitudes and beliefs is their negative effect on the society's collective capacity for responding to its pressing problems.

In essence, Heilbroner's analysis suggests that the values that have held primacy in our culture are in the process of losing their validity and vitality. The individualistic ethic, with its emphasis on competitiveness and contradiction of the spirit of collective enterprise, provides little sense of social purpose or shared goals. The cluster of values associated with individualism may prove themselves to be unsatisfying to the individual and unstable for the larger society. More specifically, the stress on personal achievement, the relentless pressure for advancement, and the acquisitive drive that signals the way to success in our society are critical weaknesses in our present way of life.[17]

Other values rooted in the very nature of industrial civilization also have dehumanizing and problematic consequences. Efficiency often seems an end in itself, resulting in a tendency to subordinate human evaluations to those based on technical criteria. Quantitative modes of thought prevail; people live by the clock and adjust their lives to machine-paced schedules and routines. The drive to dominate and master the physical environment has not only created significant health hazards but destroyed important recreational resources as well. Aesthetic aspects of life have become secondary to technical achievement and standards.

If these elements of our value system are no longer well suited for the current conditions of life, they are even less suited for life in the future. Competitive individualism, the struggle for status, and the deification of efficiency do not appear capable of enhancing individual happiness, underlying the worth of the individual, or enriching the emotional and aesthetic content of life.

Changing Social Values: Tyranny by Technology

Emerging trends in the nature and content of social values have always occupied a prominent place in the thinking of social analysts. Recently, a considerable amount of scholarly attention has been directed at the impact of technology on the values held by the members of a society. Philosopher Herbert Marcuse has argued that technological society enslaves us, creating but one narrow dimension for human existence.[18] The French social critic, Jacques Ellul, insists that technology is not a neutral instrument that serves human purposes; technology ignores and has come to supersede human values, establishing the priority and primacy of means over ends.[19] These and other thinkers of our time emphasize the role of technology in our lives as a fundamental shaping force. Moreover, there are no indications that this trend will be reversed. A look to the future of social problems must therefore consider the impact of technology's intrusion into more and more spheres of our lives.

The effect of technology on social values is neither a direct nor a simple one. Values emerge out of the concrete realities of day-to-day living and are shaped by the institutional structures that organize major spheres of social activity. Technology has produced profound changes in our values primarily because it has produced fundamental social institutions.[20] Indeed, the technological apparatus we have erected often appears to have developed a life of its own, suggesting its own solutions to problems which are in turn evaluated according to technological criteria.

Sociologist Robert Nisbet has identified four distinct technological processes that have an impact on social values and institutions.[21] *Abstraction* refers to the separation of moral values from social contexts which are important and meaningful to the individual. Scientific and technological norms are abstract and impersonal, and their effect is to make moral values seem less urgent, less important as guides to behavior. The personal and intimate character of behavior is replaced by an impersonal, calculating, utilitarian frame of mind.

Generalization is closely related to the process of abstraction; both refer to transformations in moral and normative standards accompanying the spread of technology. Basic social norms typically arose in closely knit community contexts, where they were concrete and meaningful for individuals in their daily lives. With the advance of technology and the emergence of mass society, norms that once were rooted in small, community-type collectivities became generalized into mass norms. General, rather than particular, principles came to serve as guides for conduct.

Individuation denotes the fragmentation and atomization of traditional community structures and primary social relationships. The abstractness and impersonality of technological societies, along with their greater mobility and diversity, promote within the individual feelings of separation from the community.

Rationalization refers to the tendency to bring greater and greater areas of thought and conduct under the formal rules of bureaucratic administration. Informal, individual decision making in the areas of religion, education, and government has been increasingly replaced by centralized, impersonal, administrative decision making. Rationalization has become deeply embedded in modern society, with significant implications for the values of individuality and personal autonomy. "The very progress of modern administrative techniques," writes Nisbet, "has created a problem in the maintenance and nurture of individual thought and action."[22]

Technological ideas, values, and goals will continue to exert their influence on the social values and institutions of the future. Where they come into conflict with widely held social norms and take precedence over those norms, they may become a disorganizing force in society. Further, when technology is deeply embedded in the workings of society, it may act to retard social change by reducing normal and healthy conflict within institutions. Conflict is minimized or managed through the processes of rationalization, generalization, and abstraction. In this manner, technology undermines important social values; individuality, autonomy, and the ability of the individual citizen to influence the decision-making process are all jeopardized. The impact of technological hardware and modes of thought on basic social processes and structures represents a primary contributing factor to the broad problem of human alienation.

Philip Slater, who also has addressed the question of the appropriateness of certain contemporary values for future society, shares Heilbroner's views concerning the deleterious effects of the core value of "competitive individualism,"[23] The technology-based value system, argues Slater, is fundamentally antihumanistic. It sanctions the spending of billions of dollars to discover ways of killing more efficiently, yet spends very little to find ways of improving the quality of life. The values of competition and personal gain foster a preoccupation with self and create a widening schism between the individual and society. Slater warns us to turn away from

> our exaggerated moral commitment to the "virtues" of striving and individual achievement. The mechanized disaster that surrounds us is in no small part a result of our having deluded ourselves that a motley scramble of people trying to get the better of one another is socially useful instead of something to be avoided at all costs. It has taken us a long time to realize that seeking to surpass others might be pathological, and trying to enjoy and cooperate with others healthy, rather than the other way around.[24]

Public Purpose versus the Planning System

Of the institutions that will shape the direction and quality of life in the future, those in the economic and political spheres are likely to maintain their primacy. As we have seen, the existing structures and functions of these institutions are major contributing factors to several current problems. They tend to serve the interests of the wealthy and the powerful to the detriment of other segments of society, and in so doing they contribute to the problems of inequality and poverty and the related problems of restricted opportunities in education and employment; and they will continue to be a primary vehicle through which human activity is organized to deal with large-scale problems.

But this must be considered in the light of our earlier assertion that the current civilizational malaise derives in large part from the feeling that major institutions are no longer responsible to the needs and desires of the individual, the feeling that the average citizen counts very little in the decision-making process. A crucial issue for the coming age, therefore, is whether our institutions will move in the direction of greater or lesser responsiveness to the concerns of the citizenry.

The trends toward centralization and concentration of power in our society discussed in Chapter 6 ride on deep economic, technological, and political undercurrents; and these propelling forces show no signs of altering their direction. This is not to say that concerted public action is incapable of modifying these trends, but only that efforts to bring about change will encounter and must cope with deeply rooted historical processes. Economist John Kenneth Galbraith argues that the key to understanding emerging institutional trends lies in the uneven development of the economic system, which has resulted in a relatively small number of giant firms dominating the economy as well as the political system.[25] These huge corporate organizations, which comprise what Galbraith terms the "planning system," are the piviotal centers of power in our society, and their influence increasingly shapes social relationships and permeates vast areas of human conduct. Thus the central political issue of the coming age would appear to be conflict between the public purpose and the goals and interests of the planning system.

Although the corporate sector does engage in planning that extends beyond the immediate future, its planning is for private rather than public purposes. Giant firms seek to increase their size and eliminate uncertainties in their operation, but their planning is not necessarily rational in the long run. Production priorities often make little sense; consumer demand is contrived and manipulated through advertising, and goods are produced with little regard for real need or usefulness. Long-range planning for the public as a whole tends to be ignored by both corporate and government decision makers.

Traditional economic theory treats such problems as pollution and the depletion and pillage of natural resources as "externalities," excluding these public concerns from the decision-making calculus. This absence of long-range public planning is a matter of substantial concern, especially in light of the problems which will emerge or be exacerbated by the inevitable decline in economic growth. As Heilbroner has noted: "The myopia that confines the present vision of men to the short-term future is not likely to disappear overnight, rendering still more difficult a planned and orderly retrenchment and redivision of output."[26]

The manner in which the rewards of major institutions are to be distributed constitutes a recurring problem for all social systems. Sociologist Herbert Gans argues that the most critical problem facing our society in the decades ahead is the need for more economic and political equality.[27] Because of inflation and the reduced rate of economic growth, many segments of our society face the prospect of a decline in their standard of living. Economists speak of a "ratchet effect" to indicate people's resistance to any movement downward from a standard of living to which they have grown accustomed. As a means of preserving the higher living standards they have achieved in the post–World War II period, the middle strata especially may demand a redistribution of wealth and income in the direction of greater equality.

During the 1960s and early 1970s, students, workers, members of minority groups, and other segments of society expressed a demand for more control over conditions that affect their lives. Although these protest movements have subsided recently, Gans believes that the demands themselves continue to exist and will surface again politically in the future. Groups that have been relegated to a marginal position in the political process will no longer be content to allow decisions that have a substantial impact on their lives to be made by a handful of corporate and government policymakers. The popular discontent over the centralization of policymaking may eventually translate into a movement toward greater political equality.

The view that the future will see a movement toward equality in political and economic institutions is held by many observers of the current scene, but this view is by no means shared by all social analysts. Heilbroner warns that as resource and environmental limitations eventually lead to a deterioration of the world economic situation and an intensification of conflict between the "have" and the "have-not" countries (over, for example, the distribution of world food supplies between the population-heavy Third World countries and the industrialized nations), there is a danger of a drift toward authoritarian political structures. He suggests that democratic institutions have inherent difficulties in managing social tensions and that authoritarian structures would hold out the possibility of a superior capacity to mobilize both national resolve and national resources for effectively dealing with crisis situations.

As the histories of the United States, or Switzerland, or modern Scandinavia all illustrate, democracies can provide stable and strong government. . . . Yet, even in these cases, strong leaders provide a sense of psychological well-being that weak ones do not, so that in moments of crisis and strain demands arise for the exercise of strong-arm rule. As the histories of ancient and modern democracies illustrate, the pressure of political movement in times of war, civil commotion, or general anxiety pushes *in the direction of authority,* not away from it. These tendencies may be short-lived, or may give rise to totalitarian governments that in time collapse, but I do not think that one can deny that these pressures are a persistent fact of political life.[28]

Compounding this tendency is what appears to be a general belief in our society that centralized authority is able to deal with crisis and unrest more successfully than less authoritarian structures.[29] In the long run, a continuing movement toward centralization of power is at least as likely as—and perhaps more so than—a movement toward more egalitarian structures.

Preparing for Future Problems: Simplistic and Realistic Remedies

As noted in the first chapter of this volume, social problems have two dimensions; they reflect objective social conditions as well as people's beliefs about and subjective assessments of those conditions. In part because of the subjective aspect of social problems, many different and conflicting viewpoints are in evidence concerning the manner in which we ought to deal with problematic conditions. These divergent modes of thought reflect people's beliefs about the origin of social problems and about what is possible and probable in the future. Some modes of thought remain lodged within the same myopic framework that has dominated our thinking and our responses to social problems in the past. Others take a longer perspective, focusing on what changes must take place if the society of the future is to provide and sustain a high quality of life for its members.

There appears to be an undercurrent of thought in our society that a return to a simpler way of life would alleviate the widespread disenchantment with major institutions and the accompanying feelings of individual powerlessness. Adherents of this view suggest that great benefits would follow from a rebirth of the traditional community. They believe that the anonymous, impersonal urban structures that characterize modern life need to be replaced by more intimate collectivities, in which the members share common values and the individual has a distinct place that provides a clear-cut identity. This mode of thought has found expression in the recent attempts at communal living, but it is also evident among other segments of the population. The calls for neighborhood schools and a return of decision-making power to states and localities seem to have at their core a belief that "mass society" is the basic generative force of social problems. In a sense, this belief is both accurate and naive—accurate because many social problems are indeed rooted in the increasing complexity of modern society but naive because it fails to recognize that urbanization, industrialization, and modernization are long-standing and powerful historical trends which cannot be reversed without great social convulsions.

Another response to social problems might well be termed a "Band-Aid" or "crisis-management" approach, and it is especially prevalent in large-scale government decision making. Here problems are confronted only when they have reached such proportions that action is imperative; even then, proposals for dealing with problems tend to focus on piecemeal ameliorative programs. The problem of one-fifth of our society living in poverty amidst unprecedented affluence did not evoke serious and ameliorative action until the urban riots and unrest of the early 1960s. Suddenly, a War on Poverty was declared to reduce the inflammatory potential of the situation, and a plethora of government agencies and fragmentary programs were established. There are many who question whether this Band-Aid approach is capable of providing effective long-range solutions.

Similarly, the problem of unemployment becomes a matter of grave national concern only when it reaches the "unacceptable" level of 8 to 10 percent. This, of course, implies that it is acceptable for millions of people who want to work to be denied employment—as long as their numbers remain below the crisis level. Such a superficial approach ignores the basic fact that in our society work tends to be equated with personal worth. As a result, *any* unemployment tends to be disruptive of both individual and family life in psychological as well as material ways. Further, piecemeal government programs such as temporary public works projects do not get at the roots of the problem of providing and allocating enough employment in the long run for all those who wish to work. To a very great extent, this type of thinking and this mode of responding stem from the absence of comprehensive and long-range social planning. Such thinking lends itself to a fatalistic attitude that in the future we will simply drift from one major crisis to another.

Technological Utopianism

Most Americans seem to assume that somehow, before it's too late or before things become too bad, technology will provide the solutions for our most critical problems. We seem possessed by a naive faith that technologies can be devised to deal effectively with pressing personal and social problems. Many people, for example, are not really too concerned about future energy shortages, for in the back of their minds lurks the promise that technology will eventually provide an unlimited supply of energy from nuclear power or solar conversion. The world population problem, it is often believed, can be managed by increasing the food supply through the development of new high-yield seeds for major crops. Mental disorders too, many feel, will ultimately be controlled or eliminated by the development of new drugs. It has even been suggested that a solution to the problem of crime could be achieved by installing centrally connected television monitors on the streets of high-crime areas.[30] Technological utopianism, as we shall refer to such thinking, is attractive because if offers simple, quick, and easy solutions to complex social problems.

The growth of technological forms of thought parallels other developments in our society, but at the same time it is emerging as a topic of serious concern. In responding to socially rooted problems, solutions that fit into a technological framework tend to be given priority over those that depend more upon human resources. Such solutions are often felt to be more practical, more immediate, and more manageable from the point of view of decision makers in the large bureaucracies that deal with social problems. The problems that have been discussed as types of deviant behavior represent one area that is particularly amenable to technological forms of thought.

> The theory used to recruit physicians and deploy chemical technology in the war against social deviance, crime, misbehavior, alcoholism, mental illness, drug addiction, [and] overanxiety . . . derives from the determination that these conditions are analogous to medical problems and therefore can be solved through medical means. Once a human problem is identified as a disease, the stage is set for mobilizing the technological apparatus for discovering its cure.[31]

Thus we attempt to cure the problem of drug addiction with methadone, the problem of alcoholism with Antabuse (a drug that causes extreme nausea if alcohol is consumed after its ingestion), and the problem of mental disorders by the sustained administration of powerful psychoactive agents. But technological "cures" tend to be modeled after the simple cause-and-effect notions of machine technology and ignore a multitude of more basic factors contributing to problems.

It has been emphasized throughout this book that social problems are embedded in political, economic, and social contexts; these problems are not purely technological and neither can be their solutions. Technological utopianism is not only naive but also potentially dangerous. It is naive, for example, to cling to the comforting belief that technology will eventually create limitless energy supplies and allow us to maintain our existing lifestyles when there are definite energy production limits posed by the capacity of the earth's environment to withstand rising temperature levels caused by energy-producing technologies. What is dangerous in this outlook is that it lends itself to a sense of complacency, to a view that things will get better and problems will be corrected without requiring major social adjustments and concerted human effort.

Many writers give technology the leading role in shaping the future. Harrison Brown claims, however, that "the main bottlenecks facing humanity, the primary problems which must be solved, are far less technological in nature than they are social, economic, and political."[32] Those who see technology as the savior of the human race fail to consider the extent to which technology has not been used to solve current problems because of social, economic, and political factors. Brown points out that we already have the technology necessary to provide enough food to feed the hungry of the world, but little is being done to accomplish this. We already have the technology necessary to achieve energy independence, but little is being done to accomplish this. The reasons for these failures to act lie in the social, economic, and political situation of the United States today. The solutions would cost money and would damage industries with much invested in the status quo.

Moreover, serious moral and ethical questions are raised by the application of advanced technological methods to human problems. The social sciences have already developed procedures which permit the control of human behavior in limited ways; and there are indications that it will be even more possible to control behavior in the years ahead.[33] For example, behavior modification programs have been implemented in some prisons, hospitals, and schools in an attempt to change or eliminate troublesome and undesirable behavior. This technique is based on controlling the reward structure of a person's environment so that "desirable" conduct is reinforced and "undesirable" conduct eliminated.[34] Behavior modification holds out the promise of a simple technical solution to problem behavior, yet it ignores what some feel to be the more important question of what has caused a person to behave contrary to accepted norms.

There is yet another question raised by the possibility of scientific behavior control. Who controls the controllers? How does one draw the line between controlling harmful behavior and engineering mass conformity? Technological forms of thought base decisions on efficiency rather than upon humanitarian values. To vest greater and greater power in the hands of technological specialists and planners raises the Orwellian prospect of expert control over societal decision making.

Equality

In recent years a growing number of social analysts have come to the conclusion that comprehensive and long-range solutions to social problems must involve fundamental changes in the organization of our society. Founded on the theory that unequal access to societal rewards gives rise to many of our most pressing problems, these proposals center around changes in institutional structures to provide greater equality.

Equality in the sense spoken of here does not mean that all people should be equal in all respects, for this is impossible and patently absurd, as novelist Kurt Vonnegut, Jr., has illustrated in *Welcome to the Monkey House,* an insightful futuristic vision of a society in which a Handicapper General is responsible for making all persons literally equal.[35] What it does mean is that ability and need—rather than social class or race or sex—should determine the distribution of social rewards and that each individual should have the opportunity to realize his or her own potential. For it is resources, particularly economic ones, that largely determine a person's life chances in our society, and it is access to these basic resources that must be equalized.

Christopher Jencks, author of a major and controversial report on education and social equality, states the case forcefully:

In America, as elsewhere, the general drift over the past 200 years has been toward equality. In the economic realm, however, the contribution of public policy to this drift has been slight. As long as egalitarians assume that public policy cannot contribute to economic equality directly . . . progress will remain glacial. If we want to move beyond this tradition, we will have to establish political control over the economic institutions that shape our society. This is what other countries usually call socialism. Anything else will end in the same disappointment as the reforms of the 1960s.[36]

Those who concur with this analysis argue that the goal of equality can be achieved only through a public policy that reduces the present concentration of power and economic resources in a small, privileged stratum of society. Such a policy is aimed at extending to all segments of society the ability to exercise real power over conditions which affect their lives.

According to Herbert Gans, who has outlined a detailed program for redistributing wealth and political power in our society, which he feels is well suited to the specific nature of contemporary American society,[37] redistributive policies must focus not only on equality of opportunity but more centrally on what is termed "equality of results." That is, new social policies must directly promote equality in the areas of income, political power, education, and the social worth of jobs. The consequences of implementing such a proposal with regard to social problems cannot be predicted with any certainty. Obviously, poverty as it is now defined would be eliminated.

Gans also believes that a whole cluster of problems related to poverty and inequality would be reduced: street crime, drug addiction, alcoholism, and mental illness. The tensions and strains that often disrupt family life would be reduced by higher incomes and better jobs. Individuals who are now marginal to the political process would have an opportunity to acquire more political influence. And finally, Gans argues that internal political antagonisms would decline because "conflicts can be compromised fairly if the society is more egalitarian, if differences of self-interest that result from sharp inequality of income and power can be reduced."[38]

History has shown that major social transitions such as that proposed by Gans must contend with institutional inertia as well as with resistance from vested interests. In light of the historical trends in the direction of centralization and concentration of power and the entrenchment of interests that benefit from the present distribution of resources, the possibility of a smooth transition to a system of greater equality is unlikely. Moreover, the individualistic ethic and the striving for upward mobility are ingrained in the American value system, and personal acquisitiveness is deeply rooted in our economic and political structures. But perhaps the most important barrier to be overcome is the myopia that prevents us from seriously addressing our long-term prospects and considering their alternatives.

Challenge of the Future: Changing Our Values and Our Ways

A change in institutional structures such as the egalitarians propose is almost always—and perhaps must be—accompanied by changes in social value systems. But regardless of whether they foresee basic economic reorganization ahead, a great many observers of the long-range prospects for our society feel that substantial changes in our value systems and life-styles must necessarily occur in the decades ahead if the quality of life is not to deteriorate.

Competitive individualism, so central and so deeply ingrained in our present way of life, may no longer be a suitable value when collective social action will be required to meet a vast array of challenges, problems, and crises. Such competition is not conductive to the development of a sense of social purpose and shared goals that will obviously be needed in the future. The struggle for individual achievement promotes social fragmentation and antagonisms. If widespread discontent and chaos are to be avoided, we shall need to develop a consciousness of being part of a larger organization of people.[39] In a very real sense, the public must take precedence over the private. We shall need to recognize that the members of society in some sense share a common economic destiny, for the depletion of vital resources will affect rich and poor alike. And mass unemployment gives rise to a whole cluster of social problems from which other segments of the population will be unable to insulate themselves.

Changes in our consumption patterns and values will also be required. Conspicuous consumption will be too costly to continue into the future. We shall have to turn away from junk products, wasteful packaging, and novel gadgets that require massive advertising to impress on us that they might, in fact, have some true utility. Further, we will need to reassess our commitment to technological "progress." Slater argues that we must develop a "human-value index" that assesses the ultimate worth of a product or invention in terms of its total impact on human life—that is in terms of human and social goals rather than technical criteria.[40]

He suggests that our efforts to bring about needed changes should have two thrusts: a short-term effort to redirect existing institutions and a long-term attempt to alter motivation. The former should include an assessment of every institution and every social program "to determine whether it encourages social consciousness or personal aggrandizement."[41] The latter must be directed toward rewarding motivations other than greed and personal acquisitiveness; that is, we must come to allocate rewards on the basis of a person's contribution to the general social welfare.

Perhaps the greatest challenge of the future is inherent in a question posed by Heilbroner. Whether we shall be able to summon the collective resolve to bring about the painful changes in our attitudes and actions the future demands is a question only we—not as selfish individuals but as a people—can answer.

When men can generally acquiesce in, even relish, the destruction of their living contemporaries, when they can regard with indifference or irritation the fate of those who live in slums, rot in prison, or starve in lands that have meaning only insofar as they are vacation resorts, why should they be expected to take the painful actions needed to prevent the destruction of future generations whose faces they will never live to see?[42]

Summary

There is growing concern that the future may hold social problems greater than we know today. Confronting the future is not always pleasant, but our failure to do so now may condemn subsequent generations to a society marked by instability, disorganization, and personal unhappiness.

Breakdowns in social and cultural mechanisms for maintaining order in a social system have been referred to as crisis tendencies. Three categories of such tendencies have been identified for the future: ecological balance, anthropological balance, and international balance.

Crises in the ecological balance—the relationship between people and outer nature—stem from the constraints imposed on society by the limitations of the environment. Crises in the anthropological balance arise when the inner nature is exploited beyond endurable limits or when the socialization of the individual is in excess. Crises in the international balance spring from possibilities for conflict or cooperation that result from routing international relations. Institutional structures that society has created to deal with contemporary problems will determine how new crisis tendencies are to be handled in the future.

Robert Heilbroner has identified a number of prominent themes in current social attitudes and assessed their implications for the future. He argues that the mood of our times is one of pervasive anxiety about the future. Who will control events? And what will be the impact of these events on individual happiness and well-being? Sources of our present discontent include the recoginition that civilization is not so advanced as we thought, the lessening of confidence in the inevitable progress of civilization, and the increasing inability of material improvement to satisfy the human spirit. Heilbroner's analysis questions the continuing viability of values that have held primacy in our culture. The stress on personal achievement, the pressure for advancement, and the acquisitive drive that symbolizes success in our society are viewed as critical weaknesses. Traditional values that have been the very roots of industrial society no longer appear capable of satisfying individual, emotional, and aesthetic needs.

The impact of technology on the values of contemporary industrial society is also being questioned. Its increasing influence in our lives appears to be a growing trend and will be a significant problem for the future. Four distinct technological processes that influence social values and institutions have been identified: *abstraction*, the separation of moral values from social contexts; *generalization*, the replacement of general rather than particular principles as guides for conduct; *individuation*, the breakdown and isolation of traditional community structures and primary social relationships; and *rationalization*, the tendency to encompass greater areas of thought and conduct under the formal rules of bureaucratic organization. These processes are seen as hindrances to individual thought and action.

Harrison Brown has demonstrated that the importance of economic and political institutions in shaping the quality of life in the future will remain significant. As these institutions are currently structured, they tend to serve the interests of one segment of society over another. A crucial question for the future is whether these institutional arrangements will show greater responsiveness to the concerns of all citizens. Present trends indicate that there will be continuing conflict between the public good and the interests of those who dominate major institutions. Herbert Gans has argued that the most critical problem facing our society in the future is the need for more economic and political equality.

Largely because of the subjective aspect of social problems, opinions differ as to the manner in which we should deal with problematic conditions. Some believe that the problem of disenchantment with social institutions and the feeling of individual powerlessness can be solved if we return to a simpler way of life. They argue that the anonymous, impersonal structure of modern civilizations should be replaced by more intimate collectivities— traditional communities where all share common values and each has a distinct place in the social order.

The implementation of this belief may allay the development of those problems noted in the increasing complexity of modern society, but it appears to be impossible in the face of strong historical trends toward urbanization, industrialization, and modernization. Another popular way of responding to social problems is through crisis management or the implementation of piecemeal ameliorative programs when action becomes imperative. Many question the ability of this approach to provide effective long-range solutions to social problems.

Technological utopianism, the belief that technology will provide solutions for our critical problems, is also popular in American society, probably because it offers simple, quick, and easy solutions. Although such solutions are often thought to be more practical and manageable, they are modeled after the simple cause-and-effect notions of machine technology and ignore all the individual and social factors contributing to the problems. Some believe that technological utopianism is also a dangerous way of responding to problems, since it perpetuates complacency based on a blind faith that solutions will inevitably be found as a result of some technological breakthrough. Serious moral and ethical questions are also generated by this approach. Although we may be technologically capable of controlling human behavior, we have not yet determined how much control is legitimate or who should do the controlling.

Many proposals for solving our social problems center around changes in institutional structures that will provide greater equality. This means that the distribution of social rewards should depend upon abilities and needs and that each individual should have the opportunity to reach his or her own potential. Implementing greater equality in institutional structures can be accomplished only by basic changes in our social values, which may be the only way of maintaining the existing quality of life in the decades ahead. In such changes, painful though they will be, lie the challenge and the hope of the future.

Notes

[1]Daniel Bell, "The Year 2000—The Trajectory of an Idea," *Toward the Year 2000: Work in Progress,* ed. Daniel Bell (Boston: Beacon Press, 1969), p. 1.

[2]Harrison Brown, *The Human Future Revisited* (New York: Norton, 1978), p. 64.

[3]Jurgen Habermas, *Legitimation Crisis* (Boston: Beacon Press, 1975), p. 2.

[4]Ibid., p. 27.

[5]Ibid., p. 41–44.

[6]Dennis Wrong, "The Oversocialized Conception of Man in Modern Society," *American Sociological Review* 26 (April 1961), 183–193.

[7]Erving Goffman, *Asylums* (New York: Doubleday, 1961).

[8]Haberman, *Legitimation Crisis,* p. 43.

[9]Murray Edelman, *The Symbolic Users of Politics* (Urbana: University of Illinois Press, 1964).

[10]C. Wright Mills, *The Causes of World War III* (New York: Simon and Schuster, 1958), p. 53.

[11]Ibid., p. 47.

[12]Hannah Arendt, *On Revolution* (New York: Viking Press, 1965), p. 8.

[13]Robert L. Heilbroner, *An Inquiry into the Human Prospect* (New York: Norton, 1974).

[14]Ibid., p. 15.

[15]Ibid., p. 16.

[16]Ibid., p. 21.

[17]Ibid., p. 70.

[18]Herbert Marcuse, *One-Dimensional Man* (Boston: Beacon Press, 1964).

[19]Jacques Ellul, *The Technical Society* (New York: Knopf, 1964).

[20]Jack Douglas, ed., *Technological Threat* (Englewood Cliffs, N.J.: Prentice-Hall, 1971), pp. 37–38.

[21] Robert Nisbet, "The Impact of Technology on Ethical Decision-Making," *Technological Threat,* pp. 39–54.

[22] Ibid., p. 52.

[23] Philip Slater, "The Pursuit of Loneliness: American Culture at the Breaking Point," *The Solution of Social Problems,* ed. Martin S. Weinberg and Earl Rubington (New York: Oxford University Press, 1973), pp. 40–53.

[24] Ibid., p. 48.

[25] John Kenneth Galbraith, *Economics and the Public Purpose* (Boston: Houghton Mifflin, 1973).

[26] Heilbroner, *Inquiry into the Human Prospect,* p. 132.

[27] Herbert J. Gans, *More Equality* (New York: Random House, Pantheon Books, 1973).

[28] Heilbroner, *Inquiry into the Human Prospect,* pp. 108–109.

[29] Ibid., p. 109.

[30] Richard Quinney, *Critique of Legal Order: Crime Control in Capitalist Society* (Boston: Little, Brown, 1973), pp. 128–129.

[31] Arnold Bernstein and Henry L. Lennard, "The American Way of Drugging," *Society* 10 (May/June 1973), 16.

[32] Brown, *The Human Future Revisited,* p. 239.

[33] Douglas, *Technological Threat,* p. 105.

[34] Perry London, *Behavior Control* (New York: Harper & Row, 1969); Michael A. Shapiro, "The Uses of Behavior Control Technologies: A Response," *Issues in Criminology* (Fall 1972), 55–93.

[35] Kurt Vonnegut, Jr., *Welcome to the Monkey House* (New York: Dell Publishing/Delacorte Press, 1968).

[36] Christopher Jencks et al., *Inequality: A Reassessment of the Effect of Family and Schooling in America* (New York: Basic Books, 1972), p. 265.

[37] Gans, *More Equality.*

[38] Ibid., p. 23.

[39] Heilbroner, *Inquiry into the Human Prospect,* p. 140.

[40] Slater, "The Pursuit of Loneliness," p. 46.

[41] Ibid., p. 51.

[42] Heilbroner, *Inquiry into the Human Prospect,* p. 143.

Appendix
Understanding Social Research

631

Most people assume that scientists who study physical phenomena follow deliberate and painstaking procedures of investigation, using
special scientific tools and sophisticated measuring devices. But many fail
to realize the importance and function of a similarly scientific approach in
the professional study of social phenomena, categorizing social research as
a pseudoscientific guessing game that lacks the precision and logic of "real"
scientific inquiry. These people often claim that social research provides the
same information an average person could derive from common sense, intuition, and traditional authoritative sources of information.

It is quite true that important variables related to the study of social patterns or social problems are, by nature, less easily controlled than those of a
chemical experiment. But this does not invalidate the usefulness of a scientific approach in the study of social behavior, nor does it substantiate the
notion that one person's observations about social phenomena are as good
as anyone else's. In fact, social researchers have discovered that many of
the most commonly held assumptions and interpretations of social reality
are merely the product of traditional prejudices, misperceptions and unenlightened guesswork which fail to concur with the knowledge gained
through even the most basic methods of scientific inquiry. If knowledge is to
be regarded as a prerequisite for understanding, the investigative methods
of social science are a means both necessary and pertinent to clarification of
social problems.

The Scientific Method

The process of scientific investigation is more than a set of rules that guides the search for facts and relationships among them. It begins with the investigator's ideas about the phenomena to be studied, ideas from which questions are formulated that will define the research. If the ideas and conceptions are vague and unfocused, it may be necessary to conduct exploratory research about a particular subject to obtain more specific objectives for future research. On the other hand, there may already be a specific hypothesis which needs to be tested, one that is based on certain elements in the scientist's overall conception of phenomena. The social researcher, for example, who has several ideas about the ways in which people relate on an interpersonal level, may use these ideas to formulate a hypothesis which suggests a relationship among variables in human interaction (one such hypothesis might be that people in close proximity develop feelings of liking for one another).

The purpose of the research (whether it is exploratory or the testing of a specific hypothesis) determines the research design and the most suitable methods and techniques of investigation. The research design enables the social scientist to approach phenomena objectively and to avoid making any value judgments. Furthermore, if the investigation is unsatisfactory, the original design can be used as a reference in deciding which procedural changes might yield better results.

In plotting out a research design, the scientist determines the type of study to be conducted. An *ex post facto investigation* involves sifting through data previously collected or observed in past studies for factors which may at least partially account for the relationship among certain variables in presently observed phenomena. In a *cross-sectional study*, the social scientist observes certain variables as they operate among representative members of a population at a specific point in time. A *longitudinal study*, on the other hand, may examine those same variables over an extended period of time in order to determine and describe possible trends; or it may involve observations made before and after specific factors have been introduced into a social situation in order to determine their effects.

In deciding which type of study to utilize, the researcher must also consider the type of data to be sought and the ways in which the variables can be controlled in order to test the hypothesis. These are important considerations, since the researcher does not wish to be deflected by extraneous or inaccurate information. In order to actually gather the facts, the scientist may utilize one or a combination of research methods appropriate to the scope and limitations of the research. Sample surveys, questionnaires, interviews, participant-observer studies, case studies, and controlled experimentation are just some of these methods. The coding of data —the way data are organized and systematized—is also planned in the research design and enables the researcher to analyze those factors pertinent to the study. The actual techniques used in analyzing data may be designed to include various mathematical computations and statistical procedures.

Equipped with a basic research plan, the scientist can finally proceed to gather facts. In the course of doing so, it may become evident that the methods of investigation are inadequate or that certain kinds of data are simply unavailable. This may compel a modification of the research design. In analyzing and interpreting data, the researcher seeks to relate the facts that have been uncovered to those ideas which originally inspired the research. This often involves correlating variables in order to discover what (if any) significant relationships exist among them. It is quite possible that the findings may necessitate a modification of the original hypothesis or even a total rejection of it. Regardless of the outcome, the social scientist realizes that facts must be recorded as they have presented themselves and not fabricated or deliberately misrepresented in order to prove the original hypothesis. In other words, empirical evidence is the social researcher's guiding principle in formulating a generalization.

The final task of the scientist is a report of the findings, presented in the most precise method possible. Affective or colorful language is strictly avoided, since the strength of the scientist's conclusions rests on the clarity and objectivity of the data. The report itself may be utilized by other researchers as support for their own investigations or as a departure point for further studies on the subject. And in the case of sociological research, it may also be used by policy makers in determining which areas of the social environment demand public concern and in devising programs that are responsive to specific social problems.

Types of Social Research

Whatever the fundamental goal of social researchers—whether to uncover basic principles and patterns of social behavior, to delineate social problems and develop practical procedures for improving the quality of social life, or a combination of both—they are dependent upon a research methodology that includes the collection and analysis of social data. Not all techniques of data gathering are used as frequently or successfully as others, nor are they all equally precise or applicable to the testing of certain hypotheses. Social scientists must utilize their training and experience in deciding which techniques are appropriate to their particular inquiries and in judging the validity of information gained through these techniques.

Controlled Experimentation

A technique of data gathering that most people automatically associate with the scientific method is experimentation. Whether the experiment is conducted in the laboratory or the field, the fundamental purpose is the same: to arrange a comparison of two sets of circumstances that are equal (constant) in all variables except one.

For instance, in one study researchers attempted to test the hypothesis that delinquency might be prevented in a potentially delinquent boy if he received intense friendly counseling on a one-to-one basis with an adult.[1] The researchers set up experimental and control groups consisting of 325 subjects each. Both groups contained an equal number of predelinquent (potentially delinquent) and non-predelinquent boys. Individual boys were matched on the basis of age, delinquency-prediction rating, health, intelligence, and other relevant variables, so that each group contained equivalent samples. During a period of from four to eight years, the boys in the experimental group received adult counseling, whereas the boys in the control group received no counseling. Within a few years after the end of the program, the researchers compared official records of the boys in both groups and found that counseling had had no significant effect on delinquency.

Controlled experimentation is an effective method for testing hypotheses which involve causal relationships among variables. While such experimentation is common in the physical sciences, only recently has it been employed by social researchers, partly due to the expense it involves. In the delinquency study, a large staff of professionals was needed to screen the boys before adequate sample groups could be created and to provide one-to-one counseling for the experimental group. The size of the group and the length of time of the experiment required considerable sums of money.

Other limitations of controlled experimentation (such as the intervention of factors which are unaccounted for and which may affect the outcome of the experiment) are inherent in the nature of social research. For example, some counselors left during the middle of the delinquency study, requiring a change in counselors for the boys in the experimental group. There is no way to assess the impact this change may or may not have had on individual boys. Furthermore, there is no way to make certain that each boy received the same counseling services; in fact, in this experiment no attempt was made to standardize the counseling services provided to the subjects in the experimental group. Such factors limit the usefulness of any conclusions drawn from this type of experimentation.

Sample Survey

A major technique for gathering empirical data on attitudes, values, opinions, and behavior is the sample survey. It is commonly utilized by political campaigners and advertisers to obtain some indication of those qualities people are seeking in a candidate or a product and the way people are affected by different types of campaigns and commercials. The sample survey has been useful in both quantitative analysis (for example, in estimating the *number* of people who will vote Democratic or Republican) and qualitative analysis (for example, in determining the *type* of person who is attracted to the Democratic or Republican party).

In social research, the sample survey has provided considerable empirical data that are useful in conjunction with other research methods, such as case studies. The term *sample* refers to any group of people who have been chosen as representative members of the population under study. In a national voting survey, for instance, the population would consist of all adult voters; the sample would consist of just those citizens interviewed.

Depending upon the availability of a sample group for survey investigations and the type and projected use of the data being sought, the social scientist designs a survey plan which may employ such data-gathering techniques as interviews, questionnaires, or tests. While some surveys may be conducted in such a way as to assess public opinion in response to a specific event, like the repeal of the death sentence or the invasion of a foreign country, others may be repeated at various time intervals to determine changes in the public's attitudes or values. Americans are regularly polled by the Harris and Gallup organizations to determine their opinions of the president's job performance.

The problems and limitations associated with sample surveys are in some respects similar to those that affect other methods of social research. Briefly stated, sample groups may not be as representative as the researcher thinks or would wish them to be. Responses given during a survey investigation are not always accurate or adequate. However, other sources of information can be used to test the findings of survey studies; and the surveys may, in turn, reveal certain variables that are not accounted for in controlled experiments or other methods of social research.

Case Studies

The case study is an important technique for investigating the details of social patterns, processes, and behavior. It may involve the compilation of data about the history of a single individual, a family, or a special group of individuals; or it may involve a detailed account of a specific event such as a political demonstration. Sometimes the personal case study is used as a scientific wedge to open the more complex phenomena of group behavior to analysis. For example, the history, attitudes, and practices of a single member of the Amish community in Pennsylvania could serve as groundwork for more comprehensive studies and as a dramatic and illustrative accompaniment to statistical reports.

The case study is especially useful in exploratory research. Although a single case study is adequate for only limited generalization, it may be helpful in formulating additional hypotheses and creating the design of related studies that will employ more comprehensive and objective techniques of scientific inquiry. Furthermore, since broad theories and statistical reports may not indicate the special needs of individuals within any given population, case studies of specific individuals and situations provide information essential to any practical efforts or programs to ameliorate social conditions.

Participant-Observer Studies

Intimate knowledge of various social experiences and phenomena may be gained through a type of field investigation in which the researcher functions as both a participant and an observer. Used as an alternative to or in conjunction with other research methods, participant-observer studies can provide valuable insights which would be difficult, if not impossible, to gain through other means.

Sociologist William F. Whyte, for example, conducted a study of social organization in an urban slum.[2] Whereas previous sociological theories had maintained that slum districts suffered from social disorganization. Whyte hypothesized that a slum area has a highly complex social organization. To collect his data, Whyte lived with a family in the area for eighteen months and then took his own apartment there for an additional two years. While living in Cornerville (the fictitious name of the slum), Whyte participated in many community activities. He joined clubs, dated local girls, and became a campaign worker for a local politician.

Rather than study all aspects of social organization in the slum, Whyte chose to focus on the street corner gangs living in the area. He carefully observed the behavior of gang members. Sometimes he deliberately remained on the sidelines while gang members engaged in conversation. On other occasions, he joined in their conversation in order to direct it toward topics about which he desired information, such as the status relationships among gang members. Whyte found "that in every group [in Cornerville] there was a hierarchical structure of social relations binding the individuals to one another and that the groups were also related hierarchically to one another."

A major difficulty for the researcher using the participant-observer method is maintaining credibility as a member of the group under observation. If group members suspect duplicity or bad faith, they may become hostile or exclude the researcher from their confidences. On the other hand, if group members are informed of the researcher's purpose (as in this case), they may consciously or unconsciously modify their usual behavior. Furthermore, there is the problem of quantitative analysis and verification of field observation, since the researcher may be able to make only field notes on impressions about the group. Finally, the researcher's participation risks emotional involvement and loss of objectivity.

Nevertheless, the researcher's training in scientific method will lend at least some validity to the observations, and the findings of participant-observer studies may form the basis for hypotheses that inspire further research. These studies also enable researchers to evaluate the implementation of social programs (for example, prisoner rehabilitation programs) and to study and assess the behavior and practices of those professionals and officials who administer such programs.

Interviews and Questionnaires

Although interviews and questionnaires may be used in sample surveys, they also may be used as separate tools or in conjunction with any other method of social research. Both provide for the systematization of the data being sought; and the significance of findings derived from both techniques is dependent, to a great extent, upon whether the sample of people chosen for study is truly representative.

The questionnaire is a structured instrument completed by a respondent or by an interviewer asking questions of a respondent. Since there is no way to exert personal control over the responses on a questionnaire, its design is of great importance to the social researcher. The socioeconomic level and educational background of the target population must be taken into consideration in planning the language and sentence structure of the questions. Even if the information sought is purely factual, ambiguous wording and the use of unfamiliar terminology may result in inaccurate responses by subjects. More difficult to plan for is psychological game playing on the part of the respondents. It is not uncommon for people to try to determine the researcher's intention in asking certain questions (especially those dealing with opinions and attitudes) and to give answers they believe are acceptable (or unacceptable) to the researcher. Or, lacking any firm opinion about a topic, a respondent may simply fabricate a response. Subtle use of repetitive or overlapping questions may expose duplicity and misunderstandings on the part of the respondent, although the researcher must be cognizant of these factors when evaluating the questionnaire.

Unlike the questionnaire, the interview provides an opportunity for the social researcher to evaluate responses and modify the questioning pattern while the interrogation is in progress. However, at least a general plan of questioning is formulated prior to the actual interview. It may have a highly structured format (similar to the questionnaire), in which the respondent is asked a series of questions and is required to choose one of several answers. In another case, the order and type of questions asked may be controlled while the respondent is allowed to formulate replies in any fashion. Or the researcher may dispense entirely with formal questions and simply follow a topic outline. This last interview format is especially useful if the researcher has little in-depth data about the subject under inquiry. It encourages the respondent to volunteer any information pertinent to the topic, some of which the researcher may not otherwise know how to elicit.

The Use of Records

Utilizing the techniques of experimentation, survey, interview, and observation, the social researcher gathers data pertaining to a single event or phenomenon in time or to social conditions and changes within an extended time period. A considerable amount of sociological research also involves the comparison of data in the form of already existing records from different sources and time periods.

For example, one sociologist suspected a relationship between substandard housing conditions and juvenile delinquency.[3] In his study, he correlated delinquency rates in 155 census districts in Baltimore (available from court records) and data from the Bureau of the Census relating to housing units in the same districts. By controlling different variables, such as race and income, while comparing the statistical data, he discovered that home ownership was the one variable that remained significant throughout. His conclusion was that home ownership was indicative of family stability. This was interpreted as a partial explanation for the fact that lower delinquency rates were found in areas where home ownership was the major housing characteristic.

The Interpretation of Data

Quantitative measurement of data is a major activity of the social researcher, no matter which of the previously mentioned research methods are employed. Yet statistics and other quantified data are useful in describing and comparing phenomena only insofar as they are handled skillfully and with scientific objectivity; misinterpreted, they may suggest false conclusions and misleading generalizations. A good grasp of the concepts and problems of scientific measurement is therefore essential to the study of social problems.

Sampling Methods

Drawing a sample can be one of the most important steps in any research program and a necessary concomitant to any of the major research methods that are used to obtain data. Information obtained from a sample is used as the basis for making inferences about the particular population group from which it is drawn. Samples are necessary because the total population is often too large to study. But there may be problems, not only in planning but also in evaluating studies based on sampling.

"Scientific" studies based on absurdly small samples are often used to influence public opinion. An advertiser may state that in a recent survey of doctors, nine out of ten recommended a certain brand of cough medicine. Yet if the survey happens to have included only ten doctors, any self-respecting statistician would be obliged to view the results as a chance occurrence. A sample is simply not adequate unless it is large enough to preclude chance occurrences; the researcher who wishes to obtain valid data must be able to establish that further sampling would not significantly modify the results.

An even more important and difficult problem than that of size is finding a sample that is truly representative. If a sample is chosen without any specific system, it will not serve a valid purpose—even if it includes thousands of cases, a high percentage of which yield positive results in support of a hypothesis. There are two basic methods that can be used to draw a sample: the random method and the proportional representation method. Both techniques may involve problems for the researcher.

The random sample is comprised of people who are chosen randomly from the population under study—for example, every thirtieth name in a phone book or every other house in a particular community. In some ways, the random method is the most accurate and easiest technique for choosing a sample group. Yet this method can be costly and time-consuming, especially if contact with random group members is difficult to achieve or sustain for the duration of the study. For instance, some group members chosen on a random basis may well have erratic work schedules or other characteristics and life-styles that make it difficult for the researcher to interview them.

The other technique of sampling is based on proportional representation of each type of individual in the population group under study. Residence, income, profession, ethnic background, and education are some of the variables the sample may reflect in percentages comparable to the larger population group from which it is drawn. The obvious difficulty is choosing and controlling those variables that are relevant to the investigation. If the variables are not carefully considered, information from the sample group may lead to inaccurate inferences about social behavior in the large population. Sometimes data from previous studies are available as a guide in organizing this kind of sample group, but quite often the researcher is obliged to expend considerable time and energy in making preliminary tests in order to determine those factors relevant to the study.

Averages

The term *average* is casually and commonly used by most people. Unfortunately, the "average" person often uses the term as a convenient disguise for imprecise information. The social researcher, on the other hand, recognizes it as a useful statistical device that makes it possible to describe and compare people, events, and various aspects of social phenomena. In scientific terminology, an average refers to the most central mathematical tendency of whatever group or social phenomenon being studied. There are three types of averages: the mean, the mode, and the median.

The *mean,* commonly equated with the term *average,* is the total sum of values divided by the total number of cases from which those values are derived. For example, suppose a researcher is calculating the mean annual income of a group of ten high school graduates. The income figures for this group are:

$5000	$5500	$5500	$5500	$6000
$6500	$6500	$7500	$9000	$9500

To arrive at the mean, the researcher determines the total income of the group ($66,500) and divides by the number of cases (ten). The result is the mean income of $6650.

The mean is often a good indicator of central tendency (a value representing the entire distribution) since it utilizes all the values available from the collected data. It can be misleading, however, if the distribution includes extreme cases. If the $9500 top income in the example above were $35,000, the mean income would be $9200, hardly a figure typical for the group. For this reason, social researchers often use the mode and the median as measurements of central tendency, since neither is affected by extremes in distribution.

The *mode* is that value in a series of values which most frequently occurs. In the example above, the mode would be an income of $5500. The *median* is the midpoint in a series of values when those values are arranged in numerical order. The median is therefore flanked on both sides by an equal number of values when there is an odd-numbered series of values. If there is an even-numbered series of values, the median is the mean of the two middle values. In the example above, the median is $6250 (the mean of the two middle values—$6000 and $6500).

In using averages, the social researcher must determine which of these three measures of central tendency best fits the needs of the study and the data under consideration. Unless the data contain extreme cases, the mean is the best measurement, since it takes into account the values of all cases.

Correlation

Correlations are mathematical statements that indicate the degree to which two sets of variables are related. A common error is to equate correlation with causation, thereby suggesting relationships among variables that may not exist. It is true that a statistical correlation may eventually provide evidence for a causal relationship, but the relationship cannot be claimed until certain questions have been posed and satisfactorily answered.

Before causation can be considered, it must be established that a true relationship between variables exists—that two factors vary together significantly. The first step, then, is to determine whether a certain factor occurs significantly more (or less) frequently in the specific group being studied than it does in the general population. For example, before a researcher can begin to determine whether a valid association exists between heredity and alcoholism, it is necessary to compare the percentage of *all alcoholics* with living or dead alcoholic relatives to the percentage of *all people* who have living or dead alcoholic relatives. The researcher must then determine the *coefficient of correlation,* a measurement of the two variables which involves complicated mathematical procedures. For our purpose, it will suffice to state that there may be a positive correlation, in which two factors vary together in the same direction, or a negative correlation, in which two factors vary proportionately but in opposite directions. Even if a relationship between two factors seems to exist, this does not prove causation; nor does it indicate which factor is the cause and which one the effect. The researcher must still examine several possible relationships before suggesting a pattern of causation. For example, if a correlation between alcoholism and organic malfunctions is established, it may be the case that (1) inherited organic malfunctions cause alcoholism, (2) alcoholism causes organic malfunctions, (3) other factors are responsible for the incidence of both alcoholism and organic malfunctions, or (4) alcoholism and inherited organic malfunctions are independent factors and only coincidentally associated.

Obviously, if more than two variables are involved, establishing what is cause and what is effect is even more difficult. The complexity of the interactions may preclude any definitive statements about correlation, much less causation. Yet holding all but one variable constant (assuming this is possible) may suggest a correlation which is mathematically accurate but which is only a partial and simplified description of available data. Investigation into social problems such as juvenile delinquency, for example, might yield partial correlations suggesting some simple causal relationships. On the other hand, such correlations may seem to negate the relationship between a specific factor and delinquency. In a real-life situation, however, very subtle and complex interactions among many variables probably produce the particular social problem under study, and conclusions drawn on the basis of limited data, partial controls, and statistically impressive correlations are tenuous at best.

Notes

[1]Edwin Powers and Helen L. Witmer, *An Experiment in the Prevention of Delinquency: The Cambridge-Somerville Youth Study* (New York: Columbia University Press, 1951).

[2]William F. Whyte, *Street Corner Society: The Social Structure of an Italian Slum* (Chicago: University of Chicago Press, 1943).

[3]Bernard Lander, *Towards an Understanding of Juvenile Delinquency* (New York: Columbia University Press, 1954).

GLOSSARY

Abstraction   separation of moral values from social contexts that are important and meaningful to the individual.

Alienation   a feeling of noninvolvement in and separation from one's group or society, through feeling powerless and/or seeing values and norms shared by others as meaningless.

Anomie   normlessness, or state of confusion produced by sudden or dramatic changes in the social structure.

Assimilation   the process by which members of one group discard their unique cultural traits and adopt those of another group.

Automation   a kind of technology in which a production process (often manufacturing) is carried out by a set of self-regulating machines rather than directly by people.

Battered-child syndrome   term used to describe the medical condition of severely abused children.

Behavior modification   treatment whereby the therapist teaches the patient to substitute new responses for those displayed to the patient's disadvantage in the past.

Birthrate, crude   figure derived by dividing the number of births in one year by the population count in the middle of the year, then multiplying by a thousand to show the figure per thousand people.

Bureaucratic institutionalism   the growth of bureaucracies as the predominant mode of organization in both public and private associations.

Closed marriage   the merging of husband and wife into a single entity.

Competitive individualism   a cultural preference for competing for personal gains rather than cooperating for group or societal benefits.

Conglomerate   a company consisting of a number of subsidiaries in a variety of unrelated industries.

Control group   in a scientific experiment, the group which is like the experimental group in every way except that it does not receive the experimental treatment.

Corporate state   a condition in which the institutions of government and the economy are intimately related.

Correlation   a mathematical statement that indicates the degree to which two sets of variables are related.

Cultural pluralism   see *pluralism*.

Culture lag   the time lag between the occurrence of a phenomenon and the change in social relationships or ideas required to accommodate it.

Culture of poverty   a way of life among the poor that transcends time and place, thus making for remarkable similarities in such things as family patterns, value systems, and interpersonal relations.

Cybernation   simultaneous use of computers and automation for the organization and control of material and social processes.

Death rate, crude   figure derived by dividing the number of deaths in one year by the population count in the middle of the year, then multiplying by a thousand to show the figure per thousand people.

De facto   in reality or fact.

De jure   according to law.

Demography   the science of counting people.

Deviant behavior   behavior that varies significantly from the social norms established for persons occupying a particular position in the social structure.

Differential association theory   theory that criminal behavior is learned through interaction with a group that offers rewards to the learner and helps the learner build an identity.

Differential social organization   varying patterns of roles, statuses, norms, and values which predominate in a group.

Discrimination   unequal treatment of equal people because of their membership in certain social groups or categories.

Ecosphere   nature's rhythms and cycles.

Ecosystem   intricate web of relationships between all living things and the physical environment they share.

Emigration   movement out of a country.

Entail   the system of limiting inheritance of property to a specified, unalterable succession of heirs.

Ethnic minority   a group that differs from the dominant group in terms of cultural background and traditions.

Ethnic relations   patterns of interaction between members of minority and majority groups.

Ethnocentrism   belief in the superiority of one's own group over other groups in the society.

Experimental group   in a scientific experiment, the group the researcher subjects to experimental treatment, the effect of which is determined by comparing this group to the control group.

Extended family   three or more generations of family living together as a single, large household.

Fecundity   the biological capacity for childbearing.

Fertility   the actual number of births to women of childbearing age.

Fixed income   an assessment of one's income in absolute dollars or specific cash income.

Frustration-aggression theory   theory holding that a person who is blocked from satisfaction of needs or desires will respond by striking out—at the obstacle, if it is known and not too threatening, otherwise at a substitute victim.

Generalization   transformation in moral and normative standards accompanying the spread of technology.

Generalized other   concept referring to the society or community whose values and expectations an individual observes and follows.

Group therapy   treatment involving groups of eight to ten people, in which a secure social situation is used to get them to seek help as well as help others.

Human-value index   a criterion that assesses the ultimate worth of a product or invention in terms of its total impact on human life, that is, in terms of human and social goals rather than technical ones.

Hypothesis a statement relating two or more variables, expressed in such a way that scientific methods can be used to test it.

Immigration movement into a country.

Incidence rate the number of persons per unit of population recently diagnosed as having a particular disorder during a specified period.

Individuation fragmentation and atomization of traditional community structures and primary social relationships.

In-migration movement into an area within a country.

Labeling theory viewpoint that deviance is a consequence of the way society treats an offender rather than a quality of one's behavior.

Latent social problems harmful social conditions that have yet to be generally acknowledged.

Legitimacy a belief by group members that an action is proper, justified, and appropriate to the circumstances.

Manifest social problems problems that have been acknowledged by the decision makers and that society has taken measures to solve or somehow ameliorate.

Mean the total sum of values divided by the total number of cases from which those values are derived.

Median the midpoint in a series of numerical values, when those values are arranged in a low-to-high order.

Megalopolis a highly urbanized area in which cities and towns are run together in an almost unbroken chain of dense settlements.

Metropolitan federation a form of government in which certain powers are delegated to a consolidated group of cities with each individual city government retaining only partial independence.

Migration geographical movement of people, especially that resulting in a permanent change of residence.

Migration, crude rate of net difference between the rate of immigration and the rate of emigration.

Minority group category of people who possess imperfect access to positions of equal power and to the corollary categories of prestige and privilege in the society.

Mode the value in a series of scores which occurs most frequently.

Mortality death.

Multinational corporation business establishment with extensive investments in production or distribution in several countries.

Multiversity the contemporary large university with its enormous bureaucracy, rigid specialization, and multiple functions.

Negative income tax a guaranteed income program in which low-income persons would be paid an annual amount by the federal government based on initial income and exemptions.

Neurosis mental disorder characterized by high levels of anxiety and emotional discomfort that disrupt normal interaction, family life, and occupational performance.

"No fault" divorce divorce in which the blame is not placed on either partner and neither one assumes a "guilty" role.

Norm a cultural rule defining expected behavior.

Nuclear family   a married couple and their children.

Oligopoly   the domination of an industry by a few producers.

Open classroom   educational atmosphere in which the teacher becomes a "resource person" who provides the students with many educational activities from which to choose.

Open marriage   term given to new rules and style of marriage in which each partner is free of many traditional customs and expectations as well as of rigid sex-role definitions.

Out-migration   movement out of an area within a country.

Pluralism   a condition wherein society is composed of a number of interdependent ethnic or racial groups, each maintaining a degree of autonomy.

Population change, crude rate of   difference between the crude birthrate and the crude death rate.

Poverty index   concept used by the Social Security Administration that reflects different consumption requirements of families, based on their size and composition, sex and age of the family head, and farm or nonfarm residence.

Power elite   those who occupy the top positions in the corporate, governmental, and military sectors.

Prejudice   an attitude based on stereotypes; emotional prejudgment of members of a social group or category.

Prevalence rate   the number of persons per unit of population diagnosed as having a specific disorder during a given time.

Primary contacts   human contacts characterized by intimate, face-to-face relations

Primogeniture   the system of inheritance in which all property is given to the eldest son.

Proprietary hospitals   hospitals operated for profit.

Psychedelic drugs   those psychoactive drugs that primarily affect the way the mind processes information (well-known examples are LSD and peyote).

Psychoactive drugs   those drugs that affect the central nervous system in such a way that physical functions, emotional states, and consciousness are altered.

Psychoanalysis   a treatment of mental illness that relies on intensive sessions between analyst and patient, generally extending over a three- to four-year period.

Psychosis   mental disorders characterized by unusual behavior, gross distortion of reality, and an inability to function adequately either all or part of the time.

Psychosomatic   refers to the body's response to stressful mental states.

Psychosurgery   brain surgery performed on social deviants without evidence of organic impairment for the purpose of changing behavior patterns.

Psychotherapy   treatment of mental illness through the use of various techniques such as verbal analysis, persuasion, challenge, and suggestion, depending upon the orientation of the therapist.

Race relations   patterns of interaction between members of minority and majority groups.

Racial minority   a group that differs from the dominant group in terms of physical or biological characteristics.

Rationalization tendency to bring greater and greater areas of thought and conduct under the formal rules of bureaucratic administration.

Relative income an assessment of one's income in relation to that of others.

Research design methods and techniques of investigation best suited to answering the particular questions posed.

Role expected behavioral pattern attached to a particular status.

Role model a person whose behavior in a role is taken by another person as an ideal, or pattern to imitate, in performing the same role.

Sample any group of people who have been chosen as representative members of the population under study.

Secondary contacts see *segmental contacts*.

Segmental contacts secondary contacts characterized by casual, compartmentalized, less than intimate relationships.

Segregation social and/or residential separation, based on people's membership in social groups or categories and enforced by law and/or custom.

Separatism doctrine arguing for complete separation of the races, advocated especially by some black Americans who desire economic, social, educational, and geographic independence of whites.

Social change changes in social relationships and culture.

Social disorganization a condition wherein certain social standards and rules lose their meaning and relevance because they fail to provide predictable expectations to serve as guidelines for social conduct.

Social problems those conditions identified by sociological analysis of the organization and functioning of a society as having a negative impact on individual and social well-being.

Social processes special patterns of interaction which occur regularly and uniformly and thus constitute distinctive patterns.

Socioeconomic status social rank, as indicated by a combination of two or more social and economic observations, such as income, occupation, education, and occupational prestige.

Standard Metropolitan Statistical Area (SMSA) a county or group of counties containing at least one city of 50,000 or more that provides many services and jobs for the whole area; a U.S. Bureau of Census term.

Stigmatization a process in which a person is identified or assigned as a member of a socially undesirable category, resulting in disqualification from full social acceptance.

Synanon the first therapeutic community for drug addicts, started in California by a former alcoholic who applied the philosophy and techniques of Alcoholics Anonymous to a small group of addicted persons on a 24-hour-a-day live-in basis.

Technological utopianism an assumption by Americans that technology will provide the solution for our most critical problems.

Total institution a place where many individuals are subject to the tight control of a formal organization; exit, contact with the outside world, privacy, and personal decisions are all highly restricted or impossible.

Value conflicts the conflicting values held by disparate groups of a heterogeneous population.

Voluntary hospitals hospitals affiliated with medical schools as teaching hospitals.

Work ethic the traditional American emphasis on productive activity as both highly important and valuable in and of itself.

Zero population growth the situation which results when the increase in population through births and immigration is equal to population loss through deaths and emigration.

Chapter 11

Chapter 12

Chapter 13

Chapter 14

Chapter 15

Chapter 16

Index